The Battle of Mohács, 1526

History of Warfare

Editors

Kelly DeVries (*Loyola University Maryland*)
Aimée Fox (*King's College London*)
John France (*Swansea University*)
Paul Johstono (*The Citadel, South Carolina*)
Frederick Schneid (*High Point University, North Carolina*)

VOLUME 146

The titles published in this series are listed at *brill.com/hw*

The Battle of Mohács, 1526

Edited by

Norbert Pap

BRILL

LEIDEN | BOSTON

Cover illustration: Türkenschlacht bei Mohatsch from Ehrenspiegel des Hauses Österreich (Buch VII) - BSB Cgm 896, Augsburg, 1559 [BSB-Hss Cgm 896], Bildnr. 760-761. With kind permission of the Bayerische Staatsbibliothek, München. Available online: https://daten.digitale-sammlungen.de/0010/bsb00103106 /images/index.html?id=00103106&groesser=&fip=eayayztsewqfsdrfsdrxdsydxdsydxdsydqrs&no=10&seite=760/
https://daten.digitale-sammlungen.de/0010/bsb00103106/images/index.html?id=00103106&groesser=&fip=eayayztsewqfsdrfsdrxdsydxdsydxdsydqrs&no=9&seite=761/

Chapter Thirteen has been made with the support of the OTKA Project, no. K 146585 entitled Hungary and the Western Balkans. The starting year is 2024.

Library of Congress Cataloging-in-Publication Data

Names: Pap, Norbert, 1969- editor.
Title: The Battle of Mohács, 1526 / edited by Norbert Pap.
Description: Leiden ; Boston : Brill, [2024] | Series: History of warfare, 1385-7827; volume 146 | Includes index.
Identifiers: LCCN 2024028780 (print) | LCCN 2024028781 (ebook) | ISBN 9789004695825 (hardback) | ISBN 9789004707498 (ebook)
Subjects: LCSH: Mohács, Battle of, Hungary, 1526. | Hungary–History–Turkish occupation, 1526-1699.
Classification: LCC DR507 .B38 2024 (print) | LCC DR507 (ebook) | DDC 943.9/041–dc23/eng/20240621
LC record available at https://lccn.loc.gov/2024028780
LC ebook record available at https://lccn.loc.gov/2024028781

Typeface for the Latin, Greek, and Cyrillic scripts: "Brill". See and download: brill.com/brill-typeface.

ISSN 1385-7827
ISBN 978-90-04-69582-5 (hardback)
ISBN 978-90-04-70749-8 (e-book)
DOI 10.1163/9789004707498

Copyright 2024 by Koninklijke Brill BV, Leiden, The Netherlands.
Koninklijke Brill BV incorporates the imprints Brill, Brill Nijhoff, Brill Schöningh, Brill Fink, Brill mentis, Brill Wageningen Academic, Vandenhoeck & Ruprecht, Böhlau and V&R unipress.
All rights reserved. No part of this publication may be reproduced, translated, stored in a retrieval system, or transmitted in any form or by any means, electronic, mechanical, photocopying, recording or otherwise, without prior written permission from the publisher. Requests for re-use and/or translations must be addressed to Koninklijke Brill BV via brill.com or copyright.com.

This book is printed on acid-free paper and produced in a sustainable manner.

Contents

Preface VII
List of Figures and Tables IX
Notes on Contributors XIII

Introduction: Exploring Research Challenges on the Battle of Mohács 1
   Norbert Pap

PART 1
The Armies and the Battle

1   Süleyman and Hungary: Conquest, Ideology and Memory   15
    Pál Fodor

2   The Main Scenes   47
    Norbert Pap, Máté Kitanics and Péter Gyenizse

3   The Hungarian and Ottoman Forces at the Battle of Mohács   83
    Máté Kitanics, Pál Fodor and Norbert Pap

4   Ottoman Turkish Handguns   125
    Norbert Pap, Pál Fodor and Máté Kitanics

5   The Battle and Its Aftermath   171
    Norbert Pap and Máté Kitanics

PART 2
The Overall Landscape

6   Geomorphology of the Mohács Plain and Its Environs   217
    Péter Gyenizse, Dénes Lóczy and Gábor Varga

7   Reconstruction of the Drainage of the Mohács Plain and Its Implications for the Battle of Mohács   238
    Péter Gyenizse, Dénes Lóczy and Gábor Varga

PART 3
The Battle Arena

8   Localizing the Central Area of the Battle of Mohács: Search for the Medieval Settlement of Földvár   271
    Norbert Pap, Máté Kitanics and Péter Gyenizse

9   Critical Comments on the Available Military Archaeology Topographic Data   306
    Máté Kitanics, Norbert Pap, Sándor Konkoly and Erika Hancz

10 Where and How Did King Louis II Die?   357
    Norbert Pap, Péter Gyenizse and Máté Kitanics

PART 4
Spaces of Remembrance

11 Hünkâr Tepesi (Törökdomb): the Ottoman Memorial Place of the Battle   417
    Norbert Pap, Pál Fodor, Máté Kitanics, Tamás Morva, Gábor Szalai, Erika Hancz and Péter Gyenizse

12 Landscape, Artistic Representation, Memorials: Remembrance of the Location of the Battle of Mohács in 1526   448
    Júlia Papp

13 Memorial Politics and the Sites of the Battle of Mohács   494
    Norbert Pap

Index   527

Preface

The story behind the book dates back to October 2016. Our research team celebrated the localization of the Ottoman mausoleum (*türbe*) of Sultan Süleyman (1520–1566) in Szigetvár. We had a very successful period, between 2013 and 2015 we found and excavated the symbolic *türbe* of the ruler who died in 1566 during the siege of Szigetvár. The mausoleum and the adjacent buildings were searched in vain for more than 100 years.

It was at this dinner that the idea of our new project was raised by our late colleague János Hóvári, a distinguished Ottomanist, historian. For more than a hundred years, a debate has been going on in Hungary among historians and other researchers about the place where the crucial event of the period, the Battle of Mohács (1526), took place.

To turn the idea into a project, money was needed (as always). In the end, this was provided by the Hungarian Academy of Sciences and its Excellence Collaboration Programme. The studies started in 2018. The social environment and reception of the türbe project in Szigetvár and the battle project of Mohács were very different. The research at the türbe was met with rather incredulous amazement in Hungary, while the battlefield research at Mohács was accompanied by furious debate.

Nevertheless, the investigations were done, just before the tragic COVID-19 pandemic. In retrospect, we were lucky. We could finalize the project in time, the participants survived the disease, and the closures provided the peace of mind needed for summarizing the results.

After several preliminary studies, work on the manuscript of this volume started in 2021. Looking back through my correspondence, I received a reply to my email from Kelly DeVries in early March 2021. He wrote that the subject was very exciting and of great interest not only to him but also to what he believes is a wide audience. The topic of this volume fits well into the History of Warfare series.

The work took much longer than I had originally thought. As usual, much was discovered while writing. It was one of the most intellectually exciting and transformative periods of my life. For all this, I owe an infinite debt of gratitude to my collaborators, especially to Pál Fodor and Máté Kitanics.

Along the way, we have had help from many institutions, whose generous funding has made it possible to carry out this project: the Hungarian Academy of Sciences, the Szentágothai János Research Centre of the University of Pécs, the HUN-REN Research Centre for the Humanities and the Hungarian Scientific Research Fund – OTKA K 146585. Thanks to Nándor Zagyi for assisting us with some practical issues regarding this publication, such as the bibliographies, and indexing. We would also like to thank the late János Hóvári for the original idea and his support during the research. Thanks also to Marcella Mulder, who provided quick and fair assistance with the administrative aspects of the volume.

Norbert Pap
Pécs, April 2024

Figures and Tables

Figures

1.1 Portrait of Sultan Süleyman   16
2.1 Mohács Island on a map (1720–1725)   48
2.2 The smaller Mohács branch and the larger Baracska branch of the Danube on Ignácz Müller's map of 1769   49
2.3 The main stations of Louis II's and Süleyman's armies to Mohács, along the Danube   52
2.4 The surroundings of the Island of Mohács with the main sites mentioned in the sources   55
2.5 Mohács on the map of the Military Survey I (1783)   58
2.6 Mohács on the Danube   61
2.7 The location of the treasure trove found in Duna Street [Kálvin köz] in Mohács   63
2.8 The assumed location of the Kölled fort at the crossing (ca. 1696) by Marsigli   64
2.9 Bozuk kilise (Buziglica) at the ruins of Géta monastery (Ketu) and the crossroads to Mohács and to Merse and Majs   68
2.10 Cross-section of the swamp showing elevation differences at the Vizslak Meadow   70
2.11 "Deep Ditch", or "valley", an ancient river bed on the battlefield   72
2.12 The main scenes of the battle   73
2.13 Result of visibility analysis on the Mohács Plain   74
4.1 The *tabur cengi*, the Ottoman order of battle, 1526, Battle of Mohács   141
4.2 Janissaries with handguns accompanying Sultan Murad III   147
5.1 Depiction of the Battle of Mohács, 1559, Augsburg   177
5.2 The site of the Battle of Mohács   187
6.1 Location of the investigated area in Europe   219
6.2 Microtopography in the Mohács Plain   223
6.3 Geomorphological surfaces of the study area   223
6.4 Topographical section of natural levees on both banks of the Béda-Danube and scroll-bar systems   225
6.5 Photos of the floodplain   226
6.6 The flood-free terrace presented in photos   227
6.7 Topographical section of Látóhegy and its environs   228
6.8 Topographical section of the Sátorhely Ridge   229
6.9 The paleobed near Sátorhely and its topographical sections   231
6.10 The paleomeander near Sátorhely on photographs   231

6.11	Geomorphological map of the northern Mohács Plain	233
6.12	The hills bordering the terrace from the west presented in photos	234
7.1	Location of the Danube and Mohács in Europe	239
7.2	Drainage of the Mohács Plain today	240
7.3	The present-day main channel of the Danube	240
7.4	Changes of the Danube channel north of Mohács between 1808 and 1880	244
7.5	Results of map comparisons with the aim of reconstructing the late 17th century course of the Danube	246
7.6	The channel sections linked to Lake Riha and the one-time bend	247
7.7	Drainage map of the Mohács Plain in the first half of the 19th century	249
7.8	The incised narrow bed of the Csele Stream next to the confluence with the Danube	253
7.9	The Dolina, a slight depression east of the fiberboard plant	254
7.10	The plain section of the Lajmér Stream with waterlogged areas	256
7.11	Low-lying, watery, swampy, waterlogged places in the Hungarian part of the Mohács Plain	261
7.12	Swampy, watery, wet soil areas on the flood-free terrace	262
8.1	Map of possible sites of village Földvár on the battlefield of Mohács	272
8.2	The boundaries of the estate of Földvár west of the Danube according to the 1338 inspection of landmarks	275
8.3	Distance data from the medieval Mohács according to Brodarics	289
8.4	The Mohács Plain in 1700	292
8.5	The three chambers along the Borza Stream	298
8.6	The Borzathw Valley (Borza Lake Valley) in 1476	299
8.7	Geophysical survey of chamber I–III	299
9.1	Site plan of mass graves I and II excavated in 1960	309
9.2	The siege of Arad by the Christian armies, 1658	310
9.3	Size distribution of projectiles from the Majs area	323
9.4	Size distribution of projectiles from the area of Mohács Island	324
9.5	Archeological finds of the Mohács Plain and Mohács Island, by groups	332
9.6	Map of the archaeological finds and sites of the Mohács Plain and Mohács Island	332
9.7	Mass grave No. I during excavation	346
10.1	Danube sections below the mouth of the Csele Stream	376
10.2	The Danube section downstream the confluence of the Csele Stream	379
10.3	Places related to the name of water with the prefix Fekete or Kara in the vicinity of Mohács	380
10.4	The dry bed of a former river valley called *Dolina*: passage to the Danube	381
11.1	Törökdomb (Turkish Hill) on maps	429
11.2	Turkish Hill in 1926	431

11.3	The eastern part of the Turkish Hill with archeological objects	432
11.4	Find (cross) belonging to the chapel built on top of the Turkish Hill	434
11.5	Swampy landscape on the eastern side of Turkish Hill (April 2018)	436
11.6	North-south section of Turkish Hill and its surroundings	437
11.7	East-west section of Turkish Hill and its surroundings	437
11.8	Stylised 3D reconstruction of Turkish Hill and its surrounding	438
12.1	The Battle of Mohács. Detail of the *Tabula Hungariae* (1528)	451
12.2	Antal Marastoni and Károly Rusz: "The mill of the Csele Stream near Mohács (grave of King Louis II)"	461
12.3	István Dorffmaister: Louis II (1787)	464
12.4	József Borsos: The Battle of Mohács in 1526 (1837)	465
12.5	Mihály Bartalits: The plan of Louis II's monument (1846)	471
12.6	János Mihalovits: The death of Louis II (1843)	473
12.7	Memorial statue of the Battle of Mohács near Mohács (1874)	475
12.8	Károly Cserna: The battlefield at Mohács (1896)	477
12.9	Károly Zelesny: The monument at Mohács (1897)	477
12.10	György Kiss: The death of Louis II on the monument of the Battle of Mohács (c. 1895)	479
12.11	Barnabás Holló: The death of Louis II (end of the 19th century)	480
12.12	Bertalan Árkay: Plan of the votive church in Mohács	483
12.13	Pál Kő: Statue of Süleyman I (1976)	485
12.14	Pál Kő: Statue of Louis II (1976)	486
13.1	Soma Orlai Petrich: Discovery of the Body of King Louis II (1851)	501
13.2	József Szűcs in the Filmhíradó (1976) and a labour movement worker statue	516
13.3	Colonel Lajos Négyesi, János B. Szabó, and József Szűcs at the Mohács National Memorial (2018)	519

Tables

2.1	Süleyman I's journey from Mohács to Buda	53
2.2	The spread of news of the battle in the days after 29 August 1526	75
3.1	Troop numbers of the armies facing each other at Mohács	116
4.1	Variants of the dirhem in the Islamic World	133
4.2	Types and characteristics of treasury handguns in the first half of the 16th century	135
4.3	Ottoman janissary handgun data	136
4.4	Turkish small arms exhibited at the "National Exhibition of the Millennium" in Budapest, 1896	136
4.5	Light arquebuses, collected by Balázs Németh	149

4.6	Experimental firing data of the 16th–17th century handguns	152
5.1	Chronology of the day of the battle (29 August)	178
5.2	Ottoman loss data in primary and memorial sources	190
8.1	Data on village Földvár	281
8.2	Explanation of some names on the 1700s estate map	293
9.1	Parameters of the cannonballs found at Black Gate	317
9.2	Quantitative and percentage distribution of the size categories of projectiles found at Majs and Mohács Island	324
9.3	Archaeological finds and sites of the Mohács Plain and Mohács Island	328
9.4	Documented hostilities and encampments on the plain and the Mohács Island (1526–1711)	341
10.1	The most reliable (earliest) sources on the king's death	360
10.2	Environmental features of the place of death of King Louis II in the 16–18th century memory sources	392
13.1	The truth of József Szűcs' claims in 1976 and 2021	514

Notes on Contributors

Pál Fodor
PhD, DSc, is a research professor and honorary director general at the HUN-REN Research Centre for the Humanities, Institute of History. He is the president of the Hungarian Historical Society. He has published extensively on early Ottoman history, the social, economic, and military structure of the Ottoman Empire (up to the end of the 17th century), Ottoman political thought and Ottoman–Hungarian political relations. He is the author and editor of more than ten books and more than four hundred articles including In Quest of the Golden Apple: Imperial Ideology, Politics, and Military Administration in the Ottoman Empire (2000), The Unbearable Weight of Empire: The Ottomans in Central Europe – a Failed Attempt at Universal Monarchy (1390–1566) (2016), The Business of State: Ottoman Finance Administration and Ruling Elites in Transition, 1580s–1615 (2018), 16. ve 17. Yüzyıl Osmanlı Kaynaklarında Sultan Süleyman'ın Sigetvar'daki Türbe Kasabası (2021).

Péter Gyenizse
PhD, is an associate professor at the Institute of Geography and Earth Sciences, University of Pécs. He is a geographer and GIS expert. In recent decades carried out landscape change and landscape reconstruction studies in Hungary, especially in South Transdanubia. In addition, he examines the impact of natural features on settlement development and creates city classification GIS models.

Erika Hancz
MA, has graduated in Archaeology and Turcology in the University of Szeged, Hungary. Then she continued her post graduate studies in the Eötvös Loránd University in Hungary. Since 2007 she is working at the University of Pécs, Faculty of Archaeology as a research fellow. She is majoring in Ottoman archaeology, especially architecture and ceramics. She is the leader archaeologist of the excavations in Szigetvár-Turbék, where the symbolic tomb of Sultan Suleiman the Magnificient was found with other buildings, inside of a former palisade castle and village which was built by the Ottoman Turks. She also write her articles mainly from this topic.

Máté Kitanics
PhD, is a research fellow of the Szentágothai Research Centre, University of Pécs. Since 2012 he has been a member of the Zrínyi-Szulejmán Research Group, which identified and excavated the former Tomb of Sultan Suleiman and the nearby mosque and dervish monastery at Turbék near Szigetvár. Since

2018, he has been involved in the research project 'Mohács 1526–2026 – Reconstruction and remembrance', which focuses on landscape reconstruction and historical geography of the Battle of Mohács in 1526. His broader research interests include the historical and ethnic geography of the Carpathian Basin and the Balkan Peninsula.

Sándor Konkoly
MSc, is a graduate geographer from the University of Pécs, Hungary. His field of research is historical geography and archaeological geology. In his work using interdisciplinary research methods, he deals with the historical geography of the Mohács Island and localization of its hidden fortified objects. In 2015, Zoltán Magyary's Board of Trustees of the Office of Public Administration and Justice awarded his professional and scientific achievements with the National Excellence Award. In 2021 he became involved in the Mohács battlefield research with his analytical investigations. He is a PhD student at the Doctoral School of Earth Sciences of the University of Pécs, and is a member of the Pécs Military History Working Committee of the Hungarian Academy of Sciences.

Dénes Lóczy
PhD, DSc, is a graduate of Eötvös Loránd University, Budapest. At present he is professor of physical geography at the University of Pécs. His main fields of study are floodplain geomorphology, ecology and restoration; land evaluation and sustainable farming. He was Alexander von Humboldt Fellow in Germany. Now he is president of the Hungarian Geographical Society and Honorary Fellow of the International Association of Geomorphologists.

Tamás Morva
MSc, graduated as a geographer from the University of Pécs in 2013, and then studied geoinformatics as an MSc and PhD student. He has published in several areas of geography, later mainly in the field of landscape reconstruction and complex GIS-based classification systems. He is also interested in the interaction between natural and social geographical factors, in cartography and geomorphology.

Norbert Pap
PhD, Dsc, is a research professor of historical and political geography at the Szentágothai Research Centre and full professor at the Institute of Geography and Earth Sciences, University of Pécs. He has been working in Szigetvár since 2010, leading the research team concerning the death and the burial place of Sultan Suleiman since 2012. Moreover, his research activities cover the presence of Islam in East-Central Europe, furthermore the relationships between

the Balkans and Hungary. The project studied the Battle of Mohács (1526) started in 2018. He has written more than four hundred scientific publications to date. He is the author of ten books so far.

Júlia Papp

PhD, DSc, is an art historian and senior research fellow at the Research Centre for the Humanities, Institute of Art History, Budapest. She graduated from the Eötvös Loránd University in Budapest. Her main research areas are Hungarian fine arts in the 18–19th centuries and European artwork reproduction (photographs, plaster casts) in the 19th century. She published the oeuvre catalogue of the engraver Johann Blaschke in 2012, and she was the editor of the academic handbook about 19th century fine arts (2018). She organized several exhibitions (for example about the education of women in Hungary, the photographs of Roger Fenton, and artwork reproductions in the 19th century). Since 2018 she has been researching the 16–19th century fine art depictions of the Battle of Mohács in 1526 and King Louis II, who died in the battle.

Gábor Szalai

MSc, is a historical and political geographer, PhD candidate at the University of Pécs. He is a member of the Zrínyi-Szulejmán Research Group since 2015 and the "Mohács 1526–2026 – Reconstruction and Remembrance" Program since 2017. His fields of research cover the study of social, ethnic and religious geographies, sociogeography, including the study of local, mixed ethnic society of villages, and the government-organised population exchanges following World War I and their geopolitical consequences to this day.

Gábor Varga

PhD, graduated from the Janus Pannonius University of Pécs with a degree in geography. Here, at the same institution, but now at the University of Pécs, he obtained a PhD in geomorphology. Currently, he is Head of the Department of Physical and Environmental Geography at the Institute of Geography and Earth Sciences, Faculty of Sciences. His research interests focus on general surface evolution, landslide processes and forms, and periglacial geomorphology of the Carpathian Basin.

INTRODUCTION

Exploring Research Challenges on the Battle of Mohács

Norbert Pap

In connection with the research on the Battle of Mohács, future generations must face numerous problems beyond the interpretation of written historical sources. The battle holds enormous symbolic significance in Hungarian history and has become a kind of overarching narrative. It marks a milestone that separates the first five 'glorious' centuries of the thousand-year-old Christian Hungarian state in the Carpathian Basin from the following five 'catastrophic' centuries. The memory of the medieval Hungarian Kingdom with its imperial possibilities is still alive in the Hungarian historical consciousness. It is a historical fact that contemporary Hungary was a significant middle power. The end of the era is unequivocally linked in Hungarian historical tradition to the defeat of the Hungarian army and the death of King Louis II in the battle. The Battle of Mohács has repeatedly appeared and continues to appear as a reference point in public discourse or in the interpretation of current national catastrophes.

It follows from the above that thinking and analysing the battle cannot escape from memory-political considerations and their interdependent structure that is capable of remembrance and forgetfulness. Over the past centuries, the role of the actors has been reinterpreted many times, and new perspectives have emerged concerning the events. The treatment of historical data has occasionally become problematic according to the current ideological considerations. Based on the above, the fundamental question is to identify what is a scientific assertion based on evidence regarding the battle and what is a politics of memory overlay.

The research of the Battle of Mohács began at the end of the 19th century. Over the approximately 130 years that have passed since then, progress in the different disciplines has been uneven. Knowledge of the location of military clashes has expanded to a lesser extent in historical research, while to a greater extent in earth sciences and archaeology. The image of the Battle of Mohács underwent the most significant transformation during the 400th-anniversary commemorations when previous interpretation mostly based on current national narratives and local folk traditions first gained scientific foundations.

Hypotheses and military explanations developed in the 1920s still form the basis of current perceptions of the battle. The intensive research of the 1960s and 1970s deepened some aspects, but did not change the overall picture of the combat fundamentally.

In the past century, new scientific methods have emerged that allow and force us to rethink and reconsider our ideas about the course of the battle. Natural sciences, particularly earth sciences, have played a key role in this change. Over the past five centuries, changes in the landscape and climate raise questions about the differences between present and past conditions. Do we understand the environmental references in the contemporary and later descriptions? How did the actual drainage system and vegetation of the 16th century affect military planning that time? The battlefield today is a well-maintained agricultural landscape, where it is unlikely that we will find the former elements of the environment because they have been erased by the changes of the past five centuries. Modern geospatial methods offer a key to understanding and reconstructing the 16th-century landscape and environmental conditions. This allows us to model the landscape around 1526 as well as earlier and later periods, which can provide valuable reference points that are based on scientific research, independent of memory tradition, and free from errors in narrative sources, emotional and political biases.

1   Why Is Historical Geographical Research Needed?

Those who are not versed in the historical geography, especially in hydrogeography, of the Carpathian Basin cannot comprehend how the anti-Ottoman wars of the 15th–17th centuries unfolded in the region. The opposing sides had to not only contend with each other but also with the environment. The drainage system, in particular, posed significant challenges for any troops fighting in the region. This was no different in 1526.

The reason for the need for modern historical geographical reconstruction of the Mohács Plain lies in the fact that despite the extensive literature spanning about 130 years on the battle, a consensus has not yet been reached on the description of the battle or the topographical interpretation of the Christian and Ottoman positions: the camping, marching, and fighting locations have seen extremely diverse interpretations. The locations in question have been interpreted and placed in scientific debates, but typically, they have been evaluated from the perspective of the current landscape, removed from their complex geographical environment, and without taking into account the changes in the landscape over time.

The group of 20th-century authors who dealt with the topic consisted of military officers specializing in terrain and military operations – the most influential of whom were Jenő Gyalókay (after World War I) and Géza Perjés (after World War II) – whose topographical perspective was primarily shaped by their own military terrain training and geographical thinking of their time. This battlefield perspective was static, leading them to project their own battlefield experiences onto the landscape they knew, which, however, was not the same as it was in the early 16th century. This military tradition, concerned only with a narrow range of factors that helped or hindered military activities – such as topography and hydrography – failed to sufficiently consider the dynamic state of these factors and the larger-scale changes that occurred in the landscape over time. This resulted in a unique problem in that while the earth sciences made a significant progress in the 20th century, leading to revolutionary theoretical and methodological renewal, researchers on the battlefield failed to fully exploit the theoretical and practical possibilities of earth sciences of their own time: they were not at all familiar with the real geographical environment of the 16th-century battlefield and did not sufficiently understand the changes that had occurred since then.

Scientific discoveries of the 20th century, such as plate tectonics and climate change, which are largely responsible for the transformation of the environmental conditions surrounding the Mohács Plain, or the effects of anthropogenic surface shaping, did not become part of the considerations in research related to the terrain and the battlefield environment.

The concepts that defined the Battle of Mohács were primarily born in three main periods: the two decades before World War I, the 1920s, and the 1960s and 1970s. There is no evidence that the authors who dealt with the history of the battle during these periods took into account climatic, geological and morphological changes, anthropogenic geomorphic impacts, and the possibility of significant landscape transformation resulting from these factors. By examining historical maps, they did see some differences between the former and their own era, but practically the only question they asked themselves was whether the Danube has eroded the former battlefield by now?

It was suggested that the battlefield could have been moved to Mohács Island due to the changes in the riverbed. "The claim has been repeatedly made that the battlefield of Mohács no longer exists because the Danube has completely washed it away, so that the battlefield is now either in the Danube basin or on Mohács Island." Finally, they were reassured that it was not: "nothing is missing from the area where the army of King Louis II fought Sultan

Süleyman."[1] By now, it is a well-known and accepted view that a colder and wetter climate period called the Little Ice Age (LIA) occurred at the end of the Middle Ages and during the early modern period, which had an impact on human life.[2] In Europe, the emergence of the LIA theory and related local studies brought about revolutionary findings for our investigation period. The first research results appeared in the United States during the outbreak of World War II,[3] and therefore, the 1940s were lost for research in Hungary due to the war conditions. West of the Iron Curtain, in the 1950s and 1960s, investigations in this direction gained momentum. The first significant scientific publications on the topic were released in the early 1970s.[4]

In the Soviet-dominated alliance system, ideological and political constraints prevailed on the issue,[5] which prevented the development of a publicly receptive intellectual environment for the application of Western findings and scientific results. The theory only began to emerge in Hungary in the 1980s, but it only gained widespread recognition in the 1990s. It was only in 1999 that the first comprehensive analysis of the issue was published.[6]

---

1 Jenő Gyalókay, *A mohácsi csata* [The Battle of Mohács] (Budapest: Királyi Magyar Egyetemi Nyomda, 1926), p. 212.
2 Prior to that, in the 9th–13th centuries, by contrast, there was a drier, warmer period ('the Medieval Warm Period'). It was during this period that the Viking settlements of Greenland were established. In Árpád-era Hungary, the climate also became warmer and drier during this period. Cf. András Vadas and Lajos Rácz, "Éghajlati változások a Kárpát-medencében a középkor idején," [Climate change in the Carpathian Basin during the Middle Ages] *Agrártörténeti Szemle* 51 (2010), no. 1–4, pp. 39–62.
3 Although there were some precursors to the idea of climate change, the idea has long gone unheeded. One of the first papers was written by Matthes. François E. Matthes, "Report of Committee on Glaciers, April 1939," *Eos, Transactions American Geophysical Union* 20 (1939), no. 4, pp. 518–523.
4 Emmanuel Le Roy Ladurie, *Times of Feast, Times of Famine: A History of Climate Since the Year 1000* (Garden City, NY: Doubleday, 1971); Hubert Horace Lamb, *Climate: Present, Past and Future* (London: Methuen, 1972); Hubert Horace Lamb, *Climate, History and the Modern World* (London: Routledge, 1995).
5 For a long time, the Soviet leadership sought ways to change the course of the major Siberian rivers (Ob, Yenisei), ignoring natural conditions. In the Stalinist view, nature is almost unchanging at the scale of human society, and environmental issues were almost neglected. In the 1960s Khrushchev was very intensively involved in the issue, and even long after his downfall the planning process to implement the plan continued. Cf. Michael Overman, *Water: Solutions to a Problem of Supply and Demand* (Garden City, NY: Doubleday,1969), p. 183. In the 1960s and 1970s, the political circumstances outlined above did not create a conducive intellectual environment for discussing or even raising the issue of landscape change and climate change.
6 Lajos Rácz, *Magyarország éghajlattörténete az újkor idején* [The climatic history of Hungary in the early modern era] (Szeged: Juhász Gyula Felsőoktatási Kiadó, 2001).

The theory of plate tectonics had a fate similar to that of climate change. It emerged in the Western countries in the 1960s, but only much later did it surface in the scientific community of the countries belonging to the Soviet sphere of influence. In Hungary, the theory was met with significant resistance, and it was only after scientific debates in the 1970s that it gained acceptance.[7] However, it only became widely accepted in the 1980s.

The significance of this for the Mohács Plain and the Mohács Island was that it was only through plate tectonics that the characteristic feature of the area, that the plates carrying the plain and the island rise and fall, could be explained. This, in turn, fundamentally influenced the course of the Danube, as well as of its tributaries and other smaller watercourses, the characteristics of sedimentation, and the landscape pattern.[8]

Anthropogenic impacts also played an important role in the changes to the landscape. The process was generally known, and perhaps some of its elements were given too much importance compared to natural processes. River regulation, the expansion of large-scale agriculture that determined the appearance of the plain, and the abolition of the '*notch*' system[9] in floodplains are among the main human impacts. The consequences affecting the battle area include significant changes to local drainage patterns in the terraced plain of Mohács, the drainage of swamps and wetlands, the channelization of watercourses, the almost complete eradication of natural vegetation, and the radical alteration, rounding and partially smoothing of the micro-topography. The consequences of the process for the local society and the landscape along the Danube were thoroughly elaborated by the ethnographer Bertalan Andrásfalvy, with serious impact on related sciences, in the 1970s and 1980s.[10] It seems that in the

---

[7] The geophysicist Lajos Stegena and the paleontologist Barnabás Géczy were the first proponents, but it was only much later that geology and related sciences began to apply it in their studies.

[8] Over the last ten thousand years, the area has subsided by tens of metres, although not uniformly over time. This means that over the last 500 years, the subsidence has had a significant impact on sediment transport and deposition.

[9] According to the ethnographer Andrásfalvy's definition, a "notch" (in Hungarian: fok) is "a man-made ditch cutting through natural levees and during high stages allowing water flow out over the entire floodplain and during recession back to the channel." Bertalan Andrásfalvy, *A Sárköz és a környező Duna-menti területek ősi ártéri gazdálkodása és vízhasználatai a szabályozás előtt* [Ancient floodplain farming and water uses of the Sárköz and the surrounding Danube areas before the regulation] (Vízügyi Történeti Füzetek) 6 (Budapest: Vízügyi Dokumentációs és Továbbképző Intézet, 1973).

[10] Bertalan Andrásfalvy, *Duna mente népének ártéri gazdálkodása Tolna és Baranya megyében az ármentesítés befejezéséig*, [The floodplain economy of the people of the Danube in Tolna and Baranya Counties until the end of the regulation works] (Tanulmányok Tolna megye történetéből) VII (Szekszárd: A Tolna Megyei Tanács Levéltára, 1975).

research on the battle and of the landscape that hosted this battle, these insights were not taken into account.

The investigations carried out by geographers concerning Baranya County and the Danube Valley, as well as the town of Mohács, were continuous throughout the 20th century. Among these works, Márton Pécsi's work on the geomorphology of the Danube valley[11] and the Mohács monograph by Antal Lehmann and Ferenc Erdősi[12] stand out, as well as Gyula Gábris' study on the Mohács Plain.[13] The geographical literature has dealt extensively with the course alignment and geomorphic action of the river, the factors of settlement and the development of Mohács town, which provided important contributions to understanding the use of the landscape. These works could have served as important references for the interpretation of the battlefield, but the conclusions were still not drawn. The basic views on the Battle of Mohács had already been firmly established before the revolutionary scientific discoveries mentioned above, so they did not play a part in scientific debates concerning the battle – up to now.

The successive generations who relied on the battlefield interpretations of Jenő Gyalókay and Géza Perjés, who also debated with them and among each other on many issues, did not fundamentally question their assessment of the landscape, which may have been influenced by their recognized professional expertise in military and terrain issues. Both of them were military officers, with Gyalókay having gained experience in the World War I, while Perjés made use of his experiences in the World War II.

The lack of interdisciplinary dialogue and knowledge of international battlefield research eventually led to a significant amount of fiction being included in the historical thinking about the location of the battle. This idea is not entirely new. Gábor Gyáni's 2006 essay also raises the possibility that, in relation to the main source, Brodarics's chronicle, at least part of the account is fictional or fictionalized: he believes that the battle cannot be objectively reconstructed.[14]

---

11 Márton Pécsi, *A magyarországi Duna-völgy kialakulása és felszínalaktana* [The formation and morphology of the Danube Valley in Hungary] (Földrajzi Monográfiák) 3 (Budapest: Akadémiai Kiadó, 1959).
12 Ferenc Erdősi and Antal Lehmann, *Mohács földrajza* [Geography of Mohács] (Mohács: Mohács *Városi Tanács V.B. Művelődési Osztálya*, 1974).
13 Gyula Gábris, "A mohácsi csatamező," [The battlefield of Mohács] *Föld és Ég* 15 (1980), no. 8, pp. 249–252.
14 According to Gyáni, Brodarics's account is a "fictionalised account" and "Brodarics's chronicle actually gives us a fictional narrative of the events around Mohács." Gábor Gyáni, "Elbeszélhető-e egy csata hiteles története? Metatörténeti megfontolások," [Is it

Based on the same sources, some historians placed the battle in the northern part of the plain, while others placed it in the central or a few on the southern part. Their historical analysis did not, or only exceptionally, cover the physical reality in the 16th century. Each historian-storyteller pictured the battlefield according to their own narrative, either taking into account geographical circumstances or not, and sometimes reinterpreted them to meet the demands of the drama.

Military historians tried to identify the references of written primary sources to the elements of the environment in a landscape that has lost its original properties, which has inevitably led to misunderstandings and, in part, to a multitude of extreme interpretations that also contradict each other. The approach solely relying on written historical sources cannot resolve the interpretation of the battle.

2 Mohács Debates

Interpreting the battle and predicting its consequences, with sharp differences of opinion, started as early as the end of 1526, not least because a civil war broke out in the country as a direct corollary of the battle. Mohács has been an important reference point for thinking about national issues since the 19th century, becoming a unit of measure for national tragedies. It became a basis for comparing the failures of the defeated anti-Habsburg freedom fights, the 1920 Trianon Treaty, and the Soviet occupation of the country. The highly politicized thinking about Mohács grew into thinking about the 'Mohácses'. This circumstance influenced the research and researchability of the issue. There has never been harmony between scientific research and memory politics in the past century: it was interpreted differently during the Austro-Hungarian dualism, which was experienced as a 'silver age', than in the Horthy era, the Hungarian Soviet system, and that continued after the regime change in 1990. There have always been tensions between research results and the discourse surrounding them, and compliance with current ideological expectations has been decisive in public discourse. However, there is also a continuity, as Mohács has been perceived as a turning point in every era.

The research on Mohács was accompanied by heated debates of variable intensity for 130 years, often with ad hominem arguments, questioning characters not opinions. The so-called Mohács debate was one of the significant

possible to tell the authentic story of a battle? Metahistorical considerations] *Hadtörténelmi Közlemények* 119 (2006), no. 1, p. 125.

historian discussions in the post-World War II period, which lasted for decades but was most intense in the 1960s and 1970s, and continued with less intensity in the 1980s. Many claim that it has never really ended. Not only professional historians, but also representatives of related professions participated in the debate which became highly politicized and increasingly focused on their own age. under the pretext of Mohács. Within the limited freedom of the Hungarian communist/socialist system, this opened up numerous opportunities for the scientific community and artistic circles to demonstrate – in connection with Mohács – Hungarian patriotism against internationalist socialism.

After a quieter period around the turn of the millennium, the Mohács debate entered a new chapter in the 2010s. This time, outside the circle of professional historians, medical doctors István Nemes and Balázs Tolvaj entered the debate, whose findings provoked sharp reactions from experts on the subject.[15] They questioned the narrative about the death of King Louis II. The authors expressed doubts about the historical description of the condition of the king's corpse and believed that there were still questions to be clarified in this regard. Did the search team find the king's corpse in October 1526? If it was not his corpse, then what really happened to King Louis II? Or could there be something wrong with the description? The reactions were strong, as the questions touched on the foundations of the Mohács issue. In the artistic representation of the battle, the discovery of the king's corpse has been a strong iconographic symbol for centuries but it is also one of the favourite topics of conspiracy theories.

Even before the debate about the corpse of King Louis II could be settled, a new, equally emotionally charged research project was launched. This time, the 120 million HUF grant from the Hungarian Academy of Sciences' Excellence Collaboration Programme made it possible to start the three-year research project 'Mohács 1526–2026 – Reconstruction and Memory,' led by Pál Fodor and Norbert Pap, producing a series of new results, including some that have stirred up considerable controversy.[16] It is worth recalling the aim of the project. The

---

15   István Nemes and Balázs Tolvaj, "II. Lajos magyar király (1506–1526) holttestének megtalálása. Az 1926-ban írt igazságügyi orvosszakértői vélemény elemzése és újraértelmezése," [The discovery of the body of King Louis II of Hungary (1506–1526). Analysis and reinterpretation of the forensic expert opinion written in 1926] *Orvosi Hetilap* 155 (2014), no. 12, pp. 475–480. See also *"Nekünk mégis Mohács kell ..." II. Lajos király rejtélyes halála és különböző temetései,* ["We still need Mohács…" The mysterious death and various funerals of King Louis II] eds. Gábor Farkas Farkas, Zsolt Szebelédi, and Bernadett Varga (Budapest: Magyar Tudományos Akadémia Bölcsészettudományi Kutatóközpont, Országos Széchényi Könyvtár, 2016).

16   See https://www.mohacs.btk.mta.hu.

funding was not only intended for traditional historical research, but also for interdisciplinary studies using innovative methodological tools producing novel results and possibly supporting socio-economic development projects. However, the main task was to discover the peculiarities of the battlefield.

3   From Fictional to Scientifically Based Battle Descriptions

Historical research of spatial and temporal relations must go beyond the use of written sources. These are the facts that appeared as evidence in the minds of people in a given historical time, the authors of the source texts. The perception of the time passing is based on the annual, monthly, and weekly routines of the given community, along with the religious holidays and the order of agricultural work. The physical environment is also well known, and the extremely slow changes are no different to constancy to the authors of the sources, so we usually do not receive information about them when reading their texts. The changes over centuries can already be significant, but it is difficult to get an idea of their magnitude and rate from documents in the archives. However, using other methods, such as analysing measurable trends, evaluating changes on historical maps, and modelling using geographic information systems (GIS), we can get closer to reconstructing the geographical conditions of each period also reflected in references in the written sources.

The research methodology applied in the book is based primarily on the theoretical and methodological achievements of the earth sciences in recent decades: data provided by modern remote sensing tools (satellite imagery, analysis of aerial photographs), geophysical surveys, the possibilities offered by geoinformation modelling, and the significantly expanded source material offered by the archival digitisation programme.

During the research, we aimed to reconstruct the contemporary topography, hydrography, land use, and vegetation cover of the Mohács region. It was possible to obtain data on the conditions of the road network of the time. It was also important to determine which crossing points could have formed major bottlenecks in the movement of troops. Landscape reconstruction was also significant in determining which dry, solid surface areas were suitable for battle, and which areas were floodplains, wet meadows, and swamps. The environmental reconstruction work also provided an important contribution to localizing some of the landforms and anthropogenic landscape elements mentioned in historical sources.

Through scrutinising the geographical names of the literary sources and descriptions of the battle, we aimed to localise the main geographical positions. The method was to collect and analyse the geographical locations and topological relations from all available primary sources and contemporary descriptions. If they confirmed previous data and fitted in the reconstructed landscape, they were approved as relevant locations. Furthermore, we also examined whether these results correlated with archaeological data and local folk traditions.

The chapters of the book deal with the following main topics:
- *'Mohács' and politics.* As a starting point, the significance of the Battle of Mohács is examined in Ottoman imperial concepts and politics in 1526. It is followed by presenting the Törökdomb (Turkish Hill) at Mohács as an Ottoman victory monument and the first Christian memorial. Mohács also produced significant iconography, which is dealt with separately. In the last chapter, we looked at the role of the battlefield area in 20th- and early 21st-century politics of memory.
- *Changes in the environment over the last 500 years.* We attempted to localise the main parts of the battlefield and its wider surroundings that appear in historical sources by combining environmental reconstruction and historical source analysis. We surveyed flood-free surfaces suitable for combat versus water-covered, marshy areas, the movements and locations of armies – in a separate chapter. The analysis also focuses on the influence of the Danube River, its floodplain swamps and crossing points, as well as military camps, and the complex problem of the town of Mohács, which served as a port and river crossing point.
- *Földvár.* The location and the characteristics of Földvár, the most mysterious village in Hungarian military history, as described by eyewitness and chronicler István Brodarics, where the Ottoman artillery was stationed during the battle, has been debated for hundred years. We clarified these issues and explained why this village played such an important role in the events.
- *The death of the king.* The possible manner and place of the death of the Hungarian and Czech king, Louis II is presented.
- *Archaeology.* Using archaeological topography, we managed to decipher some important features of the clashes and the significant challenge of distinguishing between the characteristics of the nine military operations/battles that took place on the studied territory between 1526 and 1711. The analysis sheds light on the unique connections between archaeology and the politics of memory. The five mass graves of the battle are not only a place of remembrance but also a site of scientific research and political debates.
- *Ottoman Handguns.* Small firearms played a decisive part in the Ottoman victory, but there has been much debate about them. Our approach in this case was also interdisciplinary. We analysed not only the reports from

written sources, but also data from the collections of preserved weapons, shooting experiments with replicas of 16th-century small firearms, and geochemical aspects. These results indicate that the Battle of Mohács in 1526 belongs to the series of great 16th-century battles (such as Chaldiran in 1514, Pavia in 1525, Marj Dabiq in 1516, Ridaniya in 1517, Nagashino in 1575, etc.) where infantry equipped with handguns was of great, sometimes decisive importance.

– *The armies and the battle.* There has been much discussion about the participants in the battle, which we also reviewed, determining the numbers, the nature, role and location of the units. We also had to deal with questions related to dating. Clarifying the peculiarities of the timekeeping of the era, the issues of interpretation of astronomical phenomena, and the dating of events before the 1582 Gregorian calendar reform brought us closer to determining the events of the day of the battle not only in geographical space but also in (micro)chronological terms. As a result, we were able to create a new reconstruction of the course of the 29 August 1526 battle based on the events described in sources, in a way which was not possible before.

Bibliography

Andrásfalvy, Bertalan. *Duna mente népének ártéri gazdálkodása Tolna és Baranya megyében az ármentesítés befejezéséig.* [The floodplain farming of the people of the Danube in Tolna and Baranya counties until the end of the flood relief] Tanulmányok Tolna megye történetéből VII. Szekszárd: A Tolna Megyei Tanács Levéltára, 1975.

Andrásfalvy, Bertalan. *A Sárköz és a környező Duna-menti területek ősi ártéri gazdálkodása és vízhasználatai a szabályozás előtt.* [Ancient floodplain farming and water uses of the Sárköz and the surrounding Danube areas before the regulation] Vízügyi Történeti Füzetek 6. Budapest: Vízügyi Dokumentációs és Továbbképző Intézet, 1973.

Erdősi, Ferenc and Antal Lehmann. *Mohács földrajza.* [Geography of Mohács] Mohács: Mohács Városi Tanács V.B. Művelődési Osztálya, 1974.

Farkas, Gábor Farkas, Zsolt Szebelédi, and Bernadett Varga eds. *"Nekünk mégis Mohács kell…" II. Lajos király rejtélyes halála és különböző temetései.* ["We still need Mohács…" The mysterious death and various funerals of King Louis II] Budapest: Magyar Tudományos Akadémia Bölcsészettudományi Kutatóközpont, Országos Széchényi Könyvtár, 2016.

Gábris, Gyula. "A mohácsi csatamező." [The battlefield of Mohács] *Föld és Ég* 15 (1980): 249–252.

Gyalókai, Jenő. *A mohácsi csata.* [The Battle of Mohács] Budapest: Királyi Magyar Egyetemi Nyomda, 1926.

Gyáni, Gábor. "Elbeszélhető-e egy csata hiteles története? Metatörténeti megfontolások." [Is it possible to tell the authentic story of a battle? Metahistorical considerations] *Hadtörténelmi Közlemények* 119 (2006): 121–133.

Lamb, Hubert Horace. *Climate, History and the Modern World.* London: Routledge, 1995.

Lamb, Hubert Horace. *Climate: Present, Past and Future.* London: Methuen, 1972.

Le Roy Ladurie, Emmanuel. *Times of Feast, Times of Famine: A History of Climate Since the Year 1000.* Garden City, NY: Doubleday, 1971.

Matthes, François E. "Report of Committee on Glaciers, April 1939." *Eos, Transactions American Geophysical Union* 20 (1939): 518–523.

Nemes, István and Balázs Tolvaj. "II. Lajos magyar király (1506–1526) holttestének megtalálása. Az 1926-ban írt igazságügyi orvosszakértői vélemény elemzése és újraértelmezése." [The discovery of the body of King Louis II of Hungary (1506–1526). Analysis and reinterpretation of the forensic expert opinion written in 1926] *Orvosi Hetilap* 155 (2014): 475–480.

Overman, Michael. *Water: Solutions to a Problem of Supply and Demand.* Garden City, NY: Doubleday, 1969.

Pécsi, Márton. *A magyarországi Duna-völgy kialakulása és felszínalaktana.* [The formation and subsurface structure of the Danube Valley in Hungary] Földrajzi Monográfiák 3. Budapest: Akadémiai Kiadó, 1959.

Rácz, Lajos. *Magyarország éghajlattörténete az újkor idején.* [The climatic history of Hungary in the early modern era] Szeged: Juhász Gyula Felsőoktatási Kiadó, 2001.

Vadas, András and Lajos Rácz. "Éghajlati változások a Kárpát-medencében a középkor idején." [Climate change in the Carpathian Basin during the Middle Ages] *Agrártörténeti Szemle* 51 (2010): 39–62.

PART 1

The Armies and the Battle

CHAPTER 1

Süleyman and Hungary: Conquest, Ideology and Memory

Pál Fodor

1   Conquest

Sultan Süleyman (Figure 1.1) ruled for 46 years (1520–1566), and although there were several changes in the composition of the ruling elite, the rationale of imperial politics – except in the last ten years – displayed astonishing continuity. This is an important point to make because – although there are more sources from his age than from any previous time – we have no personal correspondence or any other source of direct information from him or his innermost circle about his personal opinions, ideas or long-term goals. Researchers are therefore reduced to inferring from the sultan's deeds what he had on his mind and what he aimed to achieve.

Immediately we bump into a thorny question: did the Ottoman state and Sultan Süleyman himself have long-term ideas which historians, borrowing from military strategists, tend to label 'grand strategy'? If they did, what strategic role did they assign to Hungary? This is an unavoidable question: Süleyman led his first military campaign on Hungary (1521, Belgrade), lost his life during another Hungarian campaign (1566, Szigetvár) and launched most of his wars against Hungary and the Habsburg Monarchy (1526, 1532, 1541, 1543, 1552, etc.).

In the more recent literature (following the path set by Edward Luttwak, Geoffrey Parker and others) it has principally been Gábor Ágoston who has begun to examine the suitability of this model for Ottoman history. As he puts it, the 'grand strategy' is nothing other than "a global vision on the geopolitics of states and their military, economic and cultural capabilities".[1] It is this vision which determines the empire's long-term policy and the mobilization of its economic and human resources to attain present political goals. According to Ágoston, we are not able to speak of a unified strategy stretching over centuries. And yet there clearly were methods which the House of Osman employed

---

1   Gábor Ágoston, "The Ottomans: From Frontier Principality to Empire," in The Practice of Strategy: From Alexander the Great to the Present, eds. John Andreas Olsen and Colin S. Gray (Oxford: Oxford University Press, 2011), p. 107.

FIGURE 1.1　Portrait of Sultan Süleyman.
SOURCE: UNKNOWN PAINTER (AROUND 1600). HISTORICAL PHOTOGRAPHIC COLLECTION _0438. HUNGARIAN NATIONAL MUSEUM.

consistently over a prolonged period of time: dynastic marriages, the inclusion of local elites and military organizations, the flexible organization of provincial administration and taxation, and forced resettlement. It is perhaps first in the case of Sultan Süleyman that we can discern the contours of a 'grand strategy'.[2] For the most part, I myself am in accord with these, but I would contend that some kind of 'long term strategy' can be seen to emerge from the Ottoman political leadership much earlier, the key elements to which were as follows: 1) the crushing of the small Balkan states; 2) the ousting of the Italian (Latin) trading nations; 3) the subjugation of the Muslim Turkish states of Asia Minor; 4) the isolation and gradual destruction of Byzantium, and the capture of Constantinople.[3] In Europe, after 1453, Hungary would come to take centre stage in the Ottoman Turkish conquest plans, if at the time this was still shared with some Mediterranean and Near East targets. But as these latter areas would gradually come under Ottoman control, so would Hungary rise up the list of countries to be conquered, until it was top of the list. The reasons for this were equally ones of foreign and domestic politics and of economics and ideology.

Let us first look at the *foreign policy factors*. From the late 15th century, the Ottomans saw more and more clearly that, with the decline of the crusader spirit and the papacy's ability to assert its interests, a division had developed in the Western world which could be exploited. Above all, the wars in Italy from the end of the 15th century onwards, the Valois–Habsburg rivalry that unfolded after the election of Charles V as emperor and then engulfed the West for half a century, the birth of Protestantism, etc., provided the opportunity to draw such conclusions. It was also reassuring to the Ottoman Porte that, from the turn of the century onwards, the European powers saw her not only as a religious enemy but as a potential ally, as one of the players in Europe's power struggles, and actively sought her friendship. From the 1520s the Habsburgs' advance in Italy also inspired the Ottomans to a much more active western role, for, as I will discuss in a moment, they had plans of their own in this area.

To turn to the *economic factors:* the greater part of the Ottoman state's resources and income originated from the Balkans, and although, following

---

[2] Gábor Ágoston, "'The Most Powerful' Empire: Ottoman Flexibility and Military Might," in Empires and Superpowers: Their Rise and Fall, eds. Georg Zimmar and David Hicks (Washington, DC: Society for the Preservation of the Greek Heritage, 2005), pp. 127–171, particularly pp. 154–157; Gábor Ágoston, "Information, Ideology, and Limits of Imperial Policy: Ottoman Grand Strategy in the Context of Ottoman–Habsburg Rivalry," in *The Early Modern Ottomans: Remapping the Empire,* eds. Virginia H. Aksan and Daniel Goffman (Cambridge: Cambridge University Press, 2007), pp. 76–77. Gábor Ágoston, *The Last Muslim Conquest: The Ottoman Empire and Its Wars in Europe* (Princeton, Oxford: Princeton University Press, 2021), p. 334.

[3] Pál Fodor, *The Unbearable Weight of Empire: The Ottomans in Central Europe – A Failed Attempt at Universal Monarchy (1390–1566),* 2nd ed. (Budapest: Research Centre for the Humanities, Hungarian Academy of Sciences [=HAS], 2016). In the first part of the essay I summarize my principal findings in this book.

the conquest of the Near East, the significance of this area would diminish, it retained its primary role.[4] The Ottomans had thoroughly explored and were fully informed about the more developed Central European lands, and assumed that their acquisition would be financially advantageous, or at least not cost more than the maintenance of their existing northern Balkan frontiers.

Of the factors relating to *domestic politics*, the most important would seem to be the pressure exerted by the troops stationed in Rumelia. By all accounts, there did exist a 'Rumelian lobby' whose demands and methods were not unlike those of the Ottoman military élite in Bosnia and Hungary in the years prior to the Long War of 1593–1606.[5] In both cases many decades had passed since any great imperial campaigns had been launched against Hungary or Croatia. The borderlands would be destroyed by the constant incursions and skirmishes. Soldiers, desirous of prebends and loot, and whose numbers were liberally inflated by the presence of volunteers, were ever more impatiently waiting for new occupations of territory from where to extend their raids to more and more new areas fresh for exploitation. Süleyman's turn to the West was also inspired by the public mood in Ottoman society. His subjects were sick and tired of decades of wars against Muslims; his soldiers wished to fight on European territories that promised richer pickings.

2 Ideology

All these intentions were strongly supported, even encouraged, by the very complex ideological reasons that have long provided the legal basis for Western conquests. Jihad, the imperative of holy war, was not even the first of these, though ever more evidence suggests that Süleyman conceived of the wars of the dynasty as true 'religious wars' and felt waging them to be a

---

4 Erol Özvar, "Transformation of the Ottoman Empire into a Military-Fiscal State: Reconsidering the Financing of War from a Global Perspective," in *The Battle for Central Europe: The Siege of Szigetvár and the Death of Süleyman the Magnificent and Nicholas Zrínyi (1566)*, ed. Pál Fodor (Budapest, Leiden, and Boston: Research Centre for the Humanities HAS and Brill, 2019), pp. 38–39; cf. Pál Fodor, "The Military Organization and Army of the Ottoman Empire (1500–1530)," in *On the Verge of a New Era: The Armies of Europe at the Time of the Battle of Mohács*, eds. János B. Szabó and Pál Fodor (Mohács 1526–2026: Reconstruction and Remembrance) (Budapest: Research Centre for the Humanities HAS, 2021), pp. 96–97.

5 Pál Fodor, "Ottoman Policy towards Hungary, 1520–1541," *Acta Orientalia Academiae Scientiarum Hungaricae* 45 (1991), no. 2–3, pp. 292, 334–336; Pál Fodor, "Prelude to the Long War (1593–1606): Some Notes on the Ottoman Foreign Policy in 1591–1593," in *The Great Ottoman Turkish Civilization* 8, eds. Güler Eren et al. (Ankara: Yeni Türkiye, 2000), pp. 297–301.

personal obligation.⁶ Kemalpaşazade, one of the empire's intellectual pillars, stated, recalling a personal meeting with Süleyman I in late 1526, that the ruler firmly believed that "his success in this jihad [the victory at Mohács] … was due to the assistance of divine mercy and that the driving into slavery of the army of evil unbelievers and their beys and their unprecedented and unrepeatable defeat on the battlefield were thanks not to human efforts but to the power of the eternal."⁷ At the same time, having acquired control of the Near East and established a protectorate over the holy places of Islam, Süleyman and the Ottoman power elite (which retained the same principles even as its composition changed) increasingly defined the Ottoman state and dynasty as the true caliphate.⁸ In this role, the sultan as God's vicar was assigned the task of enforcing religious law and protecting Sunni Islam from the threats of Christianity and the Kizilbash 'sect' (that is, Safavid Iran).⁹

Since the turn of the 15th century, the Ottoman sultans had considered themselves to be descendants of the world conqueror Alexander the Great; by the second half of the 15th century, this conviction had become state ideology

---

6 See, for example, his report about the Battle of Zsarnó (Serbian Žrnov/Avala, Turkish Havale/Güzelcehisar near Belgrade), in which the troops stationed along the border crushed John Szapolyai's army, written in a highly solemn, religious tone in mid-May 1515, when he was still heir to the throne: İstanbul, Topkapı Sarayı Müzesi Arşivi, E. 5438. English translation: Pál Fodor, "Wolf on the Border: Yahyapaşaoğlu Bali Bey (?–1527): Expansion and Provincial Elite in the European Confines of the Ottoman Empire in the Early Sixteenth Century," in Şerefe: Studies in Honour of Prof. Géza Dávid on His Seventeenth Birthday, eds. Pál Fodor, Nándor E. Kovács, and Bence Péri (21st-Century Studies in Humanities) (Budapest: Research Centre for the Humanities HAS, 2019), pp. 77–79. See further the testimony of Chancellor Celalzade Mustafa, a chief architect of the imperial project of Süleyman: Kaya Şahin, Empire and Power in the Reign of Süleyman: Narrating the Sixteenth-Century Ottoman World (Cambridge Studies in Islamic Civilization) (New York: Cambridge University Press, 2013), passim.

7 Kemal Paşa-zâde, Tevarih-i Âl-i Osman. X. Defter, haz. Şefaettin Severcan (Türk Tarih Kurumu Yayınları) XVIII/13 (Ankara: Türk Tarih Kurumu, 1996), pp. 319–320.

8 This claim was articulated as early as 1524: Feridun M. Emecen, "Sultan Süleyman ve Hilafet: 1524," in Kanuni Sultan Süleyman ve Dönemi: Yeni Kaynaklar, Yeni Yaklaşımlar/Süleyman the Lawgiver and His Reign: New Sources, New Approaches, eds. M. Fatih Çalışır, Suraiya Faroqhi, and M. Şakir Yılmaz (İstanbul: İbn Haldun Üniversitesi, 2020), pp. 45–57. Cf. Hulusi Yavuz, "Sadrıâzam Lütfi Paşa ve Hilafet Meselesi," Marmara Üniversitesi İlâhiyat Fakültesi Dergisi 5–6 (1987–1988/1993), pp. 27–54.

9 Colin Imber, Ebu's-su'ud. The Islamic Legal Tradition (Edinburgh: Edinburgh University Press, 1997), pp. 73–76. On the important role of Sufism in the Ottoman conception of sovereignty and caliphate and in Ottoman political thought, see HüseyinYılmaz, Caliphate Redefined: The Mystical Turn in Ottoman Political Thought. (Princeton: Princeton University Press, 2018).

and continued as an important legitimizing and motivating force during Süleyman's early decades.[10]

But the Byzantine legacy, and the legal demands derived from this, would become even more significant. With the occupation of Constantinople in 1453, the sultans became the heirs of the Byzantine (Roman) emperors, and they claimed that, as 'Turkish-Roman padishahs' (*basileus kai autokrator/amiras Turkorhomaion*), they were the sole rulers of the world, just as the Roman and Eastern Roman emperors had once been.[11] *Gurbetname*, a work composed shortly after the Battle of Mohács, states that the only legitimate Roman emperors were the ones who ruled from Constantinople.[12] Thus Süleyman had from the first moment set his sights on Italy and on Charles V, who also desired to acquire the peninsula; his imagination (and that of İbrahim Pasha, who motivated him) was transfixed by the conquest of Italy and world dominance. This is why Süleyman would also consider it his obligation, once in control of the imperial city (*sedes imperii*) to restore the Roman Empire and establish the third Rome. And this is why Süleyman referred to himself as *sahib-kıran* (world conqueror) and, in line with the apocalyptic mood of the time, as *mahdi* (saviour) and *müceddid* (renewer), that is, ruler of the last age.[13]

A perfect synthesis of ideologies associating the Ottomans with Alexander the Great, the legacy of Byzantium and the apocalyptic expectations is Beharî's *Fethname-i Gaza-i Ungurus/Kıyametname*, an epic poem (*mesnevi*) composed in Hungary right after the Battle of Mohács in 1526. Beharî had himself fought in the battle, and his main message – possibly widely shared in the sultan's court – was that the clash between the Ottoman Empire and Hungary was a

---

10   Caroline Sawyer, "Sword of Conquest, Dove of the Soul: Political and Spritual Values in Aḥmadī's "Iskandarnāme," in *The Problematics of Power: Eastern and Western Representations of Alexander the Great*, eds. M. Bridges and J. Ch. Bürgel (Schweizer Asiatische Studien) 22 (Bern, Berlin, etc: Peter Lang, 1996), pp. 135–147; cf. Pál Fodor, "The Formation of Ottoman Turkish Identity," in *Identity and Culture in Ottoman Hungary*, ed. Pál Fodor and Pál Ács (Studien zur Sprache, Geschichte und Kultur der Türkvölker 24) (Berlin: Klaus Schwarz Verlag, 2017), pp. 26–27, 39.

11   Fodor, ibid, p. 38.

12   İsmail Hami Danişmend, "Gurbet-nâme-i Sultan Cem İbni Sultan Muhammed Hân Tâbe Serâhumâ ve Caale-i Cennete Mesvâhuma," *Fatih ve İstanbul* 2 (1954), pp. 211–270. On *Gurbetname* authored most likely by an Italian-speaking convert who was close to the court, see Tijana Krstić, *Contested Conversion to Islam: Narratives of Religious Change in the Early Modern Ottoman Empire* (Stanford, California: Stanford University Press, 2011), pp. 78–79, 84–88, 95, and 193.

13   Şahin, ibid, pp. 1–12, 53–57, 61–62, 67–68, and 188–191. For an overview of the titles of Ottoman rulers, see Ágoston, *The Last Muslim Conquest*, pp. 335–339. On the close relationship between the title and role of the mahdi and the caliph, see Yılmaz, *Caliphate Redefined*, 282–283, 285.

cosmic struggle between East and West, one of the decisive events preceding the Last Judgment. East is represented by Süleyman, the new Alexander, the Sun moving from the east westward to extend its radiance on the entire world and establish the reign of Islamic law (*şeriat*) and thus initiate the final period of history.[14] The ceremonial yataghan made for Süleyman by the court goldsmith Ahmed Tekelü after the Battle of Mohács conveyed the same message: on its blade a *simurg* (Süleyman) and a dragon (Louis II) fight, symbolising the struggle between Islam and Christianity, between light and darkness – and the *simurg* is the victor.[15]

But on the path to Italy, to Rome or to Vienna there stood a frustratingly stubborn country referred to as *Ungurus*, which for more than a century had not only resisted, but even struck back quite forcefully. For this reason, in the 15th century and the beginning of the 16th century, Hungary occupied a special place in Ottoman politics and imagination. It became an arch-enemy in the same way that the Ottoman Empire itself had become a sworn nemesis of Hungary in the early 15th century. The Ottomans saw the Hungarians as the organizers of the crusades, who were constantly striving to eliminate the empire and Islam in general. Neighbouring Hungary, as the only power capable of resistance, thus became a symbol of the whole Christian world and – after 1453 – assumed the role previously assigned to Byzantium. This is why Ottoman chronicles from the second half of the 15th century refer to the Hungarians as 'Byzantines' (*Beni Asfer*, the yellowish/red people), and this is why the Hungarians appear with such emphasis in Ottoman legends concerning Constantinople.[16] Hungary and Croatia were the first *kızıl elma*s, or golden apples, to be acquired in the Latin world. The *kızıl elma* is well known as a symbol of Ottoman world domination, but it also represented the great European cities (Buda, Vienna, Rome, etc.) that the Ottomans wished to occupy.[17]

---

14   Balázs Sudár, "A végítélet könyve. Oszmán elbeszélő forrás a mohácsi csatáról," *Történelmi Szemle* 52 (2010), no. 3, pp. 399, 403, 405, and 410; cf. Agâh Sırrı Levend, *Ġazavāt-nāmeler ve Mihaloğlu Ali Bey'in Ġazavāt-nāmesi* (Türk Tarih Kurmu Yayınlarından) XI/8 (Ankara: Türk Tarih Kurumu, 1956), pp. 45–46.
15   István Vígh, "Szülejmán jatagánja és a mohácsi csata," *Hadtörténelmi Közlemények* 117 (2004), no. 2, pp. 730–738.
16   Fodor, "The Formation of Ottoman Turkish Identity," p. 40.
17   Pál Fodor, "Ungarn und Wien in der osmanischen Eroberungsideologie (im Spiegel der Târîḫ-i Beç ḳrâlı, 17. Jahrhundert)," *Journal of Turkish Studies* 13 (1989), pp. 81–98; In Turkish: "Osmanlı Fetih İdeolojisinde Macaristan ve Viyana: Tarih-i Beç Kralı (17. yy.)", Pál Fodor, *Kızıl Elma* (İstanbul: Yeditepe, 2020), pp. 65–102.

3   Main Military Events in Hungary (1521–1566)

From what we have seen it is evident that an attack on Hungary in 1521 was part of a global strategy underpinned by the ideologies of conquest detailed above. The Ottoman leadership appears to have considered the Hungarian 'front' to have been much more important than all the others – in Iran, the Indian Ocean and the Mediterranean. Süleyman, it seems, judged his economic and military strength to have been sufficient for a successful attack on the Latin world that would turn the old dream of his dynasty into reality.

The breakthrough into the West did indeed begin in promising fashion.[18] The occupation of Buda did not succeed at first, but that of Belgrade did (1521). Despite unexpected domestic difficulties, by the end of 1524 the sultan had ordered a new Hungarian campaign to be arranged, and if İbrahim Pasha had not spent so long in Egypt, the Battle of Mohács (or of who knows where) might have taken place a year earlier. The triumph at Mohács (1526) dispelled any doubts, but also thoroughly misled the ruler and his entourage. It led him to believe that henceforth nothing and no one would be able to stand in his way, and this in turn led him ever more often to read the situation incorrectly. Even the failure of the two sieges of Vienna (1529, 1532) and the growing need for reinforcements on the other fronts would only temporarily distract him from returning to the implementation of his grand plan. It would take him many years (until the second half of the 1540s) to understand that he had made a miscalculation, and had overestimated his strength. After gaining victories in the 1530s on the Iranian front as well as on the Mediterranean front against Emperor Charles V, Süleyman again headed towards Central Europe, where he attempted to continue where he had left off in 1532. In 1541 he occupied Buda, and established the first Ottoman province in Hungary in order to bring his supply lines closer to Vienna. He had originally planned to incorporate the Szapolyai-run part of the country in full, and to capture the leaders of the pro-Turkish party, but after acquiring the Hungarian capital his intentions changed. He passed over control of Transtibiscan region ('Tiszántúl') and Transylvania (reduced to an Ottoman *sancak*), both of which were incidental to the main direction of the conquest, nominally to John Sigismund (in reality to his guardian, Friar George), while he left 'Temesköz' – the region around Temesvár (also as a *sancak*) – in the hands of Péter Petrovics. King Ferdinand would also express an interest in the eastern part of Hungary, believing as he

---

18   For a succinct summary of Süleyman's principal military campaigns, see also János B. Szabó, "The Ottoman Conquest in Hungary: Decisive Events (Belgrad 1521, Mohács 1526, Vienna 1529, Buda 1541)," in *The Battle for Central Europe,* ed. Fodor, pp. 261–275.

did that, as Hungary's legitimately elected ruler, everything pertaining to the Holy Crown was rightly his. As such, the future of these regions depended on the result of the inevitable clash between the two great powers – a clash that would also serve to decide the fate of the whole of Central Europe.[19]

The first act of the struggle took place in 1542. German imperial troops besieged Ottoman Pest, but would suffer a humiliating defeat.[20] In the following year, the sultan again marched against Vienna. Although he would make significant gains during his campaign (acquiring, among others, Pécs, Székesfehérvár and Esztergom, it was at this time that he effectively established Ottoman dominion in Hungary), he did not manage to get as far as his chief target of Vienna. This did not curb his enthusiasm, however, and in the second half of 1544 he set about preparing for a historic campaign greater than those before it. Yet, on 12 April 1545, he halted these protracted and very costly preparations, determining that the campaign be 'adjourned'. It is still not entirely clear why he brought this decision. It is possible he was ruffled by the enormous costs of his campaigns of the previous few years, both on land and at sea, by the tensions rife within the ruling family, by cooperation between Georgia and Iran, and by the peace treaty signed in September 1544 between Emperor Charles V and King Francis I of France. In summer 1547 Süleyman signed a treaty with the Habsburg brothers in which he insisted on including the fiction that all of Hungary belonged to him, though he accepted Ferdinand's *de facto* authority in the areas which were really under Habsburg control. Süleyman's 'great plan', namely the conquest of Hungary and the West, had already failed on the battlefield many years before, perhaps at the end of the 1520s or the beginning of the 1530s; now he was merely stamping this failure with his official seal. When he set off on his last Hungarian campaign in 1566, his only objective can have been damage limitation: with the occupation of Szigetvár and Gyula, he attempted to stabilize the Principality of Transylvania he had created in 1553–1556 and the Ottoman dominion in Hungary and Croatia.[21] His success was thus confined to territories far distant from Vienna or Rome, and fell well short of his original intentions. I am therefore of the opinion that both

---

19 On this recently, see Pál Fodor and Teréz Oborni, "Between Two Great Powers: The Hungarian Kingdom of the Szapolyai Family," in *A Forgotten Hungarian Royal Dynasty: The Szapolyais*, ed. Pál Fodor and Szabolcs Varga (Mohács 1526–2026: Reconstruction and Remembrance) (Budapest: Research Centre for the Humanities, 2020), pp. 127–161.

20 On the sieges of Buda and Pest in 1540–42, see *Buda oppugnata. Források Buda és Pest 1540–1542. évi ostromainak történetéhez,* ed. Péter Kasza (Mohács 1526–2026: Reconstruction and Remembrance) (Budapest: Research Centre for the Humanities), 2021.

21 On Süleyman's last campaign in a European context, see Fodor ed., *The Battle for Central Europe*.

the sultan's final victory and the fortress of Szigetvár itself, which would soon become one of the sacred centres of the Ottoman world, can be seen as symbols of the failure of Ottoman ambitions to attain universal rule.

4   Memory

The wars and conquests of Süleyman I in Hungary almost immediately became objects of Ottoman politics of memory. The sultan himself was intent on promoting it by several means. Having entered Buda on 11 September 1526, he issued an order on 15 September that "The armoury and other goods in the royal palace, and the extremely large cannon and the rest of guns and zarbzens, as well as the bronze figure on a column outside, in front of the palace, and his sons inside [the palace]" be carried to the ships and transported to Istanbul.[22] Kemalpaşazade gives a clear account of the background to the order:

> These guns ... had been left behind by Sultan Mehmed during the siege of Belgrade [in 1456]. ... That was when they got into the hands of the evil-doing unbelievers who took them to the seat of their king as mementos of the war and kept them since those old times in proof of their victory and warning symbol of that terrible war. And diverse nations would come to view them, who would herald it far and wide what they had seen and heard about them. ... The above mentioned statues ... transported to Istanbul, were set on stone columns and their sight served as a reminder ... And in this way, the works of those depraved people were turned against them, and their goal was thwarted, for the implements they had intended as mementos were put to the opposite purpose.[23]

---

22   Anton C. Schaendlinger, *Die Feldzugstagebücher des ersten und zweiten ungarischen Feldzugs Süleymans I* (Beihefte zur WZKM) 8 (Wien: Verband der wissenschaftlichen Gesellschaft Österreichs, 1978), pp. 86–87/54.

23   Kemal Paşa-zâde, *Tevarih-i Âl-i Osman, X. Defter*, pp. 316–317. On the bronze statues destroyed in 1536 following the execution of İbrahim Pasha, see Árpád Mikó, "Imago Historiae," in *Történelem – Kép. Szemelvények múlt és művészet kapcsolatából Magyarországon / Geschichte – Geschichtsbild. Die Beziehung von Vergangenheit und Kunst in Ungarn,* ed. Árpád Mikó and Katalin Sinkó (Veröffentlichungen der Ungarischen Nationalgalerie) 2000/3 (Budapest: Magyar Nemzeti Galéria, 2000), pp. 42–46; Gülru Necipoğlu, "The Aesthetics of Empire: Arts, Politics and Commerce in the Construction of Sultan Süleyman's Magnificence," in *The Battle for Central Europe,* ed. Fodor, pp. 127–131.

Süleyman's gain was thus not confined to victory on the battlefield. He also took previously-captured implements of war that were symbols of Hungarian self-confidence and set them up in public in his own capital to proclaim his victory to the world.

In the following years and decades, Süleyman extended his rule to about one third of Hungary. Djamis and mosques soon appeared in the conquered castles and towns – initially mostly in the form of converted churches, later as new buildings – as a sign that the area was now under the rule of Islam. There were 99 localities in Ottoman Hungary with at least one imperial mosque, and many had several. Most of these, understandably, bore the name of Süleyman, although they were often referred to by his royal title *Hünkar*.[24]

A Hungarian spy's report of 1544 reveals that in the previous year, after capturing the town and fortress of Székesfehérvár, Süleyman visited the tomb of King Louis II in the church where Hungarian kings were crowned and buried, and covered it with a cloth of silk. When this valuable fabric was stolen shortly afterwards,

> The sultan sent an inspector to survey Hungary in 1544. Which inspector, upon arriving in Fehérvár, examining everything faithfully and thoroughly in accordance with the emperor's order to determine whether the cloth of silk [pall?] which the emperor had placed on the tomb of King Louis when he first attended a prayer in that church was in place, did not find the cloth, and moreover, found the tombs of all the other kings ravaged, and reported this to the sultan. The sultan immediately despatched a messenger by whom he conveyed the strict order to find the person who had dared to remove the cloth from its place.[25]

The astonishing gesture may have been calculated to enhance Süleyman's nimbus in two different ways: it propagated his humaneness even among the enemy while at the same time letting the wide world know that he had gained victory in the battlefield of Mohács over a great king worthy of high esteem.[26] There is no knowing what impressions these acts made, but one of the greatest Hungarian chroniclers of the late 16th century certainly painted a surprisingly

---

24 Balázs Sudár, *Dzsámik és mecsetek a hódolt Magyarországon* (Monumenta Hungariae Historica, Elenchi) (Budapest: MTA Bölcsészettudományi Kutatóközpont, 2014), pp. 62, 78.
25 National Archives of Hungary, 1544.
26 He applied the same device in 1521 after the capture of Belgrade: he donated robe of honours to the surviving Hungarian defenders led before him: Schaendlinger, *Die Feldzugstagebücher*, pp. 48/20–21.

favourable picture of Süleyman. Ferenc Forgách (1535–1577) wrote about the sultan's decision to go to war personally in 1566, despite his old age, and about his death:

> When the chief administrators expressed a different opinion in the council, he allegedly declared that it was not they who had earned him the glory of respect and renown. 'That one is mine,' he said, 'and is a possession that will remain through my life and even after I have passed from this mortal life into immortal life; I beg the great Allah to seal it with the final outcome of my life devoted to his faith, with a fortunate victory on enemy soil in the land of the foe, under the walls of the city of Vienna.' These are notable words, worthy of such a great ruler ... I wish that the good Christians would not only hear them with their ears but would also take them to heart. In the event, he died at Szigetvár as a man whose place is among the great strategists of ancient times.[27]

Another ploy to propagate the memory of victories at Belgrade and Mohács, and over Hungary as a whole, was the timing of the occupation of Buda (1541). There can be no doubt, despite the lack of documentary evidence, that Süleyman deliberately sent his janissaries to take in the castle on – of all dates – the 29th of August. The Ottoman state administration was well aware of the Christian calendar and even used some of its elements. For example, taxation and waging wars had multiple connections to the days of St George and St Demetrius. They also knew that 29 August was the day of the beheading of St John the Baptist, a Christian saint for whom Muslims had great respect: his grave in Damascus has been preserved to this day in what is now the Omayyad great mosque, initially erected as a church dedicated to St John. After 1453 the right upper arm and skull of St John (and lots of other Christian relics and Byzantine imperial insignia) were moved to the treasury of Sultan Mehmed, who conquered Constantinople. It is recorded that the sultan sometimes lit a candle in front of them as a sign of his deep reverence. It is also true that in 1484 his son Bayezid II, out of political considerations, donated the saint's hand to the Knights of Rhodes, whom Süleyman, after defeating them, permitted to take the hand to Cyprus in 1523. When that island was taken by the Ottomans in 1571, the relic was returned to the treasury of the Porte, and it can still be viewed there. Well aware of – and having adopted several elements of – the

---

27   Ferenc Forgách, "Emlékirat Magyarország állapotáról Ferdinánd, János, Miksa királysága és II. János erdélyi fejedelemsége alatt," transl. István Borzsák, in *Humanista történetírók*, ed. Péter Kulcsár (Budapest: Szépirodalmi Kiadó, 1977), pp. 843–844.

Byzantine imperial traditions, the sultans must have known that the reliquary containing the finger of St John the Baptist was used during the coronation of the Byzantine emperors. During his preparations for taking and entering Buda, Süleyman would naturally have taken account of the corresponding days in the Christian calendar and been reminded of the triumphant days of 29 August in 1521 and 1526. He would then have seen the opportunity to deepen the humiliation of the infidel Hungarians by crowning his series of victories on the same day they had started twenty years before, the day of the beheading of the Christian saint.[28]

Many historical works in prose and verse were written to disseminate Süleyman's self-image and propaganda – often upon his encouragement or commission – at the same time as, or shortly after, the military events. These 'accounts of holy wars' or 'accounts of conquests' (*gazavatname*s, *fethname*s) often bearing the title *Süleymanname*, narrated the story of single campaigns (Belgrade, Rhodes, Moldavia, Esztergom, Szigetvár, etc.) or several successive campaigns.[29] (None covered all the sultan's campaigns). Outstanding among them are Bostan's *Süleymanname*,[30] Celalzade Mustafa's *Tabakatü'l-Memalik ve*

---

28   Pál Fodor, "Az oszmán-törökök szerencsenapja: augusztus 29. / Osmanlı Türklerinin Uğurlu Günü: 29 Ağustos," in *Félhold és kereszt. Konferencia és kiállítás a Fővárosi Szabó Ervin Könyvtárban 2001. október 17. / Hilal ve Haç. Başkent Szabó Ervin Kütüphanesinde Bilimsel Konferans ve Sergi* (Budapest: Fővárosi Szabó Ervin Könyvtár, 2002), pp. 23–30/129–137. Cf. Paolo Giovio, *Historia sui temporis* (1551, excerpt), Hungarian translation by Gábor Petneházi, in *Buda oppugnata*, ed. Kasza, p. 173: "this month (August) was, by some secret prophecy, the most fortunate for military enterprise of all for him..."; cf. ibid. p. 180.

29   For a still authoritative overview, see Abdülkadir Özcan, "Historiography in the Reign of Süleyman the Magnificent," in *The Ottoman Empire in the Reign of Süleyman the Magnificent*, Vol. II, ed. Tülay Duran (İstanbul: The Historical Research Foundation Istanbul Research Center, 1988), pp. 167–222; recently see Filiz Duman, "XVI. Yüzyılda Yazılan Fetihnâmeler ve Gazavâtnâmeler: Bibliyografya Çalışması," in *Filoloji Alanında Teori ve Araştırmalar II*, ed. Gülnaz Kurt (Ankara: Gece Kitaplığı, 2020), pp. 289–315. The fact that Suleiman's positive image was often echoed by foreign diplomats, travellers and observers (as we have seen in Forgách) suggests that the Ottoman elite successfully communicated this image to the outside world; on this, see Suraiya Faroqhi, *Another Mirror for Princes: The Public Image of the Ottoman Sultans and Its Reception* (Istanbul: The Isis Press, 2008), pp. 53–85, particularly pp. 63–67.

30   It is still unpublished; cf. Hüseyin Gazi Yurdaydın, "Bostan'ın Süleymannâmesi (Ferdî'ye Atfedilen Eser)," *Belleten* 19 (1955), no. 74, pp. 137–202; Rhoads Murphey, "Polemic, Panegyric, and Pragmatism in Ottoman Historical Writing Produced during the Early Years of Sultan Suleyman's Reign," in *Kanûnî Sultan Süleyman ve Dönemi*, eds. Çalışır et al., pp. 267–297.

Derecatü'l-Mesalik,[31] Celalzade Salih's *Tarih-i Sultan Süleyman/Süleymanname* and its continuation,[32] and Matrakçı Nasuh's compilation of several parts which is notable for its novel, topographic approach.[33] In mid-century, pursuing his cultural rivalry with Iran, Süleyman set up the office of şehnameci, whose incumbent was assigned the task of extolling the greatness of the Ottoman ruler in epic poems in Persian, modelled on Firdausi's *Shahnama*.[34] His last – Szigetvár – campaign was immortalized by especially many works in prose and verse including Feridun Ahmed Bey's and his follower Seyyid Lokman's chronicles – both of them richly embellished with miniatures.[35] The authors ('literati-historiographers') of the mentioned works deemed it their main task

---

31 Published with a thorough introduction by Petra Kappert, *Geschichte Sultan Süleymān Ḳānūnīs von 1520 bis 1557 oder Ṭabaḳāt ül-Memālik ve Derecāt ül-Mesālik von Celālzāde Muṣṭafā genannt Ḳoca Nişāncı* (Verzeichnis der orientalischen Handschriften in Deutschland) Supplementband 2 (Wiesbaden: Franz Steiner Verlag, 1981). Latin script transcription and facsimile: Funda Demirtaş, *Celâl-zâde Mustafa Çelebi, Tabakâtü'l-Memâlik ve Derecâtü'l-Mesâlik*, PhD dissertation (Kayseri: Erciyeş Üniversitesi 2009).

32 Seyid Ali Topal, *Celalzâde Salih Çelebi'nin Tarih-i Sultan Süleyman İsimli Eseri*, PhD dissertation (Ankara: Ankara Üniversitesi, 2008); Seyid Ali Topal, "Celalzade Salih Çelebi'nin Hayatı ve Eserleri," *Çukurova Üniversitesi İlahiyat Fakültesi Dergisi* 11 (2011), no. 1, pp. 109–128; Celalzâde Salih Çelebi, *Târîh-i Sefer-i Zafer-Rehber-i Alaman. [Kanunî Sultan Süleyman'ın Alaman Seferi (1532)]*, ed. Fatma Kaytaz (İstanbul: Çamlıca, 2016); cf. Fatma Kaytaz, "Târih-i Sefer-i Zafer-Rehber-i Alaman Adlı Eserinin Tanıtımı Dolayısıyla Celâlzâde Salih'in *Süleymannâme*'si Hakkında Bazı Yeni Çıkarımlar," *Osmanlı Araştırmaları* 43 (2014), pp. 145–163.

33 For some parts of it, see Naṣūḥü's Silāḥī (Maṭrāḳçī), *Beyān-ı Menāzil-i Sefer-i 'Irāḳeyn-i Sulṭān Süleymān Ḫān*, ed. Hüseyin Yurdaydın (Ankara: Türk Tarih Kurumu, 1976); Davut Erkan, *Matrâkçi Nasûh'un Süleymân-nâmesi (1520–1537)*, Yüksek Lisans Tezi (İstanbul: Marmara Üniversitesi, 2005); cf. Davut Erkan, "Matrakçı Nasûh'un Hayatı ve Eserleri Üzerine Notlar," *Osmanlı Araştırmaları* 37 (2011), pp. 181–197.

34 Christine Woodhead, "An Experiment in Official Historiography: The Post of Şehnāmeci in the Ottoman Empire, ca. 1555–1605," *Wiener Zeitschrift für die Kunde des Morgenlandes* 75 (1983), pp. 157–182.

35 Erika Hancz, "A Nagy Szulejmán szultán utolsó hadjáratát megörökítő önálló művek, az ún. Szigetvár-námék és szerzőik," in *A becsvágy igézetében. V. Nemzetközi Vámbéry Konferencia*, ed. Mihály Dobrovits (Dunaszerdahely: Lilium Aurum, 2008), pp. 95–123; Nicolas Vatin, *Ferîdûn Bey, Les plaisants secrets de la campagne de Szigetvár. Édition, traduction et commentaire des folios 1 à 147 du Nüzhetü-l-esrâri-l-ahbâr der sefer-i Sigetvâr (ms. H 1339 de la Bibliothèque de Musée de Topkapı Sarayı)* (Neue Beihefte zur Wiener Zeitschrift für die Kunde des Morgenlandes) 7 (Wien: Lit, 2010); *Nüzhet-i Esrârü'l-Ahyâr der Ahbâr-ı Sefer-i Sigetvar. Sultan Süleyman'ın Son Seferi*, eds. H. Ahmet Arslantürk and Günhan Börekçi, proof-reading Abdülkadir Özcan (Zeytinburnu Belediyesi Kültür Yayınları) 26 (İstanbul: Zeytinburnu Belediyesi, 2012); István Nyitrai, *Seyyed Lokman Kiegészítése és a perzsa történeti eposz az Oszmán Birodalomban*, PhD dissertation (Budapest: ELTE University, 2005).

to extol Süleyman and his dynasty and to justify his conquests and his leading role within the Islamic world. Like Kemalpaşazade cited earlier, nearly all conveyed the message that the sultan had a divine mission to fight the infidels and heretics and that his successes were guaranteed by the Almighty's support. Celalzade, for instance, evaluated the victory at Mohács in the following words:

> To none of the former sultans or old khans was such great conquest granted; never since the beginning of the world had two most glorious padishahs been pitted against one another with armies like the sea. This event belongs to the wonders and rarities of the world; praise be to Allah that it was granted to the fortunate padishah, the refuge of religion. It was clearly the gift of boundless divine mercy and the infinite goodness of God that in two or three hours more than two hundred thousand abominable souls fell into the dust but only some one hundred and fifty people of the Islamic nation were martyred. Undoubtedly, the army, the refuge of Islam, was assisted by hosts of invisible saints and holy souls. God-fearing and saintly holy warriors and some righteous pious souls say that his holiness the Prophet ... with the holy souls of all his noble companions ... took part in this brilliant war of faith.[36]

The memory of Süleyman's presence and military activity in Hungary remained vivid after his death. The places he stayed during battles and sieges, and places he passed by or where his tent was put up were particularly enveloped in reverence. Most of them were high points or hills, and even in the 16th century were already regarded by Ottoman Turks as sacred sites, usually named *Hünkâr tepesi* (Sultan's, or Emperor's Hill). Probably the first was a hill in Belgrade, dedicated in memory of the siege and conquest of 1521. Writing about Sultan Mehmed III's entry to Belgrade in 1596, a contemporary Ottoman chronicler recalled:

> The imperial tent has since long ago been set up on the sacred place known by the name Sultan's Hill (*Hünkâr depesi*). Of [the ruler's] predecessors,

---

36 Kappert, *Geschichte Sultan Süleymān Ḳānūnīs*, 150a. Demirtaş, *Celâl-zâde Mustafa Çelebi*, 204–205. Neither did the later chroniclers Mehmed Zaim (1578) and İbrahim Peçevi (prior to 1645) forget to emphasize the uniqueness of the victory at Mohács: Ayşe Nur Sır, *Mehmed Za'îm, Câmi'ü't-tevârîh*, Vol. I, PhD dissertation, (İstanbul: Marmara Üniversitesi, 2007), pp. 355–356; *Tarih-i Peçevî*, Vol. I, (İstanbul: Matbaa-i Amire, 1281/1864), pp. 97–98. For the date of Peçevi's death (1645), see İbrahim Pazan, "Copies of Peçevi History Manuscripts and Determination of Peçevi İbrahim Efendi's Death Date," in *Ankara International Congress of Scientific Research–VIII, June 9–11 2023 / Ankara, Türkiye*, ed. Abdulmecit Güldaş (Ankara: IKSAD Yayınevi, 2023), pp. 8–14.

his highness the late and deceased Sultan Süleyman khan of a fortunate life, the conqueror of the well-protected Belgrade – may he rest in peace! – had a station there. During campaigns to Hungary, the imperial tents are pitched up on that pleasant and fortunate site.[37]

The sacrality of the place was also strengthened by the fact that in 1566 the imperial tent complex of Süleyman, who had died under Szigetvár and was being transported to Istanbul, was erected there, and a funeral ceremony was held in front of it with the participation of the new ruler, Selim II.[38] The great conqueror's example was – as Ottoman chroniclers record – followed by subsequent rulers (such as Mehmed III) and also by the grand viziers and commanders-in-chief (*serdar, serasker*) appointed to lead military campaigns. For instance, Grand Vizier Sinan Pasha, as he marched towards Vienna in 1594, Saturcı Mehmed Pasha, determined to take Nagyvárad in 1598, and the military leaders of the late 17th century-campaigns had their tents pitched on Sultan's Hill at Belgrade so that the great ruler's spirit should promote their cause.[39] Evliya Çelebi claims that east of the castle of Esztergom, vineyards and orchards that had been planted in place of the perished archiepiscopal town extended at one edge to the "hill of Süleyman khan" (*Süleymân Hân depesi*); from this it is evident that one of the sites associated with the great ruler from the time of the successful siege of 1543 was also marked by the name of "Sultan's Hill".[40] By the same token, Evliya Çelebi describes a "castle of Süleyman khan/shah's tent" (*kal'a-i çârbâğ-ı cihân, ya'nî otağ-ı Süleymân Hân*, and *kal'a-i otağ-ı Süleymân Şah*) in the vicinity of Schwechat near Vienna: this was allegedly the site of the sultan's tent complex for the (failed) siege of Vienna in 1529. The traveller adds that after the retreat it fell into the hands of the Germans, who – with an

---

37   *Topçular Kâtibi 'Abdülkâdir (Kadrî) Efendi Tarihi (Metin ve Tahlîl)*, Vol. I, yayına haz. Ziya Yılmazer (Türk Tarih Kurumu Yayınları) III/21 (Ankara: *Türk Tarih Kurumu*, 2003), p. 135.

38   Selânikî Mustafa Efendi, *Tarih-i Selânikî*, Vol I, haz. Mehmet İpşirli (İstanbul Üniversitesi Edebiyat Fakültesi Yayınları) 3371 (İstanbul: İstanbul Üniversitesi Edebiyat Fakültesi, 1989), pp. 49–51.

39   Kâtib Çelebi, *Fezleke [Osmanlı Tarihi (1000–1065/1591–1655)]*, Vol. I, neşre haz. Zeynep Aycibin (İstanbul: Çamlıca, 2016), pp. 41, 142; Lajos Fekete, "Hódoltságkori oszmanli-török helyneveink," *Századok* 57–58 (1923–1924), p. 616. Maps surviving from the time of the late-17th-century wars suggest that this elevation was somewhere in the foreground of the mountain and fortress of Zsarnó/Žrnov (see supra note 7) south of Belgrade. Cf. Željko Škalamera and Marko Popović, "Novi podaci sa plana Beograda iz 1683," in *Godišnjak Grada Beograda*, Knj. 23 (Beograd: Muzej Grada Beograda, 1976), pp. 33–58.

40   Evliyâ Çelebi b. Derviş Mehemmed Zıllî, *Evliyâ Çelebi Seyahatnâmesi, VI. Kitap. Topkapı Sarayı Kütüphanesi Revan 1457 Numaralı Yazmanın Transkripsiyonu–Dizini*, haz. Seyit Ali Kahraman and Yücel Dağlı (İstanbul: Yapı Kredi Yayınları, 2002), p. 171; Fekete, ibid, p. 616.

intention to create their own memorial place – erected a complex in the shape of the quondam camp, but with durable materials.[41] (This building was the Neugebäude, built by Emperor Maximilian II and abandoned by the mid-18th century and had nothing to do with Süleyman's tent complex. The Ottoman legend about it probably dates from the first half of the 17th century. In the second half of the century, the Ottomans had already clearly identified it as a sacred site associated with Süleyman).[42]

Of the numerous Sultan's/Emperor's Hills in Hungary, the mound on the battlefield of Mohács was by far the most important, as a memorial was built on it in the 17th century. It reminded passing Muslims that, as later tradition held, the sultan used to pray or direct the military manoeuvres from there (neither can be proven). The main source on the creation of the shrine of commemoration is İbrahim Peçevi:

> As the fortunate padishah of Islam arrived at the tall hill called Sultan's Hill on the plain of Mohács, he dismounted his horse, ascended the hill and sat on a throne. I, a poor feeble-minded person, traversed the area with youthful zeal under the pretext of hunting for goshawks before the one thousandth year [19 October 1591–7 October 1592] and God the Most High wot, I climbed that hill twice or three times because I thought it would bring me luck, for a padishah fighting for the faith prayed to heaven from there. It was indeed very high and hard to climb. Not long ago, when the late standard-bearer Hasan Pasha was the governor-general of Buda,[43] he had a simple kiosk-like edifice (*köşk şekli*) framed up and a well dug next to it.[44]

European travellers, diplomats and soldiers who happened to pass by also made mention of the memorial and resting place. Their accounts reveal that it was erected on a small elevation between the road leading from Eszék (Croatian Osijek, Ottoman Ösek) to Buda and the flood plain of the Danube,

---

41   Evliyâ Çelebi b. Derviş Mehemmed Zıllî, *Evliyâ Çelebi Seyahatnâmesi, 7. Kitap. Topkapı Sarayı Kütüphanesi Bağdat 308 Numaralı Yazmanın Transkripsiyonu–Dizini*, haz. Yücel Dağlı, Seyit Ali Kahraman, and Robert Dankoff (İstanbul: Yapı Kredi Yayınları, 2003), pp. 89–92.
42   On this, see Karl Teply, *Türkische Sagen und Legenden um die Kaiserstadt Wien* (Wien, Köln, Graz: Hermann Böhlaus Nachf., 1980), pp. 96–108.
43   He refers to Acem Hasan Pasha, who was indeed a standard bearer (*mir-i alem*) before he was transferred to the post of *beylerbeyi* of Buda from February 1630 to early October 1631: Antal Gévay, *A' budai pasák* (Bécsben: 1841), pp. 29–30.
44   *Tarih-i Peçevî*, Vol. I, p. 89.

on which – as excavations reveal – there had originally been a Roman watchtower, and which was later given the name *Šatorišće/Sátorhely*, then *Törökdomb/Türkenhügel/Turski brig* (Turkish Hill) by the South Slav, Hungarian and German inhabitants of the region. The kiosk (some contemporary observers took it for a mosque) was built of wood. There was a well nearby, and the whole memorial place was surrounded by a moat. Evliya Çelebi claims that "forty thousand" Muslim victims of the battle of Mohács were buried there and "hundreds of pious Muslims have seen and testified that on Friday night, as well as on the night of *kadr, berat* and *mirac*[45] often a light shone over these forty thousand martyrs."[46] These numbers and the light phenomenon must belong to the imaginative Evliya Çelebi's customary exaggerations. But he must be right that the place also functioned as a place of pilgrimage, because there is evidence that Bosnian Muslims visited the place to pray right up to the early 20th century.[47]

It was not at Mohács, however, but in the vicinity of Szigetvár that the most important memorial to Süleyman was established. A memorial garden was laid out on what is now the Turbék vineyard, where the sultan's tent complex was set up in 1566 and his body, after he died at early dawn on 7 September, lay underground for 42 days. Between 1574 and 1579, the site developed into a complex *lieu de mémoire* comprising a memorial türbe and, subsequently, a mosque, dervish lodge, barracks, palisade, and other buildings. What had been a military camp thus became one of the most popular destinations of pilgrimage and shrines of worship in the Ottoman world. Gradually a Muslim settlement of two 'neighbourhoods' (*mahalle*) grew up around it. The belief that the sultan's internal organs had been buried there in a golden vessel upon the orders of the grand vizier began to spread in the late 16th century and greatly increased interest in the memorial place.[48] Although the shrine fell into ruin

---

45   These nights (27 Ramazan, 14–15 Şaban and 26 Receb) are considered sacred in the Islamic religion.
46   *Evliyâ Çelebi Seyahatnâmesi, VI. Kitap,* pp. 112–113.
47   The site of *Törökdomb* (Turkish Hill) has been localized in recent years by a research team led by Norbert Pap and Pál Fodor; cf. Norbert Pap, Pál Fodor, Máté Kitanics, Tamás Morva, Gábor Szalai, and Péter Gyenizse, "A mohácsi Törökdomb," *Történelmi Szemle* 60 (2018), no. 2, pp. 325–345. The mound, which played an important role in the commemorating festivities in 1926, has mostly perished by now.
48   To this day it is a moot question whether or not Süleyman's internal organs were removed and separately interred. For example, Feridun M. Emecen, "Kānûnî Sultan Süleyman'ın Macaristan'daki Türbesine Dair Görüşler," in *Ekrem Hakkı Ayverdi. 30. Yıl Hâtıra Kitabı,* haz. Özcan Ergiydiren, İ. Aydın Yüksel, and Kemal Y. Aren (İstanbul Fetih Cemiyeti) 114 (İstanbul: İstanbul Fetih Cemiyeti, 2014), pp. 79–82; as well as Norbert Pap and Máté Kitanics, "Nagy Szulejmán szultán szigetvári türbéjének kutatása (1903–2016),"

after the Ottoman Turks were expelled, local people remembered it for a long time and only in the 20th century did it finally sink into oblivion. Remains of the memorial have been coming to light one after the other in recent years through a coordinated programme of research and excavation.[49]

Süleyman's 'Türbetown' had a combination of functions.[50] First of all it was a 'memorial' (*makam türbesi*) marking the place of the great sultan's death. It was a 'place of worship' or 'shrine' (*meşhed*) which was believed to hide the internal organs of Sultan Süleyman, a 'warrior of the faith' (*gazi*)[51] and 'martyr' (şehid). It was a 'place of pilgrimage' (*ziyaretgah*) which almost from the very first moment attracted pilgrims who subscribed to the Ottomans' fervently practised – if controversial – cult of saints from all over the Ottoman world (including chief military commanders) to seek the intercession of the sultan 'living in Paradise' as they sought success for their plans in this world or reassurance about their life in the world to come, or just hoped for a miracle.[52]

---

in *Szulejmán szultán Szigetváron. A szigetvári kutatások 2013–2016 között*, eds. Norbert Pap and Pál Fodor (Pécs: Pannon Castrum Kft., 2017), pp. 25–47; Norbert Pap and Máté Kitanic, "A sejk álma – Turbék oszmán zarándokváros története," in *Szulejmán szultán zarándokvárosa*, ed. Norbert Pap (Szigetvár-könyvek) 2 (Budapest, Pécs: Research Centre for the Humanities, University of Pécs, 2020), pp. 28–30, think it should not be flatly discarded (while the use of the gold vessel must be a legend). By contrast, it is denied by Nicolas Vatin, "On Süleyman the Magnificent's Death and Burials," in *The Battle for Central Europe*, ed. Fodor, pp. 427–443.

49   On the history of the discovery and exploration of the memorial site, see Norbert Pap et al., "Finding the Tomb of Suleiman the Magnificent in Szigetvár, Hungary: Historical, Geophysical and Archeological Investigations," *Die Erde* 146 (2015), no. 4, pp. 289–303; Pál Fodor and Norbert Pap, "In Search of the Tomb of Sultan Süleyman in Szigetvár," *Acta Orientalia Academiae Scientiarum Hungaricae* 71 (2018), no. 2, pp. 179– 195; Norbert Pap, "The Pilgrimage Town (*Türbe Kasabası*) of Sultan Süleyman at Szigetvár," in *The Battle for Central Europe*, ed. Fodor, pp. 539–552.

50   The following passage is taken slightly modified from my recent book: Pál Fodor, *16. ve 17. Yüzyıl Osmanlı Kaynaklarında Sultan Süleyman'ın Sigetvar'daki Türbe Kasabası* (İstanbul: Yeditepe, 2021), pp. 45–46.

51   In 1591 a Western traveller saw a bow and arrow displayed in Süleyman's türbe in Istanbul, reminding one of Süleyman's being a *gazi*: Gülru Necipoğlu, *The Age of Sinan: Architectural Culture in the Ottoman Empire* (London: Reaktion Books, 2005), p. 220.

52   On visiting the tombs of saints and martyrs and their role in the legitimation of conquests, see Gilles Veinstein, "Le rôle des tombes sacrées dans la conquête ottomane," in Gilles Veinstein, *Autoportrait du sultan ottoman en conquérant* (İstanbul: The Isis Press, 2010), pp. 269–284; Balázs Sudár, "The Ottomans and the Mental Conquest of Hungary," in *Identity and Culture in Ottoman Hungary*, eds. Ács and Fodor, pp. 55–67. An attempt to compile the register of sacred places of Ottoman Hungary: Mehmet Emin Yılmaz, "Osmanlı Macaristan'ında Tekkeler, Türbeler, Şehitlikler ve Mezar Taşları," *Vakıflar Dergisi* 52 (2019), pp. 157–204. Cf. further Gülru Necipoğlu, "Dynastic Imprints on the Cityscape: The Collective Message of Imperial Funerary Mosque Complexes in Istanbul," in

Finally, it was an 'ideological program' that symbolized and legitimated the imperialist politics of the Ottoman Empire, particularly the domination of Hungary and further territorial conquests. Out of all the memorial places associated with Süleyman, this expressed most powerfully the notion widely held among the Ottoman public that the fate of Süleyman and that of the Ottoman rule in Hungary were inextricably intertwined.

Accordingly, the memorials to Süleyman were only imprints of a view of the conqueror of Hungary that gained steadily wider acceptance after it evolved in the decades following his death: he personified the ideal ruler, and his long reign was the ideal period of the empire. The general crisis and gloomy atmosphere that came to a head in the 1580s greatly contributed to the process that turned a sultan who was fairly unpopular in the last decade of his life into a ruler's etalon and transformed his political, military and ideological programmes into an ideal model. The discontent caused by his sedentary way of life and erroneous personal and political decisions, and the ensuing rebellions, gradually fell into oblivion, as did the true reason for undertaking the Szigetvár campaign at an advanced age and in frail health: he was forced into it to combat the discontent. His martyr's death improved his image, but it took a long time for his reign to acquire an unequivocally positive evaluation. There are unmistakable signs from the 1590s of his being looked back on with nostalgia.[53]

Süleyman's influence upon subsequent generations can be sensed in several regards. Firstly, some rulers built their entire political identity on emulating him. In particular, Ahmed I (1603–1617), although he lacked victories on the battlefield, took each of his steps in line with his intention to revive the figure of an active, belligerent, just, law-abiding and law-enforcing ruler (the 'new Süleyman') intent on realizing global rule and the victory of the Sunna.[54] And Süleyman can

---

Cimitières et traditions funéraires dans le monde islamique / İslam Dünyasında Mezarlıklar ve Defin Gelenekleri, Vol. II, ed. Jean-Louis Bacqué-Grammont and Aksel Tibet (Türk Tarih Kurumu Yayınları) XXVI/6ª (Ankara: Türk Tarih Kurumu, 1996), pp. 23–36.

53 Halil İnalcık, "Suleiman the Lawgiver and Ottoman Law," *Archivum Ottomanicum* 1 (1969), pp. 105–106; Cemal Kafadar, "The Myth of the Golden Age: Ottoman Historical Consciousness in the Post-Süleymânic Era," in *Süleymân the Second and His Time*, ed. Halil İnalcık and Cemal Kafadar (İstanbul: The Isis Press, 1993), pp. 37–48; Feridun M. Emecen, "XVI. Asırda Hukuk: Kanuni'nin Kanunâmeleri ve Bir Mitin Doğuşu," in Feridun M. Emecen, *Osmanlı Klasik Çağında Hanedan, Devlet ve Toplum* (İstanbul: Kapı, 2018), pp. 346–349.

54 Nebahat Avcıoğlu, "Ahmed I and the Allegories of Tyranny in the Frontispiece to George Sandys's *Relation of a Journey Anno. Dom.1610*," *Muqarnas* 18 (2001), pp. 218–223; Günhan Börekçi, *Factions and Favorites at the Courts of Sultan Ahmed I (r. 1603–17) and His Immediate Predecessors*, PhD dissertation (Columbus: The Ohio State University, 2010), pp. 80–147, 234–260; Günhan Börekçi, "The Memory of Szigetvár and Sultan Süleyman in Ottoman/Turkish Culture," in *The Battle for Central Europe*, ed. Fodor, pp. 533–535.

also be demonstrated to have been the role model for Osman II (1618–1622), Murad IV (1623–1648) and Mehmed IV (1648–1687).[55] The erection of the memorial (kiosk) of Mohács during the reign of Murad IV, who led the most successful campaigns since Süleyman, could hardly be a coincidence.

Secondly, Süleyman, in addition to his influence on specific persons, had a weighty political legacy that loomed large in the mind of later generations. Süleyman's policy towards Hungary and Transylvania left a project to his successors that they were neither able nor willing to relinquish, and one that they would again and again attempt to turn into reality. The essence of this project was the occupation of Vienna and the defeat of the Habsburgs. It was with this same objective that the Ottoman troops embarked on the campaigns of 1593–1594, 1663–1664 and 1683.[56] It was during the Long War (1593–1606) that various groups of Ottoman statesmen began to use the example of Süleyman to encourage the sultans to go to war and to justify their conquests. They even attributed the use of certain tactical elements (such as the need to winter in the battlefield) to him.[57] An integral part of this conception was the idea that Transylvania was "Sultan Süleyman's invention",[58] and that the Porte alone was entitled to decide on the principality's fate, status (union with Hungary, for

---

[55] On Osman II, see Baki Tezcan, *The Second Ottoman Empire: Political and Social Transformation in the Early Modern World* (Cambridge: Cambridge University Press, 2010), pp. 79–190; on Murad IV: Caroline Finkel, *Osman's Dream: The Story of the Ottoman Empire 1300–1923* (New York: Basic Books, 2006), pp. 215–222; on Mehmed IV: Marc David Baer, *Honored by the Glory of Islam: Conversion and Conquest in Ottoman Europe* (Oxford: Oxford University Press, 2008).

[56] *Die Schlacht von Mogersdorf/St. Gotthard und der Friede von Eisenburg/Vasvár 1664. Rahmenbedingungen, Akteure, Auswirkungen und Rezeption eines europäischen Ereignisses,* ed. Karin Sperl, Martin Scheutz, and Arno Strohmeyer (Eisenstadt: Amt der Burgenländishen Landesregierung, 2016); *A szentgotthárdi csata és a vasvári béke. Oszmán terjeszkedés – európai összefogás / La bataille de Saint-Gotthard et la paix de Vasvár. Expansion ottomane – coopération européenne,* ed. Ferenc Tóth and Balázs Zágorhidi Czigány (Budapest: Research Centre for the Humanities HAS, 2017); Kahraman Şakul, *II. Viyana Kuşatması: Yedi Başlı Ejderin Fendi* (İstanbul: Timaş, 2021).

[57] Sándor László Tóth, "A szulejmáni 'ideálkép' formálódása a 15 éves háború időszakában," *Acta Universitatis Szegediensis Acta Historica* 92 (1991), pp. 51–57.

[58] The original Hungarian wording: *"mert Erdély szultán Szuliman találmánya";* Grand Mufti Esad Efendi's words to the Transylvanian envoys, 19 January 1619: Tamás Borsos, *Vásárhelytől a Fényes Portáig. Emlékiratok, levelek,* ed., introduction and notes by László Kocziány (Bukarest: Kriterion, 1972), pp. 394–395; cf. Katalin Péter, "Bethlen Gábor magyar királysága, az országegyesítés és a Porta," *Századok* 117 (1983), no. 5, p. 1045; Sándor Papp, "Bethlen Gábor, a Magyar Királyság és a Porta (1619–1629)," *Századok* 145 (2011), no. 4, pp. 944–949.

example) and scope for manoeuvre. This also led to serious wars (1658, 1660–1664, 1670s and 1680s, and 1691–1693).⁵⁹

While continuing conquest was undoubtedly the central element of Süleyman's legacy, certain peace-seeking strata of military society identified an alternative strand in Süleyman's politics that embraced negotiation and respect for frontiers. They claimed that Süleyman's example consisted just as much in the peace treaties he concluded with the Habsburgs and the fixing of borders as in territorial expansion. To unilaterally breach treaties and violate borders or launch wars without substantial reason was to fail to meet the criteria of a just war, and hence would be disapproved by Süleyman.⁶⁰ Such arguments were put forth, for example, in opposition to the campaigns of 1663–1664 and 1683, but – possibly not by chance – they were always overcome by the pro-war circles who also cited Süleyman. (As a kind of symbolic response to them, Kara Mustafa Pasha rode to the memorial *türbe* of Süleyman at Szigetvár to ask the great predecessor's spiritual assistance and blessing for the major venture against Vienna).⁶¹ Moreover, this alternative line of argument seems to have surfaced mostly after great military defeats and appears to have had to do with scapegoating rather than with comprehensive ideological considerations. In the everyday life of Ottoman Hungary, for example, the number one imperative was the transgression of the borders and their ceaseless extension at the expense of the "unbelievers". And it was due to this mentality and necessity that Ottoman soldiers had doubled or tripled the Ottoman dominion in Hungary by the last third of the 17th century⁶² – while the two great powers officially were at peace throughout much of the century.

Fortunately, scholars researching the Ottoman polity's attitude to Süleyman's legacy do not have to depend solely on the words of the high elite. There is a group of 17th-century sources which reveal the ideas of the janissary corps

---

59   János B. Szabó, "II. Rákóczi György 1658. évi török háborúja," *Hadtörténelmi Közlemények* 114 (2001), no. 2–3, pp. 231–278; Özgür Kolçak, "A Transylvanian Ruler in the Talons of the 'Hawks': György Rákóczi II and Köprülü Mehmed Pasha," in *Turkey and Romania: A History of Partnership and Collaboration in the Balkans*, eds. Florentina Nitu et al. (International Balkan Annual Conference [IBAC] Book Series) 4 (İstanbul: Türk Dünyası Belediyeler Birliği, 2016), pp. 341–359.

60   On all this, see the excellent study by Özgür Kolçak, "Paths of Glory: The Rise of the Köprülüs and the Execution of Şamizade Mehmed Efendi (1663)," in "Buyurdum ki...." – *The Whole World of Ottomanica and Beyond: Studies in Honour of Claudia Römer*, eds. Hülya Çelik, Yavuz Köse and Gisela Procházka-Eisl (The Ottoman Empire and Its Heritage, Politics, Society and Economy) 78 (Leiden, Boston: Brill, 2023), pp. 451–476.

61   Fodor, *Türbe Kasabası*, p. 46.

62   As demonstrated by Klára Hegyi, *A füleki szandzsák* (Budapest: Research Centre for the Humanities, 2019).

about conquests and about Süleyman I in a somewhat naïve, almost folkloristic form. These texts include *Hikâyet-i Kızıl Elma* (1673),[63] *Tarih-i Beç Kralı ve Feth-i Sultan Süleyman Han Gazi* (second half of the 17th century)[64] and *Merhum Sultan Süleyman Hazretlerinün Nakşivan Seferinde Vaki Olan Ayin ve Kaidelerin Beyan Eder* (arguably 17th century).[65] Towards the end of his life Süleyman was obviously unpopular among the janissaries,[66] but 100–120 years after his death – as these texts testify – he was elevated to 'celestial' heights by the same section of military society.

In the legends, he is the ruler who – in his seventh campaign – defeats the 'seven kings' supporting the king of Vienna (the seven German electors, that is, and through them the Holy Roman Empire), the hostile Hungarians siding with the Viennese king (and even the other Hungarians, themselves Ottoman vassals), the Ragusans, and later the Kizilbash shah. He is the sultan who takes part in the battle in disguise, who is ready to sacrifice his life for the victory of Islam ("this day will be the day of our Kerbela" – he utters before the decisive clash),[67] who performs functions of the commander-in-chief and 'high priest' during the fighting (praying for victory), who asks the opinion of the janissaries before every military manoeuvre (defying the disapproval of many who deem it a 'Turkish custom' [*Türk edeb*]),[68] amply rewards them after the battle, and tries to satisfy all their requests (such as their need for water supply). He is the ruler whose orders still regulate the life of the janissaries, his 'curses' (*lanet*) and 'letters of curses' (*lanetname*) falling on all those who violate the 'laws' (*kanunlar*), 'customs and rules' (*ayin ve kaideler*) he laid down.

These texts appear to reflect and sum up the central elements of Süleyman's self-perception in the form of folk tales: the importance of fighting the Christians and the Kizilbash, that is, the two kinds of heresy; the desire to capture the *kızıl elma*s; and the warrior ruler who lays down laws and rules in response to the needs of his subjects to make their lives easier and ensure the smooth running of the state. The tendency to sacralize the ruler is also

---

63 Çelenklioğlu, "Hikâyet-i Kızılalma," *Türk Kültürü* 16 (1978), no. 185, pp. 309–310.
64 İstanbul, Topkapı Sarayi Müzesi Kütüphanesi (= TSMK), Revan 1319, 151b–167a, and Revan 1320, 91a–102a. For an analysis of this source, see Fodor, "Ungarn und Wien in der osmanischen Eroberungsideologie."
65 TSMK Revan 1320, 88b–90b and the copy in the private library of the late İ. Hakkı Uzunçarşılı, 127a–130a.
66 Pál Fodor, "Sultan, Imperial Council, Grand Vizier: Changes in the Ottoman Ruling Elite and the Formation of the Grand Vizieral *telhis*," *Acta Orientalia Academiae Scientiarum Hungaricae* 47 (1994), no. 1–2, pp. 80–81.
67 TSMK Revan 1319, 151b; Revan 1320, 91a.
68 TSMK Revan 1320, 89a.

apparent, and already had a long past: in 1588, Seyyid Lokman wrote that at the end of his life Süleyman had "attained the status of spiritual pole", that is, he had become the supreme saint.[69] It is well known that Süleyman's modern Turkish epithet 'Law-giver' or 'Law-abiding' (*Kanunî*) cannot be documented earlier than the beginning of the 18th century.[70] Even though the texts in question do not use this sobriquet, the message that the great predecessor had given laws to the janissaries, had lived and abided by them himself and had personally supervised their observation, thereby creating an eternally valid order, must have greatly contributed to the birth of Süleyman's *Kanunî* epithet – which might therefore have occurred in the second half of the 17th century. This process was obviously fostered by the general nostalgia for Süleyman and his age. İbrahim Peçevi's words suggest that the desperate subjects looked to the late great sultan, as well as God, in seeking remedies for their ills: "But we rather request favour from God. And we hope for help and grace from the spiritual influence of the late and deceased Sultan Süleyman khan gazi, the greatest warrior of the faith."[71]

The important conclusion for our purpose is that in the comprehension of the janissaries and the common folk, as in the ideological constructions of the upper political and intellectual crust, the figure of Süleyman was inseparable from Hungary right up to the great defeats at the end of the century and the peace of Karlowitz (1699), which swept all related ideas away. For adherence to Süleyman's legacy eventually culminated in total failure – the loss of Hungary.

---

69 Christine Woodhead, "Perspectives on Süleyman," in *Süleyman the Magnificent and His Age: The Ottoman Empire in the Early Modern World,* eds. Metin Kunt and Christine Woodhead (London, New York: Longman, 1995), p. 176; in the original: *"derece-i aktaba vusul bulduğı meşhurdur."* [Seyyid Lokman,] *Kiyâfetü'l-İnsâniyye fî Şemâili'l'Osmâniyye* (Istanbul: The Historical Research Foundation Istanbul Research Center, 1987), 48b. In Sufism, the "pole" or "axis" (*kutb*, plur. *aktab*) is the head of the community of saints, the perfect man, the spiritual leader of the world. According to other authors, Süleyman had already reached this position in the first half of his life; Matrakçı Nasuh, for example, repeatedly refers to him as "the lord of the world and the axis of the rotation of time (*hudavend-i cihan ve kutb-i daire-i zaman)*"; see Erkan, *Matrâkçi Nasûh'un Süleymân-nâmesi,* pp. 112, 148; cf. pp. 30, 192.

70 Kafadar, "The Myth of the Golden Age", p. 41, note 7.

71 *"Ve illa bundan ziyade cenab-i bariniün inayetin rica ederüz. Ve gazilerüin serfirazı merhum ve mağfurun-leh Sultan Süleyman han gazi ruhaniyetinden imdad ve himmet umaruz." Tarih-i Peçevî,* Vol. I, p. 8.

Bibliography

Ágoston, Gábor. "The Ottomans: From Frontier Principality to Empire." In *The Practice of Strategy: From Alexander the Great to the Present*, eds. John Andreas Olsen and Colin S. Gray, 105–131. Oxford: Oxford University Press, 2011.

Ágoston, Gábor. "Information, Ideology, and Limits of Imperial Policy: Ottoman Grand Strategy in the Context of Ottoman–Habsburg Rivalry." In *The Early Modern Ottomans: Remapping the Empire*, eds. Virginia H. Aksan and Daniel Goffman, 75–103. Cambridge: Cambridge University Press, 2007.

Ágoston, Gábor. "'The Most Powerful' Empire: Ottoman Flexibility and Military Might." In *Empires and Superpowers: Their Rise and Fall*, eds. Georg Zimmar and David Hicks, 127–171. Washington, DC: Society for the Preservation of the Greek Heritage, 2005.

Ágoston, Gábor. *The Last Muslim Conquest: The Ottoman Empire and Its Wars in Europe*. Princeton, Oxford: Princeton University Press, 2021.

Arslantürk, H. Ahmet and Günhan Börekçi eds. *Nüzhet-i Esrârü'l-Ahyâr der Ahbâr-i Sefer-i Sigetvar. Sultan Süleyman'ın Son Seferi*. Proof-reading Abdülkadir Özcan. Zeytinburnu Belediyesi Kültür Yayınları 26. İstanbul: Zeytinburnu Belediyesi, 2012.

Avcıoğlu, Nebahat. "Ahmed I and the Allegories of Tyranny in the Frontispiece to George Sandys's *Relation of a Journey Anno. Dom.1610.*" *Muqarnas* 18 (2001): 203–226.

B. Szabó, János. "The Ottoman Conquest in Hungary: Decisive Events (Belgrad 1521, Mohács 1526, Vienna 1529, Buda 1541)." In *The Battle for Central Europe: The Siege of Szigetvár and the Death of Süleyman the Magnificent and Nicholas Zrínyi (1566)*, ed. Pál Fodor, 263–275. Budapest, Leiden, and Boston: Research Centre for the Humanities, Hungarian Academy of Sciences (=HAS) and Brill, 2019.

B. Szabó, János. "II. Rákóczi György 1658. évi török háborúja." *Hadtörténelmi Közlemények* 114 (2001): 231–278.

Baer, Marc David. *Honored by the Glory of Islam: Conversion and Conquest in Ottoman Europe*. Oxford: Oxford University Press, 2008.

Borsos, Tamás. *Vásárhelytől a Fényes Portáig. Emlékiratok, levelek*, ed., introduction and notes by Kocziány László. Bukarest: Kriterion, 1972.

Börekçi, Günhan. "The Memory of Szigetvár and Sultan Süleyman in Ottoman/Turkish Culture." In *The Battle for Central Europe: The Siege of Szigetvár and the Death of Süleyman the Magnificent and Nicholas Zrínyi (1566)*, ed. Pál Fodor, 523–538. Budapest, Leiden, and Boston: Research Centre for the Humanities HAS and Brill, 2019.

Börekçi, Günhan. *Factions and Favorites at the Courts of Sultan Ahmed I (r. 1603–17) and His Immediate Predecessors*, PhD dissertation. Columbus: The Ohio State University, 2010.

Celalzâde Salih Çelebi. *Târîh-i Sefer-i Zafer-Rehber-i Alaman. [Kanunî Sultan Süleyman'ın Alaman Seferi (1532)]*. Neşre hazırlayan Fatma Kaytaz. İstanbul: Çamlıca, 2016.

Çelenklioğlu, *"Hikâyet-i Kızılalma." Türk Kültürü* 16 (1978): 53–54.
Danişmend, İsmail Hami. "Gurbet-nâme-i Sultan Cem İbni Sultan Muhammed Hân Tâbe Serâhumâ ve Caale-i Cennete Mesvâhuma." *Fatih ve İstanbul* 2 (1954): 211–270.
Demirtaş, Funda. *Celâl-zâde Mustafa Çelebi, Tabakâtü'l-Memâlik ve Derecâtü'l-Mesâlik*, PhD dissertation. Kayseri: Erciyeş Üniversitesi, 2009.
Duman, Filiz. "XVI. Yüzyılda Yazılan Fetihnâmeler ve Gazavâtnâmeler: Bibliyografya Çalışması." In *Filoloji Alanında Teori ve Araştırmalar 11*, ed. Gülnaz Kurt, 289–315. Ankara: Gece Kitaplığı, 2020.
Emecen, Feridun M. "Sultan Süleyman ve Hilafet: 1524." In *Kanuni Sultan Süleyman ve Dönemi: Yeni Kaynaklar, Yeni Yaklaşımlar/Süleyman the Lawgiver and His Reign: New Sources, New Approaches*, eds. M. Fatih Çalışır, Suraiya Faroqhi, and M. Şakir Yılmaz, 45–58. İstanbul: İbn Haldun Üniversitesi, 2020.
Emecen, Feridun M. "XVI. Asırda Hukuk: Kanuni'nin Kanunâmeleri ve Bir Mitin Doğuşu." In Feridun M. Emecen, *Osmanlı Klasik Çağında Hanedan, Devlet ve Toplum*, 319–336. İstanbul: Kapı, 2018.
Emecen, Feridun M. "Kānûni Sultan Süleyman'ın Macaristan'daki Türbesine Dair Görüşler." In *Ekrem Hakkı Ayverdi. 30. Yıl Hâtıra Kitabı*, haz. Özcan Ergiydiren, İ. Aydın Yüksel, and Kemal Y. Aren, 71–86. İstanbul Fetih Cemiyeti 114. İstanbul: İstanbul Fetih Cemiyeti, 2014.
Erkan, Davut. "Matrakçı Nasûh'un Hayatı ve Eserleri Üzerine Notlar." *Osmanlı Araştırmaları* 37 (2011): 180–197.
Erkan, Davut. *Matrâkçi Nasûh'un Süleymân-nâmesi (1520–1537)*, Yüksek Lisans Tezi. İstanbul: Marmara Üniversitesi, 2005.
Evliyâ Çelebi b. Derviş Mehemmed Zıllî, *Evliyâ Çelebi Seyahatnâmesi, 7. Kitap. Topkapı Sarayı Kütüphanesi Bağdat 308 Numaralı Yazmanın Transkripsiyonu–Dizini*, haz. Yücel Dağlı, Seyit Ali Kahraman, and Robert Dankoff. İstanbul: Yapı Kredi Yayınları, 2003.
Evliyâ Çelebi b. Derviş Mehemmed Zıllî. *Evliyâ Çelebi Seyahatnâmesi, VI. Kitap. Topkapı Sarayı Kütüphanesi Revan 1457 Numaralı Yazmanın Transkripsiyonu–Dizini*, haz. Seyit Ali Kahraman and Yücel Dağlı. İstanbul: Yapı Kredi Yayınları, 2002.
Faroqhi, Suraiya. *Another Mirror for Princes: The Public Image of the Ottoman Sultans and Its Reception*. Istanbul: The İsis Press, 2008.
Fekete, Lajos. "Hódoltságkori oszmanli-török helyneveink." *Századok* 57–58 (1923–1924): 614–626.
Finkel, Caroline. *Osman's Dream: The Story of the Ottoman Empire 1300–1923*. New York: Basic Books, 2006.
Fodor, Pál. *16. ve 17. Yüzyıl Osmanlı Kaynaklarında Sultan Süleyman'ın Sigetvar'daki Türbe Kasabası*. İstanbul: Yeditepe, 2021.
Fodor, Pál. "The Military Organization and Army of the Ottoman Empire (1500–1530)." In *On the Verge of a New Era: The Armies of Europe at the Time of the Battle of Mohács*,

eds. János B. Szabó and Pál Fodor, 91–115. Mohács 1526–2026: Reconstruction and Remembrance. Budapest: Research Centre for the Humanities HAS, 2021.

Fodor, Pál. *Kızıl Elma*. İstanbul: Yeditepe, 2020.

Fodor, Pál. "Wolf on the Border: Yahyapaşaoğlu Bali Bey (?–1527): Expansion and Provincial Elite in the European Confines of the Ottoman Empire in the Early Sixteenth Century." In Şerefe: Studies in Honour of Prof. Géza Dávid on His Seventeenth Birthday, eds. Pál Fodor, Nándor E. Kovács, and Bence Péri, 57–87. 21st-Century Studies in Humanities. Budapest: Research Centre for the Humanities HAS, 2019.

Fodor, Pál. *The Unbearable Weight of Empire: The Ottomans in Central Europe – A Failed Attempt at Universal Monarchy (1390–1566)*, 2nd ed. Budapest: Research Centre for the Humanities HAS, 2016.

Fodor, Pál. "The Formation of Ottoman Turkish Identity." In *Identity and Culture in Ottoman Hungary*, eds. Pál Fodor and Pál Ács, 19–54. Studien zur Sprache, Geschichte und Kultur der Türkvölker 24. Berlin: Klaus Schwarz Verlag, 2017.

Fodor, Pál. "Az oszmán-törökök szerencsenapja: augusztus 29. / Osmanlı Türklerinin Uğurlu Günü: 29 Ağustos." In *Félhold és kereszt. Konferencia és kiállítás a Fővárosi Szabó Ervin Könyvtárban 2001. október 17. / Hilal ve Haç. Başkent Szabó Ervin Kütüphanesinde Bilimsel Konferans ve Sergi*, 23–30/129–137. Budapest: Fővárosi Szabó Ervin Könyvtár, 2002.

Fodor, Pál. "Prelude to the Long War (1593–1606): Some Notes on the Ottoman Foreign Policy in 1591–1593." In *The Great Ottoman Turkish Civilization* 8, eds. Güler Eren et al. 297–301. Ankara: Yeni Türkiye, 2000.

Fodor, Pál. "Sultan, Imperial Council, Grand Vizier: Changes in the Ottoman Ruling Elite and the Formation of the Grand Vizieral *telhis*." *Acta Orientalia Academiae Scientiarum Hungaricae* 47 (1994): 67–85.

Fodor, Pál. "Ottoman Policy towards Hungary, 1520–1541." *Acta Orientalia Academiae Scientiarum Hungaricae* 45 (1991): 271–345.

Fodor, Pál. "Ungarn und Wien in der osmanischen Eroberungsideologie (im Spiegel der Târîḫ-i Beç ḳrâlı, 17. Jahrhundert)." *Journal of Turkish Studies* 13 (1989): 81–98.

Fodor, Pál and Teréz Oborni. "Between Two Great Powers: The Hungarian Kingdom of the Szapolyai Family." In *A Forgotten Hungarian Royal Dynasty: The Szapolyais*, eds. Pál Fodor and Szabolcs Varga, 127–161. Mohács 1526–2026: Reconstruction and Remembrance. Budapest: Research Centre for the Humanities, 2020.

Fodor, Pál and Norbert Pap. "In Search of the Tomb of Sultan Süleyman in Szigetvár." *Acta Orientalia Academiae Scientiarum Hungaricae* 71 (2018): 179–195.

Forgách, Ferenc. "Emlékirat Magyarország állapotáról Ferdinánd, János, Miksa királysága és II. János erdélyi fejedelemsége alatt." Transl. István Borzsák. In *Humanista történetírók*, ed. Péter Kulcsár, 567–1039. Budapest: Szépirodalmi Kiadó, 1977.

Gévay, Antal. *A' budai pasák*. Bécsben: 1841.

Hancz, Erika. "A Nagy Szulejmán szultán utolsó hadjáratát megörökítő önálló művek, az ún. Szigetvár-námék és szerzőik." In *A becsvágy igézetében. V. Nemzetközi Vámbéry Konferencia,* ed. Mihály Dobrovits, 95–123. Dunaszerdahely: Lilium Aurum, 2008.

Hegyi, Klára. *A füleki szandzsák.* Budapest: Research Centre for the Humanities, 2019.

Imber, Colin. *Ebu's-su'ud. The Islamic Legal Tradition.* Edinburgh: Edinburgh University Press, 1997.

İnalcık, Halil. "Suleiman the Lawgiver and Ottoman Law." *Archivum Ottomanicum* 1 (1969): 105–138.

Kafadar, Cemal. "The Myth of the Golden Age: Ottoman Historical Consciousness in the Post-Süleymânic Era." In *Süleymân the Second and His Time,* eds. Halil İnalcık and Cemal Kafadar, 37–48. İstanbul: The Isis Press, 1993.

Kappert, Petra. *Geschichte Sultan Süleymān Ḳānūnīs von 1520 bis 1557 oder Ṭabaḳāt ül-Memālik ve Derecāt ül-Mesālik von Celālzāde Muṣṭafā genannt Ḳoca Nişāncı.* Verzeichnis der orientalischen Handschriften in Deutschland Supplementband 2. Wiesbaden: Franz Steiner Verlag, 1981.

Kasza, Péter ed. *Buda oppugnata. Források Buda és Pest 1540–1542. évi ostromainak történetéhez.* Mohács 1526–2026: Reconstruction and Remembrance. Budapest: Research Centre for the Humanities, 2021.

Kâtib Çelebi. *Fezleke [Osmanlı Tarihi (1000–1065/1591–1655)],* Vol. I, neşre haz. Zeynep Aycibin. İstanbul: Çamlıca, 2016.

Kaytaz, Fatma. "Târih-i Sefer-i Zafer-Rehber-i Alaman Adlı Eserinin Tanıtımı Dolayısıyla Celâlzâde Salih'in *Süleymannâme*'si Hakkında Bazı Yeni Çıkarımlar," *Osmanlı Araştırmaları* 43 (2014): 145–164.

Kemal Paşa-zâde. *Tevarih-i Âl-i Osman. X. Defter,* haz. Şefaettin Severcan. Türk Tarih Kurumu Yayınları XVIII/13. Ankara: Türk Tarih Kurumu, 1996.

Kolçak, Özgür. "Paths of Glory: The Rise of the Köprülüs and the Execution of Şamizade Mehmed Efendi (1663)." In *"Buyurdum ki...." – The Whole World of Ottomanica and Beyond: Studies in Honour of Claudia Römer,* eds. Hülya Çelik, Yavuz Köse and Gisela Procházka-Eisl, 451–476. The Ottoman Empire and Its Heritage, Politics, Society and Economy 78. Leiden, Boston: Brill, 2023.

Kolçak, Özgür. "A Transylvanian Ruler in the Talons of the 'Hawks': György Rákóczi II and Köprülü Mehmed Pasha." In *Turkey and Romania: A History of Partnership and Collaboration in the Balkans,* eds. Florentina Nitu et al., 341–359. International Balkan Annual Conference (IBAC) Book Series 4. İstanbul: Türk Dünyası Belediyeler Birliği, 2016.

Krstić, Tijana. *Contested Conversion to Islam: Narratives of Religious Change in the Early Modern Ottoman Empire.* Stanford, California: Stanford University Press, 2011.

Levend, Agâh Sırrı. *Ġazavāt-nāmeler ve Mihaloğlu Ali Bey'in Ġazavāt-nāmesi.* Türk Tarih Kurmu Yayınlarından XI/8. Ankara: Türk Tarih Kurumu, 1956.

Mikó, Árpád. "Imago Historiae." In *Történelem – Kép. Szemelvények múlt és művészet kapcsolatából Magyarországon / Geschichte – Geschichtsbild. Die Beziehung von Vergangenheit and Kunst in Ungarn,* eds. Árpád Mikó and Katalin Sinkó, 34–47. Veröffentlichungen der Ungarischen Nationalgalerie 2000/3. Budapest: Magyar Nemzeti Galéria, 2000.

Murphey, Rhoads. "Polemic, Panegyric, and Pragmatism in Ottoman Historical Writing Produced during the Early Years of Sultan Suleyman's Reign." In *Kanuni Sultan Süleyman ve Dönemi: Yeni Kaynaklar, Yeni Yaklaşımlar/Süleyman the Lawgiver and His Reign: New Sources, New Approaches,* eds. M. Fatih Çalışır, Suraiya Faroqhi, and M. Şakir Yılmaz, 269–303. İstanbul: İbn Haldun Üniversitesi, 2020.

Naṣūḥü's Silāḥī (Maṭrāḳçī). *Beyān-ı Menāzil-i Sefer-i 'Irāḳeyn-i Sulṭān Süleymān Ḫān,* neşr. Hüseyin Yurdaydın. Ankara: Türk Tarih Kurumu, 1976.

Necipoğlu, Gülru. "The Aesthetics of Empire: Arts, Politics and Commerce in the Construction of Sultan Süleyman's Magnificence." In *The Battle for Central Europe: The Siege of Szigetvár and the Death of Süleyman the Magnificent and Nicholas Zrínyi (1566),* ed. Pál Fodor, 115–159. Budapest, Leiden, and Boston: Research Centre for the Humanities HAS and Brill, 2019.

Necipoğlu, Gülru. *The Age of Sinan: Architectural Culture in the Ottoman Empire.* London: Reaktion Books, 2005.

Necipoğlu, Gülru. "Dynastic Imprints on the Cityscape: The Collective Message of Imperial Funerary Mosque Complexes in Istanbul." In *Cimitières et traditions funéraires dans le monde islamique / İslam Dünyasında Mezarlıklar ve Defin Gelenekleri,* Vol. II, eds. Jean-Louis Bacqué-Grammont and Aksel Tibet, 23–36. Türk Tarih Kurumu Yayınları XXVI/6ª. Ankara: Atatürk Kültür, Dil ve Tarih Kurumu, 1996.

Nyitrai, István. *Seyyed Lokman Kiegészítése és a perzsa történeti eposz az Oszmán Birodalomban,* PhD dissertation. Budapest: ELTE University, 2005.

Özcan, Abdülkadir. "Historiography in the Reign of Süleyman the Magnificent." In *The Ottoman Empire in the Reign of Süleyman the Magnificent,* Vol. II, ed. Tülay Duran, 167–222. İstanbul: The Historical Research Foundation Istanbul Research Center, 1988.

Özvar, Erol. "Transformation of the Ottoman Empire into a Military-Fiscal State: Reconsidering the Financing of War from a Global Perspective." In *The Battle for Central Europe: The Siege of Szigetvár and the Death of Süleyman the Magnificent and Nicholas Zrínyi (1566),* ed. Pál Fodor, 21–63. Budapest, Leiden, and Boston: Research Centre for the Humanities HAS and Brill, 2019.

Pap, Norbert. "The Pilgrimage Town (*Türbe Kasabası*) of Sultan Süleyman at Szigetvár." In *The Battle for Central Europe: The Siege of Szigetvár and the Death of Süleyman the Magnificent and Nicholas Zrínyi (1566),* ed. Pál Fodor, 539–552. Budapest, Leiden, and Boston: Research Centre for the Humanities HAS and Brill, 2019.

Pap, Norbert and Máté Kitanics. "A sejk álma – Turbék oszmán zarándokváros története." In *Szulejmán szultán zarándokvárosa*, ed. Norbert Pap, 9–84. Szigetvár-könyvek 2. Budapest, Pécs: Research Centre for the Humanities, University of Pécs, 2020.

Pap, Norbert, Pál Fodor, Máté Kitanics, Tamás Morva, Gábor Szalai, and Péter Gyenizse. "A mohácsi Törökdomb." *Történelmi Szemle* 60 (2018): 325–345.

Pap, Norbert and Máté Kitanics. "Nagy Szulejmán szultán szigetvári türbéjének kutatása (1903–2016)." In *Szulejmán szultán Szigetváron. A szigetvári kutatások 2013–2016 között*, eds. Norbert Pap and Pál Fodor, 25–47. Pécs: Pannon Castrum Kft., 2017.

Pap, Norbert, Máté Kitanics, Péter Gyenizse, Erika Hancz, Zita Bognár, Tamás Tóth, and Zoltán Hámori. "Finding the Tomb of Suleiman the Magnificent in Szigetvár, Hungary: Historical, Geophysical and Archeological Investigations." *Die Erde* 146 (2015): 289–303.

Papp, Sándor. "Bethlen Gábor, a Magyar Királyság és a Porta (1619–1629)." *Századok* 145 (2011): 915–963.

Pazan, İbrahim, "Copies of Peçevi History Manuscripts and Determination of Peçevi İbrahim Efendi's Death Date." In *Ankara International Congress of Scientific Research–VIII, June 9–11 2023 / Ankara, Türkiye*, ed. Abdulmecit Güldaş, 8–14. Ankara: IKSAD Yayınevi, 2023.

Péter, Katalin. "Bethlen Gábor magyar királysága, az országegyesítés és a Porta." *Századok* 117 (1983): 1028–1060.

Şahin, Kaya. *Empire and Power in the Reign of Süleyman: Narrating the Sixteenth-Century Ottoman World*. Cambridge Studies in Islamic Civilization. New York: Cambridge University Press, 2013.

Şakul, Kahraman. *II. Viyana Kuşatması: Yedi Başlı Ejderin Fendi*. İstanbul: Timaş, 2021.

Sawyer, Caroline. "Sword of Conquest, Dove of the Soul: Political and Spritual Values in Aḥmadī's *Iskandarnāme*." In *The Problematics of Power: Eastern and Western Representations of Alexander the Great*, eds. M. Bridges and J. Ch. Bürgel, 135–148. Schweizer Asiatische Studien 22. Bern, Berlin, etc: Peter Lang, 1996.

Schaendlinger, Anton C. *Die Feldzugstagebücher des ersten und zweiten ungarischen Feldzugs Süleymans I*. Beihefte zur WZKM 8. Wien: Verband der wissenschaftlichen Gesellschaft Österreichs, 1978.

Selânikî Mustafa Efendi. *Tarih-i Selânikî*. Vol I, haz. Mehmet İpşirli. İstanbul Üniversitesi Edebiyat Fakültesi Yayınları 3371. İstanbul: İstanbul Üniversitesi Edebiyat Fakültesi, 1989.

Seyyid Lokman. *Kiyâfetü'l-İnsâniyye fî Şemâili'l'Osmâniyye*. Istanbul: The Historical Research Foundation Istanbul Research Center, 1987.

Sır, Ayşe Nur. *Mehmed Zaʿîm, Câmiʿüʾt-tevârîh*, Vol. I, PhD dissertation. İstanbul: Marmara Üniversitesi, 2007.

Škalamera, Željko and Marko Popović. "Novi podaci sa plana Beograda iz 1683." In *Godišnjak Grada Beograda,* Knj. 23. Beograd: Muzej Grada Beograda, 1976.

Sperl, Karin, Martin Scheutz, and Arno Strohmeyer eds. *Die Schlacht von Mogersdorf/St. Gotthard und der Friede von Eisenburg/Vasvár 1664. Rahmenbedingungen, Akteure, Auswirkungen und Rezeption eines europäischen Ereignisses.* Eisenstadt: Amt der Burgenländishen Landesregierung, 2016.

Sudár, Balázs. *Dzsámik és mecsetek a hódolt Magyarországon.* Monumenta Hungariae Historica, Elenchi. Budapest: MTA Bölcsészettudományi Kutatóközpont, 2014.

Sudár, Balázs. "The Ottomans and the Mental Conquest of Hungary." In *Identity and Culture in Ottoman Hungary,* eds. Pál Ács and Pál Fodor, 55–68. Berlin, Boston: Klaus Schwarz Verlag, 2020.

Sudár, Balázs. "A végítélet könyve. Oszmán elbeszélő forrás a mohácsi csatáról." *Történelmi Szemle* 52 (2010): 389–419.

Tarih-i Peçevî. Vol. I. İstanbul: Matbaa-i Amire, 1281/1864.

Teply, Karl. *Türkische Sagen und Legenden um die Kaiserstadt Wien.* Wien, Köln, Graz: Hermann Böhlaus Nachf., 1980.

Tezcan, Baki. *The Second Ottoman Empire: Political and Social Transformation in the Early Modern World.* Cambridge: Cambridge University Press, 2010.

Topal, Seyid Ali. "Celalzade Salih Çelebi'nin Hayatı ve Eserleri." *Cukurova Üniversitesi İlahiyat Fakültesi Dergisi* 11 (2011): 109–128.

Topal, Seyid Ali. *Celalzâde Salih Çelebi'nin Tarih-i Sultan Süleyman İsimli Eseri,* PhD dissertation. Ankara: Ankara University, 2008.

Topçular Kâtibi 'Abdülkādir (Kadrî) Efendi Tarihi (Metin ve Tahlîl). Vol. 1, yayına haz. Ziya Yılmazer. Türk Tarih Kurumu Yayınları III/21. Ankara: Türk Tarih Kurumu, 2003.

Tóth, Ferenc and Balázs Zágorhidi Czigány eds. *A szentgotthárdi csata és a vasvári béke. Oszmán terjeszkedés – európai összefogás / La bataille de Saint-Gotthard et la paix de Vasvár. Expansion ottomane – coopération européenne.* Budapest: Research Centre for the Humanities HAS, 2017.

Tóth, Sándor László. "A szulejmáni 'ideálkép' formálódása a 15 éves háború időszakában." *Acta Universitatis Szegediensis Acta Historica* 92 (1991): 51–58.

Vatin, Nicolas. "On Süleyman the Magnificent's Death and Burials." In *The Battle for Central Europe: The Siege of Szigetvár and the Death of Süleyman the Magnificent and Nicholas Zrínyi (1566),* ed. Pál Fodor, 427–443. Budapest, Leiden, and Boston: Research Centre for the Humanities HAS and Brill, 2019.

Vatin, Nicolas. *Ferîdûn Bey, Les plaisants secrets de la campagne de Szigetvár. Édition, traduction et commentaire des folios 1 à 147 du* Nüzhetü-l-esrâri-l-ahbâr der sefer-i Sigetvâr *(ms. H 1339 de la Bibliothèque de Musée de Topkapı Sarayı).* Neue Beihefte zur Wiener Zeitschrift für die Kunde des Morgenlandes 7. Wien: Lit, 2010.

Veinstein, Gilles. "Le rôle des tombes sacrées dans la conquête ottomane." In Gilles Veinstein, *Autoportrait du sultan ottoman en conquérant*, 269–284. İstanbul: The Isis Press, 2010.

Vígh, István. "Szülejmán jatagánja és a mohácsi csata." *Hadtörténelmi Közlemények* 117 (2004): 730–738.

Woodhead, Christine. "Perspectives on Süleyman." In *Süleyman the Magnificent and His Age: The Ottoman Empire in the Early Modern World*, eds. Metin Kunt and Christine Woodhead, 164–190. London, New York: Longman, 1995.

Woodhead, Christine. "An Experiment in Official Historiography: The Post of Şehnāmeci in the Ottoman Empire, ca. 1555–1605." *Wiener Zeitschrift für die Kunde des Morgenlandes* 75 (1983): 157–182.

Yavuz, Hulusi. "Sadrıâzam Lütfi Paşa ve Hilafet Meselesi." *Marmara Üniversitesi İlâhiyat Fakültesi Dergisi* 5–6 (1987–1988/1993): 27–54.

Yılmaz, Hüseyin. *Caliphate Redefined: The Mystical Turn in Ottoman Political Thought*. Princeton: Princeton University Press, 2018.

Yılmaz, Mehmet Emin. "Osmanlı Macaristan'ında Tekkeler, Türbeler, Şehitlikler ve Mezar Taşları." *Vakıflar Dergisi* 52 (2019): 157–204.

Yurdaydın, Hüseyin Gazi. "Bostan'ın Süleymannâmesi (Ferdî'ye Atfedilen Eser)." *Belleten* 19 (1955): 137–202.

CHAPTER 2

The Main Scenes

Norbert Pap, Máté Kitanics and Péter Gyenizse

1 Introduction

The environment, and especially the drainage pattern, plays a very important part in understanding the Ottoman campaign of 1526 and the Battle of Mohács. In the following chapter, we will examine the main places mentioned in the sources, and the sites of the events, identify them and clarify their role. The armies marched along the Danube and its floodplains, and the configuration of flood-free and marshy lands, and above all the defensive aspects, were of fundamental significance in their camping. Transport and warships also used the river. In choosing the battlefields, the Hungarian command considered the need for a flat flood-free land suitable for cavalry maneuvers and the hydrographic features that would allow the much smaller Hungarian army to avoid being encircled. It can be said that without knowledge and reconstruction of the elements of the geographical environment of the period, the military actions described cannot be comprehended.

2 The Danube

The main watercourse in the area is the Western or Mohács branch of the Danube. The presence of the watercourse, its water level and its floods have determined the life of Mohács and its surroundings for centuries (Figures 2.1 and 2.2). After the Ottoman wars, the region was the scene of a long-lasting land dispute in the 18th century, the documents of which reveal the geography of the region. The document below, dated 1726, describes the demarcation of the estates of the bishop of Pécs and Prince Eugene of Savoy (in Hungarian usage Jenő Savoyai) between the western and eastern branches of the Danube on the Mohács Island:

> All these having been faithfully and humbly delivered to us, we have graciously decreed and determined that the boundaries of the island territory belonging to the bishop of Pécs, as the landlord of the town of

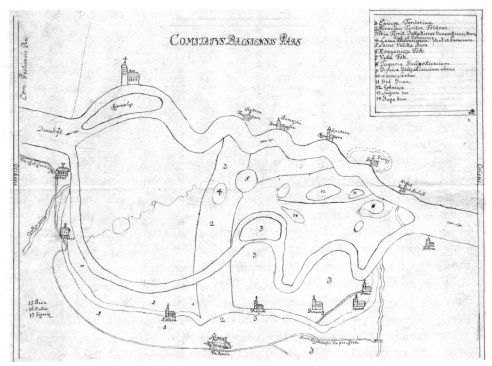

FIGURE 2.1   Mohács Island on a map (1720–1725). The wider Baracska branch to the east (top of the figure), the narrower Mohács branch (i.e. the Little Danube) to the west (bottom of the figure).
SOURCE: SÁMUEL MIKOVINY, COMITATUS BACSIENSIS PARS. MTA TK MO. NO 1.

Mohács and the estate of Kölked, be separated from the island territory belonging to Prince Eugene, as the landlord of the estates bordering on Dályok, Izsép, Márok and Darázs with the Little Danube on this side, based on the use of land as attested and shown until 1722; be completely separated, mutually distinguished (from both sides), by the Vidafok rivulet flowing from the Little Danube into Lake Velika, or Lake Siroka Bara, and from there by another rivulet called Konyenicza, which flows into the greater part of the Danube, the boundary being drawn by the estuaries and lakes just mentioned, so that half of them are attached to the one, and the predetermined parts are attached to the other half, with a proportional right of fishing in the same places, and in this way, the rivulet known as Vidafok, Lake Siroka Bara, and the other rivulet, (called)

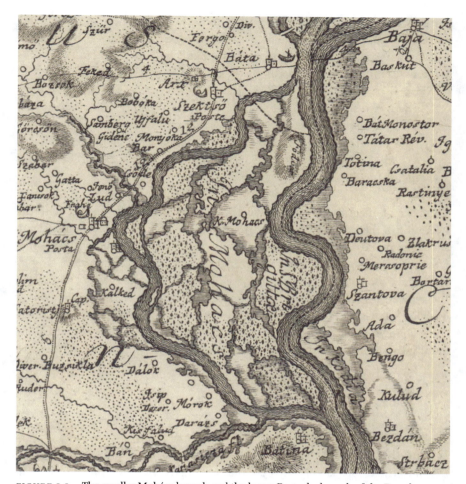

FIGURE 2.2   The smaller Mohács branch and the larger Baracska branch of the Danube on Ignácz Müller's map of 1769.
SOURCE: MAPPA GEOGRAPHICA NOVISSIMA REGNI HUNGARIAE DIVISI IN SUOS C... [B IX A 513]. INSTITUTE AND MUSEUM OF MILITARY HISTORY.

Konyenicza on the same island shall be considered to be distinguishing boundary of said parts.[1]

The width of the Mohács Danube, still called the Little Danube in the source, is today the narrowest at the ferry crossing, between the town and the island

---

1 *Királyi Könyvek* [Royal Books], 35.156/b. p. 421. See https://archives.hungaricana.hu/hu/libriregii/.

ferry, at almost 250 metres, while at the mouth of the Csele Stream and before the Cigány-zátony [Cigány Shoal] it is the widest, at around 700–800 meters.[2] But it was not always so. In the past, the main branch of the river was the Baracska Danube, which flows along the eastern side of Mohács Island.

> The eyewitness of the fights, István Brodarics also mentions this in his account of the battle. The Danube splits into two channels just above Báta the larger channel splits the Trans-Hungarian region into flat fields, the smaller one washes the banks of Báta and Mohács, and both arms merge below Mohács, forming an island.[3]

This relative magnitude was reversed by the end of the 18th century with the widening of the western branch due to certain tectonic and morphological reasons. The process, which eventually resulted in the Mohács branch becoming wider and the Baracska branch narrower, can be traced on maps.[4]

Overall, the shift of the Danube's main channel to the western branch in the 17th and 18th centuries resulted in the formation of the present wider Mohács branch and a decrease in the water flow of the eastern branch. All these changes are mainly due to geological causes (uplift and settlement along fault lines) rather than to human influences.

3   Roads to Mohács

3.1   *King Louis II from Buda to Mohács*

To reach the battlefield, the Hungarian and Ottoman armies advanced along the Danube. The troops largely used the roads along the river, mainly the 'via militaris'. Most of the supplies were carried by hundreds of ships. The flood plains and the wide bends in the river forced the troops to make considerable detours.

The army of King Louis II left Buda on 20 July 1526 and his troops were stationed in dozens of places before reaching Mohács. The stops at the settlements

---

2 Ferenc Erdősi and Antal Lehmann, *Mohács földrajza* [The Geography of Mohács] (Mohács: Mohács Városi Tanács V.B. Művelődési Osztálya, 1974).

3 István Brodarics, *Igaz leírás a magyaroknak a törökkel Mohácsnál vívott csatájáról* [A true account of the battle between the Hungarians and the Turkish Emperor Süleyman at Mohács (1528)], in *Örök Mohács: szövegek és értelmezések,* eds. János B. Szabó and Gábor Farkas Farkas (Budapest: Bölcsészettudományi Kutatóközpont, 2020), p. 312.

4 Gábor Faludi and László Nebojszki wrote a paper on this process in the Hidrológiai Közlöny [Hydrological Bulletin]. Faludi Gábor and Nebojszki László, "A Mohácsi-sziget kialakulása és vizeinek történelmi változásai," [The formation of Mohács Island and the historical changes in its waters] *Hidrológiai Közlöny* 88 (2008), no 4, pp. 47–57.

of Érd, Ercsi, Adony, Pentele (today Dunaújváros), Földvár, and Paks were located on the banks of the Danube, the road closely following the riverbed along these stretches. After Paks, the troops marched to Tolna, where they had an extended rest, as this was the agricultural town designated as the assembly point for the troops and the place where intensive discussions were held on how to deal with the situation. From here, the army made a significant detour to the west to bypass the joint floodplain of the Danube and the small Sárvíz River. From the town of Szekszárd, the troops stopped twice before reaching Báta. The road then followed the river until Mohács, although including some steep sections.

The whole march lasted for more than a month (Figure 2.3). The king arrived in Mohács on 25 August. In some camps, they stayed for a long time, waiting for troops to arrive from other parts of the country. The king sent out orders, letters begging for help from the allies, and urgent messages to the magnates who were too slow to assemble. He made great efforts to raise an army of adequate numbers and equipment to fight the Ottomans, but as we shall see, he succeeded only partially.

After Tolna, an important meeting took place in the Monastery of the Holy Blood, the most prestigious pilgrimage site of the medieval Kingdom of Hungary, in Báta. A Diet was held there between 16–19 August. Beyond being practical, camping in Báta was an important part of spiritual preparation.

4 Sultan Süleyman's Road from Constantinople to Mohács and Buda

Süleyman left Constantinople on 23 April. The main stations of the Ottoman army's march were Filibe (Plovdiv) (22 May), Niš (9 June), Nándorfehérvár (Beograd) (8 July), Pétervárad (Petrovaradin) (13–27 July), Újlak (Ilok) (1–8 August), Eszék (Osijek) (14 August), Mohács (29 August) (Figure 2.3). The journey was along the old military route and the troops were accompanied by a considerable flotilla on the Danube after Beograd. The Ottoman campaign diary reports several instances of extreme weather conditions (rain, hail) during the journey. The longest period of forced encampment was during the siege of Pétervárad, which lasted for about two weeks. Clashes with Tomori's retreating troops did not cause the Ottomans any major difficulties.

The Ottoman troops advanced with a gap of one or two days following Tomori. The minimal difference is shown by the fact that when Süleyman reached the Drava (at Eszék/Osijek), 14 August), the retreating Hungarian troops crossed the Danube at Kölled (Kolut) and encamped near Krassó (12–13 August).

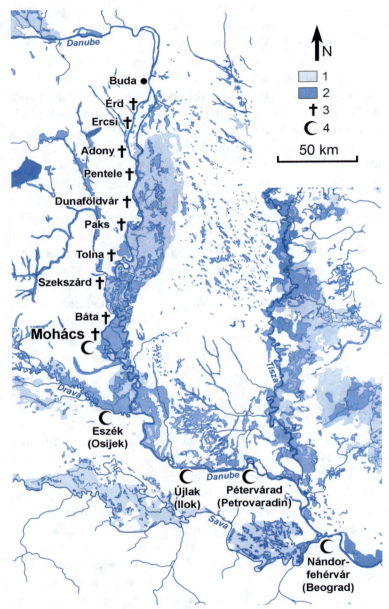

FIGURE 2.3 The main stations of Louis II's and Süleyman's armies to Mohács, along the Danube. Edited by Péter Gyenizse. Legend: 1 = seasonally waterlogged area; 2 = permanently waterlogged area; 3 = stations of Louis II's army; 4 = stations of Süleyman's army. Source of the map used as background: The water-covered and flooded areas of Hungary before the start of flood relief and drainage works [B IX b 255].
SOURCE: INSTITUTE AND MUSEUM OF MILITARY HISTORY.

After the Battle of Mohács, Süleyman used the same route to Buda – the *via militaris* of Roman origin – as Louis II's army from Buda to Mohács. The Ottoman army was capable of marching 22–25 kilometres daily. Thus the 192–195 km from the camp at Mohács to Buda would be covered in eight days. They reached Buda only on the 10th day (11 September), as they had a rest on the second day. At this time, before crossing the Sárvíz River, the troops were reorganised, and the prisoners were executed or released. Looking at the daily stretches, the probable locations of the Ottoman camps corresponded very closely to those of Louis II (Table 2.1). We can therefore assume that these places were ideal for camping, water supply and forage.

TABLE 2.1   Süleyman I's journey from Mohács to Buda. Edited by Norbert Pap

Date	Events of the day	Estimated distance (km)	Station
03.9	Monday: At Mohács, Ottoman military set fire to the palace, finally crossing a "lake" "whose waters beat the horse's tail", there was only a bridge, and they camp relatively early for the afternoon prayer (around 4 pm)	22	Báta
04.9	Tuesday: Having rest, killing or releasing useless prisoners, prohibiting raiding, sending messengers, putting the troops together	0	Next to the Sárvíz, near the monastery of Báta
05.9	Wednesday: The troops cross three bridges, station at a medium distance. Crossing the Sárvíz River at several points	45	Close to Szekszárd
06.9	Thursday: continue past the town of "Tolis" (Tolna), stopping on the banks of the Danube	75	Between Tolna and Paks
07.9	Friday: Ottoman troops pass a "big town" ([Duna]Földvár) and stay near the Danube. It is a medium distance station	100	North to Földvár
08.9	Saturday: no data	122	Pentele
09.9	Sunday: no data	145	Adony
10.9	Monday: no data	165	Érd-Batta
11.9	Tuesday: arrival to Buda	190	Under the walls of Buda
12.9	Wednesday: Having rest, the emperor marches into Buda	0–5	March on Buda

5   The Journey of Pál Tomori's Army

The commander of the southern Hungarian territories was Pál Tomori Archbishop of Kalocsa, a Franciscan monk. He was an experienced commander who tried to hold back and slow down the advancing Ottoman army. During these operations, he had about 3000 cavalrymen and about 40 warships (pinnaces or so-called *naszád*s). His troops were experienced and battle-hardened, but he had serious difficulties in financing the fighting throughout the year.

After the fall of the fortress of Pétervárad (the siege took place between 13–27 July), his troops crossed to the left bank of the Danube. His army retreated, in such a way that it did not take up the fight with the main Ottoman forces, but using the cover of the river and its floodplain, trying to hamper the Ottoman advance by small attacks, mainly using the warships. According to the written sources, he was fully aware of the hopelessness of a frontal confrontation and had also assessed the destructive superiority of the Ottoman army. The geographical environment played an important role in his strategy and tactics. Moving northwards, he was confronted with the question of what to do, where, and how he could and should engage the Turks.

King Louis II called a Diet at Báta in the Monastery of the Holy Blood (16–19 August). On 12 or 13 August, Tomori, on the king's orders, took his army across the Danube, or more precisely across the main branch of the river (Figure 2.4). According to sources, this took place at Kölled (Kolut).[5] The archbishop went to the Diet with a small escort, leaving his troops – his cavalry, which had almost doubled in size by the time after other troops of the southern noblemen, and the crew of his warships joined – near the marshes of the Krassó. The further position of the army could still change depending on the outcome of the discussions at the Diet.

They decided in Báta that Tomori and György Szapolyai, Count of Szepes (the brother of János Szapolyai, voivode of Transylvania and later king) would be the commanders-in-chief of the Hungarian army. Both were very hesitant, stressing that they were not ready for the task. At the same time, it is also clear

---

5   *1504–1566 Memoria rerum: A Magyarországon legutóbbi László király fiának legutóbbi Lajos királynak születése óta esett dolgok emlékezete (Verancsics-évkönyv)*, [Chronicle of Antal Verancsics...] ed. József Bessenyei (Bibliotheca Historica) (Budapest: Magyar Helikon, 1981). Excerpt republished in *Örök Mohács*, eds. B. Szabó et al., p. 401. Three years later, in 1529, János Szapolyai crossed the river in the same way when he went to Mohács and paid homage to Sultan Süleyman.

THE MAIN SCENES 55

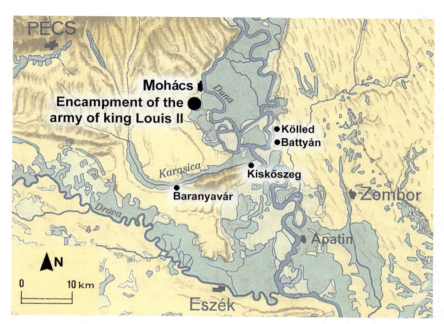

FIGURE 2.4   The surroundings of the Island of Mohács with the main sites mentioned in the sources. Edited by Péter Gyenizse. Kölled (Kolut) is the place where Tomori's army crosses the main branch of the Danube; Baranyavár is the crossing of the Karasica Stream; Kiskőszeg (Batina) is a crossing on the Danube, the place near which the Ottoman flotilla anchored. Source of the map used as background: The water-covered and flooded areas of Hungary before the start of flood relief and drainage works.
SOURCE: INSTITUTE AND MUSEUM OF MILITARY HISTORY [B IX B 255].

from the accounts that there was much debate about what should be done, and what position to take, with the hope of success.

Before the Diet, the leaders believed that Süleyman should be stopped at the Drava, but by then (14 August) the sultan had already reached Eszék (Osijek), a significant city at the river. The news of the movements of the Ottoman troops was brought by Tomori, since his troops were in contact with the advancing Ottomans and he alone was able to make a proper reconnaissance. If the Ottoman army were able to cross the river, then according to the contemporaries the situation was hopeless and the king and the army should escape – as the only good option. Although it was much discussed, neither the 'Battle of Drava' took place nor the army and the king began to flee northwards. Finally, Mohács was selected as the rallying point for the troops.

Brodarics describes the place as follows:

> The village or town of Mohács is quite well known, surrounded on all sides by a vast plain, unbroken by hill or forest. To the west lies the town of Pécs, as we have said, quite illustrious before this defeat, and to the north the above-mentioned Báta to the east the smaller branch of the Danube, and to the south, at a distance of more than four miles, the Drava River, from which to Mohács there are partly vineyard hills and partly certain marshy places.[6]

Tomori had two options – before 12 August – when he received the royal order to bring his troops back across the Danube. The first was to use the Battyán (Bezdán) – Kiskőszeg (Batina) Danube crossing and utilise the swampy floodplain of the Karasica Stream as a defence line, occupying its northern side to protect the crossing. This would have been a break with his earlier tactic of deploying his troops in a direct attack against the advancing Ottoman main force, which he had already realised was hopeless. If no attempt was made to halt the Ottoman advance at the wide Drava, how reasonable was it to do the same at the much narrower stream?

As it turned out, he did not opt for the Battyán (Bezdán) plain, but – as we mentioned above – crossed the Danube at Kölled 10 kilometres further north. His troops encamped opposite the royal camp, on the other side of the swamp called Krassó, south of Mohács, for about two weeks. Finally, on 27 August, he led his retreating troops to the south of Mohács, across the marsh to the royal camp four kilometres from the town.

6   Mohács and the Floodplains

To evaluate the situation of the town of Mohács and the sites of the Battle of Mohács, we have to distinguish three levels of elevation along the Danube. In this region, low floodplains are defined as areas that are 5–6 meters above the Danube 0 point. This level was already flooded by the Danube at a slightly higher than mean water level before flood relief work, so it was only dry at low water levels. Maps of the past centuries show that the low floodplain was mostly covered by marshland, reeds, and waterlogged areas. They can be found on both the eastern and western sides of the Mohács Danube. Fishing and

---

6   Brodarics, "Igaz történet," [A true account] in *Örök Mohács*, eds. B. Szabó et al., p. 312.

gathering (floodplain farming) were a typical form of farming here. The higher parts were used as pasture in the summer. Before water regulation works, no residential buildings were erected in these low-lying areas.

The high floodplain level is formed by land surfaces rising 8–9 meters above the Danube at its 0 point. Water was able to enter these areas only during major floods. A higher level of floodplain can only be observed in small patches around Mohács. In fact, the older eastern half of Mohács, along the Danube, is also situated on the higher flood plain. The factors that populated the ancient core of the town include several physical geographical features. The first one is the Danube itself, then a narrow branch of the river, with many opportunities for use. Parallel to it, the Buda-Eszék/Osijek road runs along the edge of a flood-free terrace. But why was the largest riverside town in the region built on this stretch of the Danube? Because the town is located where the steeply sloping higher bank of the Danube declines, and a higher floodplain surface is wedged between the higher terrace and the river. It was still mostly a flood-free surface, which made it easier to load vessels and get on and off ferries. Further to the south, the floodplain terrace moves away from the river, making the wide marshy floodplain impossible to cross.[7] Another natural feature is that the old core of the town, which lies on a high floodplain, is separated from the western, higher part by a deeper area of a former Danube branch. The undeveloped low-lying area is clearly visible on the map of the Military Survey I (Figure 2.5), for which the accompanying description reads: "... the Rókus Chapel, which lies on the road from New Mohács to Old Mohács, and where the small embankment raised at the marshy stream rests on the palisade [in der Plank], is built from solid material."[8] This water was used to protect the town from the west, as can be seen on Ottendorf's map of 1663. Its line can still be followed from the Sokác-rév through Bajcsy-Zsilinszky, Tomori and Tompa Mihály streets. We also know the name of this swampy watercourse that separated the two parts of the city: Büdös-árok [Büdös Ditch]. It originated from the present spring in Gólya Street, ran southwards to the Bég Stream, and from there its waters flowed to the floodplains towards Kölked.[9]

---

7   Although the Béda Danube approaches Kölked 900 metres away, the area between the village and the river was very marshy before the regulation of waterways. To the south, the next port of call is on the other side of the Karasica Stream, at Kiskőszeg (Batina).

8   *Első katonai felmérés*, 1783 [Military Survey I, 1783] col. 12. sect. 33 Baranya County; Klára T. Mérey, *Baranya megye települései az első katonai felmérés idején* [Settlements of Baranya County at the time of the Military Survey I] (Tanulmányok és források Baranya megye történetéből) 12 (Pécs: Baranya Megyei Levéltár, 2004), p. 109.

9   *Baranya megye földrajzi nevei* 11. kötet, [Geographical names in Baranya County.] ed. János Pesti (Pécs: Baranya Megyei Levéltár, 1982), p. 457.

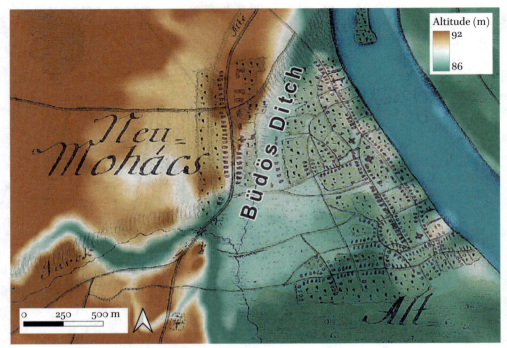

FIGURE 2.5 Mohács on the map of the Military Survey I (1783), coloured based on a relief model. The deeper area of the former Danube branch (the Büdös Ditch) separating "Alt" (Old) and "Neu" (New) Mohács is clearly visible. Edited by Péter Gyenizse.
SOURCE: ELSŐ KATONAI FELMÉRÉS, 1783 [MILITARY SURVEY I, 1783].

South of Mohács, the higher and lower surfaces of the floodplains widen considerably between the Danube and the flood-free terrace. A vivid picture of the state of the marshy areas on the western side of the Danube in the early 19th century can be seen in one of the descriptions of the Danube region, which was mapped from a military point of view:

> The swamps of Mohács and Kölked start at Mohács and go as far as Izsép. This is largely made up of wet meadows, overgrown with bulrushes and reeds. It is filled with small pools and divided by moats. In the middle, there is a drier area where the village of Kölked stands on a small hill. There is only a small part that can be scythed back at the edges. This swamp is sometimes completely flooded by the Danube. Only in dry summers do parts of it dry out, and in winter it freezes completely. This swamp is accessible only by two known routes, namely from Mohács to Kölked and from Dállyok to Izsép, but only in very dry weather and only

on foot or by light vehicles [*leichte Fuhrwerk*]. The area of this swamp is nearly a square mile. In order to make this area usable, an embankment needs to be built along the right bank of the Danube to withstand the highest water levels and ice tides.[10]

The Island of Mohács always had and still has a completely separate and specific drainage pattern. In previous centuries, the deepest part of the former Danube riverbeds, the Danube bottom, always had some water left over for most of the year because of the high ground-water level.

The flood-free terrace surface is separated from the higher floodplain by a characteristic scarp at 90–100 metres above sea level. It is not located on the island, but in the vicinity of Mohács, and it stretches several kilometres westwards from the Danube and the higher floodplain surface to the semicircular Ridge of Bár-Lánycsók-Nagynyárád-Majs. The Mohács terraces, covered with good fertile soil and free from flooding, are now mainly used for arable farming. However, maps of the previous centuries show that there were waterlogged wetlands in the shallow valleys of smaller streams that crossed the terrace, which were previously used mainly for grazing. Through the regulation of streams, the extent of the wetlands has now been significantly reduced. The flood-free terrace was also the route for major roads in the area, including the millennium-old Danube military road, where traffic was only disrupted by waterlogged stream beds.[11] Today, four small watercourses flow through the terrace (Csele, Jenyei, Bég and Borza Streams).

7 The Christian Army Camps: Mohács, "near Krassó", Kölked

There are a number of written sources on the Christian army's camps in the surrounding of Mohács. Camp sites were the area along the Danube at Mohács, in the Mohács Plain near Kölked and the camp of Tomori's army near Krassó.

The town of Mohács played an important role in the preparations for the battle. Brodarics informs us that the transport ships arrived here, and the king

---

10   Österreichisches Staatsarchiv K VII. k. 116. Topographische Beschreibung des westlichen Theils von Hungarn zwischen der Donau und der Drau. I. Abtheilung 3-ten Ternion. "*Gedrängte Beschreibung der Flüsse, Seen, Sümpfe und Moräste, dann der bestehenden und Projectirten Canäle. Militärische Bemerkung*"; Klára T. Mérey, *A Dél-Dunántúl földrajza katonaszemmel a 19. század elején* [The geography of South Transdanubia from the soldier's point of view in the early 19th century] (Geographia Pannonica Nova) 1 (Pécs: Lomart Kiadó, 2007), pp. 100–101.

11   T. Mérey, *Baranya megye települései*, [Settlements of Baranya County] pp. 107–113.

spent one or two days in the house of the bishop of Pécs on the bank of the Danube in Mohács, until the ships carrying camping equipment arrived, taking advantage of the high water level. The troops were camped in the higher-lying areas around the town, mainly to the south along the Mohács-Eszék/Osijek road. He also informs us that, during the preparations for the battle, Tomori's camp united with the royal army below Mohács. Istvánffy writes that the camp may have been two to three thousand steps south of Mohács,[12] while the papal nuncio, Antonio Giovanni da Burgio, describes it as being near Mohács.[13] The latter wrote on 5 September[14] that, after the battle, the Ottomans advanced to Mohács, to the former camp area.

The logistical requirements, the need for drinking water and the terrain conditions determined the locations of the camps. The banks of the Danube where the ships arrived and where the crossing point was located, as well as the point from which considerable quantities of drinking water had to be extracted, certainly have been secured by camps, as were the strategic roads and their intersections in the area. It is believed that the camps may have been set up along the Eszék/Osijek road further south on the bank of the Danube at Mohács, following the natural layout of the terrain, during the preparations before the battle. This is evidenced by Brodarics's description of passing through a devastated camp as he fled northwards. In the days before 29 August, partly because of the arrival and attacks of the Ottoman cavalry, the camps were united under Mohács.

7.1 *The Danube Bank at Mohács*

In Maximilian Brandstetter's painting of 1608 (Figure 2.6), we see several types of ships moored on the banks of the Danube at Mohács or floating on the river. During the Ottoman rule one of the ports of the Ottoman Danube flotilla was located here in Mohács.[15] However, according to a description from 1733, there

---

12   Miklós Isthvánffy, "A magyarok történetéből, 1622 (Részlet)," [From the History of the Hungarians, 1622 (Excerpt)] in *Örök Mohács*, eds. B. Szabó et al., p. 453.

13   Antonio Giovanni da Burgio, "Antonio Giovanni de Burgio pápai követ levele Jacopo Sadoleto pápai titkárnak, Buda, 1526. augusztus 25.," [Letter from papal ambassador Antonio Giovanni da Burgio to papal secretary Jacopo Sadoleto, Buda, 25 August 1526] in *Örök Mohács*, eds. B. Szabó et al., p. 122.

14   Antonio Giovanni da Burgio, "Antonio Giovanni de Burgio pápai követ levele Jacopo Sadoleto pápai titkárnak, Pozsony, 1526. szeptember 5.," [Letter from papal ambassador Antonio Giovanni da Burgio to papal secretary Jacopo Sadoleto, Pozsony, 5 September 1526] in *Örök Mohács*, eds. B. Szabó et al., p. 131.

15   Vass, "Mohács város hódoltságkori történetének török forrásai," [Turkish sources of the history of the city of Mohács during the Ottoman occupation] in *Baranyai helytörténetírás*, ed. Szita, pp. 15–48.

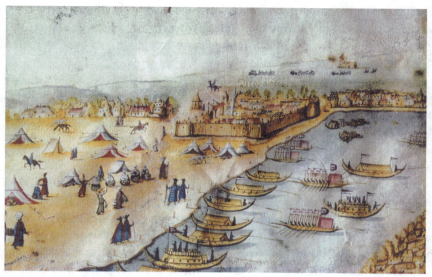

FIGURE 2.6 Mohács on the Danube. The creator is Maximilian Brandstetter, who made it during his trip to Constantinople in the beginning of the 17th century, as one of the illustrations in his diary. This is proven by the fact that the description of Mohács mentioned by János Jajczay on the back of the watercolor matches the text about Mohács in Brandstetter's known copy of his diary. See János Jajczay, "Törökkori Mohács," [Mohács in the Turkish period] Élet és Tudomány 24 (1969), no. 32, p. 1490, pp. 1524–1525, and Karl Nehring, Adam Freiherrn zu Herbersteins Gesandschaftsreise nach Konstantinopel. Ein Beitrag zum Frieden von Zsitvatorok (1606) (München: R. Oldenbourg Verlag, 1983), pp. 96–97.
SOURCE: HISTÓRIA 20 (1998), NO. 2, BACK COVER IMAGE.

was not much vessel traffic on the Little (Mohács) Danube: "… the downstream vessels rarely come here, but would rather go to the other side of the Island of Mohács, on the Great Danube."[16]

According to the sources, the port of Mohács did not play a very important role in the later period, because shipping was mostly carried out on the wider, deeper eastern branch. The town did not have a fortification at that time, it

---

16   Ádám Fricsy, "A pécsi klérus birtokainak településügyi összeírása 1733-ban," [Settlement census of the estates of the clergy of Pécs in 1733] in *Baranyai helytörténetírás 1978*, ed. Szita László (Pécs: Baranya Megyei Levéltár, 1979), p. 169.

was only built in the 1560s by the Ottoman authorities.[17] However, the town was important in 1526: it was the centre of the region, as the crossing point of the Danube. The cargo ships from Buda and Vienna arrived here, as well as Tomori's warships from the south.

What were these warships like? In the 16th century, boats came in several types and were known by a variety of names. The most common Hungarian Danube flotilla warship was the pointed-nosed, flat-bottomed, 23–24m long, 4.5m wide, 1.1m draught, pinnace. They were usually moved by 18–20 oarsmen, but there was also a proportionally smaller, so-called semi-pinnace, driven by 10 oarsmen.[18]

There were similar ones among the Ottoman Turkish ships. However, as the Ottomans were primarily seeking to dominate the Mediterranean, they had a much larger and more varied fleet of ships, both purely sailing (*yelkenli* or galley-type vessels) and rowing and sail-powered (*çektiri*). (Due to the requirements of river navigation and warfare, the latter type was most likely brought along for the 1526 campaign.) The ships with oars, called *çektiri* were divided into two groups as the large fleet ships and the narrow fleet ships.[19]

The large fleet ships are *baştarda*, *kadırga* (galley), *kalyata* and *frigate*. The *baştarda* and *kadırga* were too big for the Danube. The Ottoman galley was 42–43 meters long and had a crew of 350, the *baştarda* even much bigger. The *kalyata* (see Venetian *fusta*) was a ship of 32–34 meters, had cannons and 220 people during the war. The smaller *frigate* (*firkate*) – often used on the rivers – was half the size of the *kalyata* and had a crew of 80–100.[20] These smallest warships were fast, maneuverable and easy to operate that is why pirates used them. In the western sources was known as *brigantine*. The sources mentioned these two last types of ships in 1526.

The narrower fleet ships – which may have accounted for the bulk of the Turkish ships in the 1526 campaign – were used both as warships and for

---

17 Frigyes Kőnig and István Pánya, "A mohácsi török palánkvár," [The Turkish palisade fortress in Mohács] in *Várak, kastélyok, templomok,* ed. Pál Kósa (Kökény: 2018).

18 Jenő Szentkláray, *A dunai hajóhadak története* [History of the Danube flotillas] (Budapest: M. Tud. Akadémia Történelmi Bizottsága, 1885); Károly Csonkaréti and László Benczúr: *Haditengerészek és folyamőrök a Dunán* [Sailors and river guards on the Danube] (Budapest: Zrínyi Kiadó, 1997).

19 Bostan, Idris, *Ottoman Maritime Arsenals and Shipbuilding Technology in the 16th and 17th centuries.* (2007) Foundation for Science and Technology and Civilisation 12 p. https://muslimheritage.com/uploads/Ottoman_Maritime_Arsenals.pdf See more detailed descripton in Bostan, Idris, *Osmanlı Bahriye Teşkilâtı: XVII. Yüzyılda Tersâne-i Âmire* [Ottoman Naval Organisation: the Main Maritime Arsenal in the Seventieth Century] Ankara, 1992. pp. 14–29.

20 Bostan, Idris, 2007. pp. 12–13.

transport. These included the *karamürsel*, part warship and part transport, the *şayka*, believed by the Turks to be of Hungarian origin, the *işkampoye*, used for sending messages, and the *üstüaçık, aktarma* and *çekeleve*, used for both transport and patrol.[21]

Besides the sources, archaeological evidence also confirms camping around Mohács. It can be said that the bank of the Danube at Mohács had a unique character, so it is reasonable to assume that it played a major part in the military operations of 1526 (Figure 2.7). Its importance is best illustrated by a treasure trove, the location of which is marked on a map (Figure 2.8). This was found in Duna Street [formerly Kálvin köz], Mohács, in 1969. The 45,000 silver denarii found in the two jars were counted by the archaeologist Attila Kiss, who brought them to the museum. Some of the coins date from the time of Louis II, and previous studies have linked them to the Battle of Mohács. They were found in a place that was not inside the town at the time: they were buried around 100–120 metres south of the moat surrounding the town. It is likely that this large quantity of high-quality coins was transported to the site for military expenditure, and was most likely buried in two tents set up by the officers of the Hungarian army.

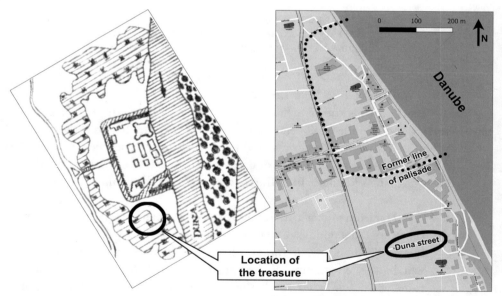

FIGURE 2.7   The location of the treasure trove found in Duna Street [Kálvin köz] in Mohács on Ottendorf's map of 1663 and Openstreetmap showing current conditions. Edited by Péter Gyenizse.

21   Ibid. 13 p.

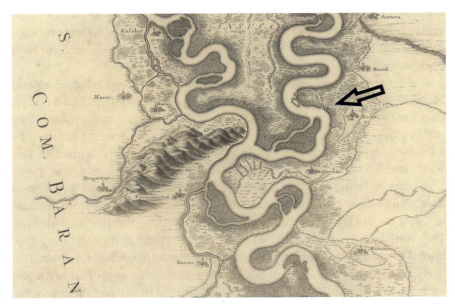

FIGURE 2.8   The assumed location of the Kölled fort at the crossing (ca. 1696) by Marsigli (the arrow shows the crossing point on the river).
SOURCE: MARSIGLI (1696/1726). MAPPA GENERALIS IN QUA DANUBII FL. CAETIUM MONTEM INTER ET B ... [S 80 – PRINTED MAPS – NO. 1/1–19.]. HUNGARIAN NATIONAL ARCHIVES.

7.2   Tomori's Camp "near Krassó"

The Tomori army is known to have been camped near the Krassó marshes after crossing the Danube at Kölled (Figures 2.4 and 2.8). The troops arrived here around 12–13 August. This army, originally consisting of 3000 horsemen and 40 *naszád*s, had swelled to 5000 or 6000 men by this time, with the arrival of other magnates's banderia from the southern parts of the country.

> ... not far from Mohács (there is) a water, or rather a marsh, which we may therefore call a puddle, or a river, the people call it Krassó, beyond which five or six thousand of Tomori's horsemen camped, partly from those who had gone with him from the beginning, partly from those who later came with Péter Perényi and others, who were led from the other side of the Danube to the inner side, by order of the king, to join the royal army. So, having taken up his camp with his comrade-in-chief near Mohács, and having also carefully pitched the camp as Gnoienski had prescribed, each man having his own position, he returned with Péter Perényi to his

own who were encamped across the water, in order that he might, if he could persuade them, bring them with him to the royal camp.[22]

The Kölled crossing (Figure 2.8) may have been of great significance in Tomori's operations because it combined several advantages. Before the fort of Kölled on the left bank, it had a consolidated bank on both sides of the Danube. The 40 warships could dock here and transfer troops, as ordered by the king. At the same time, if, as was a strong possibility, the decision to retreat had been taken at Báta, the army could have returned to the left bank of the river and continued its march northwards.

7.3   The Royal Camp at Kölked

On the king's orders, the troops were united in a larger camp near Mohács on 27 August (Figure 2.4). The final encampment before the battle is reported by several sources. The camp was set up by the *"the Polish Gnoienski"*, one of the leaders of the mercenary troops, whose skills were highly valued. Ursinus Velius described the camp as follows:

> The site of the royal camp was a flat and open field near the marshes. The gently rising hill prevented them from seeing the enemy camp. The wagons, which had been encircled as a fortification, formed a wall, so that the camp looked like a walled city.[23]

The troops of Tomori, Péter Perényi and other noblemen with smaller troops also arrived here. These Southlanders were not keen to leave their previous location. "… Tomori went to his own camp, which we are told was close by, and there with great difficulty he induced his men to retire a little and allow themselves to be united with the royal army"[24] after they had left their former camp near Krassó. "… half a mile below Mohács our camp met theirs, without, however, mingling with them, but leaving a little distance between the two camps"[25] – Brodarics wrote. It seems that some of the leaders of this army tried to keep their separation, as written sources indicate some tension with the leaders of the troops in the royal camp.

---

22   Brodarics, "Igaz történet," [A true account] in *Örök Mohács*, eds. B. Szabó et al., p. 312.
23   Caspar Ursinus Velius, "A mohácsi csata. 1530 körül (töredék)," [The Battle of Mohács. Around 1530 (fragment)] in *Örök Mohács*, eds. B. Szabó et al., pp. 348–354.
24   Brodarics, "Igaz történet," [A true account] in *Örök Mohács*, eds. B. Szabó et al., p. 315.
25   Ibid. p. 315.

8   The Ottoman Camps: Papas Irmağı/Krassó, the Site of the Battle, Kölked

The Ottoman army, after crossing the Drava in the middle of the month, camped on 28 August on the north side of the Karasica stream, near Baranyavár. The Ottoman flotilla was moored nearby at Kiskőszeg (Figure 2.4).

On the morning of 29 August, from the camp near Karasica, the Rumalian troops led by Grand Vizier İbrahim Pasha reached the Borza Valley and began to make camp in the early afternoon (Figure 2.11). Brodarics reported: "In front of us was a long hill in the shape of a theatre auditorium, beyond which the Turkish emperor was setting up his camp."[26] Velius' report confirms this: "The camp of the Turks was pitched opposite, at the foot of the mount.[27] The distance between the two was two miles."[28] "… The slight rise of the hill[29] prevented them from seeing the enemy's camp." The location of the camp is clearly identifiable as the flat area of the Majs alluvial cone that remained dry before the basin rim. On the night of the battle, the sultan retires here around midnight.

On the next day of the battle, 30 August, the sultan's camp moved further north, beyond the battlefield, where it would spend four days. This location was either the same as or close to the former royal camp. It was the site of the execution of 1500 or 2000 Christian prisoners of war on 31 August.

9   The Geographical Content of Historical Sources Describing the Battle Sites

The findings on the environment of the battle are based primarily on István Brodarics's account of the battle, which provides the most detailed and useful information. He describes the geography in a vivid, graphic way. However, other written documents that are available may add important information to Brodarics's description, or even confirm it on certain points. On the other

---

26   Ibid. p. 318.
27   Mount here was the name given to the sudden rise (20 to 40 m) of the basin margin surrounding the plain.
28   Two Italian miles equals 4 km. Caspar Ursinus Velius, "A mohácsi csata. 1530 körül (töredék)," [The Battle of Mohács. Around 1530 (fragment)] in *Örök Mohács,* eds. B. Szabó et al., p. 353.
29   Caspar Ursinus Velius, "A mohácsi csata. 1530 körül (töredék)," [The Battle of Mohács. Around 1530 (fragment)] in *Örök Mohács,* eds. B. Szabó et al., p. 353. This is the low-lying Sátorhely Ridge, also mentioned above by in Brodarics's account.

hand, on the sites the chancellor did not visit or for which he only mentions second-hand information, other participants' accounts may be more accurate.

9.1   Roads

The Ottoman army arrived in the Mohács Plain from the south, across the Karasica Stream. They used the Roman military road for lining up their troops (Figure 2.11). From the description by the Ottoman Turkish chronicler Lutfi Pasha, we know that they then crossed a difficult swampy area, which he called *"Papas ırmağı".*[30] The crossing point was at Baranyavár.

One of the geographical cornerstones of the Battle of Mohács is that – according to the account of İbrahim Peçevi – the Ottoman forces were divided at *Bozuk Kilise*. This name means "Ruined Church" in Ottoman Turkish. The place seems to be the remains of the monastery of Géta.[31] After the Ottoman period the place was called – after the Turkish name – as Buziglica. A map from 1700 shows the ruins of the monastery and the crossroads in question, next to Géta (Ketu) (Figure 2.9).

The main forces continued to push forward onto the battlefield, while the cavalry of Bali and Hüsrev Beys moved west and carried out an outflanking operation to the north of the plain to get behind the Christian army in the area of Bácsfalu.[32] After the split, the main army marched northwards up the eastern side of the plain along the line of the former Roman military road.

---

30   *Török Történetírók* II. [Turkish Historiographers II.] Ed. József Thury (Budapest: Magyar Tudományos Akadémia, 1896), p. 14.

31   In the printed text of İbrahim Peçevi's chronicle, the name *Pusu Kilisesi* (meaning: Church of Ambush) figures. See Ibrahim Pecsevi, "Krónika (1648 előtt)," [Chronicle (before 1648)] in *Örök Mohács,* eds. János B. Szabó et al., pp. 463–477. This was already identified by József Thúry in 1896 as the place known as Buziglica. See *Török történetírók II.* [Turkish chroniclers II.] (Budapest: Magyar Tudományos Akadémia, 1896), pp. 112–278. We think that the name comes from the Ottoman Turkish *Bozuk Kilise* (meaning Ruined Church) which can be identified with the ruins of the monastery of Géta. Thus, the name Buziglica is a slavicized form of the Ottoman Turkish word. Buziglica is located between Géta and Dályok. We have some clues to identify its contemporary location. Pusziklitza can be seen on the 1772 agricultural map of the settlement of Majs, north of the Géta elevation [Getta], south of Udvar (Charten von der ka[mmer]al Ortschaft Mays... Hungarian National Archives [= MNL] S 11–N.o. 830:43. On the Military Survey I (1783), the inscription Gusaklicza w. h. (w. h. = tavern) is located directly next to the main road from Baranyavár to Mohács, around 2.5 km south of Udvar and 3 km west of Dályok. In the Military Survey II (1858), Buziklicza P. (P. = praedium) and Buziklicza Wald (Wald = forest) are shown in the same area, east of the Géta praedium, which is also indicated. In this location, the inscriptions J. H. Buziglica (J. H. = hunting lodge) and Buziglica-Wald appear on the Military Survey III (1880).

32   The remains of Bácsfalu, destroyed during the Battle of Mohács, were excavated near Lánycsók. László Papp, "A mohácsi csatahely kutatása," [Research into the battlefield of

FIGURE 2.9   Bozuk kilise (Buziglica) at the ruins of Géta monastery (Ketu) and the crossroads to Mohács and to Merse and Majs, Universum dominium Siklossiense modo divisum in quator partes, nempé Celsissum Diu [!] Dni] Dni Principis Eugeny de Sabaudia, Excell.mi Dni D: Aeneae Comitis Campi Marechallia Caprara, et Ex. Dni Comitis Veterani necnon R[ever]end[issi]mi Dni Dni Epp[iscop]i Jány Anno Domini [1]700.
SOURCE: HTTPS://MAPS.HUNGARICANA.HU/HU/OSZKTERKEPTAR/2142/

The army of Bali and Hüsrev moved north-west along the roads of the higher terraces (Merse, Majs).

In addition to military considerations, there was also an environmental reason for splitting the army. The eastern side of the Mohács Plain was originally higher, and the western side was filled up later. The watercourses that flowed eastwards from the hilly area to the plains slowly filled the land in front of the valleys with their sediment, but also spread out, creating extensive areas of marshy, swampy and boggy land. Therefore, it can be seen that the alluvial fan in front of the eastern side of the Majs, which is the main focus of the present analysis, is surrounded by wet, marshy areas to the north and east, and bogs to the south. To the east, the waters then return to well-defined channels, making it much easier to cross them. The Romans built the military road in the eastern part of the plain because it was the most stable area. The western plain, with the exception of the alluvial fans, was difficult to pass in wet weather. It may have been passable only during the dry season. To the west of the plain, on the higher ground of the basin margin, it was again possible to pass, so there was a road there, but it was far from ideal, as those who passed it had to descend

Mohács] in *A Janus Pannonius Múzeum évkönyve 1960*, ed. János Dombay (Pécs: Janus Pannonius Múzeum, 1961), p. 202.

into valleys carved out by watercourses emerging from the plain, and the high water level obviously made it difficult to cross them. Then one had to climb up the basin margin again and so on, all the way to (Nagy) Nyárád.

The infantry and artillery of the Ottoman main army therefore advanced on the eastern side of the plain, while some cavalrymen led by Bali and Hüsrev followed the more difficult western road. The Buziglica junction (Figure 2.9) is therefore of particular importance and illustrates why the main army had to use the military road.[33] This is how the Ottomans reached the battlefield.

9.2   Swamp/Vizslak Meadow

Brodarics described the location of the battle as follows:

> As we have said above, this place is a vast, wide plain, not broken by woods, shrubs, water or hills, but on the left, between it and the Danube, there was muddy, marshy water, covered with dense sedge and reeds where many people later perished.[34]

In addition to Brodarics, a Czech source[35] also reported that a deep swamp lay directly next to the battlefield. Among the Ottoman Turkish chroniclers, Kemalpaşazade also notes[36] that the battle took place west of the Danube marshes. Brodarics, the Czech source and Kemalpaşazade all mention that many Christians perished in this swamp after the battle.

The sources mention standing water[37] with mud, swamp, sedge and reed. These features fit the marshland on the right bank of the Danube, the so-called

---

33   The extensive wetland to the west of Sátorhely, northeast of Majs, was drained in the 19th century, while the draining of the marshy area south of Majs was only completed in the 1950s.

34   Brodarics, *Igaz leírás*, [A true account] in *Örök Mohács*, eds. B. Szabó et al., pp. 317–318.

35   "Egy cseh úr levele a Santa Clara-kolostor főnöknőjéhez, 1526 november," [Letter from a Czech nobleman to the Mother Superior of the Santa Clara Convent, November 1526] in *Örök Mohács*, eds. B. Szabó et al., pp. 207–216.

36   Kemálpasazáde, "Mohácsnáme, 1526 és 1534 között (Részletek)," [Mohácsname, between 1526 and 1534. (Excerpts)] in *Örök Mohács*, eds. B. Szabó et al., pp. 326–338.

37   The marsh near the battlefield, which is regularly mentioned in the sources, appears as muddy, swampy water. Istvánffy, for example, called it a swampy lake. Isthvánffy, "A magyarok történetéből," [From the History of the Hungarians] in *Örök Mohács*, eds. B. Szabó et al., pp. 444–462. Athanasio Georgiceo describes it as a lake, i.e. standing water: "... and on the left a very large lake with waterfowl, although there was water in only a few places. This lake is usually flooded by the Danube at high tide..." István György Tóth, "Athanasio Georgiceo álruhás császári megbízott útleírása a magyarországi török hódoltságról, 1626-ból," [Disguised imperial envoy Athanasio Georgiceo's travelogue on the Turkish occupation of Hungary in 1626] *Századok* 132 (1998), no. 4, p. 854.

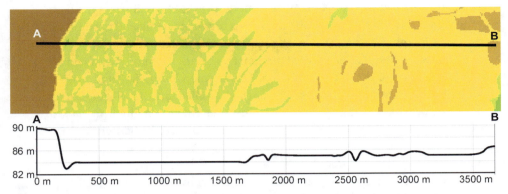

FIGURE 2.10   Cross-section of the swamp showing elevation differences at the Vizslak Meadow. Edited by Péter Gyenizse.

Vizslak Meadow.[38] All the more so because its western rim is closed by a steep slope of around 4–6 metres (Figure 2.10). This significant difference in levels is illustrated by the Czech source mentioned above: "Many sank in the swamp, one after the other fell into it."[39]

9.3   Deep Ditch

In addition to the Danube wetland, we should mention another environmental element that is prominent in the descriptions. This is a ditch or 'valley' near the marsh along which the battle took place. This is a former riverbed, which has been filled with sediment over time and is barely visible to the naked eye today, but can be easily identified by instruments and remote sensing methods: It runs from Nagynyárád to the swamp across the plain in a northwest-southeast direction (Figure 2.11). The valley in question is mentioned in the description of the battle as follows:

> At last, however, not only fear but smoke filled everything, and obstructed vision; so most of our troops were forced to go down into the valley, next to those marshy waters, but those who remained behind fought bravely and unceasingly in the face of the guns. In any case, those who had retreated to the valley to resume the fight later could no longer stand the

---

38   The Vizslak Meadow today lies to the east of the village of Sátorhely.
39   "Egy cseh úr levele," [Letter from a Czech nobleman] in *Örök Mohács,* eds. B. Szabó et al., p. 210.

power and smoke of the guns, while most of the army was also on the run meaning they had to flee too.[40]

So, next to the marshy water, emphasized in several places, was the valley which, it seems, provided cover for the Christian soldiers. This surface formation is also mentioned in the Czech source:

> ... there was a deep ditch full of water and next to it a deep marsh [...]. In some places, the ditch was so full of people and horses that it looked as if a bridge had been built across it. The cruel Turks pursued them so fiercely and pushed them into the water and the ditch, completely surrounding the Christians, such that those who escaped, with God's help, had to cut their way through the Turks.[41]

On the battlefield, another valley on the right flank also appeared in the description: "... the enemy's armies in the valley that spread out to our right, under the hills, were moving silently, betrayed only by their spearheads."[42] The Ottoman cavalry did not advance in the valley mentioned above, but in the Valley of the Borza, where the spearheads were visible, as cover by the terrain was only 3–4 meters.[43]

The Ottoman Turkish chronicler Lutfi Pasha also reported on a ditch that started from the marsh and crossed the plain: "... a spy has reported that the unbelievers, besides being so numerous, have dug a large ditch, one end of which stretches up to a hill and the other to the Danube, and it is impossible to pass through it."[44] The ditch or valley in question is very different from the meandering valleys of the active watercourses of the plain. The former riverbed, which is nearly 5 kilometres long and 50–70 metres wide, runs in gentle curves of a kilometre scale, may have appeared man-made to those

---

40   Brodarics, *Igaz leírás*, [A true account] in *Örök Mohács*, eds. B. Szabó et al., p. 320.
41   "Egy cseh úr levele," [Letter from a Czech nobleman] in *Örök Mohács*, eds. B. Szabó et al., p. 210.
42   Brodarics, *Igaz leírás*, [A true account] in *Örök Mohács*, eds. B. Szabó et al., p. 318.
43   Péter Gyenizse, Norbert Pap, Máté Kitanics, and Tamás Morva, "A mohácsi csata helyszínének pontosítását célzó beláthatósági vizsgálatok eredményei," [The results of visibility surveys to clarify the site of the Battle of Mohács] in *Az elmélet és gyakorlat találkozása a térinformatikában x.*, ed. Vanda Éva Molnár (Debrecen: Debreceni Egyetemi Kiadó, 2019), pp. 101–108.
44   Lutfi pasa, "Az Oszmán-ház története (a kezdetektől 1554-ig), 1550-es évek (Részlet)," [History of the Ottoman House (from the beginning to 1554), the 1550s (Excerpt)] in *Örök Mohács*, eds. B. Szabó et al., p. 405.

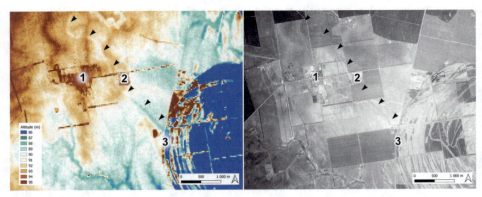

FIGURE 2.11 "Deep Ditch", or "valley" is an ancient river bed on the battlefield. Edited by Péter Gyenizse. Legend: 1 = Sátorhely village; 2 = memorial park; 3 = Turkish Hill (Törökdomb). Arrows show the 'Deep Ditch'.
SOURCE: BASED ON EU COPERNICUS GLO−30 DEM.

observing the site from a distance (Figure 2.11). Moreover, in its immediate vicinity, Christian armies did carry out earthwork. This is evidenced by the fact that the mass graves excavated in the 1960s and 1970s may originally have been depressions designed for military purposes. Together, these may explain why the scouts believed the ditch to be artificial. The historians of the period, who relied on Brodarics's chronicle, had other sources and local knowledge. Among them, Miklós Istvánffy also stressed the importance of the 'ditch' or 'valley': "Some of our horsemen retreated into the valley between the hill and a nearby marshy lake…"[45]

In his description, István Brodarics mentioned two other important geographical places in connection with the battlefield, a hill and a village: "In front of us there was a long hill, like a stage, behind which there was the camp of the Turkish emperor; at the bottom of the hill, there was a small village with a church, named Földvár. This was where the enemy set up their canons."[46] The low, curved hill was the Sátorhelyi-hát (Sátorhely Ridge). The location of the village has been identified in the Borzató Valley,[47] as the analysis clarified its position.

---

45 Isthvánffy, "A magyarok történetéből," [From the History of the Hungarians] in *Örök Mohács*, eds. B. Szabó et al., p. 457.
46 Brodarics, *Igaz leírás*, [A true account] in *Örök Mohács*, eds. B. Szabó et al., p. 457.
47 See Chapter Eight.

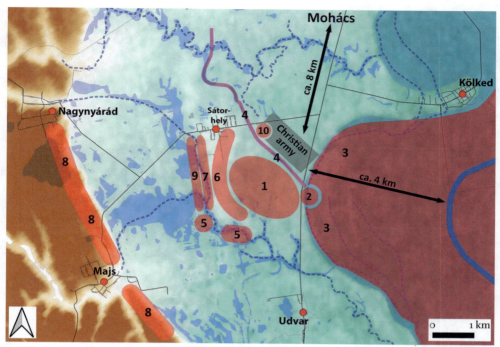

FIGURE 2.12   The main scenes of the battle. Legend: 1 = battle arena; 2 = Hünkar tepesi/Ottoman victory monument; 3 = Vizslak Meadow; 4 = Deep Ditch; 5 = Földvár; 6 = Sátorhely Ridge; 7 = road in the Valley of Borza; 8 = "mount"; 9 = forest next to Földvár; 10 = shooting positions/mass-graves. Edited by Norbert Pap, designed by Péter Gyenizse.

9.4   The Sátorhely Ridge and the Shining Spearheads

The Sátorhely Ridge played an interesting role in the battle. According to Brodarics, an Ottoman cavalry regiment tried to outflank the Christian army from the west.[48] He claims that the soldiers themselves could not be seen, the movement of the Ottoman warriors was revealed by the spearheads and the light reflected by them. The regiment moved to the north behind a low elevation. This low hill was the Sátorhely Ridge, which is only a few meters higher than the plain. We made a visibility analysis using the QGIS software tool.[49] We placed three assumed cavalry observers in the eastern, central and western parts of the Christian army. Their eye height was fixed at 2.5 meters. The purple colour in Figure 2.13 shows the areas that could not be seen by the observers

---

48   Brodarics, *Igaz leírás*, [A true account] in *Örök Mohács*, eds. B. Szabó et al., p. 318.
49   Zoran Čučković (2018): Depth below horizon: new (old) functionality for QGIS viewshed analysis. https://landscapearchaeology.org/2018/depth-below-horizon/.

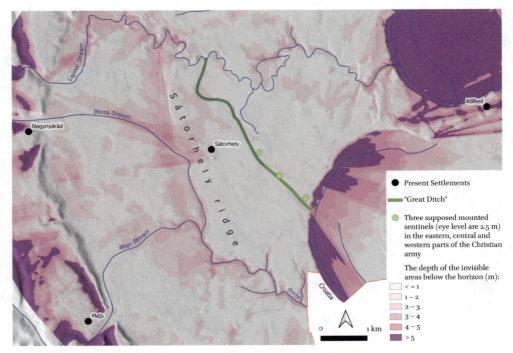

FIGURE 2.13 Result of visibility analysis on the Mohács Plain. Edited by Péter Gyenizse.

because they were obscured by the low mound. It can be concluded that the Sátorhely Ridge hid the horses and riders from the Christian sentinels in most places, but the horsemen's spearheads could extend above the ridge in several places.

9.5 Anthropogenic Elements of the Landscape: Christian Shooting Positions on the Battlefield

The most significant find associated with the Battle of Mohács was uncovered by the archaeologist László Papp in the early 1960s. During the excavation, two mass graves were found east of the settlement of Sátorhely. In preparation for the 450th anniversary commemorations, a memorial park was created around the mass graves on the initiative of the local community. Three more mass graves were then found.[50] The five mass graves contain between a thousand and two thousand soldiers who died in battle. Given their particular shape and their position in relation to each other, it has been suggested that the graves may have been originally dug as shooting positions and only subsequently

---

50   Borbála Maráz, "A mohácsi csatatér régészeti leletei," [Archaeological finds from the battlefield of Mohács] *Honismeret* 4 (1976), no. 4, pp. 23–25.

used as graves. The five depressions form a structural unit with the previously identified 'ditch', the former dry riverbed, as they were formed along a line running roughly parallel to it.

10   Escape Routes

The picture of the post-battle flight is difficult to unravel, and with little substantive description, our findings are primarily based on inferences about possible directions of passage (Table 2.2). Nightfall and the onset of the storm brought an end to the fighting and offered the survivors a chance to escape. The forested hilly terrain surrounding the Mohács Plain gave those with local knowledge a good chance of survival.

TABLE 2.2   The spread of news of the battle in the days after 29 August 1526. Edited by Norbert Pap

	After Mohács, where can a survivor and/or the news of the battle get to?	When?	Spread of information and likely escape route
The court learns of the defeat (Burgio)	Buda	30 August at midnight	Northern direction
Ulrich Czettritz	Neszmély	31 August	Heading north, but crossing the smaller Danube branch
István Brodarics	Pozsony (Bratislava)	4 September	Northern direction
Information from Johann Fugger, a merchant in Venice	Letter from Buda Letter from Vienna	31 August 5 September	Northern direction
Captain Giovanni Aidebech and 5–6 wounded persons arrive	Vienna	2–3 September	Northern direction
Count Albrecht Schlick	Buda	9 September	Northern direction
Luca Corvato and Thomaso Ungaro on a cavalry reconnaissance	Via Mágocs (Baranya County) They meet wounded persons	After 3 September (maybe 5 September)	Northern direction

TABLE 2.2 The spread of news of the battle in the days after 29 August 1526. (*Cont.*)

	After Mohács, where can a survivor and/or the news of the battle get to?	When?	Spread of information and likely escape route
Venetian merchant Lantieri	He meets traders from the south at Babócsa (Somogy County)	31 August	Western direction
Information requested by Domenico da Cividale and Jacomo da Cavali	Hosszúpereszteg (Vas County)	1–2 September	Western direction
Fazio di Savoia	Graz	(Before) 17 September	Western direction
Radics Bosics (Radič Božić), Pál Bakics (Pavle Bakić), János Filléres, Ambrus Fogarasi, the Danube naszáds and some refugees	Not known	Not known	Heading north up the Danube

In the vast majority of cases, the only thing we can determine from the sources is when the news reached each of the geographical locations, but we cannot typically plot the specific routes (except for the pinnaces, which travelled on the river).

In his description, Brodarics did not mention his own escape route. All we know is that, at least initially, he was heading north through the devastated camp, but he does not tell us anything about the rest of his journey. In his letter of 6 September, he reported that he reached Pozsony (Bratislava) only on the sixth day after the battle, on 4 September, but had been captured by Bohemian mercenaries before that. So, his escape route was ultimately northwards, but the six-day trip might have included a major detour.

The Royal Chamberlain Ulrich Czettritz [Zetritz] fled north, but as he had first successfully crossed a tributary of the Little Danube, his route had to pass partly through the Island of Mohács. He met the Queen at Neszmély on 31 August 1526.

The news of the defeat was received at midnight on 30 August by the papal nuncio Burgio at the court in Buda,[51] less than a day after the battle ended. The northward direction of the refugees is undoubted, but it is not known for sure which of the three possible routes they could have taken.

Johann Fugger, a merchant living in Venice, learned of the battle from a letter from Buda dated 31 August 1526, but it was not even clear to him on which day it was fought.[52] He learned of the king's death from a letter from Vienna dated 5 September.

Captain Giovanni Aidebech arrived in Vienna with news of the battle, with five wounded persons on 2–3 September.[53] Apparently, on the fourth or fifth day after the battle, the news reached the city with them.

A Bohemian source describes the hardships of a lucky escape from Mohács to Buda:

> ... but Albrecht still had a hard time afterwards, for he was half a mile from the battle when his horse fell and fell out from under him, because it was wounded. He thought that if he stayed there, he would not be safe from the Turks. He was also worried about the Hungarians, and asked a nobleman [who was with him] to stay with him, but he refused, because he was afraid, and rode off. Albrecht had no horse and was left all alone, so he threw off his armour and walked on. God willing, however, the nobleman's horse died, and he joined him less than a quarter of a mile away. Then, as Albrecht had a very fine gold ring, he bought a small horse for it, and paid an extra ten forints, though the horse was not worth a penny. He rode on it, and then he went on foot while the nobleman rode, and that's how they got to Buda.[54]

---

51 da Burgio, "Antonio Giovanni de Burgio pápai követ levele ... Pozsony," [Letter from papal nuncio Antonio Giovanni da Burgio ... Pozsony] in *Örök Mohács*, eds. B. Szabó et al., pp. 131–132.

52 "Johann Fugger értesülései Buda, 1526. augusztus 29–31.; Bécs, szeptember 5. (kivonat)," [Information from Johann Fugger Buda, 29–31 August 1526, Vienna, 5 September 1526] in *Örök Mohács*, eds. B. Szabó et al., p. 125.

53 "Josef Estaierhez írt level, Bécs 1526. szeptember 2–3. (kivonat)," [Letter to Giuseppe Estaier, Vienna, 2–3 September 1526] in *Örök Mohács*, eds. B. Szabó et al., p. 126.

54 "Egy cseh úr levele," [Letter from a Czech nobleman] in *Örök Mohács*, eds. B. Szabó et al., pp. 213–214.

The source describes the escape of Count Albrecht Schlick (1486–1548) from the Battle of Mohács. However, apart from the fact that they walked on foot and rode on horseback, and the direction of travel was north, he did not give a precise route. They seem to have headed straight for Buda and arrived safely. Another thread of the story is that they later went on to Pozsony.

On 3 September, the cavalry soldiers Luca Corvato and Thomaso Ungaro were commissioned by the Friulian governor to investigate what had happened at Mohács. In the village of Mágocs in Baranya County, they met many of the wounded soldiers who told them about the circumstances of the defeat in battle.[55]

The Venetian merchant Lantieri met merchants from Zrin at Babócsa in Somogy County on Friday, 31 August.[56] He was told about the defeat in battle by them. Babócsa lies to the west of Pécs on the northern bank of the Drava River, but traders from Zrin could have obtained this information from further south, at most the day before. In this case (given the short time frame), we should definitely expect westbound refugees, i.e. there were certainly survivors who fled towards Pécs and then across the Drava.

News of the circumstances of the king's death reached Graz before 17 September. Fazio di Savoia, a Venetian spy, reported on it in a letter based on information from messengers.[57]

According to an Italian report, news of the lost battle reached Hosszúpereszteg, near Sárvár in Vas County, relatively early, in early September.[58] According to the source, the two reporters left the settlement for Italy on 2 September. They received the news of the defeat before departure. It is possible that a survivor arrived in the village. The first group of refugees reached nearby Vienna only at around the same time. The likelihood of the appearance of refugees is further strengthened by the fact that the source is not yet certain of the king's death, so, the information is unlikely to have come from Pozsony. This may prove that there was a westward escape route.

---

55   Agostino da Mula, "Agostino da Mula jelentése, Udine, 1526. szeptember 25. (részletek)," [Account of Agostino da Mula, Udine, 25 September 1526 (excerpts)] in *Örök Mohács* eds. B. Szabó et al., pp. 163–165.

56   Francesco Lanteri, "Francesco Lanteri Antonio Lanterihez írt levele Pettau, 1526. szeptember 3. (részlet)," [Letter from Francesco Lanteri to Antonio Lanteri Pettau, 3 September 1526 (excerpt)] in *Örök Mohács*, eds. B. Szabó et al., p. 130.

57   Fazio di Savoia, "Fazio di Savoia jelentése, Graz, 1526. szeptember 17. (kivonat)," [Account of Fazio di Savoia, Graz, 17 September 1526 (excerpt)] in *Örök Mohács*, eds. B. Szabó et al., p. 155.

58   Information requested by Domenico da Cividale and Jacomo da Cavali Republic of Venice, 13 September 1526. In: *"Nekünk mégis Mohács kell…"*, eds. Farkas et al., p. 182.

In conclusion, the Christian army suffered huge losses, at least 16,000–18,000 soldiers died on the battlefield. Two thousand of the infantry remained, most probable the lighter-armed Hungarian archers. The river flotilla troops probably suffered no casualties at all. Most of the heavy cavalry, partly because they were most directly affected by the fighting and partly because they found it much harder to escape, perished there. A significant part of the light cavalry escaped. Of those who took part in the battle, we know most of the story of those who belonged to the elite. It is through their deaths or even their escape that posterity will judge the fate of the rest of the army.

Bibliography

B. Szabó, János and Gábor Farkas Farkas eds. *Örök Mohács: szövegek és értelmezések.* Budapest: Bölcsészettudományi Kutatóközpont, 2020.

Bessenyei, József ed. *1504–1566 Memoria rerum: A Magyarországon legutóbbi László király fiának legutóbbi Lajos királynak születése óta esett dolgok emlékezete (Verancsics-évkönyv).* Bibliotheca Historica. Budapest: Magyar Helikon, 1981.

Bostan, İdris. *Osmanlı Bahriye Teşkilâtı : XVII. Yüzyılda Tersâne-i Âmire.* [Ottoman Naval Organisation: the Main Maritime Arsenal in the Seventieth Century] Ankara: Türk Tarih Kurumu Basımevi, 1992. pp. 14–29.

Bostan, Idris. *Ottoman Maritime Arsenals and Shipbuilding Technology in the 16th and 17th centuries.* (2007) Foundation for Science and Technology and Civilisation 16 p. https://muslimheritage.com/uploads/Ottoman_Maritime_Arsenals.pdf.

Brodarics, István. "Igaz történet a magyarok és Szulejmán török császár mohácsi ütközetéről (1528)" [A true account of the battle between the Hungarians and the Turkish Emperor Süleyman at Mohács] In *Örök Mohács: Szövegek és értelmezések*, eds. János B. Szabó and Gábor Farkas Farkas, 301–325. Budapest: Bölcsészettudományi Kutatóközpont, 2020.

Burgio, Antonio Giovanni da. "Antonio Giovanni de Burgio pápai követ levele Jacopo Sadoleto pápai titkárnak, Buda, 1526. augusztus 25." [Letter from papal nuncio Antonio Giovanni da Burgio to papal secretary Jacopo Sadoleto, Buda, 25 August 1526] In *Mohács*, ed. János B. Szabó, 92. Budapest: Osiris Kiadó, 2006.

Burgio, Antonio Giovanni da. "Antonio Giovanni de Burgio pápai követ levele Jacopo Sadoleto pápai titkárnak, Pozsony, 1526. szeptember 5." [Letter from papal ambassador Antonio Giovanni da Burgio to papal secretary Jacopo Sadoleto, Pozsony, 5 September 1526] In *Örök Mohács: Szövegek és értelmezések*, eds. János B. Szabó and Gábor Farkas Farkas, 131–132. Budapest: Bölcsészettudományi Kutatóközpont, 2020.

Csonkaréti, Károly and László Benczúr: *Haditengerészek és folyamőrök a Dunán.* [Sailors and river guards on the Danube] Budapest: Zrínyi Kiadó, 1997.

Egy cseh úr levele a Santa Clara-kolostor főnöknőjéhez, 1526 november. [Letter from a Czech nobleman to the Mother Superior of the Santa Clara Convent, November 1526] In *Örök Mohács: Szövegek és értelmezések,* eds. János B. Szabó and Gábor Farkas Farkas, 207–216. Budapest: Bölcsészettudományi Kutatóközpont, 2020.

Erdősi, Ferenc and Antal Lehmann. *Mohács földrajza.* [The Geography of Mohács] Mohács: Mohács Városi Tanács V.B. Művelődési Osztálya, 1974.

Faludi, Gábor and László Nebojszki. "A Mohácsi-sziget kialakulása és vizeinek történelmi változásai." [The formation of Mohács Island and the historical changes in its waters] *Hidrológiai Közlöny* 88 (2008): 47–57.

Fricsy, Ádám. "A pécsi klérus birtokainak telepítésügyi összeírása 1733-ban." [Settlement census of the estates of the clergy of Pécs in 1733] In *Baranyai helytörténetírás 1978,* ed. Szita László, 151–204. Pécs: Baranya Megyei Levéltár, 1979.

Gyenizse, Péter, Norbert Pap, Máté Kitanics, and Tamás Morva. "A mohácsi csata helyszínének pontosítását célzó beláthatósági vizsgálatok eredményei." [The results of visibility surveys to clarify the site of the Battle of Mohács] In *Az elmélet és gyakorlat találkozása a térinformatikában X.,* ed. Vanda Éva Molnár, 101–108. Debrecen: Debreceni Egyetemi Kiadó, 2019.

Isthvánffy, Miklós. "A magyarok történetéből, 1622 (Részlet)." [From the History of the Hungarians, 1622 (Excerpt)] In *Örök Mohács: Szövegek és értelmezések,* eds. János B. Szabó and Gábor Farkas Farkas, 444–462. Budapest: Bölcsészettudományi Kutatóközpont, 2020.

Jajczay, János. "Törökkori Mohács." [Mohács in the Turkish period] *Élet és Tudomány* 24 (1969): 1490, 1524–1525.

Johann Fugger értesülései, Buda, 1526. augusztus 29–31.; Bécs, szeptember 5. (kivonat). [Information from Johann Fugger, Buda, 29–31 August 1526, Vienna, 5 September 1526] In *Örök Mohács: szövegek és értelmezések,* eds. János B. Szabó and Gábor Farkas Farkas, 125. Budapest: Bölcsészettudományi Kutatóközpont, 2020.

Josef Estaierhez írt levél Bécs 1526. szeptember 2–3. (kivonat). [Letter to Giuseppe Estaier Vienna, 2–3 September 1526] In *Örök Mohács: szövegek és értelmezések,* eds. János B. Szabó and Gábor Farkas Farkas, 126. Budapest: Bölcsészettudományi Kutatóközpont, 2020.

Kemálpasazáde. "Mohácsnáme, 1526 és 1534 között (Részletek)." [Mohácsname, between 1526 and 1534. (Excerpts)] In *Örök Mohács: Szövegek és értelmezések,* eds. János B. Szabó and Gábor Farkas Farkas, 326–338. Budapest: Bölcsészettudományi Kutatóközpont, 2020.

Kőnig, Frigyes and István Pánya. "A mohácsi török palánkvár." [The Turkish palisade fortress in Mohács] In *Várak, kastélyok, templomok,* ed. Kósa Pál, 24–29. Kökény: 2018.

Lanteri, Francesco. "Francesco Lanteri Antonio Lanterihez írt levele Pettau, 1526. szeptember 3. (részlet)." [Letter from Francesco Lanteri to Antonio Lanteri Pettau, 3

September 1526 (excerpt)] In *Örök Mohács: szövegek és értelmezések,* eds. János B. Szabó and Gábor Farkas Farkas, 130. Budapest: Bölcsészettudományi Kutatóközpont, 2020.

Lutfi pasa, "Az Oszmán-ház története (a kezdetektől 1554-ig), 1550-es évek (Részlet)." [History of the Ottoman House (from the beginning to 1554), the 1550s (Excerpt)] In *Örök Mohács: Szövegek és értelmezések,* eds. János B. Szabó and Gábor Farkas Farkas, 404–409. Budapest: Bölcsészettudományi Kutatóközpont, 2020.

Maráz, Borbála. "A mohácsi csatatér régészeti leletei." [Archaeological finds from the battlefield of Mohács] *Honismeret* 4 (1976): 23–25.

Mula, Agostino da. "Agostino da Mula jelentése Udine, 1526. szeptember 25. (részletek)." [Account of Agostino da Mula Udine, 25 September 1526 (excerpts)] In *Örök Mohács: szövegek és értelmezések,* eds. János B. Szabó and Gábor Farkas Farkas, 163–165. Budapest: Bölcsészettudományi Kutatóközpont, 2020.

Nehring, Karl. *Adam Freiherrn zu Herbersteins Gesandschaftsreise nach Konstantinopel. Ein Beitrag zum Frieden von Zsitvatorok (1606).* München: R. Oldenbourg Verlag, 1983.

Papp, László. "A mohácsi csatahely kutatása." [Research into the battlefield of Mohács] in *A Janus Pannonius Múzeum évkönyve 1960,* ed. János Dombay, 197–253. Pécs: Janus Pannonius Múzeum, 1961.

Pecsevi, Ibrahim. "Krónika (1648 előtt)," [Chronicle (before 1648)] In *Örök Mohács: szövegek és értelmezések,* eds. János B. Szabó and Gábor Farkas Farkas, 463–477. Budapest: Bölcsészettudományi Kutatóközpont, 2020.

Pesti, János ed. *Baranya megye földrajzi nevei* II. kötet. [Geographical names in Baranya County.] Pécs: Baranya Megyei Levéltár, 1982.

Savoia, Fazio di. "Fazio di Savoia jelentése Graz, 1526. szeptember 17. (kivonat)." [Account of Fazio di Savoia Graz, 17 September 1526 (excerpt)] In *Örök Mohács: szövegek és értelmezések,* eds. János B. Szabó and Gábor Farkas Farkas, 155. Budapest: Bölcsészettudományi Kutatóközpont, 2020.

Sudár, Balázs. "Török fürdők a hódoltságban." [Turkish baths in Ottoman Hungary] *Történelmi Szemle* 45 (2003): 213–263.

Szentkláray, Jenő. *A dunai hajóhadak története.* [History of the Danube flotillas] Budapest: M. Tud. Akadémia Történelmi Bizottsága, 1885.

T. Mérey, Klára. *A Dél-Dunántúl földrajza katonaszemmel a 19. század elején.* [The geography of South Transdanubia from the soldier's point of view in the early 19th century] Geographia Pannonica Nova 1. Pécs: Lomart Kiadó, 2007.

T. Mérey, Klára. *Baranya megye települései az első katonai felmérés idején.* [Settlements of Baranya County at the time of the First Military Survey] Tanulmányok és források Baranya megye történetéből 12. Pécs: Baranya Megyei Levéltár, 2004.

Thury, József ed. *Török Történetírók* II. [Turkish Historiographers II.] Budapest: Magyar Tudományos Akadémia, 1896.

Tóth, István György. "Athanasio Georgiceo álruhás császári megbízott útleírása a magyarországi török hódoltságról, 1626-ból." [Disguised imperial envoy Athanasio Georgiceo's travelogue on the Turkish occupation of Hungary in 1626] *Századok* 132 (1998): 837–858.

Török történetírók II. [Turkish chroniclers II.] Budapest: Magyar Tudományos Akadémia, 1896.

Vass, Előd. "Mohács város hódoltságkori történetének török forrásai." [Turkish sources of the history of the city of Mohács during the Ottoman occupation] In *Baranyai helytörténetírás 1976,* ed. László Szita, 15–48. Pécs, Baranya Megyei Levéltár, 1976.

Velius, Caspar Ursinus. "A mohácsi csata 1530 körül (töredék)." [The Battle of Mohács around 1530 (fragment)] In *Örök Mohács: szövegek és értelmezések,* eds. János B. Szabó and Gábor Farkas Farkas, 348–355. Budapest: Bölcsészettudományi Kutatóközpont, 2020.

CHAPTER 3

The Hungarian and Ottoman Forces at the Battle of Mohács

Máté Kitanics, Pál Fodor and Norbert Pap

1   Introduction

Over the past century there has been much debate about the numbers and equipment of the two armies that met at Mohács, as well as about the chances of victory for the Christian side. In order to have a clear picture, we need to review the structure and characteristics of the armed forces of the two sides, based on the written sources that tell of the campaign and the battle within it. In the following chapter, we will attempt to build a coherent picture by examining and presenting the positions of the decades-long debate. At the same time, a full review of the literature on the subject would be beyond the scope of this paper.

2   The Hungarian (Christian) Armed Forces

On 29 August 1526, 29,000–32,000 Hungarians, Croats, Serbs, Czechs, Moravians, Poles and Germans gathered on the plain of Mohács. Of these, 16,000 to 17,000 were cavalrymen, the rest were infantry soldiers, artillerymen and boatmen.

But who could have been the nucleus of this Hungarian army, joined by the foreign fighters? In the period, the Hungarian king's customary banderium consisted of 1000 men, while royal governors (the voivode of Transylvania, the comes of Seklers [Székelys], the Croatian ban, the count of Temes County) and ecclesiastical dignitaries (archbishops, bishops, certain abbots, provosts and chaplains) were usually required to take part in the campaign alongside the monarch with a full banderium of 400 men or a half banderium of 200.[1] From

---

[1]   Uladislai II. decretum a. 1498. *"Banderia archi-episcoporum, episcoporum, abbatum, praepositorum, capitulorum: et numerus equitum.; De regali banderio, et regiorum officialium."* Articulus 20, 21. Sándor Kolosvári et al., *Corpus Juris Hungarici: 1000–1526. évi törvénycikkek* [Articles of law for the years 1000–1526] (Budapest: Franklin-Társulat, 1899), p. 606. The

the end of the 15th century, we also know by name the dozens of secular magnates who were obliged to fight alongside the king and the prelates. Among them was the Serbian despot who served the Hungarian king and who was obliged to provide 1000 heavy cavalrymen and 1000 hussars.[2]

We also know from the decrees of the first half of the 1520s that landowners were obliged to field one horseman for every ten plots of land equipped at least with a lance and a shield or a bow and quiver. And some northern counties of Hungary sent infantrymen with handguns in a similar way.[3] The obligations of the clergy with secular goods and possessions were essentially not different from those of the landed nobility.[4] In addition to the above, there were also the minor landowners with one plot of land who 'served with their blood' in the army as infantry soldiers or cavalrymen.[5] Then, in 1526, in the face of increased danger and in preparation for the campaign, the king was required to arm a larger banderium than had been expected up to that time. The prelates, barons and wealthy nobles were asked to make greater sacrifices than usual in order to provide troops (heavy cavalry, light cavalry, arquebusiers) and were obliged to go to war in person. In case of emergency, all serfs or a well-armed fifth of them were to be called to arms.[6]

If we look at the military laws of the period from the end of the 15th century to the Battle of Mohács, it is clear that most of the measures relating to military service and the troops to be fielded concern the cavalry. In this regard, it is mainly in the proportion of heavy cavalry to light cavalry that we see a correction from time to time. From the above we can also conclude that the

---

archbishop of Esztergom had to provide two banderia (800 men), but there were also some clergymen who had to arm only 50 or 100 horsemen. The total number of horsemen to be provided by royal officers and ecclesiastical dignitaries at this time was 8950.

2 Uladislai II. decretum a. 1498. *"De dominis baronibus, qui cum viris ecclesiasticis banderiatis exercituare, seu militare tenebuntur."* Articulus 22. Kolosvári et al., *Corpus Juris Hungarici*, pp. 606 and 608. The Serbian despot Stjepan Berislavić did not take part in the Battle of Mohács.

3 Ex Ludovici II. decr. a. 1523. *"Domini, et nobiles de singulis decem sessionibus, unum equitem dare tenentur."* Articulus 19 and 31. Kolosvári et al., *Corpus Juris Hungarici*, p. 814, p. 834.

4 Ex Ludovici II. decr. a. 1523. Exercituandi Spiritualium modus. Articulus 42. Kolosvári et al., *Corpus Juris Hungarici*, p. 820.

5 *"Nobiles unius sessionis, exercituantium more, equestres, vel pedestres, ad expeditionem vadant."* Articulus 20. See further Articulus 31. Kolosvári et al., *Corpus Juris Hungarici*, p. 814 and 834.

6 Ludovici II. decr. a. 1526. *"Rex, ad expeditionem se praeparet: et gentem paratam habeat.; Belli onus solitum, quo majori poterunt apparatu; omnes assumere debent.; Coloni, per singula capita assumantur in bellum; in extrema necessitate.; Apparatum belli, quo majorem poterunt, levent."* Articulus 8–11. Kolosvári et al., *Corpus Juris Hungarici*, p. 842. The levy of the fifth part was calculated on the basis of the taxable plots of land.

cavalry played a prominent role in the military organisation of the late medieval Kingdom of Hungary. It is no coincidence that the choice of location for the battle of 1526 was also adapted to this arm of service. The battle was fought on the field of Mohács, which was not divided by water, trees or bushes, and was chosen to be suitable for a cavalry charge, or even a heavy cavalry charge.

In the Hungarian diet's decrees of the late 15th and early 16th centuries, the number of references to infantrymen in comparison to cavalry is small. There is a Hungarian expert on the Battle of Mohács who, in connection with this, has pointed out that "The laws governing military organization give some guidance on the proportions of cavalry, but provide no hint of why infantry comprised half of the Hungarian army in 1526."[7] However, the statement needs to be nuanced. First of all, it was not a purely Hungarian army, but a Christian army fighting against the Ottomans, which, in addition to the soldiers of the Hungarian crown, was made up mainly of Czechs, Moravians, Poles and Germans. Less than half of this Christian army, 12,000 to 13,000, were footmen. Of these, some 6000–7000 were from the Czech, Moravian, Polish and German lands, the remainder coming from the territories under the jurisdiction of the Hungarian crown. As can be seen, therefore, those to whom the mentioned laws governing the organisation of the army could apply did not make up about half of the total army, but only amounted to about half of the total infantry.

In addition to cavalry and infantry, artillery was also part of the Christian army. The casting, maintenance and professional handling of cannons was expensive and required great skill. In the case of a field battle, the guns were transported to the battlefield on land by animal-drawn carts or by water, depending on the geographical position, or, as at the Battle of Mohács, by a combination of the two. It also required a lot of money and good organisation. In 1526, King Louis II of Hungary and Bohemia proved wanting in both. He had few cannons compared to the Ottomans, and some of these were only brought into fighting condition just before the battle, while others were sent from abroad, from Vienna, to help. Even in this dimension, preparations for battle were rather disorganised and slow. Moreover, it seems that the Hungarian side did not attach as much importance to it as the Ottoman army.

---

7 János B. Szabó, "The Military Organization and Army of the Kingdom of Hungary (1490–1256)," in *On the Verge of a New Era: The Armies of Europe at the Time of the Battle of Mohács* eds. János B. Szabó and Pál Fodor (Budapest: RCH Eötvös Loránd Reserch Network, 2021), p. 163.

A special natural challenge of the anti-Turkish struggles of the 15th–17th centuries was to hold up the Ottoman conquerors on the natural routes of Central Europe, the Danube and its tributaries, and to maintain a substantial river flotilla to this end. The southern Slav and Hungarian boatmen formed a distinct social group in the towns along the rivers. During the period, they usually numbered between 1000 and 2000 people. Their vessels included the naszád (boat), the half-naszád and even smaller boats. Their clothing typically consisted of a hat, sleeveless doublet, baggy trousers and boots. Their remuneration also contained a piece of broad-cloth to dress themselves. It is possible that some of them wore armour, but their main defensive weapon was the shield, which they wore strapped to their arms even when rowing. The cannon was an important weapon. However, the use of small arms in water skirmishes was very different from that on land. For a long time, the Danube boatmen were averse to handguns, preferring the bow. The matchlock ignition was impractical on water, in wet, humid and foggy conditions. So the arquebus, which was generally used in close combat, only really caught on with them when it became simpler and easier to use. The bow was therefore used alongside the arquebus until the end of the 16th century. Their basic weapons also included the lance, the sword, the mace, the spontoon (fokos) and the pickaxe.[8]

According to some calculations, the military potential of the Kingdom of Hungary at the beginning of the 16th century was some 50,000–60,000 men.[9] In 1521, when the Ottoman campaign threatened the country, some reports put the number of men in arms at more than 70,000, including foreign auxiliaries and the peasants of the southern borderland.[10] However, as we shall see, the size of the force that was eventually assembled at Mohács in 1526 was much smaller than these figures, at about half that number.

8   Jenő Szentkláray, *A dunai hajóhadak története* [History of the Danube flotillas] (Budapest, M. Tud. Akadémia Történelmi Bizottsága, 1885), 433 p.
9   András Kubinyi, "Magyarország hatalmasai és a török veszély a Jagelló-korban (1490–1526)," [The magnates of Hungary and the Turkish threat in the Jagiellon era (1490–1526)] in *Közép-Európa harca a török ellen a 16. század első felében,* ed. István Zombori (Budapest: Magyar Egyháztörténeti Enciklopédia Munkaközösség (METEM), Historia Ecclesiastica Hungarica Alapítvány, 2004), pp. 117–146.
10 János B. Szabó, "The Military Organization and Army of the Kingdom of Hungary (1490–1256)," in *On the Verge of a New Era: The Armies of Europe at the Time of the Battle of Mohács* eds. János B. Szabó and Pál Fodor (Budapest: RCH Eötvös Loránd Research Network, 2021), p. 154.

3   The Ottoman Forces

The army of the Ottoman Empire has been extensively and thoroughly researched.[11] We also have a clear picture of the organisation of the army, the units and the financial structures that enabled the army to be maintained.

At the beginning of the 16th century, the backbone of the Ottoman army was formed by the provincial light cavalry (sipahis), who rendered military service in return for revenue grants (timar, dirlik). They were equipped with swords, lances, bows, arrows, coats of mail, helmets, and some of them, mainly from the coastal provinces, served in the navy.

In the year 1527–1528, 27,868 timar-holding sipahis were registered. The timariots went to war year by year and accompanied by their mounted armed retainers (cebelü) whose number depended on the income of their prebends. Their total number was estimated at between 50,000 and 100,000 in the whole of the empire. At the same time, some of this huge number, especially those with modest livelihood, were assigned to the defence of the territory where their estates were located. Hence, during the campaigns, mobilisation was limited to a smaller number.

The other main part of the army was the sultan's salaried household troops (kapıkulu ocakları), which consisted of the janissary elite infantry and of the six household cavalry regiments. The janissaries were typically recruited into the army through the *devşirme*, the forced levy of boys from among the Christian families in the empire. These children were prepared for military service through long years of training. The janissary novices were admitted into the corps as the janissary soldiers got too old or died. In the year 1524–1525, the number of janissaries was 9390 and the number of novices 4961 (14,351 in total). In the year following the "Buda campaign", i.e. 1527–1528, the number of janissaries fell to 7886 and the number of novices to 3553 (11,439 in total).

A distinctive piece of clothing was their tall headgear with a flap. Their armament most often included a light coat of mail, sabre, shield, lance and, originally, bow and arrow. From the 1440s, they were increasingly equipped with handguns, and after the Mamluk war (1485–1491) of Sultan Bayezid II they were furnished with highly effective arquebuses. In pitched battles, they

---

[11]   On this, see e.g. Murphey Rhoads, Ottoman *Warfare, 1500–1700* (Routledge, 1998), 304 p.; Gábor Ágoston "Firearms and Military Adaptation: the Ottomans and the European Military Revolution, 1450–1800," *Journal of World History* 25 (2014), no. 1, pp. 85–124; Pál Fodor, "The Military Organization and Army of the Ottoman Empire (1500–1530)," in *On the Verge of a New Era: The Armies of Europe at the Time of the Battle of Mohács* eds. János B. Szabó and Pál Fodor (Budapest: RCH Eötvös Loránd Research Network, 2021), pp. 91–115.

formed an impenetrable wall in front of the sultan, and were also regularly deployed in the most dangerous fortress sieges.

In 1524–1525, the six court cavalry regiments (sipahi oğlanları, silahtar, garibs of the left and of the right, and ulufecis of the left and of the right) totalled 5997, while in 1527–1528, their number was 5088. These troops were under the command of six ağas and received high salaries. They not only defended the sultan's person, but also, for example, helped to collect imperial taxes.

With the spread of cannons, the Ottomans began to employ artillerymen (topçı) and gun carriage drivers (top arabacıları), while armourers (cebeci) manufactured, repaired and supplied weapons for court troops. They numbered 1676 in 1524–1525 and 2162 in 1527–1528.

In addition to these main services, auxiliary and peasant soldier units of various origins were also at the disposal of the Ottoman state. The akıncıs, azabs, yürüks, yayas, müsellems, voynuks, eflaks, and cerehors made up a total force of some 40,000–45,000 men. In addition, the Crimean Tatars and the Romanian principalities usually joined the Ottoman military enterprises with smaller forces, some estimates put the number at around 3000. The number of soldiers stationed in the imperial fortresses in the age of the Battle of Mohács was also significant, estimated at over 40,000.

In total, the Ottoman forces numbered between 170,000 and 180,000, but a large part of the total force was constantly engaged in defending the borders of the empire and maintaining internal peace. During the great campaigns, such as that of 1526, only less than half of the force was deployed: the number of troops marching to Mohács can be estimated at around 80,000.

4   The Cavalries

The number and composition of the Christian cavalry at Mohács is described by István Brodarics, Hungarian Chancellor and eyewitness chronicler of the battle. According to him, King Louis II left Buda on 20 July 1526 for the assembly point at Tolna with about 3000 cavalrymen and infantrymen, and arrived on 6 August 1526 with about 4000 mounted soldiers. Here the king was met by the Palatine (nádor) István Báthori,[12] and was joined by György Szapolyai, Count of Szepes, Pál Várdai,[13] Bishop of Eger and Ferenc Perényi, Bishop of Várad. And although Szapolyai, who became co-commander-in-chief of the

---

12   According to Brodarics, the king sent the palatine in advance from the second station after Buda, Ercsi.
13   Várdai did not participate in the battle, as the king sent him to Buda.

battle, was rumoured to be bringing a large army with him, in the end, as confirmed by Brodarics and the papal nuncio Antonio Giovanni da Burgio,[14] he appeared with only 300 horsemen in addition to his infantry. Of these, 200 were heavy horsemen and 100 were light cavalrymen. Pál Tomori, Archbishop of Kalocsa, commander-in-chief, joined by Péter Perényi, Count of Temes, with 5000–6000 horsemen, encamped separately from the former and withdrew his troops to Mohács, thus uniting the main army. A few days before the battle, Croatian ban Ferenc Batthyány appeared with a number of noblemen, including 3000 cavalrymen in addition to his infantry, while István Aczél, the Castellan of Pozsony, brought 300 well-armed soldiers, and Simon Erdődy, the Bishop of Zagreb, a little over 700.[15] In addition to those mentioned above, the cavalry was augmented by the presence of other prelates and secular magnates.

The question may of course arise, whether there could have been a significant discrepancy between the numbers expected under the regulations governing military mobilization and the actual numbers that showed up at the battlefield. The decrees of the late 15th and early 16th centuries sought to determine the number of horsemen to be provided according to the size of estates and property. Prelates and barons were also persuaded to provide heavy cavalry for the majority of their quota. However, several ecclesiastical and secular lords apparently failed to show up at Mohács with the required number of soldiers, and in many cases it was not recorded whether a half or a full banderium arrived. In addition, it is certain that the proportion of the heavy cavalry was also lower than expected. Given the high cost of equipping

---

14   Antonio Giovanni da Burgio, "Antonio Giovanni da Burgio pápai követ levele Jacopo Sadoleto pápai titkárnak Buda, 1526. augusztus 13. (részletek)," [Letter from the papal nuncio Antonio Giovanni da Burgio to the papal secretary Jacopo Sadoleto, Buda, 13 August 1526 (excerpts)] in *Örök Mohács: szövegek és értelmezések,* eds. János B. Szabó and Gábor Farkas Farkas (Budapest: Bölcsészettudományi Kutatóközpont, 2020), pp. 111–114.

15   István Brodarics, "Igaz történet a magyarok és Szulejmán török császár mohácsi ütközetéről 1528," [A true account of the battle between the Hungarians and the Turkish Emperor Süleyman in Mohács in 1528] in *Örök Mohács,* eds. B. Szabó et al., pp. 301–325. According to the translation in the quoted volume, the bishop of Zagreb would have appeared at Mohács with not 700 horsemen, but more than 70, but this is incorrect. Cf. Stephanus Brodericus, *De conflictu Hungarorum cum Solymano turcarum imperatore ad Mohach historia verissima* (Bibliotheca Scriptorum Medii Recentisque Aevorum. Series Nova) 6 (Budapest: Akadémiai Kiadó, 1985), p. 47. In another translation of Brodarics the correct number, 700, can be read: Imre Szentpétery (transl.), *Brodarics históriája a mohácsi vészről* [Brodarics's history of the Mohács diaster]. Budapest, 1903, p. 53.

them, it is not surprising that they made up only a small part of the total Christian cavalry: the strength of the heavy cavalry can be estimated at between 2000 and 2500.[16]

The 'beautiful corps' of heavy cavalry, just over 1000 men in the second battle formation was positioned directly behind the king and the high dignitaries. A considerable number of the Hungarian, Czech and Moravian magnates and their bodyguards, who were in the king's row and in the rows immediately in front of and behind the monarch, also belonged to the heavy cavalry. There were also some scattered in the first formation or column. That the heavy cavalry was the dominant feature of the battle and that it played a decisive role in the charge is confirmed not only by Christian but also by Ottoman Turkish sources. Kemalpaşazade, for example, reported of the custom of the 'tiger-like' Hungarians to cover themselves and their horses from top to toe with armour, and then, in the open field, "all of them at once, with a fierce charge, throwing

---

16   Brodarics informs us that in the second battle formation of the Christian army stood *"the beautiful corps of heavy cavalry with a thousand or so armoured men after the king and the magnates, because the rest of the cavalry belonging to this arm was scattered in the first column."* See Brodarics, "Igaz történet," [A true account] in *Örök Mohács*, eds. B. Szabó et al., p. 317. From this description alone we can infer that the slightly more than 1000 heavy cavalrymen behind the king and the high dignitaries made up the bulk of the Christian heavy cavalry; those in the first column, alongside the infantry and light cavalry, could only have been fewer in number. Other data also suggest that the number of heavy cavalry was in reality less than the number that some have suggested (4000). Burgio, the papal nuncio, wrote of only 200 heavy-armed horsemen at the time of the king's departure for Buda. See Antonio Giovanni da Burgio, "Antonio Giovanni da Burgio pápai követ levele Jacopo Sadoleto pápai titkárnak Buda, 1526. július 26.," [Letter from the papal nuncio Antonio Giovanni da Burgio to the papal secretary Jacopo Sadoleto Buda, 26 July 1526] in *Örök Mohács*, eds. B. Szabó et al., pp. 94–97. A German eyewitness to the battle, in agreement with the foregoing, reported that *"the Hungarian king has mostly German noblemen in his court / and good German soldiers / men-at-arms and others / must have been 300 / with them he went to battle".* See "Új híradás: Hogyan esett meg a magyarországi csata a török császárral. Itt volt egy ember Bécsből, és utána megírta Ottingenbe 1526.," [New News: How the battle of Hungary with the Turkish Emperor was fought. Here was a man from Vienna, and afterwards he wrote to Ottingen, 1526.] in *Örök Mohács*, eds. B. Szabó et al., pp. 221–223. Another report by Burgio tells us that, contrary to preliminary expectations (5000 men), György Szapolyai joined the king at the Tolna camp with only 1500 soldiers, including 200 heavy-armed cavalrymen armed in the Hungarian manner. See Burgio, "Antonio Giovanni da Burgio pápai követ levele ... Buda, 1526. augusztus 13.," [Letter from the papal nuncio Antonio Giovanni da Burgio ... Buda, 13 August 1526] in *Örök Mohács*, eds, B. Szabó et al., pp. 111–114. If we take into account the slightly more than 1000 heavy cavalry behind the king and the high dignitaries, the few hundred notables and their bodyguards in the rows around the king, and the heavy cavalry scattered in the first column under the command of Ferenc Batthyány and Péter Perényi, we think that we can hardly get more than the 2000–2500 mentioned above.

themselves upon any strong division, break through it just as a rushing stream tears up the side of a mountain."¹⁷ And later, while recounting the events of the battle, he wrote of the Christian cavalry clad in steel and pouring like a torrent, attacking the Ottoman army.

The majority of the cavalry, however, were not heavy but light cavalry, including hussars, who wore chain mail and helmets at most, and were equipped with shields and, among other things, lances and sabres. A considerable portion of this light cavalry was capable of rapid movement and a variety of tasks, but the more skilled and well-equipped could also be deployed in a closed formation, as at the Battle of Mohács. Among them were the battle-hardened Hungarian and Serbian soldiers from the southern counties neighbouring the Ottomans, as well as the Croatian cavalry from Slavonia. This crowd was present in both the first and second battle formations.

In the front line, the Slavonian light cavalry under Croatian Ban Ferenc Batthyány was massed on the right flank, while on the left flank, under the command of Péter Perényi, was part of the cavalry that had already fought the Ottomans at Pétervárad (Petrovaradin). However, as mentioned above, light cavalry was also part of the second formation: on the one hand, they surrounded its core, and on the other hand, this was also the original position of the hussar commander Gáspár Ráskai with his troops, who were in charge of guarding the king in the centre and rescuing him, if necessary.

The extant Christian and Ottoman sources on the battle mainly emphasise the cavalry and the individual cavalry charges by the Christians, with less mention of the infantry. According to Bernardus Vapovius, "the cavalrymen clashed with the Turks with great vigour; they fought here with such fury, so much blood was shed that it is said that rivulets of blood flowed into the Danube."¹⁸ Miklós Istvánffy reported that "some of our horsemen retreated into the valley between the hill and a nearby marshy lake to avoid the cannonballs, but at the urging of the commanders they again engaged in battle..."¹⁹ The Ottoman campaign diary recalled that "one of the troops, covered from head to foot with heavy iron and carrying an iron spike in their hands, rode recklessly and fearlessly towards the beylerbeyi of Rumelia, İbrahim Pasha, with no regard for

---

17   Kemálpasazáde, "Mohácsnáme 1526 és 1534 között (részlet)," [Mohácsname, between 1526 and 1534. (excerpt)] in *Örök Mohács,* eds. B. Szabó et al., p. 327.
18   Bernardus Vapovius, "Fragmentum Sigismundi 1526–1535," in *Örök Mohács* eds. B. Szabó et al., p. 340.
19   Miklós Isthvánffy, "A magyarok történetéből 1622 (részlet)," [From the history of the Hungarians 1622 (excerpt)] in *Örök Mohács,* eds. B. Szabó et al., p. 457.

the bullets and cannonballs that were fired."[20] Similarly, Celalzade Mustafa wrote that "all the unbelievers of the most debauched morals held their lances straight up, but when they rushed towards us, they suddenly let them down and galloped with their horses bent over their necks."[21]

The aforementioned light and heavy cavalry charges were finally broken by cannon fire, or at least the fear of it, but even more so by the volleys from the handguns of the janissaries. Those of the Christian army who could fled. It is not accidental that – as some accounts reveal – several lords, such as Palatine István Báthori and Royal Cup-bearer János Bánffy, left the battlefield alive on fresh horses given to them by their servants, to replace their fallen horses.[22] However, it did matter who was a light cavalryman and who was a heavy cavalryman. Since the former outnumbered the latter, their losses were greater in terms of numbers. Proportionally, however, the heavy cavalry suffered a heavier blow, as even those who survived the clash found it harder and slower to leave the battlefield, and the pursuers caught up with them. Antonio Giovanni da Burgio wrote immediately after the battle[23] that only a small part of the heavy cavalry had escaped, while an intelligence report of September 1526[24] complained that the majority of the light cavalry had survived the battle. Another example is a letter written about the battle by a Czech nobleman in November 1526, also detailing the fate of three Czech knights, Albrecht, Albin and Stefan Schlick. Stefan, one of the counts of Schlick, arrived in Mohács with his men and equipment long before the battle. Albrecht and Albin joined them later, leaving their armour and war horses behind in the rush. As it turned out, Albrecht and Albin were lucky "… that they had no armour and no heavy war horses, otherwise they would not have been able to escape…". The author of

20 "Az 1526. évi hadinapló 1526 (részlet)," [The 1526 campaign diary (excerpt)] in *Örök Mohács*, eds. B. Szabó et al., p. 245.
21 Dzselálzáde Musztafa, "Az országok osztályai és az utak felsorolása, 1560-as évek (részlet)," [The echelons of the dominions and the hiearchies of destinations, 1560s (excerpt)] in *Örök Mohács*, eds. B. Szabó et al., p. 415.
22 Isthvánffy, "A magyarok történetéből," [From the history of the Hungarians] in *Örök Mohács*, eds. B. Szabó et al., pp. 457 and 444–462.
23 Antonio Giovanni da Burgio, "Antonio Giovanni da Burgio pápai követ levele Jacopo Sadoleto pápai titkárnak Pozsony, 1526. szeptember 5.," [Letter from the papal envoy Antonio Giovanni da Burgio to the papal secretary Jacopo Sadoleto Pozsony, 5 September 1526] in *Örök Mohács*, eds. B. Szabó et al., pp. 131–132.
24 "Hírszerzői jelentés Magyarországgal kapcsolatban, Pettau, 1526. szeptember 20.," [Intelligence report on Hungary Pettau, 20 September 1526] in *Örök Mohács*, eds. B. Szabó et al., pp. 158–159.

the letter added that "not a single infantryman escaped, not one of those who did not have a horse."[25]

It seems that the light cavalry who survived were able to leave the plain battlefield easier and faster than their heavy-amoured comrades. Most of the latter were lost. Piotr Tomicki, Archbishop of Krakow, reported[26] a total of 4000 horsemen killed, while in his memoirs Brodarics mentioned between 3500 and 4500 cavalrymen among the casualties.[27] So if these figures can be given credit, roughly a quarter of the total Christian cavalry was destroyed.

In the Ottoman army divided into three corps (the Rumelian on the left, the sultan in the middle, the Anatolian on the right), the cavalry was the most important arm of service, smilarly to the Christian army. Of the sultan's forces, which we estimate at around 80,000, the cavalry numbered between 57,000 and 58,000. Due to the structure and maintenance of the army, the bulk of this force was made up of timariots, the main body of whom were in the Rumelian and Anatolian corps. Research puts the total number of these *sipahi*s and their retainers at 45,000.[28]

Of the elite units of the imperial army, the court cavalry numbered just under 6000 in the year before the battle, organised into the six regiments mentioned above; it is unlikely that more than 5000 of them were drafted for the campaign. They played an important role in the battle, defending the sultan from the renewed attacks of the Hungarian cavalry.

We should also mention the thousands of cavalry troops of Yahyapaşa-oğlu Bali and Hüsrev Beys, the district governors of Semendria and Bosnia respectively, on the Ottoman left flank. The selected troops of Bali had a major role in destroying the Christian camp and perhaps also in driving the Christian army back. Kemalpaşazade also sang the praises of the exploits of the *akıncı*s at the Battle of Mohács, who, he said, "having slain thousands of the enemies of the faith, drove back those who survived. The first were sent to hell … and the

---

25   "Egy cseh úr levele a Santa Clara kolostor főnöknőjéhez, 1526. november," [Letter from a Czech nobleman to the Superior of the Convent of Santa Clara, November 1526] in *Örök Mohács*, eds. B. Szabó et al., pp. 208–210.

26   Piotr Tomicki, "A magyar hadsereg veszteséglistája Piotr Tomicki krakkói érsek és lengyel alkancellár iratai között 1526. október," [The list of losses of the Hungarian army in the documents of Piotr Tomicki, Archbishop of Krakow and Vice-chancellor of Poland, October 1526] in *Örök Mohács*, eds. B. Szabó et al., pp. 185–188.

27   A list of losses from 1526 gives the larger figure of 6000. See "A mohácsi csatára vonatkozó veszteséglista 1526," [The casualty list relating to the Battle of Mohács 1526] in *Örök Mohács*, eds. B. Szabó et al., pp. 218–220.

28   Gábor Ágoston, "War-Winning Weapons? On the Decisiveness of Ottoman Firearms from the Siege of Constantinople (1453) to the Battle of Mohács (1526)," *Journal of Turkish Studies* 39 (2013), pp. 140–141.

runners were caught up, some of them were captured and put on a belt, and others were slaughtered."[29] Contrary to the exaggerated figures of the chroniclers, the number of *akıncıs* who marched on the campaign can be estimated at 7000–8000.

Finally, we should mention that although we do not know their exact role and position in the Battle of Mohács, there were certainly müsellem cavalry in the Ottoman army. The mentioned campaign diary tells us that in the campaign some müsellem beyis were appointed as supervisors at a bridge construction over the Danube in Buda.[30]

5   The Infantry

The aforementioned Czech and Moravian infantrymen were of outstanding combat value in the studied period. In March 1526, Louis II wrote letters to Archduke Ferdinand of Austria and King Henry VIII of England urging them to send money to recruit infantrymen which, as he said, was the most important thing. The monarch wanted to enlist "very brave infantrymen" from the territory of the Kingdom of Bohemia to fight the Turks.[31] In the end, the Czech, Moravian and Polish soldiers were recruited with papal money, arranged by the papal nuncio in Hungary, Antonio Giovanni da Burgio. The nuncio's frequently written reports reveal that it was only with great difficulty that he succeeded in conscripting soldiers and captains. On 18 June, Burgio wrote that "His Holiness has five thousand soldiers in Hungary, including the thousand at Pétervárad..."[32] Of the latter 1000, 500 were cavalrymen and 500 infantrymen. Since almost all of the latter had fallen at the siege of Pétervárad, we can calculate

---

29   Kemálpasazáde, "Mohácsnáme," in *Örök Mohács,* eds. B. Szabó et al., p. 331.
30   Along with them, two *yaya/piyade* district governors from Anatolia are mentioned in the list of participants: Feridun M. Emecen, "Mohaç 1526. Osmanlılara Orta Avrupa'nın Kapılarını Açan Savaş," in Feridun M. Emecen, *Osmanlı Klasik Çağında Savaş. İstanbul: Timaş,* 2010, p. 211.
31   II. Lajos, "II. Lajos magyar király levele VIII. Henrik angol királynak Buda, 1526. március 25.," [Letter of Louis II, King of Hungary to Henry VIII, King of England Buda, 25 March 1526] in *Örök Mohács,* eds. B. Szabó et al., pp. 38–39; II. Lajos, "II. Lajos magyar király levele Ferdinánd ausztriai főhercegnek Buda, 1526. március 25.," [Letter of Louis II, King of Hungary to Ferdinand, Archduke of Austria Buda, 25 March 1526] in *Örök Mohács,* eds. B. Szabó et al., pp. 37–38.
32   Antonio Giovanni da Burgio, "Antonio Giovanni da Burgio pápai követ levele Jacopo Sadoleto pápai titkárnak Buda, 1526. június 18.," [Letter from the papal envoy Antonio Giovanni da Burgio to the papal secretary Jacopo Sadoleto Buda, 18 June 1526] in *Örök Mohács,* eds. B. Szabó et al., p. 72.

with no more than 4000 papal infantrymen on the battlefield of Mohács. This figure is in strong agreement with the one recorded by István Brodarics, who claimed that a total of 4000 infantrymen, well equipped in every respect and in the papal mercenary corps, were in the line at the assembly point at Tolna before the battle. According to the chancellor, the 1500 Poles led by Captain Lenard Gnoienski particularly excelled in military prowess, while 1300 were under the command of Annibale de Este di Padovana Cartagine.

Some of the Christian arquebusiers may have been among the papal mercenaries. This is also proven by the fact that on 5 August 1526, Louis II wrote to the papal nuncio asking him to bring gunpowder from Vienna, so that in case of need, neither the papal infantrymen under the command of Ambrus Sárkány, nor Annibale de Este di Padovana Cartagine's men, or the Poles should suffer any shortage.[33] Count György Szapolyai of Szepes and his 1200 infantrymen also arrived in Tolna together with his mounted troops. His foot-soldiers, as Istvánffy writes, must have mainly been gunners, since the count came from the counties of northern Hungary, which, under the aforementioned 1523 decree, were obliged to send one gunner for every 10 serfs.[34] Shortly before the battle, 200 of Elek Thurzó's infantrymen arrived at the camp of Mohács, but without the treasurer, for the king had entrusted him with the protection of Queen Maria. Ferenc Batthyány, the Croatian ban, also arrived here, together with the magnates János Tahy and János Bánffy, with a total of slightly less than 3000 Slavonian infantrymen in addition to the cavalry. János Szerecsen from Tolna also brought a larger number of troops, with more than 2000 archers, mainly from the territories along the Drava River, partly from his own estates and partly from those of the Pécs chapter.[35] Finally, we should mention Bishop Fülöp Móré of Pécs, who, according to Burgio, had about 400 infantrymen.[36]

If we add up the above figures (10,800) and combine them with the group of infantrymen, including the German landsknechts, with whom the king left Buda, we can indeed conclude that the Christian army had – in concert with Brodarics's data – no more than 12,000–13,000 infantrymen. The sources also

---

[33] II. Lajos, "II. Lajos magyar király levele Antonio Giovanni da Burgio pápai követnek Paks, 1526. augusztus 5.," [Letter of Louis II, King of Hungary to the papal secretary Jacopo Sadoleto Paks, 5 August 1526] in *Örök Mohács*, eds. B. Szabó et al., p. 106.

[34] Ex Ludovici II. decr. a. 1523. Domini, et nobiles de singulis decem sessionibus, unum equitem dare tenentur. Articulus 19. Kolosvári et al., *Corpus Juris Hungarici*, p. 814.

[35] Brodarics, "Igaz történet," [A true account] in *Örök Mohács*, eds. B. Szabó et al., pp. 301–325.

[36] Burgio, "Antonio Giovanni da Burgio pápai követ levele ... Buda, 1526. június 18.," [Letter from the papal envoy Antonio Giovanni da Burgio ... Buda, 18 June 1526] in *Örök Mohács*, eds. B. Szabó et al., pp. 72–73.

give us an idea of how these foot-soldiers were deployed on the battlefield and what losses they suffered.

Most of the infantry – about 10,000 according to Istvánffy – were in the first battle formation. Several historians have pointed out that this formation was stretched out as much as possible to prevent the enemy from outflanking it. To achieve this, "infantry battalions were placed between the cavalry regiments,"[37] with "cavalry and infantry mixed,"[38] in a long line. In the second formation, as before, a much smaller group of infantry were deployed, here "one or two infantrymen took up positions on the flanks."[39] These covered the flanks. Finally, Istvánffy estimated that 2000 men, including other personnel, were left behind to guard the camp(s).

Some historians believe that the ranks of foreign infantry were "fragmented and disorganised" in the unfortunate "mixed-up" fighting,[40] "with barely a hundred men in any one place, and the three types of infantry, Hungarian, Czech and German, always mixed up".[41] Despite all this, in the last phase of the battle, thousands of Czechs, Moravians, Poles and Germans successfully organized themselves into formations, defending themselves effectively for some time afterwards. Although their heroism is undisputed, they probably had no choice, as with no horses and the enemy at their backs, they could not think of fleeing. Their units with pikes, swords and shields, and the arquebusiers who supported them, seem to have repulsed the Ottoman cavalry at first, but the janissary gunners who were sent in to support them broke their resistance. As Agostino da Mula, the governor of Patria del Friuli, put it a few days after the battle: "Although six or eight thousand Bohemian and landsknecht retreated into a square and were not broken by the Ottoman cavalry, a good group of janissary gunners attacked them and they were killed instantly, as were the others."[42] From what the source mentions, we can assume, albeit cautiously, that most of the foreign infantry did not take an active part in the attacks, and

---

37 Paulus Iovius, "Krónika a törökök viselt dolgairól Róma, 1531 (részlet)," [Chronicle about the deeds of the Turks Rome, 1531 (excerpt)] in *Örök Mohács,* eds. B. Szabó et al., p. 359.

38 Joachim Camerarius, "A Magyarországon, Mohácsnál elszenvedett vereségről és Lajos király haláláról 1541," [On the defeat at Mohács in Hungary and the death of King Louis 1541] in *Örök Mohács,* eds. B. Szabó et al., p. 371.

39 Brodarics, "Igaz történet," [A true account] in *Örök Mohács,* eds. B. Szabó et al., p. 317.

40 Jan Dubravius, "Csehország története 1552 (részlet)," [History of Bohemia 1552 (excerpt)] in *Örök Mohács,* eds. B. Szabó et al., p. 392, p. 393.

41 János Zsámboky, "Feljegyzés a mohácsi csatáról 1584 előtt," [Note on the Battle of Mohács before 1584] in *Örök Mohács,* eds. B. Szabó et al., p. 432.

42 Agostino da Mula, "Agostino da Mula jelentése Udine, 1526. szeptember 15. (átirat)," [Report of Agostino da Mula Udine, 15 September 1526 (transcript)] in *Örök Mohács,* eds. B. Szabó et al., p. 151.

that their larger masses, which remained intact, thus played a more significant role only in the final phase of the battle.

In a letter written a few days after the battle, István Brodarics remembered about 10,000 infantrymen killed,[43] while in the already mentioned list of casualties of 1526, concerning the Battle of Mohács, we read about 12,000. Whichever figure we accept the fact remains that infantry losses far exceeded those of the cavalry. Of the infantry, as we have written, very few left the battlefield alive for lack of horses.

The written records on the Ottoman infantry are clearer than those on the Christian infantry. The proportion of infantrymen in the army was much smaller than on the Christian side, and was understood to be mainly the elite Ottoman infantry, the janissaries. On the basis of the list of arms and ammunitions of the court salaried troops/janissaries (13 April 1526), which shows that 4000 handguns and 5200 bows were issued from the imperial armoury, Gábor Ágoston concluded that the janissaries were almost all present in the Mohács campaign, numbering some 9200.[44] However, it is difficult to believe that all the janissaries of the Ottoman Empire were present in the campaign and thus on the battlefield. The number of janissary gunners on the plain of Mohács must have been 4000, and the total number of janissaries assigned to the Rumelian and the household troops must have been around 8000, although a small part of them probably died in the preceding sieges or were wounded to the point of being unfit for combat.

If we look at the figures for the years before and after the campaign, we can see that the total number of janissaries and janissary novices decreased by almost 3000 from 1524–1525 to 1527–1528, including about 1500 active janissaries.[45] This suggests that at least 1500 died during the campaign, as recruits replaced those who had died, become unfit to fight or were aging. A considerable part of this loss was presumably due to the sieges, as mentioned in the campaign diary. In particular, the capture of Pétervárad may have cost much blood. In the battle of 29 August, on the other hand, they are reported to have suffered only minor losses, despite the prominent role of the janissaries in deciding the battle. Their volleys broke the charge of the Christian cavalry, just as they finally broke the resistance of the Czech, Moravian, Polish and German

---

43 István Brodarics, "Magyarország kancellárja Piotr Tomicki alkancellár püspöknek és Andrzej Krzycki przemyśli püspöknek Pozsony, 1526. szeptember 6." [Chancellor of Hungary to Vice-chancellor, Bishop Piotr Tomicki and Andrzej Krzycki Bishop of Przemyśl, Pozsony, 6 September 1526] in *Örök Mohács*, eds. B. Szabó et al., pp. 137–138.

44 Gábor Ágoston, "Firearms and Military Adaptation: the Ottomans and the European Military Revolution, 1450–1800," *Journal of World History* 25 (2014), no. 1, pp. 85–124.

45 Fodor, "The Military Organization," in *On the Verge*, eds. B. Szabó et al., pp. 91–115.

infantry, who were in a closed formation. Moreover, as already mentioned, like the court cavalry, some of the janissaries played an important role in the sultan's defence. Among them, the role of the solaks, the well-trained bodyguard of the ruler must be stressed. According to Kemalpaşazade,[46] they prevented at the last moment the Hungarian heavy cavalrymen, who had broken through the 'living wall', from making a direct attempt on Sultan Süleyman's life.

Although there is no mention of them in the sources, there were certainly other infantrymen besides the janissaries present at the Battle of Mohács. First and foremost the azabs, who mostly fought with bows and lances; their numbers in 1526 can be estimated at 7000–8000. In addition to them, we should mention the yayas, who were mostly used for auxiliary work; they must have been present in the campaign, as yaya district governors were also appointed as supervisors in the construction of the Buda bridge mentioned earlier. It is also difficult to imagine that, in addition to the above, voynuk and eflak troops from the Balkans did not join the army. However, we learn nothing from the sources about the position or role of these infantrymen, some of whom carried out important and large-scale technical and other auxiliary work in the 1526 campaign. In the Ottoman order of battle of this period, they were often placed in the front line and used to increase the mass.

On the whole, we believe that the rate of the infantry fighting in the Ottoman army was smaller than on the Christian side, but they were still slightly more in numbers.

6 The Artillery

According to the sources, Hungarian artillery did not play a significant role in the Battle of Mohács. In May 1526, the papal nuncio Burgio expressed the opinion that the Hungarians had only the will and courage to fight, but they had no commanders, ships, food supplies, weapons or artillery.[47] A similar opinion was uttered two weeks before the battle by Joannes Verzelius, who warned, among other things, of the enormous difference in artillery between the Ottoman and Christian sides.[48] But by then the core of the Hungarian artillery had already

---

46 Kemálpasazáde, "Mohácsnáme," [Mohácsname] in *Örök Mohács,* eds. B. Szabó et al., pp. 326–338.
47 Burgio, "Antonio Giovanni da Burgio pápai követ levele ... Buda, 1526. május 24. (részletek)," [Letter from the papal envoy Antonio Giovanni da Burgio ... Buda, 24 May 1526] in *Örök Mohács,* eds. B. Szabó et al., pp. 61–62.
48 Joannes Verzelius, "Joannes Verzelius pápai küldött levele Jacopo Sadoleto pápai titkárnak Buda, 1526. augusztus 13. (részletek)," [Letter from the papal envoy Joannes Verzelius

THE HUNGARIAN AND OTTOMAN FORCES AT THE BATTLE OF MOHÁCS 99

been formed. On 31 July, Burgio informed the papal secretary Jacopo Sadoleto that he had had the king's 18 cannons repaired for 600 forints.[49] These were indeed deployed on the king's departure for Mohács on 20 July:

> Order 9: on the side the infantry with artillery, followed by the 10th order: about eight hundred wagons of supplies, which will also serve as cover when they halt, with their women and equipment.[50]

The king, although he sensed the problem of quantity, began rather late, only after his departure from Buda, to urge Queen Maria to ask Archduke Ferdinand for cannons from Vienna.[51] His request seems to have been granted, as Brodarics describes the ships arriving from Buda to Mohács as carrying, in addition to the smaller and larger cannons, the nine guns sent by the Viennese. The cannons may have included those previously promised by László Szalkai, Archbishop of Esztergom,[52] and we also know from Royal Treasurer Elek Thurzó that he sent some cannons with his 200 foot-soldiers.

The question arises, of course, how many Christian guns could have been facing the Ottoman guns. What was the balance of forces in this regard? The casualty lists compiled after the battle show 85 guns, but it is quite clear that there were not that many on the battlefield. In a letter written to Piotr Tomicki, Archbishop of Krakow on 6 September, a few days after the battle, Brodarics said that "we were robbed of our camps, all our guns were left behind".[53] Then he went on to explain in more detail that some of the guns were with the troops in the battle array, some were in the camps, and some were not even unloaded

---

to the papal secretary, Jacopo Sadoleto Buda, 13 August 1526 (excerpts)] in *Örök Mohács*, eds. B. Szabó et al., p. 111.

49 Burgio, "Antonio Giovanni da Burgio pápai követ levele ... Buda, 1526. július 31.," [Letter from the papal envoy Antonio Giovanni da Burgio ... Buda, 31 July 1526] in *Örök Mohács*, eds. B. Szabó et al., pp. 101–102.

50 "A király indulásának rajza Budáról a Török ellen 1526-ban, illetve az emberek és az ellátmány, amelyet magával vitt Buda, 1526. július 20.," [A drawing of the king's departure from Buda against the Turks in 1526, and the men and supplies he took with him Buda, 20 July 1526] in *Örök Mohács*, eds. B. Szabó et al., p. 93.

51 Burgio, "Antonio Giovanni da Burgio pápai követ levele ... Buda, 1526. augusztus 6. (részletek)," [Letter from the papal envoy Antonio Giovanni da Burgio ... Buda, 6 August 1526 (excerpts)] in *Örök Mohács*, eds. B. Szabó et al., pp. 108–109.

52 László Szalkai, "Szalkai László esztergomi érsek levele Miklós besztercebányai plébánoshoz Esztergom, 1526. június 24. (részlet)," [Letter of the Archbishop of Esztergom, László Szalkai to the parish priest Miklós of Besztercebánya, Esztergom, 24 June 1526 (excerpt)] in *Örök Mohács*, eds. B. Szabó et al., p. 77.

53 Brodarics, "Magyarország kancellárja ... Pozsony, 1526. szeptember 6.," [Chancellor of Hungary ... Pozsony, 6 September 1526] in *Örök Mohács*, eds. B. Szabó et al., p. 137.

from the ships.[54] We do not know, therefore, exactly how many Christian guns were actually used in the battle. The military historian Jenő Gyalókay,[55] based on Hieronymus of Zara's report of 1526, estimated that there must have been 53 cannons on the battlefield. Some later took this data for granted.[56] Of course, the fact that only a part of the 85 cannons were used in the battle shows that not only the Ottoman but also the Christian army was not fully prepared for the beginning of the battle. At least, the artillery commander Hans von Hardegg certainly did not manage to set up all the guns in the battle lines by the time the battle was fought.

The importance of cannons for the Ottomans during this period, not only in sieges but also in field battles, is also proven by the fact that between 1522 and 1528 a total of 1127 cannons were cast, the vast majority of which were small and medium calibre field guns (zarbzen).[57] Consequently, the Ottoman artillery at Mohács greatly surpassed the enemy side not only in the number of guns, but also in the skill of its artillery corps. But what did this mean in terms of numbers?

In a letter written a few days after the battle, István Brodarics put the number of Ottoman cannons on the Mohács Plain at 400,[58] while in his memoirs he mentioned more than 300 big guns. The chancellor also pointed out that this weapon represented a greater force in the Ottoman army than the others. The number of Ottoman guns can therefore be put at 300 or a little more.

It is also an important question where the Christian and Ottoman guns were placed. The eyewitness Brodarics, in his recollection, placed the Christian guns directly behind the first rows of the first battle formation, while Istvánffy says that the guns were placed in a suitable position between the first and second battle formations. For more than a century, most scholars have agreed that the cannons were placed in the first battle formation, with the only dispute being over their position there.[59]

54 Brodarics, "Igaz történet," [A true account] in *Örök Mohács,* eds. B. Szabó et al., p. 321.
55 Jenő Gyalókay, *A mohácsi csata 1526. augusztus 29.* [The Battle of Mohács 29 August 1526] (Budapest: Királyi Magyar Egyetemi Nyomda, 1926).
56 Bálint Hóman and Gyula Szekfű, *Magyar történet* II. [Hungarian History II.] (Budapest: Magyar Királyi Egyetemi Nyomda, 1936); Lajos Bende, "A mohácsi csata," [The Battle of Mohács] *Hadtörténelmi Közlemények* 13 (1966), no. 3, pp. 532–567.
57 Gábor Ágoston, *Guns for the Sultan: Military Power and the Weapons Industry in the Ottoman Empire* (New York: Cambridge University Press, 2005), p. 83, p. 180; Fodor, "The Military Organization," in *On the Verge,* eds. B. Szabó et al., pp. 91–115.
58 Brodarics, "Magyarország kancellárja ... Pozsony, 1526. szeptember 6.," [Chancellor of Hungary ... Pozsony, 6 September 1526] in *Örök Mohács,* eds. B. Szabó et al., pp. 137–138.
59 Gyalókay, *A mohácsi csata* [The Battle of Mohács]; Bende, "A mohácsi csata," [The Battle of Mohács] *Hadtörténelmi Közlemények,* pp. 532–567.; Géza Perjés, "A mohácsi csata (1526.

However, there is still no conclusive evidence as to exactly where this location was. Stephan Gerlach visited the battlefield of Mohács 47 years after the battle, in 1573, and wrote of it: "This place is now partly waste land, partly arable. When we were there, it was full of corn. You can still see the trenches where the cannons stood and where the dead were buried."[60] A total of five mass graves containing the dead of the Battle of Mohács were found in 1960 and 1975–1976. Three of them were irregular, curved in shape, leading the archaeologists who excavated them to speculate that they may have originally been cannon emplacements. This was also the opinion of the military historian Lajos Négyesi, who saw them as the location of the artillery emplacements of the Christian left wing.[61] The above hypotheses are further strengthened by the knowledge that after the start of deep tillage with the steam plough, cannon wheel iron fittings and cannon balls were also found in the Fekete-kapu (Black Gate) field to the east of the mass graves, along with other finds from the period.[62] These, together with the location of the mass graves, may provide clues as to the position of the Christian artillery.

Some of the Ottoman artillery's one- and two-pounder cannons, designed for field combat, were placed at the left flank of the Ottoman army where the Rumelian troops lined up. The number of guns deployed here was estimated at 150 by Celalzade Mustafa, who stated that they were linked to each other with chains.[63] On the Ottoman right flank, in front of the Anatolian army, there were no guns, but the sultan's household troops who took up position in the centre, also had artillery. This, in view of the above figures, could not have been smaller than that of the Rumelian army. Although they arrived later on the battlefield, these guns were also successfully chained together, as Lutfi Pasha noted.[64] In the usual formation, the janissaries were behind the cannons, which were chained together and thus formed an almost impenetrable barrier,

---

augusztus 29.)," [The Battle of Mohács (29 August 1526)] *Hadtörténelmi Közlemények* 23 (1976) no. 3, pp. 427–468.

60 Dávid Ugnád, *Ugnád Dávid konstantinápolyi utazásai* [Dávid Ugnád's travels to Constantinople] (Budapest: Szépirodalmi Könyvkiadó, 1986), p. 121.

61 Lajos Négyesi, "A mohácsi csata," [The Battle of Mohács] *Hadtörténelmi Közlemények* 107 (1994), no. 4, pp. 62–79.

62 Norbert Pap, Péter Gyenizse, Máté Kitanics, and Gábor Szalai, "Az 1526. évi mohácsi csata helyszíneinek földrajzi jellemzői," [Geographical characteristics of the sites of the Battle of Mohács in 1526] *Történelmi Szemle* 62 (2020), no. 1, pp. 111–151.

63 Dzselálzáde Musztafa, "Az országok osztályai és az utak felsorolása 1560-as évek (részlet)," [The echelons of of the dominions and the hierarchies of destinations, 1560s (excerpt)] in *Örök Mohács,* eds. B. Szabó et al., pp. 411–419.

64 Lutfi pasa, "Az Oszmán-ház története 1550-es évek (részlet)," [History of the Ottoman House, 1550s (excerpt)] in *Örök Mohács,* eds. B. Szabó et al., pp. 404–409.

while the azabs were in front of the cannons. In the sultan's corps, behind the janissaries were the court cavalry, providing defence for the emperor, who was protected by his bodyguards, as already mentioned. As described above, the use of cannons and chains was highly deliberate, and was given great importance in the Ottoman army.

However, the question of where the Ottoman guns were placed can be supplemented by the question of how. Indeed, several of the Christian sources mention that the Ottoman guns were entrenched in some way, hidden by vegetation or set up in a depression or valley. According to Brodarics, the cannons were positioned as if in a valley, so that they caused fear rather than damage, the projectiles flying around the heads of the Christian attackers. In September 1526, Queen Maria wrote to King Sigismund of Poland that the Turks had lured the Christians to a place where there were many cannons hidden in the earth and grass.[65] The *Ehrenspiegel des Hauses Österreich* claims that as part of a battle stratagem "... thousands of sappers were made to dig in the cannons and cover them with all kinds of green vegetation."[66] Considering that at the beginning of the battle the Rumelian army had just arrived and were busy with the camping and preparations for the battle, and that the sultan's household troops came to the aid of the Rumelians during the battle, it is hard to believe that they dug hiding places and placed the cannons in the trenches as part of a battlefield tactics. However, we may lend more thought to Brodarics's comment above that the cannonballs in the valley did less damage to the Christian army than if they had been on the plain. Several other sources mention that the trajectory of the projectiles was too high. Among them, the Venetian spy Antonio Boemo wrote that the Turkish guns carried very high and therefore did little damage to the men. Nevertheless, according to him, "the Hungarian light cavalrymen took to running, seeing that the bullets were passing not far over their heads in quick succession, that they hit a few of them, and that there was such smoke that they could hardly see who was who."[67] According to the German chronicler Camerarius (1541), "the bullets flew higher, hitting only the spears

---

65 Mária, Magyarország királynéja, "Mária, Magyarország királynéja Zsigmondnak, Lengyelország királyának Pozsony, 1526. szeptember 9.," [Mary, Queen of Hungary to Sigismund, King of Poland, Pozsony, 9 September 1526] in *Örök Mohács,* eds. B. Szabó et al., pp. 140–142.

66 "Habsburg-ház dicsőségtükre Augsburg, 1559," [Ehrenspiegel des Hauses Österreich Augsburg, 1559] in *Örök Mohács,* eds. B. Szabó et al., p. 396.

67 Antonio Boemo, "Antonio Boemo velencei kém jelentése 1526. november 12. (összefoglaló)," [Report of the Venetian spy Antonio Boemo 12 November 1526 (summary)] in *Örök Mohács,* eds. B. Szabó et al., p. 201.

of some...",[68] while the Czech historian Dubravius (1552) concluded that "the cannons, however, did the Hungarians rather little harm, as the bullets missed the army".[69] Here we should mention: the aforementioned contemporaries echo the legend that the Turkish cannoneers, most of whom were allegedly Christians, turned against the Turks during the battle and deliberately aimed over the heads of the Christian army.[70] We can neither confirm nor deny this, nor can we prove whether the terrain had anything to do with the inaccurate aiming of the cannons, which were set up in a short time.

In the year before the battle, the number of the central Ottoman artillery corps (topçı) was 632. In addition, there were 516 gun carriage drivers (top arabacısı) and 528 armourers (cebeci) on the payroll.[71] The number of personnel around the cannons was some 1000, and including the armourers it amounted to approximately 1600.

Finally, let us see what role the artillery played on one side and on the other! How much did they contribute to the outcome of the battle?

As already indicated above, the available information suggests that the Christian guns played only an episodic role in the battle. Brodarics recalled: "When the battle signal was given, those who were in the first rows bravely charged at the enemy, all our guns were fired, but the enemy was hardly damaged."[72] According to the records, therefore, the cannons appear to have been used only once by the Christian army, and as the enemy may have been out of range at the time, they did not cause any significant damage.[73] By contrast, some sources report that the Ottoman guns played an important role in the outcome of the battle. These suggest that the unprecedented number of ordnance, the cannon fire and its sound, the smoke and the projectiles whizzing around the heads of the attackers had a demoralising effect on the Christian army, mainly due to their psychological impact. According to Burgio,

---

68   Camerarius, "A Magyarországon, Mohácsnál elszenvedett vereségről," [On the defeat at Mohács in Hungary] in *Örök Mohács,* eds. B. Szabó et al., p. 372.
69   Dubravius, "Csehország története," [History of Bohemia] in *Örök Mohács,* eds. B. Szabó et al., p. 393.
70   János B. Szabó and Gábor Farkas Farkas ed., Örök Mohács. Szövegek és értelmezések [Eternal Mohács: texts and interpretations]. Research Centre for the Humanities, Budapest, 2020, p. 411., n. 15.
71   Gábor Ágoston, *Osmanlı'da Strateji ve Askeri Güç* (İstanbul: Timaş Yayınları, 2012), p. 179.
72   Brodarics, "Igaz történet," [A true account] in *Örök Mohács,* eds. B. Szabó et al., p. 319.
73   Johannes Cuspinianus, "Johannes Cuspinianus buzdító beszéde a Szent Római Birodalom fejedelmeihez és előkelőihez 1526 vége," [An exhortatory address by Johannes Cuspinianus to the princes and nobles of the Holy Roman Empire end of 1526] in *Örök Mohács,* eds. B. Szabó et al., pp. 271–290; Isthvánffy, "A magyarok történetéből," [From the history of the Hungarians] in *Örök Mohács,* eds. B. Szabó et al., pp. 444–462.

the papal nuncio, "the sight of so many enemy guns shocked our people and paralysed them."[74] A Christian eyewitness not only confirmed that they had to fight with some 300 cannons, but also wrote that when they pressed close to the guns, the Turks "fired so fiercely that no one could stay there any longer."[75] Brodarics reported that most of the army took flight when, after repeated firing, "the force and smoke of the guns seemed intolerable."[76]

According to some accounts, the artillery of the sultan's corps seems to have performed better than the Rumelian artillery observed by Brodarics. According to a Czech source, "there was confusion in that part, a head flew here, an arm there, a horse torn in two there! They caused so much damage that the [Christians] had to flee."[77]

All in all, we can say that the Ottoman artillery surpassed the Christian one in every respect. The Ottomans used their artillery more consciously and it effectively influenced the outcome of the battle, playing a major role in defence.

7 The Hungarian and the Ottoman Fleet

The Christian boatmen did not take part in the Battle of Mohács, but they had an important role to play before the battle: to delay the advance of the Ottoman fleet as much as possible and to support the defence of the strategic fortresses along the Danube. Long before the battle, Antonio Giovanni da Burgio pointed out why it was important to maintain a sufficiently large river flotilla: "The boatmen (naszádos) are already scattered and do not want to serve. But what happens if the boatmen do not serve and leave the Danube free for the Turks? There will be no obstacle to the Turks as far as Buda"[78] – he wrote to the papal secretary at the end of March 1526. Around that time, the pay of Pál Tomori's

---

74 Burgio, "Antonio Giovanni da Burgio pápai követ levele ... Pozsony, 1526. szeptember 5.," [Letter from the papal envoy Antonio Giovanni da Burgio ... Pozsony, 5 September 1526] in *Örök Mohács*, eds. B. Szabó et al., p. 131.

75 "Új híradás: Hogyan esett meg a magyarországi csata a török császárral," [New News: How the battle of Hungary with the Turkish Emperor was fought] in *Örök Mohács*, eds. B. Szabó et al., p. 221.

76 Brodarics, "Igaz történet," [A true account] in *Örök Mohács*, eds. B. Szabó et al., p. 320.

77 "Egy cseh úr levele," [Letter from a Czech nobleman] in *Örök Mohács*, eds. B. Szabó et al., p. 209.

78 Burgio, "Antonio Giovanni da Burgio pápai követ levele ... Buda, 1526. március 29. (részletek)," [Letter from the papal nuncio Antonio Giovanni da Burgio ... Buda, 29 March 1526 (excerpts)] in *Örök Mohács*, eds. B. Szabó et al., p. 46.

boatmen, who were mainly Serbs, Croats and Hungarians serving in the southern marches, had arrived very rarely for months. The threat loomed large that they would abandon their ships, with disastrous consequences. The situation did not improve much in the following months. At the end of June, Tomori urged the king from Pétervárad to appoint additional captains to Tamás Podvinay,[79] and at the beginning of July he asked the king for new naszáds and shaykas and money to hire another 1000 people.[80]

At the same time, in the first days of July, Tomori withdrew from the fortress of Pétervárad and crossed to the left bank of the Danube, his remaining boatmen anchoring near his camp. After clashes with the soon arriving Ottoman fleet, the boatmen did not wait for the fall of Pétervárad (27 July). They retreated first to Újlak (Ilok), and then, as the fortresses along the Danube capitulated, to the anchorage at Mohács Island, from where their chances to impede the Danubian advance of the Ottomans, who were stronger in every respect, dwindled. Their numbers, equipment and fighting morale could no longer be improved by the money sent by the king to Tomori at the end of July, or by the royal letter of mercy granted to the boatmen, which included privileges and benefits. It is typical that shortly before the battle, in mid-August, their envoys went to the king, handed over their flags and declared that, as they had not received their pay for months, they were no longer willing to serve.[81]

The question arises, of course, how many Christian boatmen were there. A starting point might be that Tomori fought the Ottoman fleet at Pétervárad with 40 Christian vessels, and then retreated with them. The average number of crew on these ships was 30, equipped with long spears, swords, bows, handguns, and shields.[82] Accordingly, the Christian fleet at that time had a crew of about 1200 men. Even if some of these were scattered in August because of the irregular payment of salaries, they were partially replaced, as a few more ships from the north arrived at the anchorage of Mohács Island, also carrying

---

79   Pál Tomori, "Tomori Pál kalocsai érsek levele 11. Lajos magyar királyhoz Pétervárad, 1526. június 25." [Letter of Pál Tomori, Archbishop of Kalocsa to King Louis II of Hungary Petrovaradin, 25 June 1526] in *Örök Mohács,* eds. B. Szabó et al., pp. 78–79.
80   Tomori, "Tomori Pál kalocsai érsek levele ... Pétervárad, 1526. július elején," [Letter of Pál Tomori, Archbishop of Kalocsa ... Petrovaradin, early July 1526] in *Örök Mohács,* eds. B. Szabó et al., pp. 82–83.
81   Burgio, "Antonio Giovanni da Burgio pápai követ levele ... Buda, 1526. augusztus 15. [Letter from the papal envoy Antonio Giovanni da Burgio ... Buda, 15 August 1526] in *Örök Mohács,* eds. B. Szabó et al., p. 115.
82   Szentkláray, *A dunai hajóhadak története* [History of the Danube flotillas].

cannons.[83] The sources suggest that the supplies of the army at Mohács were also partly carried by boat on the Danube, which was greatly facilitated by having to sail downstream. Piotr Tomicki's casualty list for the battle of Mohács included 200 transport vessels, which, even if we accept the figure, must certainly include small craft, too.[84]

Just over 1000 boatmen (and an unknown number of other crews on cargo ships) were therefore certainly at Mohács on the day of the battle, but as noted above, the boatmen under Radics Bosics (Radič Božić) did not fight the Turkish fleet on the water. Although Caspar Ursinus Velius wrote[85] that by the time of the battle the Ottomans had a hundred fast ships beyond the royal camp and posed a threat, this could hardly have been the case in reality. On the one hand, it is clear from the Ottoman campaign diary and from other sources, that the Ottomans had planned to camp under Mohács on 29 August and were not planning to attack until the 30th. On the other hand, no source based on eyewitness observation confirms the appearance at Mohács of an Ottoman squadron attacking on the Danube at the time of the battle. That no Danube clash took place here is confirmed by Brodarics, who says that when they all assembled at Mohács, "there were about twenty-four or twenty-five thousand men, for the boat party, which was itself at the same place, was of no use in this war..."[86]

All in all, the role of the Christian fleet on the day of the battle seems to have been limited to supporting the flight. When defeat became clear, many of those who survived rushed to the Danube: many of them wanted to escape further north in light, swift rowing boats. One of them, according to surviving sources, was the co-commander-in-chief György Szapolyai, who, while trying to get on a boat with his horse, sank and drowned in the river.[87]

As the sources show, and as we have already mentioned, the Ottoman fleet was significantly superior. Domenico Venier (1526) wrote in his report from

83   Brodarics, "Igaz történet" [A true account] in *Örök Mohács*, eds. B. Szabó et al., pp. 301–325.; Isthvánffy, "A magyarok történetéből," [From the history of the Hungarians] in *Örök Mohács*, eds. B. Szabó et al., pp. 444–462.
84   Tomicki, "A magyar hadsereg veszteséglistája," [The list of losses of the Hungarian army] in *Örök Mohács*, eds. B. Szabó et al., pp. 185–188.
85   Caspar Ursinus Velius, "A mohácsi csata 1530 körül (töredék)," [The Battle of Mohács around 1530 (fragment)] in *Örök Mohács*, eds. B. Szabó et al., pp. 348–355.
86   Brodarics, "Igaz történet," [A true account] in *Örök Mohács*, eds. B. Szabó et al., p. 316.
87   Camerarius, "A Magyarországon, Mohácsnál elszenvedett vereségről," [On the defeat at Mohács in Hungary] in *Örök Mohács*, eds. B. Szabó et al., pp. 370–373; "Habsburg-ház dicsőségtükre," [Ehrenspiegel des Hauses Österreich] in *Örök Mohács*, eds. B. Szabó et al., pp. 395–400; Joachimus Cureus, "Gentis Silesiae Annales 1571," in *Örök Mohács*, eds. B. Szabó et al., pp. 422–427.

Rome on 21 April 1526 that the Turks were stationed not far from Nicopol and that 300 of their ships had arrived on the Danube.[88] Concerning the siege of Pétervárad, Burgio wrote about 100 ships of the size of Christian naszáds, plus 23 galleys and other vessels,[89] while the Venetian merchant Antonio di Giovanni, who lived in Buda, put the number at 23 naszáds, 200 barges (with ten men each) and a few large ships.[90] By contrast, the campaign diary's entry of 10 July reported that a Turkish fleet of 800 ships including shaykas had arrived before the army reached Pétervárad,[91] and Sultan Süleyman's letter of victory also claimed that 800 ships, loaded with brave warriors, had arrived under the fortress.[92] So, as we can see, the data on the number of Turkish ships display a wide scatter, which is not surprising, since not only warships arrived, but also parts of the supplies and equipment of the large army were transported on the Danube, just as, of course, vessels were needed for the pontoon bridges. However, despite the different figures, it seems certain that a significant number of the ships did not reach Mohács. If we are to believe Burgio, who is in many cases well informed, the number of units that penetrated deep into Hungary must have been around 100–120. Most of these seem to have been naszáds, or semi-naszáds, similar to those of the Hungarians, but they also had larger vessels, presumably floated up from the Black Sea. A Venetian spy report of 1526 mentions 30 fustas (Turkish kalyatas), as well as brigantines and pontoon boats.[93]

The Hungarian ships could only slow down the advance of the Ottoman fleet, which was larger in number and crew, but could not prevent it. Immediately before the battle, the Ottoman fleet consisted of 100 naszáds and 23 galleys,

---

88   Domenico Venier, "Domenico Venier jelentése Róma, 1526, április 21. (kivonat)," [Account of Domenico Venier Rome, 21 April 1526 (excerpt)] in *Örök Mohács,* eds. B. Szabó et al., pp. 54–55.

89   Burgio, "Antonio Giovanni da Burgio pápai követ levele …Buda, 1526. július 26.," [Letter from the papal envoy Antonio Giovanni da Burgio … Buda, 26 July 1526] in *Örök Mohács,* eds. B. Szabó et al., pp. 94–97.

90   Antonio di Giovanni, "Antonio di Giovanni Francesco di Giovannihoz írt levele Buda, 1526. július 26. (részlet)," [Letter from Antonio di Giovanni to Francesco di Giovanni Buda, 26 July 1526] in *Örök Mohács,* eds. B. Szabó et al., p. 97.

91   "Az 1526. évi hadinapló 1526 (részlet)," [The 1526 campaign diary (excerpt)] in *Örök Mohács,* eds. B. Szabó et al., p. 239.

92   Szulejmán szultán, "Szulejmán szultán két győzelmi jelentése 1526," [Sultan Süleyman's two letters of victory 1526] in *Örök Mohács,* eds. B. Szabó et al., pp. 258–263.

93   "…which amounted to thirty fustas, plus many brigantines, and long ships suitable for bridge-building, of which there were altogether more than two thousand." Boemo, "Antonio Boemo velencei kém jelentése," [Report of the Venetian spy, Antonio Boemo] in *Örök Mohács,* eds. B. Szabó et al., p. 201.

or, if we accept Velius's figures, 100 naszáds. The sources are silent, but analogies suggest that the fighting forces were largely composed of skilled azab and sipahi troops. It is clear from one or two instances that janissaries were also assigned to the ships when necessary to increase their effectiveness. Then, if the situation so required (and this was very much the case in Mohács), they were again directed to the land troops. The number of soldiers serving on the ships is not known, but if we want to estimate it, we must be careful not to double count the number of soldiers who were part of the land forces but were temporarily assigned to ships. Taking this into account, we can estimate the number of personnel remaining on the Ottoman flotilla stationed at the port before the battle, based on the number of ships (100 or 120, of which 20–30 were fustas/kalyatas, the rest shaykas), at around 5000.

At the end of August, on the eve of the battle, the Ottoman flotilla may have been stationed near Kiskőszeg (Batina), south of the mouth of the Karasica Stream. On the more than 20-kilometre stretch of Danube between Mohács and Kiskőszeg, the floodplain stretched for several kilometres on both sides, making it unsuitable for landing. After the battle, the Ottoman fleet, no longer hampered by the Hungarian warships, pushed on ahead of the land troops to Buda, perhaps inspiring Velius's report of the rapid advance of the Turkish fleet. The Hungarian ship crews made their escape first towards Buda and then towards Pozsony. This, of course, not only left the lower Danube unprotected and vulnerable, but for a time the Ottomans were able to navigate the river unhindered as far as Komárom.

8   About the Age of the Soldiers in the Battle

The origins and status of the soldiers involved in the battle have already been described above. It is also worth taking a look at the age structure. In the 1970s, Zsuzsa K. Zoffmann, an anthropologist working on the excavation of the mass graves of the fallen at the Battle of Mohács, found that most of the dead in the graves she examined, but only partially excavated, were men of 20–50 years of age and of robust build, while only a few remains of younger persons were found.[94] In 2020, one of the mass graves (No. III) was re-opened and the skeletons were excavated layer by layer. The full investigation (Zoffmann only

---

94 Zsuzsanna K. Zoffmann, *Az 1526-os mohácsi csata 1976-ban feltárt tömegsírjainak embertani vizsgálata* [Anthropological study of the mass graves of the Battle of Mohács in 1526, excavated in 1976] (Biológiai tanulmányok) 9 (Budapest: Akadémiai Kiadó, 1982).

examined the top layer of the tomb without moving the skeletons) revealed the remains of several persons under the age of 18.

In recent years, a controversy over the remains of the bodies found in the mass graves at Sátorhely has also drawn attention to the question of how old the soldiers who took part in the Battle of Mohács must have been. A glaring problem is that many remains in the mass graves at Sátorhely are judged by the modern notion of adulthood, by the standards of modern-day military requirements.

Life expectancy at birth in Europe in the 16th century was much lower than today. It is also worth noting that in Hungary, around 1505, the so-called "legal age" for men was lowered from 14 to 12 years.[95] Although this may give us a clue as to the beginning of adulthood, we must remember that in that period military service and the ability to take up arms were linked to the ability to bear arms. Of course, there was no uniform date for this, but we know, for example, that in Transylvanian Sekler (Székely) military families, service was customary from the age of 15.[96] In the case of Hungarian nobles in the 16th century, the first armed test usually took place at the age of 14–16. After their first combat experience, they were allowed to compete in their first tournament at the age of 15 or 16 and then start their independent military service.[97]

In the Ottoman Turkish world, the rules of military engagement were even stranger than the examples above.[98] Under Muslim religious law, both male and female children reached puberty at the age of 15 (lunar) years. From that time onwards, boys were also considered tax payers. In many parts of the Ottoman Empire, however, male children aged 12–14 were considered 'mature' (adult)

---

95   József Holub, "Az életkor szerepe középkori jogunkban és az "időlátott levelek," [The role of age in medieval law and the "letters of the age examination"] *Századok* 55–56 (1921–1922), pp. 32–76, pp. 212–235.

96   Ákos Egyed, "A székely hadrendszer és katonai társadalom a XVI. századig," [The Székely military system and military society up to the 16th century] *Korunk* 35 (1976), no. 4, pp. 294–300.

97   József Kelenik, "Tisztképzés vagy nemesi iskola? Gondolatok a XVI. század magyar katonai képzéséről," [Officer training or noble school? Reflections on the Hungarian military education of the 16th century] in *A magyar katonai vezető- és tisztképzés története*, eds. Ferenc Lengyel and Mihály Szántó (Budapest: HM Oktatási és Tudományszervező Főosztály, 1996), pp. 12–17.

98   Pál Fodor, Norbert Pap, and Máté Kitanics, "Kiket rejthetnek a sátorhelyi tömegsírok? – Néhány gondolat a mohácsi csata tömegsírjainak vizsgálatáról," [Who might be hidden in the mass graves of Sátorhely? – Some thoughts on the investigation of the mass graves of the Battle of Mohács] *Újkor.hu. A velünk élő történelem* (2021). Available at https://ujkor.hu/content/kiket-rejthetnek-satorhelyi-tomegsirok-nehany-gondolat-mohacsi-csata-tomegsirjainak-vizsgalatarol.

and were subject to the so-called 'bachelor tax' (resm-i kara, resm-i mücerred, ispence) or, in the case of non-Muslims, the 'poll tax' (cizye).[99] A decree from 1511, summarising the rules of the prisoner tax (pencik), also counts the age of puberty (adulthood) from the age of 12.[100] Also relevant to this study is that an imperial decree of 1536 gives the following information on the age limits for the timariot army:

- If the underage son of a (deceased) sipahi was assigned a timar, he had the right to send a man-at-arms (cebelü) to war in his stead until he grew up. But when he reached the age of ten, he had to enlist in person.
- As the campaigns had already taken place in very distant places in the years before the decree was issued, i.e. before 1536, many of the ten-year-old sipahi sons could not meet the obligation to appear in person and were therefore deprived of their timars. In order to prevent this, it was decreed that sons of sipahis sons could send a cebelü in their stead until the age of 16, and that they were only obliged to go to war in person from the age of 16.
- A son of sipahi whose father had died and who had not applied to the governor-general (beylerbeyi) for a prebend within seven years of his 12th birthday, had not attended his court regularly, and had not participated in military ventures, was later denied a timar.[101]

Based on the above, the Ottoman army at the time of the Battle of Mohács may have included 10–12 year old 'child soldiers', just as the Christian army may have included a good number of 'child soldiers' aged 15–16. The teenage dead found in the mass graves at the site of Sátorhely are therefore unlikely to be 'civilians', but rather soldiers killed in battle.

9 Discussion

The huge difference in numbers between the two armies is evident in contemporary accounts. At Mohács, the battle between David and Goliath unfolded; the question is how large the two armies were and what chances David had of victory.

---

99 Géza Dávid, "The Age of Unmarried Male Children, in the Tahrir Defters," *Acta Orientalia Scientiarium* 31 (1977), no. 3, pp. 347–357.
100 İsmail Hakkı Uzunçarşılı, *Osmanlı Devleti Teşkilâtından Kapukulu Ocakları. I. Acemi Ocağı ve Yeniçeri Ocağı* (İstanbul: 1984), p. 90; Irène Beldiceanu-Steinherr, "En marge d'un acte concernant le pengyek et les aqınğı," *Revue des Études Islamiques* 37 (1969), pp. 21–47.
101 Douglas A. Howard, "Ottoman Administration and the Tîmâr System: Sûret-i Ḳânûnnâme-i 'Osmânî Berây-i Tîmâr Dâden," *Journal of Turkish Studies* 20 (1996), pp. 46–125.

Most historians of the period now believe that the number of Christian troops gathered on the Plain of Mohács was between 25,000 and 27,000. Among the first authors, Sándor Szurmay put the number at 28,000,[102] Barna Halmay at 28,000–30,000,[103] while Jenő Gyalókay, referring to Brodarics, put the number of Christian troops at 24,000–25,000.[104] To the latter we may add that in his memoirs the chancellor did indeed say that before the battle, when they were all assembled, "there were about twenty-four to twenty-five thousand men."[105] However, if we add up the figures given by Brodarics, we get between 25,000 and 27,000 people.[106]

The issue of numbers came to the fore again in the 1970s at the 450th anniversary of the battle. At that time, Géza Perjés, considering Brodarics's figures to be wrong, put his vote in favour of an army of 50,000–60,000 men.[107] András Kubinyi drew attention to the methodological errors in the calculation, which led to the overestimation of the army.[108] However, there were other authors of the period who did the opposite: István Nemeskürty calculated a Christian army of 15,000–20,000 men, saying that it could not have been larger, since considerable armies had been left behind under the command of János Szapolyai, the voivode of Transylvania, and Croatian ban Kristóf Frangepán.[109]

Let us return to the widely accepted figure of 25,000–27,000 troops, based on the description of Brodarics. A significant problem is that, in addition to the figures actually quantified by the chancellor, his memoirs include individuals the size of whose troops is left unmentioned. The chancellor also wrote that "while the king was in Tolna, there were a large number of people gathering from almost all parts and provinces of Hungary on this side [of the Danube]

---

102 Sándor Szurmay, *A mohácsi hadjárat 1526-ban* [The Mohács campaign in 1526] (Budapest: Pesti Könyvnyomda Rt., 1901).
103 Barna Halmay, *Az 1526-iki mohácsi csata keletkezése és igazi helye. A négyszázéves évfordulóra egykoru adatok alapján* [The origins and the real place of the Battle of Mohács in 1526. Based on contemporary data for the four hundredth anniversary] (Debrecen: Magyar Nemzeti Könyv- és Lapkiadóvállalat Rt., 1926).
104 Gyalókay, *A mohácsi csata* [The Battle of Mohács].
105 Brodarics, "Igaz történet," [A true account] in *Örök Mohács,* eds. B. Szabó et al., p. 316.
106 13,000–14,000 horsemen and 12,000–13,000 infantrymen. To this must be added the boatmen who did not take part in the battle.
107 Géza Perjés, *Mohács* (Budapest: Magvető Kiadó, 1979).
108 András Kubinyi, "A mohácsi csata és előzményei," [The Battle of Mohács and its antecedents] *Századok* 115 (1981), no. 1, pp. 66–107.
109 István Nemeskürty, *Önfia vágta sebét* [Wounded by her own kind] (Budapest: Magvető Kiadó, 1983).

and beyond, which we call counties."¹¹⁰ In most cases, we do not know how many people the phrase 'a large number' might have meant in total. More recently, Gábor Szatlóczki has raised the point that Brodarics's figures are incorrect in some places and incomplete in others, i.e. the number of troops from several counties is nowhere indicated by the chancellor. According to his calculations, the Christian army could have numbered considerably more than 27,000, which, in his opinion, is also supported by the fact that some contemporary sources wrote of a Christian army of 40,000–50,000, or even 60,000.¹¹¹

The question was approached from a different point of view by Richárd Botlik, who questioned not the number of 25,000–27,000 troops, but whether all concerned had done their duty. In his opinion, less than half of the magnates turned up at Mohács, most of the counties (64%) were absent from the battle, and a total of 41,000 Transylvanian, Croatian, Czech, Moravian and Silesian fighters who could have been expected to be present were absent.¹¹² The response to this hypothesis was not long in coming. János B. Szabó and Norbert C. Tóth, reflecting on Botlik's calculations, sought to prove that it was the other way round, with the vast majority of Hungarian counties present (69%) at Mohács, as were 14 of the 19 bishops and 10 of the 15 high dignitaries (barons). It was therefore concluded that the dignitaries and officials of the Kingdom of Hungary had not run away from the task before them at all.¹¹³

The question then arises: what can the size of the Christian army have been? We can only make an estimate, starting from the assumption that Brodarics, who took part in the battle, had real information about the number of troops

---

110   Brodarics, "Igaz történet," [A true account] in *Örök Mohács,* eds. B. Szabó et al., p. 310. Some of the county armies apparently joined the royal army before the Tolna station, or became part of Tomori's army, which eventually increased to 5000–6000 men.

111   Gábor Szatlóczki (2022): *A lovag, a gyalog és a had. A Magyar Királyság hadszervezete és hadserege a mohácsi csata idején (kézirat)* [The military organization and army of the Kingdom of Hungary during the Battle of Mohács (manuscript)]. The paper was published as a manuscript. Szatlóczki claims that the editorial board of the military history journal *Hadtörténelmi Közlemények* refused to publish it without justification.

112   Richárd Botlik, *Az 1526. évi mohácsi csata árnyékseregei* E-book [The shadow armies of the Battle of Mohács in 1526] (Budapest: Szerző, 2017). Available at https://www.academia.edu/34807761/Az_1526_%C3%A9vi_moh%C3%A1csi_csata_%C3%A1rny%C3%A9kseregei_Bp_2017_Shadow_Militaries_of_the_Battle_of_Moh%C3%A1cs_1526.

113   János B. Szabó and Norbert C. Tóth, "'Árnyékboksz az árnyéksereggel' – avagy már megint mindenért Szapolyai a hibás. A magyar elit 1526. évi katonai szerepvállalásáról Botlik Richárd új könyve kapcsán," ['Shadow boxing with the shadow army' – or again, everything is the fault of Szapolyai. On the military engagement of the Hungarian elite in 1526 in the context of the new book by Richárd Botlik] *Hadtörténelmi Közlemények* 131 (2018), no. 2, pp. 287–320.

joining the royal army and, as chancellor and a survivor of the battle, he must have had a realistic idea of the losses.

The fact that the number was not much higher is confirmed by the information of Burgio, who gave the number of troops as between 25,000 and 30,000 in a letter written immediately after the battle.[114] Brodarics's figure of 25,000–27,000 (26,000–28,000 including the boatmen) should be corrected upwards by a few thousand (a total of about 29,000–32,000), taking into account that he did not assign troop numbers to several lords and did not provide figures for some counties.[115] However, the fact that only a minor correction may be necessary may indicate that several lords and counties, as already mentioned in passing, sent troops to the war below the expected numbers. The difficulties in raising the banderia, the slowness and sometimes refusal of joining the war, the delayed or often contradictory actions, which are clearly reflected by the sources, may have contributed significantly to this. In view of these factors, however, contemporary sources which reported a Christian army of 40,000 to 50,000, sometimes even 60,000, can be interpreted differently. In our opinion, they included not only the fighting troops, but also the personnel accompanying and serving them, and thus gave an (exaggerated) estimate of the strength of the army.

Finally, let us briefly address the question of the odds: could more have been done to win? The arrival of auxiliary troops still on the road would have improved the chances of the Hungarian army. At the same time, Brodarics also pointed out that once the Ottoman troops had crossed the Drava and were only two miles from Mohács, "there seemed no longer a sufficiently certain way of retreating from a very near enemy, especially from an enemy whose horses were swift and who were most capable and willing to pursue those who were fleeing."[116]

The total Ottoman army, according to Brodarics's report written immediately after the battle, was 200,000, of which he believed 80,000 were fit for war.[117] In his recollections he mentioned 300,000 and 70,000 respectively.[118] The figure of

114 Burgio, "Antonio Giovanni da Burgio pápai követ levele ... Pozsony, 1526. szeptember 5.," [Letter from the papal nuncio Antonio Giovanni da Burgio ... Pozsony, 5 September 1526] in *Örök Mohács*, eds. B. Szabó et al., pp. 131–132.
115 Since Brodarics definitely stated 12,000–13,000 infantry, the above-mentioned correction of a few thousand concerns the cavalry.
116 Brodarics, "Igaz történet," [A true account] in *Örök Mohács*, eds. B. Szabó et al., p. 315.
117 Brodarics, "Magyarország kancellárja ... Pozsony, 1526. szeptember 6.," [Chancellor of Hungary ... Pozsony, 6 September 1526] in *Örök Mohács*, eds. B. Szabó et al., pp. 137–138.
118 *Brodarics históriája* [Brodarics's history]. The fact that there is an oft-quoted Hungarian translation, where the figure of 60,000 is wrongly given instead of 70,000, was pointed out

300,000 men immediately before and after the battle is also mentioned in the letters of many contemporaries, such as Burgio,[119] Pál Tomori,[120] the Venetian merchant Ludovico Morello,[121] or Agostino da Mula,[122] but also in the work of Bernardus Vapovius.[123] This overestimated figure of 300,000, like the information of 200,000, may refer to the entire army, including auxiliary personnel. In his impressive work on military history,[124] the military historian József Bánlaky put the Turkish troops fighting at Mohács at 70,000 or slightly more, and more recently many have taken the figure of 60,000–70,000 proposed by János B. Szabó as the reference number.[125] The present authors believe that the armed, combat-ready part of the Ottoman army was somewhat more than this, around 80,000. However, whichever of these figures we choose, the Christian army did not stand much of a chance against an Ottoman army of 60,000–80,000 men. This numerical superiority was the reason why the commander-in-chief Tomori wanted to defeat the Rumelian corps before the full Ottoman army had developed, so that they would have a chance to face the later arriving corps.

We might add: on the Christian side, an army larger than the number that appeared would not have meant a much greater chance of victory. A passage from a letter by Aeneas Sylvius, later Pope Pius II, written in the mid-1450s, sheds light on this problem:

> How are we to persuade the princes who rule the Christian world to take up arms? Go on, tell all the kings to go to war. To whom will you give the high command? How will the order of battle be set up? Who understands

by Pál Fodor and András Mércz. Pál Fodor and András Mércz, "Mi is veszett Mohácsnál? Oszmán-török veszteséglista az 1526. évi hadjáratról," ['What is lost at Mohács?' An Ottoman Turkish casualty list of the 1526 campaign] *Történelmi Szemle* 65 (2023), no. 1, p. 211.

119 Burgio, "Antonio Giovanni da Burgio pápai követ levele … Buda, 1526. május 30.," [Letter from the papal envoy, Antonio Giovanni di Burgio … Buda, 30 May 1526] in *Örök Mohács*, eds. B. Szabó et al., pp. 64–65.

120 Tomori, "Tomori Pál kalocsai érsek levele … Pétervárad, 1526. június 25.," [Letter of Pál Tomori, Archbishop of Kalocsa … Petrovaradin, 25 June 1526] in *Örök Mohács*, eds. B. Szabó et al., pp. 78–79.

121 Ludovico Morello, "Ludovico Morello levele Francesco Contarininek Bécs, 1526, szeptember 24. (részlet)," [Ludovico Morello's letter to Francesco Contarini Vienna 24 September 1526 (excerpt)] in *Örök Mohács*, eds. B. Szabó et al., p. 163.

122 Agostino da Mula, "Agostino da Mula jelentése Udine, 1526. szeptember 25. (részletek)," [Report of Agostino da Mula Udine, 25 September 1526 (excerpts)] in *Örök Mohács*, eds. B. Szabó et al., pp. 163–165.

123 Vapovius, "Fragmentum Sigismundi" in *Örök Mohács* eds. B. Szabó et al., pp. 338–344.

124 József Bánlaky, *A magyar nemzet hadtörténelme* XII. [The military history of the Hungarians XII.] (Budapest: Grill Károly Könyvkiadó vállalata, 1939).

125 János B. Szabó, *A mohácsi csata* [The Battle of Mohács] (Budapest: Corvina, 2006).

the different languages? Who will rule the different customs? Who will persuade the English to make friends with the French? Who will unite the Genoese with the Aragonese? Who will reconcile the Germans with the Hungarians and the Czechs? If you take few men to fight the Turk, you are easily defeated. If many, it will be chaos.[126]

There are signs of the latter in the sources, i.e. forging units with different languages and backgrounds into a common army was a problem for the Hungarian military leadership.

However, the debate on opportunities places a disproportionate emphasis on numbers. At least just as important was the difference between the two armies in the quality of leadership, command and control, and the technological level of weaponry. We believe that it was not only the Ottoman numerical superiority of roughly two and a half times that posed a problem for the Hungarian command, but also the qualitative superiority of the Ottoman army. The latter was based on the effective use of artillery and small arms on the Ottoman side, and, in addition to the professional leadership mentioned above, on discipline, cohesion and drill.

10 Conclusion

There was a significant difference in numbers between the two armies, with the Ottomans outnumbering the Hungarians by about two and a half to one. This was particularly true of the cavalry, which was more than three times as large. Heavy cavalry had a major and decisive role to play in the Christian army, but was negligible in numbers and role in the Ottoman army. As the course of the battle revealed, advances in military technology had rendered this arm obsolete. There was also a discrepancy of more than threefold between the strengths of the opposing artilleries. In terms of warships, the Ottoman superiority was many times greater: the Turkish army had large ships that the Hungarian fleet did not have. The only service in which the difference was smaller was the infantry. However, the janissaries were much better equipped than the Christian mercenaries.

---

126 Ambrus Miskolczy, *A román középkor időszerű kérdései. Régi-új viták és közelítések* [Topical issues of the Romanian Middle Ages. Old and new debates and approaches] (Budapest: Magyarságkutató Intézet, 2021).

TABLE 3.1 Troop numbers of the armies facing each other at Mohács

	Ottoman	Hungarian
Cavalry	57,000–58,000 (of which about 500 are heavy cavalry)	16,000–17,000 (of which about 2000–2500 are heavy cavalry)
Infantry	16,000–17,000	12,000–13,000
Artillery	1600 men/300 guns	300 men/85 guns
River flotilla	5000 persons/ca. 100–120 units	1000–1200 persons/40 naszáds
Total	About 80,000	About 29,000–32,000

Overall, we can conclude that not only the considerable numerical superiority (Table 3.1) but also the qualitative difference between the two armies contributed to the Ottoman victory.

Bibliography

A király indulásának rajza Budáról a Török ellen 1526-ban, illetve az emberek és az ellátmány, amelyet magával vitt Buda, 1526. július 20." [A drawing of the king's departure from Buda against the Turks in 1526, and the men and supplies he took with him Buda, 20 July 1526] In *Örök Mohács: szövegek és értelmezések,* eds. János B. Szabó and Gábor Farkas Farkas, 92–93. Budapest: Bölcsészettudományi Kutatóközpont, 2020.

A mohácsi csatára vonatkozó veszteséglista 1526. [The casualty list relating to the Battle of Mohács 1526] In *Örök Mohács: szövegek és értelmezések,* eds. János B. Szabó and Gábor Farkas Farkas, 218–220. Budapest: Bölcsészettudományi Kutatóközpont, 2020.

Ágoston, Gábor. "Firearms and Military Adaptation: The Ottomans and the European Military Revolution, 1450–1800." *Journal of World History* 25 (2014): 85–124.

Ágoston, Gábor. "War-Winning Weapons? On the Decisiveness of Ottoman Firearms from the Siege of Constantinople (1453) to the Battle of Mohács (1526)." *Journal of Turkish Studies* 39 (2013): 129–143.

Ágoston, Gábor. *Osmanlı'da Strateji ve Askeri Güç.* İstanbul: Timaş Yayınları.

Ágoston, Gábor. *Guns for the Sultan: Military Power and the Weapons Industry in the Ottoman Empire.* New York: Cambridge University Press, 2005.

Az 1526. évi hadinapló (részlet). [The 1526 campaign diary (excerpt)] In *Örök Mohács: szövegek és értelmezések,* eds. János B. Szabó and Gábor Farkas Farkas, 235–257. Budapest: Bölcsészettudományi Kutatóközpont, 2020.

B. Szabó, János and Norbert C. Tóth. "'Árnyékboksz az árnyéksereggel' – avagy már megint mindenért Szapolyai a hibás. A magyar elit 1526. évi katonai szerepvállalásáról Botlik Richárd új könyve kapcsán." ['Shadow boxing with the shadow army' – or again, everything is the fault of Szapolyai. On the military engagement of the Hungarian elite in 1526 in the context of the new book by Richárd Botlik] *Hadtörténelmi Közlemények* 131 (2018): 287–320.

B. Szabó, János. "The Military Organization and Army of the Kingdom of Hungary (1490–1256)," in *On the Verge of a New Era: The Armies of Europe at the Time of the Battle of Mohács*, eds. János B. Szabó and Pál Fodor, 147–171. Budapest: Research Centre for the Humanities, 2021.

B. Szabó, János. *A mohácsi csata*. [The Battle of Mohács] Budapest: Corvina, 2006.

Bánlaky, József. *A magyar nemzet hadtörténelme* XII. [The military history of the Hungarians XII.] Budapest: Grill Károly Könyvkiadó vállalata, 1939.

Beldiceanu-Steinherr, Irène. "En marge d'un acte concernant le penğyek et les aqınğı." *Revue des Études Islamiques* 37 (1969): 21–47.

Bende, Lajos. "A mohácsi csata." [The Battle of Mohács] *Hadtörténelmi Közlemények* 13 (1966): 532–567.

Boemo, Antonio. "Antonio Boemo velencei kém jelentése 1526. november 12. (összefoglaló)." [Report of the Venetian spy Antonio Boemo 12 November 1526 (summary)] In *Örök Mohács: szövegek és értelmezések*, eds. János B. Szabó and Gábor Farkas Farkas, 201–204. Budapest: Bölcsészettudományi Kutatóközpont, 2020.

Botlik, Richárd. *Az 1526. évi mohácsi csata árnyékseregei* E-book. [The Shadow armies of the Battle of Mohács in 1526] Budapest: Szerző, 2017. Available at https://www.academia.edu/34807761/Az_1526_%C3%A9vi_moh%C3%A1csi_csata_%C3%A1rny%C3%A9kseregei_Bp_2017_Shadow_Militaries_of_the_Battle_of_Moh%C3%A1cs_1526_.

Brodarics históriája a mohácsi vészről. [Brodarics's history of the disaster at Mohács.], trans. Imre Szentpétery. Budapest: Lampel/Wodianer Ny., 1903.

Brodarics, István. "Magyarország kancellárja Piotr Tomicki alkancellár püspöknek és Andrzej Krzycki przemyśli püspöknek Pozsony, 1526. szeptember 6." [Chancellor of Hungary to Vice-chancellor, Bishop Piotr Tomicki and Andrzej Krzycki Bishop of Przemyśl, Pozsony, 6 September 1526] In *Örök Mohács: szövegek és értelmezések*, eds. János B. Szabó and Gábor Farkas Farkas, 137–138. Budapest: Bölcsészettudományi Kutatóközpont, 2020.

Brodarics, István. "Igaz történet a magyarok és Szulejmán török császár mohácsi ütközetéről 1528." [A true account about the battle between the Hungarians and the Turkish Emperor Süleyman in Mohács in 1528] In *Örök Mohács: szövegek és értelmezések*, eds. János B. Szabó and Gábor Farkas Farkas, 301–325. Bölcsészettudományi Kutatóközpont, Budapest, 2020.

Brodericus, Stephanus. *De conflictu Hungarorum cum Solymano turcarum imperatore ad Mohach historia verissima*. Bibliotheca Scriptorum Medii Recentisque Aevorum. Series Nova 6. Budapest: Akadémiai Kiadó, 1985.

Burgio, Antonio Giovanni da. "Antonio Giovanni da Burgio pápai követ levele Jacopo Sadoleto pápai titkárnak Buda, 1526. augusztus 13. (részletek)." [Letter from the papal nuncio Antonio Giovanni da Burgio to the papal secretary Jacopo Sadoleto, Buda, 13 August 1526 (excerpts)] In *Örök Mohács: szövegek és értelmezések,* eds. János B. Szabó and Gábor Farkas Farkas, 111–114. Budapest: Bölcsészettudományi Kutatóközpont, 2020.

Burgio, "Antonio Giovanni da. Antonio Giovanni da Burgio pápai követ levele Jacopo Sadoleto pápai titkárnak Buda, 1526. július 26." [Letter from the papal nuncio Antonio Giovanni da Burgio to the papal secretary Jacopo Sadoleto Buda, 26 July 1526] In *Örök Mohács: szövegek és értelmezések,* eds. János B. Szabó and Gábor Farkas Farkas, 94–97. Budapest: Bölcsészettudományi Kutatóközpont, 2020.

Burgio, Antonio Giovanni da. "Antonio Giovanni da Burgio pápai követ levele Jacopo Sadoleto pápai titkárnak, Pozsony, 1526. szeptember 5." [Letter from the papal nuncio Antonio Giovanni da Burgio to the papal secretary Jacopo Sadoleto Pozsony, 5 September 1526] In *Örök Mohács: szövegek és értelmezések,* eds. János B. Szabó and Gábor Farkas Farkas, 131–132. Budapest: Bölcsészettudományi Kutatóközpont, 2020.

Burgio, Antonio Giovanni da. "Antonio Giovanni da Burgio pápai követ levele Jacopo Sadoleto pápai titkárnak, Buda, 1526. június 18." [Letter from the papal nuncio Antonio Giovanni da Burgio to the papal secretary Jacopo Sadoleto Buda, 18 June 1526] In *Örök Mohács: szövegek és értelmezések,* eds. János B. Szabó and Gábor Farkas Farkas, 72–73. Budapest: Bölcsészettudományi Kutatóközpont, 2020.

Burgio, Antonio Giovanni da. "Antonio Giovanni da Burgio pápai követ levele Jacopo Sadoleto pápai titkárnak, Buda, 1526. május 24." [Letter from the papal nuncio Antonio Giovanni da Burgio to the papal secretary Jacopo Sadoleto Buda, 24 May 1526] In *Örök Mohács: szövegek és értelmezések,* eds. János B. Szabó and Gábor Farkas Farkas, 61–62. Budapest: Bölcsészettudományi Kutatóközpont, 2020.

Burgio, Antonio Giovanni da. "Antonio Giovanni da Burgio pápai követ levele Jacopo Sadoleto pápai titkárnak, Buda, 1526. július 31." [Letter from the papal nuncio Antonio Giovanni da Burgio to the papal secretary Jacopo Sadoleto Buda, 31 July 1526] In *Örök Mohács: szövegek és értelmezések,* eds. János B. Szabó and Gábor Farkas Farkas, 101–102. Budapest: Bölcsészettudományi Kutatóközpont, 2020.

Burgio, Antonio Giovanni da. "Antonio Giovanni da Burgio pápai követ levele Jacopo Sadoleto pápai titkárnak, Buda, 1526. augusztus 6." [Letter from the papal nuncio Antonio Giovanni da Burgio to the papal secretary Jacopo Sadoleto Buda, 6 August 1526] In *Örök Mohács: szövegek és értelmezések,* eds. János B. Szabó and Gábor Farkas Farkas, 108–109. Budapest: Bölcsészettudományi Kutatóközpont, 2020.

Burgio, "Antonio Giovanni da (1526h): Antonio Giovanni da Burgio pápai követ levele Jacopo Sadoleto pápai titkárnak, Buda, 1526. március 29." [Letter from the papal nuncio Antonio Giovanni da Burgio to the papal secretary Jacopo Sadoleto Buda, 29 March 1526] In *Örök Mohács: szövegek és értelmezések,* eds. János B. Szabó and Gábor Farkas Farkas, 45–46. Budapest: Bölcsészettudományi Kutatóközpont, 2020.

Burgio, Antonio Giovanni da. "Antonio Giovanni da Burgio pápai követ levele Jacopo Sadoleto pápai titkárnak, Buda, 1526. augusztus 15." [Letter from the papal nuncio Antonio Giovanni da Burgio to the papal secretary Jacopo Sadoleto Buda, 15 August 1526] In *Örök Mohács: szövegek és értelmezések,* eds. János B. Szabó and Gábor Farkas Farkas, 115. Budapest: Bölcsészettudományi Kutatóközpont, 2020.

Burgio, Antonio Giovanni da. "Antonio Giovanni da Burgio pápai követ levele Jacopo Sadoleto pápai titkárnak, Buda, 1526. május 30." [Letter from the papal nuncio Antonio Giovanni da Burgio to the papal secretary Jacopo Sadoleto Buda, 30 May 1526] In *Örök Mohács: szövegek és értelmezések,* eds. János B. Szabó and Gábor Farkas Farkas, 64–65. Budapest: Bölcsészettudományi Kutatóközpont, 2020.

Camerarius, Joachim. "A Magyarországon, Mohácsnál elszenvedett vereségről és Lajos király haláláról 1541." [On the defeat at Mohács in Hungary and the death of King Louis 1541] In *Örök Mohács: szövegek és értelmezések,* eds. János B. Szabó and Gábor Farkas Farkas, 370–373. Budapest: Bölcsészettudományi Kutatóközpont, 2020.

Cureus, Joachimus. "Gentis Silesiae Annales 1571." In *Örök Mohács: szövegek és értelmezések,* eds. János B. Szabó and Gábor Farkas Farkas, 422–427. Budapest: Bölcsészettudományi Kutatóközpont, 2020.

Cuspinianus, Johannes. "Johannes Cuspinianus buzdító beszéde a Szent Római Birodalom fejedelmeihez és előkelőihez 1526 vége." [An exhortatory address by Johannes Cuspinianus to the princes and nobles of the Holy Roman Empire end of 1526] In *Örök Mohács: szövegek és értelmezések,* eds. János B. Szabó and Gábor Farkas Farkas, 271–290. Budapest: Bölcsészettudományi Kutatóközpont, 2020.

Dávid, Géza. "The Age of Unmarried Male Children, in the Tahrir Defters." *Acta Orientalia Scientiarium* 31 (1977): 347–357.

Dubravius, Jan. "Csehország története 1552 (részlet)." [History of Bohemia 1552 (excerpt)] In *Örök Mohács: szövegek és értelmezések,* eds. János B. Szabó and Gábor Farkas Farkas, 390–394. Budapest: Bölcsészettudományi Kutatóközpont, 2020.

Dzselálzáde Musztafa. "Az országok osztályai és az utak felsorolása 1560-as évek (részlet)." [The echelons of the dominions and the hierarchies of destinations, 1560s 1560s (excerpt)] In *Örök Mohács: szövegek és értelmezések,* eds. János B. Szabó and Gábor Farkas Farkas, 411–419. Budapest: Bölcsészettudományi Kutatóközpont, 2020.

Egy cseh úr levele a Santa Clara kolostor főnöknőjéhez, 1526. november." [Letter from a Czech nobleman to the Superior of the Convent of Santa Clara, November 1526] In *Örök Mohács: szövegek és értelmezések,* eds. János B. Szabó and Gábor Farkas Farkas, 207–216. Budapest: Bölcsészettudományi Kutatóközpont, 2020.

Egyed, Ákos. "A székely hadrendszer és katonai társadalom a XVI. századig." [The Székely military system and military society up to the 16th century] *Korunk* 35 (1976): 294–300.

Emecen, Feridun M. "Mohaç 1526. Osmanlılara Orta Avrupa'nın Kapılarını Açan Savaş," in Feridun M Emecen, *Osmanlı Klasik Çağında Savaş*. *İstanbul: Timaş*, 2010, 159–216.

Fodor, Pál. "The Military Organization and Army of the Ottoman Empire (1500–1530)." In *On the Verge of a New Era. The Armies of Europe at the Time of the Battle of Mohács*, eds. János B. Szabó and Pál Fodor, 91–115. Budapest: ELKH BTK, 2021.

Fodor, Pál and András Mércz. "Mi is veszett Mohácsnál? Oszmán-török veszteséglista az 1526. évi hadjáratról." [What is lost at Mohács? Ottoman Turkish casualty list from the 1526 campaign] *Történelmi Szemle* 55 (2023): *forthcoming*.

Fodor, Pál, Norbert Pap, and Máté Kitanics. "Kiket rejthetnek a sátorhelyi tömegsírok? – Néhány gondolat a mohácsi csata tömegsírjainak vizsgálatáról." [Who might be hidden in the mass graves of Sátorhely? – Some thoughts on the investigation of the mass graves of the Battle of Mohács] *Újkor.hu. A velünk élő történelem* (2021). Available at https://ujkor.hu/content/kiket-rejthetnek-satorhelyi-tomegsirok-nehany-gondolat-mohacsi-csata-tomegsirjainak-vizsgalatarol.

Giovanni, Antonio di. "Antonio di Giovanni Francesco di Giovannihoz írt levele Buda, 1526. július 26. (részlet)," [Letter from Antonio di Giovanni to Francesco di Giovanni Buda, 26 July 1526] In *Örök Mohács: szövegek és értelmezések*, eds. János B. Szabó and Gábor Farkas Farkas, 97. Budapest: Bölcsészettudományi Kutatóközpont, 2020.

Gyalókay, Jenő. *A mohácsi csata 1526. augusztus 29.* [The Battle of Mohács 29 August 1526] Budapest: Királyi Magyar Egyetemi Nyomda, 1926.

Habsburg-ház dicsőségtükre Augsburg, 1559. [Ehrenspiegel des Hauses Österreich Augsburg, 1559] In *Örök Mohács: szövegek és értelmezések*, eds. János B. Szabó and Gábor Farkas Farkas, 395–400. Budapest: Bölcsészettudományi Kutatóközpont, 2020.

Halmay, Barna. *Az 1526-iki mohácsi csata keletkezése és igazi helye. A négyszázéves évfordulóra egykoru adatok alapján.* [The origins and the real place of the Battle of Mohács in 1526. Based on contemporary data for the four hundredth anniversary] Debrecen: Magyar Nemzeti Könyv- és Lapkiadóvállalat Rt., 1926.

Hírszerzői jelentés Magyarországgal kapcsolatban Pettau, 1526. szeptember 20. [Intelligence report on Hungary Pettau, 20 September 1526] In *Örök Mohács: szövegek és értelmezések*, eds. János B. Szabó and Gábor Farkas Farkas, 158–159. Budapest: Bölcsészettudományi Kutatóközpont, 2020.

Holub, József. "Az életkor szerepe középkori jogunkban és az "időlátott levelek." [The role of age in medieval law and the "letters of the age examination"] *Századok* 55–56 (1921–1922): 32–76, 212–235.

Hóman, Bálint and Gyula Szekfű. *Magyar történet* II. [Hungarian History II.] Budapest: Magyar Királyi Egyetemi Nyomda, 1936.

Howard, Douglas A. "Ottoman Administration and the Tîmâr System: Sûret-i Ḳânûnnâme-i 'Osmânî Berây-i Tîmâr Dâden." *Journal of Turkish Studies* 20 (1996): 46–125.

Iovius, Paulus. "Krónika a törökök viselt dolgairól Róma 1531 (részlet)." [Chronicle about the deeds of the Turks Rome, 1531 (excerpt)] In *Örök Mohács: szövegek és értelmezések,* eds. János B. Szabó and Gábor Farkas Farkas, 358–359. Budapest: Bölcsészettudományi Kutatóközpont, 2020.

Isthvánffy, Miklós. "A magyarok történetéből 1622 (részlet)." [From the history of the Hungarians 1622 (excerpt)] In *Örök Mohács: szövegek és értelmezések,* eds. János B. Szabó and Gábor Farkas Farkas, 444–462. Budapest: Bölcsészettudományi Kutatóközpont, 2020.

K. Zoffmann, Zsuzsanna. *Az 1526-os mohácsi csata 1976-ban feltárt tömegsírjainak embertani vizsgálata.* [Anthropological study of the mass graves of the Battle of Mohács in 1526, excavated in 1976] Biológiai tanulmányok 9. Budapest: Akadémiai Kiadó, 1982.

Kelenik, József. "Tisztképzés vagy nemesi iskola? Gondolatok a XVI. század magyar katonai képzéséről." [Officer training or noble school? Reflections on the Hungarian military education of the 16th century] In *A magyar katonai vezető- és tisztképzés története,* eds. Ferenc Lengyel and Mihály Szántó, 12–17. Budapest: HM Oktatási és Tudományszervező Főosztály, 1996.

Kemálpasazáde. "Mohácsnáme (részlet)." [Mohácsname (excerpt)] In *Örök Mohács: szövegek és értelmezések,* eds. János B. Szabó and Gábor Farkas Farkas, 326–338. Budapest: Bölcsészettudományi Kutatóközpont, 2020.

Kolosvári, Sándor, Dezső Márkus, Gyula Nagy, and Kelemen Óvári. *Corpus Juris Hungarici: 1000–1526. évi törvénycikkek.* [Articles of law for the years 1000–1526] Budapest: Franklin-Társulat, 1899.

Kubinyi, András. "Magyarország hatalmasai és a török veszély a Jagelló-korban (1490–1526)." [The powerful actors of Hungary and the Turkish threat in the Jagiellon era (1490–1526)] In *Közép-Európa harca a török ellen a 16. század első felében,* ed. István Zombori, 117–146. Budapest: Magyar Egyháztörténeti Enciklopédia Munkaközösség (METEM), Historia Ecclesiastica Hungarica Alapítvány, 2004.

Kubinyi, András. "A mohácsi csata és előzményei." [The Battle of Mohács and its antecedents] *Századok* 115 (1981): 66–107.

Lajos, II. "II. Lajos magyar király levele VIII. Henrik angol királynak, Buda, 1526. március 25." [Letter of Louis II, King of Hungary to Henry VIII, King of England Buda, 25 March 1526] In *Örök Mohács: szövegek és értelmezések,* eds. János B. Szabó and Gábor Farkas Farkas, 38–39. Budapest: Bölcsészettudományi Kutatóközpont, 2020.

Lajos, II. "II. Lajos magyar király levele Ferdinánd ausztriai főhercegnek Buda, 1526. március 25." [Letter of Louis II, King of Hungary to Ferdinand, Archduke of Austria Buda, 25 March 1526] In *Örök Mohács: szövegek és értelmezések,* eds. János B. Szabó and Gábor Farkas Farkas, 37–38. Budapest: Bölcsészettudományi Kutatóközpont, 2020.

Lajos, II. "II. Lajos magyar király levele Antonio Giovanni da Burgio pápai követnek Paks, 1526. augusztus 5." [Letter of Louis II, King of Hungary to the papal secretary

Jacopo Sadoleto Paks, 5 August 1526] In *Örök Mohács: szövegek és értelmezések,* eds. János B. Szabó and Gábor Farkas Farkas, 106. Budapest: Bölcsészettudományi Kutatóközpont, 2020.

Lutfi pasa. "Az Oszmán-ház története 1550-es évek (részlet)." [History of the Ottoman House 1550s (excerpt)] In *Örök Mohács: szövegek és értelmezések,* eds. János B. Szabó and Gábor Farkas Farkas, 401–409. Budapest: Bölcsészettudományi Kutatóközpont, 2020.

Mária, Magyarország királynéja. "Mária, Magyarország királynéja Zsigmondnak, Lengyelország királyának Pozsony, 1526. szeptember 9." [Mary, Queen of Hungary to Sigismund, King of Poland, Pozsony, 9 September 1526] In *Örök Mohács: szövegek és értelmezések,* eds. János B. Szabó and Gábor Farkas Farkas, 140–142. Budapest: Bölcsészettudományi Kutatóközpont, 2020.

Miskolczy, Ambrus. *A román középkor időszerű kérdései. Régi-új viták és közelítések.* [Topical issues of the Romanian Middle Ages. Old and new debates and approaches] (Budapest: Magyarságkutató Intézet, 2021.

Morello, Ludovico. "Ludovico Morello levele Francesco Contarininek Bécs, 1526, szeptember 24. (részlet)." [Ludovico Morello's letter to Francesco Contarini Vienna 24 September 1526 (excerpt)] In *Örök Mohács: szövegek és értelmezések,* eds. János B. Szabó and Gábor Farkas Farkas, 163. Budapest: Bölcsészettudományi Kutatóközpont, 2020.

Mula, Agostino da. "Agostino da Mula jelentése Udine, 1526. szeptember 25. (részletek)." [Report of Agostino da Mula Udine, 25 September 1526 (excerpts)] In *Örök Mohács: szövegek és értelmezések,* eds. János B. Szabó and Gábor Farkas Farkas, 150–152. Budapest: Bölcsészettudományi Kutatóközpont, 2020.

Mula, Agostino da. "Agostino da Mula jelentése Udine, 1526. szeptember 15. (átirat)." [Report of Agostino da Mula Udine, 15 September 1526 (transcript)] In *Örök Mohács: szövegek és értelmezések,* eds. János B. Szabó and Gábor Farkas Farkas, 163–165. Budapest: Bölcsészettudományi Kutatóközpont, 2020.

Murphey, Rhoads. *Ottoman Warfare, 1500–1700.* Routledge, 1998.

Négyesi, Lajos. "A mohácsi csata." [The Battle of Mohács] *Hadtörténelmi Közlemények* 107 (1994): 62–79.

Nemeskürty, István. *Önfia vágta sebét.* [Wounded by her own kind] Budapest: Magvető Kiadó, 1983.

Pap, Norbert, Péter Gyenizse, Máté Kitanics, and Gábor Szalai. "Az 1526. évi mohácsi csata helyszíneinek földrajzi jellemzői." [Geographical characteristics of the sites of the Battle of Mohács in 1526] *Történelmi Szemle* 62 (2020): 111–151.

Perjés, Géza. *Mohács.* Budapest: Magvető Kiadó, 1979.

Perjés, Géza. "A mohácsi csata (1926. augusztus 29.)." [The Battle of Mohács (29 August 1526)] *Hadtörténeti Közlemények* 23 (1976): 427–468.

Szalkai, László. "Szalkai László esztergomi érsek levele Miklós besztercebányai plébánoshoz Esztergom, 1526. június 24. (részlet)." [Letter of the Archbishop of

Esztergom László Szalkai to the parish priest Miklós of Besztercebánya Esztergom, 24 June 1526 (excerpt)] In *Örök Mohács: szövegek és értelmezések*, eds. János B. Szabó and Gábor Farkas Farkas, 77. Budapest: Bölcsészettudományi Kutatóközpont, 2020.

Szatlóczki, Gábor. (2022): *A lovag, a gyalog és a had. A Magyar Királyság hadszervezete és hadserege a mohácsi csata idején (kézirat).* [The military organization and army of the Kingdom of Hungary during the Battle of Mohács (manuscript)] (2022).

Szentkláray, Jenő. *A dunai hajóhadak története.* [History of the Danube flotillas] Budapest: M. Tud. Akadémia Történelmi Bizottsága, 1885.

Szulejmán szultán. "Szulejmán szultán két győzelmi jelentése 1526." [Sultan Süleyman's two accounts of victory 1526] In *Örök Mohács: szövegek és értelmezések*, eds. János B. Szabó and Gábor Farkas Farkas, 258–263. Budapest: Bölcsészettudományi Kutatóközpont, 2020.

Szurmay, Sándor. *A mohácsi hadjárat 1526-ban* [The campaign of Mohács in 1526] Budapest: Pesti Könyvnyomda Rt., 1901.

Tomicki, Piotr. "A magyar hadsereg veszteséglistája Piotr Tomicki krakkói érsek és lengyel alkancellár iratai között 1526. október." [The list of losses of the Hungarian army in the documents of Piotr Tomicki, Archbishop of Krakow and Vice-chancellor of Poland, October 1526] In *Örök Mohács: szövegek és értelmezések*, eds. János B. Szabó and Gábor Farkas Farkas, 185–188. Budapest: Bölcsészettudományi Kutatóközpont, 2020.

Tomori, Pál. "Tomori Pál kalocsai érsek levele II. Lajos magyar királyhoz Pétervárad, 1526. június 25." [Letter of Pál Tomori, Archbishop of Kalocsa to King Louis II of Hungary Petrovaradin, 25 June 1526] In *Örök Mohács: szövegek és értelmezések*, eds. János B. Szabó and Gábor Farkas Farkas, 78–79. Budapest: Bölcsészettudományi Kutatóközpont, 2020.

Tomori, Pál. "Tomori Pál kalocsai érsek levele II. Lajos magyar királyhoz Pétervárad, 1526. július elején." [Letter of Pál Tomori, Archbishop of Kalocsa to King Louis II of Hungary Petrovaradin, early July 1526] In *Örök Mohács: szövegek és értelmezések*, eds. János B. Szabó and Gábor Farkas Farkas, 82–83. Budapest: Bölcsészettudományi Kutatóközpont, 2020.

Ugnád, Dávid. *Ugnád Dávid konstantinápolyi utazásai.* [Dávid Ugnád's travels to Constantinople] Budapest: Szépirodalmi Könyvkiadó, 1986.

Új híradás: Hogyan esett meg a magyarországi csata a török császárral. [New News: How the battle of Hungary with the Turkish Emperor was fought] In *Örök Mohács: szövegek és értelmezések*, eds. János B. Szabó and Gábor Farkas Farkas, 221–223. Budapest: Bölcsészettudományi Kutatóközpont, 2020.

Uzunçarşılı, İsmail Hakkı. *Osmanlı Devleti Teşkilâtından Kapukulu Ocakları. I. Acemi Ocağı ve Yeniçeri Ocağı.* İstanbul: 1984.

Vapovius, Bernardus. "Fragmentum Sigismundi 1526–1535." In *Örök Mohács: szövegek és értelmezések*, eds. János B. Szabó and Gábor Farkas Farkas, 338–344. Budapest: Bölcsészettudományi Kutatóközpont, 2020.

Velius, Caspar Ursinus. "A mohácsi csata 1530 körül (töredék)" [The Battle of Mohács around 1530 (fragment)] In *Örök Mohács: szövegek és értelmezések,* eds. János B. Szabó and Gábor Farkas Farkas, 348–355. Budapest: Bölcsészettudományi Kutatóközpont, 2020.

Venier, Domenico. "Domenico Venier jelentése Róma, 1526, április 21. (kivonat)." [Account of Domenico Venier Rome, 21 April 1526 (excerpt)] In *Örök Mohács: szövegek és értelmezések,* eds. János B. Szabó and Gábor Farkas Farkas, 54–55. Budapest: Bölcsészettudományi Kutatóközpont, 2020.

Verzelius, Joannes. "Joannes Verzelius pápai küldött levele Jacopo Sadoleto pápai titkárnak Buda, 1526. augusztus 13. (részletek)." [Letter from the papal envoy Joannes Verzelius to the papal secretary, Jacopo Sadoleto Buda, 13 August 1526 (excerpts)] In *Örök Mohács: szövegek és értelmezések,* eds. János B. Szabó and Gábor Farkas Farkas, 111. Budapest: Bölcsészettudományi Kutatóközpont, 2020.

Zsámboky, János. "Feljegyzés a mohácsi csatáról 1584 előtt." [Note on the Battle of Mohács before 1584] In *Örök Mohács: szövegek és értelmezések,* eds. János B. Szabó and Gábor Farkas Farkas, 432–433. Budapest: Bölcsészettudományi Kutatóközpont, 2020.

CHAPTER 4

Ottoman Turkish Handguns

Norbert Pap, Pál Fodor and Máté Kitanics

1 Introduction

The two armies that marched towards Mohács in 1526 had a large number of infantry, also equipped with hand firearms. In the European armies, infantry was increasingly supplied with small arms in the early 16th century, and the dominant image of the battlefield changed from one of heavy cavalry to one of infantry with firearms. Spanish, French, Italian, German and Czech mercenary units were arranged in formations, and handgunners, alongside the pikemen, came to play an important and increasingly decisive role in the fighting.

Several sources mention that the Christian infantry troops were partly equipped with firearms at Mohács, but unfortunately few details of their armament have been found. At the same time, the unanimous testimony of several eyewitnesses and the judgment of posterity confirm that the Ottoman infantry, the janissaries, played a decisive role in the Ottoman victory. Fortunately, more is known about their weapons and their use, so we can focus on these weapons when tracing the role of firearms in Mohács.

In this chapter, we examine the following questions: What can be known about these small arms? What were their technical characteristics? How were they used?

2 The Spread of Small Arms among the Ottomans

We have very little data on the beginnings of Ottoman use of handguns. It is a question whether it is of Eastern or Western origin, and also, when it appeared in the Ottoman army. Indeed, it is not clear from the sources when and from what source the Ottomans began to arm their infantry with firearms. Several dates have been given for the first use of the arquebus, known in Turkish as *tüfek* (Turkish for *tube*): 1394, 1402, 1421, 1430, 1440 and 1442.[1] The main problem is that it is difficult to tell from the historical accounts whether they are small

---

1 Gábor Ágoston, "Military Transformation in the Ottoman Empire and Russia, 1500–1800," *Kritika: Explorations in Russian and Eurasian History* 12 (2011) no. 2, pp. 281–319.

calibre cannons or arquebuses.[2] According to an early 16th-century Ottoman historian, firearms (cannons) may have been used during the sieges of Gallipoli (1354) and Bolayır (1356).[3]

According to Marsigli's book published in 1732, the Ottoman handgun is of western origin.[4] Today, it is generally accepted that the Ottomans adopted its use from the Balkan Slavs and partly from the Hungarians. However, the situation is more complicated than that: the term *tüfek* (handgun) is not of Ottoman Turkish, but of Eastern origin. There is also a suggestion that the Ottomans adopted it from the Persians.[5] Turkish experts on the subject, however, consider it to be a Central Asian Turkic word.[6] It was also known to the Russians, who are believed to have acquired it when they captured Bolgar in 1376.[7] It has also been suggested that their expansion not only westward but also eastward may have acquainted the Ottomans with it, or that the term pre-dates firearms and refers to some earlier military technique. The eastern influence cannot be ruled out either, because the Ottomans also used firearms in their wars there, for example against the Mamluks, so this may also have had an influence on the development of the hand firearm and its use.

The origins of the Ottoman *tüfek* are therefore unclear, but nothing rules out the possibility of a multiple effect. We can suspect both eastern and western influences, but the western connection may have been the dominant one, because it was on the European side that the conflicts in which the infantry carrying handguns played a leading role were fought. Kolçak suggests that the firearm came to the fore in European territories because of the denser network of towns and fortifications, as it was initially used for sieges in the first place.[8]

In any case, during the Hungarian–Ottoman wars, the Ottomans already had small arms during the defence of Vidin (1443) or the second Battle of Kosovo (1448).[9] On the Hungarian side, handguns were also in use at that time.

---

2 Godfrey Goodwin, *The Janisseries* (Saqi Books, 2006), p. 129; Joseph Needham, *Science & Civilisation in China 7, Military Technology: The Gunpowder Epic* (Cambridge University Press, 1986), p. 443.

3 Kolçak, Özgür. *Ok, Tüfek ve At: 16. Yüzyıl Osmanlı Askerî Devrimi* Ankara: Türk Tarih Kurumu, 2023 p. 235, referring to the chronicle of Kemalpaşazade.

4 [Luigi Ferdinando,] Count Marsigli (1732): *Lo Stato militare dell'Imperio ottomanno/L'État militaire de l'Empire ottoman*, The Hague and Amsterdam, part 2, p. 15.

5 Gábor Ágoston, *Tüfek* (2011). Available at https://islamansiklopedisi.org.tr/tufek. On the basis that the gun in the Farsi is *tufeng*.

6 Kolçak, *Ok, Tüfek ve At*, pp. 235–236. Original meaning: blowgun. According to Kolçak, the firearm may have both Western and Eastern origins among the Ottomans.

7 Kolçak, *Ok, Tüfek ve At*, pp. 235.

8 Kolçak, *Ok, Tüfek ve At*, pp. 235–236.

9 Gábor Ágoston, "Firearms and Military Adaptation: the Ottomans and the European Military Revolution, 1450–1800," *Journal of World History* 25 (2014), no. 1, pp. 85–124.

In the famous Black Army of the Hungarian King Matthias I (Mátyás Hunyadi), the proportion of infantrymen armed with firearms was high compared to the average of the period, with one in four or five soldiers reportedly armed with them (sources usually report 2000 arquebusiers).[10] Sources indicate that the Hungarian army was using handguns in the early 16th century, and it is likely that some of the soldiers were armed with weapons of the Hunyadi era.[11] It can therefore be concluded that both sides were already using handguns intensively before 1526.

3 The Role of the Handgunner Corps in the Ottoman Military Organisation

Sources suggest that the weapon was not initially considered to be of great importance. Christian gun-bearing soldiers were hired for low pay and low prestige.[12] Such units first appeared in fortresses and in the peripheries of the empire. From 1445 onwards, the records of hundguns and gunners begin to become more frequent.[13] The situation changes from the mid-15th century, perhaps with the conquest of Constantinople: according to a contemporary Italian source, many janissaries were then armed with handguns.[14] It seems

---

10 For a good overview of Hungarian warfare in the pre-Mohács period (including weaponry and firearms), see Gyula Rázsó, "Mátyás hadászati tervei és a realitás," [Matthias I's military plans and reality] *Hadtörténelmi Közlemények* 103 (1990), no. 1, p. 16; Attila Zarnóczky, "Fegyverzet, katonai felszerelés, hadsereg Magyarországon Hunyadi Mátyás korában," [Arms, military equipment, army in Hungary in the time of Matthias I] *Hadtörténelmi Közlemények* 103 (1990), no. 1. pp. 31–65; András Kubinyi, "Mozgósítási és hadseregellátási problémák Mátyás alatt," [Mobilisation and army supply problems under Matthias I] *Hadtörténelmi* Közlemények 103 (1990), no. 1, pp. 66–73.

11 József Kelenik, "Szakállas puskák XVI. századi magyarországi inventáriumokban," [Hackbuts in 16th century Hungarian inventories] *Hadtörténelmi Közlemények* 35 (1988), no. 3, pp. 484–520.

12 Feridun Emecen, "Ateşli Silahlar Çağı: Askeri Dönüşüm/Devrim ve Osmanlı Ordusu," in Feridun Emecen and Erhan Afyoncu, *Savaşın Sultanları-I. Osmanlı Padişahlarının Meydan Muherebeleri,* (Istanbul: Bilge, 2018), pp. 38–81; Kolçak, *Ok, Tüfek ve At,* p. 237; Albrecht Fuess, "Why Domenico Had to Die and Black Slaves Wore Red Uniforms: Military Technology and Its Decisive Role in the 1517 Ottoman Conquest of Egypt," in *The Mamluk-Ottoman Transition: Continuity and Change in Egypt and Bilād al-Shām in the Sixteenth Century,* 2nd ed. eds. Stefan Conermann and Gül Sen, (V&R, Bonn University Press, 2022), pp. 131–154.

13 Emecen, "Ateşli Silahlar Çağı," p. 48, pp. 50–51, Kolçak, *Ok, Tüfek ve At,* pp. 234–237; Fuess, "Why Domenico Had to Die," pp. 131–154.

14 Emecen, "Ateşli Silahlar Çağı," pp. 50–51.

that the first battle in which the janissary handgunners, deployed in units of ten, already played an important role was the Battle of Terjan in 1473. This was a victory over Uzun Hasan's Turkoman cavalry army in Eastern Anatolia.[15]

The two wars fought against the Mamluks in the East (1485–1491, 1516–1517) had many lessons for the Ottoman army and weapon industry. In many ways, they can be seen as a prelude to the 1526 campaign.

The Mamluks had excellent cavalry, but they were averse to firearms. The sultans of Cairo organised a 500-strong infantry unit of black slaves (because they were the cheapest), which proved surprisingly effective. The attitude of the Eastern cavalry towards firearms is well illustrated by the serious tension that developed in the army between the cavalry and the black arquebusiers. The cavalry perceived fighting with handguns as degrading, and the sultanate had to get the support it needed for military reform from outside the system.[16]

The Mamluks resorted to western help to develop their weaponry. These were probably Italian experts. Two of them are known by name: one was called Domenico (his exact identity is not known), and the other was Ludovico de Varthema di Bologna, who became famous for his reports on his travels to the East. During the second Ottoman–Mamluk war, the latter sought the help of experts and support from the Knights of Rhodes.[17]

The Mamluks also seem to have had an excellent trade relationship with Venice for a long time, in which the Venetians' position in Cyprus played an important role. The raw materials for the production of firearms, mainly metal and saltpetre, were partly supplied by the Ottomans. So it can be seen that they depended heavily on the West for technology and even on the Ottomans for raw materials, and the volume is questionable, since there were also imports of weapons.

In Bayezid II's war against the Mamluks, the Ottomans were as yet defeated by the Mamluk arquebusiers. As a result, improvements were made,[18] and Selim I was victorious in 1516–1517: the Ottomans gained numerical and technological superiority and also made significant changes to their battle tactics. According to the sources, it was in the reign of Bayezid II that gunsmiths appeared at the sultan's court and light handguns were developed for the battlefield.

---

15   Emecen, "Ateşli Silahlar Çağı," p. 51.
16   Fuess, "Why Domenico Had to Die," p. 141.
17   Fuess, "Why Domenico Had to Die," p. 150.
18   Robert Irwin, "Gunpowder and Firearms in the Mamluk Sultanate Reconsidered," in *The Mamluks in Egyptian and Syrian Politics and Society*, eds. Michael Winter and Amalia Levanoni (Leiden and Boston: Brill, 2004), pp. 117–139.

Scholars concerned with the issue agree that the series of victories that began with Chaldiran is to be ascribed to Ottoman battle tactics, the mass use of cannons and gun-bearing janissaries. In particular, the field battles were very similar: against the Safavids at Chaldiran (1514), against the Mamluks at Marj Dabiq (1516) and Ridaniya (1517), against the Hungarians at Mohács (1526). Firearms were also used in large numbers in the siege of Rhodes (1522), which also ended in victory, and in another campaign in Iran (1533–1534).

Ágoston[19] and Fuess[20] also suggest that the use of the "wagenburg" was a decisive factor in the victory in the four field battles mentioned above. Fuess argues that although it originated with the Hussites (e.g. Harby, 1422), the Ottomans in the Balkans learned its use from the Hungarians and developed it further.

The usual Ottoman order of battle had the sultan in the centre, protected by a "mobile fortress": cannons, handgunners, wagons on either side, the infantry vanguard in the centre front, and cavalry on the flanks. This 'manière de combattre' relying on the wagon fortress was called *tabur cengi* in Ottoman Turkish.[21] Behind the cannons, which were linked by chains, the janissaries were lined up, usually in three rows. They fired in succession: while one line fired, the other charged so that that they did not interfere with each other. The usual rate of fire at that time (about a minute to load a gun) was for a corps to fire three rounds a minute, with only a third of the gunners firing at a time.

According to the usual tactics, the task of the cavalry was to lure the enemy in front of the artillery and the janissaries in the centre by executing very precise manoeuvres. The field guns fired first, followed by the janissaries firing volleys, with the larger, longer-barrelled handguns in the front rank, and then, as the enemy came closer, the smaller, shorter-barrelled guns from the rear ranks.[22] The fight was usually decided here: the attacking enemy was crushed with their small arms. According to a 16th-century Spanish source, it was not the fire of the cannons that was decisive, but the massed handgun fire, with alternating rows.[23]

---

19 Gábor Ágoston, "War-Winning Weapons? On The Decisiveness Of Ottoman Firearms from the Siege of Constantinople (1453) to the Battle of Mohacs (1526)," *Journal of Turkish Studies* 39 (2013), pp. 129–143.
20 Fuess, "Why Domenico Had to Die," p. 132, p. 148.
21 Pál Fodor, *Tabur* (2010) Available at https://islamansiklopedisi.org.tr/tabur.
22 Emecen, "Ateşli Silahlar Çağı," p. 56.
23 Emecen, "Ateşli Silahlar Çağı," p. 73.

The equipping of the cavalry with small arms, despite attempts[24] to do so, did not progress in Süleyman's time. Like the Mamluks, the Ottoman cavalry showed strong resistance to their use (the prestige of archery was higher). Apart from practical difficulties – compared to the bow, the rate of fire was low, reloading and handling the fuse while riding was difficult – mental and cultural reasons also played a role. The exclusive use of the bow thus persisted in the first two thirds of the 16th century. After that, the use of small arms was accepted, albeit slowly and reluctantly.

4 The Ottoman Hand Firearms Production in the First Half of the 16th Century

As mentioned above, the development of effective Ottoman handguns in the early 16th century reflects Western influence. It was Bayezid II who made a major effort to develop a more effective matchlock infantry than before. This involved not only improving the quality of the guns, but also training and battle tactics. Opinions are divided as to what influenced the development of the janissaries' weapons. It has long been argued that they were developed under strong Spanish influence, so that they were in fact Spanish handguns.[25] However, others opine that they were developed independently.[26]

After the defeat of the Mamluks, the Ottomans appeared in Africa. As of the 1520s, North African territories gradually came under Ottoman influence. Some experts believe that Spanish arquebuses appeared in the Ottoman army at this time.[27] There is also important technical evidence of the Spanish influence: the spread of the use of the *miquelet,* an early flintlock in the Ottoman Empire, particularly in North Africa and the Balkans. However, it did not play a role at Mohács.

The guns used at Mohács probably had an earlier, so-called "serpentine" lock ("S" or "Z" shaped firing mechanism). In fact, in the published Ottoman lists of war material, the term 'fuse' is used, as well as 'gunpowder for a matchlock

---

24 Grand Vizier Rüstem Pasha tried to equip the court cavalry with handguns, but failed. Emecen "Ateşli Silahlar Çağı," pp. 60–61.
25 Zdzislaw Żygulski, "Oriental and Levantine Firearms," in *Pollard's History of Firearms*, ed. Claude Blair (London, Macmillan, 1983), pp. 430–431; Robert Elgood, *The Arms of Greece and Her Balkan Neighbors in the Ottoman Period* (New York: Thames & Hudson, 2009), p. 10, p. 39.
26 Emecen, "Ateşli Silahlar Çağı," p. 56.
27 Żygulski, "Oriental and Levantine" p. 430, Elgood, *The Arms of Greece*, p. 39.

gun'. The origin of the serpentine firing mechanism is disputed,[28] some say it is Chinese, others say it is Central European, perhaps German, but it may have been developed by the Ottomans. However, the *miquelet* was probably not yet in use in 1526. The use of serpentine can be traced among the Ottomans for a very long time, in some cases up into the 18th century.

During the reign of Bayezid II, in the early 16th century, a central gunsmith's workshop was established in the seraglio with the help of western specialists.[29] The source of the change was the *taife-i efrenciyan*, a team of Franks, or western Europeans. Their supposed leader was, in Ottoman terms, a 'Rus', meaning 'person from the north'. He was called Garde/Gardo,[30] but nothing is known of his origin. Other *northerners* – e.g. his brother and sons – were also employed in the workshop. They seem to have expanded only slowly, with Muslims in addition to the "Russians", and then in time with Sephardic Jews expelled from Spanish territories. Before Mohács, five out of ten employees of the *cemaat-i tüfenkçiyan* were already Spanish Sephardim.[31]

When they conquered Egypt (1517), the Ottomans also gained access to the Mamluks' gun-making workshop.[32] The important role played by Mamluk matchlock corps in the first Mamluk–Ottoman war suggests that gun-making in the East was not only an Ottoman activity, but it was also pursued in Mamluk Egypt. The known western firearms makers in Mamluk service were mainly Italians. Nothing is known about the characteristics of the workshop, its personnel or its products. The circumstances suggest that western technology was used and the raw materials and semi-finished products for the manufacture of firearms were partly obtained from the Ottomans.

It seems, therefore, that the Ottomans developed standardised weapons for the janissaries through western expertise (western and "Russian", Iberian and Italian in origin), which they used very effectively after 1514. For a long time, the centre of state handgun production was the seraglio, but by the mid-16th century it had shifted to the Istanbul gun workshop and central armoury. Sources suggest that the treasury gun standards (given in karış and dirhem)[33] remained unchanged from the 1510s to the 1570s.[34]

---

28 Kolçak, *Ok, Tüfek ve At*, p. 266.
29 Kolçak, *Ok, Tüfek ve At*, p. 238.
30 Name research shows that the name 'Garde' occurs in the early modern period in British, German and French areas.
31 Kolçak, *Ok, Tüfek ve At*, pp. 238–240.
32 Kolçak, *Ok, Tüfek ve At*, p. 236.
33 The karış is a measure of length used in the Ottoman Empire, the dirhem is a measure of weight.
34 Kolçak, *Ok, Tüfek ve At*, p. 247.

5 The "Calibre" of the Ottoman Handgun, the Dirhem

According to a contemporary Ottoman chronicle,[35] in 1566 Miklós Zrínyi, who broke out of the besieged fort of Szigetvár, was hit by the janissaries with a "five dirhem" projectile. As this example shows, the mass of the projectile is the basis for the Ottomans' determination of the calibre of their handguns (in this case, the five dirhem gun).

The dirhem (which was also the name for silver coins in the Middle East at the time) is a unit of measurement for silver, dating back to antiquity (drachma). Regional standards evolved, so the dirhem had different weights in Anatolia, Egypt, the Maghreb, Syria and Iraq.

A detailed overview of these values is given in Walther Hinz's handbook.[36] However, he has already pointed out that these values are only indicative. Gábor Ágoston, in agreement with Hinz, stresses that there was no well-developed and uniform system of measurement in the Middle East and points to the many uncertainties in this area. According to Ágoston, before 1640 the Ottomans did not even attempt to standardise the system of weights and measures, and only the financial/economic crisis prompted them to do so. Until then they had retained the established measures in use everywhere in the conquered territories, but saw to it that they did not differ at least within each individual sub-province (sancak). More precisely, they introduced the names of the measures, but allowed the locals to continue to interpret them according to local standards.[37] The standardisation that began around 1640 was not an unqualified success, although it would have been necessary for the development of trade within the empire and the economy in general.

As described above, we are thus faced with the problem of what mass to expect for a dirhem value appearing in a source from the first half of the 16th century, since "Ottoman dirhem" did not exist at that time. It had evolved by the 19th century, when it was understood to be 3.2 grams.[38] In Persia, the dirhem (dirham) originally had a value of around 4–4.25 grams, which in

---

35 Selânikî Mustafa Efendi, *Tarih-i Selânikî (971–1003/1563–1595)*, Hazırlayan Mehmed İpşirli (İstanbul: İstanbul Üniversitesi Edebiyat Fakültesi, 1989), p. 34.
36 Walter Hinz, *Measures and Weights in the Islamic World* (Kuala Lumpur: ISTAC, 2003).
37 "Unification of metrology within a sancak (sub-province) was carried out by extending the use of a typical local measure to the whole sancak. A revolutionary plan for unification was proposed following the Ottoman economic crisis around 1640, and the government was advised to extend the use of Istanbul weights and measures to the provinces of the empire. The proposal, however, was not favoured." Gábor Ágoston and Bruce Masters, *Encyclopedia of the Ottoman Empire* (New York: Facts on File, 2009), pp. 595–596.
38 According to the conversion, 1 okka equals 400 dirham.

TABLE 4.1 Variants of the dirhem according to Walter Hinz, Measures and Weights in the Islamic World (Kuala Lumpur: ISTAC, 2003)

	Dirhem mass
Anatolia	3.086 g
Egypt	3.123 g
Syria	3.167 g
Iraq	3.125 g
Maghreb	3.3 g

modern times has been reduced to 3.2–3.3 grams.[39] In Orthodox Jewish legal texts, the dirhem is a recurrent unit of measurement, with a weight of between 3–3.4 grams, and, for example, one source states that in Egypt the dirhem is 3.333 grams.[40] The theoretical units of measurement used in the different Middle Eastern areas are described in the table above, based on Walther Hinz's handbook (Table 4.1).

This clearly shows that the dirhem was not a mature unit of measurement in the 16th century, but an order of magnitude that varied from region to region. Which one should we take into account? The one used in what is now Turkey (Anatolia)? Egypt, which became a major player in the empire's economy after 1517? The Maghreb, which played an important intermediary role in western shipping, trade and Spanish relations? The dirhem, used in the temporarily conquered Tebriz (Tabriz) (1514), which weighs 3.072 g and is the smallest of the dirhems, but which was widely used 100 years after Mohács? There is considerable uncertainty. Ágoston (referring to Halil Sahillioğlu) prefers the Tebriz dirhem,[41] while İnalcık prefers the Rumi dirhem (3.207 grams).[42]

The 16th-century dirhem was therefore not a standard and universally accepted unit of measurement, so automatic conversion to the size of a projectile is rather problematic. The dirhem value of 3 grams is apparently untenable.

39 See at https://www.iranicaonline.org/articles/dirham.
40 *Dictionnaire Turc-Français* (Constantinople: Imprimerie Mihran, 1911). p. 1373.
41 Ágoston (following Sahillioğlu) writes that in the 16th and 17th centuries, the Tebriz dirhem was used in coinage. He also adopts the Rumi dirhem for the size of weapons/ammunition, but only uses it from the 18th century onwards: Gábor Ágoston, *Guns for the Sultan – Military Power and the Weapons Industry in the Ottoman Empire* (Cambridge: Cambridge University Press, 2005) p. 90.
42 Halil İnalcık, "Introduction to Ottoman Metrology," *Turcica* 15 (*1983*), pp. 311–348.

A higher value, at least 3.2 grams, is worth reckoning with, if only because we have seen that Ottoman gun-making was strongly influenced by western, Iberian-Maghrebi influences. In the case of the 5 dirhem bullet that hit Zrínyi at Szigetvár in 1566, we can start from the handguns that originated in Hungary and survived in collections. As we will see below, the 5 karış[43] long barrel was typically associated with a 5 dirhem projectile. In the case of the 110–115 cm long janissary gun, we can see that its barrel is 16–17 mm in diameter. Assuming a gap of one millimetre, a projectile size of 15–16 mm in diameter corresponds to a value of 16–17 grams (1 dirhem equals or more than 3.2 grams). The question is, what kind of material and density is associated with these figures?

The 5 dirhem bullet of the 5 karış barrel length mentioned in the sources, which killed Nicholas Zrínyi at Szigetvár, could in reality have been a barrel diameter of around 17 mm, a bullet of around 16 mm, fired by a janissary from his "long" (*uzun*) arquebus, which was considered of good quality in that period.

6 Technological Characteristics of Janissary Handguns

The handguns for the court troops were designed and partly made in the central workshop. The standardisation of arquebuses had already begun in the time of Bayezid II, and was completed sometime before 1520. The following is a brief summary of the process of gun production based mainly on Kolçak's pioneering research.[44]

The essence of the handgun is the barrel, a long metal tube, and originally the barrel was called *tüfek*. Adding the stock of a handgun and the firing mechanism were separate operations. Originally, the *tüfenkhane* (gunsmith's workshop) was responsible for making the barrel only. From the mid-16th century onwards, the workshop was located on the coast, as raw materials were transported by ship, so the 'gun manufactory' had its own harbour. The furnaces of the *tüfenkhane* were used to smelt the iron ore on which the barrels were based. The barrels were made of high-quality metal. The secret lay in the way the plain steel plates were rolled/folded. The barrels folded in the Damascus (*şamî*) method were of such high quality that they were in demand in the West, too.

---

43   1 karış = 22–23 cm, so 5 karış is about 110–115 cm.
44   Kolçak, *Ok, Tüfek ve At*, pp. 257–275.

The gun-stock was procured by the *cebehane* (the central imperial armoury) and there it was combined with the gun barrel. The head armourer (*cebecibaşı*) took care of the cleaning rod (*harbî*), the firing mechanism, the powder horn, the fuse and the bullets, and he was also in charge of distributing the weapons. Gunpowder was provided by the commissioner of the city (*şehremini*). The powder and the fuse were kept in the powder box (*vezne*), which was mostly made of metal. After use, the weapons had to be cleaned, for which the cleaning rod, called *harbî* mentioned above, was used by wrapping a cloth around it. The powder and the bullet were then loaded with it.

The production centre thus endeavoured to supply all the sultan's household troops (and the fortress garrisons) with barrel, stock, firing mechanism and powder box in one package, while sending the powder and the fuse separately. In addition, the production process was constantly controlled, and the barrels were regularly test-fired. To do this, the *cebehane* also needed bullets, fuses, primer and powder.

The handguns were stored separately in dedicated depots according to calibre and length. The short guns were stored in the *harcî tüfek* store and the long guns in the *has tüfek* store. Accordingly, the barrels of the two types of infantry guns were 4 and 5 karış long (the first for the *kütah/küçük/harcî* guns, the other for the *uzun/has* guns). The stocks of the handguns were made separately, the longer and the shorter ones being of different types. There was also a larger, longer weapon (*diraz/uzun/metris tüfeği*), which was mainly used in sieges, as it could be fired from a long distance (Table 4.2).

TABLE 4.2   Types and characteristics of treasury handguns in the first half of the 16th century
1 karış = 22–23 cm; 1 dirhem = < 3,2g.

Name	Barrel length	Calibre/shot projectile
diraz/uzun/metris tüfeği	130–160 cm long	15–29 mm barrel
uzun/has tüfek	5 karış long (110–115 cm)	5 dirhem (ca. 16 g)
kütah/küçük/harcî tüfek	4 karış long (88–92 cm)	4 dirhem (ca. 13 g)

SOURCES: KOLÇAK, 2023; EMECEN, 2018

Notes: The handguns preserved in Turkish and other eastern collections are mostly long-barrelled, sometimes iron, often ornate metris tüfeğis. They do not really serve as a starting point for our present study, as their size made them less suitable for field engagements. There are also problems of dating, as it is difficult to determine the exact date of their production. Very few of these janissary handguns have preserved in Istanbul, and they are more likely to date from the 17th and 18th centuries.

Some of the preserved janissary guns, at least partly dated to the 16th century, are described by Ágoston. As can be seen, they tend to be longer, larger weapons, presumably mostly of late 16th or 17th century date. The one that most closely resembles the known standard (*uzun/has tüfeks*) is the first in the series, with a 120 cm long barrel and 16 mm calibre. The other weapons are closer to the *metris tüfeği*, probably made after 1570 (Table 4.3).

16th–17th-century janissary handguns are also preserved in Hungarian collections (Table 4.4). Based on their size distribution, the smaller guns, with a barrel length of 90 cm or slightly longer, have a 15 mm diameter, while the

TABLE 4.3   Ottoman janissary handgun data from the collection of Gábor Ágoston

Century	Firing mechanism	Barrel length (cm)	Calibre (mm)	Reg. number
16th–17th	matchlock	120	16	406
16th–17th	matchlock	150	16	8925
16th–17th	matchlock	133	19	9086
16th	miquelet/flintlock	132	19	9053

SOURCES: ÁGOSTON, GUNS FOR THE SULTAN, P. 91; ÁGOSTON, TÜFEK HTTPS:// ISLAMANSIKLOPEDISI.ORG.TR/TUFEK

TABLE 4.4   Turkish small arms exhibited at the "National Exhibition of the Millennium" in Budapest, 1896

Barrel diameter	Barrel length	Comment
	Carbiner	
	16th century	
8 mm	53 cm	16th c., long-barreled, oriental, the barrel widens at the front, p. 377.
	17th century	
16 mm	80 cm	Late 17th c., Turkish, p. 554.
	Hackbut (Hakenbüchse)	
Barrel diameter	Barrel length	Comment
	17th century	
25 mm	107 cm	Early 17th c., Turkish, p. 552.
25 mm	102 cm	17th c., Turkish (barrel), early 18th century French stock, p. 554.

OTTOMAN TURKISH HANDGUNS

TABLE 4.4 Turkish small arms exhibited at the "National Exhibition" (*cont.*)

Barrel diameter	Barrel length	Comment
Pistol		
16th century		
13 mm	33 cm	2 pc, 16th c., Turkish, p. 410.
14 mm	26 cm	16th c., Turkish, p. 600.
17th century		
16 mm	32 cm	17th c., Eastern, p. 409.
15 mm	30,5 cm	17th c. Turkish, p. 508.
15 mm	27,5 cm	2 pc, 17th c., Turkish, p. 599.
14 mm	24,3 cm	17th c., Turkish, p. 600.
18th century		
16 mm	33,7 cm	2 pc, 18th c., Turkish, p. 516.
17 mm	31,2 cm	2 pc, 18th c., Turkish, p. 430.
Handguns (including light musket and musket)		
Barrel diameter	Barrel length	Comment
16th century		
15 mm	129 cm	Late 16th c., Turkish, çakmak tüfengi,[a] p. 459.
17 mm	163 cm	Late 16th c., long musket, pp. 473–474.
20 mm	103 cm	16th c., Turkish, p. 411.
15 mm	104 cm	16th c., Turkish, p. 463.
17 mm	113 cm	16th c., Turkish janissary matchlock (tüfenk), p. 549.
19 mm	132 cm	Described as similar to the weapon described at 3026, identified as a 16th century Turkish weapon, p. 659.
17th century		
15 mm	84 cm	Early 17th c., p. 429.
15 mm	125 cm	1653 (*"I won this janczar handgun in my first battle. Under Székesfehérvár…1653"*), long, matchlock musket (tüfenk or fetil tüfengi), p. 555.
16 mm	115 cm	mid 17th c., tüfenk, heavy musket, Turkish, p. 548.

a   *Çakmaklı tüfek* = flintlock.

TABLE 4.4 Turkish small arms exhibited at the "National Exhibition" (cont.)

12 mm	117 cm	Late 17th c., Turkish, tüfenk, p. 548.
16 mm	115 cm	Late 17th c., Turkish, pp. 445–446.
20 mm	100 cm	Late 17th c., Turkish barrel and structure, p. 499.
17,5 mm	86,5 cm	17th c., Turkish, tüfenk, p. 549.
24 mm	96 cm	17th c., heavy, Turkish musket, tüfenk, pp. 550–551.
18 mm	79 cm	17th c., Turkish tüfenk, p. 551.
14 mm	87,4 cm	17th c., Turkish tüfenk, p. 447.
18 mm	102 cm	17th c., Turkish barrel, the stock from the 18th century, p. 545.
14 mm	156 cm	17th c., long, Turkish, p. 546.
20 mm	108 cm	17th c., Turkish tüfenk, p. 546.
21 mm	111 cm	17th c., musket, Turkish, the gun-stock is from 18th c., p. 546.
17 mm	86,5 cm	17th c., Turkish tüfenk, pp. 552–553.
16 mm	65 cm	17th c., short, Montenegrin, Turkish, p. 553.
15 mm	89,5 cm	17th c., Montenegrin, Turkish p. 554.
15 mm	106 cm	17th c., Turkish, p. 698.
	18th century	
23 mm	90 cm	Early 18th c., Turkish, p. 553.
16 mm	88 cm	Late 18th c. (1780), tüfenk, pp. 697–698.
15 mm	126 cm	18th c., Turkish, p. 459.
17 mm	123 cm	18th c., musket, p. 554.

Note: Specimens that were not clearly marked and therefore unsuitable for analysis (contradictory or with misspellings and therefore not clearly identifiable), or those with a double barrel were excluded from the sample.

larger guns, with a barrel length of 110 cm or slightly longer, have a 17 mm diameter. We believe that the first type can be associated with the 4 dirhem projectile, while the second type can be associated with the 5 dirhem projectile.

The sources give a clear picture of the characteristics of the Ottoman treasury handguns. Two types of them were used for field fighting, with two different calibres. There was a considerable difference in price, quality and design between the gun-stock of the *harcî* guns and the *uzun* guns, and they were probably used in different ways. The use of the stock of gun also depended to a large extent on the powder charge. It was mainly the *uzun tüfeks* (5 karış long) that could be expected to be able to penetrate the armour of heavy cavalry. As these weapons were well proven, they were used for decades after Mohács.

An Ottoman source from 1640 on the sale of second-hand firearms provides useful information on Ottoman gun types.[45] The text contains descriptions of six 'muskets'. In addition to the decoration, condition and price of the weapons, it also provides information on their physical characteristics. The length of the barrel is typically given in karış, while the bullets fired from the weapon are given in dirhems. The length of five of the guns is specified (length is missing in one case): the barrels are all 5 karış long (110–115 cm). Of the six, the calibre of four is 5 dirhems, of one is 7 dirhems and of one is 10 dirhems. This suggests that barrels of 5 karış in length and 5 dirhems in calibre may have been fairly typical in the empire even in the 17th century.

The sources also show that there were many other types of handguns in the empire, not just treasury firearms, and arms were also imported. Special guns were also found in the seraglio, for which great rewards were paid to their makers. Since they were expensive, members of the Ottoman elite were their most likely owners. However, the prohibitions on the possession of firearms make it clear that simple handguns were in the hands of the common people, too.

The sources reveal that the janissary guns were closely supervised because they were assigned a particularly important role. They were standardised, very effective weapons in skilled hands and of excellent quality. Compared with the weapons of their opponents, the western infantry of the period and the rebels from within the empire, they gave their operators a huge advantage.

7   The Material of the Projectile of the Early Ottoman Arquebus

The material of the Ottoman handguns' projectiles was also peculiar, and this also contributed to the superiority of the janissaries. The material used for the projectiles was called *sürb*, for which tin was bought.[46] The lead-tin alloy, however, is less suitable as a projectile than pure lead, which is soft and melts at

---

45   Tim Stanley, "The Ottomans and the Transmission of Gun Lock Technology," in *Cultural Encounters in the Ottoman World and Their Reflections: Essays in Honor of Prof. Dr. Filiz Yenisehirlioğlu* (Ankara: 2017), pp. 205–214.
46   We know all this from Kolçak's recent research: Kolçak, *Ok, Tüfek ve At*, p. 248.

326 degrees Celsius. The lead-tin alloy, known as solder tin, is even softer. What could be the secret of its success?

These metals harden when alloyed with antimony. In the periodic table of Mendeleev, it is the arsenic (As), antimony (Sb) and bismuth[47] (Bi) underneath each other that form a very solid crystal structure in a metallic solution with tin-lead.[48]

Lead (Pb) + tin (Sn) + antimony (Sb) is therefore an excellent projectile material. It is sufficient to add a small amount of antimony (a few per cent) to the lead and tin to harden them (density of the three materials: Pb = 11.3 g/cm³; Sn = 7.3 g/cm³; Sb = 6.7 g/cm³).[49] Later, however, as tin was expensive to obtain, the Ottomans compromised on quality and used only lead hardened with antimony.[50]

The advantage of *sürb* over lead is that although it is still quite heavy, it is better retained (it does not deform under pressure and temperature, it does not spread to almost twice its original size), so the trajectory of the projectile is more stable and the impacting projectile transfers the destructive energy in a pointwise manner. Overall, the hit is more effective and the armour-piercing effect is much more powerful.

At the same time, the density of the projectile is not 11.3 g/cm³ as it would be if it were made of lead alone, but the density of the *sürb*, which we estimate to be lower considering that the ratio of tin to antimony is estimated to be around 30%. Accordingly, the diameter of a projectile of the same weight of *sürb* is significantly larger than that of a pure lead projectile.

---

47   Bismuth can only be extracted in small quantities and, since it was discovered in 1753, it could not have played a role in the metallurgy and arms production of the period.

48   Nowadays, lead is combined with arsenic to produce hardened pellets. The lead-tin-antimony alloy is now used as a base material for high wear-resistant printing type or bearing balls. Hobby shooters using black powder prefer to use the printing "lead" in the manufacture of their own projectiles.

49   Based on today's bearing balls, the ideal composition would be around 70%–25%–5%.

50   Antimony is always found together with other metals (hence its name: *anti* (against) *monos* (alone). For a long time it was confused with lead, considered to be a lighter version of it. It is known from the literature that it is present in early modern bullets to varying degrees: József Padányi and József Ondrek, "Examining Lead Bullets from the Siege of Novi Zrin in 1664," *Journal of Conflict Archaeology* 14 (2019), no. 1, pp. 1–20; D. J. Huismann et al., "Bullets over Gennep: Using Compositional Variation in Lead Musket Balls in Battlefield Archaeology," in *39th International Symposium on Archeometry 2012.* (Leuven, 2012), p.225. It is possible that not all people were aware of the importance and role of antimony in all cases and in all places, but since lead was mined together with antimony, they may have realised that in some cases it makes lead harder.

In addition to lead, iron balls were used, especially for the larger calibres. This is a common trend in the period and can also be observed in Hungarian inventories.

FIGURE 4.1 The *tabur cengi*, the Ottoman order of battle, 1526, Battle of Mohács (the cannons are chained together).
SOURCE: KÁROLY KISS, MOHÁCS EMLÉKEZETE [MEMORY OF MOHÁCS] (BUDAPEST: EURÓPA KÖNYVKIADÓ, 1987).

8 The Use of Handguns: the Enemy, the Role of Training, Alternate Firing

Although the Ottoman military development was boosted by the experience of the eastern theatres of war (Safavids, Mamluks), it was in the western theatres, especially in Central Europe, that the Ottomans faced stronger opponents who used advanced weapon systems and more sophisticated tactics. Most importantly, unlike in Asia, Europe had seen the proliferation of thick metal body armour, which posed a serious challenge to gun-makers in the West.

The wars in Italy played an important role in the spread of handguns, and some of the antecedents of the Battle of Mohács point here in a certain sense (tactics, combat experience, technology): it was mainly here that the West was able to gain modern combat experience. One of the first European battles in which small arms played a decisive role was the Battle of Cerignola (1503).[51]

Some of the western mercenaries who marched against the Ottomans in 1526, including the *landsknecht*s, may have gained some of their experience in this area. German soldiers were also familiar with the firearms of the period and how to use them. In European theatres of war at this time, infantrymen generally fought in a closed quadrangular formation: pikemen defending against attack, soldiers using swords and shields in close combat, and handgunmen lined up in a set pattern.

The experience of the battles in northern Italy, and in particular the Battle of Pavia in 1525, was a great lesson for the military leaders of the period. The battle ended in a disastrous defeat for the French. Under fire from about 3000 handgunners of the Spanish army, 8000 French soldiers were killed and the King of France himself was taken prisoner. The heavy losses of the French heavy cavalry foreshadowed the events at Mohács. However, the sources suggest that the leaders of the Hungarian army at Mohács were unaware of this or did not consider it important to learn the lessons.

It was also on the battlefields of Italy that the new modern hundguns, later known as *muskets*, were first used in Europe: apparently for the first time in 1521, during the siege of Parma.[52] However, according to Phillips, there are sources

---

51   Tonio Andrade, *The Gunpowder Age: China, Military Innovation, and the Rise of the West in World History* (Princeton and Oxford: Princeton University Press, 2016), p. 167.
52   Moritz Thierbach, *Die geschichtliche Entwicklung der Handfeuerwaffen, edited from the originals still existing in German collections* (Dresden: 1889) (Reprinted Graz: 1975 and Saarbrücken: 2018), pp. 19–20; Thomas Arnold, *The Renaissance at War.* (Cassell, 2001), pp. 75–78.

which indicate that these weapons were already in existence in 1499.[53] The reason for this, and the background to it, is that armour makers began to develop ever thicker, stronger armour that could withstand light arquebuses. The heavy armour, which weighed about 15 kg in the first half of the 15th century, had increased to 25 kg by the 16th century.[54] However, to break through 2 mm thick armour, three times as much energy was needed as for 1 mm armour.[55] The Spanish responded by introducing a new gun that could fire much further and with much greater kinetic energy to break through armour.[56] It is difficult to distinguish the weapon from the arquebus by its name in the sources, as it was often referred to as the 'great arquebus' or 'double arquebus', and later as the 'musket arquebus'. After some time, the musket gradually replaced the name arquebus, while the name musket was extended to lighter handguns, too.

As it turned out, the more advanced firearms made the heavy cavalry almost redundant, and it slowly lost its importance from the mid-16th century. The new type of handgun cut through all the armour of the time, penetrating everything. Relatively cheap and easy to learn to use, it spread quickly and easily. It was the opposite of the traditional heavy cavalry, which was very expensive and it was very difficult to replace soldiers who were lost.

The Ottoman army on the western front had to face this type of army. In particular, the heavy cavalry in heavy plate armour appeared threatening to them. But technological and combat advances in the decades before Mohács brought a new solution. The key was to equip the janissaries with firearms and to train this highly disciplined force with advanced weaponry.

Their weapons became standardised and, through training, their efficiency of use increased. Opponents with less developed weapons and far less experience were at a disadvantage. They knew the limits of their handguns through much practice, and were able to use them more effectively than their opponents. For this reason in particular, they were careful to keep the treasury's weapons under strict control.

Among Turkish historians, there are some who believe that the art of volley firing on the battlefield is an Ottoman invention,[57] but there is no consensus on

---

53   Henry Pratap Phillips, *The History and Chronology of Gunpowder and Gunpowder Weapons (ca.1000 to 1850)* (Chennai: Notion Press, 2016).
54   Alan Williams, *The Knight and the Blast Furnace. A History of the Metallurgy of Armour in the Middle Ages and the Early Modern Period* (Leiden: Brill, 2003) p. 916.
55   Williams, *The Knight and the Blast Furnace*, p. 936.
56   Benjamin Robins, *New principles of gunnery: containing the determination of the force of gun-powder, and an investigation of the difference in the resisting power of the air to swift and slow motions* (Gale ECCO, 2010), p. 160.
57   Emecen, "Ateşli Silahlar Çağı," pp. 64–74.

the issue. There is a belief that in Europe it first appeared at the Battle of Bicocca in 1522.[58] At Mohács, however, its use by the janissaries is well-documented. It is conceivable that in several places its importance was recognised autonomously through internal development. The famous Japanese volley fire of 1575[59] indicates that volley fire as a simple tactic may have been invented in several places.[60] The main prerequisite is a disciplined, well-trained infantry equipped with standardised weapons. This is why Turkish experts believe that the systematic and thorough training that led to the use of volley fire is linked to the janissaries: the Ottomans were at the forefront in the use of regular infantry, making it one of the most highly valued branches of arm. However, the weaponry and thorough training are not sufficient to explain their success.

In the great battles, the janissaries would line up in the central "mobile fortress" (*wagenburg*) behind the cannons but in front of the sultan. This is the order of battle, which had already been successfully practised at Chaldiran and in the Mamluk wars, and which then proved its worth on the European battlefield. Precise manoeuvres by the cavalry put the enemy in the firing line of the matchlockmen, who then shot the enemy soldiers to death. It seems that this tactic was also used at Mohács.

9 Main Physical Characteristics of the Handguns Used in the Fighting in the Central European Region

During the reigns of Bayezid II and Selim I, the Ottomans were successful in confronting eastern-style armies. They faced strong armoured armies after Süleyman I came to power. Nándorfehérvár (Belgrade) (1521), Rhodes (1522), and then Mohács mark the first stages of this. In addition to the naval clashes, the Hungarian theatre of operations became a test of firearms. Thus traces of the weapon culture in question can be found mainly in the collections of the Carpathian Basin and Austria.

One might ask, in connection with the above, what kind of armour the heavy cavalrymen in Mohács were wearing: light mail armour or plate armour? Based on the accounts[61] it is clear that they wore heavy plate armour, not unlike the

---

58   Frederick Taylor, *The Art of War in Italy, 1494–1529* (Cambridge University Press, 1921), p. 52; the claim is disputed by Andrade, *The Gunpowder Age*, p. 350.
59   Battle of Nagashino. The first modern battle in Japanese military history. The infantry, equipped with arquebuses, defeat the cavalry; alternate, line-by-line firing is used.
60   Kolçak (*Ok, Tüfek ve At*, pp. 74–87) makes a similar point with convincing arguments.
61   "The four knights, Albrecht and Albin Schlick, Johann and Heinrich Kuttnawer, were in great trouble, for they had to march to battle, but they had neither horses nor armour nor anything else necessary for the battle, for they had left everything on the wagons, and they

equipment worn by heavy horsemen in the western half of the continent. Both Hungarian nobles and other Christian heavy horsemen were so equipped.[62] The main function of the Ottoman handguns (especially the *uzun* guns), was to pierce this armour, and they therefore carried weapons suitable for this purpose onto the battlefield. We wonder whether these hundguns can be found in weapon collections from the period of Hungarian–Ottoman wars?

We have the opportunity to review the technical characteristics of weapons and projectiles from the early 16th to the early 18th century, from the Ottoman and 'Kuruc' wars, on the basis of a representative sample of handguns from the former aristocratic collections of Western Hungary and Burgenland, those of Körmend, Frakno (Forchtenstein) and Kismarton (Eisenstadt).[63] For this period, the barrel lengths and calibres of more than 220 such weapons have been collected. Out of the 220, 28 date from the 16th century; 89% of these (25) were between 15 and 20 mm in diameter.

With regard to Ottoman military equipment in Hungarian relation, it is worth examining the characteristics of the Ottoman handguns (especially the janissary guns) that were preserved in the various aristocratic collections of Hungary. The following is an overview of the carbines, pistols and handguns preserved in Frakno, Kismarton and Körmend, some of which were acquired

---

had no soldiers with them, for even they were on the road." "Egy cseh úr levele a Santa Clara kolostor főnöknőjéhez, 1526. november," [Letter from a Czech nobleman to the Superior of the Convent of Santa Clara, November 1526] in *Örök Mohács: szövegek és értelmezések*, eds. János B. Szabó and Gábor Farkas Farkas, (Budapest: Bölcsészettudományi Kutatóközpont, 2020), p. 208. "...the gallant and cunning Turks resisted, and marched towards the infantry, so as not to meet the well-armoured knights..." "Egy cseh úr levele," [Letter from a Czech nobleman] p. 209; "left alone, he threw off his armour and went on foot..." "Egy cseh úr levele," [Letter from a Czech nobleman] p. 214; "...four thousand Hungarians in iron armoure were reduced to the dust of the ground." Az 1526. évi hadinapló 1526 (részlet). [The Ottoman campaign diary of 1526 (excerpt)] in *Örök Mohács*, eds. B. Szabó et al., p. 246. "The unfortunate Hungarians, who are tiger-natured and eager to fight, have the old custom, when they go to battle, of covering themselves and their horses from head to foot with armour, helmet and breastplate, so that only two eyes are visible, like smoke from the embers, or a star from behind a black cloud." Kemal Paşa-zâde, *Tevarih-i Âl-i Osman*, X. Defter, Türk Tarih Kurumu Yayınları XVIII/13, Hazırlayan Şefaettin Severcan, Ankara: Türk Tarih Kurumu, 1996, 287. In Hungarian: Kemálpasazáde, "Moháscnáme (részlet)," [Mohaçname (excerpt)] in *Örök Mohács*, eds. B. Szabó et al., p. 327.

62 A piece of armour was found in mass grave II of the Sátorhely excavation: "Along the southern edge of the bones, at a depth of 105 centimetres, part of an iron armour suit was found: a piece of a lobster-tail, right elbow joint, riveted together from three plates." László Papp, "A mohácsi csatatér kutatása," [Research into the battlefield of Mohács] in *Janus Pannonius Múzeum Évkönyve 1960*, ed. János Dombay (Pécs: Janus Pannonius Múzeum, 1961), p. 248.

63 János Szendrei ed. "A XVI–XIX. század hadtörténelmi emlékei. 1526–1848.," [Military historical relicts of the 16–19th century 1526–1848] in *Magyar hadtörténelmi emlékek az Ezredéves Országos Kiállításon* (Budapest, 1896).

as booty from the Ottomans. The firearms were selected by the curator of the Hungarian Millennium Exhibition of 1896, who put together a representative display of Hungarian and Turkish military technology of the period.

Of the Turkish handguns preserved in the collections of the Hungarian nobility, the number of 16th–18th-century items is 28, pistols 8, carbines 2 and hackbuts (Hakenbüchsen) 2. This brings the total number of firearms used as a sample to 40.

It is certainly remarkable that out of the 40 weapons, a mere three have 13 mm calibre or below: a pistol, a carbine and a gun dating from the end of the 17th century. However, these weapons could not have been on the battlefield in 1526, as the Ottoman cavalry was not armed either with pistols or with cavalry carbines. The average barrel length of the guns in the sample was 112 cm, while the average calibre was 17 mm.[64] More narrowly, the data for 16th-century weapons are as follows: average barrel length 124 cm and average calibre 17.2 mm.[65]

In the 16th century sample, we can find "trench guns" (*metris tüfeği*), at least one long (*uzun*) gun and short (*harcî*) guns. The *metris tüfeği* are 130–160 cm long. A janissary handgun with a barrel length of 5 karış has a barrel diameter of 17 mm, while one of the guns with a barrel length of about 4 karış has a barrel diameter of 15 mm and the other a barrel diameter of 20 mm.

The barrels of firearms were often used for a long time (even a century or more), and old barrels were recycled when they were fitted with more modern firing mechanisms or other stocks of guns.[66] Such recycled pieces also occur in the sample we examined. This suggests that when small arms began to be supplied en masse to the infantry, they continued to be used for many decades, up to the end of the 16th century or even beyond. Thus, these weapons continued to appear and reappear in later engagements, so their imprint can be traced not only to the 1520s and 1530s, but also much later.

The Landeszeughaus in Graz houses one of the world's largest collections of weapons from the 15th to 18th centuries. It lends itself for comparison very well. As the museum's collection covers the Central European regions involved in the anti-Turkish wars, it can be considered representative. A description of the small arms in their custody, obtained from the institution,[67] shows that

---

64   The shortest barrel was 65 cm and the longest 163 cm. The smallest caliber was 12 mm and the largest 24 mm.
65   The shortest barrel is 103 cm, the longest 163 cm, the smallest calibre is 15 mm and the largest 20 mm.
66   There are many examples of this in the above-mentioned exhibition, presented and published in 1896.
67   We would also like to thank Dr. Leopold Toifl, curator of the Landeszaughaus Graz, for his answer to our questions about the small arms they keep.

FIGURE 4.2 Janissaries with handguns accompanying Sultan Murad III.
SOURCE: HEINRICH HENDROWSKI. "BILDER AUS DEM TÜRKISCHEN VOLKSLEBEN" IN I TURCHI – CODEX VINDOBONENSIS 8626. TABLE 39. HEILIGES RÖMISCHES REICH.

from the early 16th to the mid-18th century, the calibre of small arms had hardly changed: the curators of the collection found that calibre did not play a particularly important role in the development of these weapons.

However, there was a greater variation in calibre between the different types of weapons: the hackbuts collected and preserved in Graz are mostly between 20 and 23mm, the light arquebuses around 15mm and the muskets between 18 and 20mm. Pistols are smaller by comparison, averaging 9–11 mm calibre.

What do contemporary written sources comparing Christian weapons with those of the Turks tell us? As Parry points out, Venetian reports from the late 16th century, during the reign of Murad III (1574–1595), informs the Signoria that the janissaries were almost invariably armed with arquebuses, "the Ottoman model of this gun being made with a longer barrel than was normal amongst the Christians and loaded with large bullets".[68] The depiction of Murad III and his guards shows just such weapons.[69]

9.1 What Kind of Arquebuses were the Christian Infantry that Lined up at Mohács Equipped With?

It is worth taking a closer look at the smaller calibre Western weapons from the late 15th and first half of the 16th century, which appear in the literature on the Battle of Mohács as possible infantry firearms.

Balázs Németh suggests[70] that in the early 16th century the western infantry was equipped with short-barreled (60–75 cm), small-calibre (10–13 mm) firearms, and that in the Battle of Mohács they used such weapons. The source of this claim is partly a group of artefacts from a group of short-barrelled (63–78 cm) and small-calibre (10–12 mm) gun barrels found at Kopaszi reef in Budapest, which are thought to have come from a western warship sunk in 1541.[71] In his study, the author, referring to Ágoston, speculates that the janissaries' weapons may have been of the same small calibre as the weapons he

---

68 V. J. Parry, (1960) ,Bārūd, iv. The Ottoman Empire', *The Encyclopaedia of Islam*, second edition, vol. I, Leiden and London, p. 1061.
69 Arbasino, *I Turchi*, p. 67.
70 Balázs Németh, "A mohácsi csata kiskaliberű kézi lőfegyvereinek kérdéséhez I.," [The small calibre small arms of the Battle of Mohács I.] *Hadtörténelmi Közlemények* 134 (2021), no. 1, pp. 167–227.
71 The length of the preserved barrels of the guns found at Kopaszi reef are 63.7, 64, 64.7, 66.8, 71.6, 72.1 and 77.7 cm. However, the idea that the barrels belonged to a warship that sank in 1541 is an urban legend. During the event in question, the siege of Buda in 1541, there is no written record of any Western warship having sunk. The identification was based on a misinterpretation of a German newsletter report of the time, and the finds were not recovered from a shipwreck that had been found and excavated, but from the wider area of a reef during the excavation of the Danube riverbed. The group of artefacts, if they belong together at all, dates from the 16th century, but their origin and exact date are unknown.

considers to be western. In support of his claims, he lists examples of firearms (not Turkish, but western) preserved in western collections. The Table 4.5 below shows the guns in question.

TABLE 4.5   Light arquebuses, collected by Balázs Németh

Barrel diameter	Barrel length	Handgun/arquebus Comment
		15th–16th centuries
13 mm	61 cm	It is 15th-century bronze, it was bought by the Hungarian National Museum in 1887, as it was said to have been used in the Battle of Mohács.
14 mm	no data (total length of the gun 82 cm)	Made between 1500 and 1540, in the Michael Trömner collection, landsknecht arquebus.
15 mm	62,4 cm (total length of the gun 99,8 cm)	Made between 1500–1540, in the collection of Michael Trömner, bronze, landsknecht arquebus.[a]
10,9 mm	52,1 cm (total length of the gun 78,2 cm)	Made in Nuremberg between 1512–1515, it is in the collection of the Hermitage and is made of bronze. The weapon bears the coat of arms of the Behaim patrician family of Nuremberg.
12 mm	80,65 cm	It dates from the early 16th century, and appeared at a Sotheby's auction in May 1978, made of bronze. Made in Nuremberg. The coat of arms on it suggests that it belonged to the von Schlaberndorf family of Prussia.
13 mm	63 cm	Early 16th century, bronze, sold at the April 2012 auction of Hermann Historica.
15,1 mm	75 cm (total length of the gun 105,5 cm)	Made between 1500 and 1510, German, in the collection of the Royal Armouries in Leeds, made of bronze.
12 mm	76,5 cm (total length of the gun 113,5 cm)	Made between 1520–1525, it is in the Brukenthal Museum in Sibiu.
14,5 mm	56,4 cm (total length of the gun 99 cm)	Late 15th century, early 16th century, Germany, Celle. The piece can be found in the Celle Garrisons-Museum.

SOURCE: BALÁZS NÉMETH, "A MOHÁCSI CSATA KISKALIBERŰ KÉZI LŐFEGYVEREINEK KÉRDÉSÉHEZ I.," [THE SMALL CALIBRE SMALL ARMS OF THE BATTLE OF MOHÁCS I.] HADTÖRTÉNELMI KÖZLEMÉNYEK 134 (2021), NO. 1, PP. 167–227.

a   According to the source provided by Németh, contrary to his claim, the weapon was made around 1520 and is 100 cm long. The source does not mention the length of the barrel.

What picture emerges when we look at the characteristics of the weapons?

1. The weapons shown in the table do not comprise a representative sample, as they were selected from different collections in different countries, with the sole purpose of providing examples for the author's theory. All they provide is evidence that such weapons existed.
2. Four out of the nine late 15th and early 16th-century arquebuses cited by Németh as examples from European collections are 14 mm or more in size: 14 mm, 14.5 mm, 15 mm and 15.1 mm! He also mentions one of 10.9 mm, two of 12 mm and one of 13 mm bore. Within the 'sample' of nine, there are therefore four 14–15 mm guns with the characteristics observed in the Graz collection, and corresponding to light guns.
3. Six of the nine gun barrels were made of bronze: the material is expensive. Common mercenaries were not equipped with such weapons. Moreover, two of the bronze weapons, a 10.9 mm and a 12 mm arquebus, belonged to aristocratic/patrician families, as is attested by the coats of arms that feature on them. They were probably used for self-defence/hunting.

There was no standardisation in the armament of the western infantry as there was with the janissaries. Presumably, they had a motley stock of arquebuses, and the quality and performance of these weapons was inferior to that of the janissary handguns. The tendency, on the basis of the specimens observed, is for western guns to have been shorter and perhaps slightly smaller in calibre than Ottoman guns. Despite this, they had to meet high standards: they were expected to penetrate the advanced armour of the period. This, in turn, raises the problem of 'minimum sufficiency' in terms of the powder charge and projectile.

10 Which Firearms are Suitable for Fighting Heavy Cavalry?

The question that arises for anyone studying the technological issues of the early 16th century is: what was a handgun capable of at that time? A lot depended, for example, on the right powder. Different types were developed, one type was used for cannons, another for handguns and yet another for hunting guns. There were many different recipes, many experiments to produce effective gunpowder.[72] The main difference was the grain size.[73] The gas

---

[72] Tessy S. Ritchie, Kathleen E. Riegner, Robert J. Seals, Clifford J. Rogers, and Dawn E. Riegner, "Evolution of Medieval Gunpowder: Thermodynamic and Combustion Analysis," *ACS Omega* 6 (2021), no. 35, pp. 22848–22856.

[73] Sean McLachlan, *Medieval Handgonnes: The First Black Powder Infantry Weapons* (Osprey Publishing, 2010), pp. 9–12 and 22–26; see also Kelly DeVries, *Medieval Military Technology* (Broadview Press Ltd., 1992), pp. 156–157.

released by the combustion of gunpowder evolved differently for different grain sizes and, to some extent, for different compositions.

In that era, it was not self-evident to have good quality, effective gunpowder, so the usability and effectiveness of weapons could be questionable for quite some time. Accuracy of aiming and limited range were additional problems. Nor should we forget that the use of metal armour to protect western armies in the era posed a significant challenge to small arms, as mentioned several times.

It is generally accepted that early handguns owed their usefulness to the quality of the corned powder, the proper construction of the barrel wall and the long barrel. The coarse-grained powder developed a lot of gas. Most importantly, the barrel was long, preferably a metre or more, to allow the gunpowder gas to accelerate the bullet all the way through, giving the gun a higher firing velocity and a quadratically increasing kinetic energy. This allowed the bullet to fly farther, penetrate armour and damage the body more easily, and also to aim more accurately.[74]

A study by Graz authors sought to find out the destructive power of various 16th-century weapons. It revealed that one 16th-century gun with a 15.1 mm diameter but only 76 cm long barrel could penetrate a 2 mm steel plate at 30 metres and a 1 mm steel plate at 100 metres.[75] This shows the limitations of the weapon. If a handgun with a calibre of about 15 mm could only penetrate 1 mm armour at a range of 100 metres, what could a much smaller calibre and shorter barreled weapon (e.g. the barrels found on the Kopaszi reef: 65–78 cm long, 10–11 mm in diameter) have been capable of? It is easy to see how much less. The main data from the Graz experiment are summarised in the table below.

It should also be taken into account that the weapons used in the experiment presented by Krenn et al. were authentic, but they used modern black powder for the test. Its effectiveness, however, is far superior to that of the gunpowder mixtures of the early modern period. The weapons of the time emitted a huge cloud of smoke with a high powder charge, but accelerated the projectiles more modestly. It can be concluded that the conditions under which the Austrian weapons experiments were carried out were far too ideal: the weapons of the 16th and 17th centuries were not able to achieve the efficiency shown in Table 4.6. However, these values are still useful for us because they show their upper limit. That is, they were certainly capable of less, but what they could not achieve, their predecessors could not produce in their time, either.

---

74 McLachlan, *Medieval Handgonnes,* p. 26.
75 Peter Krenn, Paul Kalaus, and Bert Hall, "Material Culture and Military History: Test-Firing Early Modern Small Arms," *Material History Review* 42 (1995), fall/autumn, pp. 101–109.

TABLE 4.6 Experimental firing data of the 16th–17th century handguns based on Krenn et al.

	Hackbuts (1571)	Hackbuts (ca. 1580–90)	Handgun (1593)	Handgun (ca. 1595)	Handgun (first quarter of the 17th c.)	Handgun (first half of the 17th c.)	Pistol (ca. 1620)
Barrel length	110 cm	165.5 cm	64.5 cm	100 cm	76 cm	67.5 cm	48 cm
Weapons mass	13.4 kg	18 kg	2.9 kg	5.48 kg	2.5 kg	3.69 kg	1.59 kg
Barrel caliber	22.1 mm	20.6 mm	13.2 mm	17.8 mm	15.1 mm	19.7 mm	12.3 mm
Average diameter of bullets fired	19 mm	20.2 mm	12.3 mm	17.2 mm	14.3 mm	17.5 mm	11.8 mm
Average weight of bullets fired	38.26 g	49.14 g	10.84 g	30.06 g	17.38 g	32.06 g	9.56 g
Mass of charge	14 g	20 g	5 g	11 g	6 g	10 g	6 g
E_0	4444 Joule	6980 Joule	988 Joule	3125 Joule	1752 Joule	2463 Joule	917 Joule
From 30 m	n.a.	n.a.	Penetrates the 2 mm steel disk	Pierces the 3 mm steel disk	Penetrates the 2 mm steel disk	Penetrates the 2 mm steel disk	Penetrates the 2 mm steel disk

	Penetrates the 2 mm steel disk	Pierces the 4 mm steel disk	Pierces the 1 mm steel disk	Penetrates the 2 mm steel disk	Pierces the 1 mm steel disk		Cannot penetrate through 1 mm steel disk
From 100 m						n.a.	
Penetration depth from 30 m into spruce	n.a.	n.a.	132 mm	190 mm	146 mm	168 mm	121 mm
Penetration depth from 100 m into spruce	153 mm	189 mm	84 mm	80 mm	93 mm	103 mm	Not interpretable

SOURCE: PETER KRENN, PAUL KALAUS, AND BERT HALL, "MATERIAL CULTURE AND MILITARY HISTORY: TEST-FIRING EARLY MODERN SMALL ARMS," MATERIAL HISTORY REVIEW 42 (1995), FALL/AUTUMN, PP. 101–109.

However, the armour that gunners of the time had to shoot through (2 mm or thicker)[76] was quite a challenge. From Töll's research it is known that the protective armour (breastplates, helmets) made in the early 16th century to protect critical body parts were even thicker, with 4–6 mm being common among them.[77]

Considering that the reactive power of the projectile does not increase in direct proportion to the length of the barrel, but quadratically, the efficiency of longer handguns could be much higher.[78] The Ottoman handguns observed were generally 40% or more longer than the Western guns tested. Thus there was a huge difference in firepower. A French eyewitness account of the Battle of Szentgotthárd in 1664 illustrates this difference:

> Count Bissy had six hundred horsemen dismounted and lined them up in a row with their carbines facing the enemy on a small road along the river bank. The difference was enormous between the firepower of the janissaries' muskets and the riders' carbines, not to mention the superiority of the Turks in numbers.[79]

It can be concluded that Ottoman handguns had a significantly larger load and projectile, as well as a longer barrel than the western arquebus barrels in the collection of Balázs Németh. This provided much greater destructive power. Once again, it should be stressed that all this could only be achieved with barrels of the right length.

---

76 Williams, *The Knight and the Blast Furnace*, p. 936.
77 László Töll, *A harci vértezetek története. (A nyugat-európai hadviselésben alkalmazott testvédelmi rendszerek fejlődéstörténete a 10. századtól a 16. század közepéig)* [The History of the Battle Armours (The History of the Development of the Body Defence Systems Used in Western European Warfare from the 10th Century to the Mid-16th Century)] (2010) Available at https://dea.lib.unideb.hu/items/92022189-1c3f-4751-9ed3-b77952902f7c. According to Kubinyi, Germany (mainly Nuremberg) was the primary arms supply centre for the Hungarian nobility. András Kubinyi, "Mozgósítási és hadseregellátási problémák Mátyás alatt," [Mobilisation and army supply problems under Matthias I] *Hadtörténelmi Közlemények* 103 (1990), no. 1, pp. 66–73.
78 László Pálfalvi and Vivien Kovács, "A pV x = állandó törvény alkalmazhatóságáról egy versenyfeladat tükrében," [On the applicability of the pV x = constant law in the light of a competition problem] *Fizikai Szemle* 71 (2021), no. 11, pp. 380–384.
79 Ferenc Tóth, "Újabb francia források a szentgotthárdi csatáról," [New French Sources on the Battle of Szentgotthárd.] *Hadtörténelmi Közlemények* 127 (2014), no. 1, p. 225.

11 The Appearance of Ottoman Small Arms Used in the Battle of Mohács in Written Sources

Sources on both sides agree that the Ottoman infantry at Mohács was well equipped with handguns. However, they do not mention the characteristics of these weapons. As for the quantity of small arms, some sources give figures in the thousands, others in the tens of thousands. These higher numbers can be attributed to the soaring imagination of the time.

The handguns of the Ottoman army marching at Mohács are documented in the inventory of weapons and armaments of the court salaried troops, including the janissaries, dated 13 April 1526. The source gives details of what army supplies were ordered to be taken for the 'imperial campaign'. This suggests two or at most three types of hand firearms; 60 guns, presumably of a larger size,[80] and 4000 handguns were intended for the janissaries. As regards the latter lot, the source notes that 1000 were of good quality (*has/uzun*), while 3000 were ordinary (*harcî*) weapons.[81] In addition, 30 × 100,000, or 3 million bullets were also taken to the campaign.[82] It is also presumed that the part of the janissaries who were not equipped with firearms used bows.[83] Ágoston calculated that the 4000 guns and 5200 bows together were equal to the number of janissaries registered in the previous years (1524–1525).[84] On the basis of other considerations, however, it is unlikely that all the janissaries were taken on the campaign. This would have been against custom and common sense, but owing to the presence of the sultan and the preparation for a decisive showdown make it likely that most of them were mobilized.

The accounts on the use of handguns show that janissaries were engaged in crucial situations and with great effectiveness. One of their deployments took

---

80 Their number suggest that they were probably suited to a specific task. In any case, Emecen ("Ateşli Silahlar Çağı", p. 55.) and Ágoston interpret them as trench guns used for castle sieges, i.e. it belongs to the category of *metris tüfeği*. They were about 130–160 cm long and 20–29 mm in diameter, but exceptionally they were also made in 35 or 45 mm. See Ágoston, "Firearms and Military Adaptation", p. 97.

81 According to the above data, they took with them 1000 good quality *uzun* (i.e. 5 karış long) guns, and 3000 *harcî* (i.e. 4 karış long ordinary) guns.

82 "Az udvari zsoldosok/janicsárok fegyver- és hadianyag listája 1526. április 13.," [The inventory of arms and war material of the court salaried troops/janissaries], 13 April 1526] in *Örök Mohács*, eds. B. Szabó et al., p. 232.

83 Ágoston, "War-Winning Weapons?", p. 141. 5200 bows were included in the list of issued weapons, with 1.4 million arrows.

84 The number of janissaries was 9390 in 1524–1525. Ágoston, "Firearms and Military Adaptation", p. 97.

place at the beginning of the battle, and two other situations can be identified in which their use was a key factor in Ottoman success.

The above figures can be compared with a passage from the battle account of the Ottoman chronicler Celalzade Mustafa:

> ... When the battle formation came within range of the guns, the Rumelian army was given one hundred and fifty zarbuzans with carriages, and four thousand handgunner janissaries were ordered to join them. These zarbuzans being bound together with chains, the janissaries were drawn up in nine rows, according to the custom of war, and the above-mentioned Bali, with a troop of lion-hearted soldiers on the left flank, withdrew from the battle order and established himself at a distance...[85]

The battle began with the heavy cavalry of the Christian force attacking the Rumelian army on the left flank. István Brodarics's account highlights the role of the Ottoman cannons.[86] Ottoman chroniclers have given very similar accounts of the beginning of the battle. Kemalpaşazade, in particular, emphasises the important and decisive role of the handgunners alongside the

---

[85] Funda Demirtaş, *Celâl-zâde Mustafa Çelebi, Tabakâtü'l-Memâlik ve Derecâtü'l-Mesâlik*, PhD dissertation, Erciyeş Üniversitesi, Kayseri, 2009, p. 199; in Hungarian: Dzselálzáde Musztafa, "Az országok osztályai és az utak felsorolása 1560-as évek (részlet)," [The echelons of the dominions and the hiearchies of destinations, 1560s (excerpt)] in *Örök Mohács*, eds. B. Szabó and Farkas, p. 415.

[86] "When the signal of battle was given, those who were in the front ranks bravely charged the enemy, firing all our guns, but to the slight detriment of the enemy. The battle was much fiercer than our numbers would indicate; more of the enemy fell than of our own, until at length, fighting with terrible violence, the enemy began to retreat, either to be worn down by our charge, or to draw us before the guns. And already András Báthori is flying to the king, that the enemy is turning back, that victory is ours, that it is our turn to advance, and that we should support our own who are pursuing the routed enemy. So we ran through the trenches and bushes, but when we reached the place where the battle had been fought a little while before, you could see the bodies of many of our men lying strewn across the field, and of still more of the enemy, and some of them half dead and barely panting. Meanwhile, while our men were confronting the enemy and bravely taking up the fight, and the king's column was at the same time galloping forward as fast as armoured men can gallop, the right wing began to sway, and from this wing many were running, frightened, I think, by the cannons which the enemy then began to fire for the first time, and this running and the thick impact of the cannon-balls, which were now flying round our heads, who were standing by the king's side, filled every one with no little fear." István Brodarics, "Igaz történet a magyarok és Szulejmán török császár mohácsi ütközetéről 1528," [A true account about the battle between the Hungarians and the Turkish Emperor Süleyman in Mohács in 1528] in *Örök Mohács*, eds. B. Szabó et al., p. 319.

cannons.[87] The campaign diary gives a shorter but similar account,[88] and a similar picture emerges from Celalzade's account[89] and Peçevi's reconstruction.[90] At Mohács, the Ottoman forces used the wagenburg (*tabur cengi*) mode of combat.

---

[87] "The wicked king who appeared on the battlefield, clad from head to foot in steel, with the devilish and evil-natured wretches with him, whose rising dust clouds covered east and west and with the world-conquering banner of the clear-minded pasha in his sights, he rushed straight to the centre of the invincible army, and, ignoring the shower of cannon-balls and gun bullets, he charged with his cavalry, which poured like a torrent, unafraid. His whole mass rushed at once upon the janissaries... When he came close to the gun carriages, the handgunners, emitting a cloud of smoke, threw their bullets skywards as if it were hailing, and thus withered the flowers of the evil enemy's life". "...The shower of bullets, falling like hail on the enemy, against which neither helmet, nor armour, nor shield could serve as protection, tore the leaves and fruit from the tree of the evildoers' useless life; their fearful masses were scattered like a scattering of stubble, and the grain of their perishable life was let loose to the winds of destruction." Kemal Paşa-zâde, *Tevarih-i Âl-i Osman*, X. *Defter*, 299–300, 304; in Hungarian: Kemálpasazáde, "Mohácsnáme (részlet)," [Mohaçname (excerpt)] in *Örök Mohács*, eds. B. Szabó et al., pp. 331–332, p. 334.

[88] "One of the troops, covered from head to foot with heavy iron and carrying iron spikes in their hands, and completely oblivious to the gun bullets and cannonballs fired, galloped boldly and fearlessly towards İbrahim Pasha, the governor-general of Rumelia." "Az 1526. évi hadinapló," [The campaign diary of 1526] in *Örök Mohács*, eds. B. Szabó et al., p. 245.

[89] "...Now the Muslims fired the zarbuzans, and the gunners fired their handguns row by row, filling the air with smoke and shaking the earth with thunder. The cries of the Muslims "Allahu Akbar!" and "Allah, Allah!" reached the highest sky, and the infidels, who were destined for hellfire, made the world noisy with their wonderful shouts. As soon as the damned infidels reached this place, they saw that the gun carriages and the matchlockmen stood before them like a fort that could not be breached; they therefore, out of necessity, evaded the gun carriages, and at the sixth sub-province's troops on the left of the pasha's sancak, near which the line of carriages ended, they rushed at the Rumelian troops, the army retreating on two sides to give way to the miserable infidels. As soon as they had penetrated into the space between the battle line and the camp baggage, the warriors of faith took the misarable infidels from two sides in the back, and a very hard fight ensued..." Demirtaş, *Celâl-zâde Mustafa Çelebi, Tabakâtü'l-Memâlik*, 199–200; in Hungarian: Dzselálzáde Musztafa, "Az országok osztályai és az utak felsorolása 1560-as évek (részlet)," [The echelons of the dominions and the hiearchies of destinations, 1560s (excerpt)] in *Örök Mohács*, eds. B. Szabó et al., p. 415.

[90] "This damned infidel [namely Pál Tomori] put a few thousand of the accursed enemy in line, and they were arrayed and came like a herd of swine, all wounded by arrows. There was no obstacle before them; heedless of the chained cannonballs of the zarbzens standing before the battle-lines of the grand vizier, of his own soldiers fallen by the gun bullets, and of the cadavers of the horses, he cut in front of the zarbzens, and at the end, perhaps where the ranks of the infantry were, he found at last a gap and a breach, through which he penetrated, and cut the army of Islam in two and separated them..." *Tarih-i Peçevi*, I, (İstanbul: Matbaa-i Amire), 1864, 93; Pecsevi Ibrahim, "Krónika, 1648 előtt (részlet)," [Chronicle, before 1648 (excerpt)] in *Örök Mohács*, eds. B. Szabó et al., p. 468.

According to these sources, it seems that the Rumelian army was deployed with 150 cannons in a line in front of the village of Földvár, near a forest. Here the janissary corps was also lined up in several rows behind the cannons, which were tied with chains. On the sides there were gun carriages. The janissaries fired volleys: one line after another. The 'hail of bullets' caused great havoc among the attackers. In keeping with the usual procedure, after the artillery, perhaps the *uzun* handguns in the front ranks of the janissaries, and later the *harcî* guns were brought into action.

In the later stages of the battle, the Christian forces fought bloody battles with the Anatolian cavalry and the sultan's household troops on the left flank (the right flank from the Ottoman point of view). In this context, the sources again report that the janissaries had to be called in when, according to Peçevi, these hangunners appeared behind the Anatolian army during the battle.[91] After the attacks on the Rumelians, the Christian army also attacked further east. There was a momentary glimmer of hope of victory when, during the attack on the sultan's bodyguard, the stormers approached Süleyman himself. Not only Peçevi's account, written well over a hundred years after the battle, but also based on sources and local tradition, but also contemporary accounts suggest that this bloody and very spirited renewed attack was stopped by the janissaries. The campaign diary, the primary source of information on the Ottoman military manoeuvres, confirms this report.[92] This janissary corps fired three or four volleys here. The description by a Czech nobleman fighting on the Christian left flank of the same place, near the "deep marsh", is consistent with this account.[93]

---

[91] "…From this side, the evildoer king himself attacked the Anatolian army with his troops, but the latter relied on the battle line of the janissaries. The janissary ghazis poured down upon them with their guns, and the followers and selected soldiers of the accursed [king] fell into the dust of destruction at that place…" *Tarih-i Peçevi*, I, (İstanbul: Matbaa-i Amire), 1864, 93; Pecsevi Ibrahim, "Krónika, 1648 előtt (részlet)," [Chronicle, before 1648 (excerpt)] in *Örök Mohács*, eds. B. Szabó et al., p. 468.

[92] "The evildoer king and the rest of his desperate army attacked the felicitous ruler and the Anatolian army. Three or four times in all, the janissary corps, with gun fire, stopped, beat and drove back the despicable infidels. At last, by the grace of God the most high and the Prophet, and with the help of the hidden saints, the people of Islam, aroused and rallying their strength, turned back the wicked, and when they had no strength to attack again, they cut them down like dogs. It was a battle and slaughter so fierce that it cannot be described." "Az 1526. évi hadinapló," [The campaign diary of 1526] in *Örök Mohács*, eds. B. Szabó et al., p. 245.

[93] "When the knights in armour arrived, the Turks fired with handguns a few more shots at them: they fired straight into the king's men, causing great damage." "Egy cseh úr levele," [Letter from a Czech nobleman] in *Örök Mohács*, eds. B. Szabó et al., p. 210.

Finally, the third and final incident where Ottoman hand firearms played a role was the end of the battle. Part of Louis II's army lay dead or wounded, some of the cavalry and infantry fled, while the rest of the Czech and German infantry fought to defend themselves by forming a square. The Ottoman cavalry were no match for them, until a group of janissaries with handguns appeared and broke their resistance.[94]

Of the three events listed, the first two seem entirely plausible on the basis of the sources on both sides, while for the third, the evidence is not particularly strong, but does not seem implausible either. Overall, we can conclude that the janissaries and their guns played a decisive role in the Ottoman victory. In the first two cases, they used the mode of combat known as *tabur cengi*, as observed in other battles, while in the third case they marched close to the infantry and broke the western infantry with their handguns (perhaps the *uzun* tüfek), which were effective at long range.

The Ottoman small arms, if used in three places, could leave a military archaeological imprint at three battlefield sites, as described above. The handgunners of the Rumelian army in the northern outskirts of the village of Földvár; the janissaries, standing alongside the Anatolian army in the centre, to the east or north-east of them, 1000–2000 metres from Földvár. The third location is more difficult to determine: north of the Ottoman lines, somewhere on the battlefield near the deep marsch, but in front of the Ottoman right flank.

Since the first two events were quite close in time, it is not exluded that Peçevi is right: the Rumelian army was supported by only two thousand handgunners, not four thousand. The other two thousand, according to the campaign diary, marched with the sultan's household troops.

The archaeological imprint of Ottoman hand firearms should be fairly consistent. According to the aforementioned weapons inventory, the guns were equipped with pre-cast projectiles (30 × 100,000 pieces). This suggests one or two calibres: one for the common guns and one for the long guns, but it is also possible that the two types of guns were fired with the same 5 dirhem projectile.[95] There is also evidence that in some early handguns, the 4 karış long common guns also fired 5 dirhem bullets, so that they differed only in length, not in calibre.

---

94 "Although six or eight thousand Bohemians and landsknechts retreated in a square, and were not broken by the Turkish cavalry, a good banderium of handgunners attacked them and they were killed instantly, as were the others". Agostino da Mula, "Agostino da Mula jelentése Udine, 1526. szeptember 15. (átirat), [Account of Agostino da Mula Udine, 15 September 1526 (transliteration)] in *Örök Mohács*, eds. B. Szabó et al., p. 151.

95 Emecen, "Ateşli Silahlar Çağı", p. 56.

The weapons were reportedly used by the janissaries in a coordinated manner, firing one after the other. If all the weapons were used and there was no significant difference in the rate of fire, all the bullets fired were either of the 4 or 5 dirhem calibre (if there were two), in proportion to the number of guns of each type. There is also good reason to believe that the projectiles were made of tin, lead and antimony, based on the *sürb*'s special recipe, and that their composition was certainly different from that of the western military.

Thus, we must assume three areas in the study area where these projectiles are concentrated and where the projectiles are expected to belong to these calibres. That is, of course, if the imprint of the Christian infantry guns do not appear in these places; but even if the projectiles of the two sides should mix, those of the janissaries will differ in size and material composition from those of the Christians.

12 About the Christian Hand Firearms at Mohács

The number of western gunners on the Mohács Plain did not reach the number of janissaries, but may have reached or even exceeded 2000. German, Czech, Polish mercenaries and the troops of some northern Hungarian counties made up the bulk of them. Little is known about their equipment compared to that of the janissaries.

We do not know about the distribution of Christian handguns in terms of gauge, but based on the practice of the time – many small workshops produced the weapons, troops came from all over Central Europe, there were many old weapons – we probably have to reckon with several different weapons and calibres. Certainly more than on the Ottoman side. It does not help that only one type of weapon is mentioned by name in the written records of the battle. According to these, 500–600 hundguns from Prague were transported to Mohács. This information appears several times, perhaps to emphasise its importance. Burgio was still equipping 500 foot soldiers for the campaign in the spring of 1526, and mentions that he was supplying them with 40 of these firearms.[96] This weapon is known in the sources as the *"barbatae pixide*

---

96   The proportion of matchlockmen in the infantry of the period was far below that of soldiers with pikes, sometimes crossbows and swords. In Matthias I's "black army", the proportion of infantrymen with arquebuses was 20–25%. For lack of data, we cannot give the exact number of Christian handgunners at Mohács, but given the proportions of the Ottoman and Christian armies and the size and nature of the infantry, their numbers were probably less than the number of janissaries carrying guns.

Pragenses". It is the typical hackbut of the 16th century in the Carpathian Basin, and is mainly recorded in the inventories of castles. It must have been over 20 mm in diameter. It seems to have been more a defensive weapon than an offensive one.

The Hungarian National Museum has three hackbuts associated with the Battle of Mohács.[97] One of them dates from the second half of the 15th century, with a length of 78 cm from the firing hole to the end of the barrel, a barrel diameter of 25 mm, and a weight of 9 kg.[98] The other hackbut weapon dates from the first half of the 16th century, is 89 cm long and has a barrel diameter of 25 mm.[99] The third weapon is believed by Géza Nagy to date from the late 15th century. It is 81.5 cm long, 18 mm in diameter and weighs only 4.14 kg. If the latter weapon can indeed be linked to the Battle of Mohács, then the weapons, which form the transition between the light arquebuses and the heavy arquebuses, may have been present in the battle.[100] On the other hand, we do not have technical information on the lighter guns used by the Christian side to equip the infantry. They were certainly of smaller calibre, but we do not know at what stage of the battle and how they were used, because the accounts are silent on this.

We think it is most likely that they were similar to the 14–15 mm barrel diameter, 60–75 cm long barreled light guns that were more widely used in the period, and that is probably how some of them came to be in Balázs Németh's collection. These are the weapons that correspond to the observations made in the collection of the Landeszeughaus in Graz.[101]

Considering how disastrous the battle was from a Hungarian, and western, point of view, it is worth comparing the firepower of the 5 karış long (110–115 cm)

---

97   Géza Nagy, "Hadtörténeti ereklyék a Magyar Nemzeti Múzeumban," [Military Relics in the Hungarian National Museum] *Hadtörténeti Közlemények* 11 (1910), no. 1, pp. 223–243.

98   Károly Kozák has a barrel length of 78.5 cm, a 24 mm gauge and a weapon 8.9 kg in weight. Károly Kozák, "A magyarországi szakállas puskák fejlődéstörténetéről," [The history of development of hackbuts (Hakenbüchsen) in Hungary] *Archeologiai Értesítő* 101 (1974), no. 2, p. 300.

99   Kozák's barrel has a total length of 88 cm, a barrel cavity length of 76.5 cm, a 24 mm bore and a weapon weight of 11.2 kg. Kozák, "A magyarországi szakállas puskák," p. 300.

100 Németh writes only very briefly about the appearance of muskets in the early 16th century. He gives as an example a 15.7 mm, 8.7 kg weapon dated 1525, which is a transition between the hackbut and the heavy arquebus. He states that there are no written sources to indicate that this transitional type of weapon was used at the Battle of Mohács. Németh, "A mohácsi csata kiskaliberű," p. 179. However, the 18 mm firearm reported by Nagy is just such a weapon.

101 We are not, of course, talking about weapons made of bronze and reflecting the needs of aristocratic families.

and 5 dirhem "calibre" janissary guns with the capabilities of the 14–15 mm calibre and 60–75 cm arquebuses of the western mercenaries. In the third phase of the battle, the slaughter of Czech and German infantry exemplifies that the thousands of western infantrymen in a quadrangular formation successfully resisted the attack of the timariot horsemen, but their resistance was quickly overcome by the appearance of the janissary handguns. Presumably, their weapons were no match for the firepower of the Ottoman handguns. However, without written sources and surviving examples of weapons, this is still conjectural. Unfortunately, there is no mention of the use of Christian handguns in battle in any of the sources currently available. They were certainly used, but it is not clear where and how. What can we conclude from the course of the battle?

In the first phase of the battle, when the Hungarian heavy cavalry was attacking the Rumelian positions towards Földvár, the Christian handguns could not be used for objective reasons. The distance between the two armies was about an Italian mile (1.6–1.8 km), and the range of the guns was no more than 300–400 metres.[102] Thus, Christian handguns could hardly have played a role in the skirmishes in the outskirts of Földvár. It also follows from the defensive positioning of the army that the task of the Christian arquebusiers was to defend against a possible Turkish attack in the order of battle at the beginning of the battle.

In contrast, the attack on the Anatolian army already involved infantrymen. Although the descriptions emphasise the cavalry attack, they also mention that the infantry also took part in the battle, and we know that they were the first to flee.[103]

In the third case – the massacre of German and Czech infantry – it is worth considering that Christian guns may have been present and used. In the infantry units in the square, arquebusiers were part of the regiment, along with pikemen and infantrymen with swords and shields, and one can assume that this was no different at Mohács.

---

102   According to the Krenn et al. experiment, the range of the arquebuses was hardly more than 370 metres. Since, as mentioned above, the Krenn team used modern black powder, while the efficiency of the powder of the time was far below that of today, it is questionable whether the handguns of the time could be fired at 370 metres. Probably not. However, Turkish positions were at least four to five times further than the maximum range of 370 metres. Krenn et al., "Material Culture".

103   "Then the Hungarians began to flee in the rear of the infantry, and the king could do nothing against the cannons, there was no hope. Then the standard-bearer of the king's army seized the banner and turned it round. This was the signal for all to flee". "Egy cseh úr levele," [Letter from a Czech nobleman] in *Örök Mohács*, eds. B. Szabó et al., p. 210.

13 Discussion

The present study touches on several issues of scientific debate. These are: to what extent is the technology of Ottoman hundguns indigenous, i.e. of Eastern or Western origin? There is a strong belief that the janissaries used Spanish handguns, or at least Spanish technology ("muskets"), while others claim that this was an independent technology of their own development. Another question is what kind and how big projectiles the janissary guns fired? Do the projectiles collected in the field near Majs, thought to have been the projectiles of the battle of 1526 for some time, meet these criteria?

The above analysis shows that janissary handguns cannot be clearly classified as "Spanish" or purely Ottoman Turkish. Although the technologies described above show a strong western influence, the weapons also display specific 'oriental' features in some respects. It seems likely that the secret of success lay in the technological 'mix'.

The Ottomans were fighting with the Spanish in the Mediterranean, so their guns were inevitably encountered. However, the mediation was more likely to be based on the reception by Bayezid II of the Sephardic gunsmiths expelled from Spain following the decree of Alhambra (1492). The use of expelled Sephardic Jews in the court gunsmith's workshop (in the 1520s, 5 out of 10 of the staff of the *cemaat-i tüfenkçiyan* were already Sephardic) indicates a link with Spanish gunsmithing culture. The Spanish kinship of the janissary gun is therefore more than conjecture. The Spanish infantry and the Ottoman janissaries achieved similar successes under similar conditions and with similar solutions, and their technological base was also partly rooted in common. The Spanish influence does not mean, however, that they could not have deviated from the Spanish model in certain respects, as they had many other examples at their disposal. In the light of recent Turkish research, the importance of western knowledge and technology in the 16th century in the central gun-making workshop in Constantinople seems quite clear. However, the Spanish influence, already assumed, may have been rather complementary to that of 'Rus' or 'Northern'. The western specialists conveyed a variety of patterns. The *serpentine* firing mechanism, for example, is probably German, while the *miquelet* is clearly known to be of Iberian origin.

There are also specific, oriental elements in handgun-making. The design of the barrel is definitely one of them. The Damascus style barrel and the use of much longer barrels than in the West are a clear departure. The Damascus barrel was more resilient and could withstand the blast. This is the basis for the less robust, lighter than western weapons, which could be used more easily, but still had a high destructive power. The Spanish "arquebus with rest" used at

Pavia only achieved the same high performance with a thicker barrel, greater weight, larger calibre and larger load.

Oriental characteristics must also be taken into account for bullets and gunpowder. The use of a tin-lead-antimony mixture (*sürb*) as a projectile material, based on its own recipe, is certainly such. It made the projectile much harder and more durable, but at the same time it gave it a high mass. Its use allowed the projectile to fly better from unthreaded barrels and to transfer energy over a smaller surface area on impact because it was not deformed on firing. The result was a more accurate hit, a stronger armour-piercing capability and a more durable barrel.

We do not know much about the recipe of Ottoman gunpowder, but the terms used by the sources make it clear that the firing mechanism used a different, finer powder than the one used in the barrels. Presumably, they realised that the larger-grained gunpowder loaded into the barrel would release more gas more quickly and would be able to exert more energy. Whether they were led to this by western experts or by their own discovery is unknown, but we think the western influence is more likely.

For some time now, historians of Ottoman handguns have been struggling with the dilemma of how to reconcile the calibres of the guns preserved in museums and collections with the calibre references in the sources, i.e. the dirhem. So the question is: what mass and what diameter of projectiles did the Ottoman arquebuses fire? The dirhem data for projectiles that appear in the sources (4, 5, 7, 10, etc.) were generally converted using the equivalence of 1 dirhem equals 3 grams, namely the density of lead. Hence the problem that it is not possible to match the 14–15 mm, 16–17 mm and 19–20 mm barrels of the peserved janissary guns with the projectiles. The bullets, calculated from pure lead with 3 grams of dirhem, are smaller than would be expected from the diameter of the barrels. There could be several reasons for the calculation error. A minor problem is that experts typically underestimated the projectiles. It is more likely that 1 dirhem = ca. 3.2 grams may have been the unit of measurement used for gun bullets during this period. The other, bigger problem was that they all used pure lead (11.3 g/cm^3), which is also a source of error, because pure lead is poorly suited to projectiles, it has to be alloyed. Thus the volume and diameter of the bullet is increased by the significantly lower density of the other materials used for alloying (tin, antimony). Once these corrections have been made, the barrel diameter and the projectile size of the janissary gun can be matched. Thus, it can be said that calculations that use pure lead to convert the diameter of the projectiles in dirhems are incorrect.[104]

---

104   Ágoston, in his overview of the janissary handguns, referring to Emecen, states two things: 1. In 1553, the guns used in the Iraqi campaign fired 5 dirhem (15 grams) bullets and came in two sizes: 4 karış, or 88 cm, and 5 karış, or 110 cm (i.e. both types fired the same size

Research into the Battle of Mohács in the 2010–2020s has been dominated by a debate about the interpretation of the small arms bullets recovered in the eastern outskirts of the village of Majs. Researchers from the Janus Pannonius Museum in Pécs collected 255 lead projectiles in a metal detector survey over an area of about 110 hectares in and around a medieval village. 70% of the projectiles were 13mm or smaller and 20% were 10 mm or smaller.[105] The projectiles are concentrated in the interior of the village. In the following, we will compare the size, size distribution and environmental characteristics of the projectiles found at Majs with the picture that emerges from the sources and the weapons of the period.

At first glance, it is obvious that the small arms projectiles recovered in the Majs area do not belong to the Ottoman weapons identified in the above analysis, nor to the western weapons used during the Battle of Mohács. Neither do the typical projectiles of the Ottoman 4 and 5 karış, 4 and 5 dirhem guns appear, and also missing are the 24–25 mm projectiles of the weapons (Prague hackbut) that we know of in the Christian army.

To what extent does the picture of the gun use sites provided by the sources correspond to what can be concluded from the group of artefacts observed by the researchers of Janus Pannonius Museum in the Majs study area?

1. Near Majs there are not three, but only one concentration area of projectiles, namely at the remains of the medieval village Majsa.
2. According to the sources, the Christian heavy cavalry on the Ottoman left flank could not break through the line of janissaries and gun emplacements at the village of Földvár, so they crossed the Ottoman front line at the wagons set up to secure the battle line from the side. Consequently, the bullets, especially the damaged and deformed bullets, should be concentrated in the village outskirts and certainly not in the village.
3. A concentration of bullets was observed within the village, between houses. This could only mean that the village area was attacked from outside with small arms fire. However, the sources describe the opposite at the Battle of Mohács: the janissaries fired outwards from the direction of the settlement, at the attacking Christian heavy cavalry. And the Christian heavy cavalry obviously could not have attacked the janissaries with small arms, because they did not have them. And we have no record of Christian infantry being used against the Rumelian army.

---

bullet). 2. He also says that in the second half of the century there is talk of janissary guns that fired 12 and 15 gram bullets, i.e. he believes their calibres were 13 and 14 mm. The dirhem he counts as 3 grams. Ágoston, "Firearms and Military Adaptation", p. 105.

[105] Gábor Bertók, Márk Haramza, and Balázs Németh, "Lövedékek egy "mohácsi" csatatérről," [Bullets from a "Mohács" battlefield] in *Eke mentén, csata nyomában: A mohácsi csata kutatásánaklegújabb eredményei*, eds. Márk Haramza et al. (Budapest: Martin Opitz Kiadó etc, 2020), pp. 121–142.

On this basis, it can be concluded that several archaeological features of the Majs area do not correspond to the primary written sources about the Battle of Mohács. Based on Konkoly's investigations, it is very likely that some of the bullets collected by the archaeologists of the Janus Pannonius Museum in the area of Majs since 1993 were fired from the handguns of the western troops camped on the island of Mohács in the late 1680s.[106]

14   Summary

Janissary handguns of the period under study were made in two main sizes, around 88–92 and 110–115 cm in length. The gauge was between 14–15 mm for the shorter ones and 16–17 mm for the larger ones. The specimens preserved in Hungary are among the larger ones, with a barrel diameter of around 17 mm.

We do not have such a clear picture for the western firearms used at Mohács. The mercenary troops were equipped with 24–25 mm hackbuts, but an 18 mm gun similar to the Spanish musket is also known, but with a considerably shorter barrel and a greater weight than the longer Ottoman gun. Light guns may have been close to the calibre of the Ottoman shorter guns, but with a shorter barrel (60–75 cm).

Comparative studies of gun barrels suggest that Ottoman gun-makers deliberately built on the considerable advantage that the long barrel represents. The longer Ottoman guns may have been more advantageous on the battlefield because they were light, and the long barrel allowed them to be fired at a greater range. Better quality gun material could carry a larger load. The longer and better quality steel barrel gave the janissary gun considerable destructive power. The harder bullets were more powerful, concentrating the energy in a pinpoint pattern, and could penetrate western armour.

To overcome the heavy cavalry, the janissaries needed weapons with a relatively large charge that could accelerate along a long stretch of barrel. Comparative studies have shown that smaller weapons (shorter barrels and smaller barrel diameters) could not do much damage to a heavy cavalryman. The difference between the destructive power of the light western gun and the 110–115 cm long (5 karış) janissary gun was significant. In the Balkan and Central European battlefields, the Ottoman army gained the upper hand over the western armies, which used shorter-barrelled, smaller calibre guns and heavy cavalry.

---

106   The Majsian projectiles are discussed in more detail in the chapter on military archaeology (see Chapter Nine).

It can be concluded that the picture of the Majs area examined by the researchers of the Janus Pannonius Museum in Pécs does not correspond to the written sources, the pattern of the archaeological finds does not reflect the events, it does not fit the pattern of the clashes during the battle. At the same time, its characteristics allow us to infer the relevant period and actors. It appears that the bullets found at Majs may have been fired during a skirmish in 1687, but were definitely fired with late 17th-century weapons. On the basis of the above, the hypothesis that the janissaries fought with short-barrelled (60–70 cm), small-diameter (10–13 mm), pistol- and carbine-type firearms at Mohács can be rejected.

In the Battle of Mohács in 1526, the Ottoman infantry with handguns, and firearms in general, played a decisive role. Both sides were equipped with small arms, but the janissary formations were superior in every respect. In addition to their advanced weaponry, their training, motivation, discipline and the fact that they used their guns for volley fire, which gave them great efficiency, may have played a role in this.

Bibliography

Ágoston, Gábor. "Firearms and Military Adaptation: the Ottomans and the European Military Revolution, 1450–1800." *Journal of World History* 25 (2014): 85–124.

Ágoston, Gábor. "War-Winning Weapons? On The Decisiveness Of Ottoman Firearms from the Siege of Constantinople (1453) to the Battle of Mohacs (1526)." *Journal of Turkish Studies* 39 (2013): 129–143.

Ágoston, Gábor. "Military Transformation in the Ottoman Empire and Russia, 1500–1800." *Kritika: Explorations in Russian and Eurasian History* 12 (2011): 281–319.

Ágoston, Gábor. *Tüfek* (2011). Available at https://islamansiklopedisi.org.tr/tufek.

Ágoston, Gábor and Bruce Masters. *Encyclopedia of the Ottoman Empire*. New York: Facts on File, 2009.

Ágoston, Gábor. *Guns for the Sultan – Military Power and the Weapons Industry in the Ottoman Empire*. Cambridge: Cambridge University Press, 2005.

Andrade, Tonio. *The Gunpowder Age: China, Military Innovation, and the Rise of the West in World History*. Princeton and Oxford: Princeton University Press, 2016.

Arnold, Thomas. *The Renaissance at War*. Cassell, 2001.

Az 1526. évi hadinapló 1526 (részlet). [The campaign diary 1526 (excerpt)] In *Örök Mohács: szövegek és értelmezések*, eds. János B. Szabó and Gábor Farkas Farkas, 235–257. Budapest: Bölcsészettudományi Kutatóközpont, 2020.

Az udvari zsoldosok/janicsárok fegyver- és hadianyag listája 1526. április 13. [The list of the court mercenaries/Janissaries with arms and war material, 13 April 1526] In

Örök Mohács: szövegek és értelmezések, eds. János B. Szabó and Gábor Farkas Farkas, 231–235. Budapest: Bölcsészettudományi Kutatóközpont, 2020.

Bertók, Gábor, Márk Haramza, and Balázs Németh. "Lövedékek egy "mohácsi" csatatérről." [Bullets from a "Mohács" battlefield] In *Eke mentén, csata nyomában: A mohácsi csata kutatásánaklegújabb eredményei,* eds. Márk Haramza et al., 121–142. Budapest: Martin Opitz Kiadó etc, 2020.

Brodarics, István. "Igaz történet a magyarok és Szulejmán török császár mohácsi ütközetéről 1528." [A true account about the battle between the Hungarians and the Turkish Emperor Süleyman in Mohács in 1528] In Örök Mohács: szövegek és értelmezések, eds. János B. Szabó and Gábor Farkas Farkas, 301–325. (Budapest: Bölcsészettudományi Kutatóközpont, 2020).

DeVries, Kelly. *Medieval Military Technology.* Broadview Press Ltd., 1992.

Dictionnaire Turc-Français. Constantinople: Imprimerie Mihran, 1911.

Dzselálzáde Musztafa. "Az országok osztályai és az utak felsorolása 1560-as évek (részlet)." [A list of classes of countries and roads 1560s (excerpt)] In *Örök Mohács: szövegek és értelmezések,* eds. János B. Szabó and Gábor Farkas Farkas, 411–419. Budapest: Bölcsészettudományi Kutatóközpont, 2020.

Egy cseh úr levele a Santa Clara kolostor főnöknőjéhez, 1526. november." [Letter from a Czech nobleman to the Superior of the Convent of Santa Clara, November 1526] In *Örök Mohács: szövegek és értelmezések,* eds. János B. Szabó and Gábor Farkas Farkas, 207–216. Budapest: Bölcsészettudományi Kutatóközpont, 2020.

Elgood, Robert. *The Arms of Greece and Her Balkan Neighbors in the Ottoman Period.* New York: Thames & Hudson, 2009.

Emecen, Feridun. "Ateşli Silahlar Çağı: Askeri Dönüşüm/Devrim ve Osmanlı Ordusu." In *Savaşın Sultanları-I. Osmanlı Padişahlarının Meydan Muherebeleri,* eds. Feridun Emecen and Erhan Afyoncu, 38–81. Istanbul: 2018.

Fodor, Pál. *Tabur* (2010) Available at https://islamansiklopedisi.org.tr/tabur.

Fuess, Albrecht. "Why Domenico Had to Die and Black Slaves Wore Red Uniforms: Military Technology and Its Decisive Role in the 1517 Ottoman Conquest of Egypt." In *The Mamluk-Ottoman Transition: Continuity and Change in Egypt and Bilā̄d al-Shā̄m in the Sixteenth Century, 2nd ed.* eds. Stefan Conermann and Gül Sen, 131–154. V&R, Bonn University Press, 2022.

Goodwin, Godfrey. *The Janisseries.* Saqi Books, 2006.

Hendrowski, Heinrich. "Bilder aus dem Türkischen Volksleben" In: *I Turchi – Codex Vindobonensis 8626. Table 39.* Heiliges Römisches Reich.

Hinz, Walter. *Measures and Weights in the Islamic World.* Kuala Lumpur: ISTAC, 2003.

Huismann, D. J., J. van Doesburg, B. J. H. van Os, A. Kroeze, S. Mooren, and J. Kniep, "Bullets over Gennep: Using Compositional Variation in Lead Musket Balls in Battlefield Archaeology." In *39th International Symposium on Archeometry 2012,* Leuven, 2012.

İnalcık, Halil. "Introduction to Ottoman Metrology." *Turcica* 15 (1983): 311–348.

Irwin, Robert. "Gunpowder and Firearms in the Mamluk Sultanate Reconsidered." In *The Mamluks in Egyptian and Syrian Politics and Society*, eds. Michael Winter and Amalia Levanoni, 117–139. Leiden and Boston: Brill, 2004.

Kelenik, József. "Szakállas puskák XVI. századi magyarországi inventáriumokban." [Hackbuts in 16th century Hungarian inventories] *Hadtörténelmi Közlemények* 35 (1988): 484–520.

Kemálpasazáde. "Mohácsnáme (részlet)." [Mohácsname (excerpt)] In *Örök Mohács: szövegek és értelmezések*, eds. János B. Szabó and Gábor Farkas Farkas, 326–338. Budapest: Bölcsészettudományi Kutatóközpont, 2020.

Kiss, Károly. *Mohács emlékezete* [Memory of Mohács]. Budapest: Európa Könyvkiadó, 1987.

Kolçak, Özgür. *Ok, Tüfek ve At: 16. Yüzyıl Osmanlı Askerî Devrimi* Ankara: Türk Tarih Kurumu, 2023.

Kozák, Károly. "A magyarországi szakállas puskák fejlődéstörténetéről." [The history of development of hackbuts in Hungary] *Archeologiai Értesítő* 101 (1974): 290–303.

Krenn, Peter, Paul Kalaus, and Bert Hall. "Material Culture and Military History: Test-Firing Early Modern Small Arms." *Material History Review* 42 (1995): 101–109.

Kubinyi, András. "Mozgósítási és hadseregellátási problémák Mátyás alatt." [Mobilisation and army supply problems under Mátyás] *Hadtörténelmi Közlemények* 103 (1990): 66–73.

McLachlan, Sean. *Medieval Handgonnes: The first black powder infantry weapons*. Osprey Publishing, 2010.

Mula, Agostino da. "Agostino da Mula jelentése Udine, 1526. szeptember 15. (transcript)." [Account of Agostino da Mula Udine, 15 September 1526 (transliteration)] In *Örök Mohács: szövegek és értelmezések*, eds. János B. Szabó and Gábor Farkas Farkas, 163–165. Budapest: Bölcsészettudományi Kutatóközpont, 2020.

Nagy, Géza. "Hadtörténeti ereklyék a Magyar Nemzeti Múzeumban." [Military Relics in the Hungarian National Museum] *Hadtörténeti Közlemények* 11 (1910): 223–243.

Needham, Joseph. *Science & Civilisation in China 7, Military Technology: The Gunpowder Epic*. Cambridge University Press, 1986.

Padányi, József and József Ondrek. "Examining lead bullets from the siege of Novi Zrin in 1664." *Journal of Conflict Archaeology* 14 (2019): 1–20.

Pálfalvi, László and Vivien Kovács. "A pV $\varkappa$ = állandó törvény alkalmazhatóságáról egy versenyfeladat tükrében." [On the applicability of the pV $\varkappa$ = constant law in the light of a competition problem] *Fizikai Szemle* 71 (2021): 380–384.

Peçevi, İbrahim. "Krónika 1648 előtt (részlet)." [Chronicle, before 1648 (excerpt)] In *Örök Mohács: szövegek és értelmezések*, eds. János B. Szabó and Gábor Farkas Farkas, 463–477. Budapest: Bölcsészettudományi Kutatóközpont, 2020.

Phillips, Pratap Henry. *The History and Chronology of Gunpowder and Gunpowder Weapons (ca.1000 to 1850)*. Chennai: Notion Press, 2016.

Rázsó, Gyula. "Mátyás hadászati tervei és a realitás." [Mátyás' military plans and reality] *Hadtörténelmi Közlemények* 103 (1990): 1–30.

Ritchie, Tessy S., Kathleen E. Riegner, Robert J. Seals, Clifford J. Rogers, and Dawn E. Riegner. "Evolution of Medieval Gunpowder: Thermodynamic and Combustion Analysis." *ACS Omega* 6 (2021): 22848–22856.

Robins, Benjamin. *New principles of gunnery: containing, the determination of the force of gun-powder, and an investigation of the difference in the resisting power of the air to swift and slow motions*. Gale ECCO, 2010.

Selânikî Mustafa Efendi. *Tarih-i Selânikî (971–1003/1563–1595)*. İstanbul: Hazırlayan Mehmed İpşirli, 1989.

Stanley, Tim. "The Ottomans and the Transmission of Gun Lock Technology." In *Cultural Encounters in the Ottoman World and Their Reflections: Essays in Honor of Prof. Dr. Filiz Yenisehirlioglu*, 205–214. Ankara: 2017.

Szendrei, János ed. "A XVI–XIX. század hadtörténelmi emlékei 1526–1848." [Military historical relicts of the 16–19th century 1526–1848] In *Magyar hadtörténelmi emlékek az Ezredéves Országos Kiállításon*. Budapest, 1896.

Taylor, Frederick. *The Art of War in Italy, 1494–1529*. Cambridge University Press, 1921.

Thierbach, Moritz. *Die geschichtliche Entwicklung der Handfeuerwaffen, edited from the originals still existing in German collections* (Dresden: 1889). Reprinted Graz: 1975 and Saarbrücken: 2018.

Töll, László. *A harci vértezetek története. (A nyugat-európai hadviselésben alkalmazott testvédelmi rendszerek fejlődéstörténete a 10. századtól a 16. század közepéig)* [The History of the Battle Armouries (The History of the Development of the Body Defence Systems Used in Western European Warfare from the 10th Century to the Mid-16th Century)] (2010) Available at https://dea.lib.unideb.hu/items/92022189-1c3f-4751-9ed3-b77952902f7c.

Tóth, Ferenc. "Újabb francia források a szentgotthárdi csatáról." [New French sources on the Battle of Szentgotthárd.] *Hadtörténelmi Közlemények* 127 (2014): 206–231.

Williams, Alan. *The Knight and the Blast Furnace. A history of the metallurgy of armour in the middle ages and the early modern period*. Leiden: Brill, 2003.

Zarnóczky, Attila. "Fegyverzet, katonai felszerelés, hadsereg Magyarországon Hunyadi Mátyás korában." [Arms, military equipment, army in Hungary in the time of Matthias I] *Hadtörténelmi Közlemények* 103 (1990): 31–65.

Żygulski, Zdzislaw. "Oriental and Levantine Firearms." In *Pollard's History of Firearms*, ed. Claude Blair London, Macmillan, 1983. pp. 425–462.

CHAPTER 5

The Battle and Its Aftermath

Norbert Pap and Máté Kitanics

1   Introduction

One might ask: is it possible to tell an objective story of a battle? Can we get a realistic picture of what happened at Mohács? We have had to face the Keeganian dilemmas of military historiography.[1]

The challenge is different in each case. The main difference is not so much the approach to the battle, but the availability of written sources. At Mohács, no written military plan or memoirs of one or other of the commanders survive, the most detailed account known to us is of a 'civilian', Bishop Brodarics. The accounts of the soldiers on both sides are very sketchy. This study is therefore more an attempt to depict the faces of the armies moving in the battlefield than to show, through the soldiers' experiences, how the battle was experienced by the commander and the common soldier. Accordingly, the 1526 Battle of Mohács will be presented as the two armies struggled with each other and mainly with the terrain and environment. The objective reality of the battlefield environment can also bring us closer to understanding the battle itself.

2   Decisive Clash

Forcing a decisive clash was an important part of both sides' plans. The Ottomans wanted to force Louis II into battle, while Hungary was to be integrated into the order of their conquests in Southeastern Europe. Their numerical and technological superiority gave them every opportunity to do so. A heavy defeat of the Hungarian army, the weakening of the ruling class and the eventual capture of the monarch could have created ideal conditions for submitting the Hungarian state into vassal status and extending Ottoman influence in the region. This scenario would have corresponded to the Balkan model of Ottoman conquest.

---

[1] John Keegan, *The Face of Battle: A Study of Agincourt, Waterloo, and the Somme* (Pimlico, 2004).

Although the Ottomans were successful in 1526, it took them fifteen years to achieve their original goal of conquest, and even then not over the whole country. First, they had occupied a narrow strip along the Danube, which in time became a broad area, and by the second half of the 17th century the conquered territory reached its maximum extent.

For the Hungarian and allied forces, a possible victory over the Ottomans promised a repeat of János Hunyadi's triumph at Nándorfehérvár (Belgrade) 70 years earlier. On that occasion, in 1456, a Hungarian army led by Hunyadi defeated Mehmed II's army on the southern border. If the feat had been repeated, it would have relieved Hungary and Central Europe of further Ottoman military pressure. For the landowners of the south, who made up a large part of the Christian army, and their military, the need to free their own region from the Ottoman threat was also important, as was the preservation of their property and wealth. As we know by now, this endeavour, among others, was not successful.

3 What to Do? Plans before the Battle

There was considerable debate in the Christian army leadership before the battle about what to do. Even earlier, in the midst of the military preparations, it had been suggested that the Ottoman army should be held up along a river valley (the Drava River in particular) on the way, but this failed to materialise due to the very slow gathering of the army and coordination problems.[2] The idea was also mooted in the army leadership, including by Louis II, that the Ottomans should not be attacked because they were greatly outnumbered, but should instead be withdrawn, even as far as Pozsony (Bratislava). But this eventually remained a minority opinion. There was also talk on waiting for the troops still en route to arrive before the clash, so that they could engage the enemy with greater force. Although the expected troops were numerous (the troops of the voivode of Transylvania, the Czech regiments still on the way, and totalling tens of thousands of troops from Slavonia and Croatia), there was no chance of them arriving in time. According to the plan if a battle was to be fought, the battle line would be secured by wagons on the flanks to counter the

---

2 Brodarics István, "Igaz történet a magyarok és Szulejmán török császár mohácsi ütközetéről 1528," [A true account of the battle between the Hungarians and the Turkish Emperor Süleyman at Mohács (1528)] in *Örök Mohács: szövegek és értelmezések*, eds. János B. Szabó and Gábor Farkas Farkas (Budapest: Bölcsészettudományi Kutatóközpont, 2020), pp. 301–325. See also in detail Chapter Two.

numerically superior Ottomans and avoid encirclement, but in the end this was not done either.³ Amid the disputes, the troops from different parts of the country slowly gathered. After a while it became obvious that many of them would not arrive on time to the designated assembly point.

In the planning process, the "southern" magnates in the Mohács military camp, who feared for their estates, finally prevailed in their position that the clash should be forced out. Another argument in favour of fighting the battle was that despite the rainy weather, which caused flooding on the intermediate rivers, the Ottoman army advanced rapidly. After overcoming resistance from the fortresses along the Danube (Pétervárad [Petrovaradin], Újlak [Ilok]), it crossed the Drava in mid-August and approached the place where the Hungarian and allied troops were massed.

In the midst of endless discussions in the Hungarian camp, it slowly became clear that it was too late to retreat, because the Ottoman cavalry outnumbered the Hungarian army, so King Louis II had lost the possibility of an orderly retreat. There was no other option, they had to fight. The most experienced leaders were consulted separately and together during the planning. The leadership of the Hungarian army remained seriously divided. The more sober-minded were aware, however, that to undertake the battle was equal to suicide.⁴

The army's order of battle was decided on 27 August: the left wing was led by Péter Perényi, Count of Temes, while the right wing was led by Ferenc Batthyány, the Croatian-Slavonian-Dalmatian ban. At the meeting in Bata (16–19 August), two commanders-in-chief were appointed to head the army: Pál Tomori, Archbishop of Kalocsa, a Franciscan monk and experienced soldier, and György Szapolyai⁵, the Count of Szepes. A cavalry regiment was organised to protect the king, led by captains Gáspár Ráskai, Bálint Török and János Kállay, so that if things went badly, they could quickly get him out of the fighting. The heavy cavalry was to play the leading role among the infantry regiments. They hoped that the Ottoman army would be no match for the Hungarian heavy cavalry attacking in a closed block.

---

3 This plan had been advocated by Lenard Gnoienski, the Polish infantry commander, and the Serbian commanders Pavle Bakić (Pál Bakics) and Radič Božić (Radics Bosics), but it was not decided until the evening of 28 August, and was in vain. See Brodarics, "Igaz történet," [A true account] in *Örök Mohács,* eds. B. Szabó et al., pp. 301–325.
4 An example is the young Ferenc Perényi, Bishop of Várad, who, according to Brodarics' account, said before the battle that the day on which the battle would take place would be dedicated to the 20,000 Hungarian martyrs who had died for Christianity. See Brodarics, "Igaz történet," [A true account] in *Örök Mohács,* eds. B. Szabó et al., pp. 301–325.
5 Count of Szepes, brother of János Szapolyai (voivode of Transylvania).

For the Ottoman command, it was not clear what they would do, where they would clash with the Hungarian army: there was some anxiety in the Ottoman Turkish sources. The main question in the planning was what to do with the attacking heavy cavalry, and it was suggested that the Hungarians were entrenched and would be difficult to break through. Louis II's army was feared as a formidable opponent.

The key role in the planning was played by Yahyapasa-oğlu Bali Bey, the leader of the outpost responsible for reconnaissance, and, as he commanded a sub-province (the sancak of Semendria [Semendire/Smederevo/ /Szendrő]) in the border region, he had great experience in fighting with the Hungarians,[6] he was an excellent and respected soldier. He also had considerable authority in the military council. The Ottoman soldiers wanted to attack. Bali, however, through his knowledge of the terrain, suggested that the battle site chosen by the Hungarian army was not really advantageous for the Ottomans, as *"the space here is too narrow."*[7] This might have been the reason why the Ottoman troops advanced very cautiously, not too fast. The planned order of battle followed the formation that had matured over the previous decades. On the left wing were the Rumelian army led by grand vizier İbrahim Pasha, on the right wing the Anatolian army led by Behram Pasha, and in the centre the sultan's household troops. The cavalry led by Bali Bey of Semendria and Hüsrev Bey of Bosnia, which had played an important role in the battle, took up positions on the left wing, slightly further away from the main Rumelian army.

According to the sources, the Ottomans were preparing, or at least Bali is recorded to have urged them, not to attack first, to use their traditional fighting methods. The advice of Bali Bey is recorded as saying: *"The best course of action, therefore, will be that, as soon as these wicked men with their whole herd rush upon us, our ranks will be split to give them way; then, as soon as they have passed between our rows with inexorable speed, we will flank them."*[8]

One might ask whether this text is not a retroactive projection of the events. We are inclined to accept its veracity because it was part of the *tabur cengi* mode of combat practised by the Ottoman army, seen at Chaldiran (1514) or in the two great battles (1516, 1517) against the Mamluks. The Ottoman army,

---

6 Pál Fodor, "Wolf on the Border: Yahyapaşaoğlu Bali Bey (?–1527)," in *Şerefe. Studies in Honour of Prof. Géza Dávid on His Seventieth Birthday,* eds. Pál Fodor, Nándor E. Kovács, and Benedek Péri (Budapest, Research Center for the Humanities, 2019), pp. 57–88.

7 Davut Erkan, *Matrâkçi Nasûh'un Süleymân-nâmesi (1520–1537)*. MA thesis (İstanbul: Marmara Üniversitesi, 2005), p. 116. We thank Pál Fodor for this reference.

8 Kemálpasazáde, "Mohácsnáme. 1526 és 1534 között (részlet)," [Mohácsname. Between 1526 and 1534 (excerpt)] in *Örök Mohács,* eds. B. Szabó et al., p. 327.

whether the suggestion was made or not, and therefore regardless of Bali's advice, prepared for it and practised it.

4   Events of the Day of the Battle

The battle took place on the day of the beheading of John the Baptist, which fell on 29 August according to the Julian calendar in use at the time. This became the memorial day of the battle when commemorations are held, but the anniversary should correctly be on 8 September since the adoption of the Gregorian calendar. This is important for us because the astronomical conditions at that time corresponded not to 29 August but to 8 September today.[9] This explains why, when reconstructing events, we have to count Muslim prayer times which are the reference points for the division of the day in Ottoman Turkish sources and also markers of the progress of events in the accounts of Western eyewitnesses, according to the early autumn of 8 September and not the late summer of 29 August. According to our research, the sun rose at 5.31 am and set at 6.31 pm on the day of the battle, as perceived by local observers.[10] The astronomical references, such as sunrise, sunset and noon, appear in both Ottoman Turkish and Western sources, as well as in some cases the time of the event in hours, which was also given by following the apparent movement of the sun.

Like so much else, the duration of the battle is a matter of debate. According to the main narrator of the battle, István Brodarics, it lasted only an hour and a

---

[9]   Norbert Pap, Péter Gyenizse, Máté Kitanics, and Gábor Szalai, "A Gergely-féle naptárreform és a csillagászati jelenségek szerepe a 15–16. századi történelmi forrásaink és eseményeink értelmezésében: a 15–16. századi történelmi események kronológiai értelmezéséhez," [The role of the Gregorian calendar reform and astronomical phenomena in the interpretation of historical sources and events of the 15th–16th centuries: towards a chronological interpretation of historical events of the 15th–16th centuries] *Balkán Füzetek* 11 (2020), pp. 1–66.

[10] The methodology is based on Péter Gyenizse, Norbert Pap, Máté Kitanics, and Tibor Szabó, "Napkelte és napnyugta adatainak modellezése történelmi események rekonstrukciójához," [Modelling sunrise and sunset data for the reconstruction of historical events.] in *Az elmélet és a gyakorlat találkozása a térinformatikában XIII*, ed. Vanda Éva Abriha-Molnár (Debrecen: Debreceni Egyetemi Kiadó, 2022), pp. 155–162. Since 1884, at the International Meridian Conference in Washington DC., time has been measured in time zones rather than in 'local time' per meridian of longitude. On 29 August 2023, sunrise in Mohács is at 6.02 am and sunset at 7.32 pm. On 8 September 2023, sunrise is at 6.15 am and sunset at 7.13 pm. It can be seen that the difference between the local time in Mohács on 29 August 1526 and the time of similar days today is about 50 minutes.

half, but according to the Ottoman campaign diary it took two hours to finish.[11] The question is, of course, whether or not the slaughter of the foreign mercenaries who were unable to flee was included in the battle. We do not know. But even so, the battle could not have lasted much longer than 2.5 hours, from 4 pm to about 6.30 pm, given that, according to the sources, night had fallen and a storm that broke out at the same time brought the fighting to an end. Of course, the events that matter to us had already begun before the clashes started and continued for some time afterwards.

The first, larger part of the day was spent with the two armies marching. The Hungarian military camp was near the Kölked landbridge, situated about half Hungarian mile (ca. 4 km) south of Mohács, in the immediate vicinity of the floodplain below Mohács. "The location of the royal camp was marked out on the flat and open fields near the marsh. The gently rising hill prevented the enemy's camp from being seen. ... The camp of the Turks was pitched opposite, at the foot of the Mount. The distance between the two was two miles"[12] – wrote the contemporary chronicler Ursinus Velius.[13] The bulk of the Ottoman army had crossed the Karasica Stream, which bordered the plain from the south, on the previous day, 28 August, and camped near the crossing point in the Baranyavár region, about two Hungarian miles (ca. 16 km) from the Christians.[14] The Hungarian army had time to deploy to the south of the camp on the chosen battlefield, as planned. According to Brodarics, they moved from the camp to the battlefield, one mile (ca. 8 km) from Mohács, near the deep marsh along the Danube.

The chancellor's account details the order of battle, including where each dignitary was placed in the order of battle. "The lines on the day of battle ... had to be so arranged as to stretch as wide as possible, the main consideration being that the enemy should not get behind us. Then the whole army was divided into two columns."[15] The army's positioning by branches of service is detailed in the chapter on the two armies in this volume.[16]

The source also mentions that the king's place had been designated in advance and refers to the fact that there had been a parade three days earlier: "... the king was led by the palatine from the place which we have mentioned

---

11   "Az 1526. évi hadinapló (részlet)," [The Ottoman campaign diary of 1526 (excerpt)] in *Örök Mohács,* eds. B.Szabó et al., pp. 235–257.
12   Two (Italian) miles equals ca. 4 km.
13   Caspar Ursinus Velius, "A mohácsi csata. 1530 körül (töredék)," [The Battle of Mohács. Around 1530 (fragment)] in *Örök Mohács,* eds. B.Szabó et al., pp. 348–354.
14   Brodarics, "Igaz történet," [A true account] in *Örök Mohács,* eds. B.Szabó et al., pp. 301–325.
15   Brodarics, "Igaz történet," [A true account] in *Örök Mohács,* eds. B.Szabó et al., p. 317.
16   See Chapter Three.

FIGURE 5.1   Depiction of the Battle of Mohács, 1559, Augsburg.
SOURCE: EHRENSPIEGEL DES HAUSES ÖSTERREICH (BUCH VII) (AUGSBURG: BAYERISCHE STAATSBIBLIOTHEK, 1559), P. 379.

as having been appointed for him, and, as he had done three days before, he led the king in front of the army, so that everyone could be assured of his presence…"[17] The fact of planning and the fact of the parade three days before suggest that the artillery and infantry positions were prepared for the day of battle.

The Table 5.1 summarizes the main events of the day of the battle, both on the Hungarian and the Ottoman side, related to each other. The timelines are partly approximate values, calculated from some of the concrete data in the sources, the Muslim prayer times mentioned and the time required to overcome the terrain.

At dawn on 29 August (Wednesday), the Ottomans proceeded first. After the morning prayer, the army began its march to line up in the area opposite the Hungarian army.[18] The front of the army took 6–7 hours to cover the 12–13 km distance from the Karasica Stream to the area of Földvár. The speed of about

---

17   Brodarics, "Igaz történet," [A true account] in *Örök Mohács,* eds. B.Szabó et al., p. 318.
18   "Az 1526. évi hadinapló" [The Ottoman campaign diary of 1526] in *Örök Mohács,* eds. B. Szabó et al., pp. 235–257.

TABLE 5.1 Chronology of the day of the battle (29 August). Edited by Norbert Pap

Time	Hungarian army	Ottoman army
Just before 5.31		After the morning prayers (fajr), the Ottoman army marched to the area of Földvár, the Rumelian army in the front, followed by the sultan with the Anatolians and the court troops.
5.31	Sunrise	Sunrise
Around 6.00	The Hungarian army marches from the camp to the battlefield in about one and a half to two hours, "just after sunrise". Parade of honours, exhortations to the army. Waiting for the enemy to attack.	
7.00–12.00		At the monastery of Géta (Bozuk Kilisze = ruined church), later called Buziglica the cavalry led by Bali Bey separate from the main army and advance to scout the terrain on the roads above the rim of the plain. On the high ground they scout the position of the Hungarian army and then return to the main army.
12.00–12.30		The front of the army arrives in the area of Földvár.
12.30–14.30		On Bali's advice, they decide not to fight and to clash the next day at dawn. They set up a camp and the sultan's tent.
Around 14.30–15.00	An Ottoman cavalry regiment is discovered, recognised by spearheads, so Gáspár Raskai's troops set out to reconnoitre and push them back.	The regiment of Bali Bey, in the cover of the low Sátorhely Ridge, try to advance west of the Hungarian army and take up a position there. Their aim is to join the expected battle from there at the right time, to attack the Hungarian troops from the flanks and the rear, and to embrace them.

TABLE 5.1   Chronology of the day of the battle (29 August). Edited by Norbert Pap (*cont.*)

Time	Hungarian army	Ottoman army
15.00–16.00	A debate begins in the command on whether to launch an attack. Some leaders would rather retreat to the camp. Finally, Tomori convinces the king to attack until the full Ottoman army is present. Meanwhile, they spend too much time arguing.	
After 15.30		The Rumelian army become visible, the movement of the Christian army – the Hungarian heavy cavalry is regrouped – is followed by the Ottoman troops, who also take up arms.
16.00	The right wing cavalry charge is launched.	The light cavalry flees from the place where the guns of the Rumelian army are.
Around 16.15–16.30	The second wave of attack, including Brodarics, is launched on the back of this success.	The heavy cavalry attack is disrupted by the janissaries' handgun fire, then the Ottoman cavalry surrounds and defeats the Christian cavalry in hand-to-hand combat.
16.30–17.00		The sultan also arrives on the plain with the Anatolian and the household troops, taking their usual positions in the order of battle.
16.00–17.00		In the meantime, Bali Bey's cavalry ravages the Christian camp, slaughters the 2000 defenders and the servants there, and then attacks Louis II's army in the rear.
17.00–17.30	An attack is launched against the Anatolian army.	The Anatolian cavalry "flees". The attacking wedge gets close to the sultan, but is repulsed by the solaks. The janissaries of the salaried household troops play a major role in stopping the attack, raining down volleys of fire on the attackers.

TABLE 5.1   Chronology of the day of the battle (29 August). Edited by Norbert Pap (cont.)

Time	Hungarian army	Ottoman army
Around 17.30–18.00	The troops – first the rear rows of the Christian infantry then some of the cavalry – begin to flee. Brodarics also flees, through the already devastated camp. The other part of the cavalry commanded by the king tries – unsuccessfully – to continue the fight.	As the front surges, Ottoman gun fire and cavalry charges push the stalwart Christian cavalry back into the dry river valley, which also provides some cover.
From 17.30 to not later than 18.30	The mercenary infantry forms a square and try to defend themselves.	The janissaries are firing on the mercenaries. The sipahi cavalry slaughters the fleeing mercenaries.
Around 18.00	The king also begins to flee.	The salaried household troops remain in place. The akıncıs continue their pursuit.
Around 18.30	A violent storm breaks out giving many people shelter and a chance to escape.	The Ottoman troops remain in formation on the battlefield as the visibility decreases and they expect that further attacks may take place.
18.31	Sunset	Sunset
From 18.15 to 19.00 at the latest	Below the village of Csele, the king drowns in the smaller, western branch of the Danube, the so-called Kis- [Little] Danube. At the time of the accident, visibility is still assured, presumably during the civil twilight (the end of the civil twilight is at 19.06) taking into consideration that the sky is covered and that it rains.	Ottoman cavalrymen chase soldiers in flight in the northern part of the plain and also on the Mohács Island.
At night	The escape continues.	The Ottoman akıncıs chase small and large groups of refugees, setting them on fire and looting them.
Around midnight		The sultan goes to his tent.

THE BATTLE AND ITS AFTERMATH

two kilometres per hour may seem slow, but the average speed of advance of the Ottoman troops was no faster on other days of the campaign either. Elsewhere they covered 22–25 km, which suggests an average of 12–13 km over half a day.

In his account, Celalzade Mustafa mentions in general terms that Bali Bey was sent in advance:

> The governor of Semendire, Yahyapasa-oğlu Bali, a war-wise hero, a lion-like wolf, a guide and leader of the champions of the faith, was sent in advance by order of the world-conquering padishah to be the vanguard of the victorious army.[19]

According to Peçevi, around *Bozuk kilise* (identified as the monastery of Géta: meaning 'ruined church'), part of the army (cavalry) led by Bali Bey moved westwards along the forested roads above the basin rim[20] and had to cross several flooded watercourses. However, this operation, apart from providing the main army with a way forward from the west, was also very useful for reconnaissance, as the basin rim provides a good view in some places, rising 40 metres above the plain. In Ottoman Turkish reports, information appears that the informant was looking at the Mohács Plain from a high point. Celalzade reported that

> When they ascended a high hill, the field of Mihach appeared, the waters of the Tuna [Danube] spread out like a sea, and on its bank stood a miserable army in battle array, covering the surface of the earth in a broad expanse, and dark and black as a cloud of punishment; its huge camp with its tents was as fearsome as the mountain.[21]

---

19   Dzselálzáde Musztafa, "Az országok osztályai és az utak felsorolása. 1560-as évek (részlet)," [The divisions of countries and the list of roads. 1560s (excerpt)] in *Örök Mohács*, eds. B. Szabó et al., p. 412.

20   İbrahim Peçevi, "Krónika. 1648 előtt (részlet)," [Chronicle. Before 1648 (excerpt)]. in *Örök Mohács*, eds. B. Szabó eta al., 463–477. "Bozuk Kilise" today Buziglica is located between Géta and Dályok. We have some clues to identify its contemporary location. Pusziklitza can be seen on the 1772 agricultural map of the settlement of Majs, north of the Géta (Getta) elevation, south of Udvar (Charten von der ka[mmer]al Ortschaft Mays... Hungarian National Archives [= MNL] S 11–N.o. 830:43. On the Military Survey I (1783), the inscription Gusaklicza w. h. (w. h. = tavern) is located directly next to the main road from Baranyavár to Mohács, around 2.5 km south of Udvar and 3 km west of Dályok.

21   Dzselálzáde Musztafa, "Az országok osztályai,"[The divisions of countries] in *Örök Mohács*, eds. B. Szabó et al., p. 413.

The account of Lutfi Pasha gives a similar picture:

> ... a spy reported that the unbelievers, besides being so numerous, had dug a great ditch, one end of which extended to a mountain, and the other to the Danube, and through which it was impossible to pass.[22]

Not only the ordinary scouts, but presumably also Bali Bey himself who took part in the deliberations of the Ottoman high command, could see with his own eyes the characteristics of the terrain and the situation of the Christian army. Given his excellent knowledge of the sources, it is quite probable that İbrahim Peçevi's information about this operation, although from the 17th century, were based on original sources. The question is: what was the Hungarian perception of this?

Brodarics wrote in his account that "... we spent the greater part of the day waiting for the enemy; he did not send out as many outposts as he used to do in easy skirmishes with ours, but kept behind those hills until then."[23] The fact that the Ottoman army untipically did not send out scouts and raiding parties may indicate that this time, unlike usual, Bali Bey solved the important task of gathering information from a higher place. One thing is certain: reconnaissance was a great success. The raiders were already in the Rumelian military camp by noon with the fresh information they had obtained.

The front of the Ottoman army arrived sometime around noon on the southern side of the battlefield at Földvár. In the course of the deliberations held at that time, Grand Vizier İbrahim Pasha decided, partly on the basis of information and advice from Bali Bey, to postpone the battle until dawn next day.[24]

Thus, part of the army set up camp, while other troops set up artillery positions and the janissaries took up positions around the village of Földvár. Brodarics reported: "In front of us was a long hill in the shape of a theatre auditorium, beyond which the Turkish emperor was camped, and from the hill a small village with a church, called Földvár, descended, and there the enemy guns were positioned."[25] The artillery was positioned at the village, on the northern side (north and east of it, according to some accounts), near a

---

22 Lutfi pasa, "Az Oszmán-ház története. 1550-es évek (részlet)," [History of the Ottoman House. 1550s (excerpt).] in *Örök Mohács*, eds. B. Szabó et al., pp. 404–409.
23 Brodarics, "Igaz történet," [A true account] in *Örök Mohács*, eds. B. Szabó et al., p. 318.
24 Kemálpasazáde, "Mohácsnáme," [Mohácsname] in *Örök Mohács*, eds. B. Szabó et al., pp. 326–338.
25 Brodarics, "Igaz történet," [A true account] in *Örök Mohács*, eds. B. Szabó et al., p. 318.

forest.²⁶ The latter may have been the communal woods where the people of the village of Földvár used to pasture their pigs at the time. On old maps, an oak, ash, elm gallery forest stretched along the Borza Stream, which fits this description well.

The akıncı and sipahi cavalry were sent by Grand Vizier İbrahim Pasha to the western side of the plain, so that when the fighting broke out they could flank the Christian troops at the right time. Presumably part of the consideration was to divide attention, and also for the akıncıs to do reconnaissance work. In the cover of the low Sátorhely Ridge, in the west of the Borza Valley, they tried to move northwards with as little conspicuousness as possible. But the Hungarian command noticed them, for the tips of the riders' spears gleamed in the cover of the low ridge.²⁷ Sometime before 3 pm, Tomori sent out against them – to reconnoitre and possibly force them to return – a cavalry regiment led by Gáspár Ráskai, originally organised to protect the king. This operation was unsuccessful, as they were unable to disperse and repel the numerically superior akıncıs and sipahis, or to protect the king. Events did not seem to have proceeded as originally planned. So the question was: how did the armies adapt to the situation?

A dispute arose in the high command of the Hungarian army around 3 pm. Contrary to expectations the enemy showed no sign of wanting to attack. Clearly, if it were up to the Ottomans, there would be no more fighting that day. Since the original plan was to stop and then defeat the Rumelian army, which was advancing and would surely attack, this behaviour forced the Hungarian command to make a decision. Postponing the battle until the next day would have meant that the entire Ottoman army had to be engaged at once, which would have deprived them of any chance for victory.

Nevertheless, some suggested waiting until next day and returning to the camp like the Ottomans:

> There were some of the leaders who, tired of the long wait, thought that we should pull back and return to camp. When the monk²⁸ heard of this,

---

26   Antonio Giovanni da Burgio, "Antonio Giovanni da Burgio pápai követ levele Jacopo Sadoleto pápai titkárnak Pozsony, 1526. szeptember 5. (részlet)," [Letter from the papal nuncio Antonio Giovanni da Burgio to the papal secretary Jacopo Sadoleto Pozsony, 5 September 1526] in *Örök Mohács*, eds. B. Szabó et al., pp. 131–132.

27   "Thus, anxious and waiting, as the sun was already setting in the west, in the valley that lay to our right, under the hills, an enemy column appeared, silently marching, betrayed only by the spearheads." See Brodarics, "Igaz történet," [A true account] in *Örök Mohács*, eds. B. Szabó et al., p. 318.

28   Pál Tomori, Archbishop of Kalocsa, Co-commander-in-chief.

he and his companion[29] immediately rushed to the king, warning him that the battle must in no way be postponed, that it was less dangerous to fight now with a part of the enemy's troops than tomorrow with the whole army, furthermore the victory was not in doubt.[30]

So Tomori forced the king to make up his mind: attack now or the chance of victory would disappear tomorrow. However, by the time this decision was made, it was 4 pm. The Ottomans had reinforced their positions and the salaried household troops, as well as the Anatolian army were closing in. According to a Dalmatian eyewitness named Zaratino,[31] the Ottomans were positioned about an Italian mile from the Hungarian army, a distance the attackers had to cover.

Opposite the Hungarian army, along the Borza Stream, behind the Sátorhely Ridge, they could observe the gaps cut in the gallery forest that grew there, where the main crossings were. These gullies, or narrow passages, were also mentioned by Brodarics, who wrote: "... [the enemy] stayed behind those hills, leaving us in doubt as to whether he intended to lure or not our men into those narrow passages..."[32] The Christian cavalry began to prepare for battle, following the royal decision, which also triggered the mobilisation of the Rumelian army. Behind the low hill indicated by Velius,[33] which obscured the Ottoman camp, Ottoman cavalry troops that had not been seen before appeared in greater numbers.

The first wave of the Hungarian army's attack was directed here, and it seemed to have succeeded, because the Rumelian light cavalry (either since the Ottomans were playing tricks or they had been defeated) fled. So the second wave of the right flank was launched, another heavy cavalry attack in which Brodarics himself took part. The right flank attack finally collapsed, not so much because of the Ottoman guns as because of the devastating handgun fire of the janissaries. It is possible that there was also a problem with the discipline of the Hungarian army, since the text refers to the looting of soldiers.

The descriptions seem to indicate that the *tabur cengi* (or wagenburg) mode of combat and the tactics proposed by Bali Bey in the Ottoman war council were

---

29 György Szapolyai, Count of Szepes, Co-commander-in-chief.
30 Brodarics, "Igaz történet," [A true account] in *Örök Mohács*, eds. B. Szabó et al., p. 319.
31 Agostino da Mula, "Agostino da Mula jelentése Udine, 1526. szeptember 15. (átirat)," [Account of Agostino da Mula Udine, 15 September 1526 (transcript)] in *Örök Mohács*, eds. B. Szabó et al., pp. 150–152.
32 Brodarics, "Igaz történet," [A true account] in *Örök Mohács*, eds. B. Szabó et al., p. 318.
33 Velius's description, quoted above, is consistent with the topographical and environmental reconstruction, and confirms that the "hill", where the village of Földvár stood, lay between the two armies, and 'slightly elevated', concealing them from each other. A separate land feature was the terrain stairway, an other hill, or 'Mount' at the bottom of which the Ottoman camp was pitched.

effective. The attacking Christian cavalry, which initially appeared successful, was eventually surrounded from all directions and suffered heavy losses. The king took part in this charge, but seems to have been rescued early enough from this lost fight. In the meantime, Bali Bey's select cavalry had bypassed the Hungarian army and ransacked the Hungarian camp, slaughtering the 2000 soldiers and additional civilian staff there. According to Peçevi, these akıncıs and sipahis then somehow joined the fight against the main army, attacking the Christian army from the north.[34]

In the meantime, the sultan arrived from Karasica Stream with the Anatolian and the salaried household troops, and took their places on the battlefield. Kemalpaşazade wrote: "Meanwhile, the innumerable troops of horsemen and footmen, servants and freemen, which accompanied the person of the world-conquering sultan and formed the surroundings of his court, the refuge of the world, had appeared."[35] The palace troops with the sultan were placed in the centre, the Anatolian army, led by Behram Pasha and composed mainly of sipahi cavalry, on the right flank. It was against the latter that another attack was launched, in which the king took part. According to eyewitnesses, this attack – unlike that on the right flank which was only a cavalry charge – was joined by infantry units.

The scenario here is somewhat similar to the one on the other wing. The Anatolian cavalry, positioned near the marshes of the Vizslak Meadow, took to flight when the attack came. We do not know whether they tricked into running away or were actually beaten. The Christian army that followed the Ottoman cavalry went against the Ottoman guns and arquebusiers set up according to the *tabur cengi* system.[36]

Here, unlike on the left wing, the Ottoman artillery corps (*topçı*) and the janissaries did effective work and wrought great havoc among the attackers, as a Christian source testifies:[37]

> Upon the mighty sultan's supreme command, the handgun-bearing janissary warriors turned on the furious enemy of tiger nature, and in a minute sent not a hundred but thousands of them to hell.[38]

---

34 Peçevi, "Krónika," [Chronicle] in *Örök Mohács*, eds. B. Szabó et al., pp. 463–477.
35 Kemálpasazáde, "Mohácsnáme," [Mohácsname] in *Örök Mohács*, eds. B. Szabó et al., p. 333.
36 "Az 1526. évi hadinapló" [The Ottoman campaign diary of 1526] in *Örök Mohács*, eds. B. Szabó et al., pp. 235–257.
37 "Egy cseh úr levele a Santa Clara kolostor főnöknőjéhez 1526. november," [Letter from a Czech nobleman to the Superior of the Convent of Santa Clara, November 1526] in *Örök Mohács*, eds. B. Szabó et al., pp. 207–216.
38 Kemálpasazáde, "Mohácsnáme," [Mohácsname] in *Örök Mohács*, eds. B. Szabó et al., p. 334.

It is not certain, however, that the order of battle in the centre was entirely in the usual order. It is an anomaly that a small group of attackers somehow reached the household cavalry defending the sultan, and only the solaks were able to repel the attack on the sultan's life.

> Three drunken heavy cavalrymen of Ahriman's stature from the infidel army, with shining spears in their hands, broke through the rows in front of them, as a zigzagging thunderbolt is wont to cleave a cloud, and rose in a terrifying manner before the sun of the caliphate's sky. However, the lion-toothed warriors surrounding the person of the padishah, waiting for battle, wounded the legs of the horses of the foolhardy and blinded the bastion-like warriors, and threw them to the ground, where they slashed them with their swords.[39]

In any case, this Christian attack also collapsed, the rear rows of the infantry being the first to flee,[40] and then some of the cavalry followed suit.

The front between the two armies began to ripple, the smoke of gun blanketing the battlefield. Some groups of the Christian cavalry, in order to build up strength, retreated to the paleo-river valley ('the Great Ditch') near the great marsh on the Danube, and then again and again attacked the enemy, but Ottoman superiority soon became overwhelming:

> The king's army, greatly disconcerted by what had been said, and almost in flight, nevertheless fought on for a long time, no longer in the wide plain, but just in front of the guns, which were so close to us that there were not even ten steps between us; at last, when not only fear but gunsmoke filled the air, and it was no longer possible to see, the greater part of the army was forced to retire into the valley which lay beside that marshy water, while those who remained behind still fought valiantly in front of the guns.[41]

The young king also took part in this fight, and sources say that his horse was wounded, but not himself.

---

39 Kemálpasazáde, "Mohácsnáme," [Mohácsname] in *Örök Mohács*, eds. B. Szabó et al., p. 334.
40 "Egy cseh úr levele," [Letter from a Czech nobleman] in *Örök Mohács*, eds. B. Szabó et al., pp. 207–216.
41 Brodarics, "Igaz történet," [A true account] in *Örök Mohács*, eds. B. Szabó et al., p. 320.

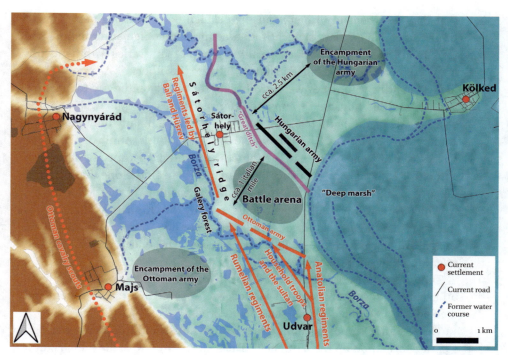

FIGURE 5.2   The site of the Battle of Mohács. Edited by Norbert Pap, designed by Péter Gyenizse.
SOURCE: BACKGROUND EUDEM AND OPENSTREETMAP.

The cavalry managed to hold out for a while longer with heavy losses, but after the hope of victory was lost, the survivors fled: "By the way, when those who had retreated into the valley returned to take up the fight, the force and smoke of the guns seemed unbearable, and the greater part of the army having fled, they were also forced to flee."[42]

However, the situation of the infantry became much worse. Only some of the Hungarian soldiers who wore light coat of mail and were familiar with the local conditions had a chance to escape and were scattered. The foreign infantrymen remained in a closed formation. As they were partially men-at-arms and unfamiliar with the local conditions, they found themselves in a hopeless situation.

The thousands of Czech, Moravian, Polish and German infantrymen resisted the sipahis surrounding them on the battlefield for a while longer. However, they were eventually broken up by the handgun fire of the janissary regiment

---

42   Brodarics, "Igaz történet," [A true account] in *Örök Mohács*, eds. B. Szabó et al., p. 320.

that had been sent in to help, and then slaughtered: "Although six to eight thousand Czech and landsknecht retreated into a rectangular formation, and were not broken by the Turkish cavalry, a group of janissaries with handguns attacked them and were killed instantly, as were the others."[43] As troops of the highest fighting value, they were involved in the attack on the Anatolian army and the salaried houshold troops, so their place must be somewhere on the eastern side of the battlefield. Few of them escaped, mainly only those who could mount on horses. This is how one of their captains, Annibale Cartagine da Este di Padovana (known in the sources as 'Cyprian') escaped by getting on a horse. It is thought that this regiment may have been the one that held out longest, lasting until about half past six in the evening, or a little bit longer, by which time the crowd had been massacred by the Ottoman soldiers. It was then that darkness began to descend, and according to several participants, then also a storm with heavy downpours arrived. This ended the fighting and offered a chance for those fleeing.

The king was no longer on the battlefield, but tried to reach safety with other runaways, but as we know he failed, was involved in a horse accident and died before nightfall.[44] He perished before 7 pm.

The Ottoman troops, including the salaried household troops, remained in a closed formation on the battlefield. The sultan stayed with his soldiers until midnight, awaiting a possible wave of attack.[45] The visibility was so bad due to the darkness and the heavy rain that it was not clear whether the battle was over or whether they should expect another charge. Meanwhile, in the northern part of the Mohács Plain, the akıncıs were hunting down small and large groups of fleeing enemies.[46]

5 The Casualties of the Fights

By the end of the day, the battlefield was littered with dead and seriously wounded. A Czech source gave an account of the battlefield: "The Turks cut off

---

43 Mula, "Agostino da Mula jelentése," [Account of Agostino da Mula] in *Örök Mohács*, eds. B. Szabó et al., p. 151.
44 The circumstances of the king's flight and death are examined in a separate chapter. See Chapter Ten.
45 Kemálpasazáde, "Mohácsnáme," [Mohácsname] in *Örök Mohács*, eds. B. Szabó et al., pp. 326–338.
46 Brodarics, "Igaz történet," [A true account] in *Örök Mohács*, eds. B.Szabó et al., pp. 301–325.

the heads of even those who had already died."[47] An Ottoman Turkish source also report: "In the place where the river of battle flowed, the heads of men lay scattered like pebbles on the banks of the river. The surface of the plain, the tops of the mounds, the tops of the heights and the openings of the valleys were covered with mutilated corpses to the end."[48] The clashes resulted in huge loss of life.

From the casualty lists it can be concluded that the infantry suffered the highest proportion of casualties within the Christian army. Both Brodarics[49] and Piotr Tomicki[50] (the Archbishop of Krakow and the Vice-chancellor of Poland) and a list of casualties also from 1526[51] wrote about this. Their total losses must have been around 10,000–12,000, and among the survivors we have to suspect more Hungarian soldiers, although there are known German and Czech survivors. All the artillery was lost and it is likely that the mortality rate among the artillery corps was also high.

The total cavalry casualties were around 4000–6000, but the largest proportion of these were suffered by the heavy cavalry. The light cavalry had a better chance of survival. In contrast, there are no known wounded among the boatmen of the Hungarian flotilla.

While credible information on Christian losses is easier to obtain and seems realistic, data on Ottoman losses is harder to find (Table 5.2). According to the entry of 29 August in the Ottoman campaign diary, 50,000 infantrymen and 4000 cavalrymen of the Christian army were killed, while only 50–60 Muslim warriors were martyred, i.e. became şehid. In his account, Celalzade Mustafa wrote of 150 dead Muslim warriors. A recent Ottoman casualty list cites 300

---

47   "Egy cseh úr levele," [Letter from a Czech nobleman] in *Örök Mohács,* eds. B. Szabó et al., p. 210.
48   Kemálpasazáde, "Mohácsnáme," [Mohácsname] in *Örök Mohács,* eds. B. Szabó et al., p. 336.
49   Brodarics István, "Brodarics István, Magyarország kancellárja Piotr Tomicki alkancellár püspöknek és Andrzej Krzycki przemyśli püspöknek 1526. szeptember 6.," [István Brodarics, Chancellor of Hungary to Vice-chancellor, Bishop Piotr Tomicki and Andrzej Krzycki Bishop of Przemyśl, Pozsony 6 September 1526] in *Örök Mohács,* eds. B. Szabó et al., pp. 137–138.
50   "A magyar hadsereg veszteséglistája Piotr Tomicki krakkói érsek és lengyel alkancellár iratai között 1526. október," [The Hungarian army's casualty list in the documents of Piotr Tomicki Archbishop of Krakow and Vice-Chancellor of Poland] in *Örök Mohács,* eds. B. Szabó et al., pp. 185–188.
51   "A mohácsi csatára vonatkozó veszteséglista, 1526," [The list of casualties relating to the the Battle of Mohács, 1526] in *Örök Mohács,* eds. B. Szabó et al., pp. 218–220.

TABLE 5.2 Ottoman loss data in primary and memorial sources. Edited by Norbert Pap

Year	Primary source	Ottoman death toll
1526	Ottoman campaign diary	50–60 people
1526	Loss data in the Bible of Budaszentlőrinc	300 persons
1526	Agostino da Mula	"In the battle, the Turks did not suffer significant losses."
Year	Memory source	Ottoman death toll
1526–1534	Kemalpaşazade	Many dead on the battlefield, but mainly the Christian
1550s	Lutfi Pasha	"a great many Muslims have been slaughtered"[a]
Around 1551	Matrakçı Nasuh	"The days of the lives of many a warrior of faith have been eclipsed, who have found themselves in the company of the martyrs and the company of the blessed."[b]
1560s	Celalzade Mustafa	150 persons
1571	Joachimus Cureus	"The Turks hardly got a scratch."[c]
1660s	Evliya Çelebi	40,000 Muslim martyrs.[d] The bodies of 40,000 martyred Muslims "… a place worth visiting. Many hundreds of pious Muslims have seen and testified that on Friday nights and on the nights of the Qadr, the Berat and the Miraj … many times the light shone upon these forty thousand martyrs."

a Lutfi, "Az Oszmán-ház története," [History of the Ottoman House] in Örök Mohács, eds B. Szabó et al., p. 407.
b Erkan, *Matrâkçi Nasûh'un Süleymân-nâmesi*, p. 116.
c Joachimus Cureus, "Gentis Silesiae Annales 1571," in *Örök Mohács*, eds. B. Szabó et al., p. 424.
d Norbert Pap, Pál Fodor, Máté Kitanics, Tamás Morva, Gábor Szalai, and Péter Gyenizse, "A mohácsi Törökdomb," [The Törökdomb of Mohács] *Történelmi Szemle* 60 (2018), no. 2, pp. 325–345.

Muslim dead.[52] Agostino da Mula, however, claimed that *"in the battle, the Turks did not suffer significant losses."*[53]

52 Pál Fodor and András Mércz, "'Mi is veszett Mohácsnál?' Oszmán-török veszteséglista az 1526. évi hadjáratról," [What is lost at Mohács? What happened at Mohács] *Történelmi Szemle* 65 (2023), no. 1, forthcoming.
53 Mula, "Agostino da Mula jelentése," [Account of Agostino da Mula] in *Örök Mohács,* eds. B. Szabó et al., pp. 163–165.

THE BATTLE AND ITS AFTERMATH

Interestingly, there is no mention of the burial of Muslim bodies in the Ottoman campaign diary. One may assume that the emphasis on the greatness of the victory did not allow any mention of their own losses. A realistic assessment of the situation is not helped by the fact that contemporary Ottoman sources tend to exaggerate Christian losses while minimising their own. For sources whose function is propagandistic, this is understandable and justifiable. In the Ottoman campaign diary, the sultan's victory reports or historical works written for the public, this intention may well have been realised.

However, the list of Ottoman losses in 1526 published by Fodor and Mércz does not align with the latter list. The text inscribed in the Bible, which was taken from the monastery of Budaszentlőrinc as booty by the Ottomans in 1526, was written down after the Ottoman army had left Hungary, probably in October, in one of the camps, based on the authors' assessment. The owner of the text (the authors suspect that it may have been the chief defterdar) made his own notes on a blank page of the Bible, copying details that were important to the Ottoman state and not intended for public interest. The simple account is devoid of propagandistic elements and – according to the authors – contains some very plausible elements. Not only does it include battlefield casualties, but even gives detailed casualty figures on a case-by-case basis. According to the list, total Ottoman casualties during the campaign were 6580.[54] The analysis also shows that the Ottoman army's casualties from the list (roughly 7000[55] dead out of an army of about 80,000, ca. 8–10%) correspond well with the usual casualty rates of battles and campaigns of the period: the record complies with the typical casualty rate of the victorious armies of the time.

However, Fodor and Mércz considered the 300 dead to be unrealistic, and believed that Ottoman losses must have exceeded this figure. The problem that arises is that if all other figures seem to be credible, and the overall campaign-wide casualty rate is realistic, and the propagandistic purpose of the text written on the blank page of the Bible is ruled out, what is the basis for claiming that the figure is inaccurate? Is this possible? Under what circumstances can the really low loss figure of 300 for Mohács be validated? Let's examine the events of the battle to see if there is any evidence of higher Ottoman casualty rate.

Among the events of the battle described above, the Ottoman cavalry dodged the attacking Hungarian army, seemed to run away, and then the attackers were

---

54 Adding up all the items on the list, the loss is less than the total amount given, only 6186 people. The question is, what could be the reason for the difference? We believe the mortality figures given at each station refer to the soldiers buried. Those who were not buried – they were "missing in action" – make up the rest of the losses.

55 Casualty figures for the entire campaign.

shot to death by the janissaries' volleys and the Ottoman centre's guns. In the endgame, the 6000–7000 Western infantrymen massed for defence are broken by janissary handgun fire and slaughtered. The events described do not, on the whole, justify a particularly large number of Ottoman victims.

But there is little mention of the wounded in the sources. The wounded on the Christian side were soon executed by the victors, while some of those on the Ottoman side had a chance to recover. When all these factors are taken into account, the total number of 300 Ottoman dead buried on the battlefield and a few thousand wounded no longer seems unrealistic. We know from the casualty list that the Ottoman army reached Buda in about ten days, but lost 100 men a day for no particular reason, as there was no fighting. Even if not all of the 1000 dead were wounded in the battle, the vast majority of them must have been. In this calculation, however, we estimate that the Ottoman losses in the Battle of Mohács may have been as high as 1200–1500. But there is another important factor that also needs to be taken into account!

The Ottoman casualty figures may have been increased to an unknown extent by the fact that the identity of the bodies was not always obvious during the burial at Mohács. The battle was fought on Wednesday, and the burial of the Christians took place largely on Sunday. The corpses were collected and their valuables taken in the 3–4 days available. In places where the dead lay mixed up and the bodies had suffered severe injuries and mutilations, it was unlikely to unambiguously distinguish Ottoman soldiers from Westerners. In Islamic law, there is also a rule for this eventuality:[56] the dead of uncertain religious background are not allowed to be buried with Muslims.

We can assume that the burial was carried out with Christian prisoners.[57] For them it made no difference who was Christian and who was Muslim. Thus some of the soldiers of the Ottoman army could have been buried in the mass graves with the Western soldiers, especially if they were Christians themselves.[58] This may be indicated by the fact that there is a batch of 300 in the casualty list that is not precisely identified, linked to exact place and occasion. They are the group of those "missing in action". We suspect that a small number of these

---

56 Ahmed al-Dawoody, "Management of the dead from the Islamic law and international humanitarian law perspectives: Considerations for humanitarian forensics," *International Review of the Red Cross* 99 (2017), no. 2, pp. 759–784.

57 Some of the Christian war prisoners were executed on 31 August, so the funerals were not carried out by them, but by those who were executed later, on 4 September.

58 If the few projectiles identified in the Sátorhely III mass grave were not found from the surface and afterwards, then the above-mentioned may explain how small calibre projectiles, not from janissary weapons, could have been found: they were from Western weapons and the victims were obviously members of the Ottoman army.

300 died at Mohács, but they have not been identified. Their bodies may have been dumped in the swamps, the Danube, or in few cases (exceptionally) in the mass graves. The total number of Ottoman soldiers who died in connection with the Battle of Mohács could therefore be around 1200 and 1500. Compared with the 14,000–18,000 dead on the Christian side, this is a difference of eleven to fifteen times the number of the Christian side, and cannot be considered unrealistically low.[59] Comparing the Battle of Mohács with other contemporary requires caution. In fact, there is only one battle of the period that is worth comparing on the basis of the unequal technical and military conditions at Mohács, and that is the Battle of Pavia in 1525. The technological difference between the two sides was particularly striking in that case. The training and equipment of the Spanish infantrymen can be compared to that of the janissaries, while that of the French heavy cavalry to that of the Hungarians. The result at Pavia was at least 8000 French soldiers killed.

The "second Battle of Mohács", i.e. the Battle of Nagyharsány (1687), which is much better documented than the one of 1526, is suitable for comparison due to its similarity in size and setting. The basic figures are similar: the combined numbers of the two sides are around 110,000 in each case. It was fought under very similar environmental conditions, with many of the losing side's troops, especially infantrymen, drowned in water and marshland. It ended in a Christian victory, with the victors suffering similarly low casualties, or even fewer. According to the Ottoman campaign diary, the combined deaths and wounded among the Christian coalition forces were only 600–700, while Ottoman casualties are estimated at over 10,000.

In the battle of 1526, most of the Ottoman casualties occurred in the endgame, during the slaughter of the infantry. The janissaries with handguns were highly instrumental in disrupting the order of battle. However, this was the only documented case of Ottoman troops coming within firing range of Westerner arquebusiers, and foreign infantrymen desperately defending themselves, with apparent Ottoman casualties. This is the place and situation where further Ottoman casualties, which may not have been recorded, can be presumed. The Ottoman death toll in this case could have been in the hundreds.

We must not forget the following: one of the characteristics of the battle is that it took place at a turning point in military technology. The use of large numbers of disciplined and well-trained janissaries, armed with effective handguns, lined up behind each other and firing volleys, and the use of large numbers of guns against a Christian army fighting with obsolete tactics, with much

---

59   Journal des campagnes du duc Charles V de Lorraine, éd. Ferenc Tóth, Paris, Honoré Champion, 2017. p. 448.

weaker artillery, less effective and fewer arquebuses, but with death-defying courage, did not justify heavy Ottoman casualties, but could have caused heavy Christian casualties. The greater loss rate of the Ottomans at Mohács is mainly due to the cavalry, especially the household cavalry, which intercepted the Christian left wing's charge against the sultan. It is certain that the sipahis and the akıncıs also suffered losses. The janissaries, on the other hand, are not at all likely to have suffered significant battlefield casualties, but rather may have suffered more during the campaign, at fortress sieges and raids.

The anomalies in the Ottoman army casualty figures are worth contextualising in the sources. Did they really fight the battle with so few casualties, or is there some kind of propagandistic effort at work here? It is also worth reviewing the sources below from the perspective of the context in which they were published.

Contemporary sources report very low death rates. Any reported figure between 50 and 300 means that the sultan's army was strong and the Hungarian army could only "scratch" it.

As we move away from the event in time, we find more data on the small Ottoman losses. At the same time, however, the losses specifically perceived in some of the Ottoman sources become more significant until we reach the description of the 40,000 martyrs mentioned by Evliya Çelebi at the "pilgrimage site" of Mohács, which recalls the battle. The significance of the higher casualty figures changes, the context of the data changes. The aim is no longer to show the strength of the sultan's army, or perhaps to exaggerate it, but to emphasize how many martyrs, or *şehid*, sacrificed their lives to conquer the territory. Their role is transformed from a casualty record into an argument for retaining the conquered territory

The Ottoman losses throughout the campaign – including the bloody castle sieges[60] – are well known. We have quite accurate data on the household military. The household cavalry must have lost at least 1000 men, while the janissaries must have lost 2000–3000 men during the "Buda campaign" of 1526. Obviously, some of the sipahis and azebs also fell, but we do not have any direct information on them. The remaining 3000–4000 are distributed in unknown proportion among the other formations of the Ottoman army. All in all, the total Ottoman death toll could reach the 7000 mentioned, of whom only a small proportion fell on 29 August.

---

60   The capture of Pétervárad (Petrovaradin) was the main casualty, with around 3000 Ottoman fighters killed, some of them janissaries.

6 The "Funeral"

The fate of the dead lying on the battlefield was usually to be buried in mass graves or sunk in the marshes of the floodplain. According to local tradition, the heroes of Mohács were buried by Dorottya Kanizsai, a noblewoman from Siklós, with her 400 paid workers. Miklós Istvánffy, the historian, remembered it like this:

> As the number of the fallen was so great, however, that not only the field but also the air[61] seemed to be spoiled and contaminated by the smell of the corpses,[62] and after the retreat of the enemy, such a great mass of dogs flocked there to devour them that the travellers say, and those who passed by could only go there with the risk of their lives, therefore Kanizsai Dóra, the widow of Imre Perényi, that pious woman, pitying the Christians who had fallen valiantly in defence of their country, hired four hundred men at her own expense to bury the bodies lying about, digging huge pits, lest wild beasts, birds and dogs should tear them to pieces and devour them.[63]

The story that links the burial of heroes to a symbolic female role raises a few questions. Miklós Istvánffy, a prominent Hungarian humanist, recorded this local tradition almost a century later. A close examination of the text reveals the following.

The author was familiar with the Greek and Latin texts that call attention to the need to eliminate the uncleanness (e.g. miasma) caused by dead bodies by burying them. As a humanist he also took the opportunity to polish his antiquarian literacy by rewriting the story of the burial of the Mohács dead with well-known and widespread topos.

The inclusion of the female figure in Istvánffy's story, written some 100 years after the battle, also seems to be a topos. The figures of women hurrying to find, weep for and bury their fallen relatives after the battles are well-known in

---

61   It is from the antiquity that contagious diseases are attributed to contaminated, miasmatic air. Robert Parker, *Miasma: Pollution and Purification in Early Greek Religion* (Oxford: Clarendon Press, 1983).

62   Miklós Isthvánffy had an estimated library of 3000 items. According to István Monok's analysis, the basic works mentioned here were to be found in his library. István Monok, *A művelt arisztokrata. A magyarországi főnemesség olvasmányai a 16–17. században* [The literary aristocrats of Hungary in the 16th–17th centuries.] (Budapest: Kossuth Kiadó, 2012).

63   Miklós Isthvánffy, "A magyarok történetéből. 1622 (részlet)," [From the History of the Hungarians. 1622 (excerpt)] in Örök Mohács, eds. B. Szabó et al., p. 460.

Balkan heroic songs about the battles against the Ottomans. The most famous of these is the case of the *Kosovar girl* from the Battle of Kosovo Polje (1389).[64] The fact that Dorottya Kanizsai married twice to the *nádor* (*palatinus*) of Hungary, the first man after the king, made her a symbolic figure: her prominent public status made her suitable to appear as the 'mother of the nation'. However, her personal involvement in the post-battle funerals and the organisation of Christian commemorations cannot be ruled out, as she had personal involvement (her foster son, Ferenc Perényi, died there) and her estate in Siklós was close to the battlefield (20 km). Apparently she had both the opportunity and the reason to visit the battlefield after the Ottomans had left, but the role attributed to her is exaggerated. However, her person and her situation in life made him particularly suited to playing a symbolic historical role, enriched by familiar topos.

The reference in the text to Dorottya Kanizsai burying the dead so that *wild animals, birds* and *dogs* would not devour them is revealing. This topos appears frequently in ancient Greek and Roman texts, as the failure to bury the deceased in this way made it impossible for them to continue their "lives" in the underworld. The most quoted and widely known reference for this is the *Iliad*. In the text of the epic, there are more than a dozen references to *dogs* feasting on the dead of battles and to *birds* eating carrion. In Sophocles' *Antigone*, the expected fate of an unburied corpse is to be eaten by scavenging *birds*. The formula in the form used by Istvánffy also appears in early Christian authors. Athenagoras deals with the fate of those lying dead on the battlefield who, because of their unburied state, became the food of *fish, beasts or birds*. According to the Christian view, even unknown persons should not be left unburied as food for beasts and birds, for they must be seen as the image and work of God.

The passage from Istvánffy's story – on the battlefield, wild dogs feast on the corpses of the fallen and you can not go past them because they are dangerous – is also a familiar medieval topos. Its origin dates back to the Battle of Hundsfeld (1109) between the Germans and the Poles.[65]

---

64 Two poems were born in the context of the Battle of Kosovo Polje (1389), whose heroes are women who are searching for their loved ones, mourning on the battlefield. "A koszovói lányka," [The girl from Kosovo] in *Jugoszláv költők antológiája*, ed. Sztoján Vujicsics D. (Budapest: Móra Kiadó, 1963), pp. 76–80., and see more "A Jugovićok anyja," [The mother of Jugović] in *Jugoszláv költők* ed. Vujicsics, pp. 81–83.

65 The Polish chronicler Wincenty Kadłubek (ca. 1150–1223) wrote of this battlefield that the dogs, which devoured many corpses, went wild, so that no one dared to go there. See *S. Orgelbranda Encyklopedia Powszechna* XII. (Warsaw: Wydawnictwie Towarzystwa Akcyjnego Odlewni Czcionek i Drukarni S. Orgelbranda Synów, 1902), p. 406.

It is interesting to note that the Ottoman Turkish traveller Evliya Çelebi also stressed the importance of protecting the bodies of Muslim martyrs from the ravages of *wild animals* when burying them on the Törökdomb (Hünkâr tepesi or Turkish Hill) in Mohács. Muslim culture is partly an heir to antiquity. Evliya himself claims to have read Greek and to have studied Hellenistic culture (which is unlikely), but he could also read Ottoman translations. It seems that his text also reflects a turn of phrase of ancient Greek considerations:

> There are ditches on the four sides of this pilgrimage site, which were dug on the order of the patron of pious foundations, Hasan Pasha, governor-general of Buda, saying 'The martyrs buried here are not to be gnawed at by animals.'[66]

There is therefore no primary source for the burial by Dorottya Kanizsai, but we do have evidence that some of the dead of the battle were buried by the local population. An example is the first temporary burial of the king, who was buried by local peasants. A body found in the cemetery of the medieval village at Újistálló Manor, near Sátorhely, and some of the dead found in the cemetery of the medieval settlement of Lajmér,[67] which were linked to the Battle of Mohács in 1526, may also be assumed to have been buried by the locals rather than the Ottomans. But what do contemporary sources say about the post-battle burials?

Sources on the Christian army hardly mention this issue, while Ottoman reports provide information on it. According to the Ottoman campaign diary, the dead were collected by the Ottoman army, and in such a way that on 1 of September the defterdar of Rumelia was ordered to organise a collection of the fallen warriors. The next day, the *grand vizier*, the *kethüda* and the *defterdar* together carried out the inspection of the dead. The diary reduced the number of fallen Christians from the previous entry (previously the total number of victims had been 54,000), and now mentions only 4,000 "armoured" and 20,000 "infantrymen." Of the 4,000 armoured – if the figure is correct – how many were cavalrymen and how many infantrymen? We think that some of them must have been infantry men-at-arms, since we estimate that the heavy

---

66   *Evliyâ Çelebi Seyahatnâmesi*, VI. Kitap, pp. 112–113. Imre Karácson, *Evlia Cselebi török világutazó magyarországi utazásai 1660–1664* [Turkish traveller Evliya Çelebi's travels] (Budapest: Gondolat Könyvkiadó, 1985), p. 192, p. 194.
67   If the three dead in one of the graves excavated in the Lajmér cemetery are indeed connected to the Battle of Mohács.

cavalry could not have numbered much more than 2,000–2,500, and there were some who survived the battle.

No data on the method of enumeration has preserved. It is possible that they counted by person, but it is also possible that they estimated the number of dead in each mass grave and then calculated the total. However, as many died by sinking into the marshes or drowning in the Danube, any figure is a rough estimate and approximation. It is also questionable whether the Ottoman officials distinguished between the bodies of the military and those of civilians who had passed with the army, or of the surrounding population. We do not really know that either. However, the data provided by Christian sources, especially by Chancellor Brodarics, certainly refers only to the military. The difference between the two figures, i.e. the 24,000 casualties from the Ottoman campaign diary and the 14,000–18,000 casualties[68] from the Christian sources of 1526, may be explained by this, in addition to methodological differences.

An important and controversial question is what justified the Ottoman army to collect the bodies of the enemy and, as a consequence, to bury the dead. It is thought that these factors may have been a combination of the quantification of a large-scale victory, the systematic collection of booty, and religious commandment.

The first aspect is the easiest to answer. In order to estimate the extent of the victory and the strength of the enemy troops still opposing, it was necessary to take an account of the dead, and of course also of the prisoners of war. There were, therefore, rational, war management reasons for this.

The other two questions, however, were influenced not only by practical considerations but also by the *şeriat*. The Islamic religious commandment to bury those killed in battle dates back to the time of the Prophet Muhammad. Muslims are obliged to bury not only their combatants but also their enemies. During the Prophet's lifetime, there were several battles (Battle of Badr in 624, Battle of Uhud in 625) in which Muslim and non-Muslim alike were victims of fighting. The practice of these battles later became a guide and a reference point for posterity.[69]

The question is, of course, how strictly did Süleyman's army respect the rules of religious law in 1526? It is not possible to answer from the current source base. However, if we look at the literature on the life of Süleyman[70] and the Süleymanic state, we can read that the young ruler, who was raised in 1520,

---

68   10,000–12,000 infantrymen and 4,000–6,000 cavalrymen.
69   al-Dawoody, "Management of the dead,", pp. 759–784.
70   M. Tayyib Gökbilgin, *Nagy Szulejmán szultán* [Sultan Süleyman the Magnificent] (Budapest: Napkút Kiadó, 2020).

made great efforts to consolidate the imperial order based on Islamic law. He sought to create a predictable state, to break down the arrogance of the elite and to discipline the army. The previous year (1525), he had crushed a janissary rebellion. The Ottoman sources point out that during the 1526 campaign the army showed exemplary discipline, not even disturbing the security of the Christian population in the marching area. There were only a few occasions when the emperor had to intervene.[71] A few minor indications from written sources suggest that the *şeriat* was at least taken into account. One such small indication is the release of old female prisoners after the battle.[72]

It cannot be denied that there were practices in the Ottoman army that are difficult to reconcile with Islam. One such practice is the practice of head cutting and collecting, which is of Central Asian origin, a practice that the Ottomans have left over from pre-Islamic times. Arab Islam does not support mutilation, which is a form of humiliation and therefore forbidden. This is an example of Islamic flexibility, of which there are many others. A study of the reconciliation of Islamic *şeriat* and Mongol-Turkish *yasa* suggests that a deeply ingrained custom among the Turkic peoples of Central Asia (such as drinking alcohol) was easily overlooked or a good explanation was found by jurists to help overlook or legitimise the violation of the rule.[73] The Ottomans' own customary law, the *kanun*, which was dominant in daily practice, supported head cutting and collecting. There are examples in the life of Sultan Süleyman of anomalies in the very law of war (especially when he was angry), and he prioritised the *kanun* over the *şeriat*. On the whole, the Ottomans seem to have followed the rules of religious law in their own way, although the legitimacy of some of their old customs was questioned and customary law sometimes superseded Muslim law in the field of warfare.

According to the prophetic tradition, Muslims were usually buried individually, but if necessity dictated, they could also be buried in mass graves. Muslims who died for the cause of Islam are called martyrs, or şehids. They did not have to be washed, but were buried in the grave as they died, covered in blood. However, it was important that the funeral should take place as quickly as possible, preferably within a day. The latter was confirmed by the account of a captured Hungarian nobleman, the Royal Chamberlain Miklós Herczeg,

---

71 Breaking the rules was punishable: death penalty.
72 The old women were of no material benefit, nor were they a threat to the army.
73 István Vásáry, "Yāsā and Sharī'a. Islamic Attitudes towards the Mongol Law in the Turco-Mongolian World (from the Golden Horde to Timur's Time)," in *Violence in Islamic Thought from the Mongols to European Imperialism Gleave,* eds. Robert Gleave and István Kristó-Nagy (Edinburgh: Edinburgh University Press, 2007).

who, after his release, gave an eyewitness account of the days after the battle. It was from him that Brodarics learned the circumstances of the execution on 31 August, and also that the Ottomans had buried their fallen soldiers before the Christian prisoners of war were executed.[74] This suggests that the date of the burial of the Muslim dead was 30 August (Thursday), which means that, according to Muslim custom, they were indeed buried within a day.

For non-Muslims, the basic rule is to ensure that their family can bury the deceased. However, if this is not possible, it is the duty of the Muslims to carry out the burial. It is not by chance that one of the *hadiths* on this subject is an Andalusian source of law, since regular clashes between Muslims and Christians were part of everyday life in the Iberian Peninsula. The Andalusian jurist Ibn Ḥazm (d. 1064) argued strongly for the burial of the dead on both sides. He argued that the rotting of bodies, or the eating and devouring of them by animals, was incompatible with Islam.[75]

The collection of loot was also based on Islamic law, and was regulated in detail. The Qur'an (8:41) and the Sunnah also deal with this issue. The booty had to be collected first and who took from it, was severely punished. It was then distributed according to the key given: in the process, four-fifhs went to the army. A large part of the booty was made up of weapons, clothing, jewellery and harness worn by the warriors. This explains why, as the Ottoman campaign diary describes, the bodies had to be collected first. The military were keen to get their share at the end of the campaign, and few were likely to risk the punishment (as we have already pointed out, the death penalty was also imposed for much lesser offences).

After the dead were collected, they were thoroughly examined, stripped and buried in suitable places (gun emplacements, artificial trenches, natural depressions). The archaeological evidence suggests that at least part of the stripping took place in the mass graves. The rule also allowed Christian prisoners to be involved to this not really pleasant practice. By analogy, it is also possible that the Ottoman technical regiments (yayas, müsellems) organised the collection and burial.

Let us return to the burial of the Christian victims linked to Dorottya Kanizsai. The story, as mentioned above, contains several ancient and medieval topos that diminish its communicative credibility. However, it is worth checking whether any similarities can be observed with the archaeological phenomena.

---

74 István Brodarics, "Brodarics István levele Krzysztof Szidłowieczki kancellárhoz, 1526. október 3.," [Letter from István Brodarics to Chancellor Krzysztof Szidłowieczki, 3 October 1526] in *Örök Mohács*, eds. B. Szabó et al., pp. 178–182.

75 al-Dawoody, "Management of the dead", pp. 759–784.

The dead were described as attracting large numbers of dogs to feast on them, making it dangerous for anyone to go near the battlefield. In contrast, the human skeletons in the mass graves at Sátorhely showed no signs of having been mauled by dogs or any other animal. We are also told that the noblewoman, driven by Christian piety, pitying the brave Christian heroes lest they should end up as prey for dogs and wild beasts, dug large pits and buried the fallen in them. According to the information available, however, the mass graves were dug as gun emplacements and shooting positions not after the battle, as the story goes, but before. In addition, the five mass graves examined during the excavations did not contain any traces or evidence of Christian piety. The bodies were thrown into the trenches without any order or consideration. Nor is it Christian piety to plunder the fallen heroes completely. And yet, on the basis of the attachments observed, there is good reason to suspect that the bodies were stripped and plundered at the graves. This may be indicated by small finds, such as the clothing clasps found in the tombs. It seems that no mass grave has yet been found that would be consistent with the story of Dorottya Kanizsai. The five mass graves at Sátorhely were most probably filled by the Ottomans with the remains of those who died in the battle.

However, the collection of human corpses, the counting, the burial was certainly not complete, only partial. There are also Ottoman Turkish sources which at least partially contradict the interpretation that the dead were buried by them. Kemalpaşazade greatly exaggerates the number of those executed and reports the unburied corpses of 10,000 'kiçi ve ulu' (small and large).[76] At the same time, the antique topos, "wolves and birds of prey", is also apparent in its wording. This again raises the question: is this authentic information or is it just another figure of speech? The relevant passage raises several questions. The number of those executed is not real, and the literary wording casts doubt on whether the information is reliable or whether it is intended to create a strong impression by using established topos. It is also possible that the Ottoman command could/would only partly have met the impossibly huge task of burial. This was well within Islamic flexibility. The effort to comply with the rule is, according to the şeriat, honourable, but what can one do if perfect implementation is not possible...

The scattered human bones found on the battlefield, and the human remains and bones that sank into and were recovered from the marshes at least suggest that some of the dead remained unburied. A small number may indeed have

---

[76] *"The carcasses of small and great were left as food for wolves and birds of prey, inviting them to this terrible feast."* Kemálpasazáde, "Mohácsnáme," [Mohácsname] in *Örök Mohács*, eds. B. Szabó et al., p. 333.

been buried by the local population. At least in the case of the dead laid to rest in Christian cemeteries, this is a plausible claim. Who knows, perhaps in the future mass graves will turn up, in which (however unlikely it may seem at the moment) Dorottya Kanizsai or some other magnates in the area buried the dead. If so, this iconic, beautiful story will be saved from the harsh, myth-busting criticism of historical, philological research.

7 The Place and Role of the Sultan's Tent and the Execution of Prisoners of War

The location of the sultan's tent played an important practical and symbolic role in the encampment of the Ottoman army. Apparently, for the military parade on 31 August (after the victory on 29 August), the execution of prisoners of war and the presentation of trophies to the army, the place near the tent became the main site of events.

Where could this tent have stood before and after the battle? Kemalpaşazade wrote that the Rumelian army arrived near the battlefield at noon:

> ... when the sun was at its zenith, and the fortunes of the stubborn enemy were declining, and the foundation of his power was crumbling, he arrived near the future battlefield, from which he could see the camp of the wicked enemy.[77]

A council was then held, and on the decision of İbrahim *grand vizier*, who had listened to the advice of Bali Bey, the work of erecting the sultan's tent begun in the early afternoon of 29 August.[78] Of this camp we know from both Velius and Brodarics that it was hidden from the Christian troops by a low rise hill (the Sátorhely Ridge), but in front of the "Mount", i.e. the pool edge surrounding the plain. The sultan retired here at midnight on the day of the battle to rest.

According to local topography, archaeological data and Ottoman Turkish sources, this camp site was somewhere in the medieval estate of Merse, south of modern Majs village, at the present-day Kiserdő of Majs. The Majs alluvial fan offered an ideal dry area for camping, while to the north and south lay a waterlogged terrain. This is confirmed by the 29 pieces 18–20 mm diameter bullets

---

77 Kemálpasazáde, "Mohácsnáme," [Mohácsname] in *Örök Mohács*, eds. B. Szabó et al., p. 326.
78 Kemálpasazáde, "Mohácsnáme," [Mohácsname] in *Örök Mohács*, eds. B. Szabó et al., p. 327.

found here, which the archaeologist who excavated them in 1967 thought were probably janissary munition. Since the janissary troops of the army that had been advancing with the Rumelian army were camped at the village of Földvár near the Borza Stream, the troops camped at the Kiserdő in Majs may indeed have been those of the janissaries who accompanied and protected the sultan. In any case, the place was suitable for encampment, and at the same time the Rumelian army formed a buffer against the enemy, thus protecting the sultan himself.

On the day after the battle, 30 August, the sultan's camp was dismantled and, according to the Ottoman campaign diary and the account of Bostan, rebuilt north of the battlefield, below Mohács where the sultan spent four more days.[79] As the army would not move on until Monday, and the Ottoman campaign diary also indicates that it rested at Mohács, the sultan's tent could be south of Mohács, but north of the battlefield. Given the terrain conditions (road system, dry terrain, water supply, public health and safety considerations), this station had to be on the site of Louis II's camp or possibly in its vicinity. It is also worth remembering that during the campaigns of the War of Reconquest (1684–1699), Christian troops camped on this site regularly. The troops had easy access to water, crossing points and harbours along the Danube at Mohács, but there was little space for camping. In contrast, at this place, on the road running south from Mohács, at the village of Kölked, there was ample space and drinking water for animals and men alike. Given the above, it is therefore highly probable that this was the site of the 31 August parade and trophy presentation.

During the battle, the Ottomans took a large number of prisoners of war. According to the eyewitness account of Miklós Herczeg, 1503 of the prisoners of war were beheaded before the victorious army was formed up, while the lives of some prisoners were spared, they were interrogated and released for ransom.[80] Ottoman sources shed light on several details. According to them, the executed were captured infantrymen and cavalrymen.[81] The beheading of

---

79 Bostan wrote: "On this day the sultan's camp, having left its place, settled a little beyond the battlefield, and remained there for four days." See Bosztán cselebi (Ferdi), "Szulejmán könyve (1520–1542) 1547 (részlet)," [The Book of Süleyman (1520–1542) 1547 (excerpt)] in *Örök Mohács,* eds. B. Szabó et al., p. 366; See more "Az 1526. évi hadinapló," [The Ottoman campaign diary of 1526] in *Örök Mohács,* eds. B. Szabó et al., pp. 235–257.

80 "On the day after the battle, one thousand five hundred of the prisoners, including most of the nobility, were gathered together and beheaded in front of the victorious army..." See Brodarics, "Igaz történet," [A true account] in *Örök Mohács,* eds. B. Szabó et al., p 321.

81 "...the horsemen and infantrymen who were captured were all led to the place of execution. The necks of these unfortunates were made the scabbard of the sword of

prisoners before the sultan is also mentioned in Bostan, but with the addition that other captives were enslaved.[82] The Ottoman campaign diary puts the number of executed at around 2000, with the beheading taking place on 31 August.[83]

There is a kind of ritual in the treatment of corpses. The heads of the slain Christian leaders, including Tomori, were displayed on spears in front of the sultan's tent, and the flags of the Christian army were lowered upside down to signify defeat. Lutfi also mentions that three piles of the cut heads of the Hungarians were demonstratively placed as a deterrent,[84] presumably also near the sultan's tent. All this seems to suggest that the mass execution of 31 August was intended to inspire the Ottoman army and demoralize the enemy. The demonstration took place near the sultan's tent, a symbolic representation of the emperor.

It is worth comparing this with the fact that a few days later, leaving Mohács and heading towards Buda, another mass execution took place on 4 September. This was also carried out with beheading, but it lacked the solemnity. Since the Christian prisoners of war had already been killed earlier, it is likely that these people were mostly captured civilians. This is also suggested by the fact that the source specifically mentions the old women who were released.[85] It seems that the number of useless prisoners was still too large and this (guarding, feeding) was an obstacle to further military operations. The purpose of this massacre, unlike the previous symbolic one, was practical, to preserve the operationality of the army.

Human remains have been found on and around the battlefield since the 19th century. Some of these may be linked to the battle of 1526, others to other

---

vengeance..." See Kemálpasazáde, "Mohácsnáme," [Mohácsname] in *Örök Mohács*, eds. B. Szabó et al., p. 337.

[82] "...more than ten thousand infidels were taken prisoner and handcuffed from horsemen and foot soldiers..." "...the prisoners of war were led by order of the padishah to the high divan, where the heads of so many wicked wretches of evil disposition were cut off, and the rest, shackled in the fetters of slavery, were left in the hands of their owners..." See Bosztán, "Szulejmán könyve," [The Book of Süleyman] in *Örök Mohács*, eds. B. Szabó et al., pp. 366–367.

[83] "Those taken alive were rounded up and beheaded, about two thousand people." See "Az 1526. évi hadinapló," [The Ottoman campaign diary of 1526] in *Örök Mohács*, eds. B. Szabó et al., p. 245.

[84] "...he gave orders to collect the heads of the slain unbelievers." See Lutfi, "Az Oszmán-ház története," [History of the Ottoman House] in Örök Mohács, eds B. Szabó et al., p. 407.

[85] "It was proclaimed in the camp that all the despicable men in the army should be put to the sword, but that the old women prisoners should not be sold, but set free. Therefore, many unbelievers were beheaded." See "Az 1526. évi hadinapló," [The Ottoman campaign diary of 1526] in *Örök Mohács*, eds. B. Szabó et al., p. 246.

military operations of the 16th and 17th centuries, as well as to the Mongolian invasion of 1241 and to civil burials in the settlements in the area.

The identification of the human remains associated with the Battle of Mohács in 1526 requires an interpretation of the events in order to identify their possible types. These types can be distinguished on the basis of characteristic wounds, the specific place and manner of death, and the religious provisions for burial. We can consider the following distinctions for the dead and human remains:
- heads collected by Ottoman soldiers in the reward system;
- the massacred 2000 guards of the Christian camp, and presumably thousands of its personnel;
- the human remains of at least 1500 soldiers beheaded on 31 August;
- the scattered bodies and body parts of soldiers killed in action;
- at the end of the battle, 6000–7000 foreign infantrymen were slaughtered;
- the Ottoman victims of the battle, about 300;
- the remains of the prisoners beheaded on 4 September.

The human remains found so far that can be associated with the battle can be included in the above types, but there are no human remains of all types. Let's see which groups can be identified by which characteristics.

According to a source, 60–80 heads found in 1910 at the chapel of St. László, on the Croatian side of the present-day Hungarian-Croatian border, south of Udvar, north of Dályok,[86] were found in a campsite of Anatolian troops. The heads were collected by the Ottoman army as a reward, so they could have been put to rest after their presentation and administration. It is not yet known where the bodies belonging to them have gone. The account of one of the participants on the Ottoman side describes one such case. Behari served as a cavalryman in the army. In his narrative poem 'The History of the Conquest of Hungary', he writes the following about the heads taken as a reward at the Battle of Mohács: "The army of the cursed king was beaten, heads were cut off with the sword, and quickly hung (on the saddle-squares)."[87] And the Ottoman statesman Koçi Bey wrote of this practice:

> Whoever distinguished himself by bringing a tongue (a prisoner of news) and a head, had his income raised by one acre for every ten acres. And the

---

86 Barna Halmay, *Az 1526-iki mohácsi csata keletkezése és igazi helye* [The origins and real place of the Battle of Mohács in 1526] (Debrecen: Magyar Nemzeti Könyv- és Lapkiadóvállalat Rt., 1926).

87 Balázs Sudár, "A végítélet könyve. Oszmán elbeszélő költemény a mohácsi csatáról," [The Book of Doom. Ottoman narrative poem about the Battle of Mohács] *Történelmi Szemle* 52 (2010), no. 3, p. 411.

timar-owner who distinguished himself exceedingly in the campaign, and brought 10 to 15 tongues or heads, received a ziamet-estate for his merits.[88]

The head of the dead person identified as a victim of the Battle of Mohács, discovered in 1961 in the medieval cemetery at the Újistálló Manor opposite the Turkish Hill (Hünkâr tepesi), was also missing, so he too can be considered a victim of Ottoman soldiers collecting heads.

Of the dead buried on or near the battlefield, the remains of the thousands of guards and staff of the Christian camp have not yet been found, nor are the whereabouts of the mass graves of at least 1500 soldiers who were executed and beheaded. Both of these sites are thought to be north of the battlefield, near the road running south from Mohács, in the area of Kölked.

During the early 20th century drainage by canals of the Vizslak Meadow on the Danube floodplain, a large number of human remains and weapons were found on the eastern edge of the battlefield. They may have been soldiers of the Christian army who were reportedly trapped by the Ottomans in the deep marshes or whose bodies were dumped in the marshes. The three young men, aged around 18, who were identified during the 1959 excavation of the medieval village cemetery of Lajmér and were laid to rest in common graves linked to the battle, were buried in a cemetery. The dead could have been soldiers or local residents, if they died during the events of 1526.

There are several theories about the origins of the dead in the mass graves discovered near Sátorhely. They have been assumed to be the guards of the camp, soldiers who died in the battle, and more recently it has been suggested that they could be the 1500–2000 executed prisoners of war mentioned in the sources.[89] If we look at the characteristics of the dead, we find a wide range of serious, fatal injuries to the heads and various parts of the body, with many decapitated, while a fair number have whole bodies, including heads.[90] All this does not correspond to the accounts of the executions, as the soldiers brought

---

88 Gyula Káldy-Nagy, "A török állam hadseregének kialakulása I. Szulejmán korára," [The creation of the army of the Turkish state for the age of Süleyman I] in *Mohács. Tanulmányok a mohácsi csata 450. évfordulója alkalmából*, eds. Lajos Ruzsás and Ferenc Szakály (Budapest: Akadémiai Kiadó, 1986), p. 179. The quotation is from the treatise of 1631 by Bey Koçi. The Ottoman statesman wrote this in retrospect to the 16th century.

89 Gábor Bertók, Réka Neményi, György Pálfi, and Béla Simon, "A mohácsi III. számú tömegsír új kutatása," [The new research of the mass grave III of Mohacs] *Magyar Régészet* 11 (2022), no. 1, pp. 44–53.

90 Zsuzsanna K. Zoffmann, *Az 1526-os mohácsi csata 1976-ban feltárt tömegsírjainak embertani vizsgálata* [Anthropological study of the mass graves of the Battle of Mohács in 1526, excavated in 1976] (Biológiai tanulmányok) 9 (Budapest: Akadémiai Kiadó, 1982).

to the execution site were uniformly decapitated and the heads were demonstratively placed in several piles. This suggests that the bodies and heads were buried separately and not together. Based on the injuries identified on the dead, it appears for the time being that they were infantrymen slaughtered by cavalry. They were partially hit from behind while running, so it is most likely that the mass graves contain mostly of the Western infantrymen slaughtered at the end of the battle.

The mass graves also contain some deaths that are different from the average. At this stage of the investigation, it appears that a minimal number of women were among the dead, perhaps brought to the site by Ottoman soldiers to collect and bury the bodies, and then eventually dumped in the grave pit for an as yet unidentified reason. During the excavation of mass grave III in 2021, two smaller calibre projectiles (between 10–13 mm) were also recovered. If they were not found in the mass graves after the Battle of Mohács, but as a consequence of the battle, their size could only have been due to the weapons of the Western infantrymen. This suggests that those who were carrying the projectiles when they entered the site must have been members of the Ottoman army who were shot by defensive gunners during the battle. They may have been buried in the mass graves deliberately or perhaps unintentionally.[91]

Although they have been searching for some time, no graves of Muslim soldiers killed in battle have been found so far. According to tradition, as recorded by Evliya Çelebi, the Muslim martyrs were buried in the area around the Turkish Hill (Hünkâr tepesi), but they were not found there during the excavation in the 1920s. Based on the events of the battle, most of them died in the southern part of the plain, so their graves should be sought near the Borza Stream. Most of their fatal injuries here were caused by blades or spears. If the Muslim tradition of burial was followed, as is assumed, they will be found in a position facing Mecca. In cases where a larger number of their deaths may have been caused by arquebuses, the bodies may be found further north, closer to the Christian positions, nearer the infantrymen with handguns.[92]

---

91 The Ottoman army included not only Muslims, but also a small number of Balkan Christian auxiliaries. The bodies of these soldiers could not be buried with the Muslim soldiers. It was also a religious rule that the dead whose religious affiliation could not be clearly established could not be buried with the Muslim soldiers. As most of the soldiers of the period were not yet in uniform, distinguishing the Ottoman Balkan fighters from the Serb, Croat and Slav soldiers of the Christian army could be problematic.

92 According to an oral tradition, until the end of the First World War, pilgrims came from Bosnia to the former *Hünkâr tepesi*, or *Törökdomb*. The pilgrims prayed here and then went to the nearby "*Black Gate*" (or Schwarzes Tor), where they also prayed. See Chapter Eleven.

Accordingly, as mentioned above, we cannot rule out the possibility that the mass graves in Sátorhely may also contain a small number of soldiers of the Ottoman army, mixed with Westerners. In the case of the Ottoman tombs, it is a thought-provoking fact, and one which is worthy of further research, that the Muslim pilgrimage to the battlefield up to the First World War involved another site, in addition to the Turkish Hill (Hünkâr tepesi): this was in the area of the Black Gate (Fekete-kapu), the same site from which some of the battle relics, weapons and cannonballs were recovered. Of the identified battle sites, the closest is the site of the massacre of the Christian infantry, where significant Ottoman losses are also believed to have occurred.

The prisoners executed by the army that had already crossed the Sárvíz River above Mohács on 4 September were presumably buried in a mass grave or in the Sárvíz swamp. They were laid together with their heads, since they were not trophies, and had no symbolic or reward value. So far, no remains of this group have been found either.

8   Summary

We believe that military geography has brought us closer to understanding the context of the battle. This concerns a different face of the battle: the battle theater. It has a significant advantage over military historiography based on only soldiers' records and recollections. This is based on natural sciences facts and is not shrouded in human subjectivity. The battlefield is objectively knowable. The struggle of man (the soldier on the battlefield) with his environment can be objectively narrated on the basis of the landscape, because one agent of this struggle – the landscape – is potentially known.

The Tomori plan was based on the assumption that the outnumbered Ottoman army's attack would be stopped in the flat, relatively narrow space between the Vizslak Meadow and the Borza Stream Valley, well suited to the operational needs of the heavy cavalry. This was to be achieved in the following way: the enemy's attack would be halted and the irresistible onslaught of the Christian heavy cavalry would overwhelm the Ottoman Turkish troops. The execution of the plan also required that the front line be wide enough to prevent being embraced. This, however, could only be achieved with great difficulty, and not satisfactorily. There were not sufficient troops to close the area, and the Hungarian rows were very long and narrow, already criticised by contemporaries. Another important condition for a glimpse of victory was that the Christian troops should engage the enemy until only the Rumelian troops had arrived on the battlefield and the entire Ottoman army had been raised.

The fact that this did not happen in the end must have been due to excellent Ottoman reconnaissance, well adapted to the conditions on the ground. The Ottomans had devised an effective plan. They wanted the entire Ottoman army to be deployed during the battle, so they did not initiate a fight. The Anatolian army on the right flank and the salaried household troops, normally positioned in the centre, deployed relatively quickly to help the Rumelians. And the cavalry led by Bali, despite the Hungarian efforts, managed to embrace the Christian army from the west. The well-rehearsed *tabur cengi* order of battle was used to crush and defeat the Hungarian army.

It is thought-provoking how much importance the Ottoman sources attach to the governor of the border district of Semendria, Yahyapaşa-oğlu Bali Bey. His active role in reconnaissance, planning, the destruction of the Christian camp and the course of the battle probably made him indispensable. It was the information gained by Bali Bey and his army of akıncıs and sipahis that enabled the Ottoman command, moving in uncharted territory, to win. However, it may be assumed that not all credit is his alone. The flattering Ottoman Turkish sources attributed the "brilliant war plan" to Grand Vizier İbrahim, but Yahyapaşa-oğlu Bali Bey was remembered as a shrewd adviser and fearless warrior, so crumbs of credit fell on him.

The plan advocated by Pál Tomori – the overwhelming counterattack after defence – was finally carried out not by the Hungarian army, but by the Ottoman army. Due to conflicts within the leadership, Tomori was forced to attack too late, which the Ottomans successfully repulsed and inflicted heavy losses on the Hungarian troops. At the same time, the decisive factor in the course of events was not initially the overwhelming numbers, but the difference in technology and organisation between the two armies: the volley fire of the janissaries, the disciplined cavalry movements and the mass deployment of guns on the Ottoman lines, which had arrived with the sultan.

The overwhelming Ottoman force became a significant factor only in the second phase of the battle, during the surge of movement between the cavalry troops. The result was a crushing Ottoman victory with minimal casualties. The Christian heavy cavalry proved to be totally inadequate against Süleyman's army. The commanders of the Hungarian army seem to have been unaware of, or failed to understand, a technical turn of events which, in the light of the outcome of the battle of Pavia the previous year, they might have been well advised to consider.

The Christian army suffered at least 14,000–18,000 casualties against the 1200–1500 Ottomans. The dead were buried partly by the Ottoman troops and partly by local civilians returning to the area after the battle. Two large-scale executions took place after the battle: first the captured soldiers and then some of the civilians who had become too numerous and an unnecessary burden to guard and supply.

Overall, the Ottoman victory, and with it the minimal loss rate, can be assessed as being largely due to qualitative, and secondarily to quantitative factors. The former were excellent reconnaissance, the use of traditional Eastern tactics, i.e. the operations of well-led cavalry troops, the mass and effective use of firearms, and only then the enforcement of a threefold stronger force. The Hungarian army had only a minimal chance of victory, but it was not a battle of equals. The self-sacrificing bravery of which we can read in the sources could not compensate for the professionalism, discipline, modern equipment and numerical superiority of the Ottoman army. Tomori's war plan would have had a chance of success only if the execution had been flawless or if the Ottoman command had made mistakes, but it did not. The result was a disastrous defeat, a huge loss of men and the death of the king. At Mohács, Sultan Süleyman I won one of the greatest victories in the history of his reign, and of the Ottoman Empire, and the Kingdom of Hungary suffered one of its greatest defeats.

Bibliography

A Jugovićok anyja. [The mother of Jugović] In *Jugoszláv költők antológiája,* ed. Sztoján Vujicsics D., 81–83. Budapest: Móra Kiadó, 1963.

A koszovói lányka. [The girl from Kosovo] In *Jugoszláv költők antológiája,* ed. Sztoján Vujicsics D., 76–80. Budapest: Móra Kiadó, 1963.

A magyar hadsereg veszteséglistája Piotr Tomicki krakkói érsek és lengyel alkancellár iratai között 1526. október. [The Hungarian army's casualty list in the documents of Piotr Tomicki Archbishop of Krakow and Vice-chancellor of Poland] In *Örök Mohács: szövegek és értelmezések,* eds. János B. Szabó and Gábor Farkas Farkas, 185–188. Bölcsészettudományi Kutatóközpont, Budapest, 2020.

A mohácsi csatára vonatkozó veszteséglista, 1526. [The list of casualties relating to the the Battle of Mohács, 1526] In *Örök Mohács: szövegek és értelmezések,* eds. János B. Szabó and Gábor Farkas Farkas, 218–220. Bölcsészettudományi Kutatóközpont, Budapest, 2020.

Al-Dawoody, Ahmed. "Management of the dead from the Islamic law and international humanitarian law perspectives: Considerations for humanitarian forensics." *International Review of the Red Cross* 99 (2017): 759–784.

Az 1526. évi hadinapló 1526 (részlet). [The Ottoman campaign diary 1526 (excerpt)] In *Örök Mohács: szövegek és értelmezések,* eds. János B. Szabó and Gábor Farkas Farkas, 235–257. Budapest: Bölcsészettudományi Kutatóközpont, 2020.

Bertók, Gábor, Réka Neményi, György Pálfi, and Béla Simon. "A mohácsi III. számú tömegsír új kutatása." [The new research of the mass grave III of Mohacs] *Magyar Régészet* 11 (2022): 44–53.

Bosztán cselebi (Ferdi). "Szulejmán könyve (1520–1542) 1547 (részlet)." [The Book of Süleyman (1520–1542) 1547 (excerpt)] In *Örök Mohács: szövegek és értelmezések,* eds János B. Szabó and Gábor Farkas Farkas, 235–257. Bölcsészettudományi Kutatóközpont, Budapest, 2020.

Brodarics, István. "Igaz történet a magyarok és Szulejmán török császár mohácsi ütközetéről 1528." [A true account of the battle between the Hungarians and the Turkish Emperor Süleyman at Mohács (1528)] In *Örök Mohács: szövegek és értelmezések,* eds. János B. Szabó and Gábor Farkas Farkas, 301–325. Bölcsészettudományi Kutatóközpont, Budapest, 2020.

Brodarics, István. "Magyarország kancellárja Piotr Tomicki alkancellár püspöknek és Andrzej Krzycki przemyśli püspöknek Pozsony, 1526. szeptember 6." [Chancellor of Hungary to Vice-chancellor, Bishop Piotr Tomicki and Andrzej Krzycki Bishop of Przemyśl, Pozsony, 6 September 1526] In *Örök Mohács: szövegek és értelmezések,* eds. János B. Szabó and Gábor Farkas Farkas, 137–138. Budapest: Bölcsészettudományi Kutatóközpont, 2020.

Brodarics, István. "Brodarics István levele Krzysztof Szidłowieczki kancellárhoz, 1526. október 3." [Letter from István Brodarics to Chancellor Krzysztof Szidłowieczki, 3 October 1526] In *Örök Mohács: szövegek és értelmezések,* eds. János B. Szabó and Gábor Farkas Farkas, 178–182. Bölcsészettudományi Kutatóközpont, Budapest, 2020.

Burgio, Antonio Giovanni da. "Antonio Giovanni da Burgio pápai követ levele Jacopo Sadoleto pápai titkárnak, Pozsony, 1526. szeptember 5." [Letter from the papal nuncio Antonio Giovanni da Burgio to the papal secretary Jacopo Sadoleto Pozsony, 5 September 1526] In *Örök Mohács: szövegek és értelmezések,* eds. János B. Szabó and Gábor Farkas Farkas, 131–132. Budapest: Bölcsészettudományi Kutatóközpont, 2020.

Celalzade Mustafa. "Az országok osztályai és az utak felsorolása 1560-as évek (részlet)." [The echelons of the dominions and the hierarchies of destinations, 1560s (excerpt)] In *Örök Mohács: szövegek és értelmezések,* eds. János B. Szabó and Gábor Farkas Farkas, 411–419. Budapest: Bölcsészettudományi Kutatóközpont, 2020.

Cureus, Joachimus. "Gentis Silesiae Annales 1571." In *Örök Mohács: szövegek és értelmezések,* eds. János B. Szabó and Gábor Farkas Farkas, 422–427. Budapest: Bölcsészettudományi Kutatóközpont, 2020.

Egy cseh úr levele a Santa Clara kolostor főnöknőjéhez, 1526. november." [Letter from a Czech nobleman to the Superior of the Convent of Santa Clara, November 1526] In *Örök Mohács: szövegek és értelmezések,* eds. János B. Szabó and Gábor Farkas Farkas, 207–216. Budapest: Bölcsészettudományi Kutatóközpont, 2020.

Ehrenspiegel des Hauses Österreich (Buch VII). Augsburg: Bayerische Staatsbibliothek, 1559.

Erkan, Davut. *Matrâkçi Nasûh'un Süleymân-nâmesi (1520–1537)*. MA thesis (İstanbul: Marmara Üniversitesi, 2005.

Fodor, Pál. "Wolf on the Border: Yahyapaşaoğlu Bali Bey (?–1527).," In *Şerefe. Studies in Honour of Prof. Géza Dávid on His Seventieth Birthday*, eds. Pál Fodor, Nándor E. Kovács, and Benedek Péri, 57–88. Budapest, Research Center for the Humanities, 2019.

Fodor, Pál and András Mércz. "'Mi is veszett Mohácsnál?' Oszmán-török veszteséglista az 1526. évi hadjáratról." [What is lost at Mohács? What happened at Mohács] *Történelmi Szemle* 65 (2023).

Gökbilgin, M. Tayyib. *Nagy Szulejmán szultán*. [Sultan Süleyman the Magnificent] Budapest: Napkút Kiadó, 2020.

Gyenizse, Péter, Norbert Pap, Máté Kitanics, and Tibor Szabó. "Napkelte és napnyugta adatainak modellezése történelmi események rekonstrukciójához." [Modelling sunrise and sunset data for the reconstruction of historical events.] In *Az elmélet és a gyakorlat találkozása a térinformatikában XIII*, ed. Vanda Éva Abriha-Molnár, 155–162. Debrecen: Debreceni Egyetemi Kiadó, 2022.

Halmay, Barna. *Az 1526-iki mohácsi csata keletkezése és igazi helye*. [The origins and real place of the Battle of Mohács in 1526] Debrecen: Magyar Nemzeti Könyv- és Lapkiadóvállalat Rt., 1926.

Isthvánffy, Miklós. "A magyarok történetéből 1622 (részlet)." [From the history of the Hungarians 1622 (excerpt)] In *Örök Mohács: szövegek és értelmezések*, eds. János B. Szabó and Gábor Farkas Farkas, 444–462. Budapest: Bölcsészettudományi Kutatóközpont, 2020.

K. Zoffmann, Zsuzsanna. *Az 1526-os mohácsi csata 1976-ban feltárt tömegsírjainak embertani vizsgálata*. [Anthropological study of the mass graves of the Battle of Mohács in 1526, excavated in 1976] Biológiai tanulmányok 9. Budapest: Akadémiai Kiadó, 1982.

Káldy-Nagy, Gyula. "A török állam hadseregének kialakulása I. Szulejmán korára." [The creation of the army of the Turkish state for the age of Süleyman I] In *Mohács. Tanulmányok a mohácsi csata 450. évfordulója alkalmából*, eds. Lajos Ruzsás and Ferenc Szakály, 163–194. Budapest: Akadémiai Kiadó, 1986.

Karácson, Imre. *Evlia Cselebi török világutazó magyarországi utazásai 1660–1664*. [Turkish traveller Evliya Çelebi's travels] Budapest: Gondolat Könyvkiadó, 1985.

Keegan, John. *The Face of Battle: A Study of Agincourt, Waterloo, and the Somme* (Pimlico, 2004).

Kemálpasazáde. "Mohácsnáme (részlet)." [Mohácsname (excerpt)] In *Örök Mohács: szövegek és értelmezések*, eds. János B. Szabó and Gábor Farkas Farkas, 326–338. Budapest: Bölcsészettudományi Kutatóközpont, 2020.

Lutfi pasa. "Az Oszmán-ház története 1550-es évek (részlet)." [History of the Ottoman House 1550s (excerpt)] In *Örök Mohács: szövegek és értelmezések*, eds. János B. Szabó and Gábor Farkas Farkas, 401–409. Budapest: Bölcsészettudományi Kutatóközpont, 2020.

Monok, István. *A művelt arisztokrata. A magyarországi főnemesség olvasmányai a 16–17. században.* [The literary aristocrats of Hungary in the 16th–17th centuries.] Budapest: Kossuth Kiadó, 2012.

Mula, Agostino da. "Agostino da Mula jelentése Udine, 1526. szeptember 15. (átirat)." [Account of Agostino da Mula Udine, 15 September 1526 (transcript)] In *Örök Mohács: szövegek és értelmezések,* eds. János B. Szabó and Gábor Farkas Farkas, 163–165. Budapest: Bölcsészettudományi Kutatóközpont, 2020.

Pap, Norbert, Péter Gyenizse, Máté Kitanics, and Gábor Szalai. "A Gergely-féle naptárreform és a csillagászati jelenségek szerepe a 15–16. századi történelmi forrásaink és eseményeink értelmezésében: a 15–16. századi történelmi események kronológiai értelmezéséhez." [The role of the Gregorian calendar reform and astronomical phenomena in the interpretation of historical sources and events of the 15th–16th centuries: towards a chronological interpretation of historical events of the 15th–16th centuries] *Balkán Füzetek* 11 (2020): 1–66.

Pap, Norbert, Pál Fodor, Máté Kitanics, Tamás Morva, Gábor Szalai, and Péter Gyenizse. "A mohácsi Törökdomb." [The Törökdomb of Mohács] *Történelmi Szemle* 60 (2018): 325–345.

Parker, Robert. *Miasma: Pollution and Purificationin Early Greek Religion.* Oxford: Clarendon Press, 1983.

Peçevi, İbrahim. "Krónika 1648 előtt (részlet)." [Chronicle, before 1648 (excerpt)] In *Örök Mohács: szövegek és értelmezések,* eds. János B. Szabó and Gábor Farkas Farkas, 463–477. Budapest: Bölcsészettudományi Kutatóközpont, 2020.

S. *Orgelbranda Encyklopedia Powszechna* XII. Warsaw: Wydawnictwie Towarzystwa Akcyjnego Odlewni Czcionek i Drukarni S. Orgelbranda Synów, 1902.

Sudár, Balázs. "A végítélet könyve. Oszmán elbeszélő költemény a mohácsi csatáról." [The Book of Doom. Ottoman narrative poem about the Battle of Mohács] *Történelmi Szemle* 52 (2010): 389–419.

Vásáry, István. "Yāsā and Sharī'a. Islamic Attitudes towards the Mongol Law in the Turco-Mongolian World (from the Golden Horde to Timur's Time)." In *Violence in Islamic Thought from the Mongols to European Imperialism Gleave,* eds. Robert Gleave and István Kristó-Nagy, 58–78. Edinburgh: Edinburgh University Press, 2007.

Velius, Caspar Ursinus. "A mohácsi csata 1530 körül (töredék)" [The Battle of Mohács around 1530 (fragment)] In *Örök Mohács: szövegek és értelmezések,* eds. Violence in Islamic Thought from the Mongols to European Imperialism Gleave, eds. Robert Gleave and István Kristó-Nagy, 348–355. Budapest: Bölcsészettudományi Kutatóközpont, 2020.

PART 2

The Overall Landscape

∴

CHAPTER 6

Geomorphology of the Mohács Plain and Its Environs

Péter Gyenizse, Dénes Lóczy and Gábor Varga

1 Introduction

Geomorphology is a discipline which examines the topography and landforms of the Earth's surface, a field of study where geology and geography overlap. Basic geomorphological research attempts to describe the shape, location, and internal structure of landforms, to classify features according to their properties, and to explore the processes that affect their development.[1]

Geomorphology influences drainage, land cover, soils and other physical factors in an area. However, it also directly or indirectly affects the socio-economic-cultural life there.

In this chapter, the scenery of the broader environs of the Battle of Mohács is scrutinized. In addition to processing literature sources, we analyzed topographic maps, aerial and satellite images, and digital elevation models with the help of GIS tools.[2] We also checked and clarified our evaluations from the above sources in the field.

2 Delineation of the Study Area

The investigated area is located in Europe, in the Pannonian basin boardered by the Alps, Carpathians and Dinarides (Figure 6.1). According to the "Landscapes" chapter of the National Atlas of Hungary (2018),[3] the study area belongs to

---

1 Dénes Lóczy and Márton Veress, *Geomorfológia I. Földfelszíni folyamatok és formák* [Geomorphology I. Processes and landforms] (Budapest, Pécs: Dialóg Campus Kiadó, 2005).
2 Péter Gyenizse, Zita Bognár, Ákos Halmai, Tamás Morva, and Bertalan Simon, "Digitális domborzatmodellek használata tájrekonstrukciós célra szigetvári és mohácsi területeken," [Using DEMs for landscape reconstruction in the areas of Szigetvár and Mohács] in *Az elmélet és a gyakorlat találkozása a térinformatikában IX.*, ed. Vanda Molnár (Debrecen: Debreceni Egyetemi Kiadó, 2018), pp. 121–128.
3 Péter Csorba, Szilvia Ádám, Zsombor Bartos-Elekes, Teodóra Bata, Ákos Bede-Fazekas, Bálint Czúcz, Péter Csima, Gábor Csüllög, Nándor Fodor, Sándor Frisnyák, Gergely Horváth, Gábor

the Danube Plain (mesoregion) of the Great Plain within the macroregion Danube-Tisza basin, and includes the group of microregions collectively called Csepel-Mohács Plain. According to this classification, the microregion Mohács Plain also comprises Mohács Island. The study area lies mainly in Hungary, but a smaller part extends into Croatia and Serbia as well.

All researchers place the location of the Battle of Mohács in the area of the Mohács flood-free terrace, although its exact place is still debated. Therefore, during our physico-geographical investigations, we mainly focus on this microregion, but since this area has been in constant contact with the surrounding microregions over the past thousands and millions of years, we also consider their geographical properties.

The boundaries of the investigated area are as follows:
– the edge of the Baranya Hills in the north and northwest;
– in the east, the line of the Baracska-Danube (Ferenc Canal);
– in the south, the Karasica Stream and the Bán Hill (Báni-hegység, Bansko brdo, Baranyahát);
– in the southwest and west, the transition is gradual towards the Lower Drava Plain.

In the course of the investigation, we drew the border at the lower edge of the hills and the new Borza Canal, which flows further south into the Karasica Stream near the village of Baranyakisfalud (Branjina). (Note that there is indeed a hilly edge in the north, but moving south, from the Nagynyárád and Majs line, we can rather conceive it as the edge of an alluvial fan plain. However, in the present study, for the sake of easier reference, we will refer to the higher ground bordering the Mohács Plain from the west as hills throughout the chapter).

The geographical landscape type of the studied microregion is a geomorphological floodplain of moderately continental climate drained during river regulation, dissected by abandoned channels in the eastern part, and a flood-free loess plain in the west.[4] Accordingly, the lowest lying parts of the area can be classified as alluvial lowland with alluvial soils. Higher floodplain levels were also formed on unconsolidated deposits, but are covered by alluvial

---

Illés, Gábor Kiss, Károly Kocsis, László Kollányi, Éva Konkoly-Gyúró, Nikolett Lepesi, Dénes Lóczy, Ákos Malatinszky, Gábor Mezősi, Gábor Mikesy, Zsolt Molnár, László Pásztor, Imelda Somodi, Sándor Szegedi, Péter Szilassi, László Tamás, Ágnes Tirászi, and Mária Vasvári, "Tájak," [Landscapes] in *Magyarország Nemzeti Atlasza* II., ed. Károly Kocsis (Budapest: MTA CSFK Földrajztudományi Intézet, 2018). pp. 112–129. Available at https://www.nemzetiatlasz.hu/MNA/National-Atlas-of-Hungary_Vol2_Ch10.pdf.

4 Péter Csorba, *Magyarország kistájai* [Microregions of Hungary] (Debrecen: Meridián Táj- és Környezetföldrajzi Alapítvány, 2021), pp. 42–43.

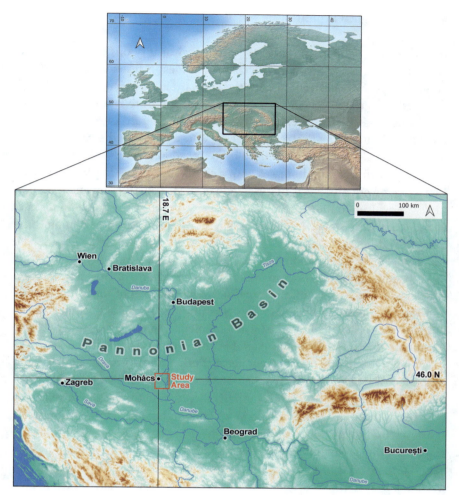

FIGURE 6.1 Location of the investigated area in Europe. Edited by Péter Gyenizse.
BASE MAP: COPERNICUS GLO-90 AND WWW.NATURALEARTHDATA.COM (ACCESSED ON 3 MARCH 2023).

soils. On the flood-free terraces and alluvial fans as well as on loess-mantled surfaces, chernozem soils of higher productivity are typical. The plain is bordered from the west by alluvial fan plains along the edge of hills which are covered with chernozem soils with loess as parent material.[5]

---

5 Csorba et. al., "Tájak".

3 Geological Evolution

As part of the Pannonian Basin, the geological history of the Mohács Plain and its surroundings was quite diverse. The oldest (Mesozoic, 252 million – 66 million years) rocks are found in the vineyard hill north of Mohács, which frames the plain from the north and northwest. There are Triassic and Jurassic limestones near the surface, as well as a volcanic (basalt) outcrop indicating movements during the Cretaceous period. These rocks are the bedrock in the range of hills along the eastern edge of the Transdanubian Hills, which flattens out from north to south, but rises with a sharp edge above the Mohács Plain. Limestones were previously quarried and used for construction and road paving.[6] Mesozoic dolomites and limestones also outcrop in the northern Mohács Island, near Váripuszta.[7] A fortress was built on this outcrop in Roman times and the Middle Ages, and later used as a stone quarry. During the Eocene and Oligocene, no sedimentation only denudation took place in the region.

In the late Miocene (about 10 million years ago), vertical movements intensified again, creating significant relief between the level of the Mohács Plain and the neighbouring hills. The area was inundated by Lake Pannon, a sea remnant, periodically filling the basin completely, In the lake sandy to clayey sediments deposited in highly variable thicknesses. By the Pliocene, Lake Pannon retreated from the area in a south-southeastern direction and dry land expanded. The Danube, which appeared in the Pannonian Basin at that time, turned from its assumed former southerly direction to the east, followed a gap between Börzsöny and the Visegrád Mountains and began to fill the intensively subsiding Great Plain basin with sediment.[8]

The general cooling that commenced in the Pleistocene (2.58 million years ago) led to a series of glacials (cold periods) and interglacials (intermediate warmer periods) in the second half of the Pleistocene, popularly called the Ice Age. The strong winds descending from the ice sheet north of the Carpathians piled up sand from the alluvial fans of the basin in dunes and blew out huge amounts of dust from them into the air. Loess was formed from falling dust

---

6 Antal Lehmann, "A terület földtörténeti kialakulása," [Geological history] in *Mohács földrajza*, eds. Ferenc Erdősi and Antal Lehmann (Mohács: Mohács városi Tanács V.B. Művelődési Osztálya, 1974), pp. 19–28.

7 Tibor Szederkényi, "A baranyai Duna menti mezozoós szigetrögök földtani viszonyai," [Geology of the isolated Mesozoic blocks along the Danube in Baranya] *Földtani Közlöny* 94 (1962), no. 1, pp. 28–32; Sándor Konkoly, "Újabb adatok Zsembéc várának lokalizációjához," [New data to locate Zsembec Castle] *Modern Geográfia* 7 (2012), no. 2, pp. 1–21.

8 Lehmann, "A terület földtörténeti kialakulása," [Geological history] in *Mohács földrajza*, eds. Erdősi et al., pp. 19–28.

bound by grassy vegetation over tens of thousands of years. The loess settled on top of the pre-existing topography smoothed depressions and irregularities of various size. Thus, topography generally became more subdued. Loess in 0.5–10 m thickness covers the hills bordering the Mohács Plain.[9]

In the glacials of cold and dry climate, the discharge of the Danube was remarkably reduced. In the area of mountains and hills, it was unable to transport its huge amount of sediment load, generated by intensive frost action, over the lowland, and deposited it in extensive alluvial fans. Gravelly and sandy river accumulations occur everywhere, even under the present-day surface of the Mohács Plain. During the wetter and warmer periods of the interglacials, however, the water volume of the rivers increased along with their ability to carry sediment load, so their channels could be deepened and widened. With this process, the former active floodplain level was turned into a flood-free terrace. Characteristic stepped, terraced river valleys, such as the Danube Valley, were created during successive cooling and warming phases.[10]

At the beginning of the Late Pleistocene (30–40 thousand years ago), the Danube split into several branches and built its alluvial fan to the east of the present area, and then shifted to the west.[11] In the second half of the Late Pleistocene, the river divided into countless distributary channels and followed roughly its current course, depositing silt with sand and sandy gravel over the Pannonian surface which subsided along the line Bár-Lánycsók-Nagynyárád-Majs. On top so-called 'wetland loess' settled. At the dawn of the Holocene, ca. 19,000 years ago, rapid warming began, which – coupled with tectonic processes – significantly increased river discharge and induced again incision that resulted in the Mohács flood-free terrace.[12] In the process, the river channel shifted a little further east and created the eastern

---

9 Márton Pécsi, *Negyedkor és löszkutatás* [Quaternary and loess research] (Budapest: Akadémiai Kiadó, 1993), pp. 275–287.

10 Gyula Gábris, "A folyóvízi teraszok hazai kutatásának rövid áttekintése – a teraszok kialakulásának és korbeosztásának új magyarázata," [A brief overview of Hungarian reseaarch on river terraces – a new explanation of terrace origin and age] *Földrajzi Közlemények* 137 (2013), no. 3, pp. 240–247.

11 Béla Bulla ed., *Magyarország természeti földrajza* [Physical Geography of Hungary] (Budapest: Tankönyvkiadó Vállalat, 1962); Béla Molnár, "Adatok a Duna-Tisza köze fiatal harmadidőszaki és negyedkori rétegeinek tagolásához és származásához nehézásvány-összetétel alapján," [Data on the division of Upper Tertiary and Pleistocene strata in the Danube-Tisza Interfluve based on heavy mineral composition] *Földtani Közlemények* 95 (1965), no. 2, pp. 217–225; Márton Pécsi, *A magyarországi Duna-völgy kialakulása és felszínalaktana* [Development and geomorphology of the Danube Valley in Hungary] (Budapest: Akadémiai Kiadó, 1959).

12 Gábris, ibid.

steep terrace edge, which detaches from the present-day Danube bank north of Mohács and continues south in the western area of the city, in the direction of Kölked-Dályok-Izsép line.[13]

Changing courses of the Danube may have been partially caused by tectonic movements Regarding the current vertical displacements in the area, István Joó's 1998 map[14] shows a subsidence of roughly 1 mm per year on Mohács Island and 0.5 mm on the Mohács Plain, where the youngest alluvial deposits of the Danube and minor watercourses are found, dated for the last 11,700 years (i.e. the Holocene).[15]

4   The Morphological Surfaces of the Mohács Plain and Its Environs

There is no doubt that the geomorphology of the mountains and hills are much more varied than those of the plains, but it would be an exaggeration to claim that lowland landscapes are utterly uninteresting for geomorphologists. Micromorphology refers to relief and landforms ranging in size from a few centimetres to a few metres.

In previous centuries, the local population had an excellent knowledge of the microrelief and their consequences under all kinds of weather and drainage conditions. For this reason, they attached great importance to even the 2–3 m differences in elevation and took advantage of the situation during settlement allocation, transport and farming (Figure 6.2).

In the Mohács Plain and its immediate environs, four surface levels can be distinguished by elevation. The geomorphological properties are markedly different from each other (Figure 6.3):
– lower and higher floodplain levels (Figure 6.3, number 1);
– flood-free terrace (Figure 6.3, number 2);
– the hilly area bordering the Mohács Plain from the north and west (Figure 6.3, number 3).

4.1   *Lower and Higher Floodplain Surfaces*
Areas located 5–6 m above the zero level of the Danube (79.195 m above sea level at the Mohács gauge), i.e. at around 84–85 m elevation, are called lower

---

13 Pécsi, ibid.
14 István Joó, "Magyarország függőleges irányú mozgásai," [Vertical movements in Hungary] *Geodézia és Kartográfia* 50 (1998), no. 9, pp. 3–9.
15 György Lovász, "Mohácsi-sík és a Nyárád–Harkányi löszvidék," [The Mohács Plain and the Nyárád-Harkány loess area] in *Baranya megye természeti földrajza*, ed. György Lovász (Pécs: Baranya Megyei Levéltár, 1977), pp. 89–91.

GEOMORPHOLOGY OF THE MOHÁCS PLAIN AND ITS ENVIRONS 223

FIGURE 6.2   Microtopography in the Mohács Plain.
PHOTO: PÉTER GYENIZSE.

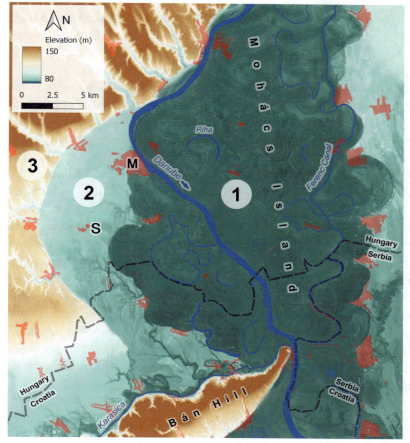

FIGURE 6.3   Geomorphological surfaces of the study area. Edited by Péter Gyenizse.
Legend: 1 = lower and higher floodplain levels (dark green); 2 = flood-free terraces (light green); 3 = hills (brown); M = Mohács; S = Sátorhely.

floodplain surfaces.¹⁶ Before river regulations they had been inundated by the Danube even at a slightly higher than mean water level; therefore, they remained dry at low water levels. Such surfaces are of Late Holocene age. Recent backwaters (permanent or temporary oxbow lakes) are characteristic of the surface, which are partly of natural origin and partly formed as a result of river regulations.¹⁷

From the evidence of the maps drawn in the past centuries, the low floodplain was mostly covered by swamps, waterlogged areas with reed-beds. Fishing and gathering related to the traditional 'notch' economy was typical. The higher ground was used as pasture in the summer. Before the regulations, humans did not settle in these low-lying areas.¹⁸

The higher floodplain surfaces rise 8–9 m above the o zero level of the Danube (i.e. 87–88 m elevation above sea level). Water could only reach them during major floods. The higher floodplain surface can be observed in patches of various size south of Mohács on the inner banks of oxbows, where extensive floodplain forests stand (e.g. the Béda Forest and the Bók Forest).¹⁹

Riverbed changes and shifts had been common over the Danube Plain until the large-scale river regulation and flow control works carried out in the 19th century. The low floodplain surface was flooded every year, while the higher floodplain surface only by occasional disastrous floods. During major floods, not only larger tributaries or meanders were created or filled up, but also smaller, usually strongly winding watercourses which drained floodwater also emerged. Between the dense network of channels, undrained flat bottoms, depressions, and saline lakes were formed.²⁰ These areas distant from watercourses, but at the same time at the lowest levels are called backswamps. In the 19–20th centuries, due to the construction of dams, most of the former geomorphological floodplain beyond the dykes became rarely affected by inundation.

Reminding of the former meandering of the Danube, the most common geomorphological feature of the floodplain is the rolling surfaces of scroll bars, consisting of point bars and swales. Point bars are arcuate aggradations not reaching above the bankfull water level built from sediment deposited on the inside of river bends. The deeper, waterlogged stripes lying between them are swales. Their arc shapes can be observed everywhere on the aerial

---

16   See at https://www.vizugy.hu.
17   Lovász, ibid.
18   Lehmann, "Mohács és környéke felszínének arculata," [Topography of Mohács and environs] in *Mohács földrajza,* eds. Erdősi et al., pp. 29–36.
19   Lehmann, ibid.
20   Pécsi, ibid.

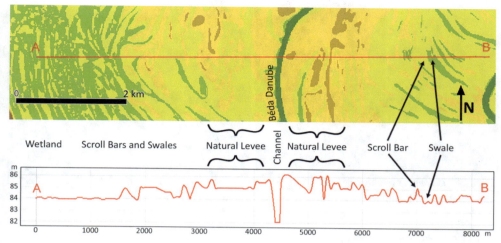

FIGURE 6.4 Topographical section of natural levees on both banks of the Béda-Danube and scroll-bar systems located farther from the riverbed. Edited by Péter Gyenizse.

and satellite images of the Danube floodplain, as well as on digital elevation models (Figure 6.4). Scroll bar systems can be used to reconstruct the most recent, several hundred or one or two thousand years old stages in the evolution of the floodplain.[21]

Landforms slightly higher than point bars are the natural levees, which accompany the channels on both banks. They owe their origin to floods. From the water leaving the channel the coarser sediment particles are directly deposited near the bed. Thus, an accumulational landform is created which rises steeper from the bed and slopes more gently in the opposite direction (Figure 6.4). The towing paths for boat navigation used to run along the natural levees accompanying the riverbed on both bank, locally even built on them. 'Notches' are the small channels that cut across the levees and connect the river and the floodplain. They played a significant part in economy (fishing, grazing, farming) during the previous centuries.

The bank stabilization and river regulation works carried out in the 19th century have very significantly transformed the surface of the floodplain. In the area protected by dams and drainage canals (between the edge of the

---

21 István Viczián, "A Duna domborzatformáló hatása Mohács környékén és az 1526. évi mohácsi csata," [Fluvial Geomorphology of the Mohács Danube Floodplain and the Battle of Mohács in 1526] in *Mohács Szimfónia. Tanulmányok a mohácsi csatával kapcsolatos kutatások eredményeiből*, eds. Szabolcs Varga and Attila Türk (Budapest: Martin Opitz Kiadó, 2022), pp. 93–114.

Lower and higher floodplain surfaces in the Vizslak Meadow

The 5–10 m high, steep edge separating the floodplain from the flood-free terrace

FIGURE 6.5   Photos of the floodplain.
PHOTO: PÉTER GYENIZSE.

geomorphological floodplain and the flood-control dykes, in the protected floodplain), since the construction of the protection works, geomorphic action has been taken over from the river by agrotechnology and today the latter governs landscape evolution. The natural watercourses are substantially reduced in number and area, they are becoming ever narrower.

4.2   *The Flood-free Terrace*

The flood-free terrace surface at an altitude of 90–100 m above sea level is separated from the higher floodplain surface by several marked ridges, which stretch in a several kilometre wide belt westward from the Danube and the floodplain until the semi-circular hill range Bár-Lánycsók-Nagynyárád-Majs-Buziglica (Figure 6.6). In the Late Pleistocene – ca. 10–15 thousand years ago – the Pannonian strata here subsided along the mentioned semicircular line. Borehole data show that the ancient Danube first deposited 6–10-m-thick sandy gravels, and then 10–12-m-thick fluvial sand on the surface which is now at 30–35-m depth and built of grey clays. Finally, at the beginning of the Holocene, this was mantled by a 9–12-m thick non-typical loess layer. However, in the Early Holocene, the area of Mohács Island sank and the river moved eastward, moving away from the semicircular rim of Bár-Lánycsók-Nagynyárád-Majs-Buziglica. In its new location, it cut its bed into the former sediment, and then carved the border of 5–10-m relative height on the line Mohács-Kölked-Dályok-Izsép, bordering the free terrace from the east, through lateral erosion.[22]

---

22   Pécsi, ibid.

The flood-free terrace south of Mohács (with the buildings of Mohács in the background)

The flood-free terrace north of Sátorhely, in the background the hills bordering it from the west

FIGURE 6.6   The flood-free terrace presented in the photos.
PHOTO: PÉTER GYENIZSE.

The terrace, covered with fertile soil, is now mainly used for farming. However, we can observe on maps from the previous centuries that in the shallow valleys of the smaller watercourses crossing the loess-mantled terrace, there occurred waterlogged areas, which were predominantly used as pastures. Due to river regulations, the extent of wetlands has been significantly reduced. The major routes ran on the free terrace, such as the thousand-year-old military road along the Danube, on which traffic was only disrupted by streambeds.[23]

Largely due to the work of waters, and to a lesser extent to the wind as geomorphic agents, microforms with a relief of a few meters have been formed on the flood-free terrace. They are either negative (often in areas of stagnant water) or positive features. A positive feature, for example, is the Látóhegy, or Látó-högy, located southwest of Mohács, next to the Mohács-Nagynyárád road (now a dirt road). "A high-lying place; it traditionally got its name from the fact that it can be seen from afar. ... You can find bricks on and around it, indicating that there was once a building and a road here." and "You can see the whole field from there."[24] It is clear from the relief section that the top of Látóhegy rises only 4–4.5 m above the surrounding terrain (Figure 6.7). Thus, local people knew the microtopography of the area well and the minimal depressions and elevations were reflected in their spatial perception, transport and

---

23   Klára T. Mérey, *Baranya megye települései az első katonai felmérés idején* [The settlements of Baranya County at the time of the Military Survey I] (Pécs: Baranya Megyei Levéltár, 2004).

24   János Pesti ed., *Baranya megye földrajzi nevei* II. [Toponymy of Baranya County II.] (Pécs: Baranya Megyei Levéltár, 1982), p. 486.

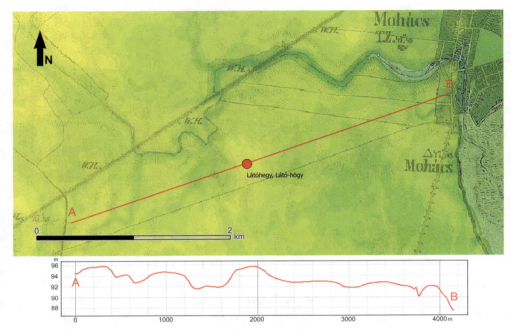

FIGURE 6.7   Topographical section of Látóhegy and its environs. Edited by Péter Gyenizse.
SOURCE OF BASE MAP: MILITARY SURVEY II (1858).

farming habits. Micro- and macro-topography influences the visibility of an area, which can be of great importance on many occasions, for instance, during a battle.

In order to settle on the plains, local people usually preferred areas close to the water, but without waterlogging. Such was the above mentioned Látóhegy, and the Sátorhely Ridge too (Figure 6.7). In its central section the free terrace is ca. 10 km wide, with the Sátorhely Ridge in the middle, but other elevations can also be observed in the area. These formerly accommodated several settlements, but today only Sátorhely is located on such an elevated terrain. The most probable theory on the formation of the ridge is that a branch of the Borza Stream coming from Nagynyárád gradually cut into the alluvial fan, which was much larger and contiguous once, and separated this outcrop from its main mass.

The negative features (depressions) of the terrace are primarily due to the geomorphic action of still existing streams, but there are also traces of watercourses active at the end of the Pleistocene.

Today the most easily noticeable and most contrasting negative forms can be associated with regulated, channelized streams: the Csele, Jenyei, Lánycsók,

GEOMORPHOLOGY OF THE MOHÁCS PLAIN AND ITS ENVIRONS

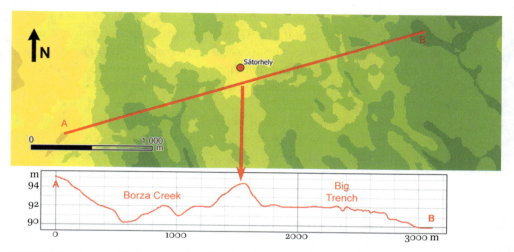

FIGURE 6.8 Topographical section of the Sátorhely Ridge with the channel of the Borza Stream to the west and the indented "Great Ditch" to the east. Edited by Péter Gyenizse.

Lajmér and Borza Streams, which now flow in artificial channels bordered by dykes on the terrace surface. However, their meandering beds active before the regulations can also be observed on contemporary maps or on current satellite images. The beds of the streams crossing the terrace are the widest and deepest along the eastern edge. The valleys of the Lánycsók and Borza Streams are 200–250 m wide and 5–6 m deep in these sections.

Aerial and satellite images taken in times of proper soil moisture content, vegetation cover, and irradiation angle also show microtopography which is hardly noticeable in the field. These include the traces of ancient watercourses, some of which may once drained to the Danube or to other major watercourses. They have been inactive for a long time and cross higher terrains of the terrace.

The material of the Mohács terrace plain was deposited by the Danube during the Late Pleistocene and possibly the Early Holocene. Its surface was certainly covered by the active branches of the river, in a way similar to the present lower and higher floodplains. The traces of the former channels have a lower sinuosity (less developed meanders) compared to now existing streams, and they mostly resemble the large bends of the present-day Danube. Consequently, the river that shaped them did not originally have a lower water flow than the Danube or its larger branch. The beds observed on satellite images are much narrower (40–70 m wide) than the main Danube branch today (400–700 m), but to our knowledge, cut-off arms are known to tend to narrow gradually after they had been abandoned, so their original widths could have been several times larger.[25] This was also observed in the case of the Rezét Dead Danube arm crossing the Gemenc Forest, where between 1896 and 2002 oxbow width was reduced from ca. 320 m to 65 m, and depth from 13 to 3 m.[26] It is therefore no coincidence that the ancient, filled, smoothed floodplain features had escaped the attention of researchers for a long time, because they are difficult to detect in the field.

The paleobed running to the east of Sátorhely village is also a long-stretching, but now only around one metre deep indentation. In our opinion, this was most likely the valley mentioned in István Brodarics' account of the battle:

> In the end, however, not only fear, but also smoke covered everything and obstructed vision; therefore, our soldiers were forced to go down to the valley, next to the marshy water, but those who remained behind fought bravely in front of the guns.[27]

In a border demarcation description from 1338, it is presumably referred to as the "Great Ditch", and in Lutfi Pasha's account as an artificial ditch that extends from the Danube to the hills.[28] The nature of the dry bed in question strongly differs from the highly sinuous, meandering beds of the active watercourses of the plain. The former bed, nearly 5 km long with gentle bends and 50–70 m width, may have seemed artificial to distant observers (Figure 6.9). In Brodarics' description, we can read about a swamp and water in the valley, which can still be found locally in the form of spots of inland water on satellite images. What was the depth of the ditch five centuries ago, before the start of large-scale and intensive cultivation? At the moment, we cannot say this exactly, but it is assumed that it had a more marked appearance and was probably deeper than at present. Today it is not a striking landform for the observer in the field (Figure 6.10).

25 Willem H. J. Toonen, Maarten G. Kleinhans, and Kim M. Cohen, "Sedimentary architecture of abandoned channel fills," *Earth Surface Process and Landforms* 37 (2011), no. 4, pp. 459–472.
26 Enikő Anna Tamás and Béla Kalocsa, "A Rezéti-Duna feltöltődésének vizsgálata," [Investigation of the infilling of the Rezét Danube] in *Élet a Duna-ártéren – természetvédelemről sokszemközt*, ed. Orsolya Somogyvári (Pécs: Duna-Dráva Nemzeti Park, 2003), pp. 43–49.
27 István Brodarics, *Igaz leírás a magyaroknak a törökkel Mohácsnál vívott csatájáról* [True account of the Battle of Mohács between Hungarians and Turkss] (Budapest, Magvető Könyvkiadó, 1983), p. 52.
28 Norbert Pap, Máté Kitanics, Péter Gyenizse, Gábor Szalai, and Balázs Polgár, "Sátorhely vagy Majs? Földvár környezeti jellemzői. A mohácsi csata centrumtérségének lokalizálása," [Sátorhely or Majs? Environmental characteristics of Földvár. Localizing the central area of the Battle of Mohács] *Történelmi Szemle* 61 (2019), no. 2, pp. 209–246.

FIGURE 6.9　The paleobed near Sátorhely and its topographical sections. Edited by Péter Gyenizse. In the top left corner the densely meandering channel of the ancient Lajmér Stream is visible, the bends of the ancient channel are much wider. Numbers indicate the sites of topographical sections. S = Sátorhely; T = Turkish Hill.
SOURCE OF BACKGROUND SATELLITE IMAGE: GOOGLEEARTH.

FIGURE 6.10　The paleomeander near Sátorhely on photographs. The ditch appears as a waterlogged zone across the agricultural field and road southwest of the Mohács National Memorial (left) and this very shallow abandoned channel is indicated by tractor tracks in a wheat field east of Sátorhely (right).
PHOTO: PÉTER GYENIZSE.

Features similar to this can be observed elsewhere on the terrace surface. However, the spatial distribution of these linear structures is not uniform. They are more common south of the Lajmér Stream as well as in the eastern terrace section. Their appearance is usually fragmentary, few long sections, such as the "Great Ditch" near Sátorhely, are detectable. In particular, we can see many fossil channel traces south of Udvar. We assume that the difference observed in the distribution of these forms can be attributed to the fact that the relative relief of the hills bordering the terrace diminishes towards the south, and completely disappears south of Buziglica. Therefore, more sediment had to be transported from the valleys of the more prominent hills to the plain, especially to its western half, better mantling the ancient riverbeds. Moving towards the south, the Majs Valley can be considered the last significant one. South of its alluvial fan, such relict fluvial features are spread all over the entire width of the terrace.

North of the Lajmér Stream, two negative topographical features are only known that could have once been riverbeds. One is the Büdös Ditch, which once separated medieval Mohács from the rest of the terrace (however, this may be younger than the beds mentioned so far). And the other, most probably, is the Dolina stretching along the northern border of the terrace, which even today reaches the Danube at the fiberboard plant of Mohács. From time to time, the Dolina could also function as the drainage route of the Jenyei water into the Danube.

In addition to the former and current beds of watercourses other lower-lying and waterlogged spots can also be found on the terrace surface. As it can be observed in the Vizslak Meadow belonging to the floodplain or in the embayment between Mohács and Kölked, the low-elevation areas typically lie in the eastern terrace foreland. Gyula Gábris mentioned a similar phenomenon at the junction of the hills and the flood-free terrace (at the western terrace edge). He explains the formation of waterlogged spots between the alluvial fans of the streams in the foreground of the hills with the following argumentation. As a result of the downcutting of the streams arriving from the hills, wide valley gaps opened on the high bluff, in front of which flat alluvial fans were built from the material transported out of the valley.[29] The alluvial fans filled up the old depression located in front of the edge along some sections of the hilly terrain, thus transforming it into a series of marshy spots of various size with reed vegetation, separated from each other (Figure 6.11).

Today, it is more difficult to detect the differences in microtopography. The excellent, chernozem-type soils formed on the terrace surface are intensively cultivated. As a consequence, the smoothing effect of tillage and rainwater is enhanced. The large-scale field cultivation of the 20th century planated the terrace surface, reducing and eliminating the differences in microtopography, which were extremely important in previous centuries, through tillage operations.

4.3   *Hilly Areas*
Completely different in pattern and origin are from the floodplain and the terrace the surface features in the hilly area that bounds the terrace in a semicircle

---

[29]   Gyula Gábris, "A mohácsi csatamező," [The battlefield of Mohács] *Föld és Ég* 15 (1980), no. 8, pp. 249–252.

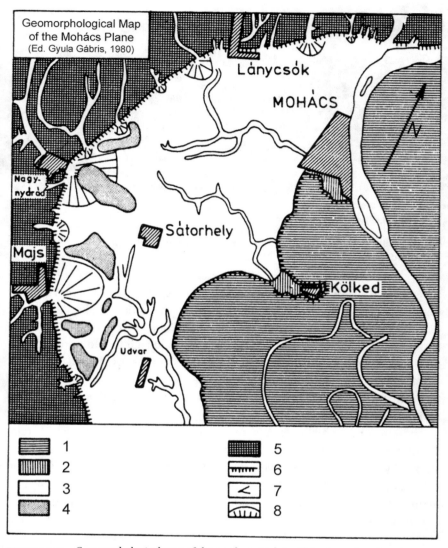

FIGURE 6.11   Geomorphological map of the northern Mohács Plain. Legend: 1 = lower floodplain; 2 = higher flood plain; 3 = flood-free terrace; 4 = waterlogged flats; 5 = Baranya Hills; 6 = high bluffs; 7 = valleys; 8 = alluvial fans.
SOURCE: GYULA GÁBRIS, "A MOHÁCSI CSATAMEZŐ," [THE BATTLEFIELD OF MOHÁCS] FÖLD ÉS ÉG 15 (1980), NO. 8, PP. 249–252.

in the northwest and west. (As mentioned before, its southern part can be considered an alluvial fan plain, rather than hills.) The relative relief here amounts to 60–70 m in the north, ca. 30 m in Nagynyárád-Majs area, but only 15 m at Buziglica (Figure 6.12).

The edge of the hills bordering the terrace from the west, between Nagynyárád and Majs

Detail of the edge of the hills northwest of Mohács

FIGURE 6.12   The hills bordering the terrace from the west presented in photos.
PHOTO: PÉTER GYENIZSE.

Its evolution history is also completely different from that of the previously described areas, which belong to the Great Hungarian Plain. After Lake Pannon receded and its basin was filled, subsidence stopped and uplift of various extent started. In the Pleistocene and Holocene in addition to fluvial erosion, other external agents (wind, frost, etc.) significantly shaped its surface. It was covered by a loess blanket during the Pleistocene glacials. Even at this time, the valleys of the streams running from the Geresd Ridge dissected this region into separate hill ranges.

The surrounding higher terrain descends to the Mohács terrace with a relatively high-angle slope, similar to the high bluffs along the Danube, which are classically built of loess. According to Gyula Gábris, when undercutting by the Paleo-Danube ended, a high bluff, significantly steeper than today, was formed in the Late Pleistocene and been gradually destroyed over the past millennia.[30]

Gyula Gábris made an attempt to determine the extent of the destruction of the high bluff since the Battle of Mohács. To this end he bored auger holes near the former village of Merse. The archaeological remains of the village were covered by about 180 cm thick sediment, which was deposited after the Battle of Mohács. In a similar way, the level of infilling could be established at several points. As it can be inferred from the cross-section and slope angle calculations, there has been no significant change in slope angle since 1526. Thus, the geomorphology and appearance of the hilly area that borders the

---

30   Gábris: ibid.

terrace from the west, where the Battle of Mohács took place, has not changed significantly in recent centuries.

5 Summary

According to the current state of research, the Battle of Mohács took place in the Mohács Plain, or more precisely, on the flood-free terrace surface. This statement is in full accordance with the contemporary description by István Brodarics:

> As we said above, in this place there is a huge, wide plain, not broken by forest, shrubs, water, or hills, only on the left side, between it and the Danube there was a muddy swamp, thickly overgrown with sedges and reeds, where many mortals later perished.[31]

So the battle took place neither on the hilly terrain nor on the otherwise flat floodplain. It is clear from Brodarics' description that the floodplain area along the Danube, unlike today, was not drained and the swampy terrain was unsuitable for military operations.

Although the Mohács terrace is a perfectly flat plain, we were able to observe several remarkable micromorphological features on its surface. These are both positive (elevations, ridges, alluvial fans) and negative (stream valleys, paleobeds) features created by rivers and the wind. Some of them played an important part in the Battle of Mohács. For instance, the "Great Ditch" behind which the Christian armies lined up was, in our assumption, a paleochannel. But Brodarics also remarked that at the beginning of the battle, a part of the Ottoman army was hidden from sight by a small mound. These microtopographical features can now be easily detected using GIS software. These investigations will be treated in other chapters of the book.

Bibliography

Brodarics, István. *Igaz leírás a magyaroknak a törökkel Mohácsnál vívott csatájáról.* [True account of the Battle of Mohács between Hungarians and Turks] Budapest, Magvető Könyvkiadó, 1983.

---

31   Brodarics, ibid, p. 46.

Bulla, Béla ed. *Magyarország természeti földrajza*. [Physical Geography of Hungary] Budapest: Tankönyvkiadó Vállalat, 1962.

Csorba, Péter. *Magyarország kistájai*. [Microregions of Hungary] Debrecen: Meridián Táj- és Környezetföldrajzi Alapítvány, 2021.

Csorba, Péter, Szilvia Ádám, Zsombor Bartos-Elekes, Teodóra Bata, Ákos Bede-Fazekas, Bálint Czúcz, Péter Csima, Gábor Csüllög, Nándor Fodor, Sándor Frisnyák, Gergely Horváth, Gábor Illés, Gábor Kiss, Károly Kocsis, László Kollányi, Éva Konkoly-Gyúró, Nikolett Lepesi, Dénes Lóczy, Ákos Malatinszky, Gábor Mezősi, Gábor Mikesy, Zsolt Molnár, László Pásztor, Imelda Somodi, Sándor Szegedi, Péter Szilassi, László Tamás, Ágnes Tirászi, and Mária Vasvári. "Tájak." [Landscapes] In *Magyarország Nemzeti Atlasza* II., ed. Károly Kocsis, 112–129. Budapest: MTA CSFK Földrajztudományi Intézet, 2018. Available at https://www.nemzetiatlasz.hu/MNA/National-Atlas-of-Hungary_Vol2_Ch10.pdf.

Gábris, Gyula. "A folyóvízi teraszok hazai kutatásának rövid áttekintése – a teraszok kialakulásának és korbeosztásának új magyarázata." [A brief overview of Hungarian reseaarch on river terraces – a new explanation of terrace origin and age] *Földrajzi Közlemények* 137 (2013): 240–247.

Gábris, Gyula. "A mohácsi csatamező." [The battlefield of Mohács] *Föld és Ég* 15 (1980): 249–252.

Gyenizse, Péter, Zita Bognár, Ákos Halmai, Tamás Morva, and Bertalan Simon. "Digitális domborzatmodellek használata tájrekonstrukciós célra szigetvári és mohácsi területeken." [Using DEMs for landscape reconstruction in the areas of Szigetvár and Mohács] In *Az elmélet és a gyakorlat találkozása a térinformatikában* IX., ed. Vanda Molnár, 121–128. Debrecen: Debreceni Egyetemi Kiadó, 2018.

Joó, István. "Magyarország függőleges irányú mozgásai." [Vertical movements in Hungary] *Geodézia és Kartográfia* 50 (1998): 3–9.

Konkoly, Sándor. "Újabb adatok Zsembéc várának lokalizációjához." [New data to locate Zsembec Castle] *Modern Geográfia* 7 (2012): 1–21.

Lehmann, Antal. "A terület földtörténeti kialakulása." [Geological history] In *Mohács földrajza*, eds. Ferenc Erdősi and Antal Lehmann, 19–28. Mohács: Mohács városi Tanács V.B. Művelődési Osztálya, 1974.

Lehmann, Antal. "Mohács és környéke felszínének arculata." [Topography of Mohács and environs] In *Mohács földrajza*, eds. Ferenc Erdősi and Antal Lehmann, 29–36. Mohács: Mohács városi Tanács V.B. Művelődési Osztálya, 1974.

Lóczy, Dénes and Márton Veress. *Geomorfológia I. Földfelszíni folyamatok és formák*. [Geomorphology I. Processes and landforms] [Budapest, Pécs: Dialóg Campus Kiadó, 2005.

Lovász, György. "Mohácsi-sík és a Nyárád–Harkányi löszvidék." [The Mohács Plain and the Nyárád-Harkány loess area] In *Baranya megye természeti földrajza*, ed. György Lovász, 89–91. Pécs: Baranya Megyei Levéltár, 1977.

Molnár, Béla. "Adatok a Duna-Tisza köze fiatal harmadidőszaki és negyedkori rétegeinek tagolásához és származásához nehézásvány-összetétel alapján." [Data on the division of Upper Tertiary and Pleistocene strata in the Danube-Tisza Interfluve based on heavy mineral composition] *Földtani Közlemények* 95 (1965): 217–225.

Pap, Norbert, Máté Kitanics, Péter Gyenizse, Gábor Szalai, and Balázs Polgár. "Sátorhely vagy Majs? Földvár környezeti jellemzői. A mohácsi csata centrumtérségének lokalizálása." [Sátorhely or Majs? Environmental characteristics of Földvár. Localizing the central area of the Battle of Mohács] *Történelmi Szemle* 61 (2019): 209–246.

Pécsi, Márton. *Negyedkor és löszkutatás.* [Quaternary and loess research] Budapest: Akadémiai Kiadó, 1993.

Pécsi, Márton. *A magyarországi Duna-völgy kialakulása és felszínalaktana.* [Development and geomorphology of the Danube Valley in Hungary] Budapest: Akadémiai Kiadó, 1959.

Pesti, János ed. *Baranya megye földrajzi nevei* II. [Toponymy of Baranya County II.] Pécs: Baranya Megyei Levéltár, 1982.

Szederkényi, Tibor. "A baranyai Duna menti mezozoós szigetrögök földtani viszonyai." [Geology of the isolated Mesozoic blocks along the Danube in Baranya] *Földtani Közlöny* 94 (1962): 28–32.

T. Mérey, Klára. *Baranya megye települései az első katonai felmérés idején.* [The settlements of Baranya County at the time of the Military Survey I] Pécs: Baranya Megyei Levéltár, 2004.

Tamás, Enikő Anna and Béla Kalocsa. "A Rezéti-Duna feltöltődésének vizsgálata." [Investigation of the infilling of the Rezét Danube] In *Élet a Duna-ártéren – természetvédelemről sokszemközt,* ed. Orsolya Somogyvári, 43–49. Pécs: Duna-Dráva Nemzeti Park, 2003.

Toonen, Willem H. J., Maarten G. Kleinhans, and Kim M. Cohen. "Sedimentary architecture of abandoned channel fills." *Earth Surface Process and Landforms* 37 (2011): 459–472.

Viczián, István. "A Duna domborzatformáló hatása Mohács környékén és az 1526. évi mohácsi csata." [Fluvial Geomorphology of the Mohács Danube Floodplain and the Battle of Mohács in 1526] In *Mohács Szimfónia. Tanulmányok a mohácsi csatával kapcsolatos kutatások eredményeiből,* eds. Szabolcs Varga and Attila Türk, 93–114. Budapest: Martin Opitz Kiadó, 2022.

CHAPTER 7

Reconstruction of the Drainage of the Mohács Plain and Its Implications for the Battle of Mohács

Péter Gyenizse, Dénes Lóczy and Gábor Varga

1   Introduction

The Danube and the minor watercourses of the study area have exerted a powerful impact on the daily life, economy, and trade of Mohács and the surrounding settlements for centuries. According to historical sources, during the Battle of Mohács, the branches of the Danube River, the Danube floodplain and the streams crossing the flood-free terrace surrounded by wetlands were highly influential. However, the regulation of the Danube and the drainage of wetlands have completely transformed the face of the landscape over the last two centuries.

This chapter was prepared in the framework of multidisciplinary research on the Battle of Mohács, so its purpose is not simply a traditional hydrogeographical description of the Mohács Plain, but primarily the investigation of the hydrological elements that may have had an impact on the battle. The chapter strongly relies on the interpretation of maps drawn in the past centuries and we have also tried to broaden our view of past drainage conditions in the area through remote sensing and GIS analyses.

2   The Danube

The Danube is the second longest river in Europe and has been an important international waterway for centuries. It issues in Germany, in the Black Forest, and travels 2850 km in southeastern direction to the Black Sea. At the beginning of the 21st century the town of Mohács is located approximately between the river kilometre marks 1445 and 1450, i.e. about halfway between the source and the mouth (Figure 7.1).

The town of Mohács and the site of the Battle of Mohács are located on the west bank of the Danube, on its flood-free terrace. To the east of them lies Mohács Island, which is bounded by the Mohács-Danube river arm to the west and the Baracska-Danube branch (today Ferenc Canal) to the

FIGURE 7.1 Location of the Danube and Mohács in Europe. Edited by Péter Gyenizse.
SOURCE OF BASE MAP: OPENTOPOGRAPHY.ORG

east. The whole of Mohács Island belongs to the floodplain of the Danube (Figure 7.2).

2.1 The Mohács-Danube and its Course before the River Regulations

Today the Mohács-Danube is the narrowest at the ferry crossing between the town and the island (270 m), while at the confluence of the Csele Stream, it is 700 m wide, and in front of the Cigány Bar, 775 m wide. This was not always the case in the past centuries, when for a long time the Baracska-Danube (today Ferenc Canal) on the eastern side of Mohács Island was the main river channel (Figure 7.3). In the 17–18th century descriptions, the expansion of the western river arm began during the life-times of the informants,[1] while its rate in the 19–20th centuries can already be easily traced on maps which are becoming more and more accurate in this period.[2]

---

1 Gábor Faludi and László Nebojszki, "A Mohácsi-sziget kialakulása és vizeinek történelmi változásai," [Origin of the Mohács Island and historical changes of its waters] *Hidrológiai Közlöny* 88 (2008), no. 4, pp. 47–57; Norbert Pap, Péter Gyenizse, Máté Kitanics, and Gábor Szalai, "Az 1526. évi mohácsi csata helyszíneinek földrajzi jellemzői," [Geographical properties of the scenes of the 1526 Battle of Mohács] *Történelmi szemle* 62 (2020), no. 1, pp. 111–151.
2 Norbert Pap, Péter Gyenizse, Máté Kitanics, and Gábor Szalai, "II. Lajos halálának helye," [Localising the death of Louis II] *Történelmi szemle* 62 (2020), no. 1, pp. 73–109.

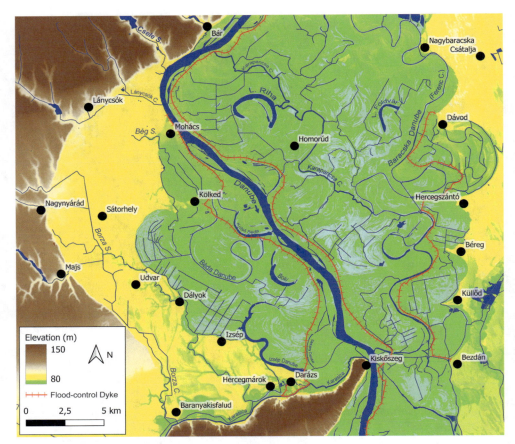

FIGURE 7.2 Drainage of the Mohács Plain today. Edited by Péter Gyenizse. Legend: C = Canal; L = Lake; S = Stream.
SOURCES OF THE DATA USED: OPENSTREETMAP.ORG, COPERNICUS GLO-30 DEM.

FIGURE 7.3 The present-day main channel of the Danube provided with massive bank protection (left) at Mohács and the contracted previous main channel, the present Ferenc Canal (right) at Nagybaracska.
PHOTO: PÉTER GYENIZSE.

The transfer of the water discharge of the Danube to the western arm created the broad Mohács arm, while the discharge of the eastern arm was heavily reduced. All these changes could be attributed to natural causes, since in the 17th and 18th centuries hardly any planned and large-scale water management intervention took place. Pál Zoltán Szabó[3], Márton Pécsi[4], and then Antal Lehmann[5] attribute the relocation of most of the flow to the western arm to neotectonic movements, i.e. uplifts and subsidences along faultlines. However, recent studies indicate that natural cycles in fluvial sediment transport and deposition activity could also have caused such a change.[6]

The Hungarian section of the Danube can be subdivided into several stretches of different channel pattern. Due to the hard, armored bed formed of rolled gravel dowstream Budapest, the river meanders only slightly, but in the lower Hungarian section tends to show higher sinuosity (well-developed meanders).[7] Recurrent floods also significantly contribute to meander formation. On the Hungarian section of the Danube, late-winter ice jams are very destructive, but sometimes the early-summer ice jams can also inflict severe damage.[8]

Andrea Kiss and József Laszlovszky documented Danube floods during the period under study. Between the late 1470s and the early 1500s, there usually occurred an ice-free or an ice-jam flood every other year. From 1585 three serious events are cited and such events were also common in the 1560s and

---

3 Pál Zoltán Szabó, "A Délkelet-Dunántúl felszínfejlődési kérdései," [Surface formation issues in Southeastern Transdanubia] *Földrajzi Értesítő* 6 (1957), no. 4, pp. 397–419.
4 Márton Pécsi, *A magyarországi Duna-völgy kialakulása és felszínalaktana* [Formation and morphology of the Hungarian Danube Valley] (Budapest: Akadémiai Kiadó, 1959), p. 184.
5 Antal Lehmann, "A terület földtörténeti kialakulása," [The geological history of the area] in *Mohács földrajza*, ed. Ferenc Erdősi (Mohács: Mohács városi Tanács V.B. Művelődési Osztálya, 1974), pp. 19–28.
6 Krisztina Sebe, Gábor Csillag, Piroska Pazonyi, and Zsófia Ruszkiczay-Rüdiger, "Quaternary evolution of the Danube River in the central Pannonian Basin and its possible role as an ecological barrier to the dispersal of ground squirrels," *Historical Biology* 30 Sep 2019, pp. 1–20. Available at https://www.tandfonline.com/doi/full/10.1080/08912963.2019.1666838 (2020. 07. 31.).
7 Enikő Tamás and Béla Kalocsa, "Alluviális árterek morfológiai összehasonlítása," [Morphological comparison of alluvial floodplains] in *Élet a Duna-ártéren - természetvédelemről sokszemközt*, ed. Orsolya Somogyvári (Pécs: 2003). Available at http://bite.sugovica.hu/ed2003/cikk/kalocsa_morfo.htm (2020. 07. 29.).
8 Gábor Faludi and Attila Szádeczky, "Az 1956. évi jeges árvíz a Duna magyarországi déli szakaszán," [The ice flood of 1956 in the southern part of the Danube in Hungary] *Hidrológiai Közlöny* 84 (2002), no. 5, pp. 293–304; Sándor Láng and Ferenc Probáld, "Az 1965. évi dunai nyári árvíz," [The Danube summer flood of 1965] *Földrajzi Közlemények* 91 (1967), no. 1, pp. 45–54.

1570s.[9] It is probable that the floods of the 16th century promoted the transfer of discharge into the Mohács arm. More detailed investigations also pointed out that the year 1526 had a wetter-than-average summer in the Pannonian Basin, which resulted in higher-than-average water levels on the Danube and its tributaries. The lower floodplain surfaces of the Danube were presumably inundated at the time of the battle. However, a significant but not destructive flood was recorded for 1526 in the chronicles.[10]

Flood control and river regulation issues first attracted the attention of water management experts in 1816, when the simultaneous floods of the Tisza, Körös and Maros Rivers affected Szeged and in 1838, during the dramatic and destructive Pest flood. These events induced large-scale river regulation and flood-control works in the Pannonian Basin.[11] The classical objective of river regulation is to ensure the passage of water, sediment load and river ice without causing damage. In the lower Hungarian section of the Danube, the regulatory works performed out of economic necessity started already in the period before hydrographic mapping (1823–1830) and continued with some interruptions until the turn of the century. As a consequence, at first the previously intense meander formation only reduced in rate, and then completely ceased. During the regulations, the Hungarian section of the Danube downstream Budapest became shorter by more than 100 km (as a result of meander cutoffs).[12] According to the data of Ferenc Erdősi, in the study area the Bok Bend was cut off in 1814, the inner Béda Bend in 1820, and the Mocskos Bend in 1821.[13] The National Atlas of Hungary demonstrates that since the construction of flood-control dykes, the Mohács Island is exposed to medium flood risk,

---

9 Andrea Kiss and József Laszlovszky, "14th–16th-Century Danube Floods and Long-Term Water-Level Changes in Archaeological and Sedimentary Evidence in The Western and Central Carpathian Basin: an Overview with Documentary comparison," *Journal of Environmental Geography* 6 (2013), no. 3–4, pp. 1–11.

10 Andrea Kiss, "A kis jégkorszak, a Spörer minimum és Mohács," [The Little Ice Age, the Spörer Minimum and Mohács] in *Mohács Szimfónia. Tanulmányok a mohácsi csatával kapcsolatos kutatások eredményeiből,* eds. Szabolcs Varga and Attila Türk (Budapest: Martin Opitz Kiadó, 2022), pp. 17–46.

11 Gábor Varga, Szabolcs Ákos Fábián, István Péter Kovács, and Ferenc Schweitzer, "Gondolatok a Kárpát-medencei folyók árvizeiről," [Thoughts on the floods of the rivers of the Carpathian basin] *Földrajzi Közlemények* 142 (2018), no. 4, pp. 291–308.

12 Béla Kalocsa and Enikő Tamás, "A folyamszabályozás morfológiai hatásai a Dunán," [The morphological effects of flow regulation along the Danube] in Élet a Duna-ártéren - természetvédelemről sokszemközt, ed. Orsolya Somogyvári (Pécs: 2003). Available at http://bite.sugovica.hu/ed2003/cikk/kalocsa_morfo.htm (2020. 07. 29.)

13 Ferenc Erdősi, *A társadalom hatása a felszínre, a vizekre és az éghajlatra a Mecsek tágabb környezetében.* [The impact of society on the surface, waters and climate in the wider environment of Mecsek] (Budapest: Akadémiai KIadó, 1987).

while the protected floodplains on the west bank of the Danube are of low flood risk.[14]

To reconstruct the course of the Mohács-Danube in 1526 with absolute precision is now almost impossible since fluvial geomorphic action has completely reshaped the floodplain topography since then. In the stretch from Báta to Mohács, the contemporary riverbed probably ran very close to the edge of the bluff or the flood-free terrace. The lateral erosion of the river channel shifting in western direction is clearly shown on 19th-century maps (previously no sufficiently accurate maps had been drawn). The lateral channel wandering did not have an equal rate along all stretches. Between 1808 and 1880, the area around the mouth of the Csele Stream was only slightly affected, but along the stretch downstream, between the confluence and Mohács, the bank was intensively undercut. The outer curve of the meander bend shifted 200–300 m to the west in 72 years, destroying a significant section of the main road to Buda which ran on the flood-free terrace surface (Figure 7.4). Due to the massive bank protection structures built at the end of the 19th century and in the 20th century, the bankline of the Danube has essentially remained unchanged in this section since 1880. A minor alteration can be observed within the town of Mohács in the last half millennium. The eastern part of Mohács was also washed away by the Danube during the studied period, about 50 m of the area of the palisades earthworks fort built in 1559 was destroyed.[15] Relying on the Roman-era Altinum fortress and watchtower (Turkish Hill, Törökdomb, Figure 7.7) and the Avar finds from the 6–8th century, István Viczián believes that the alignment of the terrace edge in the section downstream Mohács has not changed significantly over the last half millennium. He claims that the terrace margin was constantly undercut until the end of the 4th century by the active riverbed in the embayment between Mohács and Kölked and in the Vizslak Embayment downstream Kölked until the end of the 8th century.[16] Later, the

---

14　József Szabó, Ferenc Schweitzer, Gergely Horváth, Zita Bihari, Szabolcs Czigány, Szabolcs Fábián, Gyula Gábris, Krisztina Iványi, Attila Kerényi, József Lóki, Donát Magyar, Gergely Mányoki, Zsolt Molnár, Gábor Négyesi, László Pásztor, György Pátzay, Ervin Pirkhoffer, Mária Szabó, Árpád Szentiványi, Gergely Szövényi, László Tóth, Orsolya Udvardy, Gábor Varga, and György Varga, "Természeti veszélyek," [Natural hazards] in *Magyarország Nemzeti Atlasza*, ed. Károly Kocsis (Budapest: Magyar Tudományos Akadémia, Csillagászati és Földtudományi Kutatóközpont, Földrajztudományi Intézet, 2018), pp. 156–167.

15　Frigyes Kőnig and István Pánya, "A mohácsi török palánkvár," [The Turkish palanquin fortress in Mohács] in *Várak, kastélyok, templomok. Évkönyv 2018*, ed. Pál Kósa (Kökény: 2018), pp. 24–29.

16　István Viczián, "A Duna domborzatformáló hatása Mohács környékén és az 1526. évi mohácsi csata," [Fluvial Geomorphology of the Mohács Danube Floodplain and the Battle of Mohács in 1526] in *Mohács Szimfónia*, eds. Varga et al., 93–114.

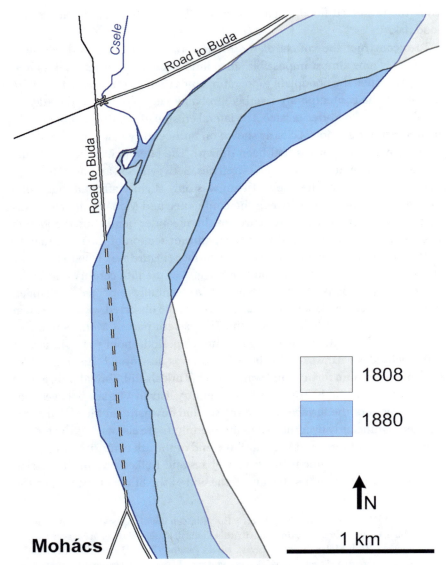

FIGURE 7.4 Changes of the Danube channel north of Mohács between 1808 and 1880. Edited by Péter Gyenizse.
MAP SOURCES: MNL OL S_12_-_DIV._XIII._-_NO._370., AVAILABLE AT HTTPS://MAPS.HUNGARICANA.HU/HU/MOLTERKEPTAR/5409/VIEW/?BBOX=-767%2C-3423%2C4662%2C-966,1808 MILITARY SURVEY III, 1880.

river moved away from the edge. Thus, at the time of the Battle of Mohács, the edge of the terrace already had its current position.

Few accurate descriptions and maps of the Danube section between Mohács and Kiskőszeg have survived from the period before regulation and flood-control works. The first useful maps date from the late 17th century and early 18th century. There are more maps available from the end of the 18th and beginning of the 19th century. Among them navigation maps stand out for their accuracy.

In the course of the research, we performed a comparative investigation of some early map representations in order to locate the course and dimensions of the Mohács Danube around 1685. For this study, we compared four maps:[17]
– the so-called Karlsruhe map dated around 1685;[18]
– Marsigli's map of 1726;[19]
– the map drawn by Eisenhut in 1791[20] (which, in our opinion, shows the course of the Danube more accurately than the Military Survey I); and
– the map sheets of the Military Survey II (1858).

We consider the reconstruction of the Danube channel in 1685 important because it shows the situation in which the transfer of water discharge capable of geomorphic action into the Mohács arm only had begun a few decades before. It can, therefore, be assumed that the Danube channel had occupied a similar position at the time of the Battle of Mohács.

However, when drawing conclusions, we must take into account some facts of physical geography and geodesy-cartography. Although the theodolite with a telescope and the triangulation methodology were already known in the second half of the 17th century, the physical conditions of the Danube section downstream Mohács made accurate surveying very difficult. We can, therefore, rightly assume that some details visible on earlier maps can only be accepted with appropriate criticism.

---

17   The authors thank Máté Kitanics for his help in collecting the maps.
18   Unknown author, *Topographischer Entwurff der umliegenden Gegend bey Sectzu (Seetsche, Dunaszekcsö in Ungarn)* (Around 1685) Available at http://www.landesarchiv-bw.de/plink/?f=4-4105632-1.
19   Luigi Ferdinando Marsigli, *A Duna Bécs és Giorgio közti szakaszának térképe* [Map of the section of the Danube between Vienna and Giorgio] (Haag, fig). Institute and Museum of Military History, B IX b 112. Available at https://maps.hungaricana.hu/hu/HTITerkeptar/2088/ (It can be assumed that the map is based on Marsigli's survey at the end of the 17th century).
20   G. J. Eisenhut, *Mappa exhibens inundationem Insulae Mohatsiensis ... 1791*. Hungarian National Archaives S_11_-_No._1441. Available at https://maps.hungaricana.hu/hu/MOLTerkeptar/2985/.

We extracted the necessary details from the selected maps and superimposed them on one another at the same scale (Figure 7.5). Since map styles greatly differed, we elaborated a standardized method for comparison. In all cases, the centerlines of the river arms were depicted with a skeleton line of uniform thickness. According to their geometry, the skeleton lines were divided into elementary straight or curved sections. During the comparison, we did not primarily focus on the size of the individual elements, but rather on their shape and morphology. Comparing the sequential order of these elements can help identify the details of the 1685 map, the earliest which can

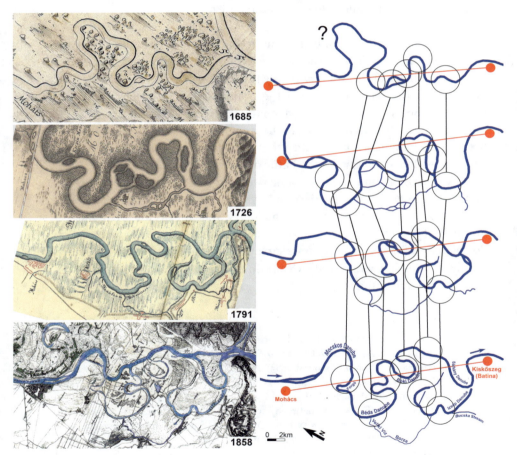

FIGURE 7.5   Results of map comparisons with the aim of reconstructing the late 17th century course of the Danube. Edited by Péter Gyenizse. The relationships between several elementary components can be identified on the sketch maps from different dates (black circles and lines). On the line for 1685, a question mark indicates a meander, then active but later cut-off (Lower Danube, Figure 7.6).

RECONSTRUCTION OF THE DRAINAGE OF THE MOHÁCS PLAIN

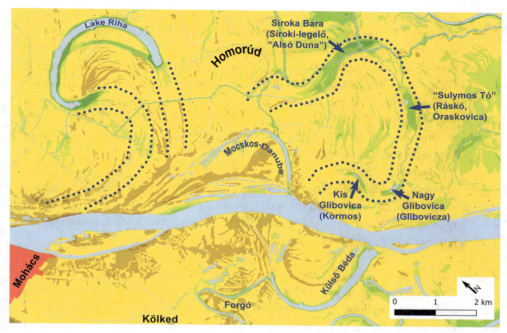

FIGURE 7.6   The channel sections linked to Lake Riha and the one-time bend which may be called Lower Danube on the digital elevation model. Edited by Péter Gyenizse.

be interpreted. In the meantime, we naturally also had to take into account that the Mohács-Danube channel had also changed. We marked Mohács and Kiskőszeg (Batina) with a red dot on the sketch maps.

The order of the details and elements of the Danube in 1685 can be better identified starting from Kiskőszeg, because moving in the other direction a difficulty arises immediately after Mohács. The Izsép-Danube near Kiskőszeg, then the Bok-Danube, and the Béda-Danube, or more precisely, their presumed antecedents, can also be recognized in this early representation. However, south of Mohács (on the right in the figure), a meander remarkably large in comparison to the others and apparently with an east-northeast alignment appears as a striking feature. The question is whether this fact can only be attributed to the distortion of the map, or does it show a previously existing meander that has been cut off since then?

To solve this issue, satellite images and the digital elevation model of the area were studied in detail. If this was really a river channel, an earlier meander, its relatively recent traces have to be visible on these spatial data sources. A deep-lying and youthful oxbow, or a trace of a former bed were sought on Mohács Island. There were two candidates for this: Lake Riha and a large riverbed remnant located south of today's Homorúd (for the sake of simplicity, let's extend the name Lower Danube found in the Donau Atlas to the entire feature).[21] In the area of the Lower Danube, there are also four wetlands with stagnant water, which are distinguished by names on the maps: Siroka Bara (Siroki pasture, "Lower Danube"), "Sulymos Tó" (Ráskó, Oraskovica); Great Glibovica (Glibovicza); Little Glibovica (Kormos).[22] It is the Lower Danube, not Lake Riha, that clearly corresponds to the drainage conditions shown on the 1685 map. Whether due to natural or artificial cutoff, Lake Riha already existed on the island at that time. Based on the 1685 map, we attempted to reconstruct the course of the Mohács Danube arm in the 17th century (Figure 7.7, dashed black line).

It can be concluded that the current bed of the Danube between Mohács and Kiskőszeg has little to do with that solely formed by the river before the regulations. When researching the Battle of Mohács, you have to reckon with a narrower, but much longer and more sinuous river bed.

2.2 Hydrography of the Lower and Higher Danube Floodplain Surfaces

From a hydrological point of view, the floodplain means the land strip along a river where flooding is expected at present with a certain frequency.[23] Protected floodplains are formerly active floodplains where now flood-control structures prevent inundation. Geomorphology considers the floodplain as a dynamic phenomenon, and takes into account the nature of geomorphic evolution. The geomorphological floodplain thus delimited is accordingly much larger than the hydrological one. From a geomorphological point of view, the floodplain is a group of alluvial landforms that accompany the river channel beyond the banks. It covers all areas with a characteristic assemblage of features of fluvial origin, including scroll bars, natural levees, abandoned riverbeds, backswamps.[24]

The floodplain of the investigated area comprises Mohács Island and the embayments on the right bank of the Danube.

---

21   Rauchmüller, *Donau Atlas. Hydrographische Donau Karte von Peterwardein bis Orschova* (Buda: 1834). Available at https://maps.hungaricana.hu/hu/HTITerkeptar/2121/.
22   Rauchmüller, Donau Atlas...; Military Survey II; Military Survey III; 1:10.000 Topography Map.
23   Dénes Lóczy, "Az árterek geomorfológiai osztályozásai a nemzetközi szakirodalomban," [Geomorphological classifications of flood plains in the international literature] *Földrajzi Közlemények* 137 (2013), no. 2, pp. 105–120.
24   Dénes Lóczy, "Folyóvízi felszínformálás," [Fluvial geomorphology] in *Geomorfológia, I. Földfelszíni folyamatok és formák*, eds. Dénes Lóczy and Márton Veress (Budapest, Pécs: Dialóg Campus, 2005), pp. 17–130.

RECONSTRUCTION OF THE DRAINAGE OF THE MOHÁCS PLAIN

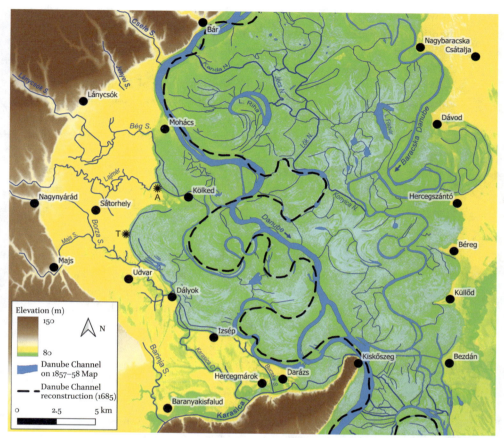

FIGURE 7.7　Drainage map of the Mohács Plain in the first half of the 19th century. Edited by Péter Gyenizse. Legend: C = Canal; N = "Notch"; S = Stream; A = Altinum; T = Turkish Hill. Maps used for the work: A Duna-mappáció, a Duna folyó magyarországi szakaszának térképei (1819–1833) az osztrák határtól Péterváradig. [The Danube Mapping, maps of the Hungarian section of the Danube River (1819–1833) from the Austrian border to Petersburg] DVD-ROM (Pécs: 2006); Baranya Vármegye föld abrosza. [Map of Baranya County] [B IX a 1441] 1938 https://maps.hungaricana.hu/hu/HTITerkeptar/949/; Second Military Survey (1857–1858).

Until 1870, Mohács Island was often flooded. The island slopes slightly from northwest to southeast. The passage of floodwaters also follows this direction on the island. The old beds ("notches") ensured that the area could be naturally drained. Numerous lakes and swampy depressions extended across the lower floodplain surface, making it difficult to cross. Its largest standing water is Lake Riha, which could be cut off from the Mohács-Danube arm. The exact time of the cut-off is not known: Dániel Szávoszt-Vass puts this event to the period between the 6–17th centuries,[25] and István Pánya believes that it is already mentioned as a lake in a 1339 document.[26] Based on our previously presented reconstruction investigation, we also see that it must have been detached from the Danube before 1685.

The 18–19th century maps show the southern half of Mohács Island as a much more marshy area than the northern part. There were several settlements in the north in the Middle Ages,[27] and it was noted that in the dry season they can be crossed by carriages, not just on foot.[28] There were also many pastures and gardens in the northern section.

South of Mohács, the higher and lower floodplain levels widen significantly between the Danube and the flood-free terrace. A vivid description of the early 19th century conditions of the marshy embayments on the west bank of the Danube is provided by Klára T. Mérey:[29]

> The marshes in Mohács and Kölked start at Mohács and continue to Izsép. They largely consist of wet meadows overgrown with bulrush and reeds. It is full of small puddles and divided by ditches. In the middle there is a drier area where the village of Kölked stands on a small hill. It only has a small meadow on the edges. This marsh is sometimes completely flooded

---

25   Dániel Szávoszt-Vass, "Támpontok a Mohácsi-Duna medrének 1526-os rekonstrukciójához," [Reference Points for the Reconstruction of the Mohács-Danube riverbed in 1526] in Mohács Szimfónia, eds. Varga et al., pp. 79–92.

26   István Pánya, "A Mohácsi-sziget középkori topográfiája," [Medieval topography of the Mohács Island] *Történeti földrajzi közlemények* 8 (2020), no. 3–4, pp. 105–120.

27   Sándor Konkoly, "Újabb adatok Zsembéc várának lokalizációjához," [New data for the localization of the castle of Zsembéc] *Modern Geográfia* 7 (2012), no. 2, pp. 1–21; Sándor Konkoly, "Középkori vár vagy római erőd? Rejtélyes nyomok a Mohácsi-szigetről," [Medieval castle or Roman fortress? Mysterious clues from Mohács Island] in *Ingenia Hungarica 1. Kárpát-medencei Szakkollégiumi Konferencia*, ed. László Horváth (Budapest: 2015), pp. 177–204; Sándor Konkoly, "Sembech középkori várának lokalizációja. A geográfia eszközeivel egy történeti rejtély nyomában," [The location of medieval castle of Sembech. In pursuit of a historical mystery with the tools of geography] in *Opuscula historica 1. Tanulmányok a XIV. és XV. Eötvös Konferenciákról*, ed. Bálint Ternovácz (Budapest: ELTE Eötvös József Collegium, 2015), pp. 13–44; István Pánya, "A Mohácsi-sziget középkori topográfiája," [Medieval topography of the Mohács Island] *Történeti földrajzi közlemények* 8 (2020), no. 3–4, pp. 105–120.

28   Klára T. Mérey, *Baranya megye települései az első katonai felmérés idején* [The settlements of Baranya County at the time of the Military Survey I] (Pécs: Baranya Megyei Levéltár, 2004), pp. 108–126.

29   Klára T. Mérey, *A Dél-Dunántúl földrajza katonaszemmel a 19. század elején* [The geography of Southern Transdanubia from a soldier's point of view at the beginning of the 19th century] (Geographia Pannonica Nova) 1 (Pécs: Lomart Kiadó, PTE TTK Földrajzi Intézet, 2007), pp. 100–101.

by the Danube. Only in dry summers do some parts dry out and in winter it freezes completely. By the way, this marsh can only be visited on two known roads, namely from Mohács to Kölked and from Dállya to Izsép, but only in very dry weather and only on foot or by light vehicles. ... At the end, he notes that this swamp is completely useless from a military point of view.

The traditional human utilisation of Danubian floodplains took the form of exploiting 'notch' systems. According to the ethnographer Andrásfalvy's definition, a 'notch' (in Hungarian: fok) is 'a man-made ditch cutting through natural levees and during high stages allowing water flow out over the entire floodplain and during recession back to the channel.'[30] The system dates back to the 13th century at least. Primary channels lead floodwater to the plain and a network of secondary ones link oxbows, meander swales and backswamps to them in order to ensure water storage and prevent the seasonal desiccation of the floodplain.

The traditional floodplain economy had a range of advantages for the local population:[31]

1. At flooding water left the channel in a tranquil flow and spread over the floodplain almost uniformly. Devastation by flood waves could be avoided.
2. During high water stages and well after the flood began to recede, water could be stored in the floodplain. When it was no longer needed, it could be conducted through the notches gradually back into the main channel. The damage by stagnant water of deteriorating quality on vegetation and fish stock could be eliminated.
3. Flooding of a floodplain section created spawning grounds with optimal depth of inundation. Thus the reproduction of fish stocks was ensured. Fishing in the notches provided protein-rich nutrition even in times of food shortage.
4. An immediate economic use is manifested in keeping meadows well-watered all the year round for mowing and grazing and in increasing the fertility of alluvial soils by the deposition of nutrient-rich mud. Vegetable gardens and orchards could be established in the floodplain.
5. The artificial canals between oxbows, swales and backswamps also functioned as waterways across otherwise inaccessible areas.

---

30 Bertalan Andrásfalvy, *A Sárköz és a környező Duna-menti területek ősi ártéri gazdálkodása és vízhasználatai a szabályozás előtt* [Ancient floodplain economy and water management in the Sárköz and the areas adjacent to the Danube] (Vízügyi Történeti Füzetek) 6 (Budapest: Vízügyi Dokumentációs és Tájékoztató Iroda, 1973).
31 Andrásfalvy, ibid.

Interpreting maps from the first half and middle of the 19th century, the drainage in the investigated area two hundred years ago was reconstructed. The 1857–1858 the Danube channel is depicted on the map sheets of the Military Survey II. The "notches" Kanda, Jécs, Lök and Konyica were particularly important on the island at that time (Figure 7.7).

The water regulation and drainage works that started at the beginning of the 19th century have completely transformed the drainage of the Danube floodplain. The Ferenc Canal was built on the eastern margin of the floodplain in 1802, and the Baracska-Danube arm was blocked from the north in 1870. Starting in 1825, ever higher flood-control embankments were erected along the Danube. On the island and in the western embayments, in 1899, flood-control and land drainage associations were founded, which until the middle of the 20th century had governed the drainage of an area of 370 km^2 and prevented waterlogging there through digging hundreds of kilometres of canals.[32]

River regulation and land drainage measures have achieved their objectives: the hazard of ice-jam floods has been remarkably reduced and a waterway of required dimensions could be ensured. The flood-control structures prevent flooding of the protected floodplain, safeguard settlements and industrial facilities, and enable agricultural cultivation. However, the water supply of water bodies in the active floodplain (abandoned channels, wet meadows) is deteriorating due to the combined effects of main channel incision and sediment deposition over the active floodplain. Due to the unidirectional change in water balance, desiccation processes can be observed which are unfavorable for the typical floodplain vegetation as well as for the reproduction of amphibians and fish. Foraging places for waterfowl are no more guaranteed year after year.[33]

---

32   Zoltán Károlyi, "A Duna-völgy vizeinek szabályozása," [Regulation of the waters of the Danube Valley] in *A magyar vízszabályozás története II.,* ed. Dénes Ihrig (Budapest: Országos Vízügyi Hivatal, 1973); *A magyarországi Duna-szakasz és kisebb mellékvizei* [The Hungarian section of the Danube and its smaller tributaries] (Magyarország hidrológiai atlasza) I/9 (Budapest: Vízgazdálkodási Tudományos Kutató Intézet, 1962), pp. 134–181.

33   Kalocsa et al., A folyamszabályozás [The morphological effects] in Élet a Duna-ártéren, ed. Somogyvári; András Hervai, *A Mohácsi-sziget talajvíz rendszerének átalakulása a tájátalakítások* következményeként. PhD-értekezés [The transformation of the groundwater system of Mohács Island as a consequence of landscape changes. PhD thesis] (Pécs: PTE TTK, 2020); András Hervai, Dávid Nagy and Sándor Konkoly, "Landscape transformations on Mohács Island following river regulations," *Podravina* 37 (2020), no. 19, pp. 47–60.

3 Streams on the Flood-free Terrace

3.1 *The Csele Stream*

The best-known watercourse of the area, the Csele, only crosses the Mohács Plain in a short section, on its northern edge (Figures 7.2 and 7.7). In the work of Klára T. Mérey (2004), we can read that at the end of the 18th century: "… the Csely (or Csele) Stream is 4-feet wide and 1–2-feet deep, swampy terrain. It has a clay and sandy bed. A bridge built at the mill of the Csely Stream allows crossing. The stream is passable for both cavalry and infantry."[34]

The Csele Stream enters the area from the northwest, from the Baranya Hills, while also collecting the waters of the Himesháza Ditch and the Szebény Watercourse. Its catchment area is about 87 km², and its maximum water flow is estimated at 34 m³/s.[35] Leaving its 50–200 m wide, wet valley floor, it runs about 700 m through the northernmost corner of the Mohács Plain. Meanwhile, it cuts deeper and deeper into the loess-mantled terrace surface before reaching the sinking level of the Danube (Figure 7.8). Around the confluence, in the area called Gyurgyóv,[36] the terrace surface is slightly lower today. According to the evidence of the Military Survey II map sheet (1858), the stream did not run straight to the Danube, but rather meandered, splitting into several branches

FIGURE 7.8   The incised narrow bed of the Csele Stream next to the confluence with the Danube.
PHOTO: PÉTER GYENIZSE

---

34   T. Mérey, *Baranya megye települései*, [The settlements of Baranya County] pp. 108–126.
35   Zoltán Dövényi ed., *Magyarország kistájainak katasztere* [Cadastre of the landscap units of Hungary] (Budapest: MTA Földrajztudományi Kutatóintézet, 2010).
36   János Pesti ed., *Baranya megye földrajzi nevei II*. [The geographical names of Baranya County II] (Pécs: Baranya Megyei Levéltár, 1982), pp. 351–583.

at the confluence. The bend near the confluence can already be seen as cut off on the map sheet of the Military Survey III (1880). The widening of the Danube and undercutting the high bank may have played a major part in destroying the bend near the confluence.

3.2 The Catchment of the Jenyei Water

The Jenyei Water Stream (also called canal or ditch) issues in the Baranya Hills, near the village Székelyszabar. Jenei or Paprika Mill stands at the gate of the marshy valley leading to the plain. On the maps of the Military Survey I (1783) and Military Survey II (1858), the stream did not reach the Danube, but disappeared in the marshy wetland overgrown by grasses between the mill and the town of Mohács, its course was interrupted and its water leaked away (Figure 7.7). Towards the northeast from the valley gate, from the mill to the confluence with the Csele Stream, there is a subsidence area which can be clearly identified on the DEM and which could have been the bed of the Jenyei Stream once (Figure 7.9). Its middle section is called the Dolina (meaning valley in Slavic), a waterlogged terrain where animals used to be watered.[37] It is assumed to be aligned along an ancient valley. Around 1936, it was channelized jointly with the Lánycsók Stream, and since then it flows into the Danube at the industrial district in the northern part of Mohács.[38]

3.3 The Lánycsók Stream Catchment

The Lánycsók Stream issues from several headwaters in the Baranya Hills. Its catchment area is 90 km², and its highest estimated flood discharge is

FIGURE 7.9   The Dolina, a slight depression east of the fiberboard plant.
PHOTO: PÉTER GYENIZSE

---

37   Pesti ed., *Baranya megye földrajzi nevei*, [The geographical names of Baranya County] pp. 351–583.

38   Pesti ed., *Baranya megye földrajzi nevei*, [The geographical names of Baranya County] pp. 351–583.

estimated at 36 m³/s.³⁹ It appears on maps and in written sources under different names: Lánycsók Stream, Maráza-Lánycsók Stream, Bácsfa Stream, Bég Stream, Betschwar Jarek, Mühl Bach (Mill Stream). It entered the plain from a valley south of Lánycsók, formerly called Csotala Grund, and then, roughly to the east, reached the Danube floodplain at Mohács (Figure 7.7). In the lower section, wet sections were recorded in several places in the bed of the stream, better known as Bég Stream.

In a late 18th century description: "The mill stream has flat banks that do not rise anywhere. The riverbed is marshy, it has drinking water for the animals, it never dries up, it runs overbank in spring and autumn."⁴⁰

The channel section where the stream leaves the valley is relatively straight. In the western section it was probably regulated as early as the early 19th century. However, it can be observed on the satellite images that the channelized main branch is connected to two parallel, winding arms from the south, which only occasionally conducted water in the 18th and 19th centuries.

The stream bed is crossed by the road leading from Mohács to Nagynyárád. A 18th-century military expert wrote the following about it: "The road towards Nyárád is rarely dry but crosses marshy meadows, which cannot be traversed with heavy weapons (batteries) due to the soft ground."

In 1902, the Kölked Flood Control Association relocated the confluence of the Lánycsók Stream above Mohács. The Jenyei water was also diverted into this channel⁴¹ (Figure 7.2). Its lower section used to be wet, but now it is cut from its water supply and only functions as a rainwater drainage ditch.

3.4 *The Lajmér Stream*

The stream was named after the medieval village of Lajmér, which once lay on its banks.⁴² It is located between the catchment of two sizeable streams (the Lánycsók and the present-day Borza Streams) of the Mohács flood-free terrace (Figure 7.7). This leads to the delicate situation that since the early 20th century water regulations it has not received water supply from the hills, it has dried up and its bed was converted to ploughland around 1938.⁴³ Despite tillage, the former bed is clearly visible on the DEM and satellite images (Figure 7.10).

---

39 Dövényi ed., *Magyarország kistájainak katasztere*. [Cadastre of the landscap units of Hungary].
40 T. Mérey, *Baranya megye települései*, [The settlements of Baranya County] pp. 108–126.
41 Pesti ed., *Baranya megye földrajzi nevei*, [The geographical names of Baranya County] pp. 351–583.
42 Pesti ed., *Baranya megye földrajzi nevei*, [The geographical names of Baranya County] pp. 351–583.
43 Pesti ed., *Baranya megye földrajzi nevei*, [The geographical names of Baranya County] pp. 351–583.

FIGURE 7.10 The plain section of the Lajmér Stream with waterlogged areas. Legend: A = Altinum.
SOURCE: GOOGLE EARTH SATELLITE IMAGE FROM 2006.

The stream meandered through the Mohács terrace from east to west, then crossed the thousand-year-old war road at the Kölked Tavern and reached the Danube floodplain next to the former Roman fortress (Altinum, Castle Hill). Its water must have fed the marshes near the terrace margin in the past.

The water regime of the stream must have been very extreme. Several waterlogged areas were recorded along the watercourse. For example, according to the informants, the "Lajmíri big pit" was a pond which flooded the road in rainy weather, so horse-drawn carriages had to make kilometre-long diversions.[44] On the Military Survey I map sheet, the Leimer and Teicho lakes were accommodated in the riverbed, but it was recorded as dry during the summer.[45]

Analyzing the written descriptions and the maps we concluded that most of the wet areas around the Lajmér Stream which made traffic difficult were close to the hills and near the confluence. The middle part of the plain section of the stream only obstructed traffic parallel to the stream and to a lesser extent along the roads crossing it.

3.5 The Borza Stream

The most prominent watercourse of the Mohács terrace, the Borza meandered through the area in a northwest-southeast direction (Figure 7.7). Its catchment area is 138 km², and its maximum estimated flood discharge is 37 m³/s.[46]

---

[44] Pesti ed., *Baranya megye földrajzi nevei*, [The geographical names of Baranya County] pp. 351–583.
[45] T. Mérey, *Baranya megye települései*, [The settlements of Baranya County] pp. 108–126.
[46] Dövényi ed., *Magyarország kistájainak katasztere*. [Cadastre of the landscap units of Hungary].

It originally had two more important arms, (1) the Versend Stream (Mill Stream) coming from the Nagynyárád Valley, which was actually known as Barza or Borza, and (2) the Malomárok (Majs Stream) coming from the Majs Valley. They probably flowed down the alluvial fans in variable directions, then reached the actual Borza Valley, where they flowed southeast in the markedly incised, winding bed. The stream reached the Danubian floodplain and the Veliki water flowing there on the north side of Dályok village, but it had an outflow that was active with higher water stages northeast of Udvar. The course of the latter can be partially or entirely artificial.

We can read the following about Nyárád in a document from the end of the 18th century:

> The ribbon of the stream flowing through the village is 3 to 6 feet wide and 2 to 3 feet deep. It has flat banks. It inundates the streets when it floods. ... In case of flooding, the infantry cannot cross it at all, for the cavalry crossing involves danger. ... The meadows are dry on higher terrain and marshy in the valleys.[47]

It can be claimed that the Borza Valley west-southwest of Sátorhely was a broad wetland, wider than 300 m in rainy weather. It is not by chance that it appears in the 18th century description of Sátorhely as

> when mentioning the meadows, it is noted that they are marshy to the north. The road to Nyarad is also of poor quality – because of the swamps and the 'inconvenient' meadows.[48]

Downstream the former Borza Manor, the wet floodplain of the stream is only 100–250 m wide, further downstream (as far as Dályok) it slightly cuts into its floor and the width of the wet area is reduced to 50–100 m. It is no coincidence that the Buda-Eszék main road also crosses it here, instead of further to the west.

Today the Borza drainage system shows a completely different picture. It was heavily channelized in the second half of the 20th century to conduct its water southwards through mostly man-made canals. The stream flows into the Karasica at Baranyakisfalud. In its upper section it receives the water of the Lajmér Stream, which starts north of Nagynyárád (Figure 7.2).

---

47 T. Mérey, *Baranya megye települései,* [The settlements of Baranya County] pp. 108–126.
48 T. Mérey, *Baranya megye települései,* [The settlements of Baranya County] pp. 108–126.

3.6 The Karasica and Its Tributaries

On the southern border of the study area runs the Karasica, which is mentioned in the contemporary descriptions related to the Battle of Mohács as a watercourse with a marshy floodplain extending significantly to the south of the battlefield (Figure 7.7).

The Karasica Stream (Karašica in Croatian) issues in Baranya County, at the foot of the Eastern Mecsek. Leaving the village of Illocska it enters into Croatia, where the Kamenjak Hills force it to turn east-northeast. It used to have a confluence with the Danube at Darázs, nowadays it is at Kiskőszeg (Batina).

In the investigated area, the Karasica had a wide, swampy floodplain even in the past centuries. The 18th–19th century descriptions by military experts perfectly pinpoint its military significance.

> From Baranyavár to Darázs, the banks of the Karasicza are very marshy ... Between Villány and Darázs, the entire valley is marshy, densely overgrown with sedges, reeds and thickets.[49]
>
> ... it can only be crossed on designated bridges and roads. ... During heavy rains, it floods fields and meadows, ... The meadows are dry, but those next to the Karasitza are swampy.[50]
>
> From Pócsa to Darázs, the water of this river was channelled, but it is still somewhat unregulated until Villány, ... From Darázs to the confluence, where the water flows in a natural channel, the entire valley – between the Danube and the mountain at Battina – is under water in spring and during other rains. ... Bridges with embankment roads lead across it in the lower section, among others at Baranyavár (Eszék-Buda main road), Bán, Kisfalud, Podolya, Csibogád and Darázs. Neither foot soldiers nor horsemen can cross between Darázs and Battina.[51]

The riverbed of the Karasica marshy valley was already regulated in the 1800s in installments. In 1899 the Lower Karasica Valley Water Drainage Association was formed and between 1900 and 1905 the riverbed was repaired and maintained up to the confluence with the Villány-Pogány Stream.[52]

49　T. Mérey, *A Dél-Dunántúl földrajza*, [The geography of Southern Transdanubia] pp. 100–101.
50　T. Mérey, *Baranya megye települései*, [The settlements of Baranya County] pp. 108–126.
51　T. Mérey, *A Dél-Dunántúl földrajza*, [The geography of Southern Transdanubia] pp. 100–101.
52　Károlyi: *A Duna-völgy vizeinek szabályozása*, [Regulation of the waters of the Danube Valley] in *A magyar vízszabályozás története*, ed. Ihrig.

Based on the analysis of maps and satellite images, it is claimed that the Karasica floodplain, 500 m wide, but in some embayments extended to a half kilometre, is covered with water and swamps during the rainy season.

The description from the 18th century reveals that its tributaries were considered insignificant and problem-free from a military point of view. Probably because they did not have a wide floodplain farther from the Karasica, they did not obstruct traffic. There are no factors impeding traffic or farming on the interfluvial flat surfaces, apart from spots of various size covered with inland water.

The westernmost of the three streams worth mentioning is the Branjina Stream (Kisfalud Stream), whose course may have partially reflected a faultline on the western margin of the Mohács Plain and the lateral erosion of the Danube in the Late Pleistocene. The source of the stream was originally in the Buziglica forest. This area is the southernmost point of the abovementioned wetland zone in the foreground of Nagynyárád and Majs. These swampy areas could have hindered travelling on the Buda-Eszék main road between Udvar and Buziglica. In the second half of the 20th century, the nature of the stream changed, when the water of the Borza Stream was conducted here from the north through an artificial ditch. In addition to the original meandering stream, another straight channel was also carved (Figure 7.2). Both streams reach the Karasica at Baranyakisfalud.

The other two northwest-southeast aligned watercourses had a special evolution as the Early Holocene lateral erosion of the Danube essentially washed away their upper sections. It can be observed on maps and satellite images that the middle section, the so-called Karasica Canal or Ditch west of Izsép starts from the Danube floodplain as a completely developed channel and flows into the Karasica near Hercegmárok. In all likelihood, this was originally the lower section of the Borza Stream. The Bucska (Buckó) Stream rising east of Izsép and flowing into the Karasica between Hercegmárok and Darázs attests to a similar evolution.

4 A Search for Deeper-lying and Waterlogged Areas in the Mohács Plain Influencing the Reconstruction of the Scene of the Battle

The descriptions present rainy weather before and after the Battle of Mohács. This facilitated not only the overbank flow of the Danube and the tributary streams, the wetting of the floodplain, but also the formation of stagnant inland water spots and very muddy, "deep soil" terrains further away from the watercourses. The extensive wetlands could hinder the movement of the medieval army with heavy weaponry and maneuvers in the battle.

In the Mohács Plain, the elevation of the terrain closely governs groundwater level. On the Mohács terrace with an average elevation of 90 m and above, the average groundwater level is 6–9 m below the surface, while in the floodplain areas at 85 m, it is only at 2–4 m depth. The annual groundwater cycle depends on weather and climate. The level is lowest in the winter months (there is little precipitation and more snow), highest in early summer. The impermeable clay layers between the sandy sediments accumulated by the Danube or larger streams lie relatively close to the surface, so during rainy weather high groundwater levels are common, even inland water inundations and stagnant waters are formed.[53]

For the spatial localization of the areas prone to inland water, we first collected the localities defined as low-lying, swampy, wet, pond, floodplain, and reed-covered areas. from the second volume of the book The geographical names of Baranya County, edited by János Pesti.[54] Such spots are represented by blue circles in Figure 7.11.

Based on the map representations, it can be concluded that, as expected, most low-lying and wet areas are located on the lower or higher floodplain surfaces of the Danube. In addition, several wetlands are linked to the Valley of the Lajmér Stream, and a few scattered names indicating wetlands are also found east of Mohács and around Majs.

In the next step, we digitized the water levels on the Mohács terrace, marshy, wet, inland water areas and wet meadows from maps and satellite images (Figure 7.12).

Having surveyed and mapped the swamps, wetlands, and inland water spots, a more differentiated picture of Mohács terrace was achieved. South of Mohács the following areas of larger exrension needed for the Battle of Mohács, and those which remained sufficiently dry even after a prolonged rainy period could be identified:

– the interfluve between the Bég and Lajmér Streams,
– the area east of Sátorhely,
– the area between Udvar and Dályok,
– the area between Izsép and Hercegmárok and
– the area between the Karasica Ditch and the Kisfalud (Branjina) Stream.

---

53 Antal Lehmann, "Mohács és környéke felszínének arculata," [The appearance of the surface of Mohács and its surroundings] in *Mohács földrajza*, ed. Erdősi, pp. 29–36.
54 Pesti ed., *Baranya megye földrajzi nevei*, [The geographical names of Baranya County] pp. 351–583.

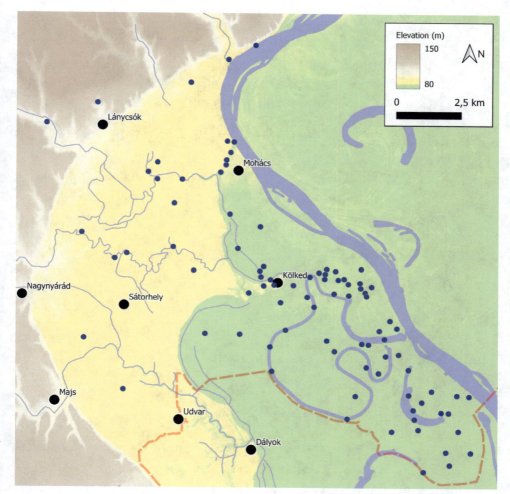

FIGURE 7.11 The dark blue dots mark low-lying, watery, swampy, waterlogged places in the Hungarian part of the Mohács Plain. Edited by Péter Gyenizse based on Geographical names of Baranya County II.
SOURCE OF BACKGROUND MAP: OPENSTREETMAP.ORG, COPERNICUS GLO-30 DEM.
THE POINTS CAN REPRESENT OBJECTS OF DIFFERENT SIZE, FROM A FEW SQUARE METRES TO EVEN SEVERAL SQUARE KILOMETRES.

The western section of the terrace, close to the hills, from Lánycsók to Buziglica, especially the environment of the Majs alluvial fan, was regarded unsuitable for warfare.

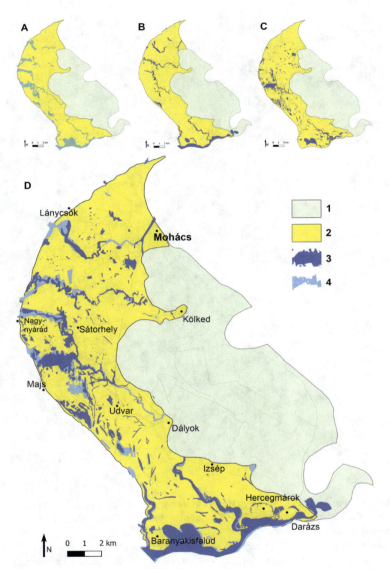

FIGURE 7.12 Swampy, watery, wet soil areas on the flood-free terrace. Legend: 1 = lower and higher floodplain surfaces (in the 16th century mainly swamps); 2 = flood-free terrace; 3 = inland and stagnant water spots, wet areas; 4 = wet meadows; A = wet meadows on the sheets of the Military Survey II; B = inland water spots, wetlands on the 1941 and 1951 Military Survey sheets; C = inland water spots, wetland areas on Google Earth satellite images between 2006 and 2017; D = summary diagram of the previous three maps. Edited by Péter Gyenizse.
SOURCE OF BACKGROUND MAP: OPENSTREETMAP.ORG.

5   Conclusions

The hydrography of the Mohács Plain has undergone a significant transformation over the past centuries. In the century after the Ottoman Occupation, the Mohács Danube, still unregulated at that time, formed a broad meander belt, bounded by backswamps on the lower floodplain surfaces and woods and pastures on the higher floodplain terrain. The flood-free terrace was also crossed by streams flowing in their natural beds. In this close-to-natural environment drainage conditions strongly influenced both the daily life and the farming practices of local people and the traffic opportunities for travellers coming from far-away lands – or even the course of an event of such a great importance as the Battle of Mohács.

In the first part of our analysis, using primarily cartographic and GIS methods, we succeeded in reconstructing the 1685 alignment of the Danube arm between Mohács and Kiskőszeg. Compared to the present-day highly regulated riverbed, this was much longer and certainly narrower. The medieval Hungarian and Ottoman boats trying to enter the port of Mohács followed the pre-regulation channel, but the meander bends were not yet developed to the extent which can be seen on 19th-century maps. During the analysis, we managed to identify an abandoned bed on Mohács Island which was depicted as a still active navigation route on the Karlsruhe map of 1685. We also established that Lake Riha must have already been a cut-off oxbow of the Danube by 1685.

For the minor watercourses, it can be claimed that they run through their alluvial fans after leaving the valley. In the areas next to the hills, no single clearly defined bed can be identified, because they have descended from the alluvial fan in ever changing directions over the past millennia, abandoning their own deposits.

The waters flowing in different directions from the alluvial fans of the streams and the smaller valleys maintained wetlands on the flood-free terrace close to the hills between Nagynyárád and Buziglica. On these surfaces, the waterlogged areas made traffic difficult and warfare with the heavily armed military futile.

From a transportation point of view, it can be stated that the biggest obstacles were the Danube and the Karasica, but in wet weather the middle section of the Borza Stream could also hinder travel. The Csele, Lánycsók and Lajmér Streams, as well as the lower section of Borza and the three tributaries of the Karasica appeared as slight to medium obstacles.

The venue of the Battle of Mohács was chosen by the Hungarian military leadership. An army of predominantly heavy cavalry presumably needed a large plain with firm ground to fight the battle. Obviously, neither the lower nor the higher floodplain surfaces of the Danube met this requirement, but there were also wetter spots on the flood-free terrace. Reconstructing the locations of these areas from maps and satellite images, we found that south of Mohács there are fewer swampy, wet, "deep soil" areas on the eastern section of the flood-free terrace. The larger flat interfluvial surfaces between the streams may have been the most suitable sites for fighting the battle.

Bibliography

A Duna-mappáció, a Duna folyó magyarországi szakaszának térképei (1819–1833) az osztrák határtól Péterváradig. [The Danube Mapping, maps of the Hungarian section of the Danube River (1819–1833) from the Austrian border to Petersburg] DVD-ROM. Pécs: 2006.

A magyarországi Duna-szakasz és kisebb mellékvizei. [The Hungarian section of the Danube and its smaller tributaries] Magyarország hidrológiai atlasza I/9. Budapest: Vízgazdálkodási Tudományos Kutató Intézet, 1962.

Andrásfalvy, Bertalan. *A Sárköz és a környező Duna-menti területek ősi ártéri gazdálkodása és vízhasználatai a szabályozás előtt.* [Ancient floodplain economy and water management in the Sárköz and the areas adjacent to the Danube] Vízügyi Történeti Füzetek 6. Budapest: Vízügyi Dokumentációs és Tájékoztató Iroda, 1973.

Baranya Vármegye föld abrosza. [Map of Baranya County] [B IX a 1441], 1938. Available at https://maps.hungaricana.hu/hu/HTITerkeptar/949/.

Dövényi, Zoltán ed. *Magyarország kistájainak katasztere.* [Cadastre of the landscap units of Hungary] Budapest: MTA Földrajztudományi Kutatóintézet, 2010.

Eisenhut, G. J. *Mappa exhibens inundationem Insulae Mohatsiensis ... 1791.* Hungarian National Archaives S_11_-_No._1441. Available at https://maps.hungaricana.hu/hu/MOLTerkeptar/2985/.

Erdősi, Ferenc. *A társadalom hatása a felszínre, a vizekre és az éghajlatra a Mecsek tágabb környezetében.* [The impact of society on the surface, waters and climate in the wider environment of Mecsek] Budapest: Akadémiai Kiadó, 1987.

Faludi, Gábor and László Nebojszki. "A Mohácsi-sziget kialakulása és vizeinek történelmi változásai." [Origin of the Mohács Island and historical changes of its waters] *Hidrológiai Közlöny* 88 (2008), 4: 47–57.

Faludi, Gábor and Attila Szádeczky. "Az 1956. évi jeges árvíz a Duna magyarországi déli szakaszán." [The ice flood of 1956 in the southern part of the Danube in Hungary] *Hidrológiai Közlöny* 84 (2002): 293–304.

Hervai, András. *A Mohácsi-sziget talajvíz rendszerének átalakulása a tájátalakítások következményeként. PhD-értekezés.* [The transformation of the groundwater system of Mohács Island as a consequence of landscape changes. PhD thesis] Pécs: PTE TTK, 2020.

Hervai, András, Dávid Nagy, and Sándor Konkoly. "Landscape transformations on Mohács Island following river regulations." *Podravina* 37 (2020), 19: 47–60.

Kalocsa, Béla and Enikő Tamás. "A folyamszabályozás morfológiai hatásai a Dunán." [The morphological effects of flow regulation along the Danube] In Élet a Duna-ártéren – természetvédelemről sokszemközt, ed. Orsolya Somogyvári. Pécs: 2003. Available at http://bite.sugovica.hu/ed2003/cikk/kalocsa_morfo.htm (2020. 07. 29.).

Károlyi, Zoltán. "A Duna-völgy vizeinek szabályozása." [Regulation of the waters of the Danube Valley] In *A magyar vízszabályozás története II.*, ed. Dénes Ihrig. Budapest: Országos Vízügyi Hivatal, 1973.

Kiss, Andrea. "A kis jégkorszak, a Spörer minimum és Mohács." [The Little Ice Age, the Spörer Minimum and Mohács] In *Mohács Szimfónia. Tanulmányok a mohácsi csatával kapcsolatos kutatások eredményeiből*, eds. Szabolcs Varga and Attila Türk, 17–46. Budapest: Martin Opitz Kiadó, 2022.

Kiss, Andrea and József Laszlovszky. "14th–16th-Century Danube Floods and Long-Term Water-Level Changes in Archaeological and Sedimentary Evidence in The Western and Central Carpathian Basin: an Overview with Documentary comparison." *Journal of Environmental Geography* 6 (2013), 3–4: 1–11.

Kőnig, Frigyes and István Pánya. "A mohácsi török palánkvár." [The Turkish palanquin fortress in Mohács] In *Várak, kastélyok, templomok. Évkönyv 2018*, ed. Pál Kósa, 24–29. Kökény: 2018.

Konkoly, Sándor. "Középkori vár vagy római erőd? Rejtélyes nyomok a Mohácsi-szigetről." [Medieval castle or Roman fortress? Mysterious clues from Mohács Island] In *Ingenia Hungarica 1. Kárpát-medencei Szakkollégiumi Konferencia*, ed. László Horváth, 177–204. Budapest: 2015.

Konkoly, Sándor. "Sembech középkori várának lokalizációja. A geográfia eszközeivel egy történeti rejtély nyomában." [The location of medieval castle of Sembech. In pursuit of a historical mystery with the tools of geography] In *Opuscula historica 1. Tanulmányok a XIV. és XV. Eötvös Konferenciákról*, ed. Bálint Ternovácz, 13–44. Budapest: ELTE Eötvös József Collegium, 2015.

Konkoly, Sándor. "Újabb adatok Zsembéc várának lokalizációjához." [New data for the localization of the castle of Zsembéc] *Modern Geográfia* 7 (2012), 2: 1–21.

Láng, Sándor and Ferenc Probáld. "Az 1965. évi dunai nyári árvíz." [The Danube summer flood of 1965] *Földrajzi Közlemények* 91 (1967): 45–54.

Lehmann, Antal. "A terület földtörténeti kialakulása." [The geological history of the area] In *Mohács földrajza*, ed. Ferenc Erdősi, 19–28. Mohács: Mohács városi Tanács V.B. Művelődési Osztálya, 1974.

Lehmann, Antal. "Mohács és környéke felszínének arculata." [The appearance of the surface of Mohács and its surroundings] In *Mohács földrajza*, ed. Ferenc Erdősi, 29–36. Mohács: Mohács városi Tanács V.B. Művelődési Osztálya, 1974.

Lóczy, Dénes. "Az árterek geomorfológiai osztályozásai a nemzetközi szakirodalomban." [Geomorphological classifications of flood plains in the international literature] *Földrajzi Közlemények* 137 (2013): 105–120.

Lóczy, Dénes. "Folyóvízi felszínformálás." [Fluvial geomorphology] In *Geomorfológia, I. Földfelszíni folyamatok és formák,* eds. Dénes Lóczy and Márton Veress 17–130. Budapest, Pécs: Dialóg Campus, 2005.

Marsigli, Luigi Ferdinando. *A Duna Bécs és Giorgio közti szakaszának térképe.* [Map of the section of the Danube between Vienna and Giorgio] (Haag, fig). Institute and Museum of Military History, B IX b 112. Available at https://maps.hungaricana.hu/hu/HTITerkeptar/2088/.

Pánya, István. "A Mohácsi-sziget középkori topográfiája." [Medieval topography of the Mohács Island] *Történeti földrajzi közlemények* 8 (2020), 3–4: 105–120.

Pap, Norbert, Péter Gyenizse, Máté Kitanics, and Gábor Szalai. "Az 1526. évi mohácsi csata helyszíneinek földrajzi jellemzői." [Geographical properties of the scenes of the 1526 Battle of Mohács] *Történelmi szemle* 62 (2020): 111–151.

Pap, Norbert, Péter Gyenizse, Máté Kitanics, and Gábor Szalai. "II. Lajos halálának helye," [Locating the death of Louis II] *Történelmi szemle* 62 (2020): 73–109.

Pécsi, Márton. *A magyarországi Duna-völgy kialakulása és felszínalaktana.* [Formation and morphology of the Hungarian Danube Valley] Budapest: Akadémiai Kiadó, 1959.

Pesti, János ed. *Baranya megye földrajzi nevei II.* [The geographical names of Baranya County II] Pécs: Baranya Megyei Levéltár, 1982.

Rauchmüller. *Donau Atlas. Hydrographische Donau Karte von Peterwardein bis Orschova.* Buda: 1834. Available at https://maps.hungaricana.hu/hu/HTITerkeptar/2121/.

Sebe, Krisztina, Gábor Csillag, Piroska Pazonyi, and Zsófia Ruszkiczay-Rüdiger. "Quaternary evolution of the River Danube in the central Pannonian Basin and its possible role as an ecological barrier to the dispersal of ground squirrels," *Historical Biology* 30 Sep (2019): 1–20. Available at https://www.tandfonline.com/doi/full/10.1080/08912963.2019.1666838 (2020. 07. 31.).

Szabó, József, Ferenc Schweitzer, Gergely Horváth, Zita Bihari, Szabolcs Czigány, Szabolcs Fábián, Gyula Gábris, Krisztina Iványi, Attila Kerényi, József Lóki, Donát Magyar, Gergely Mányoki, Zsolt Molnár, Gábor Négyesi, László Pásztor, György Pátzay, Ervin Pirkhoffer, Mária Szabó, Árpád Szentiványi, Gergely Szövényi, László Tóth, Orsolya Udvardy, Gábor Varga, and György Varga. "Természeti veszélyek." [Natural hazards] In *Magyarország Nemzeti Atlasza,* ed. Károly Kocsis, 156–167. Budapest: Magyar Tudományos Akadémia, Csillagászati és Földtudományi Kutatóközpont, Földrajztudományi Intézet, 2018.

Szabó, Pál Zoltán. "A Délkelet-Dunántúl felszínfejlődési kérdései." [Surface formation issues in Southeastern Transdanubia] *Földrajzi Értesítő* 6 (1957): 397–419.

Szávoszt-Vass, Dániel. "Támpontok a Mohácsi-Duna medrének 1526-os rekonstrukciójához." [Reference Points for the Reconstruction of the Mohács-Danube riverbed in 1526] In *Mohács Szimfónia. Tanulmányok a mohácsi csatával kapcsolatos kutatások eredményeiből*, eds. Szabolcs Varga and Attila Türk, 79–92. Budapest: Martin Opitz Kiadó, 2022.

T. Mérey, Klára. *A Dél-Dunántúl földrajza katonaszemmel a 19. század elején*. [The geography of Southern Transdanubia from a soldier's point of view at the beginning of the 19th century] Geographia Pannonica Nova 1. Pécs: Lomart Kiadó, PTE TTK Földrajzi Intézet, 2007.

T. Mérey, Klára. *Baranya megye települései az első katonai felmérés idején*. [The settlements of Baranya County at the time of the Military Survey I] Pécs: Baranya Megyei Levéltár, 2004.

Tamás, Enikő and Béla Kalocsa. "Alluviális árterek morfológiai összehasonlítása." [Morphological comparison of alluvial floodplains] in Élet a Duna-ártéren – természetvédelemről sokszemközt, ed. Orsolya Somogyvári. Pécs: 2003. Available at http://bite.sugovica.hu/ed2003/cikk/kalocsa_morfo.htm (2020. 07. 29.).

Unknown author, *Topographischer Entwurff der umliegenden Gegend bey Sectzu (Seetsche, Dunaszekcsö in Ungarn)* (Around 1685) Available at http://www.landesarchiv-bw.de/plink/?f=4-4105632-1.

Unknown author, *Universum dominium Siklossiense modo divisum in quator partes, nempé Celsissum Diu [! Dni] Dni Principis Eugeny de Sabaudia, Excell.mi Dni D: Aeneae Comitis Campi Marechallia Caprara, et Ex. Dni Comitis Veterani necnon R[ever]end[issi]mi Dni Dni Epp[iscop]i Jány Anno Domini [1]700*. Available at https://maps.hungaricana.hu/hu/OSZKTerkeptar/2142/.

Varga, Gábor, Szabolcs Ákos Fábián, István Péter Kovács, and Ferenc Schweitzer. "Gondolatok a Kárpát-medencei folyók árvizeiről." [Thoughts on the floods of the rivers of the Carpathian basin] *Földrajzi Közlemények* 142 (2018): 291–308.

Viczián, István. "A Duna domborzatformáló hatása Mohács környékén és az 1526. évi mohácsi csata." [Fluvial Geomorphology of the Mohács Danube Floodplain and the Battle of Mohács in 1526] In *Mohács Szimfónia. Tanulmányok a mohácsi csatával kapcsolatos kutatások eredményeiből*, eds. Szabolcs Varga and Attila Türk, 93–114. Budapest: Martin Opitz Kiadó, 2022.

PART 3

The Battle Arena

∴

CHAPTER 8

Localizing the Central Area of the Battle of Mohács: Search for the Medieval Settlement of Földvár

Norbert Pap, Máté Kitanics and Péter Gyenizse

From István Brodarics' account of the Battle of Mohács, we know that a village called Földvár played an important role in determining the scene of the battle.[1] The location of the village has been the subject of debate for nearly 100 years. There is an extensive literature on the possible locations of the village of Földvár on the plain of Mohács. The exact site, where the clash was centred, has been the subject of much speculation, both in academic literature and in lay writings. An article by Márta N. Ipoly, published in 1977,[2] gives an overview of the topography of the different theories with the attached map (Figure 8.1). On her map, she indicates 15 different sites, once called 'Földvár', clustered in two main locations on two flat areas that appeared to be suitable as battlefields.

On the plain, six sites are located close to each other, near the settlement of Sátorhely, and two further sites at some distance to the south-east, near the Vizslak Meadow. Another possible battle locality was assumed to be along the western slope, southeast of Majs, where some authors have suggested seven possible Földvár sites. Since the publication of the N. Ipoly study, a sixteenth candidate has been suggested. It belongs to the second group of settlement sites; since the 1990s, its proponents have considered the medieval village remains northeast of the Catholic Church of Majs to be Földvár.[3] Where might the confirmed site of this settlement be? Where was the village estate extended?

---

1 "In front of us there was a long hill, like a stage, behind which there was the camp of the Turkish emperor; at the bottom of the hill there was a small village with a church, named Földvár." Brodarics István, *Igaz leírás a magyaroknak a törökkel Mohácsnál vívott csatájáról* [A true account of the Battle of Mohács between the Hungarians and the Turks] (Budapest, Magvető Könyvkiadó, 1983), p. 46.
2 Márta N. Ipoly, "A mohácsi csata és csatatér megválaszolatlan kérdései," [Unanswered questions about the Battle of Mohács and the battlefield] *Hadtörténelmi Közlemények* 24 (1977), no. 2, pp. 206–222.
3 Lajos Négyesi, "A mohácsi csata," [The Battle of Mohács] *Hadtörténelmi Közlemények* 107 (1994), no. 4, pp. 62–79.

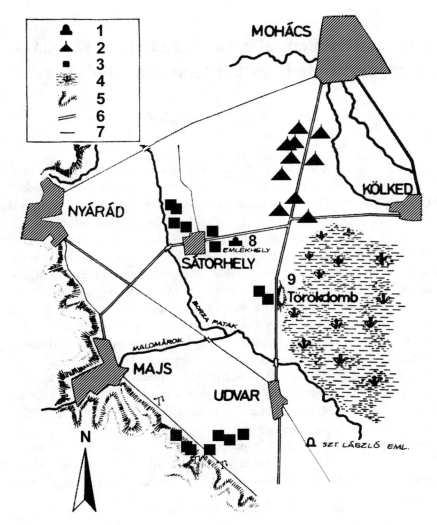

FIGURE 8.1 Map of possible sites of village Földvár on the battlefield of Mohács. Legend:
1 = Mohács Memorial; 2 = potential Hungarian camp sites;
3 = potential sites of Földvár village; 4 = swamp; 5 = the rim of plain; 6 = main roads; 7 = other roads.
SOURCE: MÁRTA N. IPOLY, A MOHÁCSI CSATA. [THE BATTLE OF MOHÁCS] P. 208.

1 Different Approaches, Different Methods

In 1926, during the period of enthusiasm coinciding with the 400th anniversary of the battle, a major turning point in the scientific debate on the location of Földvár took place. Until the 1920s, most scholars agreed that the site of the settlement was none other than the later Sátorhely estate.[4]

First, Lieutenant Endre Gergely suggested that the village in question should be looked for elsewhere, then Lieutenant Colonel Jenő Gyalókay wrote a study entitled *Földvár*, in which he summarized the debates of the time and developed his own position.[5] He considered that the arguments against continuity between the former village and the 18th century manor – apart from the name-joining – were all well-founded. Thus he argued that the site should be located somewhere south of the Borza Stream. Also in 1926, Captain Barna Halmay came forward with his ideas. At the same time as Gyalókay, he also came to the conclusion that Földvár was somewhere south of Sátorhely.[6]

Jenő Gyalókay wrote in his study that the battle was not fought in the Sátorhely area[7]. He did not specify exactly what he meant, but the context suggests that he was referring primarily to the archaeological investigations carried out by Endre Gergely at Törökdomb (Turkish Hill). However, he also mentioned the name of Halmay, who, he said, had reached the same conclusion independently of others.[8]

Indeed, before the 400th-anniversary, Endre Gergely led excavations at Turkish Hill, but the results were disappointing: he found no remains of the Ottoman dead – mentioned by Evliya Çelebi[9] – and identified only Roman and

---

4   István Kápolnai Pauer, "A mohácsi hadjárat 1526-ban," [The Mohács military campaign in 1526] *Hadtörténelmi Közlemények* 2 (1889), pp. 177–208., pp. 441–462.; Leopold Kupelwieser, *Die Kämpfe Ungarns mit den Osmanen bis zur Schlacht bei Mohács, 1526* (Vienna, Leipzig: Wilhelm Braumüller, 1899); Béla Németh, "A mohácsi vésztől a török kiűzetéséig," [From the Mohacs disaster to the expulsion of the Turks] in *Baranya multja és jelenje* II, ed. Ferenc Várady (Pécs: Pécsi Irodalmi és Könyvnyomdai Részvénytársaság, 1897), pp. 393–496.; Sándor Szurmay, *A mohácsi hadjárat 1526-ban* [The Mohács military campaign in 1526] (Budapest: Ludovika Akadémia, 1901); Tivadar Ortvay, *A mohácsi csata elvesztésének okai és következményei.* [The reasons for and consequences of losing the Battle of Mohács.] (Budapest: Magyar Tudományos Akadémia, 1910); Gyula Hummel, "Földvár," *Dunántúl*, 23 July 1926.

5   Endre Gergely, "Ásatások a mohácsi csatatéren (1924, 1925)," [Excavations on the Mohács battlefield (1924, 1925)] in *Mohács emlékkönyv 1926*, ed. Imre Lukinich (Budapest, Királyi Magyar Egyetemi Nyomda, 1926), pp. 349–360; Jenő Gyalókay, "Földvár," *Hadtörténelmi Közlemények* 27 (1926), pp. 290–300; Jenő Gyalókai, "A mohácsi csata," [The Battle of Mohács] in *Mohács emlékkönyv*, ed. Lukinich, pp. 193–276.

6   Barna Halmay, *Az 1526-iki mohácsi csata és igazi helye* [The Battle of Mohács in 1526 and its real location] (Debrecen: Magyar Nemzeti Könyv- és Lapkiadóvállalat Rt., 1926).

7   Gyalókay, "Földvár," pp. 291–293.

8   Cf. Halmay, *Az 1526-iki mohácsi csata* [The Battle of Mohács].

9   Evliyâ Çelebi b. Derviş Mehemmed Zıllî, *Evliyâ Çelebi Seyahatnâmesi. 6. Kitap. Topkapı Sarayı Kütüphanesi Revan 1457 Numaralı Yazmanın Transkripsiyonu–Dizini*, eds. Seyit Ali Kahraman and Yücel Dağlı (İstanbul: Yapı Kredi Yayınları, 2002), pp. 112–113. Earlier incomplete and

a few medieval finds. In Gergely's opinion, this completely destroyed the raison d'être of the battlefield centred on the site of Sátorhely and he suggested that the battlefield and the village of Földvár should be sought elsewhere.

The artillery officer Gyalókay was looking for a high ground that would meet his expectations of his "inner image" of the battle. As he considered Sátorhely too "flat", he expected more pronounced terrain as a possible battle site, based on Brodarics's account. He believed that the settlers who moved to the wasteland of Földvár (*praedium*), as mentioned in the 18th-century sources, could not have known anything about the long-destroyed settlement, and there was no continuity in the naming, so that the medieval village could not have been there. He believed that only beyond the Borza, to the south and west, were there sites that could be considered as battlefields (Figure 8.2). However, the remains of Földvár in his model were not found in these places, so he could not reconstruct the battlefield without contradictions.

György Györffy concluded in the 1960s, on the basis of medieval documents, that Ipoltlaka-Földvár was located on the north-eastern side of the Borza Stream. West of the Stream he marked the settlements of Nyárád, Bátya, Nagymajsa and Kismajsa.

The next generation of battle researchers developed Gyalókay's ideas further. Géza Perjés[10] assumed the battle to be farther south, on the edge of the plain, while Lajos Bende[11] reconstructed the battle on the edge, but closer to the Danube. Apart from the above, several other sites have been subject to naive interpretations, typically in the southern part of the plain.

Gyalókay's discontinuity thesis was not altered by the fact that some of the victims searched in Gergely's research were found in five mass graves near Sátorhely in the 1960s and 1970s. The archaeologists who excavated the bodies assumed they were the remains of soldiers guarding the Christian camp. The archaeologist László Papp, who identified the first two mass graves, had a particular view, since he identified the site of the village of Földvár as identical with the medieval settlement excavated near the present-day Újistálló. At the same time, he also placed the village, considered to be the centre of the battle,

---

incorrect Hungarian translation: Imre Karácson, *Evlia Cselebi török világutazó magyarországi utazásai (1660–1664)* [Turkish traveller Evliya Çelebi's travels in Hungary] (Budapest: Magyar Tudományos Akadémia, 1904), p. 192, p. 196. For the relevant new translation, see Norbert Pap, Pál Fodor, Máté Kitanics, Tamás Morva, Gábor Szalai, and Péter Gyenizse, "A mohácsi Törökdomb," [The Törökdomb in Mohács.] *Történelmi Szemle* 60 (2018), no. 2, pp. 332–333.

10   Géza Perjés, *Mohács* (Budapest: Magvető Könyvkiadó, 1979).
11   Lajos Bende, "A mohácsi csata," [The Battle of Mohács] *Hadtörténelmi Közlemények* 13 (1966), no. 3, pp. 532–567.

LOCALIZING THE CENTRAL AREA OF THE BATTLE OF MOHÁCS

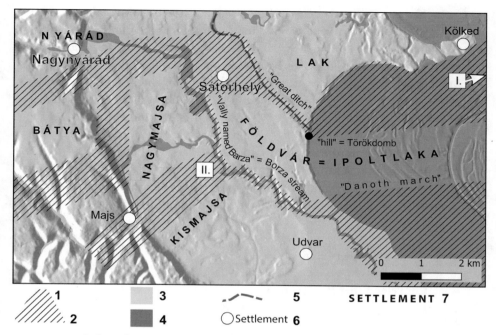

FIGURE 8.2   The boundaries of the estate of Földvár west of the Danube according to the 1338 inspection of landmarks. Edited by Péter Gyenizse. Legend: 1 = boundary section geographically easy to locate with some uncertainty; 2 = boundary section geographically less easy to locate with greater uncertainty; 3 = flood-free terrace of the Baranya Hills and the Mohács Plain; 4 = stream valleys and the marshy, water-covered floodplain of the Danube River; 5 = the former riverbed, now largely filled up; 6 = the centres and names of the present-day settlements; 7 = the land, the administrative area of the settlements named in the inspection of landmarks in the title of the figure; I = Örvény-fok [Ewrem], east of Kölked, beyond the boundary of the map; II = the road from Nagymajsa to Ipoltlaka probably crossed the Borza Stream below the section where the Majs Watercourse (not the same as the present Malomárok) flows into the Borza.

on the hillside south of Majs, on the site of the destroyed settlement of Merse. On this point, he said that Brodarics was wrong about the name.[12] Although medieval weapon remains were found, again no breakthrough was made.

On the map of the late 15th century, the historian Pál Engel depicts the estate of Földvár as being bordered by Kerekegyháza, Bátya, Majs in the west, Lajmér in the north, Dályok in the south and Vízlak in the east.

---

12   László Papp, "A mohácsi csatatér kutatása," [Research into the battlefield of Mohács] in *Janus Pannonius Múzeum Évkönyve 1960*, ed. János Dombay (Pécs: Janus Pannonius Múzeum, 1961), pp. 197–253.

In the 1990s, technological advances – notably the use of metal detectors – opened up a new era in research. First the military historian Lajos Négyesi, then archaeologists Gábor Bertók, Máté Szabó, Éva Szajcsán and Csilla Gáti, excavated and collected artifacts and weapon remains related to the Battle of Mohács at a new site northeast of Majs and published their findings in a series of studies in the mid-1990s and after 2009.[13] They also examined the remains of a previously identified village.[14] These experts concluded that it was the medieval village of Földvár.

In summary, from the 1920s onwards, there was a consensus in the papers that the remains of Földvár were located somewhere south or west of Sátorhely, and there was no substantive debate about whether Sátorhely had a medieval predecessor and whether Sátorhely could be the same as Földvár.[15]

2   The Medieval Estate

Gyalókay's claim that the centre of the battle was south of the Borza Stream also reveals the argument that the boundaries of the estate of Földvár were formed in the Middle Ages. This is how he writes about it: "This area, called Földvár, was divided in 1338 as a result of a lengthy land dispute. Its northern part – 'Lak seu Wyfolou' – remained the property of the Bechey family, the previous owners. Its southern part was given to the Abbey of Szekszárd. In old times it was called Ipoltlaka, in 1338 it was called Feuldwar. The Borza (then Barza) Stream marked the boundary between the two estates. It is therefore

---

13 Máté Szabó, Gábor Bertók, Csilla Gáti, and Éva Szajcsán, "A mohácsi csatatér kutatása – az első országos fémkeresős szakmai hétvége és tanulságai," [Exploring the battlefield of Mohács – the first national metal detection weekend and lessons learned] *Magyar Régészet* (2016), Summer pp. 1–7. Available at http://files.archaeolingua.hu/2016NY/Szabo_et_al_H16NY.pdf. (Accessed 28 April 2018).

14 Janus Pannonius Museum Archaeological Repository (= JPM RA) Majs 1167–83. 3. He published his theory in 1969 in Régészeti Füzetek [Archaeological Bulletin] with the following claim: "We have found the site of the medieval village of Majsa, a few hundred metres from the eastern side of the present-day village, with a size of around 400 metres from north to south." Papp László, "Majs," in *Az 1968. év Régészeti Kutatásai. Régészeti Füzetek* I. 22., ed. Alice Sz. Burger (Budapest: Népművelési Propaganda Iroda, 1969), p. 83.

15 Bende, "A mohácsi csata," [The Battle of Mohács]; Ferenc Szakály, *A mohácsi csata* [The Battle of Mohács] (Budapest: Akadémiai Kiadó, 1975); Perjés, *Mohács*; János B. Szabó, *A mohácsi csata* [The Battle of Mohács] (Budapest: Corvina, 2006); Gábor Bertók and Balázs Polgár, "A mohácsi csatatér és a középkori Földvár falu régészeti kutatása," [Research into the battlefield of Mohács and the archaeological study of the medieval village of Földvár] *Hadtörténelmi Közlemények* 124 (2011), no. 3, pp. 919–928.

certain that the whole territory of Földvár – from 1338 onwards – lay south of the Borza, and therefore the village in question must have been there, south of the stream."[16]

According to the hypothesis of the present study, the settlement in question was located on a small plain close to and west of the marshy area of the Danube. Since Földvár survived for hundreds of years, even under wartime conditions, the village's geographical location factors must have been so strong that its inhabitants repeatedly found it worthwhile to rebuild. The extensive estate of which it was the centre suggests that it may have had good transport links, not least as confirmed by the events of the battle. The medieval documents mention it several times and, in addition to the ownership, we have a fairly clear picture of the boundaries of the estate and its relations with neighbouring estates. Since previous research has drawn different conclusions from the same set of documents, it is advisable to follow very closely the references made in the original documents to stable natural elements of the geographical environment and objects already excavated by archaeologists, and to identify them as precisely as possible.

The first documented mention of Földvár in the form of Ipoltlaka dates back to 1223.[17] In 1337, the chief magistrate Pál announced that in 1223, Tábor's son Gergely confessed to stealing from the treasury of the Szekszárd Abbey, and therefore King Andrew II gave Gergely's *praedium* of Ipoltlaka to the Szekszárd Abbey. Subsequently, it was expropriated from the church and the name Ipoltlaka was changed to Földvár [Feuldwar]. Imre Becsei claimed that it came into his possession as a royal donation. The Becsei family denied this –that they were usurping the property of the Szekszárd Abbey – saying that Földvár never had the name Ipoltlaka. They finally conceded that Ipoltlaka, or Földvár, belonged to the Szekszárd Abbey, but since it was surrounded by their own land, they asked for a clear definition of its boundaries.[18] Two complementary boundary inspections were carried out. The boundaries of the Nagymajsa estate were clarified in a boundary inspection charter in January 1338.[19]

---

16 Gyalókay, "Földvár," p. 291.
17 Imre Nagy et al. eds., *A zichy és vásonkeői gróf Zichy család idősb ágának okmánytára I–XII.* [The documents of the elder branch of the Zich and Vásonkeő Count Zichy family I–XII] *Codex diplomaticus domus senioris comitum Zichy de Zich et Vasonkeo.* (Budapest: Magyar Történelmi Társulat, 1871–1931).
18 *Archives of Anjou-era documents.* I-. Eds. Tibor Almási et al. Budapest-Szeged, 1990-. XXI. no. 654. pp. 374– 376.
19 The field inspection took place in January 1338. National Archives of the Hungarian National Archives (=MNL OL) Diplomatic Archives (=DL), 87074 (Esterházy hg. cs. lt. rep. 96.1.1).

According to the investigation, the boundaries of the Nagymajsa estate were defined along the road leading west from the Borza Valley, between Ipoltlaka and Nagymajsa. The survey is described as starting from Földvár in the east, Kismajsa in the south and Nagymajsa in the north. The border runs westwards for an unclear distance and then turns northwards. To the north of Nagymajsa lies Bátyaföld, bounded first along its southern border and then by the Nagymajsa border to the east. To the north, the border also touches the Nyárád estate, where the description ends.

The boundaries of the Becsei estates of Lak and Nagymajsa with Földvár were also clarified by a boundary inspection in January 1338. This shows that the eastern boundary of Nagymajsa, which is missing from the above description, is the Borza Valley itself. The Becsei estate (Lak in the north, Majsa in the west) was separated from the estate of the Abbey of Szekszárd as follows:

> ... the estate once called Ipoltlaka, now called Földvár, is separated by boundary markings as follows: the first and main boundary marking begins on the west side of the Great Danube[20] above two willow trees, below which there are two mounds as boundary markings, one of which separates the estate of the Szekszárd Abbey, once called Ipoltlaka, now called Földvár, from the south, and the other separates, from the north, the Lak estate of the above-mentioned masters Töttös and Vesszős; thence, passing the above-mentioned boundary markings and proceeding westwards on the Danube island,[21] the boundary reaches two poplar trees, below which there are two mounds as boundary markings, one of which, on the south, separates the above-mentioned estate [i.e. Földvár] of the Abbey of Szekszárd, and the other separates the former estate [Lak] of the above-mentioned masters Töttös and Vesszős to the north; then, heading west, it goes up to two willow trees, under which there are two mounds as boundary markings, and these separate the estates [i.e. the Földvár estate of the Abbey of Szekszárd to the south, and the Lak estate of the Töttöss family to the north] in the above-mentioned way; and then it heads straight on, crossing the Little Danube[22] in a western

---

20   Before the 18th century, the Great Danube flowed along the eastern side of Mohács Island, which was also known as the Old Danube. This was the main branch of the river, but by the end of the 18th century, the western branch had become the main branch. The fact that the branch running towards the Great Plain, i.e. the eastern branch, is the larger, while the branch near Mohács is the smaller, was also reported by Brodarics in his work on the Battle of Mohács. See Brodarics, *Igaz leírás*, [A true account] p. 32.

21   The Island of Mohács.

22   The term 'Kis-Duna' [Little Danube] denoted the Szekcső or Mohács branch of the Danube in the period.

direction, reaching two willow trees, where there are two mounds as boundary markings, and these separate estates in the above-mentioned way; then [the boundary] continues straight westwards, and, passing several mounds as boundary markings, comes to the Danoth marsh,[23] also called Örvény-fok [Ewrem],[24] from which it goes straight westwards to [a] mountain,[25] where there are two mounds as boundary markings, which separate the estates in the manner mentioned above; [then] it proceeds westwards to the Great Ditch,[26] where there are two mounds as boundary markings, one very old, to the south, separating the above-mentioned estate of the Abbey of Szekszárd, and the other, new, on the north, separating and bounding the above-mentioned estate of masters Töttös and Vesszős; thence, passing through a large field, it comes to two mounds as boundary markings, which separate the estates as above. Continuing along this field, it comes to two mounds as boundary markings, which [also] demarcate estates in the manner already mentioned, and [from here] it continues westwards, crossing several mounds as boundary markings and then reaching a valley called Barza,[27] in which there are two mounds as boundary markings, one of which separates the above-mentioned estate of masters Töttös and Vesszős called Nagymajsa to the west, and the other separates the above-mentioned estate [Földvár] of the Abbey of Szekszárd to the east; thence it turns southwards in this valley, and passing through the road from the village of Majsa[28] to the village of Ipoltlaka or Földvár, it comes to three mounds as boundary markings, which separate the estates at the road as follows: the first on the east separates the above-mentioned estate of the Abbey of Szekszárd,

---

23 Danoth or Danóc Marsh is the medieval name of the later Vizslak Meadow. As the former town of Danóc [Danovác] was located near Izsép, in the 18th century Izsép was sometimes called Danovác.
24 The later Vizslak Meadow. The name Örvény [Ewrem] appears in János Pesti's volume *Geographical Names of Baranya County* under the Örvény-fok entry and is said to be in the area between Mohács and Kölked. János Pesti, *Baranya megye földrajzi nevei* II. [Geographical names in Baranya County] (Pécs: Baranya Megyei Levéltár, 1982), p. 493, p. 536.
25 Györffy and later Lajos Bende identify it as Turkish Hill, which contains the remains of a Roman *burgus* (watchtower) on the western edge of the swamp (Örvény [Ewrem], *Danóc Marsh, Vizslak Meadow*).
26 The former riverbed, which flows into the swamp (*Ewrem, Danóc Marsh, Vizslak Meadow*), is now a filled riverbed that stretches along the northern side of the battlefield, in front of Turkish Hill and crosses the plain in a south-east–north-west direction towards Nagynyárád. Györffy also mentions the importance of the ditch west of Turkish Hill as a boundary.
27 The valley is known as Barza (brza = fast), later the bed of the Borza Stream.
28 The medieval Majs.

the other on the south demarcates the already mentioned estate of the nobles of Kismajsa, and the third from the north, which separates the above-mentioned estate of the Imre family, namely masters Töttös and Vesszős, called Nagymajsa; this is how the boundaries of the above-mentioned estate, once called Ipoltlaka, now known as Földvár, end."[29]

The boundary was drawn to separate the Földvár, which was to be returned to the Szekszárd Abbey, from the Becsei estates (Lak in the north and Nagymajsa in the west), but it was not completely demarcated, as this was not the aim. The border section followed the following line: starting from the eastern edge of Mohács Island, it crossed the main branch of the Danube, the Mohács tributary of the Little Danube, to the west. Continuing along the swamp of the Danube (also known as Ewrem), it reached a hill (Turkish Hill), then, heading west, it first reached a large ditch (*magnum Aruk*), then, passing through the "large field", it reached the valley of the Borza Stream to the west and along its bed to the south to the Kismajsa estate, which closed the Nagymajsa estate to the south (Figure 8.5).

Some clues about the north-western border of the manor of Földvár can be found in the text of the 1338 boundary survey. According to the description, the western edge of the floodplain is the boundary of Turkish Hill, the "Great Ditch" northwest of Turkish Hill, the valley of the middle section of the Barza/Borza Stream turning south and southeast, and finally the northern upper section of the Borza River flowing east from the Nyárád Valley, connecting the manors of Nagymajsa, Nyárád and Földvár. The landscape features listed above show the north-western border of Földvár from Turkish Hill towards Nyárád, with a south-east-north-west slope. Lak is not a regular (rectangular) landscape unit, but extends from the west (from the Borza) to the east, as far as Mohács Island. In the northern part of Lak, the Becsei estate of Kerekegyháza probably extended as far as the Danube, although in this case, it is a mystery exactly how far, since Kölked extends into the floodplain as a foothill surrounded by marshy areas to the north and south. This may suggest that Kerekegyháza was further north during the period.

Gyalókay's claim that the Becsei family's estate would have been divided into two and the southern part given to the Szekszárd Abbey is incorrect. On the contrary, the Borza Stream served as a border between the eastern part of the Becsei and the western part of the Szekszárd Abbey estate. Although he made several correct statements about the topography of the area, which were confirmed by later investigations, Gyalókay ignored the clear references in the documents to the role of the Borza Stream as a separator and therefore erred in

---

29   *A zichi és vásonkeői gróf Zichy-család* [The Count Zichy family of Zich and Vásonkeő], I. 528–529. Its original: MNL OL DL 76567.

his identification of Földvár. He did not know the geography of the area at the time, and this misled his geographic positioning in several respects. A further serious distortion was that the sources he analysed did not describe the location of the settlements, but the estates with the same names as the settlements.

3 The Village

Medieval and early modern sources give a picture of this settlement on the plain of Mohács. Who lived in the village? What were the environmental factors that influenced the population of the area? What were the stages in its historical development? (Table 8.1).

TABLE 8.1 Data on village Földvár

Year	The physical nature of the settlement	Inhabitants[a]	Other data
1327[b]	Village with a chapel	-	Priest of the settlement
1338[c]	Is mentioned	-	The boundaries of the estate are inspected
1478[c]	Is mentioned	-	Is affected by legal action
1526[d]	Village with church, houses	-	-
1546 Ottoman survey register[e]	-	35 heads of family	The village has no priest, Sudár says it is likely that it no longer had a parish, the church may have been damaged

[a] Population estimates were made with 4–6 persons per family.
[b] László Koszta, "A pécsi káptalan kiadatlan oklevelei (1325–1339)," in Baranyai történetírás 1992/1995, ed. László Szita (Pécs: Baranya Megyei Levéltár, 1995), pp. 10–11.
[c] Norbert Pap, Máté Kitanics, Péter Gyenizse, Gábor Szalai, and Balázs Polgár, "Sátorhely vagy Majs? Földvár környezeti jellemzői – A mohácsi csata centrumtérségének lokalizálása," [Sátorhely or Majs? Environmental characteristics of Földvár. Localizing the central area of the Battle of Mohács] Történelmi Szemle 61 (2019), no. 2, pp. 209–246.
[d] Brodarics István, Igaz leírás a magyaroknak a törökkel Mohácsnál vívott csatájáról [A true account of the Battle of Mohács between the Hungarians and the Turks] (Budapest, Magvető Könyvkiadó, 1983).
[e] Balázs Sudár, "Földvár falu a török korban," [The Village of Földvár in the Ottoman Era] Történelmi Szemle 62 (2020), no. 1, 153–168.

TABLE 8.1   Data on village Földvár (cont.)

Year	The physical nature of the settlement	Inhabitants[a]	Other data
1552 Ottoman survey register[e]	-	33 heads of family	
1555[f]	"Market town"[g] with church	-	"Presents a bleak picture"
1565 Ottoman survey register[e]	-	16 heads of family	-
1570 Ottoman pall-tax register[h]	11 houses	44–66 inhabitants	-
1580 Ottoman survey register[e]	-	11 heads of family	-
1583 Ottoman pall-tax register[i]	9 houses	36–54 inhabitants	-
1590 Ottoman survey register[e]	-	12 heads of family	-
1675[c]	Is mentioned	-	-
1687[j]	A village seized for the treasury	"Because of the gathering camps set up there", the inhabitants fled to forests, mountains and swamps	-

[f] Hans Dernschwam's Tagebuch einer Reise nach Konstantinopel und Kleinasien (1553/55). Ed. Franz Babinger (München, Leipzig: 1923), p. 267; Cf. Hans Dernschwam, Erdély. Besztercebánya. Törökországi útinapló. [Transylvania. Besztercebánya. Turkish Travel Diary] (Budapest: Európa Könyvkiadó, 1984), pp. 492–493.
[g] Although the source describes it as a market town, we do not know for sure whether it really was.
[h] József Fölker, Mohács története [The history of Mohács] (Mohács: Rosenthal Márk Könyvnyomdája, 1900), p. 188.
[i] Magyarországi török kincstári defterek II. 1540–1639. [Turkish treasury defters in Hungary II.] Ed. Ernő Kammerer (Budapest: Athenaeum R. Társ. Könyvnyomdája, 1890), p. 606.
[j] Lajos Nagy, "A Császári Udvari Kamara pécsi prefektúrájához tartozó terület 1687-ben" [The area belonging to the Prefecture of the Imperial Court Chamber of Pécs in 1687]. in Baranyai helytörténetírás 1978, ed. László Szita (Pécs: Baranya Megyei Levéltár, 1979), p. 21.

TABLE 8.1 Data on village Földvár (cont.)

Year	The physical nature of the settlement	Inhabitants[a]	Other data
1696[c]	25 plots held in socage	Between 100 and 200 inhabitants	400 acres of good arable land; 100 acres of scything fields; 150 acres of acorn forest; no mill or water; Kiskőszeg-Földvár two and a half hours' away; 2.5 hours' circumference; former landlord: Adam Zrínyi, Ottoman Turkish landlord: Kara Osman; adjacent to: Merse, Bezedek, Danóc, Kölked
1698[f]	Is mentioned	-	Paid 6 forints in tax

The village was inhabited in the Árpád-era, originally called Ipoltlaka. In the 14th century it was already called Földvár. Over the centuries of its existence, its main owner was the Szekszárd Abbey, but at one time it was also owned by the Becsei family. It was a place with a church or chapel, so there is good reason to believe that it stood out from the average villages. The patron saints of its parish were St. Peter and the Virgin Mary.[30] Aside from the church, we can assume the presence of residential houses typical of the Árpád and late medieval periods in the village until the Battle of Mohács. An estimate of the number of inhabitants is based on the number of plots/houses and the number of heads of households. There is good reason to believe that the village was briefly deserted in 1526. However, since it soon reappears in the sources

---

30   Péter Timár, *Magyarország középkori településeinek és egyházainak topográfiai adattára II*. [Topographical database of the medieval settlements and churches of Hungary II.] (Szeged: Timár Péter, 2019), pp. 183–184; András Mező, *Patrocíniumok a középkori Magyarországon* [Patrociniums in medieval Hungary.] (Budapest: Magyar Egyháztörténeti Enciklopédia Munkaközösség (METEM), 2003), p. 368, p. 420.

as a place paying taxes, it seems that the inhabitants who fled rebuilt it after the campaign. It is questionable, however, if they settled in the same place as before, or whether they rebuilt their houses some distance from the original. Since a source from 1555 mentions the once more prosperous Földvár with its church,[31] we can assume that the village was rebuilt on the old site or in its immediate vicinity.

According to the unbroken series of data at our disposal, the settlement continued to exist in the second half of the 16th century and into the 17th century, although its population fluctuated. The names of the Ottoman defters give us the impression that Földvár was inhabited by Hungarians and (partly Magyarized) Croats, and by Vlachs. Accordingly, it is likely that the village was religiously divided, with Protestants living there at the time alongside Catholics and Orthodox people. In any case, it is remarkable that, unlike several other surrounding settlements, Földvár had no Catholic parish priest,[32] and its church, which survived for some time after the Battle of Mohács, was eventually destroyed. We can conclude that the Catholic community at the time of the conquest was not large enough to require the appointment of a local parish priest by the church, nor was it a religious community of such a size and population that it could have been able to renovate and maintain the church.[33]

Agriculture on the Földvár estate was dominated by arable farming and livestock breeding, while in the areas along the Danube it was floodplain farming. In 1573, Stephan Gerlach Snr saw a 'wasteland' or 'field with grain' on the site.[34]

---

31 *Hans Dernschwam's Tagebuch*. Cf. Dernschwam, "Erdély," [Transylvania].
32 Sudár, "Földvár falu," [The village of Földvár].
33 There are many sources from the period showing that Catholic services were held even in damaged churches. Here we will mention only one example from Mohács, when Athanasio Georgiceo, a traveller, attended a Catholic mass in a suburban church at the invitation of the local parish priest Don Simone Matkovich: "...he celebrated a mass in a very large church outside the market town, which had a roof only on one corner, where the mass was said, although these poor Catholics had already bought the material to cover the roof." As can be seen, the Bosnian Catholic community living in the suburbs had enough strength to renovate and maintain their church. István György Tóth, "Athanasio Georgiceo álruhás császári megbízott útleírása a magyarországi török hódoltságról, 1626-ból," [Disguised imperial envoy Athanasio Georgiceo's travelogue on the Turkish occupation of Hungary in 1626] *Századok* 132 (1998), no. 4, p. 854.
34 László Szalay, *Adalékok a magyar nemzet történetéhez a xvi-dik században*. [Additions to the history of the Hungarian nation in the sixteenth century.] (Pest: Ráth Mór, 1859), p. 222. Cf. its more recent translation (with minor stylistic differences): *Ungnád Dávid Konstantinápolyi utazásai*. [Dávid Ungnád's travels in Constantinople.] (Budapest: Szépirodalmi önyvkiadó, 1986), p. 121.

In the Ottoman Turkish period, some of the inhabitants of Földvár rented vineyards in Szajk village, but also paid a cask tax, which suggests that they were involved in wine trading,[35] and perhaps also in selling drinks on site.

In 1696, 400 acres of good arable land, 100 acres of hayfields, 150 acres of acorn forest and 25 plots held in socage are mentioned in Földvár.[36] On this basis, the village appears to have survived the great storms of the reconquest war and, for a time, had a population. We believe the settlement was completely depopulated in 1704 due to the raids by Serbian and Hungarian Kuruc troops. But the question arises again: was the 18th-century centre of the praedium of Földvár, the nucleus of the settlement later called Sátorhely, established on the same site as the 16th and 17th century Földvár?

We can say it is very likely that the change in the farming system and the structure of the estate, and the factors that revived the new economic and village centre, should be seen elsewhere. But first, let us look at what we know about the 18th and 19th-century Földvár praedium and its centre, which belonged to the estate of Bellye.

According to the sources, it seems that horse breeding in the area began as early as the first half of the 18th century, during the ownership of Eugene of Savoy (Jenő Savoyai), and shepherding became the dominant land use, with sheep breeding also becoming increasingly important. Indeed, a document from 1736 referred to the grazing of horses and sheep on the land as an old, common practice.[37] In connection with the latter, we should also note that after the Kuruc wars, with the arrival of German settlers in Baranya and Tolna counties, a new breed, the Cikta, began to replace the previously typical Racka sheep. It seems that, in the following decades, developments were also tailored primarily to the needs of horse and sheep breeding. Originally, the centre of what was later Sátorhely was built as a horse stable in 1768, and we also know that in 1780, there were two sheep pens at its farming centre.[38] With the disappearance of horse breeding here and the spread of the Merino sheep from the 1770s and 1780s, sheep breeding became dominant in the territory of the praedium of Földvár for a while.[39]

---

35   Sudár, "Földvár falu," [The village of Földvár].
36   Pap et al., "Sátorhely vagy Majs?" [Sátorhely or Majs?].
37   Ibid.
38   Ibid.
39   However, we can add that for a short period between 1775 and 1780, sheep breeding was temporarily relegated to the background. HU MNL OL E 156 - a. - Fasc. 123. - No. 025. pp. 25–26.

Further information can be obtained by analysing contemporary maps (1766, 1767, 1770).[40] As previously, hayfields and grazing lands accounted for the largest proportion in the new land use pattern, with the northern half of the estate occupied by a continuous scything field and the central and eastern half by a large, continuous pasture. The arable land, concentrated in the southwestern part of the estate and at the southern tip, was cultivated by the people living in Majs and Dályok. The woods and wooded groves were mainly north of the arable lands cultivated by the people of Majs in the north-western part of the lowland (Hung. *puszta*) while a 'wild pear orchard' is also known to have been present in the southeastern part of the estate. A 'garden' was also cultivated in the western part of the grassland. In 1828, thanks to the developments that began in the 1770s and 1780s, it was described as a "rational economy" and in addition to the fields divided into equal parts and bordered by lines of trees and the meadows irrigated "in the Lombardy way", the 8,000-strong Merino flock of sheep was also mentioned.[41] From the second half of the 19th century onwards, the estate was clearly dominated by cattle breeding.

Based on the above, we can identify the economic centre of the praedium of Földvár and the conditions for the development of Sátoristye/Sátorhely. Here, at the intersection of roads close to the administrative centre of Nagynyárád and Majs, the stables for horse breeding and the sheep pens, which also protected the valuable livestock from predators, were built in a safe, dry place. These were joined by additional farm buildings, and later by residential buildings of various sizes. Although the village started to grow, and in 1828 there were 128 Catholics, 30 Orthodox and 12 Protestant people living there, it was to become an independent administrative unit under the name of Sátorhely only much later, in the mid-20th century.

The name of the new settlement around the economic centre, which was formed by keeping horses, sheep and cattle, was Földvár or Földvárpuszta in Hungarian at the end of the 18th century, and Sátoristye in Croatian and Serbian. Over time, the name Sátoristye became more and more common, and in the 20th century, as a result of the name Magyarization policy, it became the present name Sátorhely, which is a simple Hungarian translation of Sátoristye: tent place. Where does the name come from?

Folklore collected in the 19th century associates this with the battle of 1526. It was explained as the site of the tents of the Ottoman army, and therefore a

---

40   Ibid.
41   Elek Fényes, *Magyarországnak és hozzákapcsolt tartományoknak mostani állapotja statisztikai és geográfiai tekintetben I.* [The present state of Hungary and its associated provinces in statistical and geographical terms.] (Pest: Trattner–Károlyi, 1839), pp. 50–51.

campsite. In reality, however, Sátoristye was the local Christian name for the site of the Ottoman victory monument (later Törökdomb) from the second half of the 17th century until the mid-18th century. It was given by the South Slavic-speaking inhabitants who called the place after the wooden pavilion (Turkish *köşk*), a large tent-shaped building that stood there between 1630–31 and 1687.[42] Legend has it that the sultan's tent was pitched there at the time of the battle, so the Turks built the tent-like pavilion here in his memory. So the name is based on a misunderstanding. Since the livestock farm was established near this place in the second half of the 18th century, it was named after it, while the name of the mound became the aforementioned Turkish Hill (Turski Brig/Türken Hügel/Törökdomb).

Since the new settlement was established in the area of Földvár *praedium* (Földvárpuszta), the name Földvárpuszta was justified, which was in line with the naming practice. The two names, Sátoristye and Földvár(puszta), were linked and even reinforced each other. Both referred to the battle, so the legitimacy of the village as the site of the battle was strong in the 19th century.

4 The Place of Földvár Village in the Central Part of the Mohács Plain in the Early Modern Period

The exact location of the medieval village can be found in the geographical indications of 16th and 17th-century sources. Firstly, the sources of the Battle of Mohács and secondly, the documents of the wars of liberation (1684–1699) provide us with a clue.

By all indications, the sultan's army was deployed at the village of Földvár on 29 August 1526 to engage the Christian army that was stationed north of this place. Since the line of the Christian army was marked out for us by the paleo river bed, the "Great or Deep Ditch" described by Brodarics, which also appears in 14th-century sources, and the location of the Ottoman artillery is known to have been deployed at the village of Földvár, we have a good starting point for the location of the two armies. According to Jacomo Zaratino,[43] who served in the regiment of the Croatian ban in the battle, the two armies were positioned about an Italian mile (about 1.6–1.8 kilometres) apart before the

---

42 See Chapter Eleven.
43 "Thus, at the said place, at one o'clock in the afternoon, skirmishes began between armies only an Italian mile apart". "Levél Velencébe, Cividale, 1526. szeptember 15.," [Letter to Venice, Cividale, 15 September 1526] in *Mohács*, ed. János B. Szabó (Budapest: Osiris Kiadó, 2006), p. 100.

battle. The question is whether we have data on a settlement in this area that corresponds to what we know about Földvár, and whether the fragmentation of the space and the location of important sites of the battle can be matched to each other.

An excavation carried out by László Papp in 1967 on a village/settlement remains east of the Borza manor suggests that a settlement existed there in the Middle Ages, the location of which corresponds to the descriptions of Földvár. Below we verify how well this site stands up to the test of known conditions and whether its character is compatible with our knowledge of the village.

If we look at the distance data provided by Brodarics for the battle of 1526, the segmentation of the space from Mohács southwards to Karasica River is as follows:

- the Christian camp is located half a mile[44] south of the medieval town of Mohács. This piece of data points west along the line of Kölked, north of the mass graves excavated near Sátorhely, around 2.7 kilometres from them, and around 4 kilometres from the medieval Mohács;[45]
- the "Deep Ditch" marking the northern boundary of the medieval Földvár estate, and Brodarics's definition of its position at the time of the battle as a wide and deep "valley" (a river paleo bed) stretching to the left to the deep marshes of the Danube River, is our next place of interest. This is about 6.7 kilometres from the medieval Mohács near the mass graves. It is also important that, along this road, some 200 metres north of the "valley", five mass graves of victims of the battle were excavated in the 1960s and 1970s;
- according to Brodarics, the site of the battle was around a mile,[46] or around 8 kilometres,[47] from Mohács. This place corresponds to the broad area or the "wide field" between the village and the "Deep Ditch";

---

[44] "So the next day, around half a mile below Mohács, our army met theirs…" Brodarics István, "Igaz történet a magyarok és Szülejmán török császár mohácsi ütközetéről (1528)," [A true account of the battle between the Hungarians and the Turkish Emperor Süleyman at Mohács (1528)] in *Mohács*, ed. B. Szabó, p. 146. Brodarics's mile has already been the subject of debate among researchers. Gyalókay estimated it at 8.353 kilometres. Gyalókay, "Földvár." Barna Halmay set it at 7.5 kilometres. Halmay, *Az 1526-iki mohácsi csata* [The Battle of Mohács]. We worked with an approximate mileage of 8 kilometres. However, it should be pointed out that Brodarics had neither an instrument, nor an accurate map, so his data can only be considered estimates, with a tolerance of a few hundred metres.

[45] Between 3.75 and 4.2 kilometres.

[46] "The place where the army was stationed was a mile from Mohács, and half a mile from the Danube River, which flows by it." Brodarics, *Igaz leírás*, [A true account] p. 46.

[47] Between 7.5 and 8.4 kilometres.

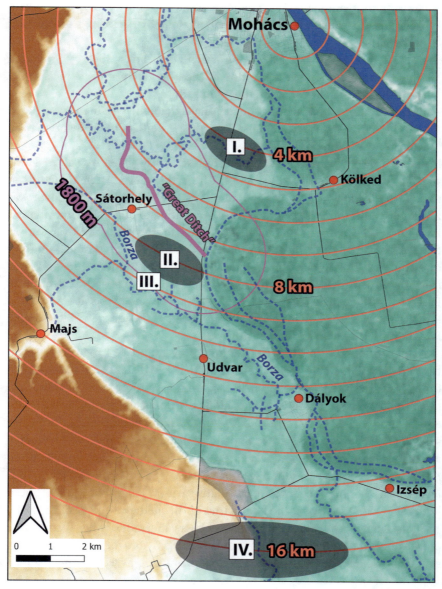

FIGURE 8.3   Distance data from the medieval Mohács according to Brodarics. Edited by Péter Gyenizse. Legend: I = Hungarian army encampment half a mile from Mohács; II = battlefield one mile from Mohács; III = medieval village remains; IV = Ottoman army encampment before 29 August 1526, two miles from Mohács.

SOURCE OF BACKGROUND: EUDEM AND OPENSTREETMAP.

- the southern border of the medieval estate of Földvár was the Borzató Valley, (in the vicinity of 18th-century Borza manor), at 10 km from Mohács of the time;
- from the deep and wide valley (the "Deep Ditch") described by Brodarics, which is approximately the location of the Christian army, the village (the site of the Turkish lines) lay an Italian mile away;[48]
- finally, Brodarics believed that on 28 August 1526, the Ottoman camp stood two Hungarian miles, or about 16 kilometres,[49] south of the Hungarian royal camp, towards the Karasica.[50]

It would be worth carrying out a control test, as suggested by Balázs Sudár, starting from the opposite direction, i.e. from the south. After the Ottoman period, the bishop's survey of 1696 mentions that the village of Földvár was 2.5-hours' walk from Kiskőszeg (Batina). According to Sudár, the information from the source indicates that the distance data for the road to Földvár were as follows: Csibogát is one and a quarter hour from Kiskőszeg, Danóc is another three quarters of an hour from Csibogát, and Földvár is another half an hour from Danóc. In his calculations, he assumed a journey speed of 8–9 km/h. Based on this, the distance between Földvár and Kiskőszeg was at least 20 km. From this, Sudár concluded that, given the speed of the journey, Földvár must have been in the wider vicinity of Udvar.

As part of our control study, we counted the number of road sections on the early modern road network. Based on this, the distance of about 20 km from Kiskőszeg at a speed of 8 km/h (2.5 hours) does not point to Udvar. On the other hand, after travelling 20 km along the Borza Stream, we arrive in the administrative area of Sátorhely. If we do the same operation at the higher speed of 9 km/h as suggested by Sudár, the distance covered will be greater, around 2.5 kilometres longer (22.5 km). Continuing the journey from south to north, we arrive in the present-day built-up area of Sátorhely. So it makes a difference whether the speed we are calculating with is 8 km/h or 9 km/h, but in both cases we will arrive at the boundaries of the medieval village of Földvár.

Sudár's claim that Földvár must have been located east of Merse, northwest of Dályok, in the wider surroundings of Udvar, is only broadly true, because, as stated above, the written sources and historical maps, as well as the distance

---

48   Although we do not know from which part of the valley the Italian mile should be calculated, the distance between the southern part of the Sátorhely Ridge and the northern side of Borza from the "Great Ditch" is typically 1,800 ±300 metres, which on average corresponds to the figure given in the source.
49   Between 15 and 16.8 kilometres.
50   "Meanwhile the Turkish emperor, with his huge army of three hundred thousand men, was only two miles away." Brodarics, *Igaz leírás*, [A true account] p. 52.

data indicate the administrative area of today's Sátorhely, the former estate of Földvár. The distance from Udvar, marked by him, to Kiskőszeg, is about 18 kilometres. Therefore, this village does not match the distance or speed data provided by Sudár.

5 The Village of Földvár on a Map from 1700

The Ottoman Turkish period of the Mohács Plain ended in 1687 with the Battle of Nagyharsány. The war of liberation against the Ottoman Turks started in 1684 and ended with the Peace of Karlowitz[51] in 1699. The end of the 17th century marked the beginning of a new era in the area in every respect. The Muslim population of the Ottoman era left, followed by new waves of settlers who transformed the landscape and changed the geographical naming. A comprehensive toponymic study of the area offers exciting conclusions.[52]

Orthodox and Catholic Slavs from the south and later Germans and other minorities from the north settled in Mohács and the surrounding villages. Serbs were granted privileges by the Habsburgs.

The Habsburgs tried to stabilize control over the liberated Hungarian territories, but a large part of the mainly Protestant Hungarians did not accept this. Between 1703 and 1711, an uprising broke out against them, which in Hungarian history is known as the Rákóczi's War of Independence, and its participants are known as the Kuruc.

An analysis of a map[53] below dated 1700, has provided important results in deciding the "Földvár dispute" (Figure 8.4). It provides a visual record of the settlement system of the transitional period after the liberation from the Ottoman Turks but before the Kuruc Wars. This is important for us because, during this short period, most of the inhabitants of the Mohács Plain spoke South Slavic languages.

In the year before the 1700 map was drawn (1699), Prince Eugene of Savoy, the victorious commander of the War of Liberation, was granted the territory of the Bellye dominium by the emperor in recognition of his merits.[54] The

---

51   The Banat (the area around Temesvár [Timişoara]) was later liberated and returned to Hungary under the terms of the Peace of Pozsarevac (1718).
52   Pap, Norbert, Kitanics, Máté, Ács, Marianna, Reményi, Péter. Geo-History of the Toponymy of Mohács Plain, sw Hungary. In: O'Reilly, Gerry (ed.) *Place Naming, Identities and Geography: Critical Perspectives in a Globalizing and Standardizing World.* Springer International Publishing, Cham, 2023 pp. 383–411.
53   Source: Universum dominium Siklossiense... (1700).
54   Pap et al., "Sátorhely vagy Majs?" [Sátorhely or Majs?].

FIGURE 8.4 The Mohács Plain in 1700. Excerpt from Celsissum Diu [! Dni] Dni Principis Eugeny de Sabaudia, Excell.mi Dni D: Aeneae Comitis Campi Marechallia Caprara, et Ex. Dni Comitis Veterani necnon R[ever]end[issi]mi Dni Dni Epp[iscop]i Jány Anno Domini [1]700.
SOURCE: HTTPS://MAPS.HUNGARICANA.HU/HU/OSZKTERKEPTAR/2142/

map played an important role in defining the new boundaries of the estates: it separates the bishop's estates around Mohács from the prince's estates further south and shows the villages belonging to the latter. The names of the settlements are not standardised but reflect the way the mapmaker interpreted the geographical names of his time and displayed them on the map. In addition to Latin, the map uses Hungarian, German and French terms for the names and the various inscriptions. The network of settlements is also structured in a way by the marking of churches and buildings: places with churches are higher in the hierarchy. The names of the settlements are mostly similar to their later names (Table 8.2), with two important exceptions: Guilue and Utvar.

The common 'ö' sound, or more precisely letter, in Hungarian, and the consonant shift cause problems for non-Hungarians when describing certain words. This is true for the spelling of both names. However, Guilue/Kölked is well defined by its location on a marshy area, by the fact that it is a Hungarian settlement that survived the Ottoman Turkish conquest and by the fact that it still exists in the same place: it is easier to decipher the term. Thus, in the case of Guilue/Kölked, the 'k' became 'g'and the 'ö ' became 'u'.

The case of the name Utvar is different from that of Kölked because its identification is problematic. There is now a village of a slightly similar name, Udvar, in the area to the east of the location marked on the 1700 map. The

TABLE 8.2   Explanation of some of the names on the 1700s estate map

Place names on the map, inscriptions	The place names today
Bata	Báta
MOHATS	Mohács
Insula St Brigita	Eastern side of the Mohacs Island
Duodecin navigia bellica IMPERIALIA	12 imperial warships
Isip	Izsép, today Topolje in Croatia
Dalyok	Dályok, today Duboševica in Croatia
Donovitz	Danóc used to be a village
Guilue	Kölked
(F)Utvar	Földvár, a destroyed village that no longer exists
Mais	Majs
Morse	Merse, a destroyed village that no longer exists (only in the name of an outskirt)
Orman	Ormány, a destroyed village that no longer exists (only in the name of an outskirt)
Beszedeg	Bezedek
Ketu	Géta, in the Middle Ages there was a monastery and a village here, (only in the name of an outskirt)
Lok	Lak, a destroyed village that no longer exists, (only in the name of an outskirt)

SOURCE: PAP ET AL., 2023.

latter, however, was only established in the second half of the 18th century by German settlers along the Mohács-Eszék road, on the western, wooded part of the Dályok estate (the latter is also marked on the map), with the that time name Udvar(d). We suspect that the name "Utvar" as it appears on the map of 1700 is in fact none other than "Földvár" itself.] Why?

The name "Földvár" is quite common in the Hungarian-inhabited areas of the Carpathian Basin. Its meaning is "Earth Castle", actually a kind of fortified place of ancient or medieval origin, of which there are many in the area. The late 17th-century spelling of these placenames may help to clear up the "mystery" of the 1700 map.

The military engineers who surveyed and mapped the liberated territories during the war (1683/84–1699) came across the name Földvár several times. The most notable ones still in existence today are (Duna)Földvár and (Tisza)Földvár, which are important towns in Hungary.

The renowned military expert and cartographer of the period, Luigi Ferdinando Marsigli, faced the problem of name transcription several times in his works. During the war, he worked in Hungary. The aforementioned (Duna)Földvár also appeared in his maps and descriptions as Feudvar and Fudvar. Furthermore the name of the former Hungarian (Tisza and later Bács)Földvár along the Tisza River, Bačko Gradište in Serbia, was recorded exactly as it appears on the above map of 1700, i.e. as Utvar. In addition, a water name, *Udvar Palus* (Udvar[i]-tó [Lake Udvar(i)]), was also indicated on the island of Mohács.[55] However, this body of water is none other than *Lacus Földváriensis* (Mikoviny, 1720–1725), i.e., Lake Földvár(i), which was once part of the Földvár estate, so the name is directly related to the village.[56] Based on these observations it can be stated that the mysterious Utvar on the mentioned map of 1700 is the Croatianized/Serbianized form of the Hungarian geographical name Földvár, and consequently Utvar is identical to the long sought-after Földvár.] How can the name change be reconstructed? On the map (Figure 8.4), "Utvar" is shown east of "Mais", north of "Ketu", on the southern side of the Borza Stream, as part of the Bellyei dominium of Eugene of Savoy. The method of mapping in this period was a field survey: the engineer obtained his data by questioning the elders of the settlements. During this period (1687–1704), the proportion of Catholic and especially Orthodox Slavs in this area was very high, and, according to the written sources, seems to have been predominant. Therefore, when recording the names of settlements, it is necessary to take into account the practice and rules of the local adoption of Hungarian names by the South Slavs.[57]

The maps and descriptions of the military engineer Marsigli, drawn up in the same period, as already mentioned, offer us a primary point of reference. As mentioned above, he recorded the Lake Földvár(i) belonging to the former Földvár estate in the form of *"Udvar Palus"*. Both names (*Utvar* on the map of 1700 and *Udvar Palus* by Marsigli) reflect the specificity of the geographical name transfer to the South Slavic ethnic groups. The South Slavic form of the Hungarian "Földvár" is *"Fudvar"* (see, among others, the example of Földvár *"Fudvar"* in Tolna County, or *"Fudvarska greda"* on the Island of Mohács).

---

55 Pap et al., "Geo-History of the Toponymy of Mohács Plain". p. 395.
56 Marsigli (1696/1726).
57 Ibid.

In cases where the informants of the military engineers are not South Slavs but Hungarians, the name Földvár is transcribed with a diphthong as "Feudvar", thus marking the 'ö' sound.[58]

Since the settlement of Udvar, south of the Földvár *praedium*, was not established by German settlers until more than half a century after the 1700 map was drawn, they got the name "ready-made", presumably from local Croats or Serbs. How?

Since Földvár was destroyed in 1704 at the latest, the Croats of nearby Dályok used the name of the devastated settlement to mark the part of the area surrounding the former village: the (f)udvar/utvar "border" towards Földvár (Utvar/Udvar). So when the German settlers arrived decades later and the land was demarcated for them, they were given landed property in the named area, after which they named their village. Thus the settlement and its estate "Udvard" is formed from the area called *'Ud/tvar'*. It is conceivable, and even probable, that the name Udvard (Udvar+d) with the suffix 'd', which the sources indicate was used for the settlement of Udvar, supports this: here the 'd' functioned as a place-name constituent, possibly with a pronunciation-stabilising effect. At that time, Földvár manor had no permanent population. The Hungarian administration thus used the original medieval name, perpetuating the geographical name Földvár. This is why the name *"Földvár praedium"* can be found on maps and documents in connection with the destroyed Földvár village, at least after 1726.[59]

6 The "Borzathw" Valley: Environmental and Archaeological Investigations

The centre of the estate, known as village Földvár, appears to have been built along the middle course of the Borza Stream,[60] on a dry area rising from the floodplain of the stream. On the western border of the manor, a crossing point was established in 1338 at the triple border of the estates of Nagymajsa, Földvár and Kismajsa. To the north of this was the stream valley, while to the south and south-east of it, according to a source from 1478, was *"Borzathw"* (Borzató,

---

58 Ibid. In Croatian and Serbian there is no 'ö', so in the case of Hungarian geographical names, the corresponding sounds are pronounced and marked with 'u'. This is how, for example, Hungarian Tököl became Tukulja, Szőkéd Sukit, Szőke Suka, Sükösd Čikuzda, Ösztyén in our study area Ustine, Földvár Fudvar and then Utvar.
59 Ibid.
60 The first mention of the estate in the form of Ipoltlaka dates back to 1223.

meaning Borza Lake), an area periodically flooded with water in rainy weather. The important road which marked the boundary in this area during the period ran along its right shore.

Shortly before the battle of 1526, an environmental description was made of the area. This document is the 1478 boundary inspection of the Merse estate (located in the southern part of the present-day administrative area of Majs), which was approved in 1520. It was a legal procedure for establishing the boundaries of Merse. According to the survey, the boundary between the Merse estate and the neighbouring estate of Kismajsa to the north ran in a west-east direction and led into the Borzató Valley. The location of the settlement of Merse is known from the excavations of László Papp in the 1960s. The border between Merse and Kismajsa ran along the alluvial fan of Majs in a west-east direction. Kismajsa (also known as *Egyházasmajsa*, i.e. the settlement had a church) probably lay in the valley behind the field, in the oldest part of the present-day village of Majs. According to the description, when the committee crossed the border, they passed from west to east, first among wild pear trees, then through a long wooded stretch, and finally through a wet, grove-like area to the Borzató Valley.

The last stretch of the Merse-Kismajsa border was on the road to the village Földvár. Since the northern side of the border was contested by the representative of Kismajsa all along the border, it is likely that this road led from Kismajsa to the village of Földvár, a considerable distance along the alluvial fan of Majs. This section was also recorded in the survey as passing alongside a 'berek' (wet grove), which corresponds well to the marshy place that was called Presztika in this area in the 18th century and was only drained along the Borza Stream in the mid-19th century.

At the Borzató Valley, the border then turned south along another road leading from east to south. For about two kilometres along this stretch, the valley of the stream consisted of a chain of small lakes and wet, marshy areas. This may have been the already mentioned Borzató Valley. Three large dry mounds emerged from this wetland during the period in question. The road ran along the border between Merse and Földvár, to the south-west of these water bodies, and may correspond to the contemporary route of the later Nagynyárád-Dalyok road, which certainly differed in alignment slightly from the present one. This is the *"Great Danoc road"* mentioned in the sources (the road was towards the medieval settlement of Danóc). This frontier was disputed throughout 1478, precisely because it was not based on a natural feature representing a sharp boundary, but could have been a wavering area.

The endpoint of this section was where they reached the former village of Kassa on the road to Danóc, and from there the border turned west. This village of Kassa was probably located in the administrative area of the present-day village of Udvar. It is known that, like Földvár, it belonged to the Szekszárd Abbey, but was situated south of it. To what extent is the analysis of the 1478/1520 source consistent with our environmental reconstruction?

Based on old maps and our field modelling, three flat, dry mounds emerged from the floodplain of the Borza Stream in the middle reaches of the watercourse, showing signs of human settlement. These dry areas were and still are part of the administrative territory of Sátorhely on the administrative maps drawn in the 19th century.

For a long time, the main problem with the use of the area was the management of the water flowing into the valley. With the onset of cooler and wetter periods (Little Ice Age) beginning here in the 15th century, continuing in the late middle ages and early modern times, the inhabitants of the area made ever greater efforts to drain the accumulated water more quickly by deepening the stream bed and reinforcing the banks to prevent flooding. This seems to be confirmed by a magnetometer survey of the former silted-up bed of the Borza Stream in 2021. It clearly shows a series of regularly spaced piles along the stream bed, spaced 8–8 metres apart in both directions, at a distance from each other of about 3.5 metres. This archaeological feature, which follows the bed, is artificial and was probably built for flood protection.[61]

According to written sources and old maps, the border may have changed to a lesser extent along this stretch, mainly due to changes in hydrological conditions. The Danóc, and later the Danube-Dályok road, played an important, even decisive role. The cadastral map of 1865 already shows the situation – after the drainage – when the boundary of the settlement of Sátorhely was settled on the levelled road (700–400 m south-west of the stream bed) and the formerly regularly flooded areas were replaced by arable land. The valley of the "Borzathw", still clearly visible on Andreas Kneidinger's 1772 agricultural map (Figure 8.5), disappeared in the mid-19th century (sometime between 1838 and 1858) as a result of drainage and canal construction.

The more varied topography, originally with more pronounced microlandforms, have been largely eroded, first by drainage, then by arable cultivation and levelling of the stream bed. The mounds have been flattened and the deeper areas filled in. The present landscape is more of an alluvial lowland

---

61   See Máté Stibrányi (2021) Sátorhely-Borza Manor. Report on the archaeological geophysical survey. Sátorhely-Budapest, 2022 22 p. Finally, this problem was solved in the 1940s and 1950s by the construction of the *Malomárok* canal and an another, smaller canal to the north of it. In the 1970s the stream bed was also eliminated when it was diverted into an artificial channel further west and its former location was largely levelled.

FIGURE 8.5 The three chambers along the Borza Stream. The map were made in 1772 by Andreas Kneidinger.
SOURCE: CHARTEN VON DER KA[MMER]AL ORTSCHAFT MAYS IN DER ... BARANYER GESPANSCHAFT ZUR HERRSCHAFT BELLYE GEHÖRIG ... [S 11 - NO. 830:43.] (MAGYAR NEMZETI LEVÉLTÁR ORSZÁGOS LEVÉLTÁRA).

character. Our research aimed at localising the village of Földvár, based on written sources and landscape reconstruction, focused on three major dry mounds located adjacent to each other along the Borza Stream.

The southernmost dry area (Figure 8.6 chamber I) deserves further investigation. So far, all we know is that a mill stood in its eastern corner, next to the Borza Stream. The date of its construction is not known, but it is certain that it is shown on maps from the second half of the 18th century, and its remains are still visible on the surface. A geophysical survey of a small area on the western edge of the outcrop has revealed archaeological remains. (Figure 8.7) However, findings on the surface recovered during the field survey suggest that this may be the result of Roman rather than medieval land use.

The central study area (Figure 8.6 Chamber II) contains not only Roman archaeological remains but also the remains of a medieval village. In 1967, László Papp identified ten Árpád-period and late medieval dwellings on the site and

LOCALIZING THE CENTRAL AREA OF THE BATTLE OF MOHÁCS   299

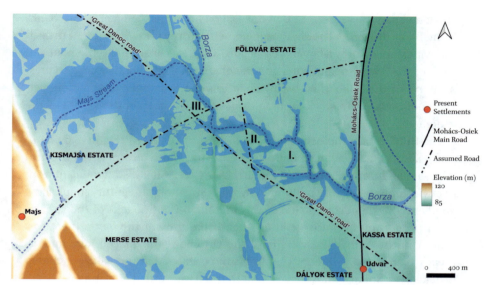

FIGURE 8.6   The Borzathw Valley (Borza Lake Valley) in 1476. Edited by Norbert Pap and Péter Gyenizse
Legend: I. = chamber I; II. = chamber II; III. = chamber III.

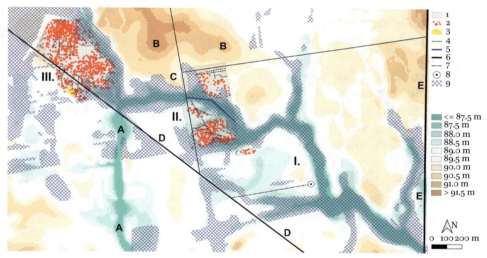

FIGURE 8.7   Geophysical survey of chamber I–III. Traces of Roman, medieval and early modern settlements (2021–2022). Edited by Norbert Pap and Péter Gyenizse. Legend: 1 = magnetometer survey area; 2 = archaeological anomalies; 3 = brick fragments on the surface; 4 = former trenches; 5 = canalised bed of Borza Stream; 6 = recent roads; 7 = hypothetical road to the mill; 8 = place of mill; 9 = wetlands; A = Borza Canal made in the 20th century; B = Sátorhely Ridge; C = Borza manor; D = Nagynyárád-Dályok road; E = Mohács-Eszék (Osijek) road.

concluded that the settlement that once stood here stretched along both banks of the Borza Stream.[62] The 2021 magnetometer survey also showed that the settlement extended over a larger area (Figure 8.7). The core of the settlement was south of the Borza Stream, but a number of archaeological finds were also present north of the established basin, albeit in a more sporadic distribution, perhaps indicative of livestock farming associated with the southern core of the settlement.

The third, northernmost area is the highest of the three (Figure 8.6 chamber III). It may have been an important crossing point. According to historical maps, a road from Majs to the stream led from here.[63] It is also significant from an environmental history point of view that 18th and 19th-century maps show woodland on the northern side of this mound, on both banks of the stream. This is important because we know that at the time of the battle there was a forest in the immediate vicinity of the Ottoman guns placed here and, as already mentioned, a late 17th century source states that the village included an oak forest. Surface finds suggest that the area was settled for a longer period. Roman, medieval and early modern pottery can be found on the surface, suggesting that traces of several settlements were mixed on the site. Accordingly, the image from the magnetometer survey carried out in 2022 revealed an intense archaeological site with several periods, with trench systems presumably dating back to the medieval period (Figure 8.7).

In 2022, the focus of the investigations was on the aforementioned map of 1700, which, confirming the above, clearly determined where the village of Földvár (Utvar on the map) may have stood. The map shows the settlement of key importance to the east of Majs, north of Géta, on the south side of the Borza Stream, just where the three adjacent higher ground levels or parcels surveyed along the Borza Stream lie.

The centre of the manor, already known from the 13th century, existed until the 17th and 18th centuries, but it is by no means certain that it always stood on the same site. Certain serious conflicts and also the expansion of the floodplain of the Borza Stream may have led to the village being renewed several times during this long period, in different places, on the well-defined higher ground of the three parcels. Until the 16th century, the village cemetery and church were the only fixed points of this system.

Further archaeological research will involve collecting surface finds from the three mounds and, after geophysical and metal detector analysis, determining what was standing exactly where within this area at the time of the

---

62 Janus Pannonius Museum, Archaeological Database, 1967, no: 1242–83.
63 Military Survey I and a map from 1838.

battle. This is particularly true for the church at Földvár, although it is noteworthy that a 1327 charter mentions a chapel at Földvár and that Brodarics, a 16th-century chronicler of the battle, also speaks of the village church. It is therefore possible that it was only a small building.

So this is the place where the Ottoman army arrived at noon on 29 August 1526. The camping took place further away from the Borzató Valley, in front of the slopes, while the artillery dug in near the wooded area at Földvár. In the gallery forest of oaks, ashes and elms there were clearings at the crossings, and the troops marched through these and across the stream.

7 Conclusion

In 1526, fighting centred on the estate of Földvár. The nature, extent and boundaries of the estate are well defined in medieval and early modern written sources. On Mohács Island, Földvár owned a valuable land rich in fishing opportunities, but its main area, where the village was situated, was located on the western side of the Béda-Danube, next to the marshy floodplain (Danóc Marsh, later Vizslak Meadow). The landlord used the flat, dry terrain for agricultural purposes. An important road, the *via militaris* (military road), dating from Roman times, ran north-south along the eastern edge of the estate. Next to the road, on the edge of the marsh, rises "Törökdomb" [Turkish Hill], on which the Romans built a watchtower. Its northern border passed along the "Great Ditch" and the "Wide Field" near the Borza Stream. The western border of the estate was formed by the Borza Stream, the most important watercourse of the plain. Along the stream a commonly-owned gallery forest was consisted of mainly of oak, ash and elm trees.

To the southwest, the important road from *Nyárád* to *Danóc* led through the Borzató Valley, and to the south, into the *Herman Forest*, another estate of the Szekszárd Abbey. In the pre-battle period, the *Danóc* road led to and through the village of *Kassa*, built on this estate.

In the Borza Lake Valley, three flat-topped, low hills rose above the marshy surface and the chain of small lakes. These, especially the upper two chambers, were settled in the medieval and early modern periods, and the area, identified as a multi-layered archaeological site, meets the identified character and specificity of Földvár in several respects. These include:
– the area along the Borza Stream, on which archaeological remains of a settlement have been identified, belonged to the estate of Földvár in the middle ages, according to the documents of 1338 and 1476, and it was a populated, inland site;

- settlement factors suggest that the village was strategically located at the crossing point of the Borza Stream, the most important watercourse of the Mohács Plain;
- the characteristics of the settlement do not contradict the demographic, environmental and economic data of medieval Földvár: they even correspond well to them;
- the exact location of the village of Utvar/Földvár is shown on the 1700 map;
- the village lies about an Italian mile from the Hungarian army position (paleo river bed), and thus matches Brodarics' description;
- the road from Kismajsa leads straight here to the east;
- the 1526 Mohács–Földvár (8 + 1.5 = 9.5 kilometres) and the 1696 Kiskőszeg (later Batina)–Földvár (2.5 hours ride = about 20–22 kilometres) distance data are in accordance with the sources.

Bibliography

B. Szabó, János. *A mohácsi csata.* [The Battle of Mohács] Budapest: Corvina, 2006.

Bende, Lajos. "A mohácsi csata." [The Battle of Mohács] *Hadtörténelmi Közlemények* 13 (1966): 532–567.

Bertók, Gábor and Balázs Polgár. "A mohácsi csatatér és a középkori Földvár falu régészeti kutatása." [Research into the battlefield of Mohács and the archaeological study of the medieval village of Földvár] *Hadtörténelmi Közlemények* 124 (2011): 919–928.

Brodarics, István. *Igaz leírás a magyaroknak a törökkel Mohácsnál vívott csatájáról.* [A True Account of the Battle of Mohács between the Hungarians and the Turks] Budapest: Magvető Könyvkiadó, 1983.

Dernschwam, Hans. *Erdély. Besztercebánya. Törökországi útinapló.* [Transylvania. Besztercebánya. Turkish Travel Diary] Budapest: Európa Könyvkiadó, 1984.

Evliyâ Çelebi b. Derviş Mehemmed Zıllî. *Evliyâ Çelebi Seyahatnâmesi. 6. Kitap. Topkapı Sarayı Kütüphanesi Revan 1457 Numaralı Yazmanın Transkripsiyonu–Dizini.* Eds. Seyit Ali Kahraman and Yücel Dağlı. İstanbul: Yapı Kredi Yayınları, 2002.

Fényes, Elek. *Magyarországnak és hozzákapcsolt tartományoknak mostani állapotja statisztikai és geográfiai tekintetben I.* [The present state of Hungary and its associated provinces in statistical and geographical terms] Pest: Trattner–Károlyi, 1839.

Fölker, József. *Mohács története.* [The history of Mohács] Mohács: Rosenthal Márk Könyvnyomdája, 1900.

Gergely, Endre. "Ásatások a mohácsi csatatéren (1924, 1925)." [Excavations on the Mohács battlefield (1924, 1925)] In *Mohács emlékkönyv 1926,* ed. Imre Lukinich, 349–360. Budapest, Királyi Magyar Egyetemi Nyomda, 1926.

Gyalókay, Jenő. "Földvár." *Hadtörténelmi Közlemények* 27 (1926): 290–300.

Gyalókai, Jenő. "A mohácsi csata." [The Battle of Mohács] In *Mohács emlékkönyv 1926*, ed. Imre Lukinich, 193–276. Budapest, Királyi Magyar Egyetemi Nyomda, 1926.

Halmay, Barna. *Az 1526-iki mohácsi csata és igazi helye*. [The Battle of Mohács in 1526 and its real location] Debrecen: Magyar Nemzeti Könyv- és Lapkiadóvállalat Rt., 1926.

Hans Dernschwam's Tagebuch einer Reise nach Konstantinopel und Kleinasien (1553/55). Ed. Franz Babinger. München, Leipzig: 1923.

Hummel, Gyula "Földvár." *Dunántúl*, 23 July 1926.

Kápolnai, Pauer István. "A mohácsi hadjárat 1526-ban." [The Mohács military campaign in 1526] *Hadtörténelmi Közlemények* 2 (1889): pp. 177–208, pp. 441–462.

Karácson, Imre. *Evlia Cselebi török világutazó magyarországi utazásai (1660–1664)*. [Turkish traveller Evliya Çelebi's travels in Hungary] Budapest: Magyar Tudományos Akadémia, 1904.

Koszta, László. "A pécsi káptalan kiadatlan oklevelei (1325–1339)." In *Baranyai történetírás 1992/1995*, ed. László Szita, 10–11. Pécs: Baranya Megyei Levéltár, 1995.

Kupelwieser, Leopold. *Die Kämpfe Ungarns mit den Osmanen bis zur Schlacht bei Mohács, 1526*. Vienna, Leipzig: Wilhelm Braumüller, 1899.

Levél Velencébe, Cividale, 1526. szeptember 15." [Letter to Venice, Cividale, 15 September 1526] In *Mohács*, ed. János B. Szabó, 100. Budapest: Osiris Kiadó, 2006.

Magyarországi török kincstári defterek II. 1540–1639. [Turkish treasury defters in Hungary II.] Ed. Ernő Kammerer. Budapest: Athenaeum R. Társ. Könyvnyomdája, 1890.

Mező, András. *Patrocíniumok a középkori Magyarországon*. [Patrociniums in medieval Hungary.] Budapest: Magyar Egyháztörténeti Enciklopédia Munkaközösség (METEM), 2003.

N. Ipoly, Márta. "A mohácsi csata és csatatér megválaszolatlan kérdései." [Unanswered questions about the Battle of Mohács and the battlefield] *Hadtörténelmi Közlemények* 24 (1977): 206–222.

Nagy, Imre et al. eds. *A zichy és vásonkeői gróf Zichy család idősb ágának okmánytára I–XII*. [The documents of the elder branch of the Zich and Vásonkeő Count Zichy family I–XII] Budapest: Magyar Történelmi Társulat, 1871–1931.

Nagy, Lajos. "A Császári Udvari Kamara pécsi prefektúrájához tartozó terület 1687-ben." [The area belonging to the Prefecture of the Imperial Court Chamber of Pécs in 1687] In *Baranyai helytörténetírás 1978*, ed. László Szita, 15–56. Pécs: Baranya Megyei Levéltár, 1979.

Négyesi, Lajos. "A mohácsi csata." [The Battle of Mohács] *Hadtörténelmi Közlemények* 107 (1994): 62–79.

Németh, Béla. "A mohácsi vésztől a török kiűzetéséig." [From the Mohacs disaster to the expulsion of the Turks] In *Baranya multja és jelenje* II, ed. Ferenc Várady, 393–496. Pécs: Pécsi Irodalmi és Könyvnyomdai Részvénytársaság, 1897.

Ortvay, Tivadar. *A mohácsi csata elvesztésének okai és következményei.* [The reasons for and consequences of losing the Battle of Mohács.] Budapest: Magyar Tudományos Akadémia, 1910.

Pap, Norbert, Máté Kitanics, Péter Gyenizse, Gábor Szalai, and Balázs Polgár. "Sátorhely vagy Majs? Földvár környezeti jellemzői – A mohácsi csata centrumtérségének lokalizálása." [Sátorhely or Majs? Environmental characteristics of Földvár. Localizing the central area of the Battle of Mohács] *Történelmi Szemle* 61 (2019): 209–246.

Pap, Norbert, Pál Fodor, Máté Kitanics, Tamás Morva, Gábor Szalai, and Péter Gyenizse. "A mohácsi Törökdomb." [The Törökdomb in Mohács] *Történelmi Szemle* 60 (2018): 332–333.

Pap, Norbert, Kitanics, Máté, Ács, Marianna, Reményi, Péter. "Geo-History of the Toponymy of Mohács Plain, SW Hungary." In: O'Reilly, Gerry (ed.) *Place Naming, Identities and Geography: Critical Perspectives in a Globalizing and Standardizing World.* Springer International Publishing, Cham, (2023) pp. 383–411.

Papp, László. "Majs." In *Az 1968. év Régészeti Kutatásai. Régészeti Füzetek* I. 22., ed. Alice Sz. Burger, 83. Budapest: Népművelési Propaganda Iroda, 1Kitanics969.

Papp, László. "A mohácsi csatatér kutatása." [Research into the battlefield of Mohács] In *Janus Pannonius Múzeum Évkönyve 1960,* ed. János Dombay, 197–253. Pécs: Janus Pannonius Múzeum, 1961.

Perjés, Géza. *Mohács.* Budapest: Magvető Könyvkiadó, 1979.

Pesti, János. *Baranya megye földrajzi nevei* II. [Geographical names in Baranya County] Pécs: Baranya Megyei Levéltár, 1982.

Sudár, Balázs. "Földvár falu a török korban." [The Village of Földvár in the Ottoman Era] *Történelmi Szemle* 62 (2020): 153–168.

Szabó, Máté, Gábor Bertók, Csilla Gáti, and Éva Szajcsán. "A mohácsi csatatér kutatása – az első országos fémkeresős szakmai hétvége és tanulságai." [Exploring the battlefield of Mohács – the first national metal detection weekend and lessons learned] *Magyar Régészet* (2016), Summer, pp. 1–7. Available at http://files.archaeolingua.hu/2016NY/Szabo_et_al_H16NY.pdf.

Szakály, Ferenc. *A mohácsi csata.* [The Battle of Mohács] Budapest: Akadémiai Kiadó, 1975.

Szalay, László. *Adalékok a magyar nemzet történetéhez a XVI-dik században.* [Additions to the history of the Hungarian nation in the sixteenth century.] Pest: Ráth Mór, 1859.

Szurmay, Sándor. *A mohácsi hadjárat 1526-ban.* [The Mohács military campaign in 1526] Budapest: Ludovika Akadémia, 1901.

Timár, Péter. *Magyarország középkori településeinek és egyházainak topográfiai adattára II.* [Topographical database of the medieval settlements and churches of Hungary II.] Szeged: Timár Péter, 2019.

Tóth, István György. "Athanasio Georgiceo álruhás császári megbízott útleírása a magyarországi török hódoltságról, 1626-ból." [Disguised imperial envoy Athanasio Georgiceo's travelogue on the Turkish occupation of Hungary in 1626] *Századok* 132 (1998): 837–858.

Unknown author, *Universum dominium Siklossiense modo divisum in quator partes, nempé Celsissum Diu* [*! Dni*] *Dni Principis Eugeny de Sabaudia, Excell.mi Dni D: Aeneae Comitis Campi Marechallia Caprara, et Ex. Dni Comitis Veterani necnon R*[*ever*]*end*[*issi*]*mi Dni Dni Epp*[*iscop*]*i Jány Anno Domini* [*1*]*700.* Available at https://maps.hungaricana.hu/hu/OSZKTerkeptar/2142/.

Ungnád Dávid Konstantinápolyi utazásai. [Dávid Ungnád's travels in Constantinople] Budapest: Szépirodalmi önyvkiadó, 1986.

CHAPTER 9

Critical Comments on the Available Military Archaeology Topographic Data

Máté Kitanics, Norbert Pap, Sándor Konkoly and Erika Hancz

1   Introduction

Since the beginning of the 20th century, archaeology has been involved in the study of the Battle of Mohács. It has become more important since the 1960s, while today it has become the most controversial and most disputed area of research.

The military archaeological phenomena observed in the 100 km² area of the Mohács Plain, but also on Mohács Island, are still and once were associated with the events of 1526. However, a thorough, critical examination of the finds and archaeological phenomena found reveals that not all of them can be linked to the 1526 battle. Some of them were found to belong to a different period, and the archaeological remains referred to in the scholarly literature on the battle have often disappeared or never existed.

The region, with its turbulent past, has undergone significant internal and external political changes over the past 130 years of research. The identity backgound of the people who carried out the research, the social status of those who found and reported the finds, and the context of the reporting are all important factors to consider when assessing and understanding the role of a find or site. Because of the enormous symbolic significance of the battle, its history and its memorial sites cannot be examined without taking into account the changing courses of memorial politics in recent decades.

2   The Sultan's/Emperor's Hill, or the Törökdomb (Turkish Hill) of Mohács

Although it is not primarily a field object of military archaeology, we cannot help mentioning here the former Sultan's or Emperor's Hill (*Hünkâr tepesi*), an anthropogenic mound later called the Törökdomb (Turkish Hill), which stretched along the edge of the Vizslak Meadow (Table 9.3/12; Figure 9.6/12). This small promontory, built by the Romans along the Danube floodplain on the Mursa-Aquincum (Eszék/Osijek-Buda) military route for a watchtower, was an important landmark for the Battle of Mohács. During the Ottoman era in 1630–1631, the Pasha of Buda had a wooden pavilion (köşk) built here as a monument to the victory, symbolically occupying the space.

The pavilion and the nearby well frequented by pilgrims and travellers, served its function until 1686, when Mohács was recaptured. During his visit to Mohács in 1663, the Ottoman Turkish traveller Evliya Çelebi also visited the enclosed site, and described it as the resting place of the Ottoman martyrs of the Battle of Mohács. After the recapture of the area by the Christians, around 1687, a chapel was built on the site of the Ottoman pavilion, which stood until the second half of the 18th century.[1]

Endre Gergely, a gendarme captain, conducted "excavations" at the hill in 1924, but found no dead bodies related to the Battle of Mohács. This fact contributed significantly to the fact that from the following years research on the battle increasingly turned towards the stepped terrain, a little more than 4.5 km southwest of the site, while several researchers suggested that the legendary Emperor's Hill should be sought elsewhere, not at Turkish Hill.[2]

The above situation was not changed by the fact that, with the start of deep ploughing, archaeological finds were discovered in the area of the Turkish Hill and in the first decades of the 1900s, a series of military relics relating to the Battle of Mohács were most probably discovered on the edge of the Vizslak Meadow and at the nearby Black Gate (Fekete-kapu/Schwarzes Tor). We might add that in 1960 the first mass graves of the battle were found at a little more than 1 km distance from Turkish Hill.

In the 1960s and 1970s, most of the material of Turkish Hill was removed, the Ottoman well was demolished and the soil was used for construction. Although there have been several theories about the location of the Emperor's Hill, in 2018, an analysis of written sources and contemporary maps proved that Turkish Hill is identical with the former Emperor's Hill.[3] In the same year,

---

1 Norbert Pap, Pál Fodor, Máté Kitanics, Tamás Morva, Gábor Szalai, and Péter Gyenizse, "A mohácsi Törökdomb," [The Törökdomb of Mohács] *Történelmi Szemle* 60 (2018), no. 2, pp. 325–345.
2 Among the sites mentioned are the bastion-like promontory 1.5 km southeast of Majs, the Merse plateau and the church hill of Nagynyárád. See Máté Kitanics, Levente Nagy, Erika Hancz, Péter Gyenizse, Gábor Szalai, László Nagy, Zsombor Klembala, Balázs Polgár, and Norbert Pap, "A Törökdomb a régészeti vizsgálatok tükrében: 1924–2020," in *Mordortól Mohácsig: A mohácsi csatatáj történeti földrajzi kutatása*, [The Törökdomb in the Light of Archaeological Investigations: 1924–2020] ed. Norbert Pap (Budapest, MTA Bölcsészettudományi Kutatóközpont, 2020), pp. 273–349.
3 Pap et al., "A mohácsi Törökdomb," [The Törökdomb of Mohács], pp. 325–345.

a metal detector survey was carried out to bring to light the remains of the Ottoman pavilion and Baroque Catholic chapel that once stood here. As a military archeological find, six lead handgun bullets were found, two of which were fired and deformed, and four of which were dropped and intact.[4] Some of the bullets were presumably left at Turkish Hill during the wars of reconquest, as Christian or western armies marching against the Ottomans on the military route camped here on several occasions in the late 17th century.[5] One of the bullets, however, was certainly made for a Turkish birdshot handgun. In 2020, a geophysical survey of the remnants of the hill and its immediate surroundings identified the encircling ditch mentioned in Ottoman and Christian sources.[6]

Overall, it can be said that Emperor's Hill and the Ottoman victory monument built on it marked the site of the Battle of Mohács in 1526 for a long time, and was an important point of reference. During the anti-Ottoman wars at the end of the 17th century, Christian troops camped in the area around the hill on several occasions. It is thought that the remains have been collected on the former hill.

2.1 The Battle's Victims and Mass Graves

The systematic investigation of the battlefield of Mohács began in the late 1950s under the leadership of László Papp, archaeologist and later director of the Janus Pannonius Museum (JPM) of Baranya County. The first results of the decade-long research appeared in April 1960, when an excavation site associated with the battle of 1526 was identified on the basis of a data provider. Eight years earlier, an excavator had unearthed human bones at a site south of Mohács, east of the village of Sátorhely. At the time (cold war period), the machine was involved in the construction of a military defence system on the Hungarian–Yugoslavian border to prevent an expected attack from Yugoslavia. However, due to the highly confidential nature of the work, the information was only made available to the authorities years later, when political relations between Yugoslavia and Hungary eased.

After the survey, excavation began in September 1960, with the digging of trenches in the areas where the scattered, crushed bones were still visible. During the excavation work, a truncated wedge, or lunar crescent, was excavated,

---

4   Kitanics et al., "A Törökdomb," [The Törökdomb] in Mordortól Mohácsig, ed. Pap, pp. 273–349.
5   See, among others, the following map illustrations: L'accampamento dal di luglio fono al di 5 di agosto infra Mohatz e Dunawar, 1687, Institute and Museum of Military History, H III c 182/28; Veldt Lager zwischen Mohaz und Baranuivar den 15. July 1691, Institute and Museum of Military History, H III c 182/37.
6   Kitanics et al., "A Törökdomb," [The Törökdomb] in Mordortól Mohácsig, ed. Pap, pp. 273–349.

14.5 m long on axis, 2.2–2.5 m wide and 1.5 m deep (No. I) (Table 9.3/15; Figure 9.6/15). Then, at the end of the month, another approximately rectangular mass grave (No. II), 8.5 m long by 2.3–2.65 m wide by 1.45–1.5 m deep, was found about 2.5 m east of the first grave (Table 9.3/15; Figure 9.6/15).

During the excavation, which only covered the upper and lateral parts of the tombs, it became clear that the battle victims, estimated at 220–230, had been dumped and thrown into the pits. Some of the corpses were complete skeletons, others were headless, but only skulls were buried. The majority of the dead were described by anthropologist Lajos Bartucz as robust males aged between 20 and 40, but exceptionally there were some older ones. The visible mortal injuries were mostly caused by sword cuts and, in one case, a battle axe. Based on the injuries, the position of the objects and the finds recovered, Papp, who led the excavation, concluded that the graves contained of fleeing Hungarian and foreign fighters associated with the Battle of Mohács in 1526. They were massacred by Ottoman cavalrymen pursuing them from the south and by the cavalry led by Báli Bey, who were charging towards the devastated Christian camp to the north.

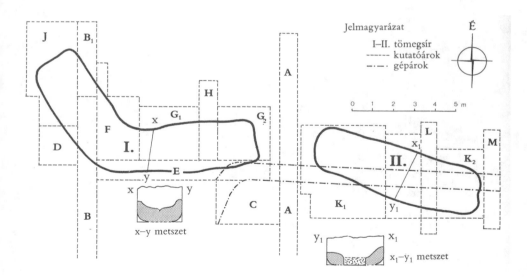

FIGURE 9.1 Site plan of mass graves I and II excavated in 1960. Legend: I–II. tömegsír = Massgrave I–II; kutatóárok = sondage; gépárok = excavated trench; metszet = cross section
SOURCE: PAPP LÁSZLÓ, "A MOHÁCSI CSATAHELY KUTATÁSA," [THE RESEARCH OF THE BATTLEFIELD OF MOHÁCS] IN MOHÁCS EMLÉKEZETE, EDS. KISS KÁROLY ET AL. BUDAPEST: EURÓPA KÖNYVKIADÓ, 1987, PP. 251–272.

In the area between the two mass graves, 8 coins – *batzen* and a *half-batzen* – from southern Germany and Salzburg were found in the trench,[7] which was filled in and then dug up again by the excavator working there in 1952. The second mass grave yielded 7 *batzen* and *half-batzen*,[8] as well as an iron rosette (*horse furniture ornament*) and the elbow part of an iron armour. In addition, both graves casted copper clothespins and cylindrical ingots, or ends of strings, twisted from copper sheet. [9]

The blunt edge of the first mass grave faced south-west (the attack was expected from there), while the second grave continued eastwards as an extension. On this basis, Papp, drawing also on Stephan Gerlach's description of 1573, suggested that the mass graves may have originally been gun emplacements, but also noted that he believed that the Christian guns may actually have been further south. Thus, he did not rule out the possibility that the sites might have been part of the *wagenburg* which was under preparation but not finished.[10] Although Papp made an attempt, he was unable to identify any other mass graves.

FIGURE 9.2   The siege of Arad by the Christian armies, 1658. Detail with the crescent-shaped gun emplacements and the military positions.
SOURCE: INSTITUTE AND MUSEUM OF MILITARY HISTORY, H III C 4.

---

7   The trench was part of the southern military defence system for a while from 1952.
8   The 15 coins were minted between 1506 and 1525.
9   Janus Pannonius Museum, Archaeological Database, 1960, 1245–83.
10 László Papp, "A mohácsi csatahely kutatása," [Research on the battlesite of Mohács] in *A Janus Pannonius Múzeum Évkönyve 1960,* ed. János Dombay (Pécs, Janus Pannonius Múzeum, 1961), pp. 197–253.

In 1975, to commemorate the 450th anniversary of the battle, a military cemetery was established around the two mass graves, with trees, flowers and statues. Three more mass graves (Table 9.3/15; Figure 9.6/15) were discovered during the construction of the Mohács National Memorial. The area around the two mass graves, which form the centre of the memorial site and were excavated in 1960, was left intact within a 15-metre radius and planted with flowers. However, in a ring-shaped strip 25 m wide from the edge of the ring, the soil was tilled to a depth of 60–70 cm to make the central part stand out. This is how the third mass grave (No. III), 4.8 m long and 3.25 m wide, was discovered at the end of October 1975, some 19 m south-east of graves I and II, and the fourth mass grave (No. IV), 4.25 m long and 1.6 m wide, was discovered in February 1976, 5 to 6 m from the third mass grave. The fifth mass grave (No. V), 11.9 m long and 2.3–3.8 m wide in its axis, was discovered in April 1976, also in the shape of a crescent, similar to the first grave, and projecting towards the south. It was also discovered accidentally, about 50 metres north-west of the centre of the park, after digging a trench for a water pipe.

The archaeologist in charge of the excavation, Borbála Maráz, believed that the regular rectangular objects III and IV were dug for burial, and she did not rule this out for the irregularly shaped tomb V.[11] In the newly, but also only partially excavated mass graves, she assumed a total of about 600–700 dead, who were thrown into the pits in a heap, as in the case of the bodies of tombs I and II. As in Papp's earlier excavation, a number of headless torsos and separate severed heads were found alongside the complete skeletons. The majority of the deceased were men aged between 20 and 50, although anthropologist Zsuzsanna K. Zoffmann identified two men aged around 17 and another between 14 and 15.[12] In most cases, death resulted from wounds by sword, for example the most common was cutting the head, but injuries on the limbs were also observed. The small number of finds consisted of copper buttons, copper and iron clothes buckles, small iron knives, iron belt buckles and iron pins. At the end of the excavation, Maráz came to the conclusion that the mass graves contained the bodies of the camp's slaughtered guards.

In 2020, the team of the Janus Pannonius Museum of Baranya County led by archaeologist Gábor Bertók, re-excavated the mass grave No. III, and then started to document and excavate the skeletons. The Department of

---

11   Borbála Maráz, "Újabb tömegsírok a mohácsi csatatéren," [More mass graves on the battlefield of Mohács] in *Mohács emlékezete,* eds. Kiss, et al., pp. 273–279.
12   Zsuzanna K. Zoffmann, *Az 1526-os mohácsi csata 1976-ban feltárt tömegsírjainak embertani vizsgálata* [Anthropologycal analysis of the mass graves of the Battle of Mohács in 1526, excavated in 1976] (Budapest: Akadémiai Kiadó, 1982).

Anthropology of the University of Szeged and the Hungarian Museum of Natural History were also involved in the investigations. Again, the finds mainly consisted of clothespins and cord endings, but also a gold coin of Matthias I (Mátyás Hunyadi) and three lead riffle bullets. Two of the latter suffered minor distortions and were determined to be between 10 and 13 mm in diameter (different figures have been published), while the third, which was badly damaged, was found to be larger than the first. It was thought that the date of burial of the lead bullets (1526) could not be disputed and that they were either from ammunition pouches left on belts or on the bodies of wounded soldiers who had been executed.[13]

Based on the examination of the skeletons, archaeologist Gábor Bertók and his colleagues were initially of the opinion that the deceased were the dead of the Christian camp. As many of them were "youth aged between 18 and 20", they could not have been soldiers in the battle, but rather auxiliary staff of the camp.[14] They later revised their interpretations and took the position that the Christian prisoners had been executed on the site of the mass graves at Sátorhely, and that the graves therefore contained people executed after the battle.[15]

It also to be noted that other dead bodies and human remains on the plain of Mohács are also linked to the Battle of Mohács in 1526. In the early 1900s, human and horse skeletons were found at the western edge of the Vizslak Meadow, near the brick kiln, with military equipments most probably related to the Battle of Mohács (Table 9.3/8; Figure 9.6/8),[16] and, according to a report, between 1925 and 1927, human bones were recovered from the wet meadow in the surrounding of Turkish Hill, while digging a drain (Table 9.3/10; Figure 9.6/10).[17] According to some reports, in 1910, 60–80 human skulls were found during earth works at the chapel of St. László, south of Udvar and north of Dályok (today Duboševica in Croatia) (Table 9.3/7; Figure 9.6/7).[18]

---

13 Gábor Bertók, Réka Neményi, György Pálfi, and Béla Simon, "A mohácsi III. számú tömegsír új kutatása," [New research on the Mohács mass grave No. III] *Magyar Régészet* 11 (2022), no. 1, pp. 44–53.

14 Olivér Kovács, *Mohácsi tömegsír: inkább a tábor halottjait rejtheti*, [Mohács mass grave: more likely to hide the camp's dead] Available at https://archeologia.hu/mohacsi-tomegsir-inkabb-a-tabor-halottait-rejtheti.

15 Bertók et al., "A mohácsi III. számú tömegsír," [The Mohács mass grave No. III] pp. 44–53.

16 Janus Pannonius Museum, Archaeological Database, 1928/1982, no. 1077–82.

17 Janus Pannonius Museum, Archaeological Database, 1961, no. 1261–83.

18 Barna Halmay, *Az 1526-iki mohácsi csata keletkezése és igazi helye* [The origins and real place of the Battle of Mohács in 1526] (Debrecen: Magyar Nemzeti Könyv- és Lapkiadóvállalat Rt., 1926).

László Papp identified a grave in 1959, north of Sátorhely, during the excavation of the medieval village cemetery of Lajmér, in which he found the skeletons of three men, aged 17–18 years, with their arms around each other and without further grave goods (Table 9.3/19; Figure 9.6/19). He believed that the dead could have been buried in the same pit under extraordinary circumstances, most probably during the Battle of Mohács, and that they were dug in the same time. Mihály Malán, the anthropologist who examined the bones, disagreed with his view, considering them to be from the 9th–12th centuries, similarly to the skeletons in other graves of the cemetery.[19]

Two years later, in 1961, Papp also conducted excavations at the Újistálló Manor opposite Turkish Hill. For decades, the site had been thought to hide mass graves, judging from the human bones occasionally found there. Although the archaeologist did not find any mass graves, he did identify a late medieval village and its cemetery. However, as in the case of Lajmér, he also brought to light a special grave. The dead man without any material objects was not lying on his back but on his stomach, and his body was buried in the direction opposite to the others. The skeleton without the skull, the right lower leg bone and the left tibia were also considered to be the dead of the Battle of Mohács because of its characteristics, which were very different from the others (Table 9.3/13; Figure 9.6/13).[20]

It is also worth mentioning that in 1960, about 140–160 m northeast of the two mass graves excavated at that time, Papp also collected human bones on the surface under the road to Sátorhely (Table 9.3/16; Figure 9.6/16). The site attracted the attention of the archaeologist because, according to the ploughman, a worker had turned out human bones there years earlier. No new mass grave was found there during the exploratory excavation, but a humerus, a metacarpal, and fragments of skull and tibia were found scattered. However, another possible dating has not, as far as we know, been checked more thoroughly. In the same year, Papp saw human bones in the fresh ploughing in two places in the S9 plough field of the Sátorhely state-owned agricultural company, namely immediately north-east of the Borza Stream and in the former Borza mansion. (Table 9.3/17; Figure 9.6/17). However, a systematic search of the sites was not carried out due to lack of time.[21]

---

19 Janus Pannonius Museum, Archaeological Database, 1959, no. 1236–83.
20 Janus Pannonius Museum, Archaeological Database, 1961, no. 1239–83; and Papp László, "Újabb kutatások a mohácsi csatatéren," [New research on the battlefield of Mohács] in *A Janus Pannonius Múzeum Évkönyve 1962*, ed. László Papp (Pécs: Janus Pannonius Múzeum, 1963), pp. 199–222.
21 Janus Pannonius Museum, Archaeological Database, 1960, no. 1245–83.

Finally, we should not forget Papp's 1968 excavation in the area around the settlement he identified as medieval Majsa, to the east of present-day Majs, south of the so-called *Malomárok*. During this excavation, he found scattered human bones and horse skeletons (Table 9.3/23; Figure 9.6/23), on which he expressed the following opinion: "… the bones are the remains of a struggle on the spot, and their scattered burial at shallow depth and without any burial order also indicates this. There can be little doubt that the remains of the fallen people of the Battle of Mohács were found here, crushed and scattered by ploughing."[22] The human bones were sent by the researcher to the Institute of Archaeology of the Hungarian Academy of Sciences for further anthropological examination. Although its outcomes are unknown, the finds were soon removed from Papp's argumentation about the Battle of Mohács.

In summary, in the early 1960s and mid-1970s, a total of five mass graves were found east of the settlement of Sátorhely, west of the Black Gate (Fekete-kapu), with an estimated 800–1000 dead bodies. The severe injuries, mainly caused by swords, and the manner of burial confirmed that the graves contained the dead of the Battle of Mohács. During the excavations, different narratives have emerged about who buried them and how. Papp, the archaeologist of the first two mass graves, was still of the opinion that the fallen were Hungarian and foreign fighters who had been slaughtered by Ottoman cavalry. He tought that the pits may have originally been the Christians' gun emplacements or, more likely, part of a planned but unfinished *wagenburg*. Borbála Maráz took the view that the mass graves contained the slaughtered guards of the Christian camp. The Janus Pannonius Musem staff, who started the re-excavation of one of the graves in 2020, also initially thought that the graves might contain the dead of the camp, but then changed their opinion and concluded that the victims were prisoners of war executed by the Ottomans. In addition to the mass graves, other human remains were found in several places on the plain of Mohács. These were found mainly on the edge of the Vizslak Meadow and near the mass graves in Sátorhely. In addition, Papp also found human bones at the site of a medieval settlement near present-day Majs, which he identified as Majsa, and which he linked, at least for a time, to the Battle of Mohács.

---

22   Janus Pannonius Museum, Archaeological Database, 1968, no. 1167–83.

3 Arm Finds from the Second Half of the 19th Century to the Period of Socialism

From the second half of the 19th century onwards, a number of artifacts associated with the Battle of Mohács were found in the Mohács Plain and on Mohács Island (Table 9.3). Some of these artifacts have been lost, many of them have survived just in descriptions, while others are still part of museum collections.

The Hungarian National Museum also has three arquebuses associated with the Battle of Mohács.[23] The first arquebus, donated to the museum by an engineer in 1865, was found on Mohács Island (Table 9.3/3; Figure 9.6/3). The fringed, round-barreled weapon dates from the first half of the 16th century, is 89 cm long and 25 mm in diameter.[24] The second hackebus, also with a fringed round barrel, arrived to the museum in 1871 as a railway consignment from Mohács (Table 9.3/4). It is dated by experts to the second half of the 15th century, it is 78 cm long from the firing hole to the end of the barrel, with a barrel of 25 mm in diameter and weighing 9 kg.[25] The third weapon, like the first, was found under the trunk of a tree on Mohács Island, between Lake Földvári and the Lök Watercourse (Table 9.3/5; Figure 9.6/5). It was donated to the museum in 1890 by a merchant of Mohács. It dates from the late 15th century, is 81.5 cm long, 18 mm in diameter, has a beard 8 cm long and weighs only 4.14 kg.

In the so-called "Danube mapping or survey", it was noted in the 1820s that the already mentioned Turkish Hill and its surroundings could hardly have been the site of the Battle of Mohács, because only a few war relics are found here.[26] However, after the advent of deep ploughing with the steam plough in the early 1900s, the opposite was reported: "Bones, spurs, horseshoes, etc., are everywhere to be found at a depth of 1½ to 2 feet, and one only has to dig around Turkish Hill with a spade to discover the site of the battlefield of

---

23   Géza Nagy, "Hadtörténeti ereklyék a Magyar Nemzeti Múzeumban," [Military relics in the Hungarian National Museum] *Hadtörténelmi Közlemények* 11 (1910), pp. 223–243.
24   Károly Kozák, who examined the weapon decades later, gives the following data: the total length of the barrel is 88 cm, the length of the barrel cavity is 76.5 cm, the diameter is 24 mm and the weight of the weapon is 11.2 kg. Károly Kozák, "A magyarországi szakállas puskák fejlődéstörténetéről," [On the history of the development of hackbut (Hakenbüchse) in Hungary] *Archaeologiai Értesítő* 101 (1974), no. 2, pp. 290–303.
25   According to Kozák, the length of the barrel cavity is 78.5 cm, the diameter is 24 mm and the weapon weighs 8.9 kg. Kozák, "A magyarországi szakállas puskák," pp. 290–303.
26   Hungarian National Archives, S 81 – No. 1/a. A Duna mappáció mérnöki iratai, [Engineering documents of the Danube mapping] p. 622.

Mohács." – wrote the amateur local historian Gyula Hummel in 1906.[27] This was confirmed by a letter from József Kalt, the keeper of the Bellye Manor, in 1928, in which he drew attention to several important finds discovered decades earlier. As already mentioned above, in the early 1900s, Kalt came across a horse skeleton and rider while digging a canal in the Vizslak Meadow east of Turkish Hill. Next to them lay a spear and a long, straight sword (*deutsches Ritterschwert*), the latter was decorated with precious stones (Table 9.3/8; Figure 9.6/8). Kalt sent the finds to Vienna.[28] During the same work, a 16th-century hilt with a truncated blade, basket-shaped, rounded hilt with a more delicate ending was also found, which is kept in the Janus Pannonius Museum (Table 9.3/9; Figure 9.6/9).[29] In 2018, Balázs Polgár, archaeologist at the Institute and Museum of Military History, took the view that the hilt was of 17th-century date, contrary to earlier expert opinion.[30] One witness placed the exact location of the artifacts on Vizslak Meadow at the manorial brick kiln north of Turkish Hill, but just south of the Black Gate Fields (*Fekete-kapu dűlő*). We should also mention here the already cited information that, according to a 1961 museum report by a witness cubist, "a great many skeletons were found" during the excavation of the canals between Vizslak and Újistálló Manor on Vizslak Meadow between 1925 and 1927 (Table 9.3/10; Figure 9.6/10). However, no one was informed of this at the time.[31] This is very important information for the localization of the battle site, especially since Kalt also reported in his letter that he had found iron cannonballs, large lead balls and pieces of swords and spears in the aforementioned Black Gate (Fekete-kapu) during deep ploughing (Table 9.3/11; Figure 9.6/11). Based on their diameter and the location of their discovery, the iron and lead cannonballs are thought to belong to the smaller calibre field guns of the Christian army (Table 9.1). Considering the calibres, they belonged mainly to falkonets and serpentinels.[32]

---

27   Gyula Hummel, "Hogy hol volt a mohácsi csata?" [Where was the Battle of Mohács?] *Mohács* 6 (1906), no. 49, pp. 2–3.
28   Janus Pannonius Museum, Archaeological Database, 1928/1982, no. 1077–82.
29   Papp, "A mohácsi csatahely," [The battle site of Mohács] in A Janus Pannonius Múzeum Évkönyve, ed. Dombay, pp. 197–253.
30   Balázs Polgár, *Oszmán-török kori csataterek régészeti kutatása Magyarországon*, PhD thesis [Archaeological research of Ottoman Turkish battlefields in Hungary] (Budapest: ELTE BTK, 2018).
31   Janus Pannonius Museum, Archaeological Database, 1961, no. 1261–83.
32   György Domokos, "Adalékok a törökkori magyar tüzérség kategória- és tipusproblémáihoz," *Hadtörténelmi Közlemények* 31 (1984) pp. 117–149.

TABLE 9.1   Parameters of the cannonballs found at Black Gate based on the JPM Archaeological Data Base (1077–82) perimeter data. Edited by Péter Gyenizse

Perimeter	Diameter (cm)	Ray	Volume (cm³)	Mass (gram)	Mass (font=0,45 kg)	Material
19.7	6.27	3.14	129.10	929.54	2.07	iron
18.7	5.95	2.98	110.42	795.05	1.77	iron
16.5	5.25	2.63	75.86	546.16	1.21	iron
16	5.09	2.55	69.17	498.00	1.11	iron
15.7	5.00	2,50	65.35	470,51	1.05	iron
15.2	4.84	2.42	59.30	426.97	0.95	iron
15.2	4.84	2.42	59.30	672.48	1.49	lead
15	4.77	2.39	56.99	410.34	0.91	iron
14.7	4.68	2.34	53.64	386.21	0.86	iron

SOURCE: PAP ET AL., 2019.

Finally, from the "heroic era" of battlefield research in Mohács, we should also mention that, according to a reporter, in the late 1940s, while ploughing in *Zsidó-puszta*, a "4 ares long and palm-wide", ornate Ottoman sword was found (Table 9.3/18; Figure 9.6/18). In 1959, the owner showed the weapon to the curator of the museum in Mohács, who noticed an oriental design on one side, "Turkish writing" on the other and a silver beating on the handle.[33]

The work of László Papp, the former archaeologist of the Janus Pannonius Museum in Pécs, which began in 1959, marked the advent of a new, intensive era of battlefield research in the Mohács Plain, when new archaeological finds were unearthed. In the early 1960s, Papp's concept of the Battle of Mohács began to crystallize. He claimed that the name of the former village at Újistálló Manor, opposite Turkish Hill, was Földvár in the Middle Ages. This Földvár, however, was not the same as the settlement Brodarics saw on the battlefield: the Chancellor confused Földvár with Majsa (near the present-day Majs), which was located under the hilly edge of the plain, or even more likely with the settlement of Merse, immediately south of Majsa. He believed that the line

---

33 Janus Pannonius Museum, Archaeological Database, 1959, no. 1234–83. The find was not ultimately added to the museum collection.

of attack of the Hungarian army centre started from the mass graves excavated in 1960, heading south-west, and then passed through the Borza Manor and Borza Elbow to the village of Merse.[34]

This was the basis of his further research in the Mohács Plain, and it was also the reason why he invested great efforts into archaeological investigations in the westernmost part of what he called the "inner battlefield", at the edge, in the vicinity of the two medieval settlement sites (Merse and Majsa). On the basis of his concept, he identified the village of Merse in 1962–1963, about 1.8 km south of the present-day village of Majs, in an archaeological excavation at the bottom of the hill range,[35] and in the 1960s, he also delimited two further medieval settlement patches in the eastern foothills of present-day Majs.[36] The relationship between them was not clarified by Papp, but he referred to the settlement south of the so-called Malomárok Watercourse as *Majsa*.

According to the contradictory statement of a tractor driver, Jakab Lencz,[37] in 1966 (1965?) a double-edged sword (Table 9.3/20; Figure 9.6/20) was unearthed in this area, about 300 metres from the settlement of Merse, while ploughing, "among horse bones", and was transported to the museum in Mohács. The Karoling-type weapon, 122.5 cm long and with a blade width of 3.5–2.5 cm, had a simple crossguard with a stick-like crossguard and a square hilt. Papp also excavated the site indicated by the informant in 1967, but found no trace of the horse skeleton. However, in one of the exploration trenches, in an area of 2–3 m^2 from a depth of 15–30 cm, a total of 29 *iron balls*, "mostly 20, some 18–19 mm in diameter, partly rusted through, and more or less polished after some cleaning, with a smooth surface" (Table 9.3/21; Figure 9.6/21) were found.[38] In 1970, the above-mentioned tractor driver, while ploughing the same field where he had turned out the sword with his plough, allegedly found a large bearded hatchet (Table 9.3/22; Figure 9.6/22).[39] He gave it to another person who showed it to the staff of the Janus Pannonius Museum as his own property in the same year.[40] However, it was not added to the museum's collection

---

34   Janus Pannonius Museum, Archaeological Database, 1961, no. 1239–83; 1967, no. 1242–83; 1968, no. 1167–83.
35   Janus Pannonius Museum, Archaeological Database, 1962–1963, no. 1157–83.
36   Janus Pannonius Museum, Archaeological Database, 1968, no. 1167–83; 1962–1963, no. 1157–83.
37   For more on the controversy, including the place and time of the occurrence, see below.
38   Janus Pannonius Museum, Archaeological Database, 1967, no. 1242–83.
39   Also in 1970, during a recent excavation, a medieval iron spur was found here. See Janus Pannonius Museum, Archaeological Database, 1970, no. 1246–83.
40   Janus Pannonius Museum, Archaeological Database, 1970, no. 1172–83.

until 1975, when it was described as a "large iron bearded axe or hatchet."[41] In 2018, archaeologist Balázs Polgár suggested that the find could be identified as a carpenter's axe.[42]

At the other site mentioned above, immediately east of the present-day Majs, south of the Malomárok, in the vicinity of the settlement identified as medieval Majsa, Papp conducted investigations in 1968. During the exploratory excavation, human and horse bones were found scattered around the site, which the archaeologist considered to be remains from the Battle of Mohács. One of the human skeletons was accompanied by a blade fragment 12 cm long and 2.5 cm wide (Table 9.3/23; Figure 9.6/23). The tractor driver who was ploughing the site at the same time (the person who found the hatchet and the double-edged sword) also found a spearhead deepened into a skull in the same place (Table 9.3/24; Figure 9.6/24), which he then handed over to the researcher.[43] The human bones found here and sent to the Institute of Archaeology of the Hungarian Academy of Sciences for further examination were, as already mentioned, not linked to the battle by Papp.

Soon after his intensive archaeological research at medieval Majsa and Merse, László Papp died in 1973 without having written a synthesis of his 11 years of research concerning the Battle of Mohács. His death marked the end of the most intensive period of battlefield research at Mohács to date. After that, it was not until the 1990s that any further archaeological research in the Mohács Plain related to the Battle of Mohács was undertaken. The fragmentary iron sword[44] (Table 9.3/14; Figure 9.6/14) found at the same time as the Mohács National Memorial was being built (1975–1976), on the southern side of the chestnud-lined road leading from the Black Gate (Fekete-kapu) to Sátorhely and thus to the mass graves, in the deepening of the road ditch, was only discovered accidentally and not as a result of systematic research. The weapon was described by the archaeologist Borbála Maráz as a "typical late 15th–early 16th-century Hungarian sword", which was broken in two at the blade.[45]

As we have seen, some of the finds from the Mohács Plain and Mohács Island are scattered, while others show a spatial concentration. Arquebuses

---

41 Janus Pannonius Museum, Archaeological Database, 1975, no. 1173–83. The object was purchased by the museum for 2000 HUF which was then the equivalent of a considerably higher than average monthly salary.
42 Polgár, "Oszmán-török kori csataterek," [Ottoman Turkish battlefields].
43 Janus Pannonius Museum, Archaeological Database, 1968, no. 1167–83.
44 The sword found here was therefore as broken as the sword(s) found at the nearby *Black Gate* in the early 20th century.
45 Maráz, "Újabb tömegsírok," [More mass graves] in *Mohács emlékezete,* eds. Kiss et al., pp. 274–279.

of the 15th–16th centuries were found on the island in the second half of the 19th century. On the eastern edge of the plain, in the nearby Vizslak Meadow, around Turkish Hill and at the Black Gate (Fekete-kapu), archaeological finds, including military equipments, were unearthed in the first decades of the 20th century, some of which are very probably related to the Battle of Mohács. Between 1959 and 1970, an intensive period began thanks to László Papp's battlefield research. In accordance with his evolving concept, his efforts were concentrated to the "mass graves-Borza Elbow-Merse-Majsa" axis, within which he focused mainly on the area around the settlements of Merse and Majsa, near the plain edge. According to highly contradictory information from one informant, a double-edged sword and a hatchet (or carpenter's axe?) were also found at Merse, while in a field excavation Papp found large calibre iron bullets. At Majsa, excavations revealed human and horse bones and a blade fragment. In addition, the same informant as mentioned above also handed over to the archaeologist in charge of the excavation a piece of spearhead he claimed to have found here. The finds were interpreted by Papp as clear evidence of the Battle of Mohács.

4   Archaeological Finds near Majs and on Mohács Island

In the 1990s, the expansion of new technologies, especially the use of metal detectors, opened a new era in the research of the battlefield of Mohács. In 1992–1993, military historian Lajos Négyesi used a metal detector to carry out a survey directly east of Majs. Here – for the third time in the research history – he discovered the settlement site north of Malomárok, which László Papp had already identified in the mid-1960s, and which József Szűcs, a local amateur collector, had also visited in the 1970s. Négyesi found a few handgun bullets, arquebuse bullets and small cannonballs, spearheads, blade fragments, spiked arrowheads, spurs and horseshoes on the settlement area and its wider surroundings. In addition to these, a *kron groschen* from the reign of King Sigismund I of Poland was also found, along with coins from other periods. Although Négyesi considered the finds to be relics of the Battle of Mohács, he failed to describe them in a way that would allow scientific conclusions to be drawn.[46]

---

46   Lajos Négyesi, "A mohácsi csata," [The Battle of Mohács] *Hadtörténelmi Közlemények* 107 (1994), no. 4, pp. 62–79. In a part of the paper, Négyesi described the results of his battlefield metal detector survey in the foreground of Majs. He published only a list of the artifacts he had collected, and thus, contrary to international standards, he did not publish

Between 2009 and 2020, the staff of the Janus Pannonius Museum, led by Gábor Bertók, collected several items and archaeological artifacts at the above-mentioned village site, which were also linked to the Battle of Mohács. During their work, they also investigated the extent of the medieval village by means of geophysical surveys. They believed that the settlement corresponded in all respects to the village of Földvár, described by Brodarics as the centre of the battle: it was situated at the bottom of a hill, and although no church was found at the village site, they concluded that the building might have stood at the top of the terrain stairs, on the site of the present-day Catholic church in Majs.[47]

Since a well-supported opinion had meanwhile developed among other battlefield researchers as to the actual location of the battle, Bertók acknowledged that the settlement they were working at could not have been the medieval village of Földvár.[48] However, like Papp's theory, they took the view that Brodarics had confused the settlement of Földvár with the medieval settlement near Majs, which they had studied. It was at this village below the

---

the parameters of the few projectiles he had found at or near the medieval settlement of Majsa. The author also seems to have linked to the Battle of Mohács finds that are common to a medieval settlement site or its immediate surroundings (e.g. horseshoes, coins, arrowheads). He has drawn far-reaching conclusions from certain types of finds and artifacts, but without the necessary evidence. For example, based on a single horseshoe found north of the settlement site and a single spur found there earlier, "according to a young man", he considered that they clearly indicated the location of the right flank and the site of the attack of the Hungarian heavy cavalry. Another such example is the single kron groschen coin of the time of Sigismund I, found on the medieval settlement site, which the author attributes to the Polish infantry of 1500 men in a rectangular formation. As the objects collected were not described in accordance with international standards, and as archaeologist Balázs Polgár stated that they were not in the collection of the Janus Pannonius Museum, it was not possible to include them in Table 9.3. and Fig. 9.6. For Polgár's comments, see Polgár, "Oszmán-török kori csataterek," [Ottoman Turkish battlefields].

47 Gábor Bertók, Máté Szabó, Márk Haramza, Éva Szajcsán, and Béla Simon, "Mohács 500 csatatérkutatási program," [Mohács 500 battlefield research programme] in *Eke mentén, csata nyomában,* eds. Márk Haramza et al. (Archaeological Studies of PPCU Institute of Archaeology) 17 (Budapest: Martin Opitz Kiadó, 2020), pp. 107–118.

48 Pap et al., "Sátorhely vagy Majs?" [Sátorhely or Majs?], pp. 209–246; János B. Szabó, "Egy Mátyás-kori oklevél és a mohácsi csata centrumában fekvő Földvár falu "rejtélye" (Egy évszázados kirakós játék új darabjai)," [One charter from Age of King Matthias and one village in the centrum of the Battle of Mohács: Földvár (New pieces from a centuries-old puzzle game)] in *Hunyadi Mátyás és kora,* eds. Attila Bárány et al. (Debrecen: MTA-DE Lendület "Magyarország a középkori Európában" kutatócsoport, 2019), pp. 149–159; András Végh and János B. Szabó, "A Mohács és Dánóc közé eső térség késő középkori birtok- és településstruktúrája," [The late medieval estate and settlement structure of the area between Mohács and Dánóc] in *Eke mentén,* eds. Haramza et al., pp. 49–73.

scarp of the terrain, or south of it, that, in their opinion, the Ottoman troops with their cavalry, janissaries and guns were deployed, receiving the attack of the Christian soldiers from the north-north-east.

The work, which has already involved dozens of volunteer metal detectorists since 2016, has resulted in a total of 6500 metal artifacts being collected, of which 400–450 were *war artifacts* military equipments, including lead and iron bullets, arrowheads, horseshoes, stirrups and spurs, bullet moulds, sword and mace fragments, axes, armour fragments and other artifacts indirectly linked to the battle by their dating, such as the number of coins and items of clothing.[49] However, only the 255 projectiles recovered have been described in more detail.[50] According to their analyses, the projectiles were located in a well-defined area in and around the former settlement (Table 9.3/26; Figure 9.6/26). 44 of them were smaller than 10 mm (17%), 128 between 10–13 mm (50%), 40 between 13–15 mm (16%), 29 between 15–18 mm (11%), 2 between 18–20 mm (1%) and 9 between 21–27 mm (4%), while 3 were larger than 30 mm (1%).

The correlation between the manufacturing technique and diameter showed that below 15 mm the cast lead balls dominates, between 15–20 mm the number of hammered balls is higher, while above 20 mm the majority of balls are made of iron. Although not supported by strong arguments, it was considered, on the basis of the abundance of circumstantial evidence and the correlation between the artifacts, written sources and geography, that the projectiles were relics of the Battle of Mohács in 1526. In the meantime, however, other research has revealed that most of the bullets found at the site of the settlement near Majs are not related to the 1526 battle.[51] This has been confirmed by the analysis of bullets from a nearby site on Mohács Island, which suggests that 95% of the finds may very well belong to a battle in the late 17th century.

Between 2008 and 2016, László Kaszur was commissioned by the Katona József Museum in Kecskemét to carry out a field survey in the northern part of Mohács Island, in the area where military camps were established during the anti-Ottoman reconquest wars at the end of the 17th century. During this examinations, projectiles (Table 9.3/6; Figure 9.6/6) and coins to help dating were recovered in the northern third of the area between Telekpuszta and Kútsebes, which covers an area of about 1.5 km². Most of the bullets are intact

---

49   Bertók et al., "Mohács 500," [Mohács 500] in *Eke mentén,* eds. Haramza et al., pp. 107–118.
50   Gábor Bertók, Márk Haramza, and Balázs Németh, "Lövedékek egy "mohácsi" csatatérről," [Bullets from a "Mohács" battlefield] in *Eke mentén,* eds. Haramza et al., pp. 121–142.
51   Pap et al., "Sátorhely vagy Majs?" [Sátorhely or Majs?], pp. 209–246.

THE AVAILABLE MILITARY ARCHAEOLOGY TOPOGRAPHIC DATA

and well-preserved, indicating a Christian military camp of short duration, with few artifacts, and not the site of an armed conflict.

The finds were analysed in 2022. As evidence of the temporary encampment of the area by the regular armed forces, a total of 319 lead and one bronze projectiles were recovered from the site on Mohács Island. The size distribution of these small arm projectiles was then compared with the size distribution of the projectiles collected at the settlement surveyed by the Janus Pannonius Museum (Figure 9.3 and 9.4; Table 9.2).

The weapon bullets from Mohács Island are distributed according to their diameter as follows: 19 below 10 mm (6%), 178 between 10–13 mm (56%), 71 between 13–15 mm (22%), 51 between 15–18 mm (16%) and 1 between 18–20 mm (0.3%). The two corresponding figures show that the size distribution is similar in both cases. From 10 mm onwards, a sharp upward trend starts, peaking just in the most contested size ranges of 11–13 mm, followed by a gradual decline down to the 18–20 mm size ranges. No size larger than 19 mm in diameter is available for the Mohács Island gun bullets, but the size distribution of the Majs bullet finds is also stable under the 18–20 mm size range. However, some projectiles larger than 21 mm in calibre still appear at Majs after a slight hiatus. It is also noteworthy that the 10–15 mm calibre projectiles show a

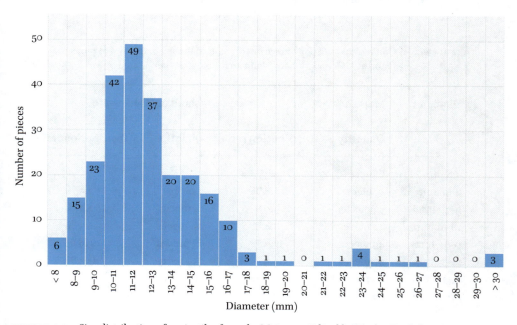

FIGURE 9.3   Size distribution of projectiles from the Majs area. Edited by Sándor Konkoly.

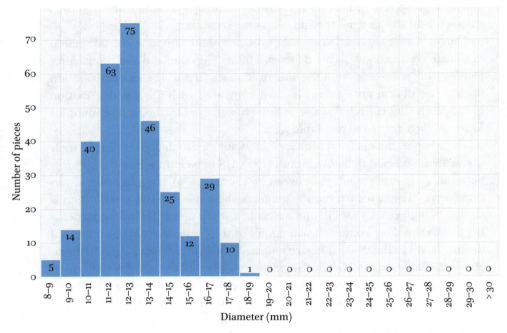

FIGURE 9.4   Size distribution of projectiles from the area of Mohács Island. Edited by Sándor Konkoly.

TABLE 9.2   Quantitative and percentage distribution of the size categories of projectiles found at Majs and Mohács Island archaeological sites. Edited by Sándor Konkoly.

Diameter	Majs site		Island of Mohács site	
	Quantity	Distribution ratio	Quantity	Distribution ratio
< 8 mm	6 pieces	2.3 %	-	-
8–9 mm	15 pieces	5.8 %	5 pieces	1.5 %
9–10 mm	23 pieces	9.0 %	14 pieces	4.3 %
10–11 mm	42 pieces	1.4 %	40 pieces	12.5 %
11–12 mm	49 pieces	19.2 %	63 pieces	19.6 %
12–13 mm	37 pieces	14.5 %	75 pieces	23.4 %
13–14 mm	20 pieces	7.8 %	46 pieces	14.3 %
14–15 mm	20 pieces	7.8 %	25 pieces	7.8 %
15–16 mm	16 pieces	6.2 %	12 pieces	3.7 %
16–17 mm	10 pieces	3.9 %	29 pieces	9.0 %
17–18 mm	3 pieces	1.1 %	10 pieces	3.1 %
18–19 mm	1 pc	0.3 %	1 pc	0.3 %

TABLE 9.2   Quantitative and percentage distribution of the size categories (*cont.*)

Diameter	Majs site		Island of Mohács site	
	Quantity	Distribution ratio	Quantity	Distribution ratio
19–20 mm	1 pc	0.3 %	-	-
21–22 mm	1 pc	0.3 %	-	-
22–23 mm	1 pc	0.3 %	-	-
23–24 mm	4 pieces	1.5 %	-	-
24–25 mm	1 pc	0.3 %	-	-
25–26 mm	1 pc	0.3 %	-	-
26–27 mm	1 pc	0.3 %	-	-
> 30 mm	3 pieces	1.1 %	-	-

similar correlation to the larger but smaller number of projectiles above 15 mm in both bullet groups.

The data also show that the difference in the percentage distribution of each size class over 10 mm between the two areas is less than 10%. Meanwhile, in the 10–13 mm and 13–15 mm diameter intervals the difference between the two projectile materials is 6%, and in the 15–18 mm size range only 4%. To this we can add that the percentage distributions are practically identical in the 11–12 mm (19%), 14–15 mm (7.8%) and 18–19 mm (0.31% and 0.39%) size ranges. It should also be noted that the proportion of projectiles with a calibre of less than 15 mm, corresponding to the size of 17th century cavalry pistols and carbines, is also the same for the two finds (83%).

The two projectile assemblies also show similarities in other projectile parameters. The proportion of cast projectiles is close and the proportion of shaped projectiles differs by only 1%. The number of cut projectiles for both the Majs and the Mohács Island projectiles is equally one.

Since a clear correlation between the small arm projectiles from the sites studied can be established, we believe that the military equipments representing the largest group of pieces at both sites investigated bear the archaeological imprint of the anti-Ottoman reconquest campaigns of the late 17th century. On the other hand, the smaller number of larger calibre bullets (13) observed in the Majs area are most probably not associated with a conflict in the late 17th century, but with a different period and a different event. In addition to their size, their very small number – only a few pieces, but of very different calibres – suggests that it would be worth considering several possibilities (small-scale 16th-century clashes) as to how they could have been deposited in the area.

Overall, we can therefore conclude the following. At the beginning of the 1990s, at the site of a single-street settlement near Majs, which had been identified decades earlier, and in its surroundings, the site exploration began and is still ongoing. Since 2016, 255 bullets have been recovered in several phases of metal detecting instrumentation. The diameter of some of the recovered projectiles is less than 10 mm, and half of the finds are in the 10–13 mm size range. In 2022, 320 projectiles collected from a late 17th-century military camp on the island of Mohács were also analyzed. A comparative analysis with the finds from the area near Majs revealed clear parallels in terms of size ranges and percentages, as well as in terms of preparation techniques. There is a strong correlation between the characteristics of the projectiles from the two areas, which suggests that the settlement site near Majs is very likely to have been predominantly the site of an armed conflict at the end of the 17th century.[52]

5 Coins Associated with the Battle of Mohács

In Mohács, two treasure finds were discovered in 1969 during road construction in the Kálvin Street (now Duna Street) (Table 9.3/2; Figure 9.6/2). The first find, containing 19,488 pieces of 10.28 kg of silver coins in cleaned condition, was hidden in a grey jug 80 cm deep. The second group of finds, at the same depth and a few metres away, contained a total of 25,997 pieces of silver coins weighing 13.62 kg in a red jar.

According to the spot tests of the time, the finds consisted of coins of Matthias I (1458–1490), Vladislaus II (1490–1516) and Louis II (1490–l526), with minimal foreign coinage.[53] The silver coins, at least the first group of finds, were examined in more detail by numismatist Balázs Nagy in 2019.[54] He found that their total quantity is unparalleled in Hungary. The processing and evaluation of the findings revealed that the number of silver coins previously recorded in the first jar had dwindled to 9,143, while the number of coins in

---

52 The small number of large calibre bullets, however, allows us to speculate that the area may have been affected by the preliminary skirmishes of the battle of 1526 or by another small-scale conflict in the 16th century.
53 Janus Pannonius Museum, Archaeological Database, 1969, no. 503–79.
54 Balázs Nagy, "Az érem és kincsleletek horizontja a mohácsi vésztől a török kivonulásáig," [The horizon of coin and treasure hoards from the Mohacs disaster to the Turkish withdrawal] in *Numophylacium Novum. Az I. Fiatal Numizmaták Konferenciája Tanulmányai*, ed. Márton Gyöngyössy (Budapest: ELTE Eötvös Kiadó, 2019), pp. 86–161.

the second jar had dwindled to 25,043. In the first coin box, 3,840 pieces of coins produced during the reign of Matthias I, 4,206 coins produced during the reign of Vladislaus II and 1,077 coins produced during the reign of Louis II were identified. The latest coins in both jugs were issued between 1520 and 1521. In this connection, Nagy pointed out that Louis II ordered the issue of new money from 1521, during which the silver denarius, which had previously been 8 lats, was replaced by a copper denarius containing 4 lats of silver. This new money, the *nova moneta*, was soon rejected, so that we can assume that the owner of the treasure trove in question intended to keep only *antiqua moneta*, i.e. more valuable coins with a higher silver content.

A study, published in 2020, explored the possible campsites of the Christian army in Mohács in the context of environmental reconstruction.[55] It was found that long before the battle, during the preparation period, the campsites of the Christian army could have been lined up along the Eszék (Osijek) road southwards from the bank of the Danube at Mohács, following the natural contours of the terrain. This was thought not only on the basis of written sources, but also for logistical and water suppy considerations. The above-mentioned treasure finds, which, according to the settlement reconstruction study, were hidden outside the settlement in 1526, were also presented as evidence of the camping near Mohács. They were buried at a distance of 100–120 metres south of the moat surrounding Mohács, where the boats that arrived here docked[56] and landed their cargo. It has therefore been suggested that the large quantity and high quality of coins, unparalleled in Hungary, may have been transported to the site for military expenditure at the Battle of Mohács and probably hidden under a tent erected there by the campers. However, the silver coins could not be dug up after the defeat of the battle.

6 "All That Glitters is Not Gold" – Finds That Do Not Exist

If we look at the archaeological finds associated with the Battle of Mohács over the last century or more, we can find the following groups:

1. *Non-existent artifacts.* Finds reported in the scholarly literature turn out after a while not to have existed. At one time or another, they became part of the public domain, sometimes part of the "Mohács canon",

---

55 Norbert Pap, Péter Gyenizse, Máté Kitanics, and Gábor Szalai, "Az 1526. évi mohácsi csata helyszíneinek földrajzi jellemzői," [Geographical features of the sites of the Battle of Mohács in 1526] *Történelmi Szemle* 62 (2020), no. 1, pp. 111–151., and see Chapter Two.
56 Contemporary map drawings and Maximilian Brandstetter's painting of Mohács from 1608 helped to identify the harbour.

theories were built on them, and various theories were confirmed. Even if the refutation is published, it will haunt the perception of the battle for a long time to come.

2. *Findings without context.* Objects that are strongly believed to be related only and exclusively to the Battle of Mohács. At the same time, however, they are either one or more of the following: their date of occurrence is uncertain or contradictory; their site is not precisely known; there are no other finds at the site that can be dated.

3. *Findings of uncertain confirmation.* There is a strong perception that they are related to the Battle of Mohács, but when the finds are re-examined, the opinion on their function and/or datings modified.

4. *Confirmed finds related to the Battle of Mohács.* Most probably they can be linked to the Battle of Mohács. They are collected by an expert or a credible person. The context of the finds is known. Their classification may be strengthened if these objects of the period are found in a well-defined area where other relics, most probably from the Battle of Mohács, have come to light in recent decades. The location of their discovery is consistent with the sources of the battle.

TABLE 9.3   Archaeological finds and sites of the Mohács Plain and Mohács Island

Finds	Location of discovery	Classification	Compatible with the sources of the battle
1. Vessels, breastplates, swords, daggers, sabres, maces, halberds, spearheads, spurs, etc.	Danube riverbed, at the former mouth of the Csele Stream	Non-existent artifacts	Cannot be interpreted
2. Two pots of silver coins (45,485 pieces)	Mohács, Kálvin lane (today Duna street)	Confirmed finds related to the Battle of Mohács	Yes
3. Arqubuse (first half 16th c.)	Mohács Island	Confirmed finds related to the Battle of Mohács	Yes
4. Arquebuse (second half 15th c.)	n.d.	Confirmed finds related to the Battle of Mohács	Yes

TABLE 9.3 Archaeological finds and sites of the Mohács Plain and Mohács Island (*cont.*)

Finds	Location of discovery	Classification	Compatible with the sources of the battle
5. Arquebuse (late 15th c.)	Mohács Island	Confirmed finds related to the Battle of Mohács	Yes
6. Coins, 320 bullets	Mohács Island	Finds not related to the Battle of Mohács[a]	No
7. 60–80 heads cut off	Chapel of St. László south of Udvar, north of Dályok (now Duboševica in Croatia)	Finds without context	Yes
8. Horse skeleton; spear; long, straight sword with precious stones	Vizslak Meadow (Vizslaki-rét), north of Turkish Hill, south of Black Gate, at the brick kiln	Confirmed finds related to the Battle of Mohács	Yes
9. Bone-bladed, basket-shaped, round-edged spear (16th or 17th c.?)	Vizslak Meadow, north of Turkish Hill, south of Black Gate, at the brick kiln	Finding of uncertain confirmation	Yes
10. "Many skeletons"	Between Vizslak and Újistálló Manor	Finds without context	Yes
11. Cannonballs, large lead balls, gun-wheel hammerings, sword and spear fragments	Black Gate	Confirmed finds related to the Battle of Mohács	Yes
12. Sultan's or Emperor's Hill: monument to Ottoman victory	Edge of Vizslak Meadow, Turkish Hill	Confirmed finds related to the memory of Battle of Mohács	Yes
13. Grave: a headless, mutilated dead body buried in a special position	In the medieval cemetery at the Újistálló Manor opposite the Turkish Hill	Confirmed finds related to the Battle of Mohács	Yes

[a] Reference sample. The finds date from the end of the 17th century.

TABLE 9.3 Archaeological finds and sites of the Mohács Plain and Mohács Island (*cont.*)

Finds	Location of discovery	Classification	Compatible with the sources of the battle
14. Fragmentary iron sword – Hungarian sword (late 15th–early 16th c.)	At the road from the Black Gate to Sátorhely	Confirmed finds related to the Battle of Mohács	Yes
15. Five mass graves: skeletons, coins, clothes buckles, armour, belt buckles, sword suspension rings, iron knives, horse tools, etc.	East of Sátorhely, west of the Black Gate	Confirmed finds related to the Battle of Mohács	Yes
16. Human bones	Directly north of the five mass graves	Finds without context	Yes
17. Human bones	On the S9 field board, south of Sátorhely, north of Borza	Finds without context	Yes
18. Decorated Ottoman sabre	Sátorhely: Zsidó-puszta	Artifact without context	Yes
19. Grave: three dead, aged 17–18, buried together	In the medieval village cemetery of Lajmér	Finding of uncertain confirmation[b]	Yes
20. Double-edged sword	At Udvar, near the Croatian border, or south of Majs, or at the medieval village of Merse?	Artifact without context	No
21. 29 "janissary" bullets, 18–20 mm diameter	South of modern Majs, at the medieval village of Merse	Confirmed finds related to the Battle of Mohács	Yes
22. Large bearded hatchet or carpenter's hatchet?	South of Majs, at the medieval village of Merse?	Artifact without context[c]	No

[b] Although Papp had always considered the deceased in the tomb to have fallen on the day of the Battle of Mohács, as indicated, the anthropologist who examined the bones considered them to be of the same age as the other 9th–12th century dead in the cemetery.

[c] According to this recent expert opinion, the find is also of uncertain confirmation.

TABLE 9.3 Archaeological finds and sites of the Mohács Plain and Mohács Island (*cont.*)

Finds	Location of discovery	Classification	Compatible with the sources of the battle
23. Horse skeletons, human skeletons, blade fragments	East of Majs, at the medieval village of Majsa	Findings of uncertain confirmation	No
24. Spearhead	East of Majs, at the medieval Majsa?	Artifact without context	No
25. "Cannonballs" made in an earthen pit	East of Majs, at the medieval Majsa	Non-existent artifacts	Cannot be interpreted
26. 400–450 findings, of which 255 projectiles[d]	East of Majs, at the medieval Majsa	Findings of uncertain confirmation[e]	No

[d] The collection of finds continued partly at the site "excavated" by Lajos Négyesi with a metal detector. For the time being, only the 255 bullets have been described in detail. If further finds from the medieval settlement of Majsa and its immediate surroundings are analysed and published, it may be possible to examine to what extent they correspond to or differ from the "usual" finds from a late medieval Hungarian settlement.

[e] The finds are identical to the reference sample and most probably date to the late 17th century.

EDITED BY MÁTÉ KITANICS

The first three groups are examined below. We believe that the common thread and driving force behind them is the same: the Battle of Mohács determined the course of Hungarian history to such an extent, and was so deeply rooted in the national public imagination, and even more so in the everyday life of the people living in the surroundings of Mohács, that not only local cubists, agricultural workers and other people, but also expert researchers tended to associate almost all war stories with the Battle of Mohács. Indeed, it seems that if there are no artifacts, they can be created mainly by hearsay or half-information, but also by imagination. This does not mean, of course, that the second and third groups of finds listed above do not contain finds that could possibly be classified as objects from the Battle of Mohacs, but overall there is a high proportion of them that may have been misidentified.

Without being exhaustive, let's look at a few examples to get a better understanding of what it's all about!

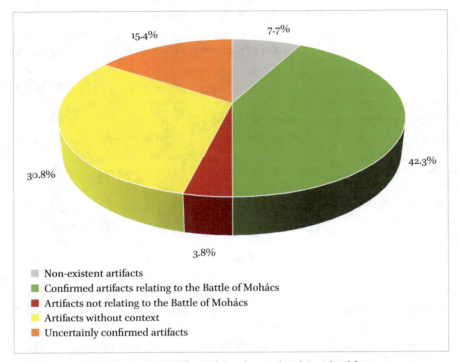

FIGURE 9.5   Archeological finds of the Mohács Plain and Mohács Island, by group. Edited by Nándor Zagyi.

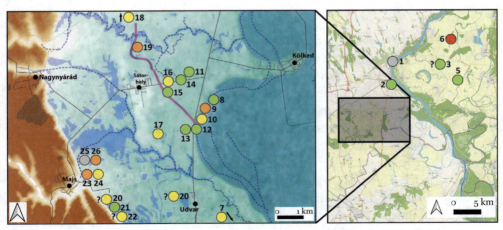

FIGURE 9.6   Map of the archaeological finds and sites of the Mohács Plain and Mohács Island. Each number follows the order of Table 9.3. The colours are recorded according to the groups shown in Figure 9.5. Edited by Máté Kitanics, designed by Péter Gyenizse.

In 1896, the historian Gyula Dudás wrote in his paper published in the *Archaeologiai Értesítő*[57] that the dredgers that had been deepening the Danube riverbed for years brought to the surface the weapons of the warriors who had drowned in the Csele Stream[58] and the Danube during the Battle of Mohács. In this connection, he mentioned the iron helmets, breastplates, swords, daggers, sabres, pikes, maces, halberds, spearheads and spurs in the collection of the engineer in charge of the dredging (Table 9.3/1; Figure 9.6/1). The account of the artifact collection has also been referenced by and incorporated into general works on the history of the Battle of Mohács. Among others, it was also referred to by the eminent military historian Jenő Gyalókay, in his summary of the Battle of Mohács, written for the 400th anniversary of the battle, entitled "The Battle of Mohács."[59] Then, in 1928, an article entitled *Leletek, melyek nincsenek* [Finds that do not exist] was published, the author of which stated that the weapons in question never existed. When asked about the artifacts at the museum in Mohács, the engineer "made the astonishing statement that it must be a mistake, because he had not found any artifacts during his work on the Danube."[60]

The area around Újistálló Manor, opposite Turkish Hill, has been considered a possible site of the mass graves of the Battle of Mohács since the first decades of the 1900s. The skeletons found here were thought to be the victims of the Battle of Mohács. In several cases they were exhumed and laid to rest in the cemetery at Sátorhely. After László Papp's excavations in 1961, it was discovered that the site of the stalls was the site of a medieval village and its cemetery,[61] which may provide an alternative explanation for the numerous human remains found during excavations here. However, as mentioned above, Papp also identified a mutilated skeleton within the cemetery during his excavation

---

57   Gyula Dudás, "Mohácsi emlékekről," [On the memories of Mohács] *Archaeologiai Értesítő* 16 (1896), pp. 430–431.
58   The Csele Stream, whose 16th century mouth later fell into the Danube riverbed due to changes in the riverbed, is an iconic place where, according to the memoirs, the fleeing king drowned. However, this assumption has been shown in recent years to be unfounded. See Norbert Pap, Péter Gyenizse, Máté Kitanics, and Gábor Szalai, "II. Lajos halálának helye," [Louis II's place of death] *Történelmi Szemle* 62 (2020), no. 1, pp. 73–110.; and see Chapter Ten.
59   Jenő Gyalókay, "A mohácsi csata," [The Battle of Mohács] (Budapest: Királyi Magyar Egyetemi Nyomda, 1926).
60   Ede Brand, "Adalékok Mohács történetéhez," [Additions to the history of Mohács] *Mohácsi Hírlap* 18 (1928), no. 41, p. 2.
61   Janus Pannonius Museum, Archaeological Database, 1961, no. 1239–83.

here, which he considered to be a body from the Battle of Mohács. This leaves us with the uncertainty as to which of the following cases we are dealing with.

1. There were never any mass graves with the dead. The skeletons of the large medieval cemetery were simply assumed to be the remains of the victims of the Battle of Mohács, which in turn included one of the dead who died in the Battle of Mohács.
2. If the entire area of the manor were to be thoroughly excavated, the former Ottoman victory monument and the site of the military road would reveal both the entire medieval cemetery and part of the dead of the Battle of Mohács.

Obviously, only extensive, professional investigations could solve the issue.

The area near the church of Majs as a site and the supposed "centre of the battle" was not forgotten after Papp's death, and a maintenance worker from Mohács, an amateur collector who had only completed elementary school, did much to preserve it. In the 1970s, József Szűcs "discovered" for the second time the medieval settlement site near Majs, north of the so-called "Malomárok", which Papp had identified in the mid-1960s. According to local newspapers, "a large quantity of Turkish cannonball remains from an earthen pit" (Table 9.3/25; Figure 9.6/25) was found there, which Szűcs interpreted as important evidence of the battle.[62] However, the location of the "cannonballs" has not been verified by a specialist, and the finds have not been published in any of the studies on the Battle of Mohács. Perhaps not by accident. The alleged cannonballs were presented by Szűcs in a film news report in 1976, which showed with great certainty that the "artifacts" did not exist, that they were not cannonballs but pieces of cinders of unknown origin.[63]

Let us look at the second group. In the 1960s, László Papp conducted research near Majs and in the surroundings of the site of village of Merse in order to prove that the area was nothing more than the "inner battlefield" of the Battle of Mohács. It is to this site that the few artifacts from this period (sword, battle axe) that were Papp's "main evidence" and that confirmed the hypothesis he had proposed, can be linked. However, the circumstances in

---

62   B. Cs., "Ágyúgolyót szánt az eke," [The plough was plowing a cannonball] *Déli Hírlap* 8 (1976), no. 241, p. 5.
63   In the same newsreel, Szűcs was said to have led Papp to the first mass graves in 1960. Contrary to this claim, László Papp in his 1960 excavation diary precisely names the tractor driver in the person of Márton Koller, a local citizen. He mentions Szűcs as having joined the fieldwork that identified the mass graves on the basis of the human bone fragments on the surface. Szűcs was also mentioned in the above-mentioned 1976 *Déli Hírlap* article as having been credited with leading archaeologists to the mass graves.

which the artifacts were found, including where they were found, were highly uncertain and controversial. Let us look at them.

All of them were recovered by the tractor driver Jakab Lencz from Majs while ploughing, so the exact locations of their discovery were not recorded by a specialist, who could have authenticated them. Papp first received information about the double-edged straight sword in 1966 from the agronomist of the agricultural cooperative in Majs that it had been found last year (1965) near the cemetery of Udvar close to the Hungarian–Yugoslavian border and had been transferred to the museum in Mohács.[64] Papp considered the information so authentic at the time that it was an important criterion in the selection of the site for the archaeological excavation near Udvar in 1966. In response to Papp's enquiries, the Mohács museum confirmed that the weapon had been found near Udvar. Nevertheless, when in 1967 Papp visited Lencz, who was working on the border of Udvar, he gave credit to the claim of the tractor driver of the Majs cooperative, who said that the weapon, accompanied by horse bones, had been found while ploughing, not in the village of Udvar, but south of the village of Majs, near the medieval settlement fort identified as Merse. However, when the archaeologist verified the claim at the site marked by Lencz, he found no trace of the horse skeleton.[65] The anomalies are reinforced, and the circumstances of the find's discovery – which has become accepted – are made even more doubtful by the fact that Papp believed, according to his 1966 excavation report, that the sword had been found in 1965.[66] In a later archaeological report (1968), however, he wrote that Lencz had found the weapon in 1966.[67] We do not know, therefore, exactly where, when and in what context one of the main pieces of "evidence" in the archaeological research of the Battle of Mohács was found.

The large battle axe was shown to an archaeologist of the Janus Pannonius Museum in 1970 by a forester named Antal Újvári, who said that it was also found by Lencz in the same place as the sword. The object, the circumstances of which were not reported by the finder but by another person, was only

---

64 "In view of the information provided by the agronomist of the cooperative, who said that a long, double-edged, large-bladed sword was found last year in the area towards the courtyard, near the courtyard cemetery, and that it was supposedly taken to the museum in Mohács, we are digging a small trench in a place that cannot be neglected for battle site research, namely around the middle of the southern double back." See Janus Pannonius Museum, Archaeological Database, 1966, no. 1159–83.
65 Janus Pannonius Museum, Archaeological Database, 1967, no. 1242–83.
66 The fact that the sword was found in 1965 was confirmed by archaeologist Borbála Maráz in a 1975 note. See Janus Pannonius Museum, Archaeological Database, 1975, no. 1173–83.
67 Janus Pannonius Museum, Archaeological Database, 1968, no. 1167–83.

added to the museum's collection years later, in the mid-1970s. It was also under interesting circumstances that Lencz handed over the *"kopjavas"* (spearhead) to Papp. He said that it was drilled into a skull and turned over by the plough next to Majs. However, the tractor driver, as he said, pulled the spearhead out of the skull and only delivered the object. He then threw the skull away and drove with his tractor over it.

Without wishing to be exhaustive, we would like to mention only the following in relation to the third group of finds. There has been more than one case in which an expert opinion contradicting the previous expert opinion was given on finds originally linked to the Battle of Mohács. As mentioned above, Papp considered the spearhead found on the edge of the Vizslak Meadow to be "a typical relic of 16th-century military dress", while archaeologist Balázs Polgár defined it as a 17th-century weapon. It was also Polgár who suggested that the large battle axe might not have been a weapon, but a carpenter's axe. Here we can mention the three dead discovered by László Papp in a common grave in the medieval village of Lajmér, who the archaeologist has classified among the casualties of the Battle of Mohács. We cannot help reminding here that the skeletons were thought by the anthropologist to be from the 9th to 12th centuries, as were the other bones in the graves, but Papp insisted on his idea until his death.[68] Finally, the debate, which will be discussed in more detail in this chapter, is also relevant here, where recent research has shown that the vast majority (95%) of the 255 bullets collected by researchers of the Janus Pannonius Museum near Majs are not from the Battle of Mohács in 1526, but are most probably the remains of a battle at the end of the 17th century. We believe that the presentation of these diametrically opposed opinions illustrates how problematic it can be to classify an artifact or group of artifacts in the study area, and in particular to link them to a single, specific event.

In conclusion, all the finds from the plain and the Mohács Island must be treated with due caution; first of all, we must abandon the view that the finds in question can only be related to the Battle of Mohács. Findings with an unverified context, often false data and tales told by locals, can seriously mislead research, and misinterpreted information can lead to erroneous theories. If, hovewer, several war-related finds are discovered in an area that complement each other in a mosaic-like way, and the site is also consistent with the sources, they are more likely to be associated with the battle of 1526.

---

68   It should be pointed out that the area was also affected by the Tatar invasion of 1241–1242, which caused severe destruction. Accordingly, it cannot be ruled out that some deaths, such as the three young people in the common grave mentioned above, may in fact be linked to the devastation of the Mongol invasion.

7 Discussions on Military Archaeological Phenomena

The interpretation of the military archaeological phenomena of the Battle of Mohács focuses on two main questions, which are the most controversial: the location of the sites of the battle, and the nature and origin of the five mass graves found in the area.

7.1 Majs or Sátorhely?

The medieval village remains in the eastern foothills of the village of Majs and the administrative area of Sátorhely enclosed by the "mass graves-Borza Stream-Vizslak Meadow" need to be examined. Although other possible sites have also been proposed in the past, the archaeological finds now raise the question of whether the Battle of Mohács in 1526 took place in the area of Majs or Sátorhely.

As already mentioned, in the 1920s, researchers' interest turned increasingly away from the area of Sátorhely, with more and more of them believing that the central area of the battle was located 4–5 km southwest, somewhere below the scarp surrounding the plain. However, these suggestions were not followed by archaeological research at that time, which only took place during the socialist period in the 1960s.

It may be recalled that in the 1960s, archaeologist László Papp made great efforts to find mass graves and human remains near the village of Majs and in the area around the medieval village of Merse to the south, which could be linked to the Battle of Mohács. However, his efforts were unsuccessful, despite a series of searches that lasted almost a decade.

At the same time, three artifacts, a double-edged sword, a 'kopjavas' (spearhead) and a hatchet, were supposedly found in this study area, which in the eyes of Papp and other researchers[69] have enhanced the value of the site and corroborated the research hypothesis. The three finds listed were associated with a lay informant of German nationality, a resident of Majs. The circumstances and places of their discovery were uncertain and, as already mentioned, the communication about them was marked by serious contradictions. To understand this, it is worth considering the circumstances of the discovery of the artifacts and the flow of information about them in the context of the internal and external politics of the time.

---

69 János B. Szabó, *A mohácsi csata* [The Battle of Mohács] (Budapest: Corvina, 2006); Négyesi, "A mohácsi csata," [The Battle of Mohács] pp. 62–79.; Márk Haramza et al. eds., *Eke mentén, csata nyomában* [Along plow, in the wake of a battle].

After the invasion of Nazi Germany in 1944, there was a transition from the harsh dictatorship of the Stalinist era (associated with Mátyás Rákosi in Hungary) to the 1956 revolution and subsequent repression, and then a slow softening of the autoritarian system after 1963. Political paranoia, however, ran throughout this period.

The Mohács Plain was first affected by the Holocaust, then by the Soviet military occupation. This was followed in 1947 by the partial lehetőségek: expulsion/relocation/deportation/removal of the population of the German villages in the Mohács Plain, and in their place by the resettlement of Hungarians expelled from Czechoslovakia and the poor Hungarian peasants of the Hungarian Great Plain, who were seen as the backbone of the communist regime. The Germans were accused of collaborating with the Third Reich authorities. Even after the, population change, the proportion of the German minority, who stayed in the area but were treated with suspicion and hostility, remained significant, especially in the villages of Majs, Udvar, Nagynyárád and to some extent Lánycsók, as well as in Mohács.

The foreign policy context is also important: the sites were located in an area heavily affected by the Cold War, in the heavily guarded Hungarian part of the Yugoslav–Hungarian border region. A defence system consisting of deep bunkers, barbed wire barriers and mine barricades was built to stop an expected attack from Yugoslavia. The area was controlled by the AVH, the secret police of the communist state. Border raids also took place and there were zones where civilians were not officially allowed to enter. There was also deep suspicion of members of the southern Slavic minorities living in the villages of the region and in Mohács. Anyone could easily be accused of being a spy for Josip Broz Tito. As a result, local public life was characterised by secrecy and a high level of mistrust, partly because of fears that those who broke strict rules, such as the ban on entering certain areas, could be severely punished. These may also have contributed to the contradictory information provided by some local reporters about the finds and where they were found.[70]

So if we examine the proposed battlefields of the area under the military defence system along the border (Majsa, Merse) to see which can be more

---

70   These political circumstances were also the reason why Papp only began excavating the first two mass graves in 1960. Mass grave No. 11 had already been cut through by a machine in 1952 while digging a trench in the military defence system, but for years no one had dared or wanted to provide the relevant museums and experts with information about the human bones that had been unearthed. Finally, as mentioned above, Papp came to the site by chance, based on the narration of Márton Koller, a coachman who was transporting him. On this, see Janus Pannonius Museum, Archaeological Database, 1960, no. 1245–83.

securely linked to the Battle of Mohács, we are left with very little. Indeed, very little can be said with certainty about the location and circumstances of the three artifacts mentioned above (sword, hatchet, spearheads). Lencz, who found them, may have had several reasons for not being honest about the place and circumstances of the discovery. For one thing, he was of German origin and worked in an area that was heavily patrolled by the border police and the secret police. On the other hand, the artifacts seem to have been exchanged, at least as indicated by the fact that the hatchet was not found by Lencz, but by another person. It is also possible that when Lencz changed his statement about the original location of the first find, i.e. the original location of the sword, this suited Papp well, since this weapon could be an important piece of evidence for his concept that the battlefield of the battle of Mohács was in the area of Majs. However, given the serious inconsistencies in the circumstances of its discovery, it is clear that the sword is unsuitable for use as scientific evidence.

If all this is taken into account, there remains only one find, or more precisely one group of finds, that has been properly documented during archaeological investigation. This group of finds is the 29 iron bullets between 18 and 20 mm, which were collected by archaeologist László Papp during an excavation with sondage. As they were found in an extremely small area of about 2–3 m² without any other projectiles in the vicinity, it can be assumed that they were dropped. The iron bullets were thought by Papp to be projectiles from "Spanish handguns" used by janissaries and were sent to the Ózd Metallurgical Works for further examination. In an interview in 1970, he claimed that laboratory tests had confirmed the dating of the finds to the time of the battle.[71]

Since the list of arms and munitions for the Mohács campaign dated 13 April 1526 shows that the janissaries were issued 30 packs of handgun bullets from the imperial armoury,[72] it is suspected that one pack of bullets was scattered over the excavation site. The artifacts were found at the so-called *"Kiserdő"* (near the medieval village of Merse), south-west of the medieval village of Földvár, in the present-day municipality of Majs, at the site where sources suggest the sultan's camp was located on the night of the battle. It is therefore very likely that the bullets can be associated with a janissary regiment of the sultan's corps.

---

71 E. H., "Huszonkilenc janicsár golyó. Ásatás a mohácsi csatatéren," [Twenty-nine janissary bullets. Digging on the battlefield of Mohács] *Dunántúli Napló* 27 (1970), no. 206, p. 3.

72 "Az udvari zsoldosok/janicsárok fegyver- és hadianyag listája, 1526. április 13.," [The list of arms and war material of the household mercenaries/janissaries, 13 April 1526] in *Örök Mohács: Szövegek és értelmezések*, eds. János B. Szabó and Gábor Farkas Farkas (Budapest: Bölcsészettudományi Kutatóközpont, 2020), pp. 231–235.

However, this group of finds does not indicate the location of the battlefield, but that of the Ottoman Turkish camp, although it does indirectly point to the possible location of the battlefield.

Let us look specifically at the archaeological sites (village remains) in the foreground of the Catholic church in Majs. László Papp, as described above, found two medieval village cemeteries near Majs in the 1960s, close to each other but separated by the so-called *"Malomárok"* water course. The medieval village site in the north was "rediscovered" in the 1970s by József Szűcs, after Papp's death. And Lajos Négyesi "discovered" the area for the third time between 1992 and 1993, when he found bullets (and other objects) on the site with a metal detector. After 2009, a new investigation was launched at the same site, with researchers from the Janus Pannonius Museum also conducting regular metal detector searches. As mentioned above, 255 small arm projectiles were collected during the investigation.

Since the village site under the terrain scarp ("hill") corresponded to the "Brodarics hill" concept, it was assumed that the artifacts collected in the 110 hectares of land could be related to the battle of 1526. For a while, the question of the centre of the battle seemed to be resolved: the battle took place at Majs. However, a new controversy arose in 2019 over the interpretation of the bullets. First, it became clear that the area around the village of Majs (the presumed Földvár), which had been discovered three times, did not correspond to the environmental descriptions of the battle or to the distance data for the site given by Brodarics, and that the density of the bullets in question (2.3 per hectare) was suspiciously low.[73] Moreover, it has been suggested that the diversity of projectile sizes was too wide (8–35 mm) and that there were few projectiles of the calibre of the weapons used in the first half of the 16th century.

According to the consensus in the scholarly literature, the projectile diameter of 8–13 mm, which accounts for 67% of the finds and is found in most of the finds near Majs, is not very characteristic of the period. The study, which was discussed with researchers from the Janus Pannonius Museum, suggested that it would be worth considering other conflicts in the area, as there are several documented cases of military operations in the area in the period 1526–1711 (Table 9.4), and it is also possible that there were undocumented clashes on the plain adjacent to the military route. It has also been suggested that there are traces of fighting much later than the Battle of Mohács, perhaps dating from the anti-Ottoman wars of liberation (1683–1699) or the anti-Habsburg

---

73   Pap et al., "Sátorhely vagy Majs?" [Sátorhely or Majs?] pp. 209–246.

THE AVAILABLE MILITARY ARCHAEOLOGY TOPOGRAPHIC DATA

TABLE 9.4   Documented hostilities and encampments on the plain and the Mohács Island (1526–1711)

Date of	Event	Title
26–29 August 1526	Three days of skirmishes preceding the Battle of Mohács and the battle itself	The sultan's campaign of 1526
19 August 1529	Sultan Süleyman's armies marching on Vienna encamp at Mohács; Hungarian King John I Szapolyai and his entourage pay homage to the sultan	The sultan's campaign of 1529
1532	Part of the Ottoman army crosses the Mohács Plain	Ottoman campaign
1541, 1543, 1566, 1683	The camping and passage of the Ottoman armies across the plain of Mohács	Sultan's campaigns
1598	"The free hajduks ... took Mohács, Szekszárd, Tolna, and as they retreated, they defeated the Turks badly..."[a]	Attack of the hajduks on Mohács
1599	Miklós Pálffy sends 1600 hajduks to Mohács to burn it down[b]	Attack of the hajduks on Mohács
1602–1603 winter	Crimean Khan Gazi Giray's soldiers wintering in Mohács devastate the area, the inhabitants flee to the island[c]	After the military events of 1602, the troops of the Crimean Tatar Khan retreat to Pécs and Mohács
1614	The sancakbeyi of Mohács is defeated by Christian troops at Koppány, and Mohács and its surroundings are devastated[d]	The military actions extended to Mohács and its surroundings

a   *Gr. Illésházy István nádor följegyzései 1592–1603* [The records of Count István Illésházy, Palatine of Hungary 1592–1603] (Monumenta Hungariae Historica. Scriptores) 7 (Pest: Magyar Tudományos Akadémia, 1863), p. 55.

b   László Szita, "Mohács gazdasági és társadalmi fejlődése a XVIII. század első felében," [The economic and social development of Mohács in the first half of the 18th century] in Baranyai Helytörténetírás. A Baranya Megyei Levéltár Évkönyve, 1976, ed. László Szita (Pécs: Baranya Megyei Levéltár, 1976), p. 53.

c   Kálmán Nagy and Erika Hancz, *Az oszmán kori Mohács* [The Ottoman Mohács] (Szülőföld Könyvkiadó, 2016), p. 101.

d   József Fölker, Mohács története [History of Mohács] (Mohács: Rosenthal Márk Könyvnyomdája, 1900), p. 37; Szita, "Mohács gazdasági és társadalmi fejlődése," [Economic and Social Development of Mohács] in Baranyai Helytörténetírás, ed. Szita, p. 53.

TABLE 9.4   Documented hostilities and encampments on the plain and the island of Mohács (*cont.*)

Date of	Event	Title
1664	Mohács and its surroundings are devastated[e]	The Winter Campaign of Miklós Zrínyi
1686	– Captain Mátyás Radonai of Zalavár burns down the part of Mohács still in Ottoman Turkish hands outside the palisade[c] – Charles of Lotharingia's troops occupied Mohács[f] – According to the report of the Calvinist superintendent István Gyimóthy, the hajduks of Veszprém and the Ottoman army of Eszék (Osijek/Ösek) alternately plundered the villages around Mohács from October 1686 to the spring of 1687[g]	Events in Baranya during the anti-Ottoman wars of liberation
1687	Camping place for Christian troops marching to and returning from Eszék; a series of small and large clashes south of Mohács during July and August[h]	The Ottoman counter-attack led by Grand Vizier Süleyman, which led to the Battle of Nagyharsány on 12 August

e   Béla Németh, "A mohácsi vésztől a török kiűzetéséig," [From the Mohács Crisis to the Turkish Expulsion] in *Baranya multja és jelenje II,* ed. Ferenc Várady (Pécs: Pécsi Irodalmi és Könyvnyomdai Részvénytársaság, 1897), p. 474.

f   Lajos Nagy, "Az 1686–1687. évi hadjárat," [The campaign of 1686–1687] in *Budától–Belgrádig. Válogatott dokumentumrészletek az 1686–1688. évi törökellenes hadjáratok történetéhez. A nagyharsányi csata 300. évfordulójának emlékére,* ed. László Szita (Pécs, Baranya Megyei Levéltár, 1987), p. 16; László Szita, "Szerbek visszavándorlása Baranya megyébe a szatmári béke utáni években," [The return of Serbs to Baranya County in the years after the Peace of Szatmár] in *Baranyai helytörténetírás 1978,* ed. László Szita (Pécs, Baranya Megyei Levéltár, 1979), pp. 87–149.

g   Ferenc Szakály, "A felszabadító háborúk történeti helyéről (Ki felelős a hódoltsági terület pusztulásáért?)" [On the historical place of the wars of liberation (Who is responsible for the destruction of the conquered territory?)] in *A török elleni visszafoglaló háborúk történetéből 1686–1688,* ed. László Szita (Pécs: 1989), pp. 25–42.

h   Lajos Nagy, "Az 1686–1687. évi hadjárat," [The campaign of 1686–1687] in *Budától–Belgrádig. Válogatott dokumentumrészletek az 1686–1688. évi törökellenes hadjáratok történetéhez. A nagyharsányi csata 300. évfordulójának emlékére,* ed. László Szita (Pécs, Baranya Megyei Levéltár, 1987), pp. 13–51.

TABLE 9.4 Documented hostilities and encampments on the plain and the island of Mohács (*cont.*)

Date of	Event	Title
1704	The Mohács Plain is almost completely depopulated, the Serbian population of Majs also flees across the Drava[i]	Invasion, then Kuruc campaign during the Rákóczi War of Independence (1703–1711)

i Lajos Nagy, "A kurucok és a rácok pusztításai Baranya vármegyében 1704 elején," [The ravages of the Kuruc and the Serbs in Baranya County in early 1704] in *Baranyai Helytörténetírás 1985–1986*, ed. László Szita (Pécs: Baranya Megyei Levéltár, 1986), pp. 13–132.

Kuruc uprising (1703–1711).[74] The debate has been going on for years and is likely to continue.

The team that collected bullets near Majs has since admitted that the village they were investigating is not a fortress. However, in their opinion, István Brodarics was wrong in naming the village; in fact, he saw the settlement under the scarps they were investigating, but confused it with Földvár (archaeologist László Papp had argued the same earlier). In order to prove that small calibre arms were used during the Battle of Mohács, they collected 10–14 mm barrels with a barrel length of 60–70 cm from European collections of the period, and they also identified tapestries and paintings depicting such weapons.[75] However, the discussion revealed that many of the small calibre handguns of the period on display are aristocratic, bronze-barrelled, special and expensive weapons, whose military use is questionable.

The known weapons of the Ottoman army of the battle were certainly larger than 13 mm, but the known weapons of the western troops, such as the 500–600 Prague hackbut (Hakenbüchse), were also much larger (about 24–25 mm). We may add that we are faced with a lack of data on the Hungarian army. Although it is possible that smaller calibre arms were present on the battlefield, we do not know at all where and how the handguns were used by the western soldiers. What we can say with certainty is that, if the area near Majs, supposed to be the site of the Battle of Mohács, were to correspond to the village of Földvár as seen by Brodarics, we should find the imprint of janissary handguns. However, their projectiles of larger calibre cannot be found there.

74 Pap et al., "Sátorhely vagy Majs?" [Sátorhely or Majs?] pp. 209–246.
75 Bertók et al., "Lövedékek egy "mohácsi" csatatérről," [Bullets from a "Mohács" battlefield] in *Eke mentén,* eds. Haramza et al., pp. 121–142; Balázs Németh, "A mohácsi csata kiskaliberű kézi lőfegyvereinek kérdéséhez I.," [The small calibre small arms of the Battle of Mohács I] *Hadtörténeti Közlemények* 134 (2021), no. 1, pp. 167–227.

It seems that the final word on this issue will be said by a series of archaeological investigations, which will include the evaluation of the battles and camp sites of the anti-Ottoman reconquest wars in the Baranya region. The physical characteristics of the projectiles found near Majs (size distribution, typical calibre, technology of manufacture) correspond well with the parameters of the projectiles left behind by the western cavalry camped at the time on Mohács Island and collected with metal detectors. This suggests that the artifacts are the remnants of an armed confrontation in the north-eastern outskirts of Majs during the War of Reconquest at the end of the 17th century. The year 1687 was the most active in the area from a military point of view. Major General Tobias von Hasslingen reports on small-scale skirmishes with Ottoman forces in the area as an aftermath to the Battle of Nagyharsány on 12 August 1687.[76] It is therefore suggested that the soldiers camped on the Island of Mohács at this time may have been one of the participants in this armed conflict near Majs, who clashed with Ottoman cavalry similarly armed (with pistols and carbines).

Let us also examine the site of Sátorhely, which is also thought to be the centre of the Battle of Mohács, enclosed by the "mass graves–Borza Stream–Vizslak Meadow", from the point of view of military archaeological evidence. As we have seen, László Papp concentrated most of his efforts on the sites below the scarps in the western part of the Mohács Plain, and only investigated smaller areas in the Sátorhely area. In recent decades, there were no trial trenching and large-scale excavations at Sátorhely.

The trend continued after Papp's death. For six decades now, archaeologists have focused on the area of Majs below the scarps, and so the results for the plain have been unbalanced. The research concentrated on Majs and its immediate surroundings has thus produced a relatively large number of finds, but their provenance, as explained above, is highly doubtful.

First of all, we have to say that there is only one group of finds in the vast plain of Mohács that can be linked to the Battle of Mohács with one hundred per cent certainty. These include the five mass graves excavated in the 1960s and 1970s, in which, according to previous research, approximately 1,000 people are buried. These mass graves, in turn, are located at a greater distance, 4.5 km as the crow flies, from Majs, the battle site assumed by researchers of the Janus Pannonius Museum. There are several other indications of related military activity in the area. As mentioned above, human bones have been found scattered around 140–160 m from the graves. In the eastern direction,

---

76 László Szita, "Tobias von Hasslingen báró vezérőrnagy hadsereg főszállásmester parancskönyve és hadinaplója az 1687. évi hadjáratról," [Command book and war diary of Baron Major General Tobias von Hasslingen, Quartermaster General of the Army, for the campaign of 1687] in *Budától Belgrádig,* ed. László Szita (Pécs: Baranya Megyei Levéltár, 1987), pp. 175–223.

a few hundred metres away, at the mound of Black Gate (Fekete-kapu), the finds suggest the presence of guns and gun emplacements. Another important additional fact is that Papp reported the presence of human remains in a field (Field S9) in two places south of the mass graves, a few hundred metres north of the Borza Stream. This suggests that further finds, and even new mass graves, may be expected in the vicinity of the five mass graves.

Another group of finds at the edge of the Vizslak Meadow is particularly significant because their testimony is compatible with written sources. Brodarics recalled that east of the battlefield there was a marshy and muddy water into which many people had drowned.[77] A more graphic Czech source from 1526 reported: "I was told by others who could barely escape that there was a deep ditch crosswise, full of water, and next to it a deep marsh. Oh, how many Christians found their death in the ditch! Many sank in the marsh, falling into it one after another."[78]

The mentioned swamp can be identified with the Vizslak Meadow (formerly Danóc Swamp). A wide, deep ditch, a paleobed, crossed the battlefield and ran out to the Vizslak Meadow at the Emperor's Hill, so that excess water could have covered the lower part of the marsh during the extreme rainfall of 1526. Since the elevation at the edge of the Vizslak Meadow, where the ground is still passable, is 90 metres above sea level, while the elevation at the edge of the swamp is only 84 metres, the 6 metre difference in level also makes sense of how those who were forced into the swamp by the Ottoman warriors could have fallen into it. On the basis of these sources and the fact that the Ottoman victory monument was built on Turkish Hill, it seems very likely that the skeletons and weapons found on the edge of the Vizslak Meadow and the finds at the nearby Black Gate (Fekete-kapu) and along the road from there to Sátorhely can be linked to the battle of 1526. Another small addition is the grave excavated at the Újistálló Manor opposite the Turkish Hill, whose mutilated skeleton Papp believed to be that of a person who died in the Battle of Mohács.

Taking all the available data together, the following emerges. In the last century or more, not as many archaeological finds have been recovered as would be expected for the size of the battle and the number of people present. One reason for this is that, apart from the 1960s and the period since 2009, no intensive archaeological research has been conducted in the area. We might add that these two more intensive periods were also mainly concentrated in the same limited area (eastern and southeastern foreground of Majs) at the

---

77 István Brodarics, "Igaz történet a magyarok és Szulejmán török császár mohácsi ütközetéről, 1528," [A true account of the battle between the Hungarians and the Turkish Emperor Süleyman at Mohács, 1528] in *Örök Mohács,* eds. B. Szabó et al., pp. 301–325.

78 "Egy cseh úr levele a Santa Clara kolostor főnöknőjéhez, 1526. november," [Letter from a Czech nobleman to the Superior of the Convent of Santa Clara, November 1526] in *Örök Mohács,* eds. B. Szabó et al., p. 210.

field site resulting in an unbalanced, spatially selective result for the plain as a whole. Meanwhile, other sites were not investigated or, if they were, only with a much smaller labour invested.

The authentic, well-described finds from the Mohács Plain, which can be classified with greater certainty as relics of the Battle of Mohács, show, in agreement with the written sources, that the centre of the battle was probably the area of Sátorhely bounded by the mass graves, the Vizslak Meadow and the Borza Stream. The assemblage of 29 handgun bullets found near the village site identified by Papp as Merse, may be modest evidence of the location of an Ottoman camp on 29 August.

7.2 *The Mass Graves Issue*

The other debate relates to mass graves. As already mentioned above, the five mass graves east of Sátorhely have been the subject of divergent opinions among the researchers. The archaeologist László Papp believed that the graves contained fleeing Christian soldiers who had been slaughtered by the Ottoman cavalrymen surrounding them from the north and south. The archaeologist Borbála Maráz, on the other hand, was of the opinion that the guards and staff

FIGURE 9.7   Mass grave No. 1 during excavation.
SOURCE: KISS KÁROLY ET AL. EDS. MOHÁCS EMLÉKEZETE, [MEMORY OF MOHÁCS] PP. 251–272.

of the Christian camp were buried in the pits. However, together with anthropologist Zsuzsanna K. Zoffmann, she also believed that the characteristics of the wounds suggested that the foot soldier victims were cut down by horsemen.

Papp also suggested that the shape of mass grave No. I is similar to that of a gun emplacement. In this connection, he also referred to a description by Stephan Gerlach, a Protestant clergyman and traveller, who, in 1573, seeing the battle site, wrote the following: "You can still see the trenches where their guns were placed and where the dead were buried."[79] However, as Papp had by this time already developed his concept of the Hungarian army's guns being positioned south of the site of the mass graves, he eventually abandoned this idea.

Borbála Maráz, when she re-examined the issue in the mid-1970s, concluded that the objects were specifically excavated as graves, so the unusual shape of mass graves I and V is no more than a coincidence.

More recent investigations have indicated that a longitudinal depression, a paleobed, can be identified to the south-west of the mass graves, parallel to the line of the mass graves, and that it is present in the sources as an environmental feature used as a cover.[80] This has again drawn attention to the fact that the mass graves may have been originally designed as shooting positions, partly for artillery and partly for infantry. In this context, the protrusion of the two crescent-shaped mass graves (No. I and V), which could be interpreted as gun emplacements, points southwards, towards the expected enemy attack. The other three nearly rectangular pits, II, III and mass grave No. IV can be interpreted as infantry positions.

As already mentioned, two small cemetery graves (Lajmér, Újistálló Manor) were identified in the 1960s, which investigations linked to the Battle of Mohács. One of their important features was that they were excavated in a hurry, with varying depths. In contrast, the excavation depth of the five mass graves was fairly uniform. The corners are rounded, the side walls are curved and the estimated depth is the same. This may suggest that the objects were dug out at the same time, by the same people, and in the same way, but in no way in a hastily manner. In addition, mass grave I starts only 2.5 m from mass grave II. It can be seen that if they had been designed as mass graves, it would have been less work to dig a single, long grave than to dig two separate objects.

The investigations of the staff of the Janus Pannonius Museum, led by Gábor Bertók, which have been ongoing since 2020, have generated new controversy

---

79   Dávid Ungnád, *Ungnád Dávid konstantinápolyi utazásai* [David Ugnad's travels in Constantinople] (Budapest: Szépirodalmi Könyvkiadó, 1986), p. 121.
80   See Chapter Eight on Földvár and Norbert Pap, Máté Kitanics, Péter Gyenizse, and Gábor Szalai, "A Mohácsi-síkon fekvő Földvár település," [The settlement of Földvár on the Mohács Plain] *Újkor.hu* (2021), Available at https://ujkor.hu/content/mohacs_foldvar.

regarding the mass graves: the question has arisen again: who are the people in the graves and how did they die? The researchers who re-opened mass grave No. III first agreed with Borbála Maráz's theory, i.e. they also believed that the people buried in the graves were those who were in the camps and had been ambushed by the Ottomans. They also argued that the graves contained a number of young people aged between 18 and 20. It was argued that these could not have been soldiers because of their age, but could only have been service personnel. It should be added, however, that at the time of the Battle of Mohács, men aged between 18 and 20 were no longer considered young at all, as there could have been "child soldiers" of 10–12 years in the Ottoman army, just as soldiers of 15–16 years in the Christian army.[81]

Bertók and his colleagues later changed their minds and voted for the graves to contain Christian prisoners executed after the battle on 31 August. On what exactly did they base their new position? On the fact that there are many severed heads in the graves, and at the same time many bodies are without their heads.

However, in relation to their newer theory, it is suggested that if the graves really contained the executed, the bodies would all be decapitated and rest somewhere else and in a different way. Indeed, according to several contemporary accounts, the Ottomans cut off the heads of all executed prisoners of war and then raised the severed heads into a gula or gulas in front of the sultan's tent.

The condition of the bodies, however, does not support such a uniform method of execution in several respects. Firstly, the bodies were found to have not only sword wounds but also wounds inflicted by a battle axe. On the other hand, lesions are varied and can be found not only on the heads but also on other parts of the body, including the limbs. The presence of severed heads is also explained by the mode of combat and the habit of "collecting heads".[82] The latter means that Ottoman soldiers collected heads during and sometimes even after battle in the hope of a reward, so that not only the heads of the living but often also those of the dead were cut off. However, it is also of particular importance in this context that a larger number of dead people whose heads were not cut off can be observed in mass graves. This also confirms that it was not execution that led to the deaths of those buried in the mass graves.

Another point of contention is that the Janus Pannonius Museum staff also found three lead bullets in the re-opened mass grave. Two of these, as mentioned above, are 10–13 mm in diameter (different figures have been published)

---

81 See Chapter Three.
82 Papp, "A mohácsi csatahely kutatása," [Research on the battle site of Mohács] in A Janus Pannonius Múzeum Évkönyve, ed. Dombay, pp. 197–253.

and one is larger, but the exact diameter of this one has not been given due to its more severe deformation than the first two. It is believed that the bullets could only have been dropped in the tomb in 1526, either from a bag of ammunition left on the belt of a prisoner of war who was executed after the battle, or by soldiers who were shot and executed in battle and then deposited in the tomb.

First, let us examine the claim that the bullets could only have been buried in the pit after the Battle of Mohács. The disturbance of mass grave No. III was documented as early as the 1976 excavation, which was attributed to the deep ploughing that had been going on at the site for decades. In addition, this mass grave was discovered when the graveyard was being formed with a bulldozer, and the machine moved or destroyed many bones. In addition, the mass grave, at least the upper layer and the sides, was excavated in 1976, then buried, and then re-excavated in 2020. The soil at the tomb has therefore been moved several times, which may have included a projectile from the topsoil that dates to the post-Battle of Mohács period. This cannot be excluded, not least because archaeologists report that the projectiles were recovered from the upper part of the tomb.

So how can the five mass graves found so far be interpreted, who are the people buried in them and how did they die? Let us look at the most likely scenario. We believe that the five objects were originally designed as gun emplacements. As already suggested by László Papp, Ottoman cavalrymen overrun Western soldiers defending or fleeing on foot in the immediate vicinity of the mass graves. The German and Salzburg coins found in the graves, the "red-brown" hair remains found, and the account of a German soldier who said that German mercenaries were led to the gun emplacements[83] suggest that these soldiers may well have been *landsknecht*s, or at least may have included *landsknecht*s among them. Evidence of a cavalry attack is not only provided by the wounds of the dead, but also by the discovery of a horse ornament from one of the graves. At the site of the mass graves, on the northern edge of the battle's central area, the heads of many of the living and dead were cut off in the massacre, as was customary for the Ottomans. The fallen were looted after the battle, and everything of value was removed from their bodies. Only heavily soiled clothes were left behind, but sometimes the dead were not searched because of their condition. In some cases, this may have left small objects that were not discovered and were later recovered during excavations.

---

83 "Új híradás: Hogyan esett meg a magyarországi csata a török császárral. Itt volt egy ember Bécsből, és utána megírta Ottingenbe (1526)," [New News: How the battle of Hungary with the Turkish Emperor Happened. Here was a man from Vienna, and afterwards he wrote to Ottingen (1526)] in *Örök Mohács*, eds. B. Szabó et al., pp. 221–223.

Burial officials could no longer always tell which the army the bodies, stripped of their clothes, badly wounded and in many cases headless, belonged to, and they may not have cared much about them.

8   Conclusions

The history of research into the military archaeology of the Battle of Mohács goes back to more than a century and is extremely complex. The area of research is very extensive and has not yet been the subject of a comprehensive archaeological study. Another disadvantage is that the area became a border zone after the First World War and a "fortified place" on the borders of sharply opposing blocs during the Cold War following the Second World War. Local society was severely traumatized first by the Holocaust and then by the population exchanges in Eastern Europe (Czechoslovak-Hungarian exchanges and German expulsions). The expelled Germans were replaced not only by Hungarians from Czechoslovakia, but also by poor peasants from the Great Plain loyal to the communist regime: the former "elite" was replaced by people with no roots in the area. The social conditions for archaeological research, such as trust-based data reporting, were shaken. The consequences are also tangible in the history of research.

The artifacts (and sites) considered to be related to the battle of 1526 were grouped according to their scientific value and their potential for consideration. It should be stressed that only 42% of the finds mentioned in the literature cited for the battle can be considered confirmed. For the rest, there are serious doubts about their relevance or they may be outright declared never to have existed. The opportunity for the inclusion of these finds is also limited by the fact that many of them are missing, untestable, and lacking documentation or having severely incomplete descriptions.

In the 1920s, it was suggested that the centre of the battle may have been in the Majs area, on the hilly terrain surrounding the plain from the west. The renewed research was essentially organised around this Majs concept. In the 1960s, László Papp believed that the remains of the battle could be found in this area through systematic fieldwork and exploratory excavations, but his efforts were unsuccessful. The failure was also recognized by some contemporaries.[84]

Nevertheless, in the same area, concentrating on the village Majs and its surroundings, new research was launched in the 1990s, first by Lajos Négyesi and

---

84   Lajos Bende, "A mohácsi csata," [The Battle of Mohács] *Hadtörténeti Közlemények* 13 (1966), pp. 532–567.

then, from 2009, by Gábor Bertók, based on the application of modern metal detecting instruments. In both cases, the investigations produced finds, but in neither case have they unearthed a significant body of artifacts with a clear link to the battle. On closer examination, most of the finds recovered in the eastern outskirts of the village of Majs in the 1960s do not belong to the relics of the battle of 1526, or are not suspected to have been originally found in this area. The handgun projectiles collected here, also from 2009, are most likely to be predominantly the remains of a cavalry clash in the late 17th century during the anti-Ottoman wars. The only group of artifacts most likely to be linked to the Battle of Mohács (29 handgun bullets, which the archaeologist linked to the janissaries) was found on the site where, according to written sources,[85] the sultan's camp of 29 August stood.

The archaeological finds (weapons and fragments, cannonballs, the victory monument of the Ottoman martyrs) that probably belong to the battle of 1526 were recovered in the area of Sátorhely. The remains of the battle casualties were also unearthed in this zone. Of particular importance are the five mass graves at Sátorhely with at least 1000 dead. These appear to be fleeing infantrymen (including foreign mercenaries, some of them German) who were killed by the Ottoman cavalrymen using cold weapons, mostly swords.

It is unlikely that they were prisoners of war demonstratively beheaded, because their wounds and injuries do not justify this, they do not correspond to the manner of execution described in the sources. Some of the bodies, after having been looted, were placed in the trenches dug by the Christian infantry on the battlefield, to be used as mass graves. Others were buried alone by the local population. Presumably, many of the victims met their destiny in marshes and watercourses, thus they were probably never buried.

Overall, it can be concluded from the examination of the finds and archaeological sites that it is unfounded to associate the immediate eastern outskirts of Majs with the central area of the Battle of Mohács in 1526. Very few finds of unambiguously 16th-century date are known from the vicinity of Majs. No more than would be expected for a village with a medieval foundation. However, the sources suggest that in 1526 the area may have been affected by the attacks in the days preceding the battle and the subsequent encampment of the Ottoman army, but the small number of relevant finds may also be linked to other minor armed conflicts in the 16th century. For all the above reasons, the battle seems to have been centred in the administrative area of Sátorhely rather than Majs.

---

85 Caspar Ursinus Velius, "A mohácsi csata. 1530 körül," [The Battle of Mohács. Around 1530] in *Örök Mohács,* eds. B. Szabó et al., pp. 348–355.

Bibliography

Az udvari zsoldosok/janicsárok fegyver- és hadianyag listája, 1526. április 13." [The list of arms and war material of the mercenaries/janissaries, 13 April 1526] In *Örök Mohács: Szövegek és értelmezések,* eds. János B. Szabó and Gábor Farkas Farkas, 231–235. Budapest: Bölcsészettudományi Kutatóközpont, 2020.

B. Szabó, János. "Egy Mátyás-kori oklevél és a mohácsi csata centrumában fekvő Földvár falu "rejtélye" (Egy évszázados kirakós játék új darabjai)." [One charter from Age of King Matthias and one village in the centrum of the Battle of Mohács: Földvár (New pieces from a centuries-old puzzle game)] In *Hunyadi Mátyás és kora,* eds. Attila Bárány et al., 149–159.

B. Szabó, János. *A mohácsi csata.* [The Battle of Mohács] Budapest: Corvina, 2006.

Bende, Lajos. "A mohácsi csata." [The Battle of Mohács] *Hadtörténeti Közlemények* 13 (1966): 532–567.

Bertók, Gábor, Réka Neményi, György Pálfi, and Béla Simon. "A mohácsi III. számú tömegsír új kutatása." [New research on the Mohács mass grave No. III] *Magyar Régészet* 11 (2022): 44–53.

Bertók, Gábor, Máté Szabó, Márk Haramza, Éva Szajcsán, and Béla Simon. "Mohács 500 csatatérkutatási program." [Mohács 500 battlefield research programme] In *Eke mentén, csata nyomában,* eds. Márk Haramza et al., 107–118. Archaeological Studies of PPCU Institute of Archaeology 17. Budapest: Martin Opitz Kiadó, 2020.

Bertók, Gábor, Márk Haramza, and Balázs Németh. "Lövedékek egy "mohácsi" csatatérről." [Bullets from a "Mohács" battlefield] In *Eke mentén, csata nyomában,* eds. Márk Haramza et al., 121–142. Archaeological Studies of PPCU Institute of Archaeology 17. Budapest: Martin Opitz Kiadó, 2020.

Brand, Ede. "Adalékok Mohács történetéhez." [Additions to the history of Mohács] *Mohácsi Hírlap* 18 (1928): 41, p. 2.

Brodarics, István. "Igaz történet a magyarok és Szulejmán török császár mohácsi ütközetéről, 1528." [A true account of the battle between the Hungarians and the Turkish Emperor Süleyman at Mohács, 1528] In *Örök Mohács: Szövegek és értelmezések,* eds. János B. Szabó and Gábor Farkas Farkas, 301–325. Budapest: Bölcsészettudományi Kutatóközpont, 2020.

Cs., B. "Ágyúgolyót szánt az eke." [The plough was plowing a cannonball] *Déli Hírlap* 8 (1976): 241, p. 5.

Debrecen: MTA-DE Lendület "Magyarország a középkori Európában" kutatócsoport, 2019.

Domokos, György. "Adalékok a törökkori magyar tüzérség kategoria- és tipusproblémáihoz." *Hadtörténelmi Közlemények* 31 (1984): 117–149.

Dudás, Gyula. "Mohácsi emlékekről." [On the memories of Mohács] *Archaeologiai Értesítő* 16 (1896): 430–431.

Egy cseh úr levele a Santa Clara kolostor főnöknőjéhez, 1526. november." [Letter from a Czech nobleman to the Superior of the Convent of Santa Clara, November 1526] In *Örök Mohács: Szövegek és értelmezések*, eds. János B. Szabó and Gábor Farkas Farkas, 207–216. Budapest: Bölcsészettudományi Kutatóközpont, 2020.

Fölker, József. *Mohács története*. [History of Mohács] Mohács: Rosenthal Márk Könyvnyomdája, 1900.

Gr. Illésházy István nádor följegyzései 1592–1603. [The records of Count István Illésházy, Palatine of Hungary 1592–1603] Monumenta Hungariae Historica. Scriptores 7. Pest: Magyar Tudományos Akadémia, 1863.

Gyalókay, Jenő. "A mohácsi csata." [The Battle of Mohács] Budapest: Királyi Magyar Egyetemi Nyomda, 1926.

H., E. "Huszonkilenc janicsár golyó. Ásatás a mohácsi csatatéren." [Twenty-nine janissary bullets. Digging on the battlefield of Mohács] *Dunántúli Napló* 27 (1970): 206, p. 3.

Halmay, Barna. *Az 1526-iki mohácsi csata keletkezése és igazi helye.* [The origins and real place of the Battle of Mohács in 1526] Debrecen: Magyar Nemzeti Könyv- és Lapkiadóvállalat Rt., 1926.

Haramza, Márk et al. eds. *Eke mentén, csata nyomában* [Along plow, in the wake of a battle] Archaeological Studies of PPCU Institute of Archaeology 17. Budapest: Martin Opitz Kiadó, 2020.

Hummel, Gyula. "Hogy hol volt a mohácsi csata?" [Where was the Battle of Mohács?] *Mohács* 6 (1906) 49, pp. 2–3.

K. Zoffmann, Zsuzsanna. *Az 1526-os mohácsi csata 1976-ban feltárt tömegsírjainak embertani vizsgálata.* [Anthropologycal analysis of the mass graves of the Battle of Mohács in 1526, excavated in 1976] Budapest: Akadémiai Kiadó, 1982.

Kitanics, Máté, Levente Nagy, Erika Hancz, Péter Gyenizse, Gábor Szalai, László Nagy, Zsombor Klembala, Balázs Polgár, and Norbert Pap. "A Törökdomb a régészeti vizsgálatok tükrében: 1924–2020." In *Mordortól Mohácsig: A mohácsi csatatáj történeti földrajzi kutatása,* [The Törökdomb in the Light of Archaeological Investigations: 1924–2020] ed. Norbert Pap, 273–349. Budapest, MTA Bölcsészettudományi Kutatóközpont, 2020.

Kovács, Olivér. *Mohácsi tömegsír: inkább a tábor halottjait rejtheti.* [Mohács mass grave: more likely to hide the camp's dead] Available at https://archeologia.hu/mohacsi-tomegsir-inkabb-a-tabor-halottait-rejtheti.

Kozák, Károly. "A magyarországi szakállas puskák fejlődéstörténetéről." [On the history of the development of hackbut (Hakenbüchse) in Hungary] *Archaeologiai Értesítő* 101 (1974): 290–303.

Maráz, Borbála. "Újabb tömegsírok a mohácsi csatatéren." [More mass graves on the battlefield of Mohács] In *Mohács emlékezete,* eds. Károly Kiss et al., 273–279. Budapest: Európa Könyvkiadó, 1987.

Nagy, Balázs. "Az érem és kincsleletek horizontja a mohácsi vésztől a török kivonulásáig." [The horizon of coin and treasure hoards from the Mohacs disaster to the Turkish withdrawal] In *Numophylacium Novum. Az 1. Fiatal Numizmaták Konferenciája Tanulmányai,* ed. Márton Gyöngyössy, 86–161. Budapest: ELTE Eötvös Kiadó, 2019.

Nagy, Géza. "Hadtörténeti ereklyék a Magyar Nemzeti Múzeumban." [Military relics in the Hungarian National Museum] *Hadtörténelmi Közlemények* 11 (1910): 223–243.

Nagy, Kálmán and Erika Hancz. *Az oszmán kori Mohács.* [The Ottoman Mohács] Szülőföld Könyvkiadó, 2016.

Nagy, Lajos. "Az 1686–1687. évi hadjárat." [The campaign of 1686–1687] In *Budától–Belgrádig. Válogatott dokumentumrészletek az 1686–1688. évi törökellenes hadjáratok történetéhez. A nagyharsányi csata 300. évfordulójának emlékére,* ed. László Szita, 13–51. Pécs, Baranya Megyei Levéltár, 1987.

Nagy, Lajos. "A kurucok és a rácok pusztításai Baranya vármegyében 1704 elején." [The ravages of the Kuruc and the Serbs in Baranya County in early 1704] In *Baranyai Helytörténetírás 1985–1986,* ed. László Szita, 13–132. Pécs: Baranya Megyei Levéltár, 1986.

Négyesi, Lajos. "A mohácsi csata." [The Battle of Mohács] *Hadtörténelmi Közlemények* 107 (1994): 62–79.

Németh, Balázs. "A mohácsi csata kiskaliberű kézi lőfegyvereinek kérdéséhez I." [The small calibre small arms of the Battle of Mohács I] *Hadtörténeti Közlemények* 134 (2021): 167–227.

Németh, Béla. "A mohácsi vésztől a török kiűzetéséig." [From the Mohács Crisis to the Turkish Expulsion] In *Baranya multja és jelenje II.,* ed. Ferenc Várady, 393–496. Pécs: Pécsi Irodalmi és Könyvnyomdai Részvénytársaság, 1897.

Pap, Norbert, Máté Kitanics, Péter Gyenizse, and Gábor Szalai. "A Mohácsi-síkon fekvő Földvár település." [The settlement of Földvár on the Mohács Plain] *Újkor.hu* (2021). Available at https://ujkor.hu/content/mohacs_foldvar.

Pap, Norbert, Péter Gyenizse, Máté Kitanics, and Gábor Szalai. "II. Lajos halálának helye." [Louis II's place of death] *Történelmi Szemle* 62 (2020): 73–110.

Pap, Norbert, Péter Gyenizse, Máté Kitanics, and Gábor Szalai. "Az 1526. évi mohácsi csata helyszíneinek földrajzi jellemzői." [Geographical features of the sites of the Battle of Mohács in 1526] *Történelmi Szemle* 62 (2020): 111–151.

Pap, Norbert, Máté Kitanics, Péter Gyenizse, Gábor Szalai, and Balázs Polgár. "Sátorhely vagy Majs? A mohácsi csata centrumtérségének lokalizálása." [Sátorhely or Majs? Locating the central area of the Battle of Mohács] *Történelmi Szemle* 61 (2019): 209–246.

Pap, Norbert, Pál Fodor, Máté Kitanics, Tamás Morva, Gábor Szalai, and Péter Gyenizse. "A mohácsi Törökdomb." [The Törökdomb of Mohács] *Történelmi Szemle* 60 (2018): 325–345.

Papp, László. "A mohácsi csatahely kutatása." [The research of the battlefield of Mohács] In *Mohács emlékezete*, eds. Károly Kiss et al., 251–272. Budapest: Európa Könyvkiadó, 1987.

Papp, László. "Újabb kutatások a mohácsi csatatéren." [New research on the battlefield of Mohács] In *A Janus Pannonius Múzeum Évkönyve 1962*, ed. László Papp, 199–222. Pécs: Janus Pannonius Múzeum, 1963.

Papp, László. "A mohácsi csatahely kutatása." [Research on the battlesite of Mohács] In *A Janus Pannonius Múzeum Évkönyve 1960*, ed. János Dombay, 197–253. Pécs, Janus Pannonius Múzeum, 1961.

Polgár, Balázs. *Oszmán-török kori csataterek régészeti kutatása Magyarországon*, PhD thesis. [Archaeological research of Ottoman Turkish battlefields in Hungary] Budapest: ELTE BTK, 2018.

Szakály, Ferenc. "A felszabadító háborúk történeti helyéről (Ki felelős a hódoltsági terület pusztulásáért?)" [On the historical place of the wars of liberation (Who is responsible for the destruction of the conquered territory?)] In *A török elleni visszafoglaló háborúk történetéből 1686–1688*, ed. László Szita, 25–42. Pécs: 1989.

Szita, László. "Tobias von Hasslingen báró vezérőrnagy hadsereg főszállásmester parancskönyve és hadinaplója az 1687, évi hadjáratról." [Command book and war diary of Baron Major General Tobias von Hasslingen, Quartermaster General of the Army, for the campaign of 1687] In *Budától Belgrádig*, ed. László Szita, 175–223. Pécs: Baranya Megyei Levéltár, 1987.

Szita, László. "Szerbek visszavándorlása Baranya megyébe a szatmári béke utáni években." [The return of Serbs to Baranya County in the years after the Peace of Szatmár] In *Baranyai helytörténetírás 1978*, ed. László Szita, 87–149. Pécs, Baranya Megyei Levéltár, 1979.

Szita, László. "Mohács gazdasági és társadalmi fejlődése a XVIII. század első felében." [The economic and social development of Mohács in the first half of the 18th century] In *Baranyai Helytörténetírás. A Baranya Megyei Levéltár Évkönyve, 1976*, ed. László Szita, 49–87. Pécs: Baranya Megyei Levéltár, 1976.

Új híradás: Hogyan esett meg a magyarországi csata a török császárral. Itt volt egy ember Bécsből, és utána megírta Ottingenbe (1526)." [New News: How the Battle of Hungary with the Turkish Emperor Happened. Here was a man from Vienna, and afterwards he wrote to Ottingen (1526)] In *Örök Mohács: Szövegek és értelmezések*, eds. János B. Szabó and Gábor Farkas Farkas, 221–223. Budapest: Bölcsészettudományi Kutatóközpont, 2020.

Ungnád, Dávid. *Ungnád Dávid konstantinápolyi utazásai* [David Ugnad's travels in Constantinople] Budapest: Szépirodalmi Könyvkiadó, 1986.

Végh, András and János B. Szabó. "A Mohács és Dánóc közé eső térség késő középkori birtok- és településstruktúrája." [The late medieval estate and settlement structure of the area between Mohács and Dánóc] In *Eke mentén, csata nyomában*, eds. Márk

Haramza et al., 49–73. Archaeological Studies of PPCU Institute of Archaeology 17. Budapest: Martin Opitz Kiadó, 2020.

Velius, Caspar Ursinus. "A mohácsi csata. 1530 körül." [The Battle of Mohács. Around 1530] In *Örök Mohács: Szövegek és értelmezések,* eds. János B. Szabó and Gábor Farkas Farkas, 348–355. Budapest: Bölcsészettudományi Kutatóközpont, 2020.

CHAPTER 10

Where and How Did King Louis II Die?

Norbert Pap, Péter Gyenizse and Máté Kitanics

The gravest political consequence of the Battle of Mohács in 1526 was the loss of the king, which plunged the country into a leadership crisis. The death of King Louis II led to succession disputes. The country was split into two parties, and its ability to defend itself was further weakened. Weeks after the disaster, contemporaries were already looking for scapegoats, and they found them. The circumstances of the horse riding accident, and in particular the fact that there was only one witness, contributed to conspiracy theories. These were mainly spread as pro-Habsburg propaganda, which emphasised the supposedly menial intentions of the Szapolyai family, and suggested that the Transylvanian voivode's path to the throne was through the murder of Louis II.

The authentic descriptions of the incident make it obvious that it was an accident. At the same time, the possible route of the king's escape and the water in which he eventually drowned have been a matter of public interest for centuries. The discovery of the body, its condition and identification marks has already been the subject of debate for some years, and focuses mainly over whether it was really the body of Louis II that was found in mid-October 1526.[1]

1 The Flight to the Danube after the Battle

The king's troop of a few men had the same considerations as all other similar groups fleeing the battlefield: to find safety as soon as possible. They had several options to choose from. Based on an analysis of the small number of known escape routes, four theoretical options were considered. They could go west or north along the military road. Turning east, they had two more options. On the one hand, they could cross the two branches of the Danube towards

---

[1] István Nemes and Balázs Tolvaj, "II. Lajos magyar király (1506–1526) holttestének megtalálása," [The discovery of the body of King Louis II of Hungary (1506–1526). An analysis and reinterpretation of the forensic medical opinion written in 1926] *Orvosi Hetilap* 155 (2014), no. 12, pp. 475–480. See also Gábor Farkas Farkas, Zsolt Szebelédi, and Bernadett Varga, eds., "Nekünk mégis Mohács kell..." *II. Lajos király rejtélyes halála és különböző temetései* [We need Mohács after all ... The death and the mysterious burials of King Louis II] (Budapest: MTA Bölcsészettudományi Kutatóközpont, Országos Széchényi Könyvtár, 2016).

Baracska in order to avoid the threat of the Ottoman Turkish cavalry raiding in the area. On the other hand, they were able to cross the small branch of the Danube and return to the right bank at Szekcső, heading north on Mohács Island in the hope by crossing the small branch of the Danube and heading north on Mohács Island, they could return to the right bank at Szekcső, confident that the Ottoman Turkish cavalry had not yet reached there.

An account from 1526 says: "The Turks chased the king and pursued him until he reached a branch of the Danube."[2] This statement seems plausible, since we have several other accounts of many people dying on the banks of the Danube as they were being pursued by the Ottoman cavalry. In his letter to the Pope, Miklós Oláh writes[3] that part of the Christian army was in danger of being killed in the Danube. According to Sultan Süleyman's letter of victory, part of the Christian army "... was drowned in the waters of the T[D]anube, like the people of Pharaoh..."[4] Kemalpaşazade also reports that some of the Christian refugees were drowned in the Danube.[5] Bostan[6] mentions that the fleeing "unbelievers" drowned in the confined space. As for the fate of the king, he writes: "... unable to help himself, he drowned into the water with his horse and arms, and joined the group that perished in the water."[7] Katib Mehmed Zaim also notes: "And the group of the unbelievers which the swords left alive, drowned in the waters of the T[D]una, like the people of the Pharaoh and Haman."[8] Camerarius says: "Only a few were taken prisoner. Szepesi,[9] while trying to jump on a boat with

---

2   Břetislav Švihovský z Rýzmberka, "Břetislav Švihovský z Rýzmberka az egyik bajor herceghez. Raby/Rabí, 1526. szeptember 16.," [Břetislav Švihovský z Rýzmberka to a Bavarian prince. Raby/Rabí, 16 September 1526] in *Örök Mohács – Szövegek és értelmezések*, eds. János B. Szabó and Gábor Farkas Farkas (Budapest: Bölcsészettudományi Kutatóközpont, 2020), p. 154.

3   Miklós Oláh, "Oláh Miklós levele VII. Kelemen pápához, Linz, 1530. február 15. (Részlet)," [Letter by Miklós Oláh to Pope Clement VII Linz, 15 February 1530 (Excerpt)] in *Örök Mohács*, eds. B. Szabó et al., pp. 346–348.

4   Szulejmán szultán, "Szulejmán szultán két győzelmi jelentése, 1526," [Sultan Süleyman's two victory reports, 1526] in *Örök Mohács*, eds. B. Szabó et al., p. 266.

5   Kemálpasazáde, "Mohácsnáme, 1526 és 1534 között, (Részletek)," [Mohácsname, between 1526 and 1534, (Excerpts)] in *Örök Mohács*, eds. B. Szabó et al., pp. 326–338.

6   Bosztán cselebi [Ferdi], "Szulejmán könyve (1520–1542), 1547 (részlet)," [Book of Süleyman (1520–1542), 1547 (excerpt)] in *Örök Mohács*, eds. B. Szabó et al., pp. 364–368.

7   According to Bostan Çelebi, the king drowned in the "Sárvíz" (Muddy Water). The main problem with the value of the source is that, although he was apparently present at the battle, he did not know and could not have known about the king's death. He is an author who could have written an authentic account of what happened on the right flank of the Ottoman army, where he was, but could only have recorded rumours of the king's death. Bosztán cselebi, "Szulejmán könyve," [Book of Süleyman] in *Örök Mohács*, eds. B. Szabó et al., p. 366.

8   Kjátib Mehmed Záim, "Történetek gyűjteménye, 1578 (részlet)," [A collection of stories, 1578 (excerpt)] in *Örök Mohács*, eds. B. Szabó et al., p. 430.

9   György Szapolyai, Count of Spiš, brother of János Szapolyai.

his galloping horse, which he could not reach, fell into the Danube and was lost in the river."[10] According to this source, one of the leaders of the army, György Szapolyai, also fled towards the Danube, but he did not survive. Dubravius confirms that György Szapolyai and László Szalkai Archbishop of Esztergom also drowned in water: "... very few died on the battlefield, but most of the nobility were either captured while fleeing or drowned themselves. The most notable of the latter were György Trencséni [Szapolyai] and László [Szalkai] Archbishop of Esztergom, who both drowned in the Danube."[11]

The above sources all testify that the flight to the east, i.e. towards the river, from the pursuing horsemen must have been quite common on the evening of the battle. Among these groups, we can also find the king, who attempted to reach safety alone with two other persons.

2 Authentic Sources on the Death of Louis II

The place of death of Louis II in 1528 is described by Brodarics as follows:

> However, he was later found in a crevice in a steep bank above Mohács, half a mile below the village of Csele. At this place, the water was higher than usual because of the flooding Danube: here he drowned with his horse, armed as he was. Others were also lost here, the bodies of András Trepka and István Aczél were found a little further on.[12]

The description therefore places the tragedy on the bank of the Danube south of the mouth of the Csele Stream, half a mile north of the centre of Mohács, south of the village of Csele. In his description, Brodarics makes two other important observations: he indicates that the Danube was flooding at the time, and that the place of death was not the riverbed but a "crevice" (*hiatus*).

---

10   Joachim Camerarius, "A Magyarországon, Mohácsnál elszenvedett vereségről és Lajos király haláláról, 1541," [About the defeat suffered in Hungary at Mohács and the death of King Louis] in *Örök Mohács,* eds. B. Szabó et al., p. 372. The story of György Szapolyai trying to escape by boat, but failing and drowning, also appears in a document of 1559. "Habsburg-ház dicsőségtükre, Augsburg, 1559," [Ehrenspiegel des Hauses Österreich, Augsburg, 1559] in *Örök Mohács,* eds. B. Szabó et al., pp. 395–400.
11   Jan Dubravius, "Csehország története, 1552 (részlet)," [The History of Bohemia, 1552] in *Örök Mohács,* eds. B. Szabó et al., p. 393.
12   István Brodarics, *Igaz leírás a magyaroknak a törökkel Mohácsnál vívott csatájáról.* [A True Account of the Battle of Mohács between the Hungarians and the Turks] (Budapest: Magvető Könyvkiadó, 1983), p. 53.

TABLE 10.1   The most reliable (earliest) sources on the king's death

Year/author	Reference to the Danube, the great river	Reference to the Csele, a stream	Swamp/pond/ overflow	Pit, muddy water
5 September 1526 Burgio[a]	"To a small branch of the Danube"			
5 September 1526 Johann Fugger[b]			"the king drowned in a pond"	
17 September 1526 Fazio di Savoia[c]			"he jumped into the swamp on horseback"	
"19 September 1526 Archduke Ferdinand of Habsburg[d]			"became lost in a marshy place"	
20 September 1526 Intelligence report[e]			"headed for the swamp ... couldn't get out"	

a   Antonio Giovanni da Burgio, "Antonio Giovanni da Burgio pápai követ levele Jacopo Sadoleto pápai titkárnak Pozsony, 1526. szeptember 5. (részlet)," [Letter from papal ambassador Antonio Giovanni da Burgio to papal secretary Jacopo Sadoleto. Pozsony, 5 September 1526] in Örök Mohács, eds. B. Szabó et al., pp. 131–132.
b   "Johann Fugger értesülései, Buda, 1526. augusztus 29–31.; Bécs, szeptember 5. (kivonat)," [Information from Johann Fugger, Buda, 29–31 August 1526; Vienna, 5 September 1526] in Örök Mohács, eds. B. Szabó et al., p 125.
c   Fazio di Savoia, "Fazio di Savoia jelentése," [The report of Fazio di Savoia. Graz, 17 September 1526] in "Nekünk mégis Mohács kell…" eds. Gábor Farkas Farkas, Zsolt Szebelédi, and Bernadett Varga (Budapest: MTA Bölcsészettudományi Kutatóközpont, Országos Széchényi Könyvtár, 2016), p. 184.
d   Ferdinánd osztrák főherceg, "Ferdinánd osztrák főherceg levele Ausztriai Margit főhercegnőnek, Linz, 1526. szeptember 18.," [Letter from Archduke Ferdinand of Austria to Archduchess Margaret of Austria. 18 September 1526] in "Nekünk mégis Mohács kell…", eds. Farkas et al., p. 184.
e   "Hírszerzői jelentés Magyarországgal kapcsolatban. Pettau, 1526. szeptember 20.," [Intelligence report on Hungary. Pettau, 20 September 1526] in "Nekünk mégis Mohács kell…", eds. Farkas et al., p. 186.

WHERE AND HOW DID KING LOUIS II DIE?

TABLE 10.1   The most reliable (earliest) sources on the king's death (*cont.*)

Year/author	Reference to the Danube, the great river	Reference to the Csele, a stream	Swamp/pond/ overflow	Pit, muddy water
29 September 1526 Thurzó[f]	"into a deep overflow of the Danube"		"to its deep overflow"	
30 September 1526 Sir John Wallop[g]	"drowned in the Danube"			
1526 Břetislav Švihovský z Rýzmberka[h]	"A branch of the Danube"			
6 October 1526 Reports by an unknown author[i]			"fell into a swamp or ditch"	
19 October 1526 Letter from Ferenc Sárffy[j]			"in a swamp"	
11 November 1526 Letter from János Szapolyai[k]				"… the mud –… the now dried-up whirlpool"

f   "Thurzó Elek tárnokmester levele I. Zsigmond magyar királynak. Pozsony, 1526. szeptember 29.," [Letter of Elek Thurzó, Treasurer to King Sigismund I of Poland. Pozsony, 29 September 1526] in "Nekünk mégis Mohács kell…", eds. Farkas et al., p. 190.

g   Sir John Wallop, "Sir John Wallop levele Thomas Wolsey kancellárnak. Köln, 1526. szeptember 30.," [Letter from Sir John Wallop to Chancellor Thomas Wolsey. Cologne, 30 September 1526] in "Nekünk mégis Mohács kell…", eds. Farkas et al., p. 191.

h   Švihovský z Rýzmberka, "Břetislav Švihovský z Rýzmberka az egyik bajor herceghez," [Břetislav Švihovský z Rýzmberka to a Bavarian prince] in Örök Mohács, eds. B. Szabó et al., p 154.

i   "Ismeretlen szerző jelentései Thomas Wolsey kancellárnak. Köln, 1526. október 6.," [Reports by an unknown author to Chancellor Thomas Wolsey. Cologne, 6 October 1526] in "Nekünk mégis Mohács kell…", eds. Farkas et al., p. 192.

j   Ferenc Sárffy, "Sárffy Ferenc győri várparancsnok jelentése II. Lajos holtteste megtalálásáról Brodarics István kancellárnak és szerémi püspöknek. Győr, 1526. október 19.," [Ferenc Sárffy, the castle commander of Győr Castle, reports the discovery of the body of Louis II to István Brodarics, Chancellor and Bishop of Szerém. Győr, 19 October 1526] in "Nekünk mégis Mohács kell…", eds. Farkas et al., p. 196.

k   János Szapolyai, "Szapolyai János levele Krzysztof Szydłowiecki lengyel kancellárhoz. Székesfehérvár, 1526. november 11.," [Letter of János Szapolyai to the Polish Chancellor Krzysztof Szydłowiecki. Székesfehérvár, 11 November 1526] in "Nekünk mégis Mohács kell…", eds. Farkas et al., p. 199.

TABLE 10.1   The most reliable (earliest) sources on the king's death (cont.)

Year/author	Reference to the Danube, the great river	Reference to the Csele, a stream	Swamp/pond/ overflow	Pit, muddy water
November 1526 Letter from a Czech nobleman[l]	"branch of the Danube"			
End of 1526 Cuspinianus[m]	"the overflow of the Danube"		"jumped into a pond created by the overflow of the Danube"	
1528 Brodarics[n]	"at this place, the water was higher than usual because of the flooding Danube"	"below a village named Csele"		"in the crevice of a steep bank"
First half of the 16th century[o] Unknown author	"in a river which in those days swelled to a wonderful extent because of the Danube" "… river, or a small branch of the Danube""			"in the muddy, silty waters of small branch of the Danube"
1530 Miklós Oláh[p]			"into a swamp on this side of Mohács"	

l   "Egy cseh úr levele a Santa Clara kolostor főnöknőjéhez, 1526. november," [Letter from a Czech nobleman to the Mother Superior of the Santa Clara Convent, November 1526] in Örök Mohács, eds. B. Szabó et al., p. 210.

m   Johannes Cuspinianus, "Johannes Cuspinianus buzdító beszéde a Szent Római Birodalom fejedelmeihez és előkelőihez, 1526 vége," [Exhortation by Johannes Cuspinianus to the princes and nobles of the Holy Roman Empire, end of 1526] in Örök Mohács, eds. B. Szabó et al., p. 276.

n   István Brodarics, Igaz leírás a magyaroknak a törökkel Mohácsnál vívott csatájáról. [A True Account of the Battle of Mohács between the Hungarians and the Turks] (Budapest: Magvető Könyvkiadó, 1983), p. 53.

o   "Ismeretlen szerző beszámolója a csatáról. 16. század első fele," [An unknown author's account of the battle. First half of the 16th century] in "Nekünk mégis Mohács kell…", eds. Farkas et al., p. 204.

p   Oláh, "Oláh Miklós levele," [Letter from Miklós Oláh] in "Nekünk mégis Mohács kell…", eds. Farkas et al., p. 158.

The question may arise: where did Brodarics get his information and what makes us think that his claims are substantiated? Unlike other events he described, in this case the chancellor was not an eyewitness but merely conveyed second-hand information.[13]

What authentic sources were available on the circumstances of the ruler's death? Only Chamberlain Ulrich Czettricz (Zetritz), who fled with the king, could have been certain about the king's death.[14] He reported the events to the queen, who was travelling westwards along the Danube, on 31 August 1526 in Neszmély. The only people who knew for sure about the death and its circumstances were the narrow circle of the court, the members of which obtained authentic information from Czettricz and later from Ferenc Sárffy, who was the person to investigate the location of the body and to verify the chamberlain's claims.[15]

There are limits to the interpretation of what happened, as neither Sárffy, nor Czettricz had all the information. In addition, Czettricz position is known only from interpretations. Their experiences of the place of death, reflected in later accounts, relate to two periods of a landscape in transition. Taking all this into account, it is necessary to carry out an analysis of the sources.

We believe that all the available authentic information on the king's death can be linked to three distinct time periods:

1. The circumstances of the king's death were first reported by Czettricz on the evening of 29 August 1526. He was the only eyewitness. We can accept his claims, but his account did not directly derive from him, but, as mentioned above, only through the interpretations of others. However, the Sárffy investigation[16] confirmed that what he said was true. The data that cannot be verified as coming from Czettricz and are very different from the reports of the narrow court elite, which rely on the Chamberlain's communication, must be treated with caution.

---

13   As chancellor, Brodarics is the addressee of the letter from Sárffy reporting the discovery of the body. As an insider, he seems certain to have heard the story of the death from Czettricz himself.
14   The Chamberlain was of Silesian Czech-German descent, so it would be more appropriate to use the name Zetritz than Czettricz, which had previously been adopted in Hungary. We thank Tibor Neumann for drawing our attention to this anomaly of transcription of the name.
15   The dozens of accompanying soldiers of the October 1526 expedition are also a possible source of information, but there is no trace of their influence on the contemporary documentation of the death.
16   Sárffy, "Sárffy Ferenc győri várparancsnok jelentése," [Report by Ferenc Sárffy, the castle commander of Győr] in *"Nekünk mégis Mohács kell..."*, eds. Farkas et al., pp. 195–198.

2. The first burial of a corpse is the second timeline. This most likely happened sometime in September. At the moment, we know the least about this. To be more precise, the funeral is one of the few certain facts we can learn from Sárffy's account. What seems certain is that the king was buried by locals near the place of death, and it is also certain that the sultan searched for the king, but his men could not find him. The detailed circumstances of the funeral are not known.
3. The third timeline, which falls between 15 and 19 October, is the time of finding the burial site and the discovery of the body. Ferenc Sárffy, the castle captain of Győr, set out with 12 soldiers and Czettricz to verify the chamberlain's credibility. Their aim was to find the monarch if possible and then take his body to the official burial site. This is the most authentic information, as Sárffy's report to Chancellor Brodarics about the expedition has survived.

3   The First Timeline: the Night of 29 August 1526

The group of sources that bear the environmental imprint of the end of August emphasizes the role of the Danube. Czettricz tells the court about what happened to him, and then apparently recounts his experiences many times to the public in September and early October 1526.

On 5 September, papal ambassador Burgio wrote his impressions of his report to Rome:

> His Majesty is said to have left the battlefield unharmed after a valiant fight, but it is not known where he headed to. That was the rumour here, which lasted for three days. But then came Ulrik Czettritz, the king's chamberlain and most trusted man, and told me that His Majesty had escaped from the battle with him and István Aczél (my friend who was in Rome in the Holy Year and had also spoken to His Holiness), and had reached a small branch of the Danube in flight [*in uno certo piccolo ramo del Dannubbio*], but when they were about to cross, the king's horse stumbled and reared up in the water, and His Majesty, whose armour was heavy and who was tired, fell and drowned in the stream. When István Aczél saw that His Majesty was in danger, he jumped after him, but he too drowned. Some say that the king went further than the stream into which the chamberlain says he drowned, but the former explanation is

more plausible, for a week has passed since the day of the battle, and still no news of His Majesty has been heard.[17]

While crossing a watercourse, which the chamberlain identifies as a small branch of the Danube, the king drowned in a riding accident. In the moments before the drowning, the horse reared up and threw the king off. This circumstance suggests that the horse was no longer swimming, but wading in the water. Aczél tried to help, but he too drowned. The watercourse was not the main branch of the Danube, but only a small secondary arm. This, as described, can only be the smaller branch of the Danube on the Transdanubian side, given the location of the battlefield.

A Czech nobleman who took part in the battle but managed to escape also reported the incident: "But the real king was also heading for some water, I hear, a branch of the Danube. The water was very flooded, and when he tried to jump over it with his horse, he fell and drowned. The poor Christian king was never to see this world again. This was told by his warden, who jumped into the water before the king, swam across and waited for him, but in vain. God have mercy on him!"[18] The letter is dated November 1526, but since it refers to Czettricz and does not mention that the body of the monarch was found, we can conclude that the information is from before 19 October. The accident happened to the king not on the main branch of the Danube, but on a secondary arm. This letter also confirms that the chamberlain's reports referred to the western branch of the Danube as the location of the accident. Czettricz also told the Czech nobleman that he had swum across this flooded watercourse (the "secondary arm") before the king, but the ruler had failed to do so. Swimming a horse implies a deeper river, not a stream. The chamberlain successfully crossed the Danube branch in question. The sources make it clear that the group was being chased: "The Turks chased the king and pursued him until he reached a branch of the Danube."[19] In a later text from 1559, we read that "Ulrich Czettrich, when he could no longer see his master and could

---

17   Burgio, "Antonio Giovanni da Burgio pápai követ levele Jacopo Sadoleto pápai titkárnak," [Letter from papal ambassador Antonio Giovanni da Burgio to papal secretary Jacopo Sadoleto] in *Örök Mohács*, eds. B. Szabó et al., p. 131.
18   "Egy cseh úr levele," [Letter from a Czech nobleman] in *Örök Mohács*, eds. B. Szabó et al., p. 210.
19   Švihovský z Rýzmberka, "Břetislav Švihovský z Rýzmberka az egyik bajor herceghez," [Břetislav Švihovský z Rýzmberka to a Bavarian prince] in *Örök Mohács*, eds. B. Szabó et al., p. 154.

not help him, made efforts to save his life because of the approaching Turks."[20] These accounts support the hypothesis that those in flight were being harassed by Ottoman raiders. Since the king and his men were fleeing on horseback, the pursuers were obviously also mounted. This seems to suggest that the immediate cause of the attempted crossing was that they were being chased by the raiding cavalry.

In his letter to the Polish king dated 29 September 1526, Treasurer Elek Thurzó, in agreement with the Czech source above, linked the place of death of Louis II to the Danube flood. According to this, the king drowned in the overflow of the Danube: "Hitherto we had hoped for better news, but alas! it is now certain that His Majesty, having fought the enemy with steadfast valour, after our regiment had faltered and our men had fled, and having received a severe wound in the battle, and having tried to escape from the enemy's hands, he slipped with his horse into a deep overflow of the Danube, and lost his life."[21]

The content of the communication is essentially the same as Czettricz's information provided elsewhere. All it says is that the king died at the Danube, nuancing the earlier account by saying that it happened not in the riverbed but in its deep overflow. The source also refers to the circumstance that the horse was injured.

In the days immediately following the battle, Johann Fugger, a merchant living in Venice, received news of the defeat of the Hungarian army from Buda on 31 August 1526, and then from Vienna on 5 September 1526, that the king had also died. "He has also received letters from Vienna, dated the 5th of the current month, which say the same, and that the king drowned in a pond, nothing more."[22] Accordingly, there was also a report of the king's death in Vienna on 5 September, which said that the king had drowned in a pond. In contrast to the earlier sources, we do not read any reference to Czettricz, and in the case of Fugger (in contrast to Thurzó) we cannot assume a direct encounter with the chamberlain. The information is very early, but the news of the king's death came by a circuitous route from Vienna to Venice. The value of these sources cannot be compared with other sources in this category, the reporters of which may have been personally informed of the circumstances of the death by the

---

20 "Habsburg-ház dicsőségtükre," [Ehrenspiegel des Hauses Österreich] in *Örök Mohács*, eds. B. Szabó et al., p. 399.
21 Thurzó, "Thurzó Elek tárnokmester levele," [Letter from Treasurer Elek Thurzó] in *"Nekünk mégis Mohács kell...,"* eds. Farkas et al., p. 190.
22 "Johann Fugger értesülései," [Information from Johann Fugger] in *Örök Mohács*, eds. B. Szabó et al., p. 125.

sole survivor. On the other hand, Fugger's account does not contradict this, and perhaps refers to the overflow that Thurzó also describes.

In a letter of 18 September 1526, written in Linz, Ferdinand of Habsburg wrote of the death of Louis II: "[the king] became lost in a marshy place and there he drowned."[23] This communication can be classified as insider information, although he was far from the source of the information and did not meet Czettricz. Contact with Vienna via the Danube was obvious, and the period between 31 August and 18 September must have provided ample opportunity for Ferdinand to obtain credible information on a matter that concerned him personally. Two other sources[24] date from almost the same period, and also give the marsh as the place of the king's death.

Sources rule out the possibility that the accident occurred in the main branch of the Danube (Old Danube). In contrast, when the above sources refer to the Danube, they are referring to a secondary arm/branch whose flooded bed formed an overflow, a swamp. Based on Brodarics's account, we know that a branch ran along the western side of Mohács Island: "The Danube splits into two channels just above Báta: the larger channel devides the Trans-Hungarian region into flat fields, the smaller one washes the banks of Bátaszék and Mohács, and both arms merge below Mohács, forming an island."[25] If the king and his retinue crossed the smaller, western branch of the Danube, which was closest to the battlefield, the overflow must have been on the eastern side of the branch, facing the island, otherwise Czettricz would not have been able to cross it successfully.

What were the environmental factors behind the experience of 29 August as recorded in the sources? By all accounts, the Danube was flooding at the time, so the riverbed and the bank were not visible. The sedimentation in the riverbed was determined by the river's sediment entrainment and transport capacity, with human interventions playing a negligible role at that time. We know that it was during this period, around the turn of the 15th and 16th centuries, that the most significant floods of all time occurred on the river.[26] When it

---

23   Ferdinánd, "Ferdinánd osztrák főherceg levele," [Letter from Archduke Ferdinand of Austria] in *"Nekünk mégis Mohács kell...,"* eds. Farkas et al., p. 184.
24   Fazio di Savoia, "Fazio di Savoia jelentése," [The report of Fazio di Savoia] in *"Nekünk mégis Mohács kell...,"* eds. Farkas et al., p. 184; "Hírszerzői jelentés," [Intelligence report] in *"Nekünk mégis Mohács kell...,"* eds. Farkas et al., p. 186.
25   Brodarics, *Igaz leírás*, [A True Account] p. 32.
26   Andrea Kiss and József Laszlovszky, "14th–16th Century Danube Floods and Long-Term Water-Level Changes in Archaeological and Sedimentary Evidence in the Western and Central Carpathian Basin. An Overview with Documentary Comparison," *Journal of Environmental Geography* 6 (2013), no. 3–4, pp. 1–11.

flooded, the water covered the sandy banks and the berms, and spilled out onto the floodplain. According to the accounts, it started to rain and it was getting dark at the end of the battle, so visibility began to deteriorate. On the Danube, there was not much to indicate that the river was fragmented between the two banks.

Based on the above, Czettricz was able to report that the refugees swam their horses in the flooded river (according to the interpretation of the Czech source), and then waded in the water (according to Burgio), while the accident itself happened not in the riverbed, but in a flooded area (in an overflow reported by Thurzó, in a pond by Fugger, and in a swamp by Ferdinand I, Fazio di Savoia and the unknown informant), where the horse reared up and threw off the king, who drowned there. By contrast, Czettricz successfully emerged from the river.

4 The Second Timeline: the First Burial of the King

Sárffy reports that the king's body was found buried in a shallow grave in mid-October. The bodies of Louis II, his horse and István Aczél were submerged in the water, which was high due to the flooding. The flood was slowly receding, the water level was falling steadily, and the bodies of those lost in the river were gradually surfacing. We do not know exactly at what rate the water receded, but it could have taken days or even a week.

The victorious Ottomans could certainly not have been the people who buried the bodies, because, although the sultan searched for the king, his men never found him. As valuables were later found in the neighbourhood, this suggests that Ottoman raiders did not looted the area. However, some of the local Christian people may have fled to the island's marshes during the battle. Among these, refugees, we can guess there were serfs who buried the monarch and then delivered his signet ring the following year.[27]

The body of the king was found and buried by unidentified persons. There is no written source on this, or none has been identified to this date. Yet this may have been the background to the local tradition of the king drowning in the Danube. It is also possible that the mention of the "notch" in the *Memoria*

---

[27] "…to the serfs who had taken the late King Louis's clothing from the field of Mohács – in our presence, they faithfully delivered it to Her Majesty the Queen, which Her Majesty had cut up in the presence of the councillors." István Báthori, "Báthori István nádor oklevele II. Lajos pecsétgyűrűjéről. Pozsony, 1527. június 24.," [Document of István Báthori, Prince of Hungary, on the signet ring of Louis II. Pozsony, 24 June 1527] in *"Nekünk mégis Mohács kell…,"* eds. Farkas et al., p. 204.

rerum may have its origins here.²⁸ In any case, it gives food for thought that, contrary to the humanists' reference to the Csele Stream, folk tradition originally maintained that the place of the king's death was the Danube.

Nagyváty was originally a settlement of small noblemen in the western part of Baranya County, where descendants of Szekler archers lived. Brodarics reports that János Szerecsen brought more than 2000 archers from the Drava River to the Battle of Mohács. These may have included the ancestors of the Nagyváty people. Sándor Solymossy published the following story in 1926:

> My grandfather told me that the whole of Nagyváty was there at the Battle of Mohács. His great-great-grandfather was the king's groom. Then, when the battle was over, the king looks back: 'Water before me, fire after me; my sweet servant, which way shall we run?' They ran on. He looks back again, he asks again: 'water before me, fire after me; my sweet servant, where shall we go?' Again, they just kept running. But for the third time, he could not ask any questions, because the Turks had caught up with him. Then the king turned his horse and headed straight for the Danube. Where he drowned.²⁹

The fire in this case represents the pursuers, the water represents the bodies of water that hinder the refugees, and finally the Danube is the place where the king dies.

The following folk song was collected in the Ormánság region, in which both the Csele Stream and the Danube appear as the place of the king's death in two consecutive verses:

> Lajos király leesett a lováról,
> Beléesett Csele-patak árkába.
> Csele-patak, Csele-patak sűrű szederindája,
> Ott veszett el a magyarok királya.
>
> Szállj le, madár, a Duna fenekére,
> Két szárnyaddal vágd kétfelé a vizet!
> Két szárnyaddal, két szárnyaddal vágd kétfelé a vizet:
> Hozd fel onnan Lajos királyt, ha lehet.

---

28   "Memoria rerum. 16. század közepe (?)," [Memoria rerum. Mid-16th century (?)] In: *"Nekünk mégis Mohács kell...,"* eds. Farkas et al., p. 214.

29   Sándor Solymossy, "Mohács emléke a néphagyományban," [The memory of Mohács in folk tradition] in *Mohácsi emlékkönyv 1526*, ed. Imre Lukinich (Budapest: Királyi Magyar Egyetemi Nyomda, 1926), p. 347.

> King Louis fell from his horse,
> Tumbling into the ditch of the Csele Stream.
> The thick bramble bushes of the Csele Stream,
> Were where the King of the Hungarians was lost.
>
> Land bird, on the bed of the Danube,
> Cut the water in two with your two wings!
> With your two wings, two wings, cut the water in two:
> Bring up King Louis from there, if you can.[30]

It seems that the two traditions concerning the place of death (the folk one, which is the Danube, and the humanist one, which is the Csele Stream, and which is spread through education) have somehow come together in this song.

5 The Third Timeline: Finding the Body of the King

Ferenc Sárffy, the castle captain of Győr, and Ulrich Czettricz, accompanied by a dozen of cavalrymen, left Győr on 11 October 1526 to verify the chamberlain's claims and find the king's body. More than six weeks had passed since the day of the battle, and the environment had changed significantly: the flood had receded completely.

The team found the body of the monarch on 18 October, according to a report by Andrea Partiba.[31] However, we doubt the accuracy of the date, as Sárffy's report was dated 19 October, in Győr. Taking into account the evidence that the news of the defeat reached Buda from Mohács in a day and a half at the end of August,[32] it seems unlikely that the reconnaissance team could have taken the king's body to Székesfehérvár in a day, before Sárffy travelled to Győr, where he wrote the report. It is more likely that the body was found somewhat earlier, on 17 October or, more likely, 16 October.

---

30   Folk song from Ormánság: https://www.youtube.com/watch?v=Gx727d6dRBs&ab_channel=Dailyretro (Download date: 9 January 2023) [Literal translation in English].
31   Andrea Partiba, "Andrea Partiba jelentése egy hadnagyhoz. Bécs, 1526. november 2.," [Andrea Partiba's report to a lieutenant. Vienna, 2 November 1526] in *"Nekünk mégis Mohács kell…,"* eds. Farkas et al., p. 199.
32   The news of the defeat (but not yet the death of the king) was received at midnight on 30 August by the papal nuncio Burgio at the court in Buda, less than a day after the battle was over. Burgio, "Antonio Giovanni da Burgio pápai követ levele Jacopo Sadoleto pápai titkárnak," [Letter from papal ambassador Antonio Giovanni da Burgio to papal secretary Jacopo Sadoleto] in *Örök Mohács*, eds. B. Szabó et al., p. 131.

Sárffy's letter, dated 19 October in Győr, reads:

> Because when we were approaching that place, and we hadn't even got there yet, Czettrich was already pointing to the place with his finger. We rushed over and saw the carcass of a horse in the marsh, and Czettrich, thinking that the body of His Majesty was there, and not caring for the marsh, jumped into the mud, and under it, he and his companions searched for the king's corpse. But he did not find it, he only found the king's weapons here.[33]

The place of the king's death is referred to as a stagnant body of water, or more precisely a marsh, and mud also figures prominently in the description. The place of death was clearly identifiable, as they had not even got there yet, when the chamberlain recognised it from a distance and pointed to it. It was only when they got very close that they saw the horse's body in the marsh. The chamberlain jumped into the mud, thinking at once that the king must have been under the horse.

János Szapolyai's letter was dated 11 November and reported on the place of the king's death as follows:

> And having arrived on the appointed day in our town, Székesfehérvár, where the body of the late, most magnificent Lord Louis, our predecessor of happy memory, King of Hungary and Bohemia, etc., lay, recently dug out of the mud – the now dried-up whirlpool into which he had carelessly fallen – and placed with great reverence in the greater church, we thought it befitting that we should first of all pay the last honours to the most distinguished prince. We therefore endeavoured to bury the earthly remains of the reigning King Louis, since his corpse, which had long been decomposing, could no longer be kept above the earth.[34]

The body was recovered "from the mud – from the now dried-up whirlpool [Ewrem]." The term "whirlpool" may have been used to refer to the mud that may have pulled the king down. The only circumstance highlighted in the letter was the presence of mud at the scene of the death.

---

33 Sárffy, "Sárffy Ferenc győri várparancsnok jelentése," [Report by Ferenc Sárffy, the castle commander of Győr] in *"Nekünk mégis Mohács kell...",* eds. Farkas et al., p. 196.

34 Szapolyai, "Szapolyai János levele," [Letter from János Szapolyai] in *"Nekünk mégis Mohács kell...",* eds. Farkas et al., p. 199.

Cuspinianus also mentions the circumstances of the king's death in his description at the end of 1526: "The disbanded army took the king along, ill-guarded by themselves, who, against everyone's expectations, jumped into a pond created by the overflow of the Danube."[35] Cuspinianus was therefore informed that the place of death was a pond, i.e. some kind of stagnant water created by the overflow of the Danube. This description fits well with the claims of Thurzó and Fugger, and places the site of the accident next to the Danube.

In the letter sent by Miklós Oláh to Pope Clement VII on 15 February 1530, we read the following: "Our king, as he tried to flee from the enemy, was driven by some misfortune into a swamp on this side of Mohács,[36] from which he could not get out, for his horse, as soon as he jerked the reins, collapsed, and there he perished miserably, with no one to help him."[37] The location is therefore a marsh north of Mohács, and it suggests that the horse played a crucial role in the accident.

This is how an apparently well-informed, unknown author described the situation in the first half of the 16th century, in an undated text: "And the king was immersed in a river, which in those days *swelled to a wonderful extent because of the Danube*. His body lay for many days in the muddy, silty water of that river, or a small branch of the Danube."[38] According to the author, the monarch was submerged in a river that had flooded to a great extent. He refers to the river in question as a branch of the Danube, which was flooding heavily at the time of the death. Taking into account that the flooding entered the main channel from the north – the tide reached the western branch around Báta – the "Danube" in this case refers to the main branch, which flowed along the eastern side of the Island of Mohács. The muddy, silty water of the small Danube branch, on the other hand, refers to the western branch. There is a direct reference in this text to the king's body lying in the muddy, silty water for days. It took a few days for the river to recede before the bodies were uncovered, but when the river did recede, the presence of mud around the bodies became obvious.

Just like the unknown author, Brodarics, too, contemplated and depicted the environment in its change. As the addressee of the letter of Sárffy, he was

---

35 Cuspinianus, "Johannes Cuspinianus buzdító beszéde," [Exhortation by Johannes Cuspinianus] in *Örök Mohács*, eds. B. Szabó et al., p. 276.

36 The term "on this side of" here is interpreted to mean above Mohács, i.e. northwards, towards Buda.

37 Oláh, "Oláh Miklós levele," [Letter from Miklós Oláh] in *Örök Mohács*, eds. B. Szabó et al., p. 348.

38 "qui illis diebus ex Danubio mirabiliter inundauerat, rex submergitur, cuius cadauer multis diebus in aqua lutulenta et limosa illius fluuii vel ramusculi Danubii jacuit…" "Ismeretlen szerző beszámolója a csatáról," [An unknown author's account of the battle] in *"Nekünk mégis Mohács kell…"*, eds. Farkas et al., p. 204.

aware of the developments, which he did not record until 1528. Below the Csele Stream, in a *"hiatus"* where the Danube's flooding caused the water to rise high: this is a narrower description of the place. This shows that when the Danube flooded, this *hiatus* was filled with water, and when the flood receded, it was no longer covered by water. It was then that the site was discovered to be a crevice or a fissure (*hiatus*). Here too, there is a sense of change in the text: both the original situation described by Czettricz and the October situation are represented, i.e. the scene is presented as having undergone a change.

The horse played a prominent role in the accident. The descriptions are based on Czettricz's account of the horse losing its balance while wading through the water, and the king losing control of the animal. The sources suggest that the horse was injured and that this may have contributed to the tragedy.[39] Louis II fell off his horse and died. That is why the chamberlain, returning with Sárffy to the place of death, immediately starts searching for the king's body in the mud under the horse.

This latter description is the most direct illustration of the fact that the water level at the place of the king's death has lowered and mud is prominent in the immediate surroundings. As the water receded, not only were the bodies found, but the king's weapons were also discovered. We believe that the valuable weapons would have been found earlier if they had been easy to see. The horse lying in the mud at the place of death, as well as several bodies found nearby (among those named: Louis II, István Aczél, András Trepka and Péter Korlátkői)[40] suggest that the incident did not take place in the riverbed but on the floodplain. If this had happened in the riverbed, the carcasses would have been washed away in the current. However, the high water levels hid them from prying eyes until the water level dropped.[41]

Some of the accounts written after 19 October 1526 describe the broader surroundings of the location of the king's death: the incident took place in a marshy area, and the specific location is described as a pond (standing water). Others describe the specific and narrow place where the body was found: the king drowned in the mud and was found in and lifted out of a depression. Compared to the descriptions from Czettricz on 29 August, the situation in mid-October, the time of the discovery of the royal body, seems to be significantly different.

---

39   Thurzó, "Thurzó Elek tárnokmester levele," [Letter from Treasurer Elek Thurzó] in *"Nekünk mégis Mohács kell...,"* eds. Farkas et al., p. 190.

40   Miklós Isthvánffy, "A magyarok történetéből. 1622 (részlet) [From the History of the Hungarians. 1622 (Excerpt)] in *Örök Mohács*, eds. B. Szabó et al., p. 460.

41   Jenő Gyalókay, A mohácsi csata. 1526. augusztus 29. [The Battle of Mohács. 29 August 1526] (Budapest: Királyi Magyar Egyetemi Nyomda, 1926) p. 59.

While the place of drowning was earlier described more broadly as a secondary arm or small branch of the Danube, and more narrowly as a Danube overflow, by mid-October the key words had increased: in addition to the river, the small branch of the Danube and the Danube otflow, the image of the swamp and the role of the silt and the depression became more pronounced. The mention of silt and depression was not at all common in the first period.

The question is: what was the reason for the change in landscape descriptions? Is there an irreconcilable contradiction, or is the difference between the descriptions of the two periods explained by the changes in environmental conditions over six weeks?

The first part of the answer to this question is contained in the letter from Ferenc Sárffy to Brodarics, when he confirms the chamberlain's earlier claims: "Let your Reverend Father be assured that all that Czettrich said at the time about the king's death was the truth, nothing but the truth."[42] How can we summarise Czettricz's main claims?

The king:
– died;
– there was an accident, not a murder;
– the incident occurred while crossing a small branch of the Danube, otherwise known as a secondary arm;
– drowned not in the streambed (running water), but in its overflow (standing water).

The above quotation suggests that evidence was sought and found, i.e. the chamberlain's claims were consistent with Sárffy's observations and experiences. The report dated 19 October thus referred back to and confirmed the previous situation.

It was therefore not necessary for Sárffy to describe the river crossing, since this fact was obvious; he was only referring back to the fact that the chamberlain was telling the truth. The other half of the answer, how the details of events fit together, can be given by reconstructing some key elements of the environment.

6   Interpreting the Elements of the Environment in the Sources

What are the general features of the environment around the Csele Stream that we can reasonably assume were still present in 1526?

---

42   Sárffy, "Sárffy Ferenc győri várparancsnok jelentése," [Report by Ferenc Sárffy, the castle commander of Győr] in *"Nekünk mégis Mohács kell…"*, eds. Farkas et al., p. 196.

The formation of the Mohács Plain and the present water system date back to the geological past. Towards the end of the Pleistocene (several hundred thousand years ago), the Danube completely filled the present-day areas between the Danube and the Tisza River, and drifted further westwards from the alluvial fan towards the Kalocsa-Baja-Zombor depression, until it finally took a north-south course similar to its present-day alignment. At the end of the last glaciation phase – around 10–15 thousand years ago – the sandy, gravelly alluvium which underlies the Holocene layers was deposited in the area.[43] In the Early Holocene, along the Lánycsók-Bár-Báta fault line running at the western edge of the Mohács Plain, the area subsided and the main riverbed suddenly took a northeast-southwest direction, closely following the feet of the hills bordering the plain. The former north-south course of the Danube is now followed only by the winding bed of the Baracska branch of the Danube, which carries smaller volumes of water. The northeast-southwest flow right at Mohács – where the river meets the Mohács terrace – takes a sudden 90° bend to the northwest-southeast to meet the Baracska Danube again further south. This latter change of direction was probably caused by the repeated subsidence of the southern part of the island, also in the Early Holocene. The island formed between the two river branchs and its area continued to subside in relation to the right bank terrace during the Early Holocene, thus becoming a permanent floodplain of the Danube.

The tectonic movement happened obviously as described above, so the elevations of the two banks of the Western Danube branch (west and east) were the same as they are today. The differences are negligible, and the 90° bend in the river was also present. This is why the river's thalweg (line of maximum flow velocity) was near the west bank, just as it is today. A map from the early 19th century (Figure 10.1/B) clearly shows how shallow the bed is in the west before the mouth of the Csele Stream and how shallow it is in the east, towards the island. The west bank of the Danube branch in Mohács appears to be higher, while the east bank is lower, for the tectonic reasons described above. The river could easily overflow when a surge came over this area, which damaged but did not flood the west bank. Channel width was less than half of what it is today, before the river was widened at the beginning of the 19th century, and it has been steadily widening ever since. In 1526, however, it was much narrower than it was even in the early 19th century.

---

43   Márton Pécsi, *A magyarországi Duna-völgy kialakulása és felszínalaktana* [The formation and subsurface structure of the Danube Valley in Hungary] (Budapest: Akadémiai Kiadó, 1959); Sándor Marosi and Jenő Szilárd eds., *A dunai Alföld* [The Danube Plain.] (Magyarország tájföldrajza) 1 (Budapest: Akadémiai Kiadó, 1967).

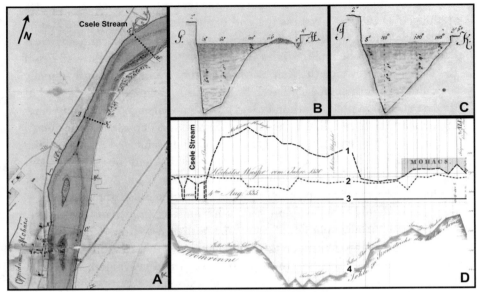

FIGURE 10.1   Danube section below the mouth of the Csele Stream, cross-sections of the riverbed (1808)(a) and longitudinal sections of the banks (1830–1840)(b). Edited by Péter Gyenizse. Legend: A = 1808 map; B = cross-section G–H; C = cross-section J–K; D = longitudinal section of the right (1) and left (2) bank edges and the bed (4) between Csele Stream and Mohács, water level on 4 August 1835 (3).
SOURCE: (A) HUNGARIAN NATIONAL ARCHIVES (= MNL OL) L S 12 DIV. XIII. NO. 370; (B) MNL OL S 80 DUNA NO. 57/1–29.

The Szekcső or Mohács branch of the Danube was known as the Little Danube.[44] By comparison, the former main branch used for navigation, the Baracska Danube on the eastern side of the island, is now only 30 metres wide. However, it may have been several hundred metres wide in the 16th century. The width of the Little Danube was small compared to today, and although by the end of the 18th century, the western branch was certainly *the* wider for tectonic and morphological reasons, even a description from 1733 tells that "...

---

44   The Mohács branch of the Danube was known as the Little Danube in the 14th century, among other things, just as it was in the 16th century or the first half of the 18th century. See National Archives of the Hungarian National Archives (=MNL OL) Diplomatic Archives (=DL), 87074. (Esterházy hg. cs. lt. rep. 96.1.1); György Szerémi, "Levél Magyarország romlásáról. 1545 körül," [Letter on the deterioration of Hungary. Around 1545] in *"Nekünk mégis Mohács kell…"*, eds. Farkas et al. pp. 209–212.; Ádám Fricsy, "A pécsi klérus birtokainak telepítésügyi összeírása 1733-ban," [Settlement census of the estates of the clergy of Pécs in 1733] in *Baranyai helytörténetírás 1978*, ed. László Szita (Pécs: Baranya Megyei Levéltár, 1979), pp. 151–204.

the downstream vessels rarely come here, but would rather go to the other side of the Island of Mohács, on the Great Danube."[45]

By the time of the Sárffy expedition in mid-October 1526, the flood on the Little Danube had certainly receded, as more than six weeks had passed since the battle. There was little water in the river, and the environmental features that separated the riverbed from the floodplain (berms, bars, flooded half-basins, basins including silt-filled depressions, and the fragmentation of the bank) became visible. The reports interpreting the situation at the end of August described crossing the narrow Danube branch, so the refugees crossed the Danube to the east, with respect to the location of the battle.

On the shallower east bank and beyond, the ponds in the floodplain were still discernible in some places in October, while the muddy-bottomed overflows may have disappeared completely. Ponds of various size, separated from each other, may have appeared as the water level was dropping.

On the western side of the Mohács branch, in the vicinity of the Csele, a 4–6 m high decaying loess wall is visible, with the river thalweg right next to it, where the bed is also the deepest. Mud pits could not have formed on this bank, and therefore could not have emerged from under the receding water. Thus, we can safely exclude this bank from the possible places of the tragedy. On the other hand, the mention of the marsh, the overflow, the lake and the mud in the sources regarding the discovery of the king's body strongly suggest the eastern bank of the Danube branch at Mohács.

The contemporary accounts of 1526, which seem reliable, give a fairly consistent picture of the place where the king's body was found. Descriptions such as "… slipped into a deep overflow of the Danube…,"[46] "… the water was higher than usual at the time due to the Danube flooding…,"[47] "… we saw the carcass

---

45   Fricsy, "A pécsi klérus birtokainak," [of the clergy of Pécs] in *Baranyai helytörténetírás 1978*, ed. Szita, p. 169. It has been suggested that the study of Lake Riha on Mohács Island might help us clarify the question of how large the Little Danube was in the 16th century, since the Riha was an ox-bow bend in the Mohács branch of the Danube. See https://dunaiszigetek.blogspot.com/2020/01/tullepni-csele-patakon.html. Some of our sources say that at that time, Lake Riha was still connected to the western branch, and it was even possible to sail up there. The problem is that Lake Riha has changed a lot since then, but it is true that its dimensions (50–150 metres in width) are an order of magnitude smaller than the present Mohács branch. Incidentally, a description of the Pécs church estates in 1733 stated that Lake Riha was only 25 acres, or slightly less than 50 metres wide. The issue will need to be examined over a longer period. However, it is clear from these fragmentary data that the Mohács branch of the Danube was much narrower and shallower, and less suitable for navigation, than it is today.

46   Thurzó, "Thurzó Elek tárnokmester levele," [Letter from Treasurer Elek Thurzó] in *"Nekünk mégis Mohács kell…"*, eds. Farkas et al., p. 190.

47   Brodarics, *Igaz leírás*, [A True Account] p. 53.

of a horse in the marsh..."[48] do not refer directly to the bed of a small branch of the Danube, but to a flooded area directly connected to the channel. What was this place and how did it come about?

The area was criss-crossed with notches and banks. A review of the 18th–19th-century maps reveals, how the western bank was destroyed decade by decade and how this area could not have been part of the floodplain – facts which support our assumption. On the opposite, eastern side of the river, the banks are much lower and overbank flow is more common.

If we look at the section downstream the confluence of the Csele Stream in a west-east cross-section, we find that the Danube flows rapidly in the west, where its sediment transport capacity is relatively high. On the west bank, we see sand bars here today, but no silt,[49] or only very small areas on the outer (landward) side of the bars. As one moves eastwards from the thalweg, the bed becomes shallower, sandbars appear, and as one approaches the bank, the presence of silt increases as flow velocity declines. In front of the east bank, thick layers of silt accumulated between the bars and the bankline.

Maps from the 19th and 20th centuries (Figure 10.2) show extensive bar formation. On the eastern side, opposite the right bank of the Csele, a wide sandbank[50] can be seen on early 19th century maps (Figure 10.2/B–C). This sandbank already existed in the 18th century, as did the 10–15 m wide water-filled area behind it (Figure 10.2/A). However, this sandbank, which was documented in the 18th and 19th centuries and still exists today, was located further east than the smaller 16th century bed, so, from these antecedents, we can infer the continued presence of the factors that underpinned the formation of sandbanks. How do these geographical circumstances compare with the events described? The river bank, formed by the high, decaying loess wall on the right, is very poorly suited for a person to get down to the river bank and to attempt to cross it (Figure 10.1/D). It may have been too high (4–6 metres), steep and friable. It was only possible to traverse by finding a suitable passage to the bank. There is just one suitable place in the area: south of the Csele, the high bank is cut by the southwest-northeast oriented dry bed of a former river valley. Presumably, this passage was also used for watering livestock.[51] It is believed that this

---

48 Sárffy, "Sárffy Ferenc győri várparancsnok jelentése," [Report by Ferenc Sárffy, the castle commander of Győr] in *"Nekünk mégis Mohács kell..."*, eds. Farkas et al., p. 196.
49 Silt is a sediment, the components of which are very light and are washed away by flowing water. The grain size of sand is between 2 mm and 0.063 mm, while the grain size of silt is between 0.063 and 0.002 mm. Kálmán Balogh ed., *Szedimentológia II*. (Budapest: Akadémiai Kiadó, 1991).
50 Belt sandbank or embankment: cross-layered sediment accumulating on the inner side of river bends in the form of parallel ridges in an arcuate arrangement.
51 Szurmay also raises the serious problem of water supply that the parties must have had in 1526. Sándor Szurmay, *A mohácsi hadjárat 1526-ban* [The Mohács military campaign

WHERE AND HOW DID KING LOUIS II DIE?

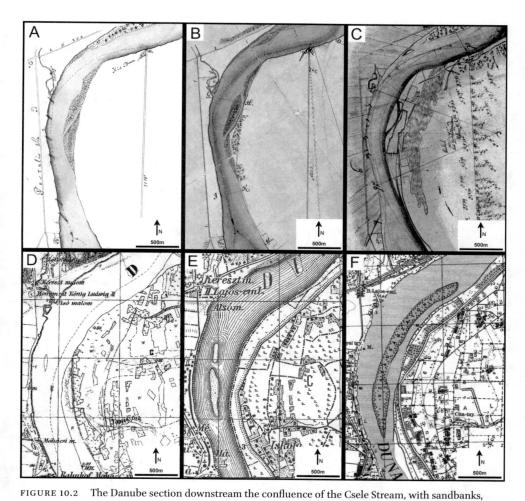

FIGURE 10.2   The Danube section downstream the confluence of the Csele Stream, with sandbanks, islands and a point bar along the eastern bank. The widening of the Danube riverbed and the removal of the western (right) bank (decay of the road and the Csele confluence) are visible. Edited by Péter Gyenizse. Legend: A = 1803; B = 1808; C = 1816; D = Military Survey III; E = 1941 Military Survey; F = 1951 Military Survey.
SOURCES: (A) MNL OL S 12 DIV. XIII. NO. 415; (B) MNL OL S 12 DIV. XIII. NO. 370; (C) MNL OL S 12 DIV. XIX. NO. 5; (D) MILITARY SURVEY III (1880); (E) 1941 MILITARY SURVEY OF HUNGARY.

in 1526] (Budapest: Ludovika Akadémia, 1901). Approaching Mohács from the north, the army had no easy access to drinking water: the streams were scarce and quickly polluted, and the Danube was the only suitable water source. The main problem is that the bank north of Mohács is, as mentioned, high and friable. There are only a few places where one can go down to the banks of the Danube to drink. These places must have been known to the officers. Of those who were with the king, Aczél (as well as Trepka) was one of those expected to know the passages to the river, as they had previously come down along the

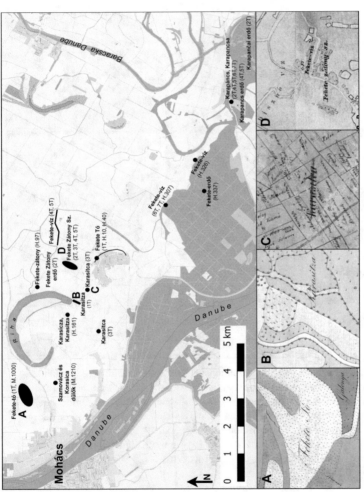

FIGURE 10.3 Places related to the name of water with the prefix Fekete or Kara in the vicinity of Mohács. Edited by Péter Gyenizse. Legend: H = Homorúd, and M = Mohács (e.g. the abbreviation H.10 stands for the 10th item at Homorúd in the book *Geographical Names of Baranya County*); Legend: 1T = Maps of the Danube survey (1827–1828); 2T = Military Survey II (1858) (1:28,800); 3T = Cadastral maps (1865); 4T = Military Survey III (1880) (1:25,000); 5T = Maps of the Kingdom of Hungary (1880–1881) (1:25,000); 6T = 1941 Military Survey (1:25,000); 7T = 1950–1951 Military Survey (1:25,000).
BACKGROUND SOURCE OF THE MAP: HTTPS://WWW.OPENSTREETMAP.ORG (DOWNLOAD DATE: 28 JANUARY 2019).

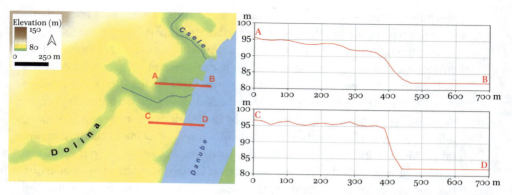

FIGURE 10.4 The dry bed of a former river valley called *Dolina*: passage to the Danube. Edited by Péter Gyenizse.
BACKGROUND SOURCE OF THE MAP: MILITARY SURVEY III (1872–1884).

passage offered the survivors the possibility to get down to the right bank of the Danube and cross it (Figure 10.4).

It seems that the king and his small retinue, with the pursuing Ottoman cavalry at their back, arrived here on the banks of the narrow Danube and fled eastwards across the river. Like other survivors, they sought refuge beyond the Danube. The accident occurred near the eastern banks of the smaller western Danube branch, in the area behind the sandbank(s), roughly opposite the confluence of the Csele, slightly to south, observing the current. At this location, there was a depression filled with water due to the flooding. This was located behind a point bar and filled in the meantime by the widening of the river.

The horse carrying the king might first have been able to swim across the smaller branch of the Danube below the confluence of the Csele, waded over the sandbank (bar) and then sank into a long, narrow, sloping depression between the bar and the bank. There, the horse must have been alarmed because it could not escape from the underwater mud and it must have reared up, burying its rider under him, who eventually drowned in the deep pit. The horse's carcass was eventually found in the mud where Czettricz had seen the king die. The high bank here may indicate that the horse could not emerge above the water, which could be due to several factors: slippery mud, the

---

Danube this way. The watering place near the Csele was easily recognisable due to the wide trail of trampled human and animal waste. It can be assumed that this passage, and the experience related to it, helped the refugees, and that it was this passage that helped Czettricz find his way back to the place of the king's death so easily and simply. Sárffy wrote that he had led those searching right to the scene of the accident.

steepness of the bank, or the fact that it was raining, which could have made even the part of the bank rising above the water slippery.

Two possibilities for the location of the king's death are suggested by environmental reconstruction and the sources. If we give credence to the 16th-century source, which suggests that the place of the king's death was a notch,[52] then he must have left the Danube bed and entered a naturally formed depression (overflow), which was used by the locals as a fishing pond (*piscina*) following human intervention (creation of a reservoir). One of the fundamental problems with these semi-natural formations was siltation, so they can be compared well with the descriptions above. However, as the area in question has been filled in the meantime, the locals no longer maintain notches, and since the Danube floods were restricted by embankments after the 19th century, there is no way to test this hypothesis.

The other possibility is that, at the point where Czettricz crossed to the other side, the depression in question (the overflow) was not dammed up. The area behind the point bar, with its width of around 10 metres, depth of 2–3 metres (Figure 10.1/B) and elongated slit shape, also matches the description of the king's place of death. If it was blocked to the north, as we can cite several examples from the last 250 years, then this body of water was also stagnant. The conditions for siltation were also present in this case, and as the water level dropped, bodies could also have emerged from this overflow.

However, the authentic sources on the king's death do not mention any fishing pond suggesting human intervention, but rather a marsh along the Danube or a standing water, lake or muddy depression without a marker. The only source referring to the notch comes from several decades after the event and from an unknown author,[53] so compared to our other documents, the claim is not particularly strong.

This makes it more likely that the king drowned in a narrow bed (crevice) in a muddy depression between the bank and the sandbank after crossing the narrow Danube at Mohács (Figure 10.3). By October, the water had receded from this area and the muddy depression had become visible. Since in the Middle Ages, the Csele estate had fishing ponds on the Danube, and several notches and lakes can be detected on 18th and 19th-century maps on the island opposite the Csele, we must assume that there were notches in the immediate vicinity of the place of death.

The allegation that the king fled eastwards across the smaller branch of the Danube is in line with Gáspár Heltai's later interpretation:

---

52   "Memoria rerum," in *"Nekünk mégis Mohács kell…",* eds. Farkas et al., p. 214.
53   Ibid.

The Turkish cavalry started to chase them, flank them, driving them into the overgrown mire of Krassó,[54] and many people perished in the mire. While running, the king caught up with Cetricz, and when they found the brook, Cetricz went before him and swam his horse through. The king followed him, and when he was about to ride out on the steep bank, the horse fell back with him, and the king was driven into the water and mud with his arms, and there the pious King Louis drowned.[55]

He also put the king's place of death near the Krassó[56] along with the deaths of other refugees (Figure 10.3)

Istvánffy mentions Brodarics's clues in his description: The incident happened above Mohács, below the village of Csele. This is how he reports it:

> ... between Mohács and the Csele, the Karasica, a swampy and muddy stream, flowing muddy with its uncertain and indefinite bed, but swollen by the waters of the Danube, which was then flooding, and the sudden downpour of rain, which fell with much ice and thunder after the battle was over ...[57]

The description "swampy and muddy stream, flowing muddy with its uncertain and indefinite bed" does not, however, fit the Csele, which flowed from the hills straight into the Danube. This describes a watercourse that flows unsteadily over flat land, which is not the case on the west bank, but is typical of the drainage pattern on Mohács Island. The Csele streambed is V-shaped, with a deep and a very defined bed, not at all an unstable water flowing with mud.

The western part of the Karasica/Krassó [Black Water] system on the Island of Mohács reached the vicinity of the presumed place of death. It also shows that the connection between the Danube and Lake Riha was provided by a notch in 1788, which can be seen opposite the village of Bár. This notch was filled in and lost its significance in the 19th century when the bend of the river

---

54   "An overgrown mire" = swamp, body of water filled with aquatic vegetation.
55   Gáspár Heltai, "Chronica az Magyaroknac dolgairúl. 1575 (részlet)," [Chronicle of the affairs of the Magyars, 1575 (Excerpt)] in *Örök Mohács*, eds. B. Szabó et al., p. 429.
56   Krassó, also known as Karasica [Black water]. On the Island of Mohács, there was a marshy area with this name that can be linked to the flight after the battle. Norbert Pap, Péter Gyenizse, Máté Kitanics, and Gábor Szalai, "Az 1526. évi mohácsi csata helyszíneinek földrajzi jellemzői," [Geographical features of the sites of the Battle of Mohács in 1526] *Történelmi Szemle* 62 (2020), no. 1, pp. 111–151.
57   Isthvánffy, "A magyarok történetéből," [From the History of the Hungarians] in *Örök Mohács*, eds. B. Szabó et al., p. 458.

at Bár was cut through, but it still appears on the topographic map of the area as a depression in the interior of the island. The close proximity of the Krassó [Karasica/Black Water] could thus explain the nomenclatural anomaly of associating the king's death with this marshy water system (Figure 10.3).

7 The Csele Stream, Fishing Ponds and Notches

It is also worth comparing our interpretation with alternative concepts. The idea of the Csele Stream as the place of death was not widely disseminated until quite late, something which István Losonczi played a major role in. In 1773, in his work *Hármas kis tükör* [Three Little Mirrors], he wrote that "The king himself was lost in the muddy waters of the Csele Stream, together with his horse, whose body was found after 2 months, and was sadly buried in Fejérvár."[58] However, the Csele Stream as a possible place of death also appears in several earlier texts (Table 10.2), such as in the chronicles of Daniel Adam z Veleslavína[59] and Mihály Cserei.[60] It is worth examining to what extent the morphological characteristics of the watercourse in question correspond to the place of the king's death as described in the sources.

This is the northernmost, rather narrow watercourse of the Mohács Plain, with a V-shaped channel that barely touches the plain. The upper section falls rapidly and only slows down in the short section on the plain. In the description of the Military Survey I at the end of the 18th century, we read: "The Csely [or Csele] Stream is 4 feet wide and 1–2 feet deep, swampy. It has a clay and sandy bed. To the northeast, at the bridge built at the mill of the Csely Stream, opposite which are remains of a ruined chapel, the water is passable for both cavalry and infantry."[61]

Extreme swelling can only be envisaged for flash floods. This 18th-century description, prior to water regulation works, does not refer to a watercourse

---

58   István Losonczi, "Hármas kis tükör. 1773," [Three Little Mirrors. 1773] in *"Nekünk mégis Mohács kell...",* eds. Farkas et al., p. 231.

59   Daniel Adam z Veleslavína, "Történeti kalendárium. 1590 (részlet)," [Historical calendar. 1590 (excerpt)] in *Örök Mohács,* eds. B. Szabó et al., pp. 439–440.

60   "...*the unhappy king fell in the Carassus, which in Hungarian is called Csele Stream, in the muddy river, and there he drowned.*" Mihály Cserei, "Erdély históriája, 1709–1712" [History of Transylvania, 1709–1712] in *"Nekünk mégis Mohács kell...",* eds. Farkas et al., p. 230. This text actually echoes Istvánffy's claim, where Carassus/Krassó is the place of death.

61   Klára T. Mérey, *Baranya megye települései az Első katonai felmérés idején* [Settlements of Baranya County at the time of the Military Survey I] (Pécs: Baranya Megyei Levéltár, 2004), pp. 109–110.

that must or can be swum across, but this was certainly not possible during flash floods.

The Csele Stream enters the area from the northwest, from the slopes of the Baranya Hills, while it also collects water from the Himesháza Ditch and the Szebényi Watercourse. Leaving its 50–200 metre-wide valley with waterlogged bottom, it covers around 700 metres across the northern, narrowing zone of the Mohács Plain. Meanwhile, it cuts deeper and deeper into the loess terraces as it reaches the Danube. Around its confluence, the terrace surface is now slightly lowered. The area is deeply cut into the loess-mantled aquifer complex and Danube deposits due to its significant west-east slope, and bears little resemblance to the area described by sources as the place of the king's death. Flash floods of the size that could have filled the riverbed would have passed on it so quickly that it is hard to imagine crossing it, or if one drowned in it, the corpse would hardy stay in the riverbed. In addition, at the scene of the death, there were four known and countless unknown bodies that were later found in the same place where they had died. Since Czettricz is known to have successfully crossed the watercourse, we can rule out the possibility that he swam across a section of the bed affected by flash flooding.

Another possibility is that the Csele was impounded back by the Danube flooding, and that this could have been the reason for the tragedy.[62] Due to terrain conditions, this backwater effect must have been very limited and felt only in the confluence area, as there was no flood protection on the river at the time, and the dams did not raise the water to the present level.[63]

This theory is also contradicted by the primary sources, which refer to a small branch or tributary of the Danube as the place of the king's death. At the same time, the army, including the king, along with Aczél and Czettricz, had already marched from north to south through this area to their station in Mohács. From the Sárvíz to the Borza, they had to cross seven Danube tributaries, of which the Csele Stream was among the smallest.[64] Some of the early

---

62   József Péteri Takáts, "Úti jegyzetek, 1797" [Travel notes, 1797] in *"Nekünk mégis Mohács kell…"*, eds. Farkas et al., p. 232.

63   The 2013 Danube record flood height was marked at the mouth of the Csele. This level was certainly not reached by the 1526 flood, because unlike in 2013, the river was not yet embanked, and the water was able to flow out towards Mohács Island, and spread out. This suggests that the water level in the Csele bed may have risen slightly near the estuary.

64   At the Csele, a rising hilltop can be seen above the short stretch of flat land. The historian's theory that the water flowed backwards in the Csele, which was swollen by the Danube, and that this is why it could be seen as a "small branch of the Danube" or the "overflow of the Danube", is unfounded not only because, before the dams were built, the flood waves were much lower than today, but also because, in this imagined situation, the river would

news reports before October 1526 (Table 10.1: Fugger, Thurzó, Ferdinand) mention a swamp, a lake, an overflow: the flooding, the rise of the water level of the Csele, assumed by some, cannot be reconciled with these historical data either. All these arguments support the conclusion that the cited watercourse could not have been the Csele Stream.

One of the reasons that made it famous may be Brodarics's iconic text that placed the location of death near the village of Csele. The village was destroyed, but the stream of the same name serves as an appropriate reminder. Over time, the details of the post-battle escape became blurred and the story was simplified. Armies moving through the area used the military road that crossed the Csele bridge. Thus, in the eyes of the contemporary intellectuals reading Brodarics, the bridge of the mill, or the immediate vicinity of the King's Bridge, gradually became the legendary site of the king's death.

By the time scientific research began to address the issue in the 19th century, it was no longer thought that the ruler had crossed the west branch of the river here, nor was there any reason seen for him to do so. By then, the Danube had multiplied its discharge in the vicinity of the confluence of the Csele Stream. By the early 19th century, it had grown to a width of around 320 metres, and today it is more than 700 metres wide. The Csele, which lay on the supposed escape route from south to north, seemed a suitable place for popular memory, especially as it crossed the military road through which both the Christian and the Ottoman armies passed. The flight northwards across the Csele has come to be seen as indisputable fact.

Jenő Gyalókay's analysis of the circumstances of the king's death was essentially intended to dispute the conspiracy theory that Louis II was the victim of an assassination attempt.[65] The military historian worked from a much smaller source base than the researchers today, but he drew a number of conclusions that are still valid. Understanding that the king could not be escorted directly towards the town of Tolna because they were being chased by Ottoman horsemen, his escorts took him towards the Danube floodplain. He wrote, however, that Burgio's and Thurzó's claims about crossing the Danube were wrong, without any particular justification, because this route would have brought the king to an island, and this violated the geographical evidence of the time.[66]

---

have flowed up the hill, which obviously defies gravity. The Csele does not behave like this in the present period of high water levels confined between embankments. This was not the case during the 2013 floods.

[65] Gyalókay, "A mohácsi csata," [The Battle of Mohács] in *Mohácsi emlékkönyv*, ed. Lukinich, p. 251.

[66] "Although "Burgio and Thurzó write about a branch of the Danube, this is a clear mistake, as the king undoubtedly wanted to escape by the road, in order to flee more quickly; and

He considered the narrow bed of the Csele Stream unsuitable for drowning.[67] He also noticed that the current confluence of the Csele is much further to the west than the former. Yet he thought the funnel-like lowermost stretch of the stream, where its current slows and deposits its sediment, may be consistent with the image of the king dying in a place covered with water. He thought that here the horse and its rider must have sunk into loose mud.[68]

It is impossible to reconstruct the exact conditions of the confluence in 1526, but based on historical maps (Figures 10.1 and 10.2), it is likely that the Csele deposited part of its sediment before reaching the Danube. There, a confluence dissected with sandbanks and short stretches of a narrow stream bed was formed, which the Danube destroyed year after year advancing from the east. Depressions covered with water may have formed, in which obviously anybody could be drowned.

It was probably not possible to descend to the Danube bank in the V-shaped stream valley on horseback. If one was somehow able to reach the stream valley, it was pointless to go as far as the confluence if one was about to continue the northward journey. There is no description or reference to this. The sources describe the crossing of a watercourse, on the other side of which there is an overflow (in the floodplain) and a swampy, muddy land. This situation is therefore not in line with the resources.

What happens if one approaches the Csele from the south, where it flows into the Danube, on its bank? The easiest access to the confluence with the Danube was at the terminus of the ancient riverbed south of the Csele, now known as the Dolina. This lower-lying area was used as a watering place by shepherds in later centuries.[69] Because of the Danube's flooding, the water was high here, and the thalweg, where the current of the water was the fastest, was close to the bank. If one wanted to swim their horse across northwards from here, one would have had to reckon with the Danube flowing from the north and the Csele flowing from the west at once. It is very doubtful that a horse can

---

if he had crossed the Danube, he would have reached one of the islands." Gyalókay, "A mohácsi csata," [The Battle of Mohács] in *Mohácsi emlékkönyv*, ed. Lukinich, p. 251.

67 "It is also certain that the accident must have happened in wide and deep water, which was also muddy, and not in the bed of a narrow stream." Gyalókay, "A mohácsi csata," [The Battle of Mohács] in *Mohácsi emlékkönyv*, ed. Lukinich, p. 251.

68 "Thus, it is unlikely that a thick but loose layer of debris and silt, covered with water, were formed in which a horse could sink." Gyalókay, "A mohácsi csata," [The Battle of Mohács] in *Mohácsi emlékkönyv*, ed. Lukinich, p. 251.

69 János Pesti ed., *Baranya megye földrajzi nevei II*. [Geographical names in Baranya County II.] I–II (Pécs: Baranya Megyei Levéltár, 1982), p. 482.

swim fast and efficiently enough to overcome the strength of these combined currents.

They would have had to travel at least 250 metres to the north on this section of the Danube, which they had to overcome partly by wading and partly by swimming. On the other hand, there is no standing water, lake or swamp on the northern bank of the Csele, so the refugees would have had to overcome a 4–6 metre high loess bank. If mass drowning had occurred here, at least some of the bodies would have been carried away by the current.[70] Based on the above reconsideration of the environment, the confluence does not correspond to the site of death shown in the sources. It is much more likely that they did not attempt to cross the Danube branch upstream, but aimed for the much closer opposite bank, so they did not have to face the counter-current. In any case, such a reconstruction of events is literally as they are presented in the sources.

The story of drowning has become much like a popular tale over time, but the events at the Csele Stream have become incompatible with early authentic sources. This was also noticed by János B. Szabó, who rejected the theory of drowning in the stream in a recent paper.[71] At the same time, B. Szabó also suggested that the king died, if not in the Csele Stream, then in its vicinity, in some swampy water, in a "fishing pond" on the right bank of the Danube.[72] In his reconstruction, the king and his retinue was fleeing north when they encountered a great commotion at the Csele bridge. Therefore, they may have tried to evade the mass of refugees not too far to the east, in the Danube floodplain.

Among the historical documents gathered by Antal Verancsics, there is an account of the death of King Louis II, according to which "King Louis fled from the battle, who indeed lost his life in the mud of a notch near the Csele."[73] Based on this, B. Szabó assumes that the nine *piscina*,[74] i.e. semi-artificial structures

---

70   If we look at it from a strictly theoretical point of view, it is the crossing from north to south on the Csele that is most similar to the tragedy described in the sources. However, as the tide receded, there was no muddy swamp in the estuary, only a much smaller stream (not stagnant water) and sandbars.

71   János B. Szabó, "II. Lajos halálának helyszíne: táj és orális hagyomány," [The place of Louis II's death: landscape and oral tradition] *Hadtörténelmi Közlemények* 132 (2019), no. 2, pp. 443–453.

72   Ibid.

73   "Memoria rerum," in *"Nekünk mégis Mohács kell...",* eds. Farkas et al., p. 214.

74   Ottó Herman, *A magyar halászat könyve I.* [The book of Hungarian fishing I.] (Budapest: K. M. Természettudományi Társulat, 1887), p. 87. The Hosszú-erdő [Long Forest] lakes, which belong to Sátoraljaújhely and are connected to the Bodrog River and get their water and fish from there, were always called *piscina* by the sources. István Tringli, *Sátoraljaújhely*

used as fishing ponds, may have provided the basis for this account.[75] The king is believed to have drowned in one of these near the Csele Stream. The most remarkable part of this assumption is that the Danube had a floodplain on its western bank near the Csele Stream. B. Szabó rightly quotes Bertalan Andrásfalvy's interpretation of the nature of notches: they are related to a floodplain.[76] However, where there is no floodplain, there can be no notches. The idea put forward by B. Szabó may be problematic, because the bank in the vicinity of the Csele Stream was high on the western side of the Danube, as can be seen on the finely detailed hydrographic map of the area before water regulation work was completed, i.e. in 1808 (Figure 10.1/A and B). Incidentally, the same high bank can be seen here today, which has been eroded, but not flooded, by the Danube during high water for thousands of years. Since the difference in height between the two banks is due to tectonic causes, which have been developing over a longer period of time, it is reasonable to assume that the same environmental situation existed in 1526.

In his book, István Tringli discussed an account of a feud in 1323 regarding the nine fishpond which belonged to the Csele estate (this document prompted first Béla Kiss and then B. Szabó to set forth the above theory).[77] Tringli writes about the incident as follows: "It is certainly not without precedent that, after Easter in 1323, the steward of Mohács took the inhabitants of the town to the village of Csele. They killed a local man with an arrow, beat up the keeper of the fishing ponds in Csele, took his clothes, seized nine ponds, which they did not return even after the nuns'legal notice arrived, but began to use them.[78] A good few years later, in 1331, the nuns first protested on behalf of the monastery

---

(Magyar Várostörténeti Atlasz) 2 (Budapest, MTA Bölcsészettudományi Kutatóközpont, 2011), p. 74.

75 János B. Szabó, following the assumption of Béla Kiss published in *Vigília* in 1976, refers to the fact that nine fishing ponds were recorded in 1323 on the Csele estate of the nuns of Nyúlsziget, (B. Szabó, "II. Lajos halálának helyszíne," [The place of Louis II's death] p. 446), and in time, these may have become marshy. He believes one of these may have been the place and cause of Louis II's death. He assumes that at least one of the fishing ponds was a notch.

76 Bertalan Andrásfalvy, *Duna mente népének ártéri gazdálkodása Tolna és Baranya megyében az ármentesítés befejezéséig*, [The floodplain farming of the people of the Danube in Tolna and Baranya counties until the end of the flood relief] (Tanulmányok Tolna megye történetéből) VII (Szekszárd: A Tolna Megyei Tanács Levéltára, 1975), pp. 159–160.

77 István Tringli, *Hatalmaskodások a középkori Magyarországon* (Kézirat). [*Power struggles in medieval Hungary*] (Manuscript).

78 Tringli, *Hatalmaskodások* [Power struggles]; MNL OL DL 2159. Published in *Codex diplomaticus Hungariae*. [= Fejér CD] VIII/2. Stud. Georgius Fejér (Buda: 1832), no. 229, pp. 495–496.

that their fishing ponds, mills and forests in Csele had been occupied by the Mohács people, and then a few months later, the bishop of Pécs presented to the royal court of justice that, by order of the nuns, the people of Csele 'had been fishing in his lakes or ponds on the Danube belonging to Mohács for three years now'.[79] It was a good indication of the value involved that the bishop said they had caused three hundred marks worth of damage."[80]

The description of the case reveals that the issue does not involve the Csele Stream: the nine lakes in question were located on the Danube. The estates of the town of Mohács, which belonged to the bishopric of Pécs, as well as the estate of the Dominican monastery of Nyúlsziget, extended to the Island of Mohács.[81] The dispute also included the forests, ship mills and fishing ponds on the border between Mohács and Csele. Tringli speculates that the flooding river may have altered the environment, and perhaps the boundaries of the two estates were not clearly defined. In fact, both parties claimed the land for themselves, from which they generated substantial profits. The fishing ponds provided most of the income, but the ship mills moored on the Danube and the forests[82] also played an important role in the lives of the locals.

Nine fishing ponds would not have fitted alongside the 700-metre-long Csele Stream (it was 100–200 metres longer at the time), which is now the Mohács Plain, and would still be clearly visible today. The Csele cuts its way through a loess plateau. Loess is a loose sediment ("yellow earth") that formed from falling dust at the end of the Pleistocene in the vicinity of large land ice sheets in cold steppe or semi-desert environments. Therefore, in places where there is such a surface, we can be sure that there has been no water cover in the last 10,000 years, because the aquatic sediments are well separated from the terrestrial loess.

In addition to water, a (fishing) pond also needs a waterproof layer to prevent water from leaking. In the studied area, this could practically only be clay. But if a lake is formed, it will accumulate lacustrine sediments. These would also be present in the sediment sequence. As there is no trace of such deposits, we cannot assume there were fishing ponds along the Csele Stream.

From the above, it is easy to see that nine fishing ponds cannot be hidden near the Csele. On the other side of the Danube branch in Mohács, in line with

---

79 "...stagna seu pisscinas suas in fluvio Danubii habitas ad Mohach pertinentes..." MNL OL DL 2668., 26080. (Fejér CD VIII/3), no. 252, pp. 557–559.
80 Tringli, *Hatalmaskodások* [Power struggles].
81 The estate of Csele also extended to the left bank of the Danube. Pesti, *Baranya megye földrajzi nevei II*. [Geographical names in Baranya County] p. 419. Even in the 19th–20th centuries (Military Survey II, Military Survey III, General Map of Hungary [around 1910], etc.), maps show e.g. the Csele Forest, which may also have belonged to the former village of Csele, on the island side.
82 See above the Csele Forest, located on the northern part of the Island of Mohács.

the 1323 source, there were plenty of such ponds on Mohács Island, and among them, there are some that were used as fishing ponds in 1323. As they generated considerable income and were a major job to maintain, we can be sure that they were kept as long as possible. Most of them certainly still existed in 1526.

We cannot say for sure, however, that the king fell into one of these. As already mentioned, the Verancsics source is not confirmed by other data, but it cannot be rejected either. What is certain is that the mud was deposited along the river at the site of the accident; and if this site was not a notch itself, it was in the immediate vicinity of these fishing ponds.

8   How Did Posterity Mark the Place of the King's Death? The Evolution of Landmarks[83]

In Table 10.2, we have gathered information on how the place of the king's death was described in secondary or memorial literature. This shows that the mentions that are known to date can be traced back to primary information. The mention of the Danube, the marsh and the mud recurs depending on who wants to emphasize what, but we can also discover other trends, such as how the context of the place was viewed in different periods.

The mention of the Danube as the actual place of death was only typical in the 16th century. In the 17th century, only the proximity of the Danube is identified as a place of drowning, but it is not directly linked to it. In addition, there are some interesting, unintentional remarks in the texts. For example, György Szerémi, who is known for his unreliability, mentions the Little Danube in the context of the escape (but not as a place of death), inadvertently referring to the difference in size between the two branches of the Danube. In the first half of the 16th century, the sources address the place of death in the context of escape.

The legitimacy of drowning in the Csele Stream was only reinforced at the end of the 16th century and only entered the canon in the 17th century, completely excluding the Danube from the interpretation. Brodarics, Szerémi, Brutus, and Istvánffy, who uses Brodarics, even emphasized the proximity of the village of Csele. However, by the 1570s, the settlement had been depopulated,[84] making it less and less suitable for use as a *landmark*.

---

83   A landmark is an object or geographical feature that helps one find their orientation.
84   Előd Vass mentions the village of Csele as a wasteland in 1574. Előd Vass, "Mohács város hódoltságkori történetének forrásai," [Sources of the history of the city of Mohács during the Ottoman occupation] in *Baranyai helytörténetírás 1975*, ed. László Szita (Pécs: Baranya Megyei Levéltár, 1976), pp. 15–48.

TABLE 10.2 Environmental features of the place of death of King Louis II in the 16–18th century memory sources

Year/author	Reference to the Danube, the great river	Reference to the Csele, a stream	Swamp/Lake	Pit, muddy water
1526 Cuspinianus[1]	"the overflow of the Danube"		"he jumped his horse into a pond created by the overflow of the Danube"	
1528 Brodarics[2]	"at this place, the water was higher than usual because of the flooding Danube"	"below a village named Csele"		"in the crevice of a steep bank"
Between 1526 and 1534 Kemalpaşazade[3]	Mounted and armed, he jumped into the water, increasing the number of those who fell or drowned in the water" (referring to the Danube)			
Summer 1528 H. Łaski/Ibrahim Pasha[4]			"shallow water" (?)	
1530 Miklós Oláh[5]			"into a swamp"	

[1] Cuspinianus, "Johannes Cuspinianus buzdító beszéde," [Exhortation by Johannes Cuspinianus] in Örök Mohács, eds. B. Szabó et al., p. 276.
[2] István Brodarics, Igaz leírás a magyaroknak a törökkel Mohácsnál vívott csatájáról. [A True Account of the Battle of Mohács between the Hungarians and the Turks] (Budapest: Magvető Könyvkiadó, 1983), p. 53.
[3] Kemálpasazáde, "Mohácsnáme," in *"Nekünk mégis Mohács kell...",* eds. Farkas et al., p. 204.
[4] "Ibrahim pasa tárgyalása Hyeronimus Łaskival. Isztambul, 1528 nyara," [Meeting of İbrahim Pasha with Hyeronimus Łaski. Istanbul, summer 1528] in *"Nekünk mégis Mohács kell...",* eds. Farkas et al., p. 206.
[5] Oláh, "Oláh Miklós levele," [Letter from Miklós Oláh] in *Örök Mohács,* eds. B. Szabó et al., p. 348.

TABLE 10.2 Environmental features of the place of death of King Louis II (cont.)

Year/author	Reference to the Danube, the great river	Reference to the Csele, a stream	Swamp/Lake	Pit, muddy water
1530 Bartoš Písař[6]			"a swamp"	
Around 1530 Paulus Iovius[7]			"swampy ditch"	
1531–1537 Ursinus Velius[8]			"sunk in a deep swamp"	
1540s Bostan[9]	"when he came to the river called Sárvíz … he plunged into the water on horseback and armed, and … he drawned in the water."			
1541 Camerarius[10]	"in a not too big and not too swift river"			"muddy water", "shallow"
1545 György Szerémi[11]	"near the Little Danube River"	"near the village of Csele"	"he fell into a swamp", "submerged in a swamp", "on the shore of a lake"	
Around 1548 Lazius[12]			"into a deep swamp"	"into mud and silt"

[6] Bartoš Písař, "Krónika a prágai felkelésről. 1530 körül," [Chronicle of the Prague Uprising. Around 1530] in *Örök Mohács*, eds. B. Szabó et al., p. 357.

[7] Paulus Iovius, "Krónika a törökök viselt dolgairól. 1531," [A chronicle of the doings of the Turks. 1531] in *Örök Mohács*, eds. B. Szabó et al., p. 359.

[8] Caspar Ursinus Velius, "Tíz könyv a magyar háborúról. 1531–1537," [Ten books about the Hungarian war. 1531–1537] in *"Nekünk mégis Mohács kell…"*, eds. Farkas et al., p. 207.

[9] Bosztán cselebi, "Szulejmán könyve," [Book of Süleyman] in *Örök Mohács*, eds. B. Szabó et al., p. 366.

[10] Camerarius: "A Magyarországon, Mohácsnál elszenvedett vereségről," [The defeat at Mohács in Hungary] in *Örök Mohács*, eds. B. Szabó et al., p. 372.

[11] Szerémi, "Levél Magyarország romlásáról," [Letter on the deterioration of Hungary] in *"Nekünk mégis Mohács kell…"*, eds. Farkas et al., pp. 209–212.

[12] Wolfgang Lazius, "Ausztria történetének tizedei. 1548 körül," [Decades of the history of Austria. Around 1548] in *"Nekünk mégis Mohács kell…"*, eds. Farkas et al., p. 212.

TABLE 10.2 Environmental features of the place of death of King Louis II (cont.)

Year/author	Reference to the Danube, the great river	Reference to the Csele, a stream	Swamp/Lake	Pit, muddy water
1552 Dubravius[13]	"in a nearby overflow of the Danube"		"into its overflow"	"he found him in the depression where the Danube tide used to recede"
1556 Knauz chronicle[14]			"in a swamp"	
1559 Ehrenspiegel des Hauses Österreich[15]			"swamp"	
First half of the 16th century Unknown author[16]	"in a river which in those days swelled to a wonderful extent because of the Danube".			"in the muddy, marshy waters of a small branch of the Danube"
Mid-16th century Memoria rerum[17]		"he lost his life in a notch, in mud near the Csele"		"notch, mud"

[13] Dubravius, "Csehország története," [The History of Bohemia] in *"Nekünk mégis Mohács kell...,"* eds. Farkas et al., p. 213.
[14] "Knauz krónika. 1556 körül (részlet)," [Knauz chronicle. Around 1556] in *Örök Mohács,* eds. B. Szabó et al., p. 394.
[15] "Habsburg-ház dicsőségtükre," [Ehrenspiegel des Hauses Österreich] in *Örök Mohács,* eds. B. Szabó et al., p. 399.
[16] "Ismeretlen szerző beszámolója a csatáról," [An unknown author's account of the battle.] in *"Nekünk mégis Mohács kell...",* eds. Farkas et al., p. 204.
[17] "Memoria rerum," in *"Nekünk mégis Mohács kell...",* eds. Farkas et al., p. 214.

TABLE 10.2 Environmental features of the place of death of King Louis II (cont.)

Year/author	Reference to the Danube, the great river	Reference to the Csele, a stream	Swamp/Lake	Pit, muddy water
Second half of the 16th century Unknown Croatian author[18]			"From the edge of the swamp, I thus waded deep", "I was pulled down by the swamp"	"sea of mud"; "stuck in the mud"
1554 Yosef ha-Kohen[19]			"in a swamp"	
1563 Michael Siegler[20]		"by the Cselepataka River"	"in a swamp"	
1566 János Zermegh[21]			"a swamp"	
1573 Stephan Gerlach Snr[22]			"he rode across the marsh", "he had already crossed, but his horse fell, and he drowned, he lost his life."	

[18] "Ismeretlen horvát szerző: Kezdődik a harc és a magyar király panasza (részlet). 16. század második fele," [Unknown Croatian author: The battle begins and the complaints of the Hungarian king (excerpt). Second half of the 16th century] in *"Nekünk mégis Mohács kell...",* eds. Farkas et al., pp. 215–218.

[19] Joszéf ha-Kohén, "Franciaország és az Oszmán Birodalom uralkodóinak krónikája, 1554," [A chronicle of the rulers of France and the Ottoman Empire, 1554] in *"Nekünk mégis Mohács kell...",* eds. Farkas et al., p. 214.

[20] Siegler, "A magyarok, az erdélyiek," [The Hungarians, the Transylvanians] in *Örök Mohács,* eds. B. Szabó et al., p. 421.

[21] János Zermegh, "Emlékirat a Ferdinánd és János, Magyarország királyai között történt dolgokról. 1556 után," [A memoir of the events between Ferdinánd and János, kings of Hungary. After 1566] in *Örök Mohács,* eds. B. Szabó et al., p. 421.

[22] "Idősebb Stefan Gerlach naplója, 1573," [Diary of Stephan Gerlach Snr, 1573] in *"Nekünk mégis Mohács kell...",* eds. Farkas et al., p. 219.

TABLE 10.2   Environmental features of the place of death of King Louis II (cont.)

Year/author	Reference to the Danube, the great river	Reference to the Csele, a stream	Swamp/Lake	Pit, muddy water
1575 Paulus Iovius[23]			"he came to a lake"	"he drowned in the waters of a two-span whirlpool"
1575 Gáspár Heltai[24]	"the overgrown mire of Krassó" (?) "when they had come to the brook"			"in water and mud"
Late 1570s Giovanni Michele Bruto (Brutus)[25]	"flooded by the Danube leaving its bed"	"at the village of Csele lying on a steep slope"		"cracked earth"
1570s Katib Mehmed Zaim[26]			"his stray body was found in a lake, drowned"	
1585 Marc'Antonio Pigafetta[27]	"not far from the Danube"	"a very narrow wooden bridge connecting the marshy areas and leading to the Danube was used for crossing", "jumped his horse into the swamp by the bridge"	"he fled towards Buda and drowned in one of those shallow swamps"	

23 Paulus Iovius, "Lajos, Pannónia és Csehország királya, 1575," [Louis, King of Pannonia and Bohemia, 1575] in *Örök Mohács,* eds. B. Szabó et al., p. 389.
24 Heltai, "Chronica," [Chronicle] in *Örök Mohács,* eds. B. Szabó et al., p. 429.
25 Ferenc Toldy ed., *Brutus János Mihály magyar királyi történetíró magyar históriája 1490–1552.* [Hungarian history of János Mihály Brutus, Hungarian royal historian 1490–1552.] (Magyar Történelmi Emlékek) 13 (Pest: Eggenberger Ferdinánd M. Akad. Könyvárus, 1867).
26 Záim, "Történetek gyűjteménye," [A collection of stories] in *Örök Mohács,* eds. B. Szabó et al., p. 430.
27 Marc'Antonio Pigafetta, "Útikönyv, 1585," [Guidebook, 1585] in *"Nekünk mégis Mohács kell...",* eds. Farkas et al., pp. 220–221.

TABLE 10.2   Environmental features of the place of death of King Louis II (*cont.*)

Year/author	Reference to the Danube, the great river	Reference to the Csele, a stream	Swamp/Lake	Pit, muddy water
1587 Reinhold Lubenau[28]	"not far from the Danube"	"next to the mill"	"he drowned in the swamp"	
1590 Daniel Adam z Veleslavína[29]		"in a muddy stream called Csele Stream"		"in the mud"
1592 David Ganz[30]		"he fell into a small river swamp" " he fell into a stream of 4–5 spans"	"swamp"	
1622 Miklós Istvánffy[31]	"swollen significantly … by the waters of the Danube"	"between Mohács and Csele, the Karasica, a swampy and muddy stream, stood in his way" (?)		"he fell into a bottomless mud of the silty brook"
1626 Athanasio Georgiceo[32]	"near the Danube"	"to a not very big stream"		
Around 1650 İbrahim Peçevi[33]		"he arrived at the swampy place known as the King's Bridge"	"swamp"	

[28] Reinhold Lubenau, "Reinhold Lubenau útleírása, 1587," [Reinhold Lubenau's travelogue, 1587] in *"Nekünk mégis Mohács kell…"*, eds. Farkas et al., pp. p. 221.

[29] Veleslavína, "Történeti kalendárium," [Historical calendar] in *Örök Mohács*, eds. B. Szabó et al., p. 440.

[30] David Ganz, "Krónika, 1592," [Chronicle, 1592] in *"Nekünk mégis Mohács kell…"*, eds. Farkas et al., p. 222.

[31] Isthvánffy, "A magyarok történetéből," [From the History of the Hungarians] in *Örök Mohács*, eds. B. Szabó et al., pp. 458.

[32] István György Tóth, "Athanasio Georgiceo álruhás császári megbízott útleírása a magyarországi török hódoltságról, 1626-ból," [Disguised imperial envoy Athanasio Georgiceo's travelogue on the Turkish occupation of Hungary in 1626] *Századok* 132 (1998), no. 4, p. 854.

[33] Pecsevi, Krónika. [Chronicle] in *"Nekünk mégis Mohács kell…"*, eds. Farkas et al., p. 247.

TABLE 10.2 Environmental features of the place of death of King Louis II (*cont.*)

Year/author	Reference to the Danube, the great river	Reference to the Csele, a stream	Swamp/Lake	Pit, muddy water
1660 Gergely Pethő[34]		"in a muddy brook known as Csele"		"muddy"
1663 Henrik Ottendorf[35]	"it flows into the Danube"	"Carassus", "barely 20 feet wide"		"very clay-filled and muddy"
1663 Jan Tomáš Pešina z Čechorodu[36]		"in swampy creek"		
Around 1663 Evliya Çelebi[37]			"sunk in a swamp"	
1664 Pál Esterházy[38]		"swampy and muddy Carasso Stream"		
1677 Jan Tomáš Pešina z Čechorodu[39]		"between Mohács and the village of Csele, to the swampy and marshy Karasica or the Csele Stream with its indeterminate bed"		"he fell into the deep silt of the muddy river" (?)

[34] Gergely Pethő, "Rövid magyar cronica, 1600," [A short Hungarian chronicle, 1600] in *Örök Mohács*, eds. B. Szabó et al., p. 478.
[35] Henrik Ottendorf, "Henrik Ottendorf útleírása, 1663," [Henrik Ottendorf's travelogue, 1663] in *"Nekünk mégis Mohács kell…"*, eds. Farkas et al., p. 227.
[36] Jan Tomáš Pešina z Čechorodu, "Ucalegon, 1663," in *Örök Mohács*, eds. B. Szabó et al., p. 480.
[37] Evlia Cselebi, "Utazások könyve. 1680 körül," [Book of travels. Around 1680] in *"Nekünk mégis Mohács kell…"*, eds. Farkas et al., p. 228.
[38] Pál Esterházy, "Mars Hungaricus, 1664," in *Örök Mohács*, eds. B. Szabó et al., p. 481.
[39] Jan Tomáš Pešina z Čechorodu, "Mars Moravicus, 1677," in *Örök Mohács*, eds. B. Szabó et al., p. 490.

TABLE 10.2 Environmental features of the place of death of King Louis II (*cont.*)

Year/author	Reference to the Danube, the great river	Reference to the Csele, a stream	Swamp/Lake	Pit, muddy water
1671 John Burbery[40]		"only the gentle Carassus flows through its middle, so slowly that its surface barely moves" "a swampy shallow"		
1677 Gáspár Hain[41]			"he drowned in the swamp"	
1709–1712 Mihály Cserei[42]		"… the unhappy king fell in the Carassus with his horse, which in Hungarian is known as the Csele Stream, in the muddy river, and there he drowned."		
1728 Pál Ember Debreceni[43]			"miserably lost in a swamp"	
1773 István Losonczi[44]		"in the muddy waters of the Csele Stream"		

[40] John Burbery, "Beszámoló Lord Henry Howard utazásáról, 1671," [An account of the journey of Lord Henry Howard, 1671] in *Örök Mohács,* eds. B. Szabó et al., p. 491–492.
[41] Gáspár Hain, "Lőcsei krónika, 1684," [Lőcse chronicle, 1684] in *Örök Mohács,* eds. B. Szabó et al., p. 492.
[42] Cserei, "Erdély históriája," [History of Transylvania] in *"Nekünk mégis Mohács kell…",* eds. Farkas et al., p. 230.
[43] Pál Debreceni Ember, "Historia Ecclesiae Reformatae, 1728," in *"Nekünk mégis Mohács kell…",* eds. Farkas et al., p. 230.
[44] Losonczi, "Hármas kis tükör," [Three Little Mirrors] in *"Nekünk mégis Mohács kell…",* eds. Farkas et al., p. 231.

TABLE 10.2   Environmental features of the place of death of King Louis II (cont.)

Year/author	Reference to the Danube, the great river	Reference to the Csele, a stream	Swamp/Lake	Pit, muddy water
1792 Márton Etédi Sós[45]		"he turned his path to the Csele Stream"	"in an ugly marsh"	"in the mud", "whirlpool"
1797 József Péteri Takáts[46]	"swollen by the flooding Danube"	"in a stream called Csele"		

45 Márton Etédi Sós, "Magyar gyász; vagy-is Második Lajos magyar királynak a mohátsi mezőn történt veszedelme, 1792," [Hungarian mourning; or the disaster of the Hungarian King Louis II in the field of Mohács, 1792] in *"Nekünk mégis Mohács kell...",* eds. Farkas et al., p. 231.
46 Péteri Takáts, "Úti jegyzetek," [Travel notes] in *Örök Mohács,* eds. B. Szabó et al., p. 571.

The first known reference (three decades after the battle, in 1563) to the Csele Stream being associated with the king's death was not that the king drowned in it, but that it was used to describe the place of death: "Following the instructions of the shield bearer Csetrics, he was found in the swampy place near the small Cselepataka River."[85] The description is illustrative: it is about a swampy place, near "Cselepataka" and not in it. The Csele flows into the Little Danube at just the point where the swamp is on the other bank. As the Csele itself is not a marshy river (although the bottom of the V-shaped bed may be muddy), it flows through the high bank into the Danube, and its confluence is constantly being eroded by the river, so no marsh can form there.[86] The stream in this case is the landmark for the place where the death occurred, alongside the river branch. What is meant here is a marshy floodplain on the eastern side of the western Danube branch, with no habitation and no elevation. It is hardly

85 Michael Siegler, "A magyarok, az erdélyiek és a szomszédos tartományok történetének kronológiája, 1563 (részlet)," [Chronology of the history of the Hungarians, the Transylvanians and the neighbouring provinces, 1563 (excerpt)] in *Örök Mohács,* eds. B. Szabó et al., p. 421.
86 If we look at the current situation, we can see that the bay is protected by a so-called spur above the estuary, so there is a well-maintained sandbar there at present, but not a marsh. When there was no spur (a kind of stone embankment perpendicular to the river), it was a steadily eroding bank, not a marsh.

possible to interpret it in any other way than the king was found at the stream, i.e. opposite its mouth.

In 1590, the Czech Daniel Adam z Veleslavína[87] is the first to mention that the king died in the bed of the Csele Stream. It is only from the mid-17th century that this concept becomes generally accepted. At this time, the context of the site is to commemorate the tragic death of the king.

The description of the aforementioned author undoubtedly still refers to the Csele Stream, just as Atanasio Georgiceo and Gergely Pethő also mention the stream. At the same time, Henrik Ottendorf, who visited the area in 1663, describes the unnamed watercourse as a river.

The Csele and the Carasica [Carasso/Carassus] begin to be more closely linked in sources from the 17th century. The picture of "Carassus" by Istvánffy, Esterházy, Jan Tomáš Pešina z Čechorodu and Burbery shows a wide, muddy and slowly flowing river. In these cases, fictitious elements are added to a real watercourse (the Csele). The description thus does not match the character of the actual watercourse (which is a narrow, confined, almost straight, barely meandering stream). Fictional elements are used to create cohesion with the contradiction between the real place by interweaving the legendary circumstances of the king's death (he crosses a river, falls into a swamp, is lifted out of the muddy water). Csele is not represented in these sources in a real and faithful way: the context changes in such a way that the texts present the legendary place of the king's death.

By the 18th century, the image of the Csele Stream as the place of death had been consolidated. In the texts of Cserei, Losonczi, Debreceni and Etédi, it also appears by name as the place of the king's death. At the same time, the geographical knowledge of this period was greatly improved compared to the 16th and 17th centuries. The Ottoman occupation ended, and the country was reconquered, both in militarily and in intellectual terms. Its geography has been explored and mapped, the vague, mystical, oriental character of the geography of the conquest has vanished. The area around Mohács was partly used by bishops and partly by secular landlords, and was intensively cultivated: knowledge of the area increased significantly. In the 18th century, it was no longer possible to describe the Csele as a river. The name of the stream became associated with the death of Louis II, which was confirmed by the construction of his first monument.[88] However, this also created a credibility

---

87 Veleslavína, "Történeti kalendárium," [Historical calendar] in *Örök Mohács,* eds. B. Szabó et al., pp. 439–440.
88 A record by József Péteri Takács (1767–1821) from 1797 has survived. In September of that year, as tutor to László Esterházy, he visited Mohács. He wrote the following about the

deficit, because there was a contradiction between the sources and the image of the stream. Péteri Takáts was already looking for an explanation: the stream swelled up from the direction of the Danube.[89]

The vast majority of the 46 sources reviewed in Table 10.2 (28) mention a swamp/standing water as the most common feature of the place where the ruler drowned. This is the most common but the least specifiable environmental characteristic as reflected in both Czettricz's and Sárffy's accounts. But perhaps even more importantly, the marshy character of the landscape around Mohács was typical of the Danube region.

As for the more specific location, 14 sources indicate that there was mud, silt or muddy water in the immediate vicinity of the body, or that the king's body was found in a muddy pit. The original source of this information is a letter from Ferenc Sárffy.

An interesting geographical anomaly appears in Bostan's description of the Battle of Mohács, which gives authentic details. The king's death is linked to a small river named Sárvíz. It flows into the narrow western branch of the Danube in the Báta area, 20 km north of Mohács. As the Ottomans regularly passed through the Sárvíz River during their campaigns, which is also reported in the Ottoman campaign diary, the chance of a typo is negligible. There is, however, a plausible explanation: in the 16th century, the Sárvíz was much wider and more navigable than today. We strongly believe that the narrower western branch of the Danube, which derived a significant part of its water from the Sárvíz, was considered by the Ottomans, who were not familiar with local hydrology, as a widened channel of the Sárvíz.

At the same, being familiar with the region may also have influenced the various views on the significance of the Csele. Peçevi[90] certainly knew the place well. He was born in Pécs, and we know that he visited the area several times while hunting. In his chronicle, he describes the place of the king's death

---

visit: "the lord bishop [László Pál Esterházy] sent me on his horse to the place where, according to common opinion, King Louis was lost. Now the stream was completely dried up because of the great drought, otherwise the water runs a mill there. One can still see there the lower marble stone of a column, which was erected long ago in memory of the sad incident, and which His Excellency wished to renew." Péteri Takáts, "Úti jegyzetek," [Travel notes] in *Örök Mohács,* eds. B. Szabó et al., p. 571.

89   "...Louis II was lost in 1526 in the stream named Csele, which was then swollen by the Danube." Péteri Takáts, "Úti jegyzetek," [Travel notes] in *Örök Mohács,* eds. B. Szabó et al., p. 571.

90   Ibrahim Pecsevi, "Krónika (részlet)," [Chronicle (excerpt)] in *"Nekünk mégis Mohács kell...",* eds. Farkas et al., pp. 236–256.

as a swampy place called the King's Bridge,[91] where he mentions that others drowned in large numbers. The northern "edge" of the plain, on the western bank of the river, was not and could not have been a swamp or a large marshy area at his time.

The King's Bridge was certainly part of the military road of the time. However, we know that in the 18th century, due to the widening Danube, the route had to be moved westwards into the area north of Mohács. So it could well be that the site of the bridge in question is now down on the bank or somewhere in the Danube riverbed. The bridge was thus located near the marshy area of the floodplain surrounding the eastern banks of the western branch, and had the same function as the Csele in other early sources: the author has marked the marsh with a known landmark, suggesting that the king died near this landmark.

In a literary piece of work, we can find another interesting testimony. In the lines of László Liszti's epic written in 1653, the place of death is suggested as a deep overbank flow. The description faithfully follows all the relevant keywords and reference points provided by Brodarics. However, it differs from it in one aspect: it also includes a tributary of the Danube (a fissure, a rift).

> Moháczhoz közelre, czak fél mért földnire, vala egy föld-hasadás,
> Kit nagy vizzel töltöt, s ugyan teli öntöt Dunabéli áradás,
> Mint egy pasványos viz, avagy mocháros iz, s mint egy Duna szakadás
>
> Cziliche falunál, s ennek határánál, vólt ez az vizbéli ér,
> Meredek partyai, s vadnak mély árkai, Duna arja hozzá fér,
> Futo Magyarokat, szegényt, s gazdagokat, itt a Török utol ér,
>
> E' föld hasadásba, s viz áradásába, Király mind lovastól hólt,
> Minden fegyverestöl, és öltözetestöl, valamint az harczon vólt,
> Sok töb társaival, s futo Magyarival, itt fel-találtatot vólt.
>
> Close to Mohácz, only half a mile away, there was a split in the ground,
> Filled with great waters, filled to the brim by the flooding Danube,

---

91   "When the defeated king, fleeing from the battle, came to a marshy place on the edge of the plain known as the King's Bridge [in the original: *Kıral köprüsi*], the crowd of fleeing infidels was so big before him that not a man, not even a dog, could have made it through them. The crowds accumulating behind them caused countless infidels to sink into the swamp, and only opened the way to the land of non-being." Pecsevi, "Krónika," [Chronicle] in *"Nekünk mégis Mohács kell..."*, eds. Farkas et al., p. 247.

> Like a stagnant water or swampy water, and like a secondary arm of the
> Danube
>
> This streamlet was at the village of Cziliche and its border,
> It has steep banks and deep beds, the flooding of the Danube reaches it,
> Running Hungarians, rich and poor are caught by the Turk here,
>
> In this split in the ground and the flooding water, the king died with his horse,
> He was found here with all his weapons and clothes as well as
> his many comrades and fleeing Hungarians who fought the battle.[92]

The reason for including the extra information is very specific, because the poet needed a rhyme at the end of the lines (*hasadás, áradás, szakadás*). For this poetic reason, a piece of geographical evidence of the period, the *"szakadás"*, i.e. the secondary arm of the Danube was included as a corollary to the landmarks.

9   Conclusions

The king's death was caused by a horse accident. The king and his two or three men escaped from the battlefield eastwards, towards the Mohács branch of the Danube, chased by the Ottoman cavalry. South of the Csele confluence, on the high bank surrounding the river from the west, there was a natural passage, which was probably also used as a watering place in the period. This is probably the route they took to cross the Danube, which is much narrower and with stronger currents than today, towards Mohács Island.

The eastern bank of the river at this point was shallow with bars. According to the medieval written sources, historical maps and local geographic nomenclature, the Csele estate also included nine notches, or *piscina*, connected to the Danube. A water system named Karasica/Krassó, or Black Water, ran through the island, close to this section of the bank.

This was the place – across the Csele confluence – towards which the refugees were heading. On the opposite bank, after swimming their horses across the riverbed, the king and his injured horse waded into a deep depression filled with a thick layer of mud, where the flooding waters were high. The horse sank into the mud, shook off its rider and both drowned in the water

---

[92] László Liszti, "Magyar Mars avagy Mohach mezején történt veszedelemnek emlékezete, 1653," [Hungarian Mars or the memory of the disaster in the field of Mohach, 1653] in *"Nekünk mégis Mohács kell…",* eds. Farkas et al., p. 227.

and mud. One of the king's escorts, István Aczél, tried to rescue him, but he himself also drowned. The king's Chamberlain, Ulrich Czettricz, swam across, rode his horse up the eastern bank and escaped. He was the only witness to the incident.

After the floods receded, the bodies were recovered and the serfs in the neighbourhood buried the king in September, in the immediate vicinity of his death. His valuables and clothing, including the royal signet ring, were delivered in mid-1527. Sultan Süleyman searched for the ruler after the battle, but his body was not found, as the flooded Danube had hidden it from raiders and scouts. The king's body was found in mid-October by a team led by the Győr castle commander, Ferenc Sárffy, on the instructions of Czettricz, and then taken to Székesfehérvár, the site of his second burial.

The place of death is described in various ways in the memory sources. A swamp, a depression filled with water, a muddy overflow, some kind of lake or standing water connected to the Danube: these were the keywords, but the possibility that the accident occurred in a notch was also raised in the literature based on memory. From the local environment it is not possible to identify the location with absolute certainty after 500 years.

The Csele Stream, the King's Bridge and the Karasica were originally *landmarks*, indicating the proximity of the place of death. Over time, the *landmarks* have undergone a major change. In the 16th century, the Danube and its surroundings appeared as the scene of the fatal accident, especially in the period closest to the time of death. In the late 16th and 17th centuries, the descriptions changed: Csele Stream appeared as a fictional site that integrated the characteristics of both a "river" and a "marsh". The transformation of the story continued into the 18th century. After the reconquest of the country, and with the accumulation of geographical knowledge, the Csele Stream version supplanted the other interpretations. The Csele Stream later became a legendary place of death, probably due to humanist intellectuals. Folk memory, on the other hand, has preserved the Danube as the actual site of drowning.

Bibliography

Andrásfalvy, Bertalan. *Duna mente népének ártéri gazdálkodása Tolna és Baranya megyében az ármentesítés befejezéséig.* [The floodplain farming of the people of the Danube in Tolna and Baranya counties until the end of the flood relief] Tanulmányok Tolna megye történetéből VII. Szekszárd: A Tolna Megyei Tanács Levéltára, 1975.

B. Szabó, János. "II. Lajos halálának helyszíne: táj és orális hagyomány." [The place of Louis II's death: landscape and oral tradition] *Hadtörténelmi Közlemények* 132 (2019): 443–453.

Balogh, Kálmán ed. *Szedimentológia II.* [Sedimentology II.] Budapest: Akadémiai Kiadó, 1991.
Báthori, István. "Báthori István nádor oklevele II. Lajos pecsétgyűrűjéről. Pozsony, 1527. június 24." [Document of István Báthori, Prince of Hungary, on the signet ring of Louis II. Pozsony, 24 June 1527] In "Nekünk mégis Mohács kell..." *II. Lajos király rejtélyes halála és különböző temetései*, eds. Gábor Farkas Farkas, Zsolt Szebelédi, and Bernadett Varga, 203–204. Budapest: MTA Bölcsészettudományi Kutatóközpont, Országos Széchényi Könyvtár, 2016.
Bosztán cselebi [Ferdi]. "Szulejmán könyve (1520–1542), 1547 (részlet)." [Book of Süleyman (1520–1542), 1547 (excerpt)] In *Örök Mohács – Szövegek és értelmezések*, eds. János B. Szabó and Gábor Farkas Farkas, 364–368. Budapest: Bölcsészettudományi Kutatóközpont, 2020.
Brodarics, István. *Igaz leírás a magyaroknak a törökkel Mohácsnál vívott csatájáról.* [A True Account of the Battle of Mohács between the Hungarians and the Turks] Budapest: Magvető Könyvkiadó, 1983.
Burbery, John. "Beszámoló Lord Henry Howard utazásáról, 1671." [An account of the journey of Lord Henry Howard, 1671] In *Örök Mohács – Szövegek és értelmezések*, eds. János B. Szabó and Gábor Farkas Farkas, 491–492. Budapest: Bölcsészettudományi Kutatóközpont, 2020.
Burgio, Antonio Giovanni da. "Antonio Giovanni da Burgio pápai követ levele Jacopo Sadoleto pápai titkárnak Pozsony, 1526. szeptember 5. (részlet)." [Letter from papal ambassador Antonio Giovanni da Burgio to papal secretary Jacopo Sadoleto. Pozsony, 5 September 1526] In *Örök Mohács – Szövegek és értelmezések*, eds. János B. Szabó and Gábor Farkas Farkas, 131–132. Budapest: Bölcsészettudományi Kutatóközpont, 2020.
Camerarius, Joachim. "A Magyarországon, Mohácsnál elszenvedett vereségről és Lajos király haláláról, 1541." [About the defeat suffered in Hungary at Mohács and the death of King Louis] In *Örök Mohács – Szövegek és értelmezések*, eds. János B. Szabó and Gábor Farkas Farkas, 370–373. Budapest: Bölcsészettudományi Kutatóközpont, 2020.
Codex diplomaticus Hungariae. Tomi VIII. Vol. II. Stud. Georgius Fejér. Budae: Typis Typogr. Regiae Vniversitatis Vungaricae, 1832.
Cserei, Mihály. "Erdély históriája, 1709–1712." [History of Transylvania, 1709–1712] In *"Nekünk mégis Mohács kell..." II. Lajos király rejtélyes halála és különböző temetései*, eds. Gábor Farkas Farkas, Zsolt Szebelédi, and Bernadett Varga, 229–230. Budapest: MTA Bölcsészettudományi Kutatóközpont, Országos Széchényi Könyvtár, 2016.
Cuspinianus, Johannes. "Johannes Cuspinianus buzdító beszéde a Szent Római Birodalom fejedelmeihez és előkelőihez, 1526 vége." [Exhortation by Johannes Cuspinianus to the princes and nobles of the Holy Roman Empire, end of 1526] In *Örök Mohács – Szövegek és értelmezések*, eds. János B. Szabó and Gábor Farkas Farkas, 271–290. Budapest: Bölcsészettudományi Kutatóközpont, 2020.

Debreceni Ember, Pál. "Historia Ecclesiae Reformatae, 1728." In *"Nekünk mégis Mohács kell..." II. Lajos király rejtélyes halála és különböző temetései,* eds. Gábor Farkas Farkas, Zsolt Szebelédi, and Bernadett Varga, 230–231. Budapest: MTA Bölcsészettudományi Kutatóközpont, Országos Széchényi Könyvtár, 2016.

Dubravius, Jan. "Csehország története, 1552 (részlet)." [The History of Bohemia, 1552] In *Örök Mohács – Szövegek és értelmezések,* eds. János B. Szabó and Gábor Farkas Farkas, 390–394. Budapest: Bölcsészettudományi Kutatóközpont, 2020.

Egy cseh úr levele a Santa Clara kolostor főnöknőjéhez, 1526. november. [Letter from a Czech nobleman to the Mother Superior of the Santa Clara Convent, November 1526] In *Örök Mohács – Szövegek és értelmezések,* eds. János B. Szabó and Gábor Farkas Farkas, 207–216. Budapest: Bölcsészettudományi Kutatóközpont, 2020.

Esterházy, Pál. "Mars Hungaricus, 1664." In *Örök Mohács – Szövegek és értelmezések,* eds. János B. Szabó and Gábor Farkas Farkas, 481. Budapest: Bölcsészettudományi Kutatóközpont, 2020.

Etédi Sós, Márton. "Magyar gyász; vagy-is Második Lajos magyar királynak a mohátsi mezőn történt veszedelme, 1792." [Hungarian mourning; or the disaster of the Hungarian King Louis II in the field of Mohács, 1792] In *"Nekünk mégis Mohács kell..." II. Lajos király rejtélyes halála és különböző temetései,* eds. Gábor Farkas Farkas, Zsolt Szebelédi, and Bernadett Varga, 231. Budapest: MTA Bölcsészettudományi Kutatóközpont, Országos Széchényi Könyvtár, 2016.

Evlia Cselebi. "Utazások könyve. 1680 körül." [Book of travels. Around 1680] In *"Nekünk mégis Mohács kell..." II. Lajos király rejtélyes halála és különböző temetései,* eds. Gábor Farkas Farkas, Zsolt Szebelédi, and Bernadett Varga, 228. Budapest: MTA Bölcsészettudományi Kutatóközpont, Országos Széchényi Könyvtár, 2016.

Farkas, Gábor Farkas, Zsolt Szebelédi, and Bernadett Varga eds. *"Nekünk mégis Mohács kell..." II. Lajos király rejtélyes halála és különböző temetései.* [We need Mohács after all ... The death and the mysterious burials of King Louis II] Budapest: MTA Bölcsészettudományi Kutatóközpont, Országos Széchényi Könyvtár, 2016.

Ferdinánd osztrák főherceg. "Ferdinánd osztrák főherceg levele Ausztriai Margit főhercegnőnek, Linz, 1526. szeptember 18." [Letter from Archduke Ferdinand of Austria to Archduchess Margaret of Austria. 18 September 1526] In *"Nekünk mégis Mohács kell..." II. Lajos király rejtélyes halála és különböző temetései,* eds. Gábor Farkas Farkas, Zsolt Szebelédi, and Bernadett Varga, 184. Budapest: MTA Bölcsészettudományi Kutatóközpont, Országos Széchényi Könyvtár, 2016.

Fricsy, Ádám. "A pécsi klérus birtokainak telepítésügyi összeírása 1733-ban." [Settlement census of the estates of the clergy of Pécs in 1733] In *Baranyai helytörténetírás 1978,* ed. László Szita, 151–204. Pécs: Baranya Megyei Levéltár, 1979.

Ganz, David. "Krónika, 1592." [Chronicle, 1592] In *"Nekünk mégis Mohács kell..." II. Lajos király rejtélyes halála és különböző temetései,* eds. Gábor Farkas Farkas, Zsolt Szebelédi, and Bernadett Varga, 222. Budapest: MTA Bölcsészettudományi Kutatóközpont, Országos Széchényi Könyvtár, 2016.

Gyalókay, Jenő. *A mohácsi csata* [The Battle of Mohács] Budapest: Királyi Magyar Egyetemi Nyomda, 1926.

Habsburg-ház dicsőségtükre, Augsburg, 1559. [Ehrenspiegel des Hauses Österreich, Augsburg, 1559] In *Örök Mohács – Szövegek és értelmezések*, eds. János B. Szabó and Gábor Farkas Farkas, 395–400. Budapest: Bölcsészettudományi Kutatóközpont, 2020.

Hain, Gáspár. "Lőcsei krónika, 1684," [Lőcse chronicle, 1684] In *Örök Mohács – Szövegek és értelmezések*, eds. János B. Szabó and Gábor Farkas Farkas, 492–493. Budapest: Bölcsészettudományi Kutatóközpont, 2020.

Heltai, Gáspár. "Chronica az Magyaroknac dolgairúl. 1575 (részlet)." [Chronicle of the affairs of the Magyars, 1575 (Excerpt)] In *Örök Mohács – Szövegek és értelmezések*, eds. János B. Szabó and Gábor Farkas Farkas, 428–429. Budapest: Bölcsészettudományi Kutatóközpont, 2020.

Herman, Ottó. *A magyar halászat könyve I.* [The book of Hungarian fishing I.] Budapest: K. M. Természettudományi Társulat, 1887.

Hírszerzői jelentés Magyarországgal kapcsolatban. Pettau, 1526. szeptember 20." [Intelligence report on Hungary. Pettau, 20 September 1526] In *"Nekünk mégis Mohács kell..." 11. Lajos király rejtélyes halála és különböző temetései*, eds. Gábor Farkas Farkas, Zsolt Szebelédi, and Bernadett Varga, 186. Budapest: MTA Bölcsészettudományi Kutatóközpont, Országos Széchényi Könyvtár, 2016.

Ibrahim pasa tárgyalása Hyeronimus Łaskival. Isztambul, 1528 nyara." [Meeting of İbrahim Pasha with Hyeronimus Łaski. Istanbul, summer 1528] In *"Nekünk mégis Mohács kell..." 11. Lajos király rejtélyes halála és különböző temetései*, eds. Gábor Farkas Farkas, Zsolt Szebelédi, and Bernadett Varga, 206. Budapest: MTA Bölcsészettudományi Kutatóközpont, Országos Széchényi Könyvtár, 2016.

Idősebb Stefan Gerlach naplója, 1573. [Diary of Stephan Gerlach Sr., 1573] In *"Nekünk mégis Mohács kell..." 11. Lajos király rejtélyes halála és különböző temetései*, eds. Gábor Farkas Farkas, Zsolt Szebelédi, and Bernadett Varga, 219. Budapest: MTA Bölcsészettudományi Kutatóközpont, Országos Széchényi Könyvtár, 2016.

Iovius, Paulus. "Krónika a törökök viselt dolgairól. Róma, 1531 (részlet)." [A chronicle of the doings of the Turks. Rome 1531 (excerpt)] In *Örök Mohács – Szövegek és értelmezések*, eds. János B. Szabó and Gábor Farkas Farkas, 358–359. Budapest: Bölcsészettudományi Kutatóközpont, 2020.

Iovius, Paulus. "Lajos, Pannónia és Csehország királya, 1551." [Louis, King of Pannonia and Bohemia, 1551] In *Örök Mohács – Szövegek és értelmezések*, eds. János B. Szabó and Gábor Farkas Farkas, 387–390. Budapest: Bölcsészettudományi Kutatóközpont, 2020.

Ismeretlen horvát szerző. Kezdődik a harc és a magyar király panasza (részlet). 16. század második fele. [Unknown Croatian author: The battle begins and the complaints of the Hungarian King (excerpt). Second half of the 16th century] In

"Nekünk mégis Mohács kell…" II. Lajos király rejtélyes halála és különböző temetései, eds. Gábor Farkas Farkas, Zsolt Szebelédi, and Bernadett Varga, 215–218. Budapest: MTA Bölcsészettudományi Kutatóközpont, Országos Széchényi Könyvtár, 2016.

Ismeretlen szerző beszámolója a csatáról. 16. század első fele." [An unknown author's account of the battle. First half of the 16th century] In *"Nekünk mégis Mohács kell…" II. Lajos király rejtélyes halála és különböző temetései,* eds. Gábor Farkas Farkas, Zsolt Szebelédi, and Bernadett Varga, 204. Budapest: MTA Bölcsészettudományi Kutatóközpont, Országos Széchényi Könyvtár, 2016.

Ismeretlen szerző jelentései Thomas Wolsey kancellárnak. Köln, 1526. október 6. [Reports by an unknown author to Chancellor Thomas Wolsey. Cologne, 6 October 1526] In *"Nekünk mégis Mohács kell…" II. Lajos király rejtélyes halála és különböző temetései,* eds. Gábor Farkas Farkas, Zsolt Szebelédi, and Bernadett Varga, 191–192. Budapest: MTA Bölcsészettudományi Kutatóközpont, Országos Széchényi Könyvtár, 2016.

Isthvánffy, Miklós. "A magyarok történetéből. 1622 (részlet)." [From the History of the Hungarians. 1622 (Excerpt)] In *Örök Mohács – Szövegek és értelmezések,* eds. János B. Szabó and Gábor Farkas Farkas, 444–462. Budapest: Bölcsészettudományi Kutatóközpont, 2020.

Johann Fugger értesülései, Buda, 1526. augusztus 29–31.; Bécs, szeptember 5. (kivonat). [Information from Johann Fugger, Buda, 29–31 August 1526; Vienna, 5 September 1526] In *Örök Mohács – Szövegek és értelmezések,* eds. János B. Szabó and Gábor Farkas Farkas, 125. Budapest: Bölcsészettudományi Kutatóközpont, 2020.

Kemálpasazáde. "Mohácsnáme, 1526 és 1534 között, (Részletek)." [Mohácsname, between 1526 and 1534, (Excerpts)] In *Örök Mohács – Szövegek és értelmezések,* eds. János B. Szabó and Gábor Farkas Farkas, 326–338. Budapest: Bölcsészettudományi Kutatóközpont, 2020.

Kiss, Andrea and József Laszlovszky. "14th–16th Century Danube Floods and Long-Term Water-Level Changes in Archaeological and Sedimentary Evidence in the Western and Central Carpathian Basin. An Overview with Documentary Comparison." *Journal of Environmental Geography* 6 (2013), 3–4: 1–11.

Knauz krónika. 1556 körül (részlet). [Knauz chronicle. Around 1556] In *Örök Mohács – Szövegek és értelmezések,* eds. János B. Szabó and Gábor Farkas Farkas, 394. Budapest: Bölcsészettudományi Kutatóközpont, 2020.

Kohén, Joszéf ha. "Franciaország és az Oszmán Birodalom uralkodóinak krónikája, 1554." [A chronicle of the rulers of France and the Ottoman Empire, 1554] In *"Nekünk mégis Mohács kell…" II. Lajos király rejtélyes halála és különböző temetései,* eds. Gábor Farkas Farkas, Zsolt Szebelédi, and Bernadett Varga, 214. Budapest: MTA Bölcsészettudományi Kutatóközpont, Országos Széchényi Könyvtár, 2016.

Lazius, Wolfgang. "Ausztria történetének tizedei. 1548 körül." [Decades of the history of Austria. Around 1548] In *"Nekünk mégis Mohács kell…" II. Lajos király rejtélyes halála és különböző temetései,* eds. Gábor Farkas Farkas, Zsolt Szebelédi, and Bernadett Varga, 212. Budapest: MTA Bölcsészettudományi Kutatóközpont, Országos Széchényi Könyvtár, 2016.

Liszti, László. "Magyar Mars avagy Mohach mezején történt veszedelemnek emlékezete, 1653." [Hungarian Mars or the memory of the disaster in the field of Mohach, 1653] In *"Nekünk mégis Mohács kell..." II. Lajos király rejtélyes halála és különböző temetései,* eds. Gábor Farkas Farkas, Zsolt Szebelédi, and Bernadett Varga, 226–227. Budapest: MTA Bölcsészettudományi Kutatóközpont, Országos Széchényi Könyvtár, 2016.

Losonczi, István. "Hármas kis tükör. 1773." [Three Little Mirrors. 1773] In *"Nekünk mégis Mohács kell..." II. Lajos király rejtélyes halála és különböző temetései,* eds. Gábor Farkas Farkas, Zsolt Szebelédi, and Bernadett Varga, 231. Budapest: MTA Bölcsészettudományi Kutatóközpont, Országos Széchényi Könyvtár, 2016.

Lubenau, Reinhold. "Reinhold Lubenau útleírása, 1587." [Reinhold Lubenau's travelogue, 1587] In *"Nekünk mégis Mohács kell..." II. Lajos király rejtélyes halála és különböző temetései,* eds. Gábor Farkas Farkas, Zsolt Szebelédi, and Bernadett Varga, 221. Budapest: MTA Bölcsészettudományi Kutatóközpont, Országos Széchényi Könyvtár, 2016.

Marosi, Sándor and Jenő Szilárd eds. *A dunai Alföld.* [The Danube Plain.] Magyarország tájföldrajza 1. Budapest: Akadémiai Kiadó, 1967.

Memoria rerum. 16. század közepe (?)." [Memoria rerum. Mid-16th century (?)] In *"Nekünk mégis Mohács kell..." II. Lajos király rejtélyes halála és különböző temetései,* eds. Gábor Farkas Farkas, Zsolt Szebelédi, and Bernadett Varga, 214. Budapest: MTA Bölcsészettudományi Kutatóközpont, Országos Széchényi Könyvtár, 2016.

Nemes, István and Balázs Tolvaj. "II. Lajos magyar király (1506–1526) holttestének megtalálása." [The discovery of the body of King Louis II of Hungary (1506–1526)] *Orvosi Hetilap* 155 (2014): 475–480.

Oláh, Miklós. "Oláh Miklós levele VII. Kelemen pápához, Linz, 1530. február 15. (Részlet)." [Letter by Miklós Oláh to Pope Clement VII Linz, 15 February 1530 (Excerpt)] In *Örök Mohács – Szövegek és értelmezések,* eds. János B. Szabó and Gábor Farkas Farkas, 346–348. Budapest: Bölcsészettudományi Kutatóközpont, 2020.

Ottendorf, Henrik. "Henrik Ottendorf útleírása, 1663." [Henrik Ottendorf's travelogue, 1663] In *"Nekünk mégis Mohács kell..." II. Lajos király rejtélyes halála és különböző temetései,* eds. Gábor Farkas Farkas, Zsolt Szebelédi, and Bernadett Varga, 227. Budapest: MTA Bölcsészettudományi Kutatóközpont, Országos Széchényi Könyvtár, 2016.

Pap, Norbert, Péter Gyenizse, Máté Kitanics, and Gábor Szalai. "Az 1526. évi mohácsi csata helyszíneinek földrajzi jellemzői." [Geographical features of the sites of the Battle of Mohács in 1526] *Történelmi Szemle* 62 (2020): 111–151.

Partiba, Andrea. "Andrea Partiba jelentése egy hadnagyhoz. Bécs, 1526. november 2." [Andrea Partiba's report to a lieutenant. Vienna, 2 November 1526] In *"Nekünk mégis Mohács kell..." II. Lajos király rejtélyes halála és különböző temetései,* eds.

Gábor Farkas Farkas, Zsolt Szebelédi, and Bernadett Varga, 199. Budapest: MTA Bölcsészettudományi Kutatóközpont, Országos Széchényi Könyvtár, 2016.

Pécsi, Márton. *A magyarországi Duna-völgy kialakulása és felszínalaktana.* [The formation and subsurface structure of the Danube Valley in Hungary] Budapest: Akadémiai Kiadó, 1959.

Pecsevi, Ibrahim. "Krónika (részlet)." [Chronicle (excerpt)] In *"Nekünk mégis Mohács kell..." II. Lajos király rejtélyes halála és különböző temetései,* eds. Gábor Farkas Farkas, Zsolt Szebelédi, and Bernadett Varga, 236–256. Budapest: MTA Bölcsészettudományi Kutatóközpont, Országos Széchényi Könyvtár, 2016.

Pešina z Čechorodu, Jan Tomáš. "Ucalegon, 1663." In *Örök Mohács – Szövegek és értelmezések,* eds. János B. Szabó and Gábor Farkas Farkas, 479–480. Budapest: Bölcsészettudományi Kutatóközpont, 2020.

Pešina z Čechorodu, Jan Tomáš. "Mars Moravicus, 1677." In *Örök Mohács – Szövegek és értelmezések,* eds. János B. Szabó and Gábor Farkas Farkas, 485–491. Budapest: Bölcsészettudományi Kutatóközpont, 2020.

Pesti, János ed. *Baranya megye földrajzi nevei II.* [Geographical names in Baranya County II.] Pécs: Baranya Megyei Levéltár, 1982.

Péteri Takáts, József. "Úti jegyzetek, 1797." [Travel notes, 1797] In *"Nekünk mégis Mohács kell..." II. Lajos király rejtélyes halála és különböző temetései,* eds. Gábor Farkas Farkas, Zsolt Szebelédi, and Bernadett Varga, 232. Budapest: MTA Bölcsészettudományi Kutatóközpont, Országos Széchényi Könyvtár, 2016.

Pethő, Gergely. "Rövid magyar cronica, 1660 (részletek)," [A short Hungarian chronicle, 1660 (excerpts)] In *Örök Mohács – Szövegek és értelmezések,* eds. János B. Szabó and Gábor Farkas Farkas, 478. Budapest: Bölcsészettudományi Kutatóközpont, 2020.

Pigafetta, Marc'Antonio. "Útikönyv, 1585." [Guidebook, 1585] In *"Nekünk mégis Mohács kell..." II. Lajos király rejtélyes halála és különböző temetései,* eds. Gábor Farkas Farkas, Zsolt Szebelédi, and Bernadett Varga, 220–221. Budapest: MTA Bölcsészettudományi Kutatóközpont, Országos Széchényi Könyvtár, 2016.

Písař, Bartoš. "Krónika a prágai felkelésről. 1530 körül." [Chronicle of the Prague Uprising. Around 1530] In *Örök Mohács – Szövegek és értelmezések,* eds. János B. Szabó and Gábor Farkas Farkas, 355–358. Budapest: Bölcsészettudományi Kutatóközpont, 2020.

Sárffy, Ferenc. "Sárffy Ferenc győri várparancsnok jelentése II. Lajos holtteste megtalálásáról Brodarics István kancellárnak és szerémi püspöknek. Győr, 1526. október 19." [Ferenc Sárffy, the castle commander of Győr Castle, reports the discovery of the body of Louis II to István Brodarics, Chancellor and Bishop of Szerém. Győr, 19 October 1526] In *"Nekünk mégis Mohács kell..." II. Lajos király rejtélyes halála és különböző temetései,* eds. Gábor Farkas Farkas, Zsolt Szebelédi, and Bernadett Varga, 195–198. Budapest: MTA Bölcsészettudományi Kutatóközpont, Országos Széchényi Könyvtár, 2016.

Savoia, Fazio di. "Fazio di Savoia jelentése. Graz, 1526 szeptember 17." [The report of Fazio di Savoia. Graz, 17 September 1526] In *"Nekünk mégis Mohács kell..."*

11. Lajos király rejtélyes halála és különböző temetései, eds. Gábor Farkas Farkas, Zsolt Szebelédi, and Bernadett Varga, 184. Budapest: MTA Bölcsészettudományi Kutatóközpont, Országos Széchényi Könyvtár, 2016.

Siegler, Michael. "A magyarok, az erdélyiek és a szomszédos tartományok történetének kronológiája, 1563 (részlet)." [Chronology of the history of the Hungarians, the Transylvanians and the neighbouring provinces, 1563 (excerpt)] In *Örök Mohács – Szövegek és értelmezések*, eds. János B. Szabó and Gábor Farkas Farkas, 420–421. Budapest: Bölcsészettudományi Kutatóközpont, 2020.

Solymossy, Sándor. "Mohács emléke a néphagyományban." [The memory of Mohács in folk tradition] In *Mohácsi emlékkönyv 1526*, ed. Imre Lukinich, 335–348. Budapest: Királyi Magyar Egyetemi Nyomda, 1926.

Švihovský z Rýzmberka, Břetislav. "Břetislav Švihovský z Rýzmberka az egyik bajor herceghez. Raby/Rabí, 1526. szeptember 16." [Břetislav Švihovský z Rýzmberka to a Bavarian prince. Raby/Rabí, 16 September 1526] In *Örök Mohács – Szövegek és értelmezések*, eds. János B. Szabó and Gábor Farkas Farkas, 154–155. Budapest: Bölcsészettudományi Kutatóközpont, 2020.

Szapolyai, János. "Szapolyai János levele Krzysztof Szydłowiecki lengyel kancellárhoz. Székesfehérvár, 1526. november 11." [Letter of János Szapolyai to the Polish Chancellor Krzysztof Szydłowiecki. Székesfehérvár, 11 November 1526] In *"Nekünk mégis Mohács kell..." 11. Lajos király rejtélyes halála és különböző temetései*, eds. Gábor Farkas Farkas, Zsolt Szebelédi, and Bernadett Varga, 199. Budapest: MTA Bölcsészettudományi Kutatóközpont, Országos Széchényi Könyvtár, 2016.

Szerémi, György. "Levél Magyarország romlásáról. 1545 körül." [Letter on the deterioration of Hungary. Around 1545] In *"Nekünk mégis Mohács kell..." 11. Lajos király rejtélyes halála és különböző temetései*, eds. Gábor Farkas Farkas, Zsolt Szebelédi, and Bernadett Varga, 209–212. Budapest: MTA Bölcsészettudományi Kutatóközpont, Országos Széchényi Könyvtár, 2016.

Szulejmán szultán. "Szulejmán szultán két győzelmi jelentése, 1526." [Sultan Süleyman's two victory reports, 1526] In *Örök Mohács – Szövegek és értelmezések*, eds. János B. Szabó and Gábor Farkas Farkas, 258–267. Budapest: Bölcsészettudományi Kutatóközpont, 2020.

Szurmay, Sándor. *A mohácsi hadjárat 1526-ban* [The Mohács military campaign in 1526] Budapest: Ludovika Akadémia, 1901.

T. Mérey, Klára. *Baranya megye települései az Első katonai felmérés idején*. [Settlements of Baranya County at the time of the Military Survey I] Pécs: Baranya Megyei Levéltár, 2004.

Thurzó, Elek. "Thurzó Elek tárnokmester levele I. Zsigmond magyar királynak. Pozsony, 1526. szeptember 29." [Letter of Elek Thurzó, Treasurer to King Sigismund I of Poland. Pozsony, 29 September 1526] In *"Nekünk mégis Mohács kell..." 11. Lajos király rejtélyes halála és különböző temetései*, eds. Gábor Farkas Farkas, Zsolt Szebelédi, and Bernadett Varga, 190. Budapest: MTA Bölcsészettudományi Kutatóközpont, Országos Széchényi Könyvtár, 2016.

Toldy, Ferenc ed. *Brutus János Mihály magyar királyi történetíró magyar históriája 1490–1552*. [Hungarian history of János Mihály Brutus, Hungarian royal historian 1490–1552] Magyar Történelmi Emlékek 13. Pest: Eggenberger Ferdinánd M. Akad. Könyvárus, 1867.

Tóth, István György. "Athanasio Georgiceo álruhás császári megbízott útleírása a magyarországi török hódoltságról, 1626-ból." [Disguised imperial envoy Athanasio Georgiceo's travelogue on the Turkish occupation of Hungary in 1626] *Századok* 132 (1998): 837–858.

Tringli, István. *Hatalmaskodások a középkori Magyarországon* (Kézirat). [*Power struggles in medieval Hungary*] (Manuscript).

Tringli, István. *Sátoraljaújhely*. Magyar Várostörténeti Atlasz 2. Budapest: MTA Bölcsészettudományi Kutatóközpont, 2011.

Vass, Előd. "Mohács város hódoltságkori történetének forrásai." [Sources of the history of the city of Mohács during the Ottoman occupation] In *Baranyai helytörténetírás 1975*, ed. László Szita, 15–48. Pécs: Baranya Megyei Levéltár, 1976.

Veleslavína, Daniel Adam z. "Történeti kalendárium. 1590 (részlet)." [Historical calendar. 1590 (excerpt)] In *Örök Mohács – Szövegek és értelmezések,* eds. János B. Szabó and Gábor Farkas Farkas, 439–440. Budapest: Bölcsészettudományi Kutatóközpont, 2020.

Velius, Caspar Ursinus. "Tíz könyv a magyar háborúról. 1531–1537." [Ten books about the Hungarian war. 1531–1537] In *"Nekünk mégis Mohács kell..." II. Lajos király rejtélyes halála és különböző temetései,* eds. Gábor Farkas Farkas, Zsolt Szebelédi, and Bernadett Varga, 207. Budapest: MTA Bölcsészettudományi Kutatóközpont, Országos Széchényi Könyvtár, 2016.

Wallop, Sir John. "Sir John Wallop levele Thomas Wolsey kancellárnak. Köln, 1526. szeptember 30." [Letter from Sir John Wallop to Chancellor Thomas Wolsey. Cologne, 30 September 1526] In *"Nekünk mégis Mohács kell..." II. Lajos király rejtélyes halála és különböző temetései,* eds. Gábor Farkas Farkas, Zsolt Szebelédi, and Bernadett Varga, 191. Budapest: MTA Bölcsészettudományi Kutatóközpont, Országos Széchényi Könyvtár, 2016.

Záim, Kjátib Mehmed. "Történetek gyűjteménye, 1578 (részlet)." [A collection of stories, 1578 (excerpt)] In *Örök Mohács – Szövegek és értelmezések,* eds. János B. Szabó and Gábor Farkas Farkas, 430–431. Budapest: Bölcsészettudományi Kutatóközpont, 2020.

Zermegh, János. "Emlékirat a Ferdinánd és János, Magyarország királyai között történt dolgokról. 1556 után (részlet)." [A memoir of the events between Ferdinánd and János, kings of Hungary. After 1566] In *Örök Mohács – Szövegek és értelmezések,* eds. János B. Szabó and Gábor Farkas Farkas, 421. Budapest: Bölcsészettudományi Kutatóközpont, 2020.

PART 4

Spaces of Remembrance

CHAPTER 11

Hünkâr Tepesi (Törökdomb): the Ottoman Memorial Place of the Battle

Norbert Pap, Pál Fodor, Máté Kitanics, Tamás Morva, Gábor Szalai, Erika Hancz and Péter Gyenizse

1 Introduction

The Mohács Plain shows traces of several military events and ambitions along with anthropogenic landscape elements. The former belligerent parties (both the winners and the losers) shaped the environment in various ways, as they erected their memorial edifices. As a result, military activities in the various periods and their memories have become interconnected and influenced each other to some extent. Some of the elements of the military landscape with symbolic content go back to at least the Roman times. Several battles were fought here in the 16th–17th centuries, and their traces were layered on top of each other, making it difficult to understand their history. From the point of view of military memory, a "hybrid" military landscape of different ages emerged. The tools, ways and scenes of remembering and reminding have changed several times in the past 500 years, highlighting different landscape elements in each case. The efforts of the local community and the central government have had an impact on the development of the cultural landscape. The economic, political and cultural consequences of this are equally important.

One of the most exciting landscape elements that characterises a long period of history is Törökdomb (Turkish Hill), a hillock hardly standing out of the surrounding Mohács Plain, a legendary and almost completely forgotten place from which, according to contemporary Ottoman sources, Süleyman the Magnificent was watching the battle and praying for victory. In this chapter, we analyse this elevation as a symbolic element of the militarized landscape in a variety of ways in terms of what roles it might have played in different historical periods, how it was used, how it shaped the memory of the battle, and what it has to say about the social changes that have taken place over the past five hundred years.

2   Research History and Methods

The changing position of researchers in connection with Turkish Hill was also shaped by views on historical tradition and local legends. Until the 1910s, the legitimacy of Turkish Hill as the place of the battles was firm; there was general consensus that the battle had taken place in its immediate vicinity.[1] Archaeological research carried out in connection with the 400th anniversary did not confirm the assumptions that the Ottomans had buried their deceased at this place.[2] Subsequently, several scholars have suggested that the battle might have taken place further south of the site known by tradition, near the Borza Stream or even further south, beyond today's borders.[3] The environment of the mass graves discovered close to nearby Sátorhely in the 1960s turned attention to a new location.[4] The Mohács Historical Memorial Site was completed on the 450th anniversary of the battle in the area where the mass graves were excavated. The memorial site became the main venue for commemorations, taking over the former role of Turkish Hill as an authentic part of the battlefield. More recently, János B. Szabó has taken the view that after the battle, the Ottoman army set up its camp north of the battlefield and Turkish Hill was

---

1   István Kápolnai Pauer, "A mohácsi hadjárat 1526-ban," [The Mohács military campaign in 1526] *Hadtörténelmi Közlemények* 2 (1889), no. 2, pp. 177–208., pp. 440–462.; Leopold Kupelwieser, *Ungarns Kämpfe mit den Osmanen bis zur Schlacht bei Mohács* (Wien, Leipzig: Wilhelm Braumüller, 1895); Béla Németh, "Baranya Szent Istvántól a jelenkorig," [Baranya County from St. Stephen to the present day] in *Baranya múltja és jelenje II.*, ed. Ferenc Várady (Pécs: Pécsi Irodalmi és Könyvnyomdai Részvénytársaság, 1897), pp. 209–730.; Sándor Szurmay, *A mohácsi hadjárat 1526-ban* [The Mohács military campaign in 1526] (Budapest: Ludovika Akadémia, 1901); Tivadar Ortvay, *A mohácsi csata elvesztésének okai és következményei* [The reasons for and the consequences of losing the Battle of Mohács] (Budapest: Magyar Tudományos Akadémia, 1910).

2   Endre Gergely, "Ásatások a mohácsi csatatéren (1924, 1925)," [Excavations on the battlefield of Mohács (1924, 1925)] in *Mohács emlékkönyv 1926*, ed. Imre Lukinich (Budapest: Királyi Magyar Egyetemi Nyomda, 1926), pp. 349–360.

3   Jenő Gyalókay, *A mohácsi csata. 1526. augusztus 29.* [The Battle of Mohács. 29 August 1526] (Budapest: Királyi Magyar Egyetemi Nyomda, 1926); Lajos Bende, "A mohácsi csata," [The Battle of Mohács] *Hadtörténelmi Közlemények* 13 (1966), no. 3, pp. 532–567; Géza Perjés, *Mohács* (Budapest: Magvető Könyvkiadó, 1979); Ferenc Szakály, *A mohácsi csata* [The Battle of Mohács] (Budapest: Akadémiai Kiadó, 1981).

4   László Papp, "A mohácsi csatahely kutatása," [Research into the battlefield of Mohács] in *A Janus Pannonius Múzeum évkönyve 1960*, ed. János Dombay (Pécs: Janus Pannonius Múzeum, 1961), pp. 197–253.

indeed the site of the sultan's tent.[5] This brought the hill back into the historical debate after a long period.

We have used several methods in our investigations. Numerous written sources mention Turkish Hill in the centuries following the Battle of Mohács in 1526, which has been the main point of reference for visitors to the battlefield for a long time. The first Hungarian map, made by scribe Lazarus (Lázár), depicts Mohács and identifies the place of battle, but there is no reference to Turkish Hill itself. Useful map material is only available from the end of the 17th century. They depict the area in more or less detail and provide important information about the relative location of the battlefield and the elements of the terrain, while their annotations reveal how the people living here related to the landscape, and what languages and place names they used. Previous archaeological research in the area has resulted in several documents that contain useful and important information on the age and human use of Turkish Hill. This was complemented by the inspection of the area and field observations. In our research, we also considered the examination of folk memory important. Since Turkish Hill was largely destroyed physically in the 20th century, our goal was to identify its original size from primary sources, descriptions and maps, through remote-sensing methods and geomorphological inspection, and we attempted to determine its physical parameters.

3 Research Findings

3.1 *Turkish Hill in Written Sources*

After the battles with the Ottomans and the sieges of cities and fortresses, the memory of the sultan's presence or his tent, including its occasional physical traces, were preserved at several places. Significant building complexes marked the site of the sultan's tent in Kosovo and Turbék next to Szigetvár, which also functioned as memorial places of the battles fought in 1389 and 1566. Additional memorial places commemorating the sultan's presence are known in Hungary. If we look at their names and the rulers they are associated with, it is easy to see that they allude to the most famous military campaigns and successes of Sultan Süleyman I in Hungary. These high grounds, which marked Süleyman's route and campsites and were seen by 16th-century Ottoman Turks as "sacred" places, were most often called *Hünkâr tepesi* (Sultan's or Emperor's Hill). The

---

5 János B. Szabó, *A mohácsi csata* [The Battle of Mohács] (Budapest: Corvina, 2006), p. 141. Cf. János B. Szabó, *Mohács. Régi kérdések, új válaszok* [Mohács. Old questions, new answers] (Budapest: HM Hadtörténeti Intézet és Múzeum, Line Design, 2015), pp. 119–132.

first one was probably created in Nándorfehérvár (Belgrade) to preserve the memory of the 1521 siege and conquest. A contemporary Ottoman chronicler recalls the following when describing Sultan Mehmed III's entry into Belgrade in 1596:

> The imperial tent has since long ago been set up on the sacred place known by the name Sultan's Hill (*Hünkâr depesi*). Of [the ruler's] predecessors, his highness the late and deceased Sultan Süleyman khan of a fortunate life, the conqueror of the well-protected Belgrade – may he rest in peace! – had a station there. During campaigns to Hungary, the imperial tents are pitched up on that pleasant and fortunate site.[6]

The sacredness of the place was also ensured by the fact that Süleyman's campsite was also set up here and was later moved to Istanbul in 1566. The sultan died near Szigetvár, and his funeral service was held here with the participation of the new ruler, Selim II.[7] According to Ottoman chronicles, the example of the great conqueror was followed not only by the later sultans (such as Mehmed III mentioned above), but also by the grand viziers and commanders-in-chief (*serdar, serasker*). Thus, for example, in the spring of 1594, Grand Vizier Sinan Pasha, who set off to attack Vienna, Saturcı Mehmed Pasha, who was prepared to take Várad in 1598, or the commanders of the campaigns in the late 17th-century wars all set up their tents on the Emperor's Hill in Belgrade (to ask the spirit of the great ruler for help).[8] According to Evliya Çelebi, vineyards and gardens were planted east of the castle of Esztergom, where the archiepiscopal see used to be, with one of their edges stretching up to the "hill of Süleyman khan (*Süleymân Hân depesi*)"; this means that one of the places of the 1543 (successful) siege associated with the great ruler was also called "the Sultan's

---

6 *Topçular Kâtibi 'Abdülkâdir (Kadrî) Efendi Tarihi (Metin ve Tahlîl)* I., ed. Ziya Yılmazer (Türk Tarih Kurumu Yayınları) III/21 (Ankara: 2003), p. 135; see also Pál Fodor's "Süleyman and Hungary" in the present volume.
7 Selânikî Mustafa Efendi, *Tarih-i Selânikî*, ed. Mehmet İpşirli (İstanbul: İstanbul Üniversitesi Edebiyat Fakültesi, 1989), pp. 49–51.
8 Kâtib Çelebi, *Fezleke I. Osmanlı Tarihi (1000–1065/1591–1655)*, ed. Zeynep Aycibin (İstanbul: Camlica Basim Yayin, 2016), p. 41, p. 142. Lajos Fekete, "Hódoltságkori oszmanli-török helyneveink," [Ottoman Turkish toponyms from the period of Turkish occupation] *Századok* 57–58 (1923–1924), no. 1–6, p. 616. Based on the maps of the late 17th-century wars, it seems that this elevation stretched south of Belgrade at the foothills of the Mountain and castle of Žarnov (Serbian Avala, Turkish Havale). Cf. Željko Škalamera and Marko Popović, "Novi podaci sa plana Beograda iz 1683," in *Godišnjak Grada Beograda*. Knj. 23 (Beograd: Muzej Grada Beograda, 1976), pp. 33–58.

Hill."[9] Similarly, Evliya Çelebi describes a place called "castle of Süleyman khan/ shah's tent" (*kal'a-i çârbâğ-ı cihân, ya'nî otağ-ı Süleymân Hân*, or *kal'a-i otağ-ı Süleymân Şah*) in the neighbourhood of Schwechat near Vienna. Allegedly, Sultan Süleyman's tent complex was set up there when he was attempting to take Vienna (in vain) in 1529, and, according to the traveller, it got into the hands of the Germans after the Ottomans had retreated; the Germans created a building complex there specifically for the purpose of establishing their own memorial place, which copied the former imperial tent complex.[10]

We believe that the special respect that surrounded the sultan's person may have led to the army's command posts receiving special attention, and the examples above suggest that they were remembered and referred to for a long time. In two places (Kosovo and Szigetvár) it is attested and elsewhere (Belgrade) it is more than likely that the site of the sultan's tent was treated as a sacred place, either in connection with his death or his place of residence.[11] Therefore, perhaps there is good reason for us to believe that this marking practice was also applied after one of the greatest and most important military victories of the 16th-century Ottoman Empire.

The "military landscape" in Mohács along with Turkish Hill appeared several times in descriptions by 16th-17th-century travellers. Hans Dernschwam saw *"Földvár, this once famous market town with its church"* in 1555, just before arriving at the station in Mohács.[12] Stephan Gerlach Snr described the area in 1573 when he travelled to Constantinople as follows:

> We came to a market town called Mohács, and as we still had plenty of time, my honorable lord and I went half a mile on a carriage up to the

---

9   Evliyâ Çelebi b. Derviş Mehemmed Zıllî, *Evliyâ Çelebi Seyahatnâmesi. VI. Kitap. Topkapı Sarayı Kütüphanesi Revan 1457 Numaralı Yazmanın Transkripsiyonu–Dizini*, eds. Seyit Ali Kahraman and Yücel Dağlı (İstanbul: Yapı Kredi, 2002), p. 171; cf. Fekete: ibid.

10 Evliyâ Çelebi b. Derviş Mehemmed Zıllî, *Evliyâ Çelebi Seyahatnâmesi. 7. Kitap. Topkapı Sarayı Kütüphanesi Bağdat 308 Numaralı Yazmanın Transkripsiyonu–Dizini*, eds. Yücel Dağlı, Seyit Ali Kahraman, and Robert Dankoff (İstanbul: Yapı Kredi, 2003), pp. 89–92. On the Austrian's complex "imitating" the sultan's camp, see the quoted study by Pál Fodor in this volume.

11 Norbert Pap, "Iszlám versus kereszténység – szimbolikus térfoglalás Szigetváron," [Islam vs. Christianity – a symbolic occupation of space in Szigetvár] in *Szulejmán szultán Szigetváron. A szigetvári kutatások 2013–2016 között*, eds. Norbert Pap and Pál Fodor (Pécs: Pannon Castrum Kft., 2017), pp. 205–242.

12 *Hans Dernschwam's Tagebuch einer Reise nach Konstantinopel und Kleinasien (1553/55). Nach der Urschrift im Fugger-Archiv*, ed. Franz Babinger (München, Leipzig: 1923), p. 267.; cf. Hans Dernschwam, *Erdély. Besztercebánya. Törökországi útinapló* [Translyvania. Besztercebánya. Turkish Travel Diary] (Budapest: Európa Könyvkiadó, 1984), pp. 492–493.

place where the last king of Hungary, Louis and his thirty-three thousand men encountered three hundred thousand Turks, and were beaten and lost. Today, this field is partly grassy and partly arable land. The heads of corn were rippling when we got there. We could still see he ditches where their beds were set up and where the dead were buried.[13]

Since there was no Ottoman victory memorial standing there at the time, the tombs and the ditches, about which we have no details, were crucial in the representation of the battle.

One hundred years after the battle, the traveller Athanasius Georgiceo visited Mohács in 1626 and crossed the 1526 battlefield on his way to Eszék (Osijek). In his travelogue, he gives the following account:

> ... on the right we saw a very beautiful landscape and on the left a very large lake with waterfowl, although there was very little water in it. This lake is usually flooded by the Danube and when the river recedes, it leaves a lot of fish behind in ponds. Next to the lake, about a mile from Mohács, there was a small hill made by janissaries when Sultan Süleyman was camping here, being entrenched, as it can still be seen today, when his people defeated the king called Louis. Half a mile away from here, we found two churches on certain hills, both lying in ruins at a beautiful location, about an Italian mile away from each other.[14]

The traveller is talking about Turkish Hill on the edge of the lake and swamp later called the Vizslak Meadow; he also mentions the legend according to which janissaries had erected it. The expression "being entrenched" certainly refers to the fact that is mentioned by many visitors to the site: the memorial was surrounded by ditches.

İbrahim Peçevi, a historiographer born in Pécs who was familiar with the site, was the first to describe the memorial place and its date of foundation in his chronicle written in the 1640s. He mentions the hill, which he calls Sultan's

---

13 László Szalay, *Adalékok a magyar nemzet történetéhez a XVI-dik században* [Additions to the history of the Hungarian nation in the sixteenth century] (Pest: Ráth Mór, 1859), p. 222. Cf. its more recent translation (with minor styptics differences): Dávid Ungnád, *Ungnád Dávid Konstantinápolyi utazásai* [Dávid Undnád's travels in Constantinople] (Budapest: Szépirodalmi Könyvkiadó, 1986), p. 121.

14 István György Tóth, "Athanasio Georgiceo álruhás császári megbízott útleírása a magyarországi török hódoltságról, 1626-ból," [Disguised imperial envoy Athanasio Georgiceo's travelogue about the Turkish occupation of Hungary, 1626] *Századok* 132 (1998), no. 4, p. 854.

or Emperor's Hill (*Hünkâr tepesi*), while recounting the story of the battle, and also tells how a kiosk was later built on it and a well dug next to it to commemorate the victory:

> As the fortunate padishah of Islam arrived at the tall hill called Sultan's Hill on the plain of Mohács, he dismounted his horse, ascended the hill and sat on a throne. I, a poor feeble-minded person, traversed the area with youthful zeal under the pretext of hunting for goshawks before the one thousandth year,[15] and God the Most High wot, I climbed that hill twice or three times because I thought it would bring me luck, for a padishah fighting for the faith prayed to heaven from there. It was indeed very high and hard to climb. Not long ago, when the late standard-bearer Hasan Pasha was the governor-general of Buda,[16] he had a simple kiosk-like edifice (*köşk şekli*) framed up and a well dug next to it.[17]

In 1663, Henrik Ottendorf, who was travelling in the region, identified the hill as being near Mohács, where he believes Süleyman's tent was set up. Like Georgiceo, he reports on a fortified site with ditches, which may have looked like this:

> Half a mile beyond Mohács, near the Danube, on an elevated hill, there is a large building made of boards, like a pleasure-house, and is surrounded by ditches. There is a deep well next to it. It was erected to honour the memory of Soliman who had set up his tent and first camp here, when he encountered King Louis and defeated him.[18]

---

15   19 October 1591–7 October 1592.
16   This refers to Acem Hasan Pasha, who was indeed standard-bearer (*mir-i alem*), before he served as *beylerbeyi* in Buda from February 1630 to the beginning of October 1631. Antal Gévay, *A' budai pasák* [The Pashas of Buda] (Bécsben: 1841), pp. 29–30.
17   *Tarih-i Peçevi*, Vol. I, p. 89; in Hungarian: Pál Fodor, "Ibrahim Pecsevi leírása a mohácsi csatáról és II. Lajos király haláláról," [İbrahim Peçevi's account of the Battle of Mohács and the death of King Louis II] in *"Nekünk mégis Mohács kell…" II. Lajos király rejtélyes halála és különböző temetései*, eds. Gábor Farkas Farkas, Zsolt Szebelédi, and Bernadett Varga (Budapest: MTA Bölcsészettudományi Kutatóközpont, Országos Széchényi Könyvtár, 2016), p. 243; cf. Fodor's study in the present volume.
18   Henrik Ottendorf, *Budáról Belgrádba 1663. Ottendorf Henrik képes útleírása* [From Buda to Belgrade 1663. Henrik Ottendorf's travelogue with pictures] (Tolna Vármegye Múltjából 7) (Pécs: Dunántúli Egyetemi Ny., 1943), pp. 54–55.

In 1663, Evliya Çelebi saw a pavilion at the place called the Sultan's or the Emperor's Hill (*Hünkâr tepesi*) where people used to pray and where Sultan Süleyman himself supposedly prayed for victory during the battle:

> This place is now called Hünkâr Depesi. Since they believe that the 'prayer is heard' they would come up here and pray. Currently, there is a wooden pavilion on the hill that was built by Vizier Hasan Pasha of Buda. It has a well abounding in water. Süleyman khan prayed with his arms open on this hill, and as all the warriors of the faith had said amen, the crusader figures of the unbelievers became visible and the skirmishers of Gazi Bali and Hüsrev Beys set out to fight with the army of unbelievers. ... Forty thousand of our faithful Muslim warriors had become martyrs, whose corpses were collected on Süleyman khan's order, and the funeral service was held for them near the fortress of Mohács on the high hill known as Süleyman Khan's Hill, with all the warriors of the faith present, where they were buried. It is currently a place of pilgrimage. There is a tall wooden pavilion at the top of this place of pilgrimage; next to it, there is a well giving water of life, where all passers-by can quench their thirst by drinking its water, praying for God's mercy on the martyrs who died on the plains of Kerbela[19] and Mohács. There are ditches on the four sides of this pilgrimage site, which were dug on the order of the patron of pious foundations, Hasan Pasha, governor-general of Buda, saying 'The martyrs buried here are not to be gnawed at by animals.' In short, it is a place that is worth a visit. Hundreds of pious Muslims have seen and testified that on Friday night, as well as on the night of *kadr, berat* and *miraj* often a light shone over these forty thousand martyrs.[20]

In his account of the 1686–1687 military campaign in Hungary, officer Giovanni Francesco Gemelli Careri describes a former wooden mosque converted into a chapel near Mohács:

> We set up our camp not far from Mohács, and the enemy did so at the place we had left, next to a former wooden mosque converted into a chapel, which was erected by Soliman in memory of the fallen King Louis

---

19 The Battle of Karbala in Iran was fought on 10 October 680 by Hussein ibn Ali against the Umayyad Caliphate, who fell with a small group of his followers. The day of the battle is the greatest (memorial) holiday of Shiites.

20 *Evliyâ Çelebi Seyahatnâmesi*, VI. *Kitap*, pp. 112–113. The mentioned nights (kadr: 27 Ramadan, berat: 14–15 Şaban and miraj: 26 Receb) are considered sacred in the Islamic religion.

and his victory, and as a token of his gratitude to the false prophet, he ordered that a dervish should pray there all the time.[21]

Also in 1687, major general Tobias von Hasslingen described the site as follows:

> We have also discovered that a wooden tent has been erected on a hill next to the marsh (visible at ^{Xm}) to commemorate the place where the Turkish sultan's tent stood when he clashed with King Louis.[22]

In his work entitled *The History of the Turks...*, Paul Rycaut (1629–1700), an English diplomat, mentions the place in connection with the battle fought at Nagyharsány in 1687:

> ... this Victory was obtained in that very Ground, where Lodowick, the last of the Hungarian kings was Slain, and his Army Routed by Sultan Soliman the Magnificent, who in Memory thereof, caused a Mosch of Wood to be Erected, and Endowed it with Eight hundred Crowns Yearly Rent, that Dervises, who are a fort of Turkish Friers, might solemnize their daily Devotions and Prayers in that place.[23]

In a country description published by András Vályi in 1799, Turkish Hill is part of the presentation of nearby Nagynyárád:"to this day, the ramparts and the hill (said to be the site of the emperor's tent), erected by human hands, are still visible."[24] In his work published in 1828 on the history of the Ottoman Empire, Joseph von Hammer-Purgstall mentions a hill near Földvárpuszta in Sátorhely, where Süleyman's tent stood. In his account, the well at the foot of the hill was called the "Török kútja" (Turkish Well) by locals and on the top of the hill, the foundations of a building were still visible at the time.[25]

---

21 Giovanni Francesco Gemelli Careri, "Beszámoló a magyarországi hadjáratokról," [An account of the Hungarian military campaign] *Hadtörténelmi Közlemények* 115 (2002), no. 2, p. 413.
22 István Kuti and András Újvári: "Mohács hadibázisának védelme 1687-ben," [Defence of military bases in Mohács in 1687] in *Előadások és tanulmányok a török elleni visszafoglaló háborúk történetéből 1686–1688*, ed. László Szita (Pécs: 1989), p. 79.
23 Paul Rycaut, *The History of the Turks. Beginning with the Year 1679* (London: 1700), p. 245. (We are indebted to Balázs Polgár for drawing our attention to this source).
24 András Vályi: *Magyar országnak leírása II.* [The History of Hungary II] (Buda: 1799), p. 689.
25 Joseph von Hammer-Purgstall, *Geschichte des osmanischen Reiches... III. ... 1520–1574*. (Pest: C. A. Hartleben, 1828), pp. 636–637.

Based on the pictures depicted in the sources, the victory monument was built along the busy Eszék-Buda road on a low elevation on the bank of a wide area of water and gallery forests along the Danube River. The memorial building was made of wood surrounded by ditches with a well next to it. Two sources indicate that the dervishes might have performed religious services at the memorial or resting place, but this is yet to be confirmed, especially in the light of other, first of all Ottoman sources. Christian sources were the first to mention that the sultan's tent must have been on this elevation, while some Ottoman sources emphasize that the sultan prayed there and did not mention a tent (although, as we have seen, the name of the Emperor's Hill is usually associated with the place of Süleyman's campsite in other sources). Some of the sources call the building a wooden mosque and emphasize its religious role by pointing out that it was supposedly transformed to a chapel during the wars of liberation. As for the function of the well, it can therefore be assumed that, in addition to providing water for travellers and their animals, it may also have had a sacral role, related to ritual ablution.

Süleyman already had a memorial place in nearby Szigetvár, at the site where he died in 1566.[26] The Süleyman memorial in Mohács was built later, but it had a similar, partly political, partly sacred function. The similarities between the two places of memory are as follows:

i. they commemorate the great Ottoman military victories (1526, 1566);
ii. they pay homage to the memory of Sultan Süleyman;
iii. they receive religious content by the fact that they are looked after by dervishes (Szigetvár) and that they serve as a place of prayer for the purpose of remembering Muslim battles (Mohács);
iv. they function as pilgrimage sites – celebrating the extension of the *darü'l-islam* (the Abode of Islam);
v. there arose a need both in Turbék and in Mohács for reclaiming the sites in a spiritual sense during the wars of liberation: a chapel was dedicated to Virgin Mary in Turbék, while sources also mention that a chapel was dedicated on Turkish Hill, but there is no credible information about a related cult.

At the same time, the differences are also significant, which result from the nature of these memorial places and the historical significance of their builders. While one of the contemporary grand viziers of the Ottoman Empire was involved in creating the monument in Turbék, "only" a frontier governor-general, that of Buda contributed to the memorial place in Mohács much later

---

26   This was Turbék, an Ottoman settlement near Szigetvár.

in the 17th century. Szigetvár is the place where the sultan died, but Mohács is "only one" of the sites of victorious battles – even if it was perhaps the most important one. Turbék had more financial resources resulting in buildings, a fortification and place of pilgrimage made from durable materials, while Mohács's "Emperor's Hill" only had a wooden building with a well, which could be much less attractive as a pilgrimage place. In spite of its more modest construction, the site in Mohács had its own significance too: it was one of the "milestones" marking the main route of Süleyman's conquests in Hungary to contemporary Muslims. Numerous Muslim pilgrimage sites have been established around the graves of various religious people (such as dervishes) in the area of the Northern Balkans and Hungary occupied by the Ottoman Turks. It is hardly a coincidence that the relatively small number of pilgrimage places of "secular" origin are related to either Süleyman or to the commanders who played a key part in breaking Hungary's resistance. This is how, in addition to the Emperor's Hills commemorating Süleyman, the burial place of Bali Bey between Semendria and Belgrade at the Lower Danube, who had a crucial role in the success at Mohács, had become a place of pilgrimage.[27] What is common in the memorial sites in Szigetvár and Mohács is that the memory of both places have survived for a long time and were filled with religious content after the Ottoman rule had collapsed.

3.2 Turkish Hill on Historical Maps

The representations of Turkish Hill (Törökdomb, Türkenhügel, Sátoristye) on maps constitute an important and special group of sources. As they were designed, in part, for military purposes or establishing property ownership, their credibility was a major factor when they were made. The symbols and legends are important visual markers of change. These maps refer back to previous stages as well as to geographical and environmental conditions.

---

27 "Praise for the pilgrimage place of the fortress of Semendria. First, on the west side of the town is a wide, high hill. There is the pilgrimage site of the martyrs. In addition, half an hour west of the town, on a high hill on the Danube towards Belgrade, is the pilgrimage site of Gazi Bali Bey. ... He was martyred in the year 933 (1526–27) and is buried in this convent. It is still a convent of the honourable dervishes, to which the men of God make pilgrimage." Evliyâ Çelebi b. Derviş Mehemmed Zıllî, *Evliyâ Çelebi Seyahatnâmesi. 5. Kitap. Topkapı Sarayı Bağdat 307 Yazmasının Transkripsiyonu–Dizini*, eds. Yücel Dağlı, Seyit Ali Kahraman, and İbrahim Sezgin (İstanbul: Yapı Kredi, 2001), p. 318. For more on this issue, see Pál Fodor, "Wolf on the Border: Yahyapaşaoğlu Bali Bey (?–1527): Expansion and Provincial Elite in the European Confines of the Ottoman Empire in the Early Sixteenth Century", in *Şerefe: Studies in Honour of Prof. Géza Dávid on His Seventeenth Birthday*, 21st-Century Studies in Humanities, eds. Pál Fodor, Nándor E. Kovács and Bence Péri, Budapest: Research Centre for the Humanities HAS, 2019, pp. 57–87.

One of the first depictions of the Turkish Hill is the engraving that records the site of the encampment of the Christian armies against the Ottomans between Mohács and Dunawar (Dunavár) from 31 July to 5 August 1687. On this small hill near the marsh a stylized roofless square building can be seen. Another example is a drawing that shows the campsite of the Christian troops encountering the Ottomans between Mohács and Baranyavár in June 1691. This hill is marked as Wachthügel (Watch-hill) right on the Danube side of the Mohács-Baranyavár main road (Figure 11.1/A),[28] referring to the original function of the place.

In the map dated between 1720 to 1725, which was made by Sámuel Mikoviny and represented Bács County, Turkish Hill is shown as the site of Süleyman's tent with the legend *"Solman Tentorii Shanzense"* (Figure 11.1/B).[29]

Another document showing Turkish Hill is Vötter's map, which can be dated to 1766[30] or possibly to the 1770s[31] with the legends *"Sháturyx"* and *"Scaturigo"*, including the symbol for a Christian chapel (Figure 11.1/C and D).

As we can see, the names of the memorial place are listed in their South Slavic form (Sháturyx,[32] Satoristi[33]), suggesting that they represent the perceptions and language use of the Southern Slav populace that survived even the Turks in the region (Figure. 11.1/C and E). Accordingly, the dominant perception in local memory was that the sultan had set up his tent on this hill. The name of Turkish Hill had ultimately lost its reference to the tent when an estate centre was built around 2.5 km away to the west, which was the basis of today's Sátorhely. The map of 1838,[34] which mentions it as the Turkish Hill, keeps the traditional name, while the estate centre mentioned before also emerges under the name of Sátoristye, "borrowing" the name and some of the memorial functions referring to the battle (Figure 11.1/E). This is why the memorial symbol of the 1526 battle (crossed swords with the date) is shown next to the village of Sátorhely on the map of Military Survey II (Figure 11.1/I).[35] The German name Türkenhügel, which is the translation of Hungarian Törökdomb, appears

---

28 H III c 182/37 – Veldt Lager zwischen Mohaz und Baranuivar den 15. July 1691. Institute and Museum of Military History.
29 MTA TK Mo. 1. – Map of Sámuel Mikoviny: Comitatus Bacsiensis Pars.
30 HU MNL OL E 156-a. - Fasc. 168. – No. 038/a. – Urbarialis census taken by István Márffy, Royal Prefect of the Hungarian Treasury (27 June 1766). Hungarian National Archives.
31 S_11_-_No._50. – Delineatio praedii Földvár in regio camerali dominio Belle ejusdemque districtu Nyaradiensi situati ... (1775 k.). Hungarian National Archives.
32 HU MNL OL E 156-a. - Fasc. 168. - No. 038/a. – Urbarialis census taken by István Márffy, Royal Prefect of the Hungarian Treasury (27 June 1766). Hungarian National Archives.
33 TK 244 – Maps of Baranya County (1769 k.). Manuscript maps, National Széchényi Library.
34 B IX a 1441 – Baranya Vármegye Föld Abrosza [Book of Maps of Baranya County] (1838). Institute and Museum of Military History.
35 Military Survey II (1806–1869).

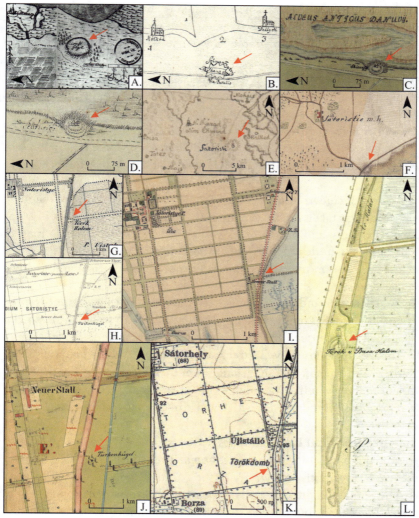

FIGURE 11.1 Törökdomb (Turkish Hill) on maps. Edited by Péter Gyenizse and Tamás Morva
Legend: A = Turkish Hill as Watchtower (Wachthügel) in 1691; B = Comitatus Bacsiensis Pars, S. Mikoviny, 1725 (?); C = Turkish Hill with the legend Sháturix and the cross on the 1766 Vötter map; D = Turkish Hill with the legend Scaturigo and the cross on a 1775 (?) map; E = Turkish Hill with the legend Sátoristi and the symbol for the chapel around 1769; F = Turkish Hill and Sátorhely (Satoristie) in Military Survey I (1783); G = Turkish Hill as Törökhalom and Sátoristye in the "Book of Maps of Baranya County" in 1838; H = Turkish Hill with the legend Türkenhügel and Satoristye in Military Survey III (1880); I = Sátoristye puszta and its surroundings in Military Survey II (1858); J = Turkish Hill as Türkenhügel on the cadastral map from 1865; K = Turkish Hill and Sátorhely in the 1941 Military Survey; L = Turkish Hill as Török or Basa Halom on the Danube mapping from the 1830s.

first in Military Survey III and is partly related to the use of names by a large number of Germans living in the area, but even more to the language use of the staff that carried out cartographical work, as well as to military language (Figure 11.1/H).[36]

In addition to the name and stylized depiction of the chapel, the map markings linked to Turkish Hill are double crosses that refer to a church/chapel. Based on the available stock of maps, it can be established that the chapel, which was probably converted from the Ottoman pavilion during the wars of liberation in 1687, as witnessed by Giovanni Francesco Gemelli Careri, might have existed until the 1770s. The chapel is no longer shown in Military Survey I (1783).

As it is not included in the relevant profile of the next Danube mapping either, which was taken in 1827 (Figure 11.1/L),[37] nor in the 1838 Book of Maps of Baranya County and on the otherwise very detailed and reliable map of Military Survey II, its destruction and abandonment can be dated to the 1770's. Any final decision on the issue requires further archaeological and archival investigations.

The most durable and lasting element of the memorial site seems to be the well built in 1630–1631 on the order of Hasan Pasha. The well of Turkish Hill is still shown in idealised form on the cadastral map made in 1865[38] (Figure 11.1/J). The well is enclosed by five trees offering shade, and the marking shows that a tired traveller can find shade and water there. Since we do not yet have information about another well dug in the area, we have to assume that the maps represent the original well, which is also referred to by many folk legends.

3.3 Archaeological Investigations on Turkish Hill

The first major archaeological investigation at Turkish Hill took place in 1924, on the eve of the 400th anniversary of the Battle of Mohács. The excavation was led by Captain Endre Gergely, who believed that the small mound next to the Eszék-Buda road could play a key role in determining the location of the Battle of Mohács. However, the excavation found mainly Roman monuments, building materials and coins, and graves near the mound, but no finds related to the Battle of Mohács.[39]

---

36 Military Survey III (1869–1887).
37 S 80 - Duna. - No. 126/1–1757 – Danube mapping (1830–1840). Hungarian National Archives.
38 Cadastral maps (19th century).
39 Gergely, "Ásatások a mohácsi csatatéren," [Excavations on the battlefield of Mohács] in *Mohács emlékkönyv*, ed. Lukinich, pp. 349–360.

FIGURE 11.2   Turkish Hill in 1926.
SOURCE: FILMHÍRADÓ (FILM NEWSREEL), NO. 132, AUGUST 1926.
AVAILABLE AT HTTPS://FILMHIRADOKONLINE.HU/WATCH
.PHP?ID=8531&FBCLID=IWAR0AZBXQ69BGFGG4BQQ8HVCHTE
_JVVKMU6NOF392IIPZADUS8ADPQZYGVW0

In 1961, archaeologist László Papp excavated directly opposite Turkish Hill, where he identified a village and its cemetery dating back to the end of the Middle Ages. One of the cemetery's dead, buried in a special position, was thought to be a casualty of the Battle of Mohács. He thought that the settlement might have been Földvár, but he did not identify it with Földvár at the centre of the Battle of Mohács. According to his theory, the chronicler István Brodarics actually saw the village of Merse and its church in the battle, but in his memoirs written in 1528 he mistakenly wrote the name Földvár instead of Merse.[40]

In 1974, during the exploration of Turkish Hill, a well, made of Roman bricks, but with distinctive pink Turkish mortar, was discovered. This was identified

---

40   László Papp, "Újabb kutatások a mohácsi csatatéren," [New research on the battlefield of Mohács] in *A Janus Pannonius Múzeum Évkönyve 1962,* ed. László Papp (Pécs: Janus Pannonius Múzeum, 1963), pp. 199–221.

FIGURE 11.3   The eastern part of the Turkish Hill with archeological objects.
PHOTO: GÁBOR SZALAI.

by the archaeologist in charge of the excavation, Attila Kiss, as the well that İbrahim Peçevi and Henrik Ottendorf had also mentioned at Császárdomb (Emperor's Hill). He collected late medieval pottery in the vicinity of the well.[41] In 1975, Roman bricks were discovered in the collapsed earth during a field survey, and in 1977 a Roman column was found here, also during quarrying.[42]

In his monograph *Ripa Pannonica*, published in 2000, archaeologist Zsolt Visy reported that he had identified traces of Roman 'opus spicatum' masonry in the section formed by earlier excavations, and the 'stone walkway and rubble' of a Roman building. He identified the remains of the Roman building as a Roman watchtower and named it Altinum 1 Burgus.[43]

The previous site inspections were followed by a more thorough non-destructive inspection in 2018 and 2020.[44] It was found that the promontory,

---

41   Janus Pannonius Museum, Archeological Database, 1974, 1248–83.
42   Janus Pannonius Museum, Archeological Database, 1977, 1280–83.
43   Zsolt Visy, "A Ripa Pannonica Magyarországon [The Ripa Pannonica in Hungary]," (Budapest: Akadémiai Kiadó, 2000).
44   Máté Kitanics, Levente Nagy, Erika Hancz, Péter Gyenizse, Gábor Szalai, László Nagy, Zsombor Klembala, Balázs Polgár, and Norbert Pap, "A Törökdomb a régészeti vizsgálatok tükrében," [The Turkish Hill in the light of archaeological investigations] in *Mordortól Mohácsig. A mohácsi csatatáj történeti földrajzi kutatása,* ed. Norbrt Pap (Budapest: MTA BTK, 2020), pp. 273–349.

later called Császárdomb and then Törökdomb, was built by the Romans. At the top of the mound, in the late 3rd and early 4th century, a square tower, or burgus, measuring 7 × 7 metres, was built of stones with a brick roof. The watchtower was part of the border defence system of the province of Valeria until the 430s, when the province came under Hun rule, and Roman administration to an end.

The majority of the medieval and early modern finds consisted of iron, bronze, copper, silvered copper and lead objects. Some of them were objects of everyday use and costume, such as a silver denarius struck during the reign of Matthias I (1458–1490), the rim of a bronze candelabrum, a narrow horseshoe with a plate and a 16th–17th-century D-shaped iron belt buckle. One of the 6 lead bullets recovered belonged to a Turkish fowling handgun. The ornamentation included various copper bands and a fragmentary lead plate with a bulging surface, the parallel of which is known from the excavation[45] of the Ottoman Turbék. The Ottoman use of the hill was also confirmed by the collection of someTurkish pink mortar in the northeastern section of the promontory, as already described by Attila Kiss. But beyond this, most of the finds could belong to the wooden buildings that once stood here, namely the Ottoman pavilion and later the Christian chapel. In addition to iron nails of various sizes, a pivot hinge that was part of a locking mechanism and a carpenter's clamp could also be found here.

The dating element was a silver-plated copper cross, 9.5 cm long and 5 cm wide, dating from the 18th century, which was found on the preserved western section of the hilltop. The hook on the upper edge of the cross and the copper band riveted to the back of the cross suggest that it was part of a chest or altar. The find provides material evidence that a chapel did indeed stand on the site of the former Ottoman pavilion from 1687 to the 1770s, as is confirmed by written sources.

It will be necessary to carry out a further authentication excavation to determine whether the perimeter trench, the various building remains and wall remains identified by the geophysical survey carried out in 2020 belong to the Roman or Ottoman period.

---

[45] Erika Hancz, "Nagy Szulejmán szultán szigetvári türbe-palánkjának régészeti feltárása (2015–2016)," [Archaeological excavation of Sultan Süleyman the Magnificent's türbe-palisade in Szigetvár (2015–2016)] in *Szulejmán szultán Szigetváron*, eds. Pap et al., pp. 89–130.

FIGURE 11.4 Find (cross) belonging to the chapel built on top of the Turkish Hill.
PHOTO: ERIKA HANCZ.

3.4 Turkish Hill in Folk Memory and Its Modern Function as A Memorial Place

There are several places that have been preserved in local memory and geographical names, including Turkish Hill, which commemorate the 1526 battle. In local languages (Croatian, German and Hungarian), the place is called Turski brig/Türkenhügel/Törökhalom/Törökdomb in the same context. According to local legends, it is an artificial mound raised by the Ottoman army during the battle, where an Ottoman victory monument was supposedly created between the old military road and the Vizslak Meadow. Legend has it that the place from where Sultan Süleyman was watching military movements was known as *Hünkâr tepesi* (Emperor's or Sultan's Hill).

According to local legend, the Turkish Well was a well where only the sultan was entitled to quench his thirst, and a soldier who once violated this regulation was executed.[46] It was used for supplying drinking water and providing a

---

46 Zsigmond Szendrey, "Mohács a magyar folklórban," [Mohács in Hungarian folklore] Ethnografia 34–35 (1923–1924), no. 1–3, p. 13. pp. 11–14.

resting place along the Eszék-Buda road near the Vizslak Meadow and tradition links it to Turkish Hill.[47]

Rumour had it that in the 19th century, 8–10 "Turks" came here every year from the direction of Eszék; "they were wailing, bowing, eating and drinking tea, and they stayed all night."[48] This tradition broke off with World War I. According to memoirs, "Turkish" (and Muslim Bosnian) visitors regularly came to this place in the 19th century and spent their time praying. The description of the visits is similar to those credibly recorded for the Tomb of Gül Baba in Budapest or the Tomb of Idris Baba in Pécs.

Turkish Hill received the greatest national and international attention in connection with the commemorations of its 400th anniversary on 29 August 1926. In addition to the central ceremony held on the Main Square in Mohács with the participation of public dignitaries, there was a ceremony held on the battlefield too, right at the place that is the focus of our study. The president of the Turán Society and former minister, Gyula Pekár and other members of the Society attended the event representing Hungary, while the Ottoman side was represented by ambassador Ridvan Bey Oğlu Hüsrev and attaché Osman Cevad Bey. After the speeches emphasizing the importance of the Turan Turkish-Hungarian brotherhood, wreaths were placed on the hill. The event was also reported by contemporary press and newsreels.[49]

3.5 Physical Characteristics of Turkish Hill

Based on the analysis of written sources and the characteristics of old maps, Turkish Hill had been an important military element in the Mohács Plain with a constantly renewed function for one and a half thousand years. The physical features of its environment are important for the historical interpretation of the site.

There is only a stylized representation of Turkish Hill from 1687 that we know of. In our study, we attempted to reconstruct the artificial hill by indicating the weight of the structures placed on it, taking into account features of the terrain and the environmental conditions.

Based on our surveys of the landscape and the reconstructions shown below, we came to the conclusion that the site was deliberately chosen by the Roman

---

47 Hammer-Purgstall, *Geschichte, III.*, pp. 636–637; Evliyâ Çelebi, *Seyahatnâmesi, VI. Kitap*, pp. 112–113.
48 János Pesti ed., *Baranya megye földrajzi nevei II.* [Geographical names in Baranya County II] (Pécs: Baranya Megyei Levéltár, 1982), pp. 489–490.
49 *Magyar Híradó*, [Hungarian News] issue no. 132, August 1926; *Pesti Napló*, 77 (1926), issue 195, 29 August.

FIGURE 11.5   Swampy landscape on the eastern side of Turkish Hill (April 2018).
PHOTO: GÁBOR SZALAI.

builders for the hill next to the Roman road surrounded by an entrenchment (with the buildings on it). The road here is close to an ancient riverbed of the Danube River. The eastern side of the *burgus* is protected by the deepest, inaccessible part of the swamp. The plain lies wide to the west with roads, arable land and villages on it. This dry, flat land surrounded by gallery forests and marshes is suitable for military operations with larger armies in the Danube backwater. Thus, the creation of this hill and the establishment of a fortified facility seem to be quite justified for monitoring the entire area.

The over-heightened terrain sections below (Figures 11.6 and 11.7) and the creative 3D reconstruction show the immediate surroundings of Turkish Hill. The Roman building was built on the edge of a terrace in a flood free zone formed in the Pleistocene era. It rises about 6 to 7 meters above the marshy eastern bank of the Danube that used to be impenetrable before drainage. The two areas are separated by a distinct edge, which has a quite steep slope that is not typical on this flatland. This high edge was formed by the Danube a few tens of thousands of years ago, and later its main branch ran either along the eastern or along the western side of the Mohács Island. During the spring floods, the flood basin was inundated every year, but the slowly flowing waters of the streamlets coming from Kölked to Dályok continued to feed the deeper water at the foot of Turkish Hill in the rest of the year. This residue of the old Danube backwater might have been much deeper and larger before drainage

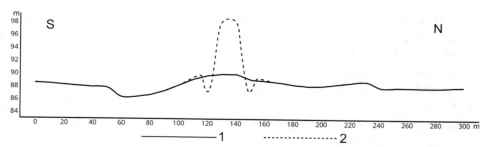

FIGURE 11.6 North-south section of Turkish Hill and its surroundings. Edited by Péter Gyenizse. By tenfold over-heightening. Legend: 1 = height of the relief today; 2 = Turkish Hill's presumed maximum height and maximum ditch depth.

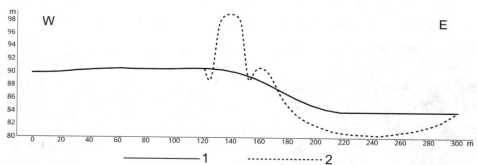

FIGURE 11.7 East-west section of Turkish Hill and its surroundings. Edited by Péter Gyenizse. By tenfold over-heightening. Legend: 1 = height of the relief today; 2 = Turkish Hill's presumed maximum height and maximum ditch depth, as well as the original estimated depth of the Danube backwater at the edge of the flood basin.

works and intensive arable cultivation. This oxbow was also located here at the time of Roman rule and in any later historical period. The terrace riser was no longer undercut by the Danube during the historical times with its branches of various size running further away. If the river channel had drifted laterally significantly in the last two thousand years, we would not see a single trace of Turkish Hill today. Today, the edge and Turkish Hill, however, do not look exactly like in the previous millennia. Natural deterioration of the riverbank has been further increased by human activity. The cutting of trees, the exploitation of land and the development of transport routes leading to the drained floodplain played a key role in this. That is why we can assume that the slope on the eastern side of Turkish Hill is now less steep than it used to be in the Roman period. Damaged soil and debris have certainly contributed to the loss of depth in the abandoned riverbed.

We do not know the exact dimensions of the *burgus,* which was part of the limes, under the Roman rule, but based on analogy, it might have been a tower with a small, approx. 7 × 7 meter square floor space standing on an artificially elevated hill of about 30 meters diameter (Figure 11.8/A). The diameter of the hill and its surrounding ditch could be measured accurately on the map sheet of the 1827 Danube mapping. The stone-paved north to south military road between Mursa and Aquincum lay roughly ten meters west of the watchtower. One thousand years later, during the Ottoman rule, the surrounding landscape showed similar characteristics. The military road remained to be as important as before, though its quality had probably deteriorated. According to certain contemporary sources, Turkish Hill might have been used as a command or observation point during the Battle of Mohács. The pavilion mentioned in our study was built on the top later (Figure 11.8/B). No significant environmental changes have occurred in the area, which has gradually become populated after

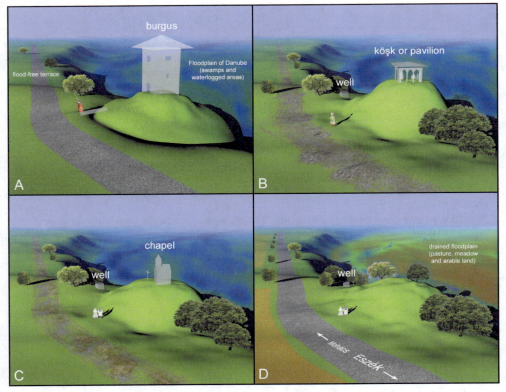

FIGURE 11.8 Stylised 3D reconstruction of Turkish Hill and its surrounding. Graphics: Péter Gyenizse. Legend: A = the Roman period; B = the Ottoman period; C = end of the 17th century; D = first half of the 19th century.

the anti-Turkish wars of liberation. The area under investigation belonged to Praedium Földvár, and both the flood-free terrace and the swampy area of the Vizslak Meadow were partly used as grazing land. According to the representation mentioned above, there might have been a small chapel on the top of Turkish Hill at the end of the 17th century (Figure 11.8/C). Landscaping works carried out in the first half of the 19th century were recorded in the Danube mappings, the Military Survey II and the 1886 cadastral map. The swampy floodplain has been drained and its area is now occupied by arable land and meadows. However, the Danube mapping sheet shows a "Flood Limit", i.e. the limit of flooding marked on the lower part of the terrace. This shows that the floodplain was under water during floods even in the first half of the 19th century. This did not endanger the terrace surfaces above Turkish Hill, where there was arable land along the paved main road among trees. The maps indicating Turkish Hill do not show any buildings, but the nearby well is still marked. This is why it could have served as a resting place for people on the road. The hill or mound, which had lost its cultic significance, was soon used for embankment and building sites (Figure 11.8/D).

3.6 "A Field of Mourning Red with Heroes' Blood"

The battleground marked the site of one of the Ottomans' greatest victories, a place that served as a campsite for their troops deployed in Hungary. This is the campsite where, in 1529, János Szapolyai I kissed the sultan's hand, twice humiliated and abased. It was not uncommon for representatives of embassies to stop en route on the battlefield, where for a long time the gun emplacements and mass graves showed the battlefields to the people passing by on the road along the Vizslak Meadow. Thus, the written sources of the period repeatedly describe the site of the battle, which over time lost the physical features that were typical of several decades after the battle.

The mound continued to serve as a memorial site of the battlefield after the wars of reconquest. In 1687, a Christian chapel was built on the site of the köşk or pavilion, which became the first Christian memorial to the battle and served as such until the 1770s.[50] In maps and descriptions from the 18th and 19th centuries, the area around Földvár, later Sátorhely (Földvárpuszta), was marked as a battlefield. This became, in the words of poet Károly Kisfaludy (1824), the *"field of mourning red with heroes' blood"*.

---

50   Norbert Pap, Pál Fodor, Máté Kitanics, Tamás Morva, Gábor Szalai, and Péter Gyenizse, "A mohácsi Törökdomb," [The Törökdomb of Mohács] *Történelmi Szemle* 60 (2018), no. 2, pp. 325–345.

4 Discussion

The number of objects referring to particular key sites of the Battle of Mohács is significant. Their common feature is strong sacredness, expressing that confrontation was motivated by factors associated with civilisation. The Battlefield Memorial Chapel in the Mohács cemetery was established in 1816 by József Király, the Bishop of Pécs, to ensure that trilingual masses commemorating anniversaries of the battle are held in Hungarian, German and Croatian. The Memorial Church on the Main Square in Mohács was built on the 400th anniversary of the battle and remains to be completed. The Mohács Historical Memorial Site in Sátorhely was completed in 1976 to commemorate the 450th anniversary near the mass graves discovered in the 1960–1970s. During the Kádár era, Hungary had an ambivalent attitude to national issues and a distinctly hostile attitude to religious issues. That is why the memorial site did not include religious symbols at the time of its establishment, but after the change of regime, a cross was erected there. The new visitor centre, which was completed in 2011, also displays a highly religious symbol, the Hungarian Holy Crown, in stylized form. Each of the commemorations emphasizes the protection of the country as well as that of Christianity and Europe. This civilisational conflict survived both in Christian as well as in Turkish and Muslim approaches. The context of the scientific debates about the battle is crucially controlled by this factor.

The place of death of King Louis II and its circumstances remain to be disputed.[51] The monument to the king, who supposedly drowned in the Csele Brook, built on the banks of the river underpinned the legitimacy of the place. The fact that the hundreds of Polish soldiers who had died in the battle already have a monument can be interpreted in the context of historical Hungarian-Polish friendship. For the time being, the thousands of Czechs and soldiers of other nations who had also fallen in battle have not yet received the same honour.

The subject of the hundred-year-long debate is where the battle itself took place, or more precisely, where its centre was. Thanks to recent research on military history, a memorial tablet (installed on a former cross) was inaugurated in honour of the battle in 1994 in the village of Majs lying on the western edge of the Mohács Plain. This was intended to support the local ambitions to see the Battle of Mohács as the "Battle of Majs", reaffirming the decisive view of

---

51 *"Nekünk mégis Mohács kell…"*, eds. Farkas et al., 336 p.

the last twenty-five years on the location of the battle.[52] However, the debate has not yet come to an end. Today's significance of the discourse on the location and function of Turkish Hill is primarily due to the "competition" among the various possible battlefields.

Turkish Hill is a prominent object of the "military landscape" in the Mohács Plain. This was the first monument to commemorate the Battle of Mohács, raised by the victors to remember and preserve the memory of the battle. Its establishment was used to express the Ottoman Empire's ambition to maintain and legitimize the rule of Islam in the given area. Balázs Polgár presumes that the memorial site was destroyed in 1687.[53] Based on the resources found and presented here, we believe that the object has continued to exist, but its function has been transformed in such a way as to symbolically counterbalance the original memorial function. When the region was liberated, the Catholic Church established a Christian chapel at the end of the 1680s, with some of its basic functions (resting place, supply of drinking water and a sacred place) preserved, although its civilisational context turned the other way. Remembrance of the battle had changed by the end of the 18th century. The chapel on Turkish Hill was abandoned before 1780 and its role was taken over by the memorial chapel built in the Mohács cemetery in 1816 and the mass celebrated there on 29 August. The estate established in nearby Sátorhely, which also built a chapel (the chapel of glorification of the Holy Cross), kept both the name Sátoristye/Sátorhely and its future legitimacy for the battle. The mass graves found here partially confirmed the site in the 20th century, although the debate of military historians about the possible locations of the battle "degraded" the village to the site of a Hungarian camp.

At the same time, the original function of Turkish Hill as a memorial site remained the same in part, as Muslims coming from Eszék (Muslims from Bosnia) continued to regard it as a sacred places and visited it from time to time. This tradition of pilgrimage survived for almost two centuries after the Ottoman period. Although pilgrimage ceased at the beginning of the 20th century, elderly people in Mohács are still telling stories about Muslim pilgrims.

---

52 B. Szabó, *A mohácsi csata*. [The Battle of Mohács]; Gábor Bertók, "Nekünk Majs kell? A mohácsi csatatér kutatása," [We need Majs? Research into the battlefield of Mohács] in *Régi idők – új módszerek,* eds. Gábor Bertók and Csilla Gáti (Budapest: Archaeolingua, 2014), pp. 161–170; Lajos Négyesi, "A mohácsi csata," [The Battle of Mohács] *Hadtörténelmi Közlemények* 107 (1994), no. 4, pp. 62–79.

53 Balázs Polgár, "Az 1526. évi mohácsi csata régészete és a kutatás újabb perspektívája," [The archaeology of the 1526 Battle of Mohács and its recent research perspectives] in *Hadi és más nevezetes történetek,* ed. Katalin Mária Kincses (Budapest: HM Hadtörténeti Intézet és Múzeum, 2018), pp. 405–415.

The debate about whether Császárdomb (Emperor's Hill) and Törökdomb (Turkish Hill) mentioned in the sources are the same or two different objects has been going on in the literature for at least one hundred years. Endre Gergely, who conducted excavations at Turkish Hill, thought that the Császárdomb of the Ottoman sources should not be found there, but on a bastion-like high ground about one and a half kilometres southeast of Majs.[54] However, he admitted that there was no evidence to support this suggestion. László Papp believed that Császárdomb was a hill three kilometres northwest of the Buziglica junction,[55] and Turkish Hill is nothing other than the sultan's campsite after the battle. According to a third assumption, Császárdomb might have been the surroundings of the church in Nagynyárád.[56] Kuti and Ujvári published passages from major general Tobias von Hasslingen's 1687 diary and believed that the location of the pavilion described there might have been the Töröksánc in Nagynyárád, and the later church was built on the site of the pavilion.[57]

The assumption by László Papp that the sultan's tent seems to have been set up on Turkish Hill after 29 August 1526[58] is reiterated by János B. Szabó in his work.[59] However, we do not consider this option to be likely. Taking into account the physical conditions of the hill – with only 70 square meters of flat space on its top that is suitable for setting up a tent – did not provide enough room for the sultan's tent. We also know from our investigations in Szigetvár[60] that the sultan's tent complex had an area of at least 1500 square meters, and 70 square meters would not have been sufficient for setting up tents, the necessary staff and guards, etc.

The various assumptions concerning the place of Császárdomb (in Merse, Nagynyárád and Sátorhely) confirm the legitimacy of different battlefield sites; the problem is that they are really only assumptions and are not supported by data pointing in these directions (since there are no such data). The scientific

---

54 Gergely, "Ásatások a mohácsi csatatéren," [Excavations on the battlefield of Mohács] in *Mohács emlékkönyv*, ed. Lukinich, pp. 349–360.
55 Papp, "A mohácsi csatahely kutatása," [Research into the battlefield of Mohács] in *A Janus Pannonius Múzeum évkönyve*, ed. Papp, pp. 197–253.
56 István Kuti and András Újvári, "Mohács hadibázisának védelme 1687-ben," [Defence of military bases in Mohács in 1687] in *Előadások és tanulmányok a török elleni visszafoglaló háborúk történetéből 1686–1688*, ed. László Szita (Pécs, 1989), pp. 75–96.
57 Kuti and Újvári, *Ibid* 79–81.
58 Papp, "A mohácsi csatahely kutatása," [Research into the battlefield of Mohács] in *A Janus Pannonius Múzeum évkönyve*, pp. 197–253.
59 B. Szabó, *A mohácsi csata* [The Battle of Mohács], p. 141.
60 Norbert Pap and Pál Fodor eds., *Szulejmán szultán Szigetváron* [Sultan Süleyman in Szigetvár] (Pécs: Pannon Castrum, 2017).

debates on Turkish Hill can be closed only when structural issues concerning the 1526 battle, such as the routes of military operations, the centre of the battle and the locations of the two armies' camps, are definitively clarified. Based on our investigations, Turkish Hill is nothing but Császárdomb itself.

5 Summary

Turkish Hill is a more than 1500 year-old, man-made and prominent element of the military landscape of Mohács. The Romans erected watchtowers (*burgu*ses) at dedicated points to control and supervise the road along the limes. Today's Turkish Hill was one of the places of these towers. The roughly 30 m long and somewhat narrower artificial hill was surrounded by a moat for defence. The at least 10-meter-tall hill and the structure built upon provided a good view of the Eszék-Buda road and the surrounding lowland.

The military road (*via militaris*) survived after the Roman times and was still in use a thousand years later. The Ottoman army led by Süleyman approached the battlefield on this road in 1526. Tradition has it that the hill played a significant role in fighting the battle. The legends and stories linked to the site mention or suggest various possibilities. It was seen as a place where the sultan prayed for victory, the place where he put up his tent or even the cemetery where the Ottoman Muslim soldiers who had fallen in the battle were buried. There is no solid evidence for any of these, and our studies show that it could not have functioned as an Ottoman cemetery or tent site. Its traditional function of controlling and observing the road suggests that it was most likely an observation point that the sultan himself might also have visited (as suggested by its Ottoman Turkish name *"Hünkâr tepesi"*), even without physical or archaeological evidence.

In 1630–1631, governor-general Hasan of Buda had a well dug and a wooden edifice built on top of the hill; according to certain (still unconfirmed) sources, dervishes were ordered to go there and pray regularly. This practice of remembrance is analogous to the use of the Süleyman monument and symbolic tomb erected in the Turbék vineyard at Szigetvár.

In 1687, the structure erected at the memorial place was transformed into a Christian chapel and was dedicated at the same time when the sacred Muslim buildings in Turbék next to Szigetvár were transformed and dedicated. It is not known how long the chapel survived and how it was used, but it was still shown on late 18th-century maps, when it disappeared finally from the maps made in the 1780s. With the establishment of a nearby estate in Sátorhely in the 1780s and the Battlefield Memorial Chapel built in 1816, the memorial function was relocated to nearby Sátorhely. When the mass graves of the Battle of Mohács were found in the 1960–1970s, this function was further strengthened.

However, Turkish Hill has survived as a legendary site. In the 18th–19th centuries, travellers found a shady resting place and water under the trees on the hill by the road. The only reminders of Ottoman times were the occasional Turkish and Bosnian Muslim pilgrims. In the first half of the 20th century, it was still in good condition and quite intact as one of the important memorial places commemorating the 400th anniversary of the 1526 battle. Thereafter, however, when the road was extended and the material of Turkish Hill was used for embankments built in Mohács, it was totally destroyed. Some of its remains can still be seen today; its partial survival is mainly due to its recent use as a triangulation point.

Situated along the busy military road, the hill occupied a prominent place among the Ottoman memorials that reminded the faithful of the successes of the holy war and the deeds of Sultan Süleyman, and carried the basic messages of the "propaganda" of the time. By exploring its history more thoroughly, we obtain a better understanding of the Ottoman Empire's ideas and actions for political mobilisation and the politics of memory in the 16th–17th centuries.

Bibliography

B. Szabó, János. *Mohács. Régi kérdések, új válaszok.* [Mohács. Old questions, new answers] Budapest: HM Hadtörténeti Intézet és Múzeum, Line Design, 2015.

B. Szabó, János. *A mohácsi csata.* [The Battle of Mohács] Budapest: Corvina, 2006.

Bende, Lajos. "A mohácsi csata." [The Battle of Mohács] *Hadtörténelmi Közlemények* 13 (1966): 532–567.

Bertók, Gábor. "Nekünk Majs kell? A mohácsi csatatér kutatása." [We need Majs? Research into the battlefield of Mohács] In *Régi idők – új módszerek,* eds. Gábor Bertók and Csilla Gáti, 161–170. Budapest: Archaeolingua, 2014.

Careri, Giovanni Francesco Gemelli. "Beszámoló a magyarországi hadjáratokról." [An account of the Hungarian military campaign] *Hadtörténelmi Közlemények* 115 (2002): 403–419.

Dernschwam, Hans. *Erdély. Besztercebánya. Törökországi útinapló.* [Translyvania. Besztercebánya. Turkish Travel Diary] Budapest: Európa Könyvkiadó, 1984.

Evliyâ Çelebi b. Derviş Mehemmed Zıllî. *Evliyâ Çelebi Seyahatnâmesi. 7. Kitap. Topkapı Sarayı Kütüphanesi Bağdat 308 Numaralı Yazmanın Transkripsiyonu–Dizini,* eds. Yücel Dağlı, Seyit Ali Kahraman, and Robert Dankoff. İstanbul: Yapı Kredi, 2003.

Evliyâ Çelebi b. Derviş Mehemmed Zıllî. *Evliyâ Çelebi Seyahatnâmesi. VI. Kitap. Topkapı Sarayı Kütüphanesi Revan 1457 Numaralı Yazmanın Transkripsiyonu–Dizini,* eds. Seyit Ali Kahraman and Yücel Dağlı. İstanbul: Yapı Kredi, 2002.

Evliyâ Çelebi b. Derviş Mehemmed Zıllî. *Evliyâ Çelebi Seyahatnâmesi. 5. Kitap. Topkapı Sarayı Bağdat 307 Yazmasının Transkripsiyonu–Dizini*, eds. Yücel Dağlı, Seyit Ali Kahraman, and İbrahim Sezgin. İstanbul: Yapı Kredi, 2001.

Gábor Farkas Farkas, Zsolt Szebelédi, and Bernadett Varga eds. *Nekünk mégis Mohács kell..." II. Lajos király rejtélyes halála és különböző temetései*. [We still need Mohács... King Louis II's mysterious death and various funerals] Budapest: MTA Bölcsészettudományi Kutatóközpont, Országos Széchényi Könyvtár, 2016.

Fekete, Lajos. "Hódoltságkori oszmanli-török helyneveink." [Ottoman Turkish toponyms from the period of Turkish occupation] *Századok* 57–58 (1923–1924): 614–626.

Fodor, Pál. "A "hitharc oroszlánja": Jahjapasa-oglu Báli Bég (?–1527). Terjeszkedés és tartományi elit az Oszmán Birodalom európai határvidékén a 16. század elején." [The lion of faithful warriors, Yahya bey Dukagjini (?–1527). Expansion and the provincial elite in the European frontier zone of the Ottoman Empire at the beginning of the 16th century] *Keletkutatás* (2019), tavasz/spring: 51–74.

Fodor, Pál. "Ibrahim Pecsevi leírása a mohácsi csatáról és II. Lajos király haláláról." [İbrahim Peçevi's account of the Battle of Mohács and the death of King Louis II] In *"Nekünk mégis Mohács kell..." II. Lajos király rejtélyes halála és különböző temetései*, eds. Gábor Farkas Farkas, Zsolt Szebelédi, and Bernadett Varga, 233–256. Budapest: MTA Bölcsészettudományi Kutatóközpont, Országos Széchényi Könyvtár, 2016.

Gergely, Endre. "Ásatások a mohácsi csatatéren (1924, 1925)." [Excavations on the battlefield of Mohács (1924, 1925)] In *Mohács emlékkönyv 1926*, ed. Imre Lukinich, 349–360. Budapest: Királyi Magyar Egyetemi Nyomda, 1926.

Gévay, Antal. *A' budai pasák*. [The Pashas of Buda] Bécsben: 1841.

Hammer-Purgstall, Joseph von. *Geschichte des osmanischen Reiches... III. ... 1520–1574*. Pest: C. A. Hartleben, 1828.

Hancz, Erika. "Nagy Szulejmán szultán szigetvári türbe-palánkjának régészeti feltárása (2015–2016)." [Archaeological excavation of Sultan Süleyman the Magnificent's türbe-palisade in Szigetvár (2015–2016)] In *Szulejmán szultán Szigetváron. A szigetvári kutatások 2013–2016 között*, eds. Norbert Pap and Pál Fodor, 89–130. Pécs: Pannon Castrum Kft., 2017.

Hans Dernschwam's Tagebuch. Einer Reise nach Konstantinopel und Kleinasien (1553/55). Nach der Urschrift im Fugger-Archiv, ed. Franz Babinger. München, Leipzig: 1923.

Kápolnai Pauer, István. "A mohácsi hadjárat 1526-ban." [The Mohács military campaign in 1526] *Hadtörténelmi Közlemények* 2 (1889): 177–208, 440–462.

Karácson, Imre. *Török történetírók III. (1566–1659)*. [Turkish historiographers III (1566–1659)] Budapest: Magyar Tudományos Akadémia, 1916.

Karácson, Imre. *Evlia Cselebi török világutazó magyarországi utazásai (1664–1666)*. [Turkish traveller Evliya Çelebi's travels in Hungary (1664–1666)] Budapest: Magyar Tudományos Akadémia, 1908.

Karácson, Imre. *Evlia Cselebi török világutazó magyarországi utazásai (1660–1664)*. [Turkish traveller Evliya Çelebi's travels in Hungary (1660–1664)] Budapest: Magyar Tudományos Akadémia, 1904.

Kâtib Çelebi. *Fezleke I. Osmanlı Tarihi (1000–1065/1591–1655)*, ed. Zeynep Aycibin. İstanbul: Camlica Basim Yayin, 2016.

Kitanics, Máté, Levente Nagy, Erika Hancz, Péter Gyenizse, Gábor Szalai, László Nagy, Zsombor Klembala, Balázs Polgár, and Norbert Pap. "A Törökdomb a régészeti vizsgálatok tükrében." [The Törökdomb in the light of archaeological investigations] In *Mordortól Mohácsig. A mohácsi csatatáj történeti földrajzi kutatása*, ed. Norbert Pap, 273–349. Budapest: MTA BTK, 2020.

Kupelwieser, Leopold. *Ungarns Kämpfe mit den Osmanen bis zur Schlacht bei Mohács*. Wien, Leipzig: Wilhelm Braumüller, 1895.

Kuti, István and András Újvári. "Mohács hadibázisának védelme 1687-ben." [Defence of military bases in Mohács in 1687] In *Előadások és tanulmányok a török elleni visszafoglaló háborúk történetéből 1686–1688*, ed. László Szita, 75–96. Pécs: 1989.

Máté, Zsolt ed. *Frontiers of the Roman Empire. The Ripa Pannonica in Hungary (RPH). Nomination statement Vol. II.* Budapest: National Office of Cultural Heritage, 2011.

Négyesi, Lajos. "A mohácsi csata." [The Battle of Mohács] *Hadtörténelmi Közlemények* 107 (1994): 62–79.

Németh, Béla. "Baranya Szent Istvántól a jelenkorig." [Baranya County from St. Stephen to the present day] In *Baranya múltja és jelenje II.*, ed. Ferenc Várady, 209–730. Pécs: Pécsi Irodalmi és Könyvnyomdai Részvénytársaság, 1897.

Ortvay, Tivadar. *A mohácsi csata elvesztésének okai és következményei*. [The reasons for and the consequences of losing the Battle of Mohács] Budapest: Magyar Tudományos Akadémia, 1910.

Ottendorf, Henrik. *Budáról Belgrádba 1663: Ottendorf Henrik képes útleírása*. [From Buda to Belgrade 1663: Henrik Ottendorf's travelogue with pictures] Tolna Vármegye Múltjából 7. Pécs: Dunántúli Egyetemi Ny., 1943.

Pap, Norbert, Pál Fodor, Máté Kitanics, Tamás Morva, Gábor Szalai, and Péter Gyenizse "A mohácsi Törökdomb." [The Törökdomb of Mohács] *Történelmi Szemle* 60 (2018): 325–345.

Pap, Norbert. "Iszlám versus kereszténység – szimbolikus térfoglalás Szigetváron." [Islam vs. Christianity – a symbolic occupation of space in Szigetvár] In *Szulejmán szultán Szigetváron. A szigetvári kutatások 2013–2016 között*, eds. Norbert Pap and Pál Fodor, 205–242. Pécs: Pannon Castrum Kft., 2017.

Pap, Norbert and Pál Fodor eds. *Szulejmán szultán Szigetváron* [Sultan Süleyman in Szigetvár] Pécs: Pannon Castrum, 2017.

Papp, László. "Újabb kutatások a mohácsi csatatéren." [New research on the battlefield of Mohács] In *A Janus Pannonius Múzeum Évkönyve 1962*, ed. László Papp, 199–221. Pécs: Janus Pannonius Múzeum, 1963.

Papp, László. "A mohácsi csatahely kutatása." [Research into the battlefield of Mohács] In *A Janus Pannonius Múzeum évkönyve 1960*, ed. János Dombay, 197–253. Pécs: Janus Pannonius Múzeum, 1961.

Perjés, Géza. *Mohács*. Budapest: Magvető Könyvkiadó, 1979.

Pesti, János ed. *Baranya megye földrajzi nevei II*. [Geographical names in Baranya County II] Pécs: Baranya Megyei Levéltár, 1982.

Polgár, Balázs. "Az 1526. évi mohácsi csata régészete és a kutatás újabb perspektívája." [The archaeology of the 1526 Battle of Mohács and its recent research perspectives] In *Hadi és más nevezetes történetek*, ed. Katalin Mária Kincses, 405–415. Budapest: HM Hadtörténeti Intézet és Múzeum, 2018.

Rycaut, Paul. *The History of the Turks. Beginning with the Year 1679*. London: 1700.

Selânikî Mustafa Efendi. *Tarih-i Selânikî*, ed. Mehmet İpşirli. İstanbul: İstanbul Üniversitesi Edebiyat Fakültesi, 1989.

Škalamera, Željko and Marko Popović. "Novi podaci sa plana Beograda iz 1683." In *Godišnjak Grada Beograda*. Knj. 23., 33–58. Beograd: Muzej Grada Beograda, 1976.

Szakály, Ferenc. *A mohácsi csata*. [The Battle of Mohács] Budapest: Akadémiai Kiadó, 1981.

Szalay, László. *Adalékok a magyar nemzet történetéhez a XVI-dik században*. [Additions to the history of the Hungarian nation in the sixteenth century] Pest: Ráth Mór, 1859.

Szendrey, Zsigmond. "Mohács a magyar folklórban." [Mohács in Hungarian folklore] *Ethnografia* 34–35 (1923–1924): 11–14.

Szurmay, Sándor. *A mohácsi hadjárat 1526-ban*. [The Mohács military campaign in 1526] Budapest: Ludovika Akadémia, 1901.

Tóth, István György. "Athanasio Georgiceo álruhás császári megbízott útleírása a magyarországi török hódoltságról, 1626-ból." [Disguised imperial envoy Athanasio Georgiceo's travelogue about the Turkish occupation of Hungary, 1626] *Századok* 132 (1998): 837–858.

Ungnád, Dávid. *Ungnád Dávid Konstantinápolyi utazásai*. [Dávid Undnád's travels in Constantinople] Budapest: Szépirodalmi Könyvkiadó, 1986.

Vályi, András. *Magyar országnak leírása II*. [The History of Hungary II] Buda: 1799.

Yılmazer, Ziya ed. *Topçular Kâtibi 'Abdülkādir (Kadrî) Efendi Tarihi (Metin ve Tahlîl) I*. Türk Tarih Kurumu Yayınları III/21. Ankara: 2003.

CHAPTER 12

Landscape, Artistic Representation, Memorials: Remembrance of the Location of the Battle of Mohács in 1526

Júlia Papp

Descriptions of the Battle of Mohács in 1526 and the death of Louis II (1516–1526) are found in numerous publications from the 16th to the 19th centuries (from the German-language newsletters that reported the battle almost immediately to literary and historical works by Hungarian and foreign authors)[1] and the representation of the tragic event in visual arts was also significant.[2] In this paper, written and visual sources (maps, country descriptions, travel journals, travel notes) are presented that depicted or mentioned the battle site as a place of remembrance. In the second part of the paper, an outline of the history of the memorials planned or actually built to commemorate the battle follows.

While chapels or other memorial symbols were often erected on the sites of medieval battles, by the early modern period, battle sites were seen as more of an accidental landscape, quickly integrated into agricultural production. These memories are most often preserved in fine art depictions of the battles. The rediscovery of the sites of famous battles and the preservation of their memory by secular or church monuments in Europe took a greater pace in the 18th century and continues unabated to this day.[3]

The virtual memory of battles of local or national significance is often part of the cultural heritage of multiple communities (e.g. of once rival ethnic groups or nations), but can also be an important element in the construction or reinterpretation of occasionally changing narratives of community identity, whether the specified battle was victorious (community pride) or tragic, lost

---

1   János B. Szabó and Gábor Farkas Gábor eds., *Örök Mohács: Szövegek és értelmezések* (Budapest: Bölcsészettudományi Kutatóközpont), 2020.
2   Júlia Papp, "Az 1526. évi mohácsi csata 16–17. századi képzőművészeti recepciója," in *Több mint egy csata: Mohács. Az 1526. évi ütközet a magyar tudományos és kulturális emlékezetben*, eds. Pál Fodor and Szabolcs Varga (Budapest: MTA Bölcsészettudományi Kutatóközpont, 2019), pp. 149–193.
3   See Ian Atherton and Philip Morgan, "The battlefield war memorial: Commemoration and the battlefield site from the Middle Ages to the modern era," *Journal of War & Culture Studies* 3 (2011), no. 4, pp. 289–304.

(community mourning). Most war memorials in recent centuries have been erected by the victors of course, but it is not uncommon to find monuments of the defeated to remind of their losses or heroic resistance (e.g. the Battle of Mohács, erected at the supposed site of the battle), or also "common" monuments, mostly erected in the spirit of reconciliation, commemorating enemy soldiers who died in the battles or the generals who led the battle, such as the Hungarian-Turkish Friendship Park in Szigetvár.

1 Maps

In 16th century maps and landscapes, brief descriptions and mostly schematic depictions of important contemporary events can often be found. These additions served a communicative function similar to contemporary illustrated newsletters (*Newe Zeyttung*) of the period. For example, a woodcut panoramic view of the Ottoman siege of Vienna in 1529, published in 1530 by the Nuremberg printer Niclas Meldeman (?–1552),[4] shows scenes of the attackers' atrocities in the area, with brief explanatory texts.[5] Some of the contemporary engravings of the Ottoman siege of Szigetvár in 1566 also contain shorter or longer descriptions of the major events of the siege, including the heroic death of Miklós Zrínyi (1508 k.–1566).[6] At the same time, on 16th- and 17th-century maps of Hungary,[7] in addition to the names of the municipalities,

---

4 Ferdinand Oppl and Martin Scheutz eds., *Die Osmanen vor Wien. Die Meldeman-Rundansicht von 1529/30. Sensation, Propaganda und Stadtbild.* (Veröffentlichungen des Instituts für Österreichische Geschichtsforschung) 74 (Wien: Institut für Österreichische Geschichtsforschung, 2020).

5 Martin Scheutz, "Die Meldeman-Rundansicht als illustrierte »Zeytung«. Der Druckort Nürnber und die kommunikative Strategie des Planes in seinen textlichen Mitteilungen," in *Die Osmanen vor Wien*, eds. Oppl et al., pp. 85–107; Yiğit Topkaya, "Eingekreiste Zeugen, auf den Kopf gestellte Märtyrer: Bilder des Grauens in Niclas Meldemans Rundansicht," in *Die Osmanen vor Wien*, eds. Oppl et al., pp. 241–258; Júlia Papp, "Die »Neuverwertung« der Illustration eines astrologischen Buches vom Ende des 15. Jahrhunderts in den deutschen Neuen Zeitungen über die Schlacht bei Mohács (1526) und die Belagerung von Wien (1529)," *Wiener Geschichtsblätter* 76 (2021), no. 2, pp. 115–133.

6 Recently see Júlia Papp, "A szigetvári hadi táj képzőművészeti ábrázolása a 16–17. században," in *Turbék. Szulejmán szultán zarándokvárosa*, ed. Norbert Pap (Budapest, Pécs: Bölcsészettudományi Kutatóközpont, 2020), pp. 451–534.

7 For the 16th and 17th century maps, I have mainly used the online version of Katalin Plihál's book. Katalin Plihál, *Kard és térkép. Hadi események és propaganda a Magyarországról megjelent térképeken. 1528–1718* (Budapest: HM Zrínyi Nonprofit Kft., 2020). Available at http://lazarus.elte.hu/kardesterkep/. For the 18th century ones I have used the website of the Moravská zemská knihovna v Brně, see https://mapy.mzk.cz/en/ with a collection of maps by

we often find textual and visual references to earlier events, even centuries earlier. These indications of battles and sieges with the Ottomans were often passed down through the maps, forming and preserving a kind of historical canon: for example, the Battle of Nicopolis (1395), the siege of Golubac (1428), the Battle of Varna (1444), the unsuccessful Ottoman siege of Nándorfehérvár (Belgrade) (1456), the capture of Nándorfehérvár (1521), the Battle of Mohács (1526), the capture of Buda (1541), the Siege of Szigetvár (1566), etc. The markings passed down on maps were also used to mark and canonize the sites of battles as memorial sites. In addition to the names of Mohács and Szigetvár, several maps also refer to the deaths of Louis II and Süleyman I (1494–1566) at these places. The fact that the vast majority of the explanations appearing next to the name of Mohács on the maps mention the death of Louis II can be interpreted as a sign of a European cult of the young king who died in battle.

Using the popular imagery of the battle between armoured Christian soldiers and horse-mounted Ottoman soldiers, a schematic battle scene near Mohács depicts the clash between the Hungarians and the Ottomans on the first known printed map of Hungary, the *Tabula Hungariae* by Lázár (Lazarus), published in 1528[8] (Figure 12.1). The lines above the battle scene commemorate the slaughter of King Louis and his companions by Süleyman: *"Hie bey dissin Kreutzlen ist Khünig Ludwig mit den seinen von Soley /manno magno / dem Zwelfftn Turkischen Kayser / erlegt wo denn. Anno 1526 die 29 Augusti."* A similar (but not identical) composition and brief description is also found on the map next to Galambóc (Golubac) where in May 1428 the Hungarian King Sigismund I (of Luxembourg) (1368–1437) unsuccessfully besieged the castle taken by the Ottomans the previous year. A map published at the expense of the Viennese humanist Johannes Cuspinianus (1473–1529) erroneously gave 1409 as the date of the Battle of Galambóc, and certainly not by accident, since 1409 is the date of the battle in Cuspinianus' exhortatory speech about the Battle of Mohács

---

Bernhard Paul Moll. I thank György Danku and Béla Szalai for their kind help in my research. See Tibor Szathmáry, *Descriptio Hungariae. Magyarország és Erdély nyomtatott térképei, 1477–1600*. (Budapest: Privately published, 1987); Lajos Szántai, *Atlas Hungaricus. Magyarország nyomtatott térképei. 1528–1850. I–II*. (Budapest: Akadémiai Kiadó, 1996); Árpád Papp-Váry, *Magyarország története térképeken* (Budapest: Kossuth Könyvkiadó, Cartographia, 2002).

8 *Tabula Hungari[a]e ad quatuor latera per Lazarum quondam Thomae Strigonien[sis] Cardin[alis] Secretariu[m]* ... (Ingolstadiani : invulgata Anno D[omi]ni 1528). National Széchényi Library, Archive of Old Prints. App. M. 136. See Katalin Plihál, *A Tabula Hungariae... Ingolstadt, 1528. Térkép és utóélete az eddigi és a jelenlegi kutatások tükrében* (Budapest: Országos Széchényi Könyvtár, Kossuth Kiadó, 2013).

FIGURE 12.1　The Battle of Mohács. Detail of the *Tabula Hungariae* (1528).
SOURCE: LAZARUS (LÁZÁR), *TABULA HUNGARIAE*, 1528. NATIONAL SZÉCHÉNYI LIBRARY, ARCHIVE OF OLD PRINTS, APP. M. 136.

(*Oratio protreptica Joannis Cuspiniani*… Vienna, 1526).[9] Further research is needed to determine whether the engravers of the woodcut map drew the two battle scenes from preparatory sketch(es) or from their own inspiration. It is nevertheless certain that, however schematic the scenes may be, they clearly show the opposing troops fighting each other and the cannons that played an important part in both battles. It also seems certain that, even if the woodcutters used sketches, they have updated the depictions: while on the copy of the map we know the nationality of the Hungarian heavy cavalry on the right side of the Battle of Mohács is indicated by the red and white [silver] striped flags held by the soldiers, in the Battle of Galambóc the Christian soldiers on the right side, facing the Ottoman light cavalry in turban, hold a flag with the two-headed eagle crest of King Sigismund.

Several new editions and versions of the Lázár map were published in Europe in the 16th century, some of which contain visual and/or textual references to the Battle of Mohács. In the *Tabula Hungariae*[10] published in Vienna

---

[9]　Péter Kasza and Géza Pálffy eds., *Brodarics-emlékkönyv. Egy különleges pártváltás a mohácsi csata után, Brodarics István szerémi pöspök búcsúlevele I. Ferdinánd királyhoz: 1527. március 18. Dévény* (Budapest: Magyar Országos Levéltár, 2011), p. 87.

[10]　Recently see Borbála Gulyás, "Donat Hübschmann magyarországi megrendelői. Négy metszet és négy miniatúra," in *Reneszánsz és barokk Magyarországon. Művészettörténeti*

in 1566 by the humanist historian János Zsámboky (Sambucus) (1531–1584), based on the Lázár map and drawn by Donat Hübschmann (1540–1583) of Leipzig using etching technique, the lamentable destruction of King Louis is mentioned near Mohács in 1526: *"Miserob: clades Lódoui: R. 1526."* In contrast, on Zsámboky's later maps (*Vngariae Loca Praecipva Recens emendata atqve edita, per Ioannem Sambvcvm...*), published in 1571 and 1579, there is no reference to the battle next to the name of Mohács, nor on some later editions of the map.

Although the map titled *Nova totius Ungariae descriptio accurata et diligens desumpta ex pluribus aliorum ...* by Matthias Zündt (1498–1572), published in Nuremberg in 1567, was mainly based on Lázár's work, it contains a reference to the battle in pictures and text a little further away from the town of Mohács, near the Drava River, but the date of the battle is wrongly given as 29 August 1520 instead of 1526: *"Künig Ludwig ist geschlagen Von dem T. K. So. 1520 den 29 Aug. Und alls verhert wie lang die ... gont."* This incorrect date was later copied onto many maps based on Zündt's work, although some, such as Alexander Mair's map *Hungariae descriptionem multis priorum correctis erroribus accurate concin[n]atam...*, published in Augsburg in 1594, show the correct year. In both Zündt's and Mair's maps, the Christian and Ottoman cavalry troops appear alongside Mohács in a similar depiction to that on the Lázár map. The text next to the name of Szigetvár, i.e. that the castle was lost and that Sultan Süleyman died here on 4 September 1566 (sic!), also had a news function on Zündt's map, describing events that had taken place a year before its publication, but on Mair's map of 1594 it was already considered a historical retrospective.

Although the map *Noua totius Hungariae, Croatiae & partis Turcicae Chorographia ...* produced in 1594 by an unknown mapmaker using Gerard Mercator's (1512–1594) *Hungaria* map of 1585, does not refer to the Battle of Mohács, the German-language explanation below the map mentions the battle, Christian casualties and the death of the Hungarian army in the description of the most important battles between the Ottomans and the Hungarians. In 1596, the *Novum Opus Geographicum ex varÿs geographicis tabulis ...* by Levinus Hulsius (1546–1606), a map of Hungary published in Nuremberg, depicted almost identical, schematic scenes of foot soldiers fighting with spears, recalling the battles of Nicopolis, Varna, Belgrade and Mohács. In the latter case, under the "battle scene" only the year of the event is given: *"An° 1526"*.

tanulmányok Galavics Géza tiszteletére I., eds. Borbála Gulyás, Árpád Mikó, and Bálint Ugry (Budapest: Bölcsészettudományi Kutatóközpont, Művészettörténet Intézet, 2021), pp. 81–83.

On the map of the Danube by the Cologne cartographer Matthias Quad (1557–1613),[11] published in 1596 and using the Lázár map as a model, we find a stylised battle scene near Mohács, but the short description of the battle on the Lázár map is not included here. The Battle of Mohács and the death of Louis II can also be found in the text on the history of Hungary at the bottom of the page. On a recently discovered late 16th-century engraved map by Wolfgang Meyerpeck, which was added to Balthasar Guerin's unpublished work on the history of Hungary (*Histoire du royaulme de Hongrie*)[12] from 1604, a schematic battle scene of the Battle of Mohács is accompanied by a handwritten text on the map, presumably by Guerin, referring to the death of the king.

Texts and images referring to earlier military events in Hungary are also found on some 17th- century maps. The map titled *Carte de la Haute et Basse Hongrie Transylvanie Moldavie Valachie Sclavonie et Croatie ...* published in Paris in 1664 and edited by Nicolas Berey, shows a schematic depiction of a cavalry skirmish next to the name of Mohács, and an explanatory text with an incorrect date of the death of Louis II. Jacob von Sandrart's (1630–1708) map of Hungary (*Neue Land Tafel von Hungarn und dessen incorporirten Kőnigreichen und Provinzen...*) published in Nuremberg in 1664, and Sigmund von Birken's (1626–1681) map of the Danube (*Danubius fluviorum Europae princeps cum omnibus accessoriis fluminibus...*), commemorate not only the king but also the death of 22,000 Christians killed in battle, under the pictogram of two crossed swords.

In later editions of Frederick De Wit's (1629 k.–1706) map *Regni Hungariae et regionum, quae ei quondam fuere unitae, ut Transilvaniae ...*, published in Amsterdam in 1686, the war's events were constantly expanded in response to the events of the liberation wars. In the September 1688 edition, next to Mohács, in addition to the battle of 1526, there is a reference to the second Battle of Mohács (Nagyharsány) in 1687. As an early example of the frequent contemporary and later salvation-historical comparisons of the first battle, which resulted in the defeat of the Christians, and the second battle, which ended in victory, the number of Christian casualties in the first battle is compared with the number of Turkish dead in the second: *"Clad. 22,000 Christ 1526. et Clad. 12,000 Tur: A° 1687."* Nicolas de Fer's (ca. 1647–1720) map titled

---

11   CELEBERRIMI TRACTUS DANUBIANI PARS PRAECIPUA AB AUSTRIAE VIENNA CONSTANTI-NOPOLIM USQUE SE PROTENDENS UNGARIAM TRANSILVANIAMQUE COMPLECTENS (Colonia/Köln: Petrus Querradt, 1596).
12   Bibliothèque nationale de France, Département des manuscrits (Français 19877). The map is found after page 249. https://gallica.bnf.fr/ark:/12148/btv1b90638902/f150.item. See Béla Szalai, *A tizenötéves háború metszeteken* (Budapest: Magyar Tudományos Akadémia Könyvtár és Információs Központ, 2021), p. 14, p. 75, p. 113, p. 189.

Le Cours du Danube …, published in Paris in 1687, also contains a reference to the most recent events. At Mohács, below the text *"Ou périt le Roy Louis, l'an 1526"*, next to Harsa Montagne (i.e. the Nagyharsány Hill) the following title is provided: *"Lieu de la déffaite des Turcs le 12 Aoust 1687."*[13] Both battle dates are also depicted on the map *Le Royaume de Hongrie Divisé en Haute, et Basse Hongrie avec l'Esclavonie* … made by Marco Vincenzo Coronelli (1650–1718) and published in Paris in 1687. For other towns, such as Siklós and Pécs, Coronelli emphatically contrasts their 16th-century Ottoman conquest with their 17th-century reconquest by the Habsburg Empire.

Explanations and depictions of earlier, mostly Ottoman-related historical events are less frequent on 18th-century maps, not only because of the increasing demand for cartographic accuracy, but also because of the diminishing Ottoman threat after the liberation wars. However, Gerard van Keulen's (1678–1726) map, published in Amsterdam around 1720 (*Nieuwe Accurate Kaert van een gedeelte van Hongarie* …), still contains numerous references to battles with the Ottomans between the 15th and 17th centuries. In addition to the pictogram of two crossed swords, the map also shows the Christian (22,000) and Ottoman (12,000) casualties of the first and second Battle of Mohács (respectively).

Popular almost from the time of the second Battle of Mohács, this topos – which saw the victory at the end of the 17th century as "reparation" for the tragic defeat of the Hungarians in the first Battle of Mohács, which resulted in the death of the young king, and as an example of divine justice – has been used in a number of literary and artistic examples. These include the commemorative medal made by Philipp Heinrich Müller (1654–1719) in 1687, during the wars of liberation, which shows on the obverse the battle scene of Christoph Fuessl's coin made around 1531 to commemorate the Battle of Mohács in 1526, and on the reverse the so-called second Battle of Mohács (Nagyharsány) in 1687.[14] This approach was also expressed, as we will see, in a pair of pictures painted by

---

13   This map also refers to the capture of Szigetvár in 1566 and the death of Sultan Süleyman there (*"Turbek ou mourut Soliman l'an 1566"*). See Norbert Pap, Máté Kitanics, Péter Gyenizse, Erika Hancz, Zita Bognár, Tamás Tóth, and Zoltán Hámori, "Nagy Szulejmán szigetvári türbéje: történeti, geofizikai és régészeti vizsgálatok," in *Szulejmán szultán Szigetváron. A szigetvári kutatások 2013–2016 között*, eds. Norbert Pap and Pál Fodor (Pécs: Pannon Castrum Kft., 2017), p. 80.

14   Géza Galavics, *Kössünk kardot az pogány ellen. Török háborúk és képzőművészet*, (Budapest: Képzőművészeti Alap Kiadóvállalata, 1986), pp. 14, 109, pict. 78; Vera G. Héri, *A törökellenes háborúk emlékérmei* (Budapest: Magyar Nemzeti Múzeum, 2009), art. 320, p. 153; Papp, "Az 1526. évi mohácsi csata," in *Több mint egy csata*, eds. Fodor et al., 175–178.

István (Stephan) Dorffmaister (1741–1797) at the end of the 18th century, depicting the lost Battle of Mohács in 1526 and the victorious Battle of Mohács in 1687.

2 Travelogues

Mohács and its surroundings were visited by several foreign travellers in the 16th and 17th centuries, and almost all of them mentioned in their travelogues the battle that ended in the disastrous defeat of the Hungarians and the death of Louis II. Hans Dernschwam (1494–ca. 1568/69), the merchant and the most important representative of the Fuggers in Hungary, joined with two of his men, at his own expense, the expedition led by Antal Verancsics (1504–1573), the Bishop of Pécs (Archbishop of Esztergom from 1569)[15] and Ferenc Zay (1498–1570), captain of the Danube navy, which started in 1553. On 22 June 1553, a diplomatic delegation left Vienna on the orders of Ferdinand I (1503–1564) and travelled to Süleyman I in Constantinople to negotiate a truce.[16] Ferdinand I also sent his senior diplomat, Ogier Ghislain de Busbecq (1522–1592), to Constantinople to continue the negotiations. Busbecq left Vienna at the end of 1554, travelling via Buda to Belgrade and arriving in Constantinople

---

15   Árpád Mikó, "Egy humanista mecénás a 16. század közepén Magyarországon: Verancsics Antal, a connaisseur," in *Mátyás király öröksége. Késő reneszánsz művészet Magyarországon (16–17. század) I.*, eds. Árpád Mikó, Mária Verő, and Anna Jávor (A Magyar Nemzeti Galéria kiadványai) 2008/3 (Budapest: Magyar Nemzeti Galéria, 2008), pp. 25–27; Éva Gyulai, "Egy közép-európai tudós portréjához: Verancsics-ikonográfia," in *Parasztok és polgárok. Tanulmányok Tóth Zoltán 65. születésnapjára*, eds. Gábor Czoch, Gergely Horváth, and Péter Pozsgai (Budapest: KORALL Társadalomtörténeti Egyesület, 2008), pp. 163–168; Éva Gyulai, "Ense opus est – Verancsics Antal emblémaverse I. Szulejmán szultánról, 1558," *Publicationes Universitatis Miskolcinensis, Sectio Philosophica* 16 (2011), pp. 129–130; Pál Ács, "»The Good and Honest Turk«. A European Legend in the Context of Sixteenth Century Oriental Studies," in *The Habsburgs and their Courts in Europe, 1400–1700. Between Cosmopolitanism and Regionalism*, eds. Herbert Karner, Ingrid Ciulisová, and Bernardo J. García García (Wien: Palatium, 2014), p. 269; Éva Gyulai, "Turcissare – Verancsics Antal török-képe," in *Humanista történetírás és neolatin irodalom a 15–18. századi Magyarországon*, eds. Enikő Békés, Péter Kasza, and Réka Lengyel (Budapest: MTA Bölcsészettudományi Kutatóközpont Irodalomtudományi Intézet, 2015) pp. 94–95; Árpád Mikó, "Egy humanista mecénás a 16. század közepén Magyarországon. Verancsics Antal (1504–1573), a műértő," *Korunk* 26 (2015), no. 1, pp. 21–22.

16   Ács, "»The Good and Honest Turk«," in *The Habsburgs and their Courts*, eds. Karner et al., pp. 269–273; Ildikó Gausz, "Tranzitirodalom a koraújkori Magyarországról. Busbecq 1554–1555. évi úti impressziói hazánkról," *Történeti tanulmányok* 23 (2015), p. 27.

on 20 January 1555.[17] As the sultan had already launched a campaign against the Persians in the summer of 1553,[18] Busbecq, together with Verancsics, Zay and Dernschamm, followed the sultan to Asia Minor. The distinguished humanists paid attention to the ancient monuments they came across on their journey, and on 29 March they discovered a stone-carved copy of the political will of Emperor Augustus (63 BC–14 AD) (*Res Gestae Divi Augusti*), the *Monumentum Ancyranum*, on the wall of a building in Ancyra (now Ankara), the former seat of the province of Galatia, the text of which was written down by Dernschwam, Verancsics and János Belsy.[19] During the negotiations with the sultan in Amasia in April 1555, they managed to reach a six-month truce under strict conditions.[20] In June 1555, the delegation returned to Constantinople, and some of them, including Dernschwam and Busbecq, travelled home, arriving in Vienna via Buda in August 1555.[21]

Dernschwam kept a detailed diary of his journey, in which he reported on his return visit to Mohács in 1555:

> But we saw the desolate sight of Földvár, this once famous market town with its church. Here was the former camp of King Louis, and Sebeg, the great camp where the king stayed. This was followed by Mohács, formerly a large market town; in it a burnt church … Then came the Csele Stream …[22]

In his memoirs of 1581 and 1582, written long after the journey, Busbecq also recounted his visit to Mohács:

> From here we came to Mohács, a place mournful over the defeat of Louis, King of Hungary. Not far from the town I saw the deep stream between the steep banks into which he and his horse had drowned and

---

17 "I arrived in Constantinople on January 20, where I met again with my earlier mentioned companions, Antal Verancsics and Ferenc Zay." Gausz, "Tranzitirodalom," p. 38.
18 Hans Dernschwam, *Erdély. Besztercebánya. Törökországi útinapló* (Budapest: Európa Könyvkiadó, 1984), pp. 174–175.
19 Ács, "»The Good and Honest Turk«," in *The Habsburgs and their Courts*, eds. Karner et al., pp. 270, 272.
20 Gausz, "Tranzitirodalom," p. 38.
21 Dernschwam, *Erdély.* pp. 55, 455–504. Busbecq later returned to Constantinople, where he served as ambassador to the Porte until 1562. After his return, he was in charge of the Imperial and Royal Library in Vienna until 1564.
22 Dernschwam, *Erdély.* pp. 492–493; Norbert Pap, Pál Fodor, Máté Kitanics, Tamás Morva, Gábor Szalai, and Péter Gyenizse, "A mohácsi Törökdomb," *Történelmi Szemle* 60 (2018), no. 2, p. 331; *Örök Mohács*, eds. B. Szabó et al., p. 400.

so perished. I do not know whether the unhappy young man ventured to confront Süleyman's large and well-trained army with a handful of his troops, chiefly unarmed peasants, through imprudence or through some unfortunate counsel.[23]

In his work *Itinerario*, published in London in 1585, the Italian traveller Marc'Antonio Pigafetta wrote about the battle and its location in detail, reporting on his 1567 trip to Constantinople:

> On 29 August 1526, Süleyman and King Louis II of Hungary clashed on the field of Mohács. The king, after a devastating blow to his army, fled by the usual route to Buda, and drowned in a shallow swamp that would not hold eight dead horses. This marsh, or swamp, was situated a good Italian mile from the battlefield, not far from the Danube, at the foot of a small hill. Between the hill and the Danube, at a distance of barely an arrow's length, are several impassable marshy areas, which can only be crossed by a very narrow wooden lane connecting the marshy areas and leading to the Danube. The king, when he tried to cross it, saw that it was full of wagons and other obstacles fleeing from battle, but he tried to break through them in a great hurry, and jumped into the marsh near the bridge, but unfortunately he and his horse drowned. The Turks say that he was found only two days after the mentioned day, and that Süleyman buried him in a temple, which we have seen not far off.[24]

The body of Louis II was actually found by a Hungarian search party several weeks after his death and buried in Székesfehérvár.

In 1573, the German theologian Stephan Gerlach (1546–1612) travelled to Constantinople as a member of David Ungnad's (1535–1600) embassy to the Porte, and in his travel diary we read of his visit to Mohács:

> As we had time, my lord drove a good half-mile by coach to the place where the last Hungarian king, Louis, with his thirty-five thousand men,

---

23　*Itinera Constantinopolitanum et Amasianum ab Augerio Gislenio Busbequio ad Solimannum Turcarum imperatorem C.M. oratore confecta. Eiusdem Busbequii de re militari contra Turcam instituenda consilium. Altera editio* (Antverpiae: Ex officina Christophori Plantini, 1582), p. 70; Gausz, "Tranzitirodalom," p. 39; *Örök Mohács*, eds. B. Szabó et al., pp. 431–432.

24　Gábor Farkas Farkas, Zsolt Szebelédi, and Bernadett Varga eds., *"Nekünk mégis Mohács kell..." – II. Lajos király rejtélyes halála és különböző temetései* (Budapest: Magyar Tudományos Akadémia Bölcsészettudományi Kutatóközpont Országos Széchényi Könyvtár, 2016), pp. 135–136, 220–221; *Örök Mohács*, eds. B. Szabó et al., pp. 433–434.

had fought three hundred thousand Ottomans. He lost the battle and died. This place is now part wasteland, part arable land. When we visited, it was full of wheat ears. You can still see the trenches where the cannons stood and where the dead were buried. ... Then we visited the place where King Louis rode across the marsh to escape from the battle. He had already crossed, but his horse fell and drowned. This was shown to us by an old Hungarian who travelled with us and had himself taken part in the battle.[25]

After completing his studies at the University of Tübingen, the German Lutheran pastor Salomon Schweigger (1551–1622) went as a travelling preacher from Vienna via Hungary to Sultan Murad III (1546–1595) in Constantinople in 1577, accompanied by Rudolf II's (1552–1612) envoy Joachim von Sintzendorff, and then in 1581 he also visited Egypt and the Holy Land.[26] His travelogue,[27] first published in 1608 and illustrated with 100 pictures of his experiences during his stay, in which he published descriptions and pictures of the life, religious customs, costumes, ceremonies, etc. of the Turks, was an important contribution to gaining a more nuanced picture of the Turks which, in contrast to the propagandistic image of the cruel, barbaric Turks, began to gain ground in Europe from the second half of the 16th century onwards.

25 "Nekünk mégis Mohács kell...", eds. Farkas et al., p. 219; Örök Mohács, eds. B. Szabó et al., p. 427. See Pap et al., "A mohácsi Törökdomb," p. 331.
26 András F. Balogh ed., Ungarnbilder im 17. Jahrhundert. Studien und Editionen der Texte: Jakob Vogel: "Vngrische Schlacht" (1626). Kapitel aus Martin Zeillers "Neue Beschreibung des Königreichs Ungarn" (1664), Salomon Schweiggers "Gezweyte neue nutzliche und anmuthige Reiß-Beschreibung" (1664) und aus Eberhard Werner Happels "Thesaurus Exoticorum" (1688) (Budapest: ELTE Eötvös József Collegium, 2013), pp. 196–197. See Gábor Farkas Farkas, "Új kérdések II. Lajos rejtélyes halálával és temetésével kapcsolatban," Magyar Könyvszemle 131 (2015), no. 4, p. 394.
27 Salomon Schweigger, Ein newe Reyßbeschreibung auß Teutschland Nach Constantinopel und Jerusalem: darinn die Gelegenheit derselben Länder, Städt, ..., der innwohnenten Völcker Art, ... Religion und Gottesdienst etc. ; insonderheit die ... gestalt deß H. Grabs, der Stadt Jerusalem ... und deß Authoris Meinung hievon ; item ... was die Röm. Keys. Maj. ... dem Türckischen Keyser ... zur Praesent ... überliefern lassen ... ; desgleichen deß Türckischen Reichs Gubernation ... und vielerley andern ... sachen ... mit 100 ... Figuren ... (Nürnberg: 1608). Several new editions of the book were published thereafter. E.g. Salomon Schweigger, Gezweyte neue nutzliche und anmuthige Reiß-Beschreibung, Die Erste nach Constantinopel und Jerusalem (Nürnberg: 1664). The modern German edition: Heidi Stein ed., Salomon Schweigger: Zum Hofe des türkischen Sultans (Leipzig: F. A. Brockhaus, 1986).

While in Buda, Schweigger visited the former royal castle,[28] and in his travel diary he recorded the still visible inscriptions from the time of King Matthias I (1443–1490) and King Vladislaus II (1456–1516),[29] as well as the astrological painting of the ceiling of the former library. In a chapter on events in Hungary in the first half of the 16th century, he also provided a detailed account of the Battle of Mohács and the tragic death of Louis II.[30] After the historical account, he goes on to describe his travels, revealing that although he had been near Mohács, he had not personally visited the town, so his knowledge was not drawn from his own experience but from historical sources.[31]

Reinhold Lubenau (1556–1631), a pharmacist and traveller from Königsberg, also visited Mohács during his trip to Constantinople in 1587. "But before we arrived, the lord sent [the ship] to port and ordered the Turks to go with us. They led us to a village called Mohács, not far from the Danube, and showed us the place near a mill where King Louis was routed by Süleyman on 29 August 1526, the king's army was defeated, and the king and his horse were overturned in the mossy place near the mill and drowned in the marsh,"[32] reads his travelogue.

---

28 Mihailo St. Popović, "Reminiszenzen an König Matthias Corvinus in den Reiseberichten des Salomon Schweigger und Reinhold Lubenau," in *Matthias Corvinus und seine Zeit. Europa am Übergang vom Mittelalter zur Neuzeit,* ed. Christian Gastgeber, (Wien: Österreichische Akademie der Wissenschaften, 2011. On his travel in Hungary see Katalin Németh S., "Salomon Schweigger útleírásának magyar vonatkozásai," in *Tarnai Andor-emlékkönyv,* ed. Gábor Kecskeméti (Budapest: Universitas Könyvkiadó, 1996); Katalin Németh S., *Magyar dolgokról. Magyar–német kapcsolattörténeti tanulmányok* (Historia litteraria) 31 (Budapest: Universitas Könyvkiadó, 2014), pp. 33–44.

29 Schweigger, *Ein newe Reyßbeschreibung.* pp. 21–22. See Árpád Mikó, "Stílus és felírat. Kőbe vésett klasszikus- és korai humanista kapitálissal írott feliratok a Mátyás- és Jagelló-kori Magyarországon," *Művészettörténeti Értesítő* 54 (2005), no. 3–4, p. 234.

30 Schweigger, *Ein newe Reyßbeschreibung.* pp. 26–27.

31 In a page note on the margin, he refers to Paolo Giovio who in his work titled *Commentario de le chose de' Turchi* (Roma, 1531) which has been published and translated several times, describes the Battle of Mohács and the death of King Louis II.

32 "Nekünk mégis Mohács kell...", eds. Farkas et al., pp. 137, 221; *Örök Mohács,* eds. B. Szabó et al., p. 439; Farkas, "Új kérdések," p. 394. *"Ehe wier aber dahin kamen, lies der Herr anlenden und befahl, den Turcken mit uns zu gehen. Die fuhreten uns nicht weidt von der Thona zu einem Dorf, Mohatsch genandt und zeigeten uns bei einer Muhlen den Ohrt, da Konig Ludowicus vom Solimanno, anno 1526 den 29. Augusti in die Flucht geschlagen, des Konigks Krigsvolck erleget und der Konigk mit seinem Pferde bei der Muhlen im Gemos gesturtzt und im Sumpf ersticket."* Wilhelm von Sahm ed., *Beschreibung der Reisen des Reinhold Lubenau I.* (Königsberg: F. Beyer, 1912), p. 91. See Ulrike Ilg, "Bebilderte Reiseberichte aus dem Osmanischen Reich in deutscher Sprache (16. bis 17. Jahrhundert)," in *Das Bild des Feindes. Konstruktion von Antagonismen und Kulturtransfer im Zeitalter der Türkenkriege.*

The mill as a memorial site of the death of Louis II was also mentioned in the diary of 12-year-old László Festetich (1785–1846), who wrote about his visit to Mohács on 8 September 1797, accompanied by József Péteri Takáts (1767–1821), presumably on the instructions or even dictation of his tutor Bishop László Pál Esterházy (1730–1799) who sent them to "… the place where, according to popular belief, King Louis fell. Now that stream was completely dried up because of the great drought, otherwise the water was running a mill there."[33] The mill, often visited by visitors to the battlefield, also appears in two paintings by István Dorffmaister depicting the Battle of Mohács, the battle painting for the bishop's summer house in Mohács[34] and the battle painting for the reception hall of the Abbey of Szentgotthárd.[35] As an indication of the continuation of the tradition in the 19th century, in 1865 the weekly newspaper *Vasárnapi Ujság* also published a woodcut illustration of the mill[36] (Figure 12.2) and the editor's suggestion to erect a monument next to the mill.[37]

Lubenau's description of his journey also mentioned a local "monument" not far from the mill: under an old oak tree, which was drying up, he found the bones and skulls of thousands of Christian soldiers. He believed that the mound, which almost completely covered the tree and was astonishing in its size, had been created as an eternal memorial to the battle. As a special manifestation of a cult of the relics, he removed moss from some of the skulls, which, after his return home, proved to be a good way of stopping the bleeding.[38] Since Lubenau, who was originally a pharmacist, would certainly have

Ostmitteleuropa. Italien und Osmanisches Reich, eds. Eckhard Leuschner and Thomas Wünsch (Berlin: Gebr. Mann Verlag, 2013), p. 64; Gausz, "Tranzitirodalom," p. 25–26.

33 National Széchényi Library, Budapest, Archive of Manuscripts, Quart. Hung. 3695, fol. 6v; Sándor Takáts, *Péteri Takáts József* (Budapest: Hunyadi Mátyás Intézet, 1890), p. 61. See Géza Galavics, "Dorffmaister István történeti képei," in *"Stephan Dorffmaister pinxit." Dorffmaister István emlékkiállítása*, eds. László Kostyál and Monika Zsámbéky (Zalaegerszeg: 1997), p. 84; *Mohács*, eds. B. Szabó et al., p. 571.

34 Oil on canvas, 553 × 271 cm. 1787. Mohács, cemetery chapel.

35 Oil on canvas, 344 × 254 cm. Budapest: Museum of Fine Arts – Hungarian National Gallery, Old Hungarian Collection, 55.387. See Galavics, "Dorffmaister István történeti képei," in *"Stephan Dorffmaister pinxit,"* eds. Kostyál et al., p. 85.

36 *Vasárnapi Ujság* 12 (1865), no. 8, 19 February, p. 89. See Katalin Sinkó, "Kontinuitás vagy a hagyomány újrateremtése? Történeti képek a 19. században," in *Akadémiai Műhely / Közgyűlési előadások / 2000 / Millenium az Akadémián I.* ed. Ferenc Glatz (Budapest: Magyar Tudományos Akadémia, 2001), p. 326; B. Szabó, *Mohács*. p. 494; *"Nekünk mégis Mohács kell…"*, eds. Farkas et al., p. 302.

37 *Vasárnapi Ujság* 12 (1865), no. 8, 19 February, p. 89.

38 Sahm ed., *Beschreibung*. pp. 91–92. Not far from the mill, "…there is an old, dried-out oak tree, around which the bones and skulls of many thousands of Christians are piled up as a perpetual reminder, so much so that the oak is almost covered with them …" Edgár

FIGURE 12.2   Antal Marastoni and Károly Rusz, "The mill of the Csele Stream near Mohács (grave of King Louis II)". Woodcut.
SOURCE: *VASÁRNAPI UJSÁG* 12 (1865), NO. 8. 19 FEBRUARY, 89.

found moss near his home also, the fact that he took this intrinsically worthless and easily obtainable substance with him from Mohács to Königsberg shows that he must have had a strong belief in its special healing powers, which were certainly linked to the memory of the heroes of Mohács.

According to a 1926 paper, the pile of bones and skulls could have been created between 1573 and 1587, as Stephan Gerlach, who visited Mohács in 1573, had not yet mentioned it.[39] As mentioned above, Gerlach did indeed visit the place where, according to local legend, "King Louis rode across the marsh to escape from battle", but he did not write about the mill. We can only speculate about the circumstances of the creation of the pile of skulls and bones, or whether the description is a literary topos linked to some other memorial site without any basis in reality. Edgár Palóczi's hypothesis that the "monument" was built between 1573 and 1587 does not seem to be well-founded, since it seems unlikely that in the 1570s – half a century after the battle – the

---

39   Palóczi, "A mohácsi csatatér régi emlékművei és ereklyéi," *Hadimúzeumi Lapok* 2 (1926), november, no. 5–7, p. 5.
   Palóczi, "A mohácsi csatatér."

bodies of thousands of Christian (!) soldiers were systematically dug up in the Ottoman-controlled agricultural area in order to place their bones around the oak tree as a mark of respect. I can think of two possible ways of getting them there. Maybe when the Ottomans buried the Christian and Muslim dead of the battle, they threw some of them to a secluded place (or multiple places), and the bodies that accidentally fell under an oak tree were left to decompose to nothing but bones. According to Ottoman historians, who sometimes exaggerate poetically, the Ottomans raised huge heaps of the enemy's corpses on the battlefield:

> The surface of the plain, the tops of the mounds, the peaks of the heights and the openings of the valleys were covered with mutilated corpses to the end. The mounds of the corpses of Satan's accomplices in the field stretched up to the sky. The surface of the field was covered with corpses, and in places mounds of corpses rose up.[40]

In the mass graves made by the Ottomans in the area of the Mohács Historical Memorial Site, there are even "... pyramids made of skulls..."[41] However, this is contradicted by the fact that the Islamic religion requires that not only own soldiers but also enemy soldiers be buried within a few days of the battle, so it is possible that the bodies were piled up as temporary signs of triumph. The fact that no animal bite marks were found on the bones of the mass graves found at Mohács also indicates a quick burial.

We cannot rule out the possibility that the bones and skulls found during agricultural work were gathered together in one place by the peasants, so as not to interfere with the cultivation of the land, and that these formed the pile of bones seen by Lubenau over half a century. It is also not certain that the traveller saw thousands of skulls and bones, as a few hundred pieces can build a big pile. It cannot be excluded that Lubenau saw the remains of victims of the mass executions carried out by the Ottomans after the Battle of Mohács or of a later clash in the area, although the large number of skulls and bones seems to contradict the latter view. However it is extremely remarkable that Lubenau interpreted the phenomenon as a memorial, the first time reporting (to my

---

40 Kemálpasazáde, "Mohácsnáme," in *Örök Mohács,* B. Szabó eds. et al., p. 336; cf. ibid. p. 266. Pál Fodor and András Mércz, "Mi is veszett Mohácsnál? Oszmán-török veszteséglista az 1526. évi hadjáratról," *Történelmi Szemle* 65 (2023), no. 2, p. 221.
41 Géza Perjés, *Mohács* (Budapest: Magvető Könyvkiadó, 1979), p. 427.

knowledge), even if possibly erroneously, a conscious effort to memorialise the battle site from the Christian side.[42]

3 Local Commemorations and Memorial Plans

In an effort to commemorate the battle and the memory of the king who died young,[43] around 1787, Bishop László Pál Esterházy of Pécs commissioned István Dorffmaister to paint the first and second Battles of Mohács (Nagyharsány) and a three-quarter-length portrait of Louis II who died in the battle, to commemorate the centenary of the victorious second Battle of Mohács[44] (Figure 12.3). The large battle portraits with semi-circular shape covers were housed in the bishop's summer residence in Mohács. Dorffmaister's portrait shows the young king wearing the gilded ornamental armour that was considered the former property of Louis II at the end of the 18th century and was exhibited in the representative room (König-Ludwigs-Saal) of the Imperial Armoury (Kaiserliches Zeughaus) on the Renngasse in Vienna.[45] It is also the armour in

---

42 The first local "memorial" to the Battle of Mohács in the physical sense is known to have been erected in the 17th century, by the victors. See Chapter Eleven.

43 Recently see Annamária Nyárs, "A mohácsi csata emlékművei a városban," *Belvedere Meridionale* 18 (2006), no. 7–8; Nóra Veszprémi, "A magyar történeti festészet kezdetei? (A mohácsi csata képi ábrázolásai a 18. század végén és a 19. század elején)," in *A magyar emlékezethelyek kutatásának elméleti és módszertani alapjai*, eds. Pál S. Varga, Orsolya Száraz, and Miklós Takács (Loci Memoriae Hungariae) 2 (Debrecen: Debreceni Egyetemi Kiadó, 2013), pp. 266–273; Zsuzsa Barbarics-Hermanik, "Türkengedächtnis in Ungarn. Die Rolle der Gedächtnisort Mohács und Szigetvár im Prozess der nationalen Identitätsbildung," in *Ein Raum im Wandel. Die osmanisch-habsburgische Grenzregion vom 16. bis zum 18. Jahrhundert*, eds. Norbert Spannenberger and Szabolcs Varga (Stuttgart: Franz Steiner Verlag, 2014), pp. 280–283; Andrea Hasanović-Kolutácz, "1526 helye és szerepe a mohácsi identitásban," in *Több mint egy csata: Mohács. Az 1526. évi ütközet a magyar tudományos és kulturális emlékezetben*, eds. Pál Fodor and Szabolcs Varga (Budapest: MTA Bölcsészettudományi Kutatóközpont, 2019), pp. 592–616.

44 Galavics, "Dorffmaister István történeti képei," in *"Stephan Dorffmaister pinxit,"* eds. Kostyál et al., pp. 84–86.

45 Recently see Júlia Papp, "Adatok II. Lajos magyar király páncélos ábrázolásaihoz," *Művészettörténeti Értesítő* 69 (2020), no. 2, pp. 269–302; Júlia Papp, "»...pugnas honeste obiit...« The armor formerly in the Viennese Imperial Zeughaus attributed to Louis II of Hungary in the Hungarian cultural history," *Zeitschrift für historische Waffen- und Kostümkunde* 64 (2022), no. 1, pp. 69–98. The armour, which played an important role in Hungarian art history and was transferred from the Kunsthistorisches Museum in Vienna to the National Museum in Budapest in 1933, and which was discovered in 1939 to have been a gift to the Polish King Sigismund Augustus II (1520–1572), was donated to Poland by the Hungarian government in late 2020.

FIGURE 12.3 István Dorffmaister: Louis II. Oil, canvas, 1787.
SOURCE: MOHÁCS, KANIZSAI DOROTTYA MUSEUM.

which Louis II can be seen on the painting of the Battle of Mohács in 1526 by Dorffmaister, as he falls from his white horse, rising almost vertically, into the marsh[46] (Figure 12.4).

---

46 Paolo Giovio (Paulus Iovius) (1483–1552) in his short biography of Louis II written in the mid-16th century, also recalled the moment of the fall with a powerful image very similar to this composition: "The king himself, losing all hope of escape, came to a lake with a

FIGURE 12.4   József Borsos: The Battle of Mohács in 1526. Reduced copy of Dorffmaister's battle picture (detail). Oil, canvas, 1837.
SOURCE: MOHÁCS, MAYOR'S OFFICE.

very high bank; when he tried to get out, his horse, which was galloping up with a straight neck, was drawn back towards him, and he fell backwards, and the weight of his horse and weapons crushed him, thus he drowned and died in the two-span whirling water." *Örök Mohács,* eds. B. Szabó et al., p. 389.

Little and contradictory information are available about the monument at the site of the Battle of Mohács, which was erected before the 19th century.[47] The poet János Batsányi (1763–1845) mentions in a poem written in 1789 a memorial column erected at the site of the battle,[48] presumably known only by hearsay, and in the travel diary of the child László Festetich from 1797 it is stated that in the vicinity of the mill where, according to popular belief, Louis II died, the lower marble stone of a memorial column is still visible, which had been erected earlier to commemorate the battle and which the bishop of Pécs wanted to have renovated.[49]

Even if László Festetich and his attendant, József Péteri Takács, could actually see the remains of the memorial column in 1797, it must have disappeared by the end of the 1810s, as it was precisely because of the absence of the memorial that Bishop József Király (1737–1825) of Pécs initiated the construction of a memorial chapel at the presumed site of the Battle of Mohács and the death of the king.[50] At the same time, he was also missing the commemoration of the victorious battle of 1687. The linking of the two Battles of Mohács as an example of divine justice is thus also found here, but unlike some earlier and contemporary manifestations of the topos, the bishop does not mention the role of the House of Habsburg in the liberation war.

In 1816, on the 290th anniversary of the battle, József Király had the single-nave, neoclassical Calvary or Battlefield Chapel of the Seven Sorrows Virgin built in the Catholic cemetery which became a place of pilgrimage by papal

---

47 According to tradition, Serbian despot Štefan Lazarević (ca. 1377–1427) had a marble memorial column erected at the site of the Battle of Kosovo between the Christian army led by Serbian forces and the Ottoman Empire in 1389. See Norbert Pap and Péter Reményi, "Encounters Between Islam and Christianity: Mohács and Kosovo Polje," in *Places of Memory and Legacies in an Age of Insecurities and Globalization,* ed. Gerry O'Reilly (Cham: Springer, 2020), pp. 285–305.

48 János Batsányi, "Székes-Fejér-Vári Professor Virág Benedek Úr' Társunkhoz Kassán, Karátson' Havában, 1789," *Magyar Museum* II/1 (1790). See Dezső Keresztury and Andor Tarnai eds., *Batsányi János Összes Művei I. Versek* (Budapest: Akadémiai Kiadó, 1953), p. 295; Attila Debreczeni, "Nemzeti nagylét, nagy temető és – Batsányi (Egy nemzeti narratíva formálódása)," in *A magyar emlékezethelyek,* eds. S. Varga et al., p. 210; *Örök Mohács,* eds. B. Szabó et al., p. 563.

49 Takáts, *Péteri Takáts,* p. 61. See Galavics, "Dorffmaister István történeti képei," in "*Stephan Dorffmaister pinxit,*" eds. Kostyál et al., p. 84; Barbarics-Hermanik, "Türkengedächtnis in Ungarn," in *Ein Raum im Wandel,* eds. Spannenberger et al., p. 281; Örök Mohács, eds. B. Szabó et al., p. 571. On the metaphorisation of Mohács as a cemetery "which foregrounds the act of remembrance and the gesture of commemorating...", see Debreczeni, "Nemzeti nagylét," in *A magyar emlékezethelyek,* eds. S. Varga et al.

50 *Örök Mohács,* eds. B. Szabó et al. pp. 576–577. See "Méltóságos és Fő Tisztelendő Király József Pécsi Püspök emléke," *Tudományos Gyűjtemény* 13 (1829), no. 4, pp. 56–60.

permission.[51] As the chapel's lookout overlooking the battlefield had cracked from heavy use, it was rebuilt to its present form between 1856 and 1860 through public donation, according to the plans of József Hild (1789–1867). In 1859, as a gift from the Bishop of Pécs, György Girk (1793–1868), two battle portraits by Dorffmaister were placed here, depicting the first and second Battle of Mohács, and a portrait of Louis II. The current form of the chapel tower was designed in 1908 by the architect Andor Pilch (1877–1936) of Pécs.

In addition to the earlier dominant ecclesiastical initiatives, from the 1830s there were also secular efforts to commemorate the Battle of Mohács and the death of the king, and in the second half of the century, emphasis also shifted to these.[52] On 1 June 1836, the town of Mohács sent a petition to Baranya County asking it to support their initiative to erect a memorial, to publish a call for donations for the planned monument in the surrounding counties and to appoint a person responsible for the matter. The document goes beyond previous local commemorations and refers to the lost battle and the death of the king as one of Hungary's greatest and saddest tragedies. The broader perspective is also hinted at by the mention of the fact that people passing through Mohács also urged the city authorities to erect a memorial statue at the site of the battle.[53]

The local initiative to erect the monument was made countrywide known by articles published in 1842 in the political newspaper *Hírnök* published in Pozsony (Bratislava) which carried domestic and international news pieces. The author of the article entitled *"On the column to be erected in memory of the Mohács disaster"*, referring to a conversation with the judge of Mohács and his colleagues in the office, says that plans were under way to install an iron statue of Louis II on horseback, which was hoped would increase the number of visitors to the town as train travel also expanded.[54] The project has also

---

51 Nyárs, "A mohácsi csata," p. 70; Barbarics-Hermanik, "Türkengedächtnis in Ungarn," in *Ein Raum im Wandel,* eds. Spannenberger et al., p. 283; Hasanović-Kolutácz, "1526 helye és szerepe," in *Több mint egy csata,* eds. Fodor et al., pp. 593–594.; János Hóvári, "A mohácsi csata két emlékéve: 1926 versus 1976," in *Több mint egy csata,* eds. Fodor et al., p. 541.

52 Barbarics-Hermanik, "Türkengedächtnis in Ungarn," in *Ein Raum im Wandel,* eds. Spannenberger et al., p. 297.

53 Pécs: Baranya County Archives of the Hungarian National Archives. IV.1.b. Baranya vármegye nemesi közgyűlésének iratai 1718/1836. A vármegye határozata: IV.1.a. Baranya vármegye nemesi közgyűlésének jegyzőkönyve 1718/1836. "In 1836, Mohács appeals to the county to ask the nearby counties to donate to the monument to be erected at the Csele Stream." József Fölker, *Mohács története* (Mohács: Rosenthal Márk Könyvnyomdája, 1900), p. 60. See Hasanović-Kolutácz, "1526 helye és szerepe," in *Több mint egy csata,* eds. Fodor et al., p. 595.

54 *Hírnök* 6 (1842), no. 10, 3 February. See *Örök Mohács,* eds. B. Szabó et al., p. 605.

been promised financial support from the County of Esztergom, presumably in response to the 1836 appeal. The representatives of Mohács had already negotiated with iron mills in Hungary and abroad, but no contractor could be found for the construction of the "colossal" statue. The journalist considers the planned project unfortunate not only because of the rapidly deteriorating material (iron) and the huge size of the statue, but also because, although the folk tradition places the site of the king's death next to the mill, it was not at all clear where he died. Instead of the equestrian statue, a building would be erected next to the bishop's summer residence, inside which would be displayed the "remains" found on the battlefield and later to be unearthed, and on top of which would be placed plaques informing travellers of the former location of the Ottoman and Hungarian camps of the battle. The contemporary press revealed that the assembly of Baranya County which included Mohács, not only took up the cause of the monument, but also wanted to submit it to the forthcoming session of the National Assembly which would have turned the local initiative into a national programme.[55]

In 1846, the efforts of the town of Mohács to erect a memorial took on a more concrete form, as the damaged documents preserved in the Baranya County Archives of the Hungarian National Archives show.[56] The town had the design of the monument to Louis II prepared by sculptor Mihály Bartalits (1808–1879) of Pécs,[57] and presented it to the county. A committee was formed for the monument, chaired by Imre Perczel, the second deputy of Baranya County, also including Eduárd Barthos, the chief judge of the town of Mohács, who presented the monument to the county. Contrary to the earlier design, and perhaps as a result of the criticism expressed in the press in 1842, the statue would not have been made of iron, but of sandstone, carved by the sculptor for a thousand silver forints. Since only 400 forints had been collected from the donations for the monument, they asked the county to send the amount they had to the town.

Esztergom County was indeed actively involved in the memorial process, as the documents and records of the assembly in the Komárom-Esztergom

---

55 *Hasznos Mulatságok* 26 (1842), no. 44, pp. 173–175. See Barbarics-Hermanik, "Türkengedächtnis in Ungarn," in *Ein Raum im Wandel,* eds. Spannenberger et al., p. 283; Hasanović-Kolutácz, "1526 helye és szerepe," in *Több mint egy csata,* eds. Fodor et al., p. 595; *Örök Mohács,* eds. B. Szabó et al., pp. 606–607.

56 Pécs: Baranya County Archives of the Hungarian National Archives. IV.101.b. Baranya Vármegye Bizottmányának iratai 958/1848.

57 Bartalits' best-known work was the series of statues of the apostles on the cathedral of Pécs, before its restoration. See Károly Sonkoly, "A pécsi székesegyház Bartalits Mihály készítette első apostolszobrai," *Janus Pannonius Múzeum Évkönyve* 29 (1984), pp. 257–301.

County Archives of the Hungarian National Archives show. Since Esztergom was the most successful in collecting donations, the council of Mohács asked for their opinion on where and in what form the monument should be implemented. The people of Mohács reported to the donor county about two ideas: one to raise a building on the battlefield to house a painting of the battle, and another to erect a statue on the spot where King Louis drowned in the stream. The archives also contain a receipt from the Mohács town treasury for the payment of 233.26 forints by Esztergom County. According to the decree of the county assembly, Esztergom County started another donation campaign which collected 190.40 forints. The document also lists the names of the donors of the new campaign together with their signatures. Although the Esztergom County assembly voted for the battlefield building, the town of Mohács decided to have a statue of Louis II on horseback made a few years later.[58] In the end, the plan was not realized: On 26 May 1848, the committee set up in 1846 decided to postpone the construction due to the turbulent political situation and to reallocate the money for other purposes.

From a formal point of view, the efforts to preserve the local memory of the battle were influenced primarily by the aforementioned paintings of István Dorffmaister, which were on display in the so-called "King's Room" of the bishop's summer house in Mohács from the end of the 18th century and in the cemetery chapel in Mohács from the second half of the 1850s. As we know from several memoirs and travelogues,[59] the room of the bishop's palace where the two battle scenes and the portrait of Louis II were placed was open to the public, and an illustration from the late 19th century shows that the battle scenes were accompanied by an armoured portrait of Louis II.[60]

The surviving draft drawing by Mihály Bartalits illustrates the 19th century recognition and popularity of István Dorffmaister's battle scene.[61] The

---

58 Esztergom Komárom-Esztergom County Archives of the Hungarian National Archives. IV.1. b, 2775/1841, 637/1842; IV.1. a, 2775/1841.

59 László Boros, "Dorffmaister Baranyában," *Művészettörténeti Értesítő* 21 (1974), pp. 279–280; Géza Galavics, "A történeti téma," in *Művészet Magyarországon 1780–1830*, eds. Hedvig Szabolcsi and Géza Galavics (Budapest: MTA Művészettörténeti Kutató Csoport, 1980), p. 165; Galavics, "Dorffmaister István történeti képei," in *"Stephan Dorffmaister pinxit,"* eds. Kostyál et al., p. 94; Veszprémi, "A magyar történeti festészet," in *A magyar emlékezethelyek*, eds. S. Varga et al. p. 264.

60 Baranya (1897), p. 372. Cf. Galavics, "A történeti téma," in *Művészet Magyarországon*, eds. Szabolcsi et al., pp. 165–166.

61 This is also indicated by the fact that the young József Borsos copied the two battle scenes and the portrait of Louis II in Mohács in 1837. József Borsos: The Battle of Mohács in 1526. Oil, canvas, 114 x 188 cm. Mohács, Mayor's Office (reduced copy of Dorffmaister's battle picture); József Borsos: Portrait of King Louis II. Oil, canvas, 107 x 73.5 cm. Hungarian

composition of the pencil sketch marked "Drawn by the sculptor Bartalits in Pécs in 1846" (Figure 12.5) bears a clear resemblance to the scene of the death of Louis II in the oil painting (Figure 12.4).

However, it seems that the pre-image used by Bartalits could not have been, or was not only Dorffmaister's painting. In 1843, a few years before Bartalits' drawing was completed, the publisher Alajos Bucsánszky (1802–1883)[62] published Pál Bedeő's (1805–1873) Hungarian history in Pozsony in both Hungarian and German, which later went through several editions.[63] The woodcuts of the richly illustrated volumes, and presumably the drawings that served as models – as can be read on the cover image and the pre-piece of the cover of later editions – were made by Bucsánszky's often-employed illustrator, János Mihalovits[64] from Pozsony. Contrary to the custom of the time, the ambitious

National Museum Hungarian Historical Gallery, 1649. Completed in 1838, the painting was transferred to the Historical Picture Gallery of the National Museum in 1949, when the Parliament Museum was closed down. György Rózsa, "A Magyar Történelmi Képcsarnok néhány újabb biedermeier képe," *Folia Archaeologica* 13 (1961), p. 292. See Ágoston Bárány, "A vándor titkai. V. levél," *Társalkodó* 6 (1837). p. 363; Galavics, "A történeti téma," in *Művészet Magyarországon,* eds. Szabolcsi et al., p. 165; Galavics, "Dorffmaister István történeti képei," in *"Stephan Dorffmaister pinxit,"* eds. Kostyál et al., p. 86; Árpád Mikó and Katalin Sinkó eds., *Történelem – kép. Szemelvények múlt és művészet kapcsolatáról* (Budapest: Magyar Nemzet Galéria, 2000), pp. 71, 114, art. IX–9, 537; Orsolya Réthelyi et al. eds., *Habsburg Mária, Mohács özvegye. A királyné és udvara 1521–1531.* (Budapest: Budapesti Történeti Múzeum, 2005), art. IX–2, 267–268; Zsuzsanna Farkas, "Die Rezeption des Malers und Fotografen József Borsos (1821–1883) einst und heute," in *Annales de la Galerie Nationale Hongroise / A Magyar Nemzeti Galéria Évkönyve 24/9, 2002–2004* (2005), pp. 9–10; Nóra Veszprémi ed., *Borsos József festő és fotográfus (1821–1883)* (A Magyar Nemzeti Galéria kiadványai) 2009/4 (Budapest: Magxar Nemzeti Galéria, 2009), pp. 167–170; Veszprémi, "A magyar történeti festészet," in *A magyar emlékezethelyek,* eds. S. Varga et al. pp. 265–266; Júlia Papp and Erzsébet Király eds., *A magyar művészet a 19. században. Képzőművészet.* (Budapest: MTA BTK, Osiris, 2018), p. 110; Stanislava Kuzmová, "The Memory of Jagiellonians in the Kingdom of Hungary, and in Hungarian and Slovak National Narratives," in *Remembering the Jagiellonians,* ed. Natalia Nowakowska (London, New York: Routledge, 2018), p. 76; Hasanović-Kolutácz, "1526 helye és szerepe," in *Több mint egy csata,* eds. Fodor et al., p. 592.

62   Gábor Kovács I., "Bucsánszky Alajos útja a kalendárium- és ponyva-tömegtermeléshez," *Magyar Könyvszemle* 101 (1985), no. 1, pp. 1–17.; Gábor Kovács I., *Kis magyar kalendáriumtörténet* (Budapest: Akadémiai Kiadó, 1989), pp. 113–119.

63   *Magyarok' története a vezérek' és királyok' képeivel* (Pozsonyban: Bucsánszky Alajos polg. könyvkötő költségén, 1843); *Geschichte Ungarns mit Abbildungen der Anführer und Könige* (Preßburg: Verlag von Alois Bucsánsky, 1843). For an unidentified German-language copy of the publication, without a title page, in the Historical Picture Gallery of the Hungarian National Museum, Book 671, see György Rózsa, *Magyar történetábrázolás a 17. században* (Budapest: Akadémiai Kiadó, 1973), pp. 77, 159; Júlia Papp, "II. Lajos magyar király fiktív páncélos ábrázolásai," *Ars Hungarica* 46 (2020), no. 4, pp. 439–440.

64   Pál Drescher, *Régi magyar gyerekkönyvek, 1538–1875* (Budapest: Magyar Bibliophil Társaság, 1934), art.142; Kovács I., "Bucsánszky Alajos," p. 7; Kovács I., *Kis magyar kalendáriumtörténet,* p. 118.

FIGURE 12.5   Mihály Bartalits: The plan of Louis II's monument. Drawing, 1846.
SOURCE: BARANYA COUNTY ARCHIVES OF THE HUNGARIAN NATIONAL ARCHAIVES, PÉCS.

master was not content with publishing a portrait of the monarchs based on Nádasdy's *Mausoleum*, which was issued in Nuremberg in 1664 and contained full-length fictitious portraits of Hungarian leaders and kings in copperplate. The portraits are arranged in a wide frame divided into several sections, in which we see vedutas, battle scenes and event scenes relevant to the life of the person portrayed. In the biographies of some of the rulers, including Louis II, there is a separate scene alongside each portrait. In an unusual fashion, the illustrator has depicted Louis II's fall to death with different depictions in the two volumes.

While the illustration in the Hungarian edition, signed J. Mihalovits, shows the young king falling from his horse jumping across the stream, the composition of the woodcut in the German edition[65] (Figure 12.6) bears a strong resemblance to the scene in Dorffmaister's painting: the king, in armour, helmet, helmet crest, carrying a sword in his belt, holding the horse's bridle with his right hand, falls backwards from his galloping horse with the same movement in both depictions, and the position of the horse's forelegs and head are identical. In my opinion, a coincidence can be ruled out, and the master who lived in Pozsony, must have seen the painting kept in Mohács (Figure 12.4) or a copy. There is an even greater similarity between Mihalovits' woodcut and Bartalits' pencil drawing. In addition to the identical composition, the two graphic works contain motif combinations that differ from the details of the painting. These include the pendant necklace worn by the king (not in the painting) and its position on the armour, the mace held in the left hand, which, unlike the oval-headed, jewelled mace in the Dorffmaister painting, is a spiked combat mace in both Bartalits' drawing and the woodcut, and the striking similarity in the geometric pattern of the horse's blanket. A similar pattern, different from Dorffmaister's, is also found on the thigh-guard in the two paintings. While in Dorffmaister's painting Louis II is recognisably wearing the mentioned armour, which he once owned and which was kept in Vienna at the end of the 18th century, the depiction of the armour in Bartalits' drawing and Mihalovits' woodcut has been stylized. The dates of the book illustration (1843) and the pencil drawing (1846) suggest that Bartalits may have been familiar with the German-language Pozsony publication and used the illustration of the death of Louis II as a model for his memorial. The image of the king falling

65 *Magyarok' története* p. 102; *Geschichte Ungarns*, p. 103. The two volumes also have different cover images. In another edition of the historical work, published a few years later (*Geschichte Ungarns mit Abbildungen der Anführer und Könige* (Pesth: Verlag von Alois Bucsánsky, 1848), p. 105.), we find a third scene, no longer depicting the fall of Louis II, but the discovery of his body. The same scene appears in a historical work published by Bucsánszky two years earlier: Lányi Károly, *Magyar nemzet történetei képekkel, a nép számára* (Posonyban: Bucsánszky Alajos, 1846), p. 154.

FIGURE 12.6   János Mihalovits: The death of Louis II. Woodcut.
SOURCE: *GESCHICHTE UNGARNS MIT ABBILDUNGEN DER ANFÜHRER UND KÖNIGE*. PRESSBURG: VERLAG VON ALOIS BUCSÁNSKY, 1843, P. 103.

backwards from his mount is also found on a relief carved by the carpenter Márton Bach from Bóly, presumably in the 1860s, on the door of the pharmacy in Mohács, which was opened in 1848 and dedicated to King Louis II.[66]

4 The 19th Century Monument

The memorial to the Battle of Mohács and the death of Louis II was eventually built upon private initiative. The obelisk-shaped monument with a lion resting on its top was erected in 1864 by Soma Turcsányi (1814–1894), a hussar lieutenant who settled in the Mohács area after the defeat of the 1848–1849 War of Independence, following years spent in prison and in hiding.[67] The donor

---

66 Nándor Parádi ed., *A mohácsi csata. Vezető a Kanizsai Dorottya Múzeum kiállításához* (A Janus Pannonius Múzeum füzetei) 19 (Pécs: Janus Pannonius Múzeum, 1980), p. 21; Hasanović-Kolutácz, "1526 helye és szerepe," in *Több mint egy csata*, eds. Fodor et al., p. 596.

67 Nyárs, "A mohácsi csata," pp. 71–72.; Barbarics-Hermanik, "Türkengedächtnis in Ungarn," in *Ein Raum im Wandel,* eds. Spannenberger et al., p. 287.; B. Szabó, *Mohács*, p. 510. See

drew a parallel between Mohács and the fall of the War of Independence: "I want our late grandchildren to never forget that only by uniting the whole nation can we avoid the tragedy of our people, because that is what happened in 1526 at the Battle of Mohács, and our fight for freedom also failed because of disunity."[68] This idea may call into question the earlier view that the creation of the monument "was probably only a local consequence of the national cult of Louis II that developed in the mid-century in an atmosphere of absolutism."[69]

Károly Halász, a military officer, published in the 26 August 1866 issue of the journal *Hazánk s a Külföld,* close to the anniversary of the Battle of Mohács on 29 August 1526, his article *"The Mourning Field of Mohács"* he quotes the poet Károly Kisfaludy (1788–1830), who said that "not even a stone shows any sign of the place of the battle". But he does mention the memorial chapel built by József Király. 50 years earlier, he writes, there was nothing in Mohács to commemorate the battle, except the bridge over the Csele Stream, which was later destroyed and "decorated with a poor quality painting of the king's death."[70] Halász describes the annual mourning celebrations on the day of the battle, at which the guilds march under their flags, crowned in the evening by a dance and patriotic speeches. He describes the obelisk-shaped memorial erected by Soma Turcsányi near the mill, whose painted metal plaque shows Louis II dismounting from his white horse. The monument's inscription is also mentioned, as well as the fact that the obelisk is topped by a carved stone lion.[71]

The monument and the oil painting – presumably on metal – of Louis II dismounting from his white horse, are also known from a contemporary depiction. In the 30 August 1874 issue of the newspaper *Magyarország és a Nagyvilág*, published on the anniversary date, an unauthorised woodcut of the monument was attached to an article entitled *"The memorial statue of the Battle of Mohács near Mohács"*[72] (Figure 12.7). The article also gave a detailed account of

---

Katalin Sinkó, "Historizmus – Antihistorizmus," in *Szemelvények múlt és művészet kapcsolatáról,* eds. *Árpád* Mikó and Katalin Sinkó (Budapest: Magyar Nemzeti Galéria, 2000), pp. 108–109.; Hasanović-Kolutácz, "1526 helye és szerepe," in *Több mint egy csata,* eds. Fodor et al., p. 596.; Hóvári, "A mohácsi csata," in *Több mint egy csata,* eds. Fodor et al., p. 541.

68 Nyárs, "A mohácsi csata," p. 71.
69 Sinkó, "Historizmus – Antihistorizmus," in *Szemelvények,* eds. Mikó et al., p. 108.
70 See Barbarics-Hermanik, "Türkengedächtnis in Ungarn," in *Ein Raum im Wandel,* eds. Spannenberger et al., p. 281.
71 *Hazánk s a külföld* 2 (1866), no. 34, 26 August, pp. 542–543. See B. Szabó, *Mohács,* p. 510; *Örök Mohács,* eds. B. Szabó et al., pp. 627–628.
72 *Magyarország és a Nagyvilág* 11 (1874), no. 35, 30 August, p. 427. Text: pp. 428–429. B. Szabó, *Mohács,* p. 511.

FIGURE 12.7   Memorial statue of the Battle of Mohács near Mohács. Woodcut.
SOURCE: *MAGYARORSZÁG ÉS A NAGYVILÁG*, 30 AUGUST 1874, P. 427.

the history of the monument, which was already in ruins at the time, pointing out that, despite all the good intentions of the patriot who financed it, a new monument worthy of the momentous event and the nation would be needed.[73] The idea of a monument that goes beyond local commemoration, worthy of the country, the nation, is therefore also present here.

The illustration clearly shows that the pre-image of the former painting was most probably the scene of the death of the king in Dorffmaister's battle painting (Figure 12.4) which is kept in Mohács. Louis II, wearing armour with a similar pattern to the one in Dorffmaister's painting, falls from his horse in the swamp with the same movement as in the Sopron painter's painting and Bartalits' pencil drawing, although here the king does not hold a mace, but the bridle with his left hand. Although the author of this paper has not found any information about the old painting of Louis II fighting "against death", which once decorated the bridge mentioned by Károly Halász and which had collapsed by 1866, it is likely that it took over the iconographic type that is well known in the town.

The monument was also depicted in two drawings by Ferenc Ujházy (1827–1921) around 1882.[74] The drawing with the inscription Csele Stream shows the monument in the background, while the drawing with the inscription "Mohács-Csele Stream monument" shows the obelisk up close.[75] Above the inscription (the text is not legible), there is a rectangular indentation with a slight curve at the top, but the drawing does not present whether it contained any depiction around 1882. The reason why the woodcut in the 1874 issue of *Magyarország és a Nagyvilág* shows a larger, roughly square panel than the indentation in Ujházy's drawing may have been that the artist wanted to depict the painting accurately, and to do so he had to show it on a larger surface.

The monument can also be seen in the drawing made by Károly Cserna (1867–1944) for the fourth volume of the millennial series *A magyar nemzet története* (History of the Hungarian Nation), edited by Sándor Szilágyi, on the age of Hunyadi and Jagiellons, but in this drawing, above the inscription on the tablet, we see only the peeling covering of the obelisk[76] (Figure 12.8). In the photograph by Károly Zelesny also (Figure 12.9), which appeared in the

---

73   *Magyarország és a Nagyvilág* 11 (1874) no. 35, 30 August, p. 429.
74   Sinkó, "Historizmus – Antihistorizmus," in *Szemelvények,* eds. Mikó et al., p. 109. Ferenc Ujházy, *Vázlatkönyv* (1882), 125 × 195 mm. Budapest: Hungarian National Gallery 1923–2027.
75   Hungarian National Gallery, Graphical Collection, in sketchbook, entitled: Vázlatkönyv, 24 lappal, 1882. (Az Írók és Művészek Egyesületének kirándulásáról), 125 × 195 mm, Hungarian National Gallery, Graphical Collection, ltsz: 1923–1027. See more Sinkó, "Historizmus – Antihistorizmus," in *Szemelvények,* eds. Mikó et al., p. 109, pict. 5.
76   Vilmos Fraknói, *A magyar nemzet története IV. A Hunyadiak és a Jagellók kora (1440–1526)* (Budapest: Athenaeum Irodalmi és Nyomdai Részvénytársulat, 1896), p. 506. See Ákos

REMEMBRANCE OF THE LOCATION OF THE BATTLE OF MOHÁCS IN 1526

FIGURE. 12.8   Károly Cserna: The battlefield at Mohács.
SOURCE: FRAKNÓI VILMOS. *A HUNYADIAK ÉS A JAGELLÓK KORA* (1440–1526). ATHENAEUM, BUDAPEST, 1896, P. 506.

FIGURE 12.9   Károly Zelesny: The monument at Mohács.
SOURCE: *BARANYA MULTJA ÉS JELENE*. EDITED BY FERENC VÁRADY. VOLUME II. PÉCS, 1897, P. 387.

late 19th century monograph on the history of Baranya County,[77] like Cserna's drawing, only the peeling plaster is visible above the inscription plate of the monument.

The official efforts to establish a memorial continued after the initiative of Soma Turcsányi had been realized. The memorial statue association, founded in 1871, was reorganised in 1883, but neither it nor the memorial committee, which had started the "most extensive nationwide donation campaign" in 1896 – by 1900, some 15,000 forints had been collected – was able to achieve the erection of a new memorial.[78] Instead, in 1896–1897, the Turcsányi monument was rebuilt from public donations. The lion obelisk is the work of Albin Jiratkó (1849–1903), the new bronze relief was made by György Kiss (1852–1919)[79] (Figure 12.10). The memorial plaque of the obelisk installed by Soma Turcsányi in the 1860s, which was probably removed during the 1896–1897 renovation, was found in the 1970s in the courtyard of a farmhouse in Mohács.[80]

The late 19th century relief by György Kiss seems to have been based on either the earlier painted metal plate of the monument or the scene of the death of Louis II in Dorffmaister's painting, but the quality of the work by the eminent academic sculptor surpasses either of these possible models. Similarities can be found both in the composition of the rearing horse and the king falling from it, as well as in the design of the armour. The contemporary press also emphasized that the sculptor commissioned by the "public of Mohács" had modelled the king's portrait and his blood on the relief, based on old memories.[81]

We also encounter the visual topos of the king falling from his galloping horse in the bronze sculpture of Barnabás Holló[82] (Figure 12.11), in the foreground

---

Szendrei, "»Mohács-kép« a Szilágyi Sándor szerkesztette millenniumi A magyar nemzet történetében," in *A magyar emlékezethelyek*, eds. S. Varga et al., p. 299.

77 Ferenc Várady ed., *Baranya multja és jelene II*. (Pécs: Pécsi Irodalmi és Könyvnyomdai Részvénytársaság 1897), p. 387. See Nyárs, "A mohácsi csata," p. 72., pict. 3.

78 Fölker, *Mohács története*, p. 60; Hasanović-Kolutácz, "1526 helye és szerepe," in *Több mint egy csata*, eds. Fodor et al., p. 598.

79 Mihály Bucsky, *Kiss György* (Pécs, Baranya Megye Tanácsa V.B., 1975), p. 161; Sinkó, "Historizmus – Antihistorizmus," in *Szemelvények*, eds. Mikó et al., p. 114; Nyárs, "A mohácsi csata," p. 71–72.; Hasanović-Kolutácz, "1526 helye és szerepe," in *Több mint egy csata*, eds. Fodor et al., p. 596.; Hóvári, "A mohácsi csata," in *Több mint egy csata*, eds. Fodor et al., p. 541. The monument was also reported in the contemporary press. Új Idők 5 (1899), no. 8, 19 February, p. 169., p. 173.; *Műcsarnok* 2 (1899), no. 10, 5 March, p. 144.

80 János Füzes, "Megtalálták Mohácson II. Lajos emléktábláját," *Dunántúli Napló* 33 (1976), 25 January https://www.kozterkep.hu/1124/ii-lajos-emlekmu.

81 *Új Idők* 5 (1899), no. 8, 19 February, p. 173.

82 Copy, the original is hidden, see Gertrúd Goda, "Holló Barnabás (1865–1917) élete és munkássága," *A Herman Ottó Múzeum Évkönyve* 44 (2005), p. 407; Gertrud Goda, *Holló Barnabás* (Miskolc: Herman Ottó Múzeum, 2016), p. 16, p. 44, p. 47, p. 56, p. 92. As far as

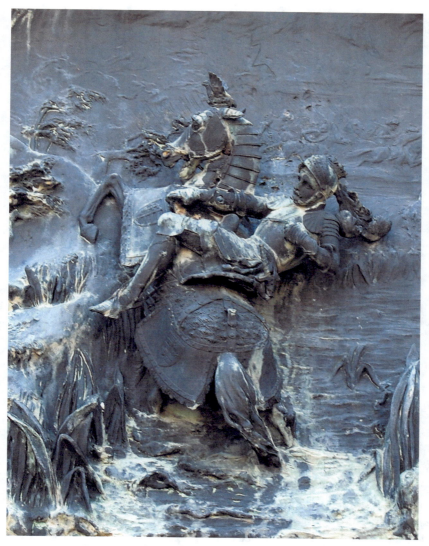

FIGURE 12.10　György Kiss: The death of Louis II. Bronze relief on the monument of the Battle of Mohács. Around 1895. Mohács.
PHOTO: TAMÁS SCHNELL.

of which the bank of the stream, covered with reeds and salt, appears just as much as in Dorffmaister's painting or in György Kiss's relief (Figure 12.10).

I know, the original sculpture is hidden somewhere, and a copy is kept in the Kanizsai Dorottya Museum in Mohács.

FIGURE 12.11　Barnabás Holló: The death of Louis II. Plaster cast, end of the 19th century.
SOURCE: HUNGARIAN NATIONAL GALLERY. 19TH–21ST CENTURY COLLECTION. DEPARTMENT OF STATUES. NO. 5236.

The sculpture, which was exhibited in 1898 at the spring exhibition of the Society of Fine Arts in Műcsarnok in Budapest,[83] was purchased by the state for the Museum of Fine Arts, and in 1904 it was deposited by the state in the Pécs City Museum, where it was still to be found in the early 1960s.[84] The Hungarian National Gallery has a plaster cast of the statue, which is half the size (70.5 cm) of the original (ca. 150 cm) and was purchased by the Museum of Fine Arts in 1918.[85] The influence of the relief by György Kiss is clearly visible on Holló's sculpture, so it seems likely that it was not directly inspired by Dorffmaister's or Borsos' painting, but by the bronze relief.[86] However, he

83　*Vasárnapi Ujság* 45 (1898), no. 17, 24 April, p. 281.
84　József Mérő, "A mohácsi csata emlékterve," *Dunántúli Napló* 19 (1962), no. 199, 26 August, p. 7.
85　Budapest: Hungarian National Gallery 5236. See *Pécs-Baranyamegyei Múzeum Egyesület Értesítője* 23 (1930), no. 1–4, p. 17.
86　A replica of the statue was on display at the permanent exhibition of the Kanizsai Dorottya Museum from 1976 to 2006. See Hasanović-Kolutácz, "1526 helye és szerepe," in *Több mint egy csata,* eds. Fodor et al., p. 612.

could have studied the armour shown at the 1896 Millennial Exhibition, either in a painting or on the plaster cast, because the cross-shaped cuts in the form of diamonds that decorate it appear in a stylised form, which are not found on Kiss's relief or on the copy of Holló's statue in the Kanizsai Dorottya Museum in Mohács.

5 Plans for a Monument in 1926

As part of the programme for the commemorative year of the 400th anniversary of the battle (1926),[87] which was strongly supported by the government, the monument next to the church was supposed to be an important element of the constructions planned for the central part of Mohács, which were only partially completed. According to the plans – as we read in the report of the secretary of the construction committee of the Mohács church[88] – a monument to the memory of King Louis on horseback was to be placed on a high platform, in front of a huge row of arches adjacent to the church. With the arcade row, the architect wanted to commemorate Hungarian patriotism: on the left side, there would have been a relief and a full-length statue of the seven bishops and nine magnates who died heroically in the first, lost Battle of Mohács in 1526, while the statues on the right side of the arcade row would have represented the leaders of the anti-Ottoman battles, especially the victorious Battle of Nagyharsány in 1687.[89] The arcade façade facing the town hall would also have been decorated with the names of 13 magnates, 12 noblemen and 50 soldiers. The reliefs depicting Balázs Paksy (?–1526) Bishop of Győr and Pál Tomori (ca. 1474–1526) Archbishop of Kalocsa had already been ordered, but were not completed due to the World War II. The right arcade row, commemorating the wars of reconquest, would have been decorated with stone reliefs of the European and Hungarian commanders of the campaign (Charles V, Duke of Lorraine, Prince Eugene of Savoy, Maximilian of Bavaria, Louis William of

---

[87] Hóvári, "A mohácsi csata," in *Több mint egy csata*, eds. Fodor et al.
[88] Kázmér Horváth, "A mohácsi csata emlékműve," *Városkultura* 9 (1936), no. 9–10, pp. 106–108. See János Tihanyi, *Tájékoztató a mohácsi csatatéri emléktemplomról.* (Budapest: 1956). Available at http://aszokfa.lapunk.hu/?modul=oldal&tartalom=1123573 Nyárs, "A mohácsi csata," p. 74; Hóvári, "A mohácsi csata," in *Több mint egy csata*, eds. Fodor et al. pp. 539–562; Hasanović-Kolutácz, "1526 helye és szerepe," in *Több mint egy csata*, eds. Fodor et al., p. 605.
[89] Hasanović-Kolutácz, "1526 helye és szerepe," in *Több mint egy csata*, eds. Fodor et al., p. 605. See Barbarics-Hermanik, "Türkengedächtnis in Ungarn," in *Ein Raum im Wandel*, eds. Spannenberger et al., pp. 291–292; Hóvári, "A mohácsi csata," in *Több mint egy csata*, eds. Fodor et al. pp. 542–543.

Baden-Baden, János Pálffy, Ádám Zrínyi, Ádám Batthyány, etc.), and the names of five magnates, ten nobles and twenty knights of the commons would have been carved in marble on the arcade façade.[90]

As we have seen, the depiction of the lost first and victorious second Battles of Mohács together was very popular in the late 17th and 18th centuries, partly as an example of divine justice and partly, in a kind of imperial perspective, to emphasize that what the Kingdom of Hungary had lost, the joint armies of the Habsburg Empire then won back. This approach was reflected in István Dorffmaister's pairs of battle paintings, as well as in the dome fresco of the parish church of Szigetvár, also by him, which depicts both the fall of Szigetvár in 1566 and its recapture in 1689. In 19th-century literature and art, partly because the religious (often with different denominations) and imperial frames of the earlier interpretations of Mohács were replaced by a national framework, the memory of the wars of reconquest faded (except for the state-commissioned works of art for the bicentenary celebrations of the 1880s), and the glorious or tragic events of national history (including the Battle of Mohács and the fall of Szigetvár) were depicted instead. It is therefore worth examining why, less than a decade after the break-up of the Austro-Hungarian Empire, the Battle of Nagyharsány in 1687 was again given such prominence in the cultural policy of the years around 1926.

That the Trianon shock influenced the design of the monument is indicated by the 25 columns of the left arcade, which were interpreted at the time as the number of counties in the country that remained after the 1920 Trianon Treaty. We find the same approach in the poem written by Béla Fischer, deputy county commissioner of Baranya County, for the inauguration of the World War memorial in Mohács in the early 1930s, in which he referred to Trianon as the heir of Mohács, which was inscribed above the names of the fallen heroes.[91]

The arcade row was built in 1937, but without the coats of arms, reliefs and the equestrian statue.[92] However, two sketches of the equestrian statue of Louis II on top of a high column in the left arcade row foreground have survived[93] (Figure 12.12). Although the drawings are very sketchy, it appears that Louis II is still sitting with his sword drawn in the saddle of the prancing horse, so the composition does not depict the fall of the king. The memorial

90 Tihanyi, *Tájékoztató*.
91 *Városkultura* 9 (1936), no. 9–10, p. 109. On the links between Trianon and Mohács in the 1926 commemorative year, see Hóvári, "A mohácsi csata," in *Több mint egy csata*, eds. Fodor et al. p. 540, p. 543, p. 548.
92 Nyárs, "A mohácsi csata," p. 74.
93 Nyárs, "A mohácsi csata," p. 74, pict. 6; Hasanović-Kolutácz, "1526 helye és szerepe," in *Több mint egy csata*, eds. Fodor et al., p. 603, pict. 15.

FIGURE 12.12 Bertalan Árkay: Plan of the votive church in Mohács.
SOURCE: HASANOVIĆ-KOLUTÁCZ, "1526 HELYE ÉS SZEREPE," IN *TÖBB MINT EGY CSATA*, EDS. FODOR ET AL., P. 603.

committee wrote to the European royal families related to the Jagiellonian dynasty in 1936, but they either did not respond or did not financially support the project. In the end, the statue was never built.[94]

---

94 Hasanović-Kolutácz, "1526 helye és szerepe," in *Több mint egy csata*, eds. Fodor et al., p. 605.

6 The Mohács Historical Memorial Site (1976)

In 1931, the Monument to the Polish Heroes was erected in Szepesi Park in Mohács to commemorate the 2000 Polish soldiers who died in battle,[95] and in 1976, on the 450th anniversary of the battle, the 20th-century monument to the battle was completed, the Mohács Historical Memorial Site which was declared a nature reserve. The cemetery-like memorial park, designed by the architect György Vadász and the horticulturalist Buda Zalay, was created on the presumed site of the former Hungarian camp, following excavations carried out in 1959–1960. In the 1960s and 1970s, several mass graves – the burial places of 1700 soldiers – were excavated and the memorial garden was built around them. The Monument's bronze gate, made of more than 10,000 bone-like elements placed under stone-clad arches, was made by József Pölöskei to commemorate the victims of the battle. The fountain in the courtyard of the atrium building is the work of Gyula Illés, and the inverted *map stone* depicting the battle site, the Hungarian and Ottoman regiments and the ruined settlements around Mohács is the work of István Bencsik. Among the headstones of the flower-shaped cemetery are the wooden statues of Louis II, Süleyman I (with a basket made of rope and the severed heads of Christians) (Figure12.13), Pál Tomori, Dorottya Kanizsai, Mary of Hungary and many anonymous heroes, as well as weapons and horse figures, the works of Pál Kő, Sándor Kiss, József Király, István Szabó, Géza Samu. On the coloured statue of Louis II, the barefaced, young monarch is not wearing armour, but holds in his right hand a shield, a symbol of battle, bearing the inscription "King Louis II 1506–1526, lived 20 years, rest in peace" (Figure 12.14). In 1990, a 10 m high wooden cross was added to the memorial, and in 2011 also a building in the shape of the Holy Crown, including an exhibition space. The park and building complex became a National Memorial in 2012.[96]

The planned memorial statue of Louis II was only completed in 2006, not as a statue on horseback but as a standing statue. Imre Varga's (1923–2019) sculpture in the square next to church in Mohács shows the king in armour but

---

[95] Hasanović-Kolutácz, "1526 helye és szerepe," in *Több mint egy csata*, eds. Fodor et al., p. 609.

[96] See István Sinkovics, János Fischer, and Gyula Ortutay, *A Mohácsi Történelmi Emlékhely*. (s. l., s. d. [1976]); László Tiszay ed., *A mohácsi Történelmi Emlékhely* (Pécs: Mecsek-Tourist Baranya m-i Idegenforg. Hiv., 1979); Gergelyné Kovács and Kálmán Papp, *Mohács-Sátorhely Történelmi Emlékhely* (Tájak, Korok, Múzeumok Kiskönyvtár) (Budapest: 1980); Nyárs, "A mohácsi csata," pp. 75–77; Hasanović-Kolutácz, "1526 helye és szerepe," in *Több mint egy csata*, eds. Fodor et al., pp. 610–611; Hóvári, "A mohácsi csata," in *Több mint egy csata*, eds. Fodor et al.

FIGURE 12.13 Pál Kő: Statue of Süleyman I. Coloured wood, 1976. Mohács National Monument.
PHOTO: TAMÁS SCHNELL.

FIGURE 12.14 Pál Kő: Statue of Louis II. Coloured wood, 1976. Mohács National Memorial.
PHOTO: TAMÁS SCHNELL.

without a helmet, wearing a funeral crown and holding a mace. On the cross next to him, 12 metres high, the coronation robe is depicted.[97]

---

97 See Norbert M. Bugarszki, *Tájékoztató a mohácsi Széchenyi térre tervezett II. Lajos emlékműről. A Várostörténeti füzetek különkiadása* (Mohács: 2002); Nyárs, "A mohácsi csata," pp. 77–81; Hasanović-Kolutácz, "1526 helye és szerepe," in *Több mint egy csata,* eds. Fodor et al., p. 608.

Acknowledgement

The study was made as part of the Mohács 1526–2026 – Reconstruction and Remembrance Program, with the support of the Tempus Public Foundation, the National Research, Development and Innovation Office (NKFIH 138702) and the Collegium Hungaricum in Vienna.

Bibliography

Ács, Pál. "»The Good and Honest Turk«. A European Legend in the Context of Sixteenth Century Oriental Studies." In *The Habsburgs and their Courts in Europe, 1400–1700. Between Cosmopolitanism and Regionalism,* eds. Herbert Karner, Ingrid Ciulisová, and Bernardo J. García García, 267–282. Wien: Palatium, 2014.

Atherton, Ian and Philip Morgan. "The battlefield war memorial: Commemoration and the battlefield site from the Middle Ages to the modern era." *Journal of War & Culture Studies* 3 (2011): 289–304.

B. Szabó, János. *Mohács. Nemzet és emlékezet.* Budapest: Osiris Kiadó, 2006.

B. Szabó, János and Gábor Farkas Farkas eds. *Örök Mohács: Szövegek és értelmezések.* Budapest: Bölcsészettudományi Kutatóközpont, 2020.

Bárány, Ágoston. "A vándor titkai. V. levél." *Társalkodó* 6 (1837): 363–364.

Barbarics-Hermanik, Zsuzsa "Türkengedächtnis in Ungarn. Die Rolle der Gedächtnisort Mohács und Szigetvár im Prozess der nationalen Identitätsbildung." In *Ein Raum im Wandel. Die osmanisch-habsburgische Grenzregion vom 16. bis zum 18. Jahrhundert,* eds. Norbert, Spannenberger and Szabolcs Varga, 275–298. Stuttgart: Franz Steiner Verlag, 2014.

Batsányi, János. "Székes-Fejér-Vári Professor Virág Benedek Úr' Társunkhoz Kassán, Karátson' Havában, 1789." *Magyar Museum* II/1, 1790.

Boros, László. "Dorffmaister Baranyában." *Művészettörténeti Értesítő* 21 (1974): 269–284.

Bucsky, Mihály. *Kiss György.* Pécs, Baranya Megye Tanácsa V.B., 1975.

CELEBERRIMI TRACTUS DANUBIANI PARS PRAECIPUA AB AUSTRIAE VIENNA CONSTANTI-NOPOLIM USQUE SE PROTENDENS UNGARIAM TRANSILVANIAMQUE COMPLECTENS. Colonia/Köln: Petrus Querradt, 1596.

Debreczeni, Attila. "Nemzeti nagylét, nagy temető és – Batsányi (Egy nemzeti narratíva formálódása)." In *A magyar emlékezethelyek kutatásának elméleti és módszertani alapjai,* eds. Pál S. Varga, Orsolya Száraz, and Miklós Takács, 208–226. Loci Memoriae Hungariae 2. Debrecen: Debreceni Egyetemi Kiadó, 2013.

Dernschwam, Hans. *Erdély. Besztercebánya. Törökországi útinapló.* Budapest: Európa Könyvkiadó, 1984.

Drescher, Pál. *Régi magyar gyerekkönyvek, 1538–1875.* Budapest: Magyar Bibliophil Társaság, 1934.

F. Balogh, András ed. *Ungarnbilder im 17. Jahrhundert. Studien und Editionen der Texte: Jakob Vogel: "Vngrische Schlacht" (1626). Kapitel aus Martin Zeillers "Neue Beschreibung des Königreichs Ungarn" (1664), Salomon Schweiggers "Gezweyte neue nutzliche und anmuthige Reiß-Beschreibung" (1664) und aus Eberhard Werner Happels "Thesaurus Exoticorum" (1688)*. Budapest: ELTE Eötvös József Collegium, 2013.

Farkas, Gábor Farkas. "Új kérdések II. Lajos rejtélyes halálával és temetésével kapcsolatban." *Magyar Könyvszemle* 131 (2015): 381–396.

Farkas, Gábor Farkas, Zsolt Szebelédi, and Bernadett Varga eds. *"Nekünk mégis Mohács kell..." – II. Lajos király rejtélyes halála és különböző temetései*. Budapest: Magyar Tudományos Akadémia Bölcsészettudományi Kutatóközpont Országos Széchényi Könyvtár, 2016.

Farkas, Zsuzsanna. "Die Rezeption des Malers und Fotografen József Borsos (1821–1883) einst und heute." In *Annales de la Galerie Nationale Hongroise / A Magyar Nemzeti Galéria Évkönyve 24/9, 2002–2004* (2005): 7–24.

Fodor, Pál and Mércz, András. "Mi is veszett Mohácsnál? Oszmán-török veszteséglista az 1526. évi hadjáratról." *Történelmi Szemle* 65 (2023): 193–235.

Fölker, József. *Mohács története*. Mohács: Rosenthal Márk Könyvnyomdája, 1900.

Fraknói, Vilmos. *A magyar nemzet története IV. A Hunyadiak és a Jagellók kora (1440–1526)*. Budapest: Athenaeum Irodalmi és Nyomdai Részvénytársulat, 1896.

Füzes, János. "Megtalálták Mohácson II. Lajos emléktábláját." *Dunántúli Napló* 33 (1976): 25 January https://www.kozterkep.hu/1124/ii-lajos-emlekmu.

G. Héri, Vera. *A törökellenes háborúk emlékérmei*. Budapest: Magyar Nemzeti Múzeum, 2009.

Galavics, Géza. "Dorffmaister István történeti képei." In *"Stephan Dorffmaister pinxit." Dorffmaister István emlékkiállítása*, eds. László Kostyál and Monika Zsámbéky, 83–109. Zalaegerszeg: 1997.

Galavics, Géza. *Kössünk kardot az pogány ellen. Török háborúk és képzőművészet*. Budapest: Képzőművészeti Alap Kiadóvállalata, 1986.

Galavics, Géza. "A történeti téma." In *Művészet Magyarországon 1780–1830*, eds. Hedvig Szabolcsi and Géza Galavics, 63–71, 163–171. Budapest: MTA Művészettörténeti Kutató Csoport, 1980.

Gausz, Ildikó. "Tranzitirodalom a koraújkori Magyarországról. Busbecq 1554–1555. évi úti impressziói hazánkról." *Történeti tanulmányok* 23 (2015): 22–40.

Geschichte Ungarns mit Abbildungen der Anführer und Könige. Pesth: Verlag von Alois Bucsánsky, 1848.

Geschichte Ungarns mit Abbildungen der Anführer und Könige. Preßburg: Verlag von Alois Bucsánsky, 1843.

Goda, Gertrud. *Holló Barnabás*. Miskolc: Herman Ottó Múzeum, 2016.

Goda, Gertrúd. "Holló Barnabás (1865–1917) élete és munkássága." *A Herman Ottó Múzeum Évkönyve* 44 (2005): 401–419.

Gulyás, Borbála. "Donat Hübschmann magyarországi megrendelői. Négy metszet és négy miniatúra." In *Reneszánsz és barokk Magyarországon. Művészettörténeti tanulmányok Galavics Géza tiszteletére I.*, eds. Borbála Gulyás, Árpád Mikó, and Bálint Ugry, 73–100. Budapest: Bölcsészettudományi Kutatóközpont, Művészettörténet Intézet, 2021.

Gyulai, Éva. "Turcissare – Verancsics Antal török-képe." In *Humanista történetírás és neolatin irodalom a 15–18. századi Magyarországon*, eds. Enikő Békés, Péter Kasza, and Réka Lengyel, 91–108. Budapest: MTA Bölcsészettudományi Kutatóközpont Irodalomtudományi Intézet, 2015.

Gyulai, Éva. "Ense opus est – Verancsics Antal emblémaverse I. Szulejmán szultánról, 1558." *Publicationes Universitatis Miskolcinensis, Sectio Philosophica* 16 (2011): 129–167.

Gyulai, Éva. "Egy közép-európai tudós portréjához: Verancsics-ikonográfia." In *Parasztok és polgárok. Tanulmányok Tóth Zoltán 65. születésnapjára*, eds. Gábor Czoch, Gergely Horváth, and Péter Pozsgai, 163–168. Budapest: KORALL Társadalomtörténeti Egyesület, 2008.

Hasanović-Kolutácz, Andrea. "1526 helye és szerepe a mohácsi identitásban." In *Több mint egy csata: Mohács. Az 1526. évi ütközet a magyar tudományos és kulturális emlékezetben*, eds. Pál Fodor and Szabolcs Varga, 563–617. Budapest: MTA Bölcsészettudományi Kutatóközpont, 2019.

Horváth, Kázmér. "A mohácsi csata emlékműve." *Városkultura* 9 (1936): no. 9–10.

Hóvári, János "A mohácsi csata két emlékéve: 1926 versus 1976." In *Több mint egy csata: Mohács. Az 1526. évi ütközet a magyar tudományos és kulturális emlékezetben*, eds. Pál Fodor and Szabolcs Varga, 539–562. Budapest: MTA Bölcsészettudományi Kutatóközpont, 2019.

Ilg, Ulrike. "Bebilderte Reiseberichte aus dem Osmanischen Reich in deutscher Sprache (16. bis 17. Jahrhundert)." In *Das Bild des Feindes. Konstruktion von Antagonismen und Kulturtransfer im Zeitalter der Türkenkriege. Ostmitteleuropa. Italien und Osmanisches Reich*, eds. Eckhard Leuschner and Thomas Wünsch, 55–75. Berlin: Gebr. Mann Verlag, 2013.

Itinera Constantinopolitanum et Amasianum ab Augerio Gislenio Busbequio ad Solimannum Turcarum imperatorem C.M. oratore confecta. Eiusdem Busbequii de re militari contra Turcam instituenda consilium. Altera editio. Antverpiae: Ex officina Christophori Plantini, 1582.

Kasza, Péter and Géza Pálffy eds. *Brodarics-emlékkönyv. Egy különleges pártváltás a mohácsi csata után, Brodarics István szerémi pöspök búcsúlevele I. Ferdinánd királyhoz: 1527. március 18. Dévény.* Budapest: Magyar Országos Levéltár, 2011.

Kemálpasazáde. "Mohácsnáme." In *Örök Mohács: Szövegek és értelmezése*, eds. János B. Szabó and Gábor Farkas Farkas, 326–338. Budapest: Bölcsészettudományi Kutatóközpont, 2020.

Keresztury, Dezső and Andor Tarnai eds. *Batsányi János Összes Művei I. Versek.* Budapest: Akadémiai Kiadó, 1953.

Kovács, Gergelyné and Kálmán Papp. *Mohács-Sátorhely Történelmi Emlékhely.* Tájak, Korok, Múzeumok Kiskönyvtár. Budapest: 1980.

Kovács I., Gábor. *Kis magyar kalendáriumtörténet.* Budapest: Akadémiai Kiadó, 1989.

Kovács I., Gábor. "Bucsánszky Alajos útja a kalendárium- és ponyva-tömegtermeléshez." *Magyar Könyvszemle* 101 (1985): 1–17.

Kuzmová, Stanislava. "The memory of Jagiellonians in the Kingdom of Hungary, and in Hungarian and Slovak national narratives." In *Remembering the Jagiellonians*, ed. Natalia Nowakowska, 71–100. London, New York: Routledge, 2018.

Lányi, Károly. *Magyar nemzet történetei képekkel, a nép számára.* Posonyban: Bucsánszky Alajos, 1846.

M. Bugarszki, Norbert. *Tájékoztató a mohácsi Széchenyi térre tervezett II. Lajos emlékműről. A Várostörténeti füzetek különkiadása.* Mohács: 2002.

Magyarok' története a vezérek' és királyok' képeivel. Pozsonyban: Bucsánszky Alajos polg. könyvkötő költségén, 1843.

Méltóságos és Fő Tisztelendő Király József Pécsi Püspök emléke. *Tudományos Gyűjtemény* 13 (1829): 4, 56–60.

Mérő, József. "A mohácsi csata emlékterve." *Dunántúli Napló* 19 (1962): 26 August.

Mikó, Árpád. "Egy humanista mecénás a 16. század közepén Magyarországon. Verancsics Antal (1504–1573), a műértő." *Korunk* 26 (2015): 17–27.

Mikó, Árpád. "Egy humanista mecénás a 16. század közepén Magyarországon: Verancsics Antal, a connaisseur." In *Mátyás király öröksége. Késő reneszánsz művészet Magyarországon (16–17. század) I.*, eds. Árpád Mikó, Mária Verő, and Anna Jávor, 25–27. A Magyar Nemzeti Galéria kiadványai 2008/3. Budapest: Magyar Nemzeti Galéria, 2008.

Mikó, Árpád. "Stílus és felírat. Kőbe vésett klasszikus- és korai humanista kapitálissal írott felíratok a Mátyás- és Jagelló-kori Magyarországon." *Művészettörténeti Értesítő* 54 (2005): 205–244.

Mikó, Árpád and Katalin Sinkó eds. *Történelem – kép. Szemelvények múlt és művészet kapcsolatáról.* Budapest: Magyar Nemzet Galéria, 2000.

Németh S., Katalin. *Magyar dolgokról. Magyar–német kapcsolattörténeti tanulmányok.* Historia litteraria 31. Budapest: Universitas Könyvkiadó, 2014.

Németh S., Katalin. "Salomon Schweigger útleírásának magyar vonatkozásai." In *Tarnai Andor-emlékkönyv*, ed. Gábor Kecskeméti, 189–200. Budapest: Universitas Könyvkiadó, 1996.

Nyárs, Annamária. "A mohácsi csata emlékművei a városban." *Belvedere Meridionale* 18 (2006): 7–8, 70–82.

Oppl, Ferdinand and Martin Scheutz eds. *Die Osmanen vor Wien. Die Meldeman-Rundansicht von 1529/30. Sensation, Propaganda und Stadtbild.* Veröffentlichungen des Instituts für Österreichische Geschichtsforschung 74. Wien: Institut für Österreichische Geschichtsforschung, 2020.

Palóczi, Edgár. "A mohácsi csatatér régi emlékművei és ereklyéi." *Hadimúzeumi Lapok* 2 (1926): November, no. 5–7, 4–10.

Pap, Norbert and Péter Reményi. "Encounters Between Islam and Christianity: Mohács and Kosovo Polje." In *Places of Memory and Legacies in an Age of Insecurities and Globalization,* ed. Gerry O'Reilly, 285–305. Cham: Springer, 2020.

Pap, Norbert, Pál Fodor, Máté Kitanics, Tamás Morva, Gábor Szalai, and Péter Gyenizse. "A mohácsi Törökdomb." *Történelmi Szemle* 60 (2018): 325–345.

Pap, Norbert, Máté Kitanics, Péter Gyenizse, Erika Hancz, Zita Bognár, Tamás Tóth, and Zoltán Hámori. "Nagy Szulejmán szigetvári türbéje: történeti, geofizikai és régészeti vizsgálatok." In *Szulejmán szultán Szigetváron. A szigetvári kutatások 2013–2016 között,* eds. Norbert Pap and Pál Fodor, 67–88. Pécs: Pannon Castrum Kft., 2017.

Papp, Júlia. "»...pugnas honeste obiit...« The armor formerly in the Viennese Imperial Zeughaus attributed to Louis II of Hungary in the Hungarian cultural history." *Zeitschrift für historische Waffen- und Kostümkunde* 64 (2022), no. 1, pp. 69–98.

Papp, Júlia. "Die »Neuverwertung« der Illustration eines astrologischen Buches vom Ende des 15. Jahrhunderts in den deutschen Neuen Zeitungen über die Schlacht bei Mohács (1526) und die Belagerung von Wien (1529)" *Wiener Geschichtsblätter* 76 (2021): 115–133.

Papp, Júlia. "A szigetvári hadi táj képzőművészeti ábrázolása a 16–17. században." In *Turbék. Szulejmán szultán zarándokvárosa,* ed. Norbert Pap, 451–534. Budapest, Pécs: Bölcsészettudományi Kutatóközpont, 2020.

Papp, Júlia. "Adatok II. Lajos magyar király páncélos ábrázolásaihoz." *Művészettörténeti Értesítő* 69 (2020): 269–302.

Papp, Júlia. "II. Lajos magyar király fiktív páncélos ábrázolásai." *Ars Hungarica* 46 (2020), no. 4, pp. 439–440.

Papp, Júlia. "Az 1526. évi mohácsi csata 16–17. századi képzőművészeti recepciója." In *Több mint egy csata: Mohács. Az 1526. évi ütközet a magyar tudományos és kulturális emlékezetben,* eds. Pál Fodor and Szabolcs Varga, 149–193. Budapest: MTA Bölcsészettudományi Kutatóközpont, 2019.

Papp, Júlia and Erzsébet Király eds. *A magyar művészet a 19. században. Képzőművészet.* Budapest: MTA BTK, Osiris, 2018.

Papp-Váry, Árpád. *Magyarország története térképeken.* Budapest: Kossuth Könyvkiadó, Cartographia, 2002.

Parádi, Nándor ed. *A mohácsi csata. Vezető a Kanizsai Dorottya Múzeum kiállításához.* A Janus Pannonius Múzeum füzetei 19. Pécs: Janus Pannonius Múzeum, 1980.

Perjés, Géza. *Mohács.* Budapest: Magvető Könyvkiadó, 1979.

Plihál, Katalin. *Kard és térkép. Hadi események és propaganda a Magyarországról megjelent térképeken. 1528–1718.* Budapest: HM Zrínyi Nonprofit Kft., 2020. Available at http://lazarus.elte.hu/kardesterkep/.

Plihál, Katalin. *A Tabula Hungariae… Ingolstadt, 1528. Térkép és utóélete az eddigi és a jelenlegi kutatások tükrében.* Budapest: Országos Széchényi Könyvtár, Kossuth Kiadó, 2013.

Popović, Mihailo St. "Reminiszenzen an König Matthias Corvinus in den Reiseberichten des Salomon Schweigger und Reinhold Lubenau." In *Matthias Corvinus und seine Zeit. Europa am Übergang vom Mittelalter zur Neuzeit,* ed. Christian Gastgeber, 231–236. Wien: Österreichische Akademie der Wissenschaften, 2011.

Réthelyi, Orsolya et al. eds. *Habsburg Mária, Mohács özvegye. A királyné és udvara 1521–1531.* Budapest: Budapesti Történeti Múzeum, 2005.

Rózsa, György. *Magyar történetábrázolás a 17. században.* Budapest: Akadémiai Kiadó, 1973.

Rózsa, György. "A Magyar Történelmi Képcsarnok néhány újabb biedermeier képe." *Folia Archaeologica* 13 (1961): 291–297.

Sahm, Wilhelm von ed. *Beschreibung der Reisen des Reinhold Lubenau I.* Königsberg: F. Beyer, 1912.

Scheutz, Martin. "Die Meldeman-Rundansicht als illustrierte »Zeytung«. Der Druckort Nürnber und die kommunikative Strategie des Planes in seinen textlichen Mitteilungen." In *Die Osmanen vor Wien. Die Meldeman-Rundansicht von 1529/30. Sensation, Propaganda und Stadtbild,* eds. Ferdinand Oppl and Martin Scheutz, pp. 85–107. Veröffentlichungen des Instituts für Österreichische Geschichtsforschung 74. Wien: Institut für Österreichische Geschichtsforschung, 2020.

Schweigger, Salomon. *Ein newe Reyßbeschreibung auß Teutschland Nach Constantinopel und Jerusalem: darinn die Gelegenheit derselben Länder, Städt, …, der innwohnenten Völcker Art, … Religion und Gottesdienst etc. ; insonderheit die … gestalt deß H. Grabs, der Stadt Jerusalem … und deß Authoris Meinung hievon; item … was die Röm. Keys. Maj. … dem Türckischen Keyser … zur Praesent … überlieffern lassen…; desgleichen deß Türckischen Reichs Gubernation … und vielerley andern … sachen … mit 100 … Figuren …* Nürnberg: 1608.

Sinkó, Katalin. "Kontinuitás vagy a hagyomány újrateremtése? Történeti képek a 19. században." In *Akadémiai Műhely / Közgyűlési előadások / 2000 / Millenium az Akadémián I.,* ed. Ferenc Glatz, 317–330. Budapest: Magyar Tudományos Akadémia, 2001.

Sinkó, Katalin. "Historizmus – Antihistorizmus." In *Szemelvények múlt és művészet kapcsolatáról,* eds. Árpád Mikó and Katalin Sinkó, 103–115. Budapest: Magyar Nemzeti Galéria, 2000.

Sinkovics, István, János Fischer, and Gyula Ortutay. *A Mohácsi Történelmi Emlékhely.* s. l., s. d. [1976].

Sonkoly, Károly. "A pécsi székesegyház Bartalits Mihály készítette első apostolszobrai." *Janus Pannonius Múzeum Évkönyve* 29 (1984): 257–301.

Stein, Heidi ed. *Salomon Schweigger: Zum Hofe des türkischen Sultans.* Leipzig: F. A. Brockhaus, 1986.

Szalai, Béla. *A tizenötéves háború metszeteken.* Budapest: Magyar Tudományos Akadémia Könyvtár és Információs Központ, 2021.

Szántai, Lajos. *Atlas Hungaricus. Magyarország nyomtatott térképei. 1528–1850. I–II.* Budapest: Akadémiai Kiadó, 1996.

Szathmáry, Tibor. *Descriptio Hungariae. Magyarország és Erdély nyomtatott térképei, 1477–1600.* Budapest: Privately published, 1987.

Szendrei, Ákos. "»Mohács-kép« a Szilágyi Sándor szerkesztette millenniumi A magyar nemzet történetében." In *A magyar emlékezethelyek kutatásának elméleti és módszertani alapjai,* eds. Pál S. Varga, Orsolya Száraz, and Miklós Takács, 287–300. Loci Memoriae Hungariae 2. Debrecen: Debreceni Egyetemi Kiadó, 2013.

Tabula Hungari[a]e ad quatuor latera per Lazarum quondam Thomae Strigonien[sis] Cardin[alis] Secretariu[m] ... (Ingolstadiani : invulgata Anno D[omi]ni 1528). National Széchényi Library, Archive of Old Prints. App. M. 136.

Takáts, Sándor. *Péteri Takáts József.* Budapest: Hunyadi Mátyás Intézet, 1890.

Tihanyi, János. *Tájékoztató a mohácsi csatatéri emléktemplomról.* Budapest: 1956). Available at http://aszokfa.lapunk.hu/?modul=oldal&tartalom=1123573.

Tiszay, László ed. *A mohácsi Történelmi Emlékhely.* Pécs: Mecsek-Tourist Baranya m-i Idegenforg. Hiv., 1979.

Topkaya, Yiğit. "Eingekreiste Zeugen, auf den Kopf gestellte Märtyrer: Bilder des Grauens in Niclas Meldemans Rundansicht," In *Die Osmanen vor Wien. Die Meldeman-Rundansicht von 1529/30. Sensation, Propaganda und Stadtbild,* eds. Ferdinand Oppl and Martin Scheutz, pp. 241–258. Veröffentlichungen des Instituts für Österreichische Geschichtsforschung 74. Wien: Institut für Österreichische Geschichtsforschung, 2020.

Várady, Ferenc ed. *Baranya multja és jelene II.* Pécs: Pécsi Irodalmi és Könyvnyomdai Részvénytársaság 1897.

Veszprémi, Nóra. "A magyar történeti festészet kezdetei? (A mohácsi csata képi ábrázolásai a 18. század végén és a 19. század elején)." In *A magyar emlékezethelyek kutatásának elméleti és módszertani alapjai,* eds. Pál S. Varga, Orsolya Száraz, and Miklós Takács, 261–273. Loci Memoriae Hungariae 2. Debrecen: Debreceni Egyetemi Kiadó, 2013.

Veszprémi, Nóra ed. *Borsos József festő és fotográfus (1821–1883).* A Magyar Nemzeti Galéria kiadványai 2009/4. Budapest: Magyar Nemzeti Galéria, 2009.

CHAPTER 13

Memorial Politics and the Sites of the Battle of Mohács

Norbert Pap

1   Introduction

The Battle of Mohács, its antecedents and consequences are still shaping the historical consciousness of Hungarians. From the 19th century onwards, it played a particularly important role in the self-image and social mindset of Hungarian society. Its commemorative function can only be compared to the Hungarian conquest of the Carpathian basin at the end of the 9th century (895/896), or the Treaty of Trianon (1920), which ended the First World War, and the Hungarian collapse of 1944–1945, even though these events are very difficult to compare. The interpretations of the lost battle are both unifying and dividing Hungarians when discussing its causes and possible ways of averting the consequences, but these questions also seem more mysterious than those of other significant events because of their Ottoman Turkish implications. The Battle of Mohács can only be compared to the struggles of other peoples of South Eastern Europe with the Ottoman Turks because their context is similar.

The Ottoman Turks, who had established a state in Asia Minor in the 13th century, managed to gain a foothold in Europe after the fall of Gallipoli. Their empire grew rapidly, conquering much of the Balkans in the 14th to 17th centuries. Meanwhile, they continued to consolidate their power by exploiting conflicts between Christian states. Murad I defeated the Serbian forces and Mehmed II captured Constantinople in 1453. And during the long reign of Süleyman I, the Ottoman army threatened Vienna. Their successors succeeded in further expanding the empire and stabilizing the Ottoman power in Central Europe for a longer period. The empire reached its greatest extent in the 17th century. After the unsuccessful siege of Vienna in 1683, a grand Christian coalition, the Holy League was formed in 1684 and successfully began to oust the Ottomans from Hungary. However, the decline of the empire and the wars of liberation against the Ottomans lasted for a long time in the Balkans, until the First World War, influencing in many ways the fate and events of Europe.

On the southern and eastern borders of Europe, there are many communities that fought fierce, long-lasting anti-Ottoman battles in the 14th–19th centuries.

These struggles played a prominent role in shaping their identity. The memory of their struggles is deeply embedded in their culture and is still present in political discourse on fundamental issues today. This period was marked by the emergence of national identities. Their first national heroes were sometimes simple warriors, or sometimes the leaders of the anti-Ottoman struggles, the commanders who heroically defended their fortresses. The lost defensive struggles of these communities during the Ottoman conquest were followed by their integration into the Ottoman Empire, which also provided the peoples of the Balkans with many opportunities over several centuries. This fact does not fit the modern national narratives of the 19th and 20th centuries, which are all about resistance and not cooperation.

The liberation of the peoples of the Balkans from Ottoman rule was a consequence of the international power shift in the 19th century. Serbs, Bulgarians, Greeks and other peoples became at once victims, heroes and pawns of international politics, but meanwhile they developed a modern concept of nationhood that is strongly anti-Ottoman but also distrustful of the Western world.

The small Southeastern European nations could not fight the extensive wars alone. The medieval and early modern states combating the Ottomans sought to forge broad alliances to mobilize Europe's resources to make the struggle meaningful. The Catholic Church, especially the papacy were highly influential in the coordination. Thus the warfare occasionally became a common European experience, and contributed to the strengthening of a common European identity.

At the same time, and at the local community level, they sometimes felt alone, abandoned, fighting with the Ottoman army in the isolated mountains and basins of the Balkans, in the plains, steppes and forests of the Carpathian Basin, which are divided by rivers and swamps. At times they surrendered in the face of overwhelming odds, but as Ottoman power began to weaken, armed rebellions often broke out. Outside the cities, in the mountains and on the islands, Ottoman rule often remained symbolic. Thus the fact that local communities sometimes fought the Ottomans for centuries led to the development of a strong regional identity. This was also the case with Mohács and Hungary.

The memory of the battles has been preserved in many forms: heroic songs in the Balkans, poems, folk tales, historical songs, ethnographic traditions as well as the historiography. Castles and fortifications became memorials themselves, or the burial places of the fallen in field battles, Ottoman mausoleums (*türbe*), Christians chapels became *lieux de mémoires*.

These cultural patterns are also clearly present in the case of Mohács, and the political communication of the successors was partly built on them. In this chapter, we review which elements of the 1526 events were used in the politics of memory related to the area: what role the battlefield and the various locations affected by the battles played in the past centuries and memory politics used them.

2   The Commemorative Role of the Great Anti-Ottoman Battles in the Balkans

The populations of the Ottoman-occupied territories experienced the conquest in different ways. In historiography, two main approaches have emerged to describe the relationship between the Ottoman Empire and Christian communities and Europe: one underlines the "civilisational conflict", while the other speaks of "interconnected history" and stresses the interaction between the two worlds.[1] In the Balkans and Central Europe, the first narrative is predominant, but the second is also present. However, the experience of civilisational conflict and interconnectedness are both present, the first more and mainly in propaganda and the second in realpolitik. Nevertheless, the legacy of the Ottoman era sets the peoples of the region against the Ottomans and also against the peoples belonging to the Islamic religion in general.

Some ethnic groups in the Balkans reacted to the Ottoman conquest by converting to Islam. These include the ancestors of today's Bosniaks, some Albanians, the Torbesh, the Gorani and some Roma. Turkish-speaking ethnic groups migrated from Anatolia to Europe, establishing the Turkish-speaking minority communities of present-day Bulgaria, Romania, Kosovo and Northern Macedonia. The (Crimean) Tatars, who are also Muslims, live alongside the Turks. For the non-Turkish Muslim communities, the Ottoman era carries a controversial legacy. Although they regard the Turks as more or less brothers, however their relationship is not free of tensions because of their participation in anti-Ottoman wars of national liberation.

---

1 Samuel P. Huntington, *The Clash of Civilizations and the Remaking of World Order* (New York: Simon & Schuster, 1996); Norbert Pap and Péter Reményi, "Encounters between Islam and Christianity: Mohács and Kosovo," in *Places of Memory and Legacies in an Age of Insecurities and Globalization. Key Challenges in Geography,* ed. Gerry O'Reilly (Springer, 2021), pp. 285–305. Maria Todorova, *Imagining the Balkans* (New York: Oxford University Press, 1997), p. 257; Arno Strohmeyer, "Clash or Go-between? Habsburg-Ottoman Relations in the Age of Süleyman (1520–1566)," in *The Battle for Central Europe: The Siege of Szigetvar and the Death of Süleyman the Magnificent and Nicholas Zrinyi (1566),* ed. Pál Fodor (Leiden, Boston, *Budapest:* Brill, Hungarian Academy of Sciences, Research Centre for the Humanities, 2019), pp. 213–239.

For Christian peoples, the experience of civilisational contact and religiously motivated struggles are dominant. This group – among present national communities – includes the Greeks, Serbs, Bulgarians, Croats, Montenegrins, Romanians and Macedonians. It is important to emphasize that the formation of nations took place on the Balkans at the latest in Europe. The Ottoman Empire was the main obstacle to the emergence of national movements and the creation of nation-states. This is also the reason why the process of nation-building has not yet been completed in many cases, and even new nations may emerge, as we could see for the case of Macedonians and the Bosniaks in the 20th century, as good examples of this. However, in the ethno-cultural contact zones, there are smaller groups of peoples for whom the process of national integration is often not yet complete. Examples of these are the Catholic Bunjevci (*bunyevác* in Hungarian) in Hungary and Serbia, or the Christian Bosniaks in Hungary.[2]

Since the nation-building processes are not yet completed, the related national mythologies are built on or even produce strong enemy images. Anti-Ottoman, anti-Turkish sentiments and political discourses are still part of present debates. In addition, conflicts often involve multiple historical actors, so their memory content is complex and contradictory. If we examine the most prominent fields of conflict, we can identify groups with unique characteristics.

The first group of clashes consists of battles of European importance and memory. However, these conflicts typically have little local or national memory (Nicopol 1396; Constantinople 1453; Lepanto 1571; Nagyharsány 1687;[3] etc.) What these battlefields have in common is that the Ottoman army engaged

---

2 Máté Kitanics and Norbert Pap, "De-bordering, Re-bordering and Integration of the Croatian Minority of Hungary," *Rocznik Instytutu Europy Srodkowo-Wschodniej/Yearbook of the Institute of East-Central Europe* 15 (2017), no. 3, pp. 91–111.

3 In the case of Nagyharsány (12 August 1687, "the second Battle of Mohács"), the battle is present in local memory. Dorffmaister's large painting can be seen in the chapel of the cemetery, the local history collection of the village includes relics of the battle, and in recent years a monument has been built, albeit a highly controversial one, where German and Austrian diplomats wreath the battle momument every 12 August, alongside local residents. However, it has not become a major memorial site in the region. The village's Calvinist Church, nearby Mohács, the castle of Siklós and many other sites and objects are of far greater importance. The main reason for this is that Hungarian participation in the Western coalition forces that fought here and liberated the area from Ottoman rule was very subordinate and small, and thus became a symbolic place of the change of Habsburg rule in Hungarian national memory, rather than the restoration of national self-determination after Ottoman rule. See János Hóvári, "A nagyharsányi csata török szemmel," [The Battle of Nagyharsány through Turkish eyes] in *Előadások és tanulmányok a török elleni visszafoglaló háborúk történetéből: 1686–1688*, ed. László Szita (Pécs: Baranya Megyei Levéltár, 1989), pp. 63–74; Ferenc Tóth, "A második mohácsi csata mítosza és valósága II.," [The myth and reality of the Second Battle of

the mostly coalition armies, predominantly Western, in a way that the local population could not typically identify with. At their place, but without them, the fighting was usually for European/imperial objectives. The consequences were endured, perhaps accepted, but the identity of the community was not decisively based on this.

In a second group, there are fateful, major battles with a strong national background and a strong local, national imprint (Kosovo Polje 1389; Mohács 1526; Udbina 1493; Malta 1565; Szigetvár 1566; Vienna 1683; etc.). In fact, these are the most important sites of memory, where the content of memory and the shaping of identity are expressed at all levels (European, national, local/regional).

A third group includes a series of local struggles with a great memorial imprint, with a high national but low international profile and little international impact (Kőszeg 1532; Eger 1552; etc.). These are the struggles that explicitly form the basis of local and regional consciousness.

The site of several of the above-mentioned prominent battles has become a memorial site. The Christian communities' resistance to Ottoman/Islamic conquest has created in their self-image a topos of the "bastion of Europe and Christianity", a sense of exceptionalism, and in many cases a sense of abandonment or victimisation. Mohács is a good Hungarian example of this.

3   The Holy War

Where did the idea of Mohács come from? The memory of Mohács was also important for the Ottomans. It was considered to be one of the greatest victories in their history. Moreover, it is associated with the name of Süleyman I, the sultan of the Ottoman Golden Age, the *'muhtesem yüzyıl'*, the Ottoman ruler who is considered the greatest and best known today. In the 17th century, during a period of decline following the prosperity of the 16th century, his person became increasingly important. His former successes seemed even brighter by comparison in the era of decline.

The day of the battle, 29 August, was significant in the history of Sultan Süleyman's reign. His army captured Belgrade from the Kingdom of Hungary on this day, and on the same day he was victorious at Mohács. In 1541, Buda was also captured by the Ottomans on 29 August. This date became the sultan's

Mohács II] in *Több mint egy csata: Mohács,* eds. Pál Fodor and Szabolcs Varga (Budapest: MTA Bölcsészettudományi Kutatóközpont, 2019), pp. 413–444.

lucky day, to which he also attached great importance on other occasions during his campaigns.

Not only the date, but also the place of the Battle of Mohács gained an important symbolic meaning. Süleyman camped at Mohács on each of his subsequent campaigns in Hungary, and in 1529, for example, it was here that he received the vassal vows of homage from Hungarian King János Szapolyai whose brother and several relatives had been massacred by Ottoman soldiers there three years earlier. After the reign of Süleyman, the Ottoman armies continued to camp in this place, which became an almost obligatory staging and camping place during the campaigns.

In 1630–1631, during the reign of Sultan Murad IV, one of the warrior sultans of the 17th century, a monument was erected on the battlefield to commemorate Süleyman and his victory in 1526. Hasan Pasha of Buda was the patron of the construction. A victory pavilion was erected, and next to it a well was created for ritual ablutions, important for Islamic religious observance, at this site south of Mohács, along the military road on the edge of the Danube floodplain marshes. The small artificial mound was formed in Roman times, when a small border watchtower (*burgus*) was built here. The Romans abandoned the site in the 5th century and it was only reused by the Ottoman Turks for the purposes of the victory monument.[4]

According to Ottoman historical tradition, Süleyman watched the battle from this small mound, which rises barely ten metres above the plain, and prayed for victory from this spot. Other sources also mention that the Ottoman dead of the battle were buried on or near this site, so that the descendants increasingly regarded it as a Muslim military cemetery. According to the written sources, a religious foundation was established to maintain it, with dervishes providing services. It functioned as a place of pilgrimage and played a role in mobilising the Muslim belivers of the empire for holy war (*jihad*) or faith war (*gaza*).

The Ottoman monument could only serve its purpose until 1687, when the Habsburg-led war for the liberation of the area, involving troops from a broad European coalition, began in 1684. It was at the time of the second Battle of Mohács at Nagyharsány (12 August 1687) that the Christian coalition forces camped near Mohács and the Jesuits, acting as the camp clergy, converted the pavilion into a Christian chapel. Thus, the Muslim Ottoman victory monument was transformed into the first Christian monument of the Battle of Mohács,

---

4 See Chapters First and Eleven.

which also served as a symbol of the reconquest. The chapel's existence can be traced back to the 1770s.

A common feature of the memorial installations is their strong sacrality, indicating that the confrontation was civilisational. The civilisational clash-point character is preserved in both the Hungarian and Christian and the Turkish and Muslim perspectives. In the narrative of the Battle of Mohács memorial sites, the idea of holy war originated with the Muslim Turks who who were the first to initiate a memorial. In the Holy League's war against the Ottomans (1684–1699), the Catholic Church represented the idea of a liberating holy war, a Christian mirror image of Islamic holy war. The battlefield memorials in Mohács (the Turkish Hill and the National Memorial built at the Mohács mass graves) thus inherited the memorial legacy of the religiously motivated war, *jihad* and the *crusade*.

In addition to historiography and military history, archaeology also became an increasingly important in the research of the battle in the second half of the 20th century. There were several reasons for this. There were serious problems with the interpretation of historical sources, because at that time there were far sparcer written sources available than at present, and ideological disputes made it difficult to reach a consensus on the events, course and consequences of the battle. The need for a different, more objective approach grew: thus battlefield archaeology emerged.

4 Mohács in the Culture of Memory and the Politics of Memory

Now, two years before 2026, the 500th anniversary of the battle, preparations are underway for the commemorations. Historical research and archaeological surveys are also in progress. What is the actual historical narrative of the battle? What was its role as a memorial site in the past, and how were the sites used by the political elites of different ideological eras? It is not easy to write a summary of this, as there is a whole library of relevant works. The latest book that attempts to comprehensively summarise the current knowledge on the subject, from the perspective of our time, is *More than a Battle* ... published in 2019,[5] which we heavily rely on in the following discussion. In this chapter we will only attempt to illustrate the trends through selected typical examples.

---

5 Pál Fodor and Szabolcs Varga eds., *Több mint egy csata. Mohács: Az 1526. évi ütközet a magyar tudományos és kulturális emlékezetben* [More than a battle. Mohács: The Battle of 1526 in Hungarian scientific and cultural memory] (Budapest: MTA Bölcsészettudományi Kutatóközpont, 2019), p. 642.

FIGURE 13.1   Soma Orlai Petrich: Discovery of the Body of King Louis II, 1851.
PHOTO: ATTILA ŐSZ. SOURCE: MUSEUM OF DEBRECEN REFORMED COLLEGE. NO. 2018.

Political reflections on the figths, related stories in Mohács were already published a few weeks after the battle. Civil war soon broke out in the country that lost its king. Some sections of society joined the Habsburg party, while others supported the rule of János Szapolyai, the voivode of Transylvania. Accordingly, the question of responsibility for the loss of the battle was seen very differently. One of the participants, Bishop István Brodarics, Royal Chancellor, wrote his influential and very popular account, *Historia verissima*[6] He initially supported Ferdinand but soon took side with John I Szapolyai. In contrast, many contemporary humanists wrote assessments of the battle in support of the Habsburgs, painting a devastating picture of the army at Mohács, and of the incompetent and divisive leadership. The assessments were not without occasional serious bias. These early writings, favourable to the Habsburgs or even to the Szapolyais, provided the basis for conspiracy theories about the events of

---

6   István Brodarics, "Igaz történet a magyarok és Szulejmán török császár mohácsi ütközetéről (1528)," [A true account of the battle between the Hungarians and the Turkish Emperor Süleyman at Mohács (1528)] in *Örök Mohács: Szövegek és értelmezések,* eds. János B. Szabó and Gábor Farkas Farkas (Budapest: Bölcsészettudományi Kutatóközpont, 2020), pp. 301–325.

almost 500 years ago, and became the arguments for blaming the participants and for making a negative assessment of the Hungarian people.

In these writings, the Jagiellonian dynasty and the king himself, as well as the Hungarian noble elite who marched into battle, were accused of incompetence. Betrayal of course also appeared among the motives. Based on this, the accusation has persisted for centuries that János Szapolyai, voivode of Transylvania, had intentionally delayed joining the battle because he already coveted the crown at that time. The blame naturally was put on the financiers of the time, namely the Fuggers. It is typical that later the blame shifted to Jews and religious arguments were also added. The Catholics attributed the defeat to the spread of Protestantism, while the Protestants blaimed it on the sins of Christianity and the papacy, and thus, seeing it as God's punishment.

Mohács, along with other symbolic places, was rediscovered in the 19th century by the intellectuals of the Reform era. Symbolic events and places were needed for the national awakening and the development of a national political and intellectual framework. Mohács was perfectly suited to these purposes. The battles against the Ottomans offered heroes and heroism in abundance. During this period, Mohács inspired plenty of literary works and works of art.[7] Among the literary works referring to the battlefield, Károly Kisfaludy's poem *Mohács*[8] stood out with its image of a "mourning field red with heros' blood".

The independence efforts of the 19th century national movement failed during the 1848–49 War of Independence. The 1849 war arms barrage and the parallels between the martyred generals executed at Arad and Mohács were apt. A series of works of art were created, and many see the fate of the Hungarian nation as allegorically represented in the person of King Louis II. In this context, the monument to Louis II was erected in 1864 on the banks of the Csele Stream.

It was the period, the second half of the 19th century, when "Mohács" became the "unit of measurement" of great Hungarian national tragedies. The question arose whether the tragedy of the Hungarian revolutionary army defeated by the Habsburgs and the Russian forces that supported them in 1849 was greater than that of the army of King Louis II, which was defeated in 1526. In one of the most famous paintings, *II. Lajos holttestének feltalálása* [Discovery the body of

---

[7] Júlia Papp, *The Battle of Mohács and Louis II in the Fine Arts of the 16th–19th centuries*. Manuscript of the MTA Doctoral Thesis (2022).

[8] Károly Kisfaludy (1788–1830), Hungarian poet; his poem *Mohács* was published in 1825 in the literary pocket-book *Auróra*, then called *Elégia*. Its opening lines became a household word: "I greet you with a sigh, a mourning field red with hero's blood, / The graveyard of our national greatness, Mohács!"

King Louis II] by Soma Orlai Petrich, some argue that the king's facial features resemble those of Sándor Petőfi,[9] the famous poet who died a heroic death at Segesvár and is a symbolic figure of the revolution.[10]

One of the most famous lyrical works, Endre Ady's poem *Nekünk Mohács kell* [We Need Mohács] was written in the years before the First World War.[11] The poet argued that the national character of Hungarians is such that their survival requires continuous national disasters.

The next great tragedy was the Treaty of Trianon (1920), the 20th-century graveyard of Hungarian national dreams. In the process of partitioning the Austro-Hungarian Monarchy, which fell apart after the First World War, the successor states did not take into account the public law framework of previous centuries, nor the map of nationalities. It has been asked whether the post-Mohács territorial division had more serious consequences for the country, which was divided into three parts, or the Trianon Peace Treaty. Mohács played a major role in the remembrance politics of the period during the 1926 commemorations. It was then that the initiative was taken to build the Votive Church in the main square of Mohács, a symbol of national unity, and it was vowed that the harmful consequences of the Trianon Peace Treaty would not take as long to eradicate as those of the Ottoman conquest.

In the follow-up to the First World War, Hungary called for a revision of the partitition at Trianon. This ultimately led to partial success: the southern territories of what is now Slovakia, Transcarpathia, Northern Transylvania, Bácska, the Baranya Triangle, Muraköz [Međimurje] and the Muravidék [Prekmurje] were returned to Hungary. For this reason, it joined Nazi Germany as an ally and was one of the last to stand by it. After the war, and partly for this reason, it lost these territories again, and was occupied by the Germans for a short time and then by the Soviets for a much longer period. Again, the question of comparison arises: was it the Ottoman Turkish or the Soviet occupation that had the greater impact? That is why, at the time of the 450th anniversary in 1976, commemorations were reduced to a local level, without even an official

---

9   Nowadays, Béla Szij and Katalin Keserű art historians argue that the face of Sándor Petőfi appears in the picture. https://magyarnemzet.hu/lugas-rovat/2023/01/visszakapta-a-debreceni-muemlek-konyvtar-a-masodik-vilaghaboru-utan-eltavolitott-tortenelmi-tablojat.

10 Sándor Petőfi (1823–1849), a significant poet of the period, a well-known actor, a symbolic figure of the revolution of 15 March 1848, who participated in the War of Independence and died in the battle against the Russian troops near Segesvár on 31 July 1849. He was considered a kind of "rock star" of the era.

11 Endre Ady (1877–1919) was one of the most important Hungarian poets and political journalists of his time. His poem *Nekünk Mohács kell* was published in 1908.

memorial year being declared.[12] At the 1976 commemoration in Sátorhely, the only speaker – Gyula Ortutay, ethnographer and politician, Secretary General of the Hazafias Népfront [Patriotic People's Front] – condemned the Hungarian leaders of the battle, praised the current successes of the Hungarian agricultural cooperative movement in his speech, but did not say a word about the Ottomans.

From the brief description it is clear that the story of the Battle of Mohács and its main characters have provided an inexhaustible amount of material for political debate for centuries. The attribution of responsibility for the Battle of Mohács, the formation of scapegoats and sometimes the fabrication of conspiracy theories have been part of the Hungarian public discourse for almost 500 years. The battle of 1526 became a basis for comparison of Hungarian national disasters, its events and consequences an example, sometimes a deterrent. The bending of historical events, extreme interpretations, the suppression of certain data, the falsification of data and the use of the battle for propaganda purposes were all common. For all these reasons, cultural imprints in the landscape were also influential, and from the second half of the 20th century onwards this became increasingly a major issue in the culture and politics of memory.

5   The Landscape of Memory

The Battle of Mohács not only caused heavy economic and human losses to the Christian states of Central Europe, but also seems to have left an indelible mark on the Hungarian national and local identity. For almost 500 years, its memory has preoccupied descendants, who have dressed up parts of the landscape around Mohács with stories, and the battle, its characters, events and places have become an essential part of local folklore.

In the place where the battle took place, which resulted in huge losses, it is estimated that around 16,000–18,000 Christian warriors were buried. The soldiers who died in the Ottoman army were also buried there. The Ottomans saw Mohács as one of the greatest victories in their history and were concerned with the place and memory of the event. Christians visiting Mohács, as well as Turkish and Bosnian Muslims, saw it as the site of the battle of 1526 and

---

12   János Hóvári, "A mohácsi csata két emlékéve: 1926 versus 1976," [Two commemorative years of the Battle of Mohács: 1926 versus 1976] in *Több mint egy csata,* eds. Fodor et al., pp. 539–562.

valued its landscape accordingly: it became a destination for commemorative journeys and partly for religious pilgrimages.[13]

At the same time, the plain of Mohács bears the imprint of several military historical events and endeavours, which are associated with anthropogenic landscape elements. The former belligerents (both victors and losers) shaped the environment in various ways, while placing their memorial structures in it. The military activities of different eras and their memories are thus interlinked and in some cases interact. Some of the symbolic elements of the battlefield date back at least to Roman times. At the same time, in the 16th and 17th centuries, several anti-Ottoman struggles were fought in the area around the battle, and traces of these battles were layered on top of each other. In terms of military memory, a 'hybrid' memorial landscape of elements from different eras has emerged. The means, modes and sites of commemoration and remembrance have changed several times over the past 500 years, with different landscape elements of the Mohács Plain being highlighted. Both local community and central government efforts have influenced the development of the commemorative elements of the cultural landscape.

Over the centuries, many monuments, Christian chapels and other commemorative structures have been erected to commemorate the battle. The Battlefield Memorial Chapel was constructed in 1816 on the initiative of the bishop of Pécs in the present-day public cemetery of Mohács. Bishop József Király – from an 18th-century local initiative and the bequest of parish priest György Makay in 1784 – decreed that every year on 29 August a memorial mass and a sermon in Hungarian, German and Croatian, in accordance with the languages of the multicultural town, should be held in memory of the Christian soldiers who died in the battle. This tradition, which has been established for more than 200 years, is the longest-standing annual commemoration in Hungarian history.

The chapel was heavily imbued with symbolism: it was built in honour of John the Baptist, the saint of 29 August, also known in Hungarian as "the neck-snapping", thus symbolising the country and nation left "without a head", referring to the death of the king and the leaders of the country. In 1859, two paintings by Stephan Dorffmaister, dating from 1787, were placed in the sanctuary. One depicts the first Battle of Mohács in 1526, the other the 100th anniversary of the second Battle of Mohács in 1687. The first is the battle of the great defeat, while the second is the battle that led to the liberation of the region from Ottoman rule. The chapel is thus a common memorial to both battles,

---

13   See Chapter Eleven.

which are linked, and, in terms of commemorative politics, an imprint of the patriotism of the Habsburgs, reflecting their merits in the anti-Ottoman struggle.

A memorial pillar was probably erected in the 18th century on the spot where, according to historical tradition, the king lost his life while fleeing. The monument to King Louis II still stands near it, north of Mohács, on the military road to Buda, on the banks of the Csele Stream. It was first erected in 1864 by Soma Turcsányi, a veteran of the 1848–49 anti-Habsburg revolution and war of independence. The monument is a reminder of the sacrifices made for the country and a strong reference to the struggle for freedom and the defence of national interests during the Habsburg oppression of 1848–1867.

During the commemoration of the 400th anniversary of Mohács in 1926, the commemorative landscape was extended with new objects.[14] The main square in the centre of the town still bears the marks of the large-scale construction of the memorial. Not only the new Votive Church, but also the orientalising design of the Town Hall building and the banqueting hall within it, hark back to the Ottoman Turkish era.

The places of commemoration on 29 August 1926: the central ceremony took place in the main square of the town, the famous Horthy speech was delivered at the Louis II monument by the Csele Stream.[15]

An interesting thread in the story is that in 1926, the only foreign delegation at the grand celebrations was Turkish. The Turkish envoy made a speech before Horthy, and then the Turkish delegation held a special commemoration at the Turkish Hill. Relations between Atatürk's Turkish Republic and the Hungarian state leadership of the time were excellent, so the commemorations placed a strong emphasis on the Hungarian–Turkish reconciliation process. By contrast, the descendants of the Christian peoples involved in the battle, the Czechs, Austrians, Germans, Croats and Serbs, did not take part: as members of the

---

14 Hóvári, "A mohácsi csata két emlékéve," [Two commemorative years of the Battle of Mohács] in *Több mint egy csata,* eds. Fodor et al., pp. 539–562.

15 Miklós Horthy was governor of Hungary from 1920 to 1944, and head of state. During the First World War, he served as a naval officer in the Austro-Hungarian Navy, during which he distinguished himself, and was later commissioned as an admiral. His famous speech in 1926 at the Louis II Memorial in Mohács is an important text in the history of Hungarian diplomacy. It expressed the aspirations of the Hungarian state to free itself from international isolation: it offered cooperation to the South Slavic peoples fighting alongside the Hungarians in the anti-Ottoman struggle.

so-called "Little Entente," they formed an enemy alliance.[16] The nuncio, on the other hand, represented the pope.

The town hall was built on the basis of a design by the Árkay brothers, because the Trianon decision to build a new state border a few kilometres to the south divided the historic Baranya County in two, and this had an impact on the settlement system. Mohács thus became relatively more important, the urban centre of the southern border region: its urbanisation accelerated, symbolised by the new town hall building.

The Kanizsai Dorottya Museum in Mohács bears the name of the noblewoman of Siklós, one of the first Hungarian female national heroes, who buried the dead of the battle according to tradition. The institution was founded in 1923, a few years before the 400th anniversary commemoration.

The foundation stone of the still unfinished Votive Church in the main square of Mohács was laid on the 400th anniversary of the battle. A bag of earth was sent from each Hungarian settlement of that time and placed at the base of the church to mark the national unity of the building. The plot was donated by the town, while the construction was partly financed by national public donations, but the building was finally consecrated unfinished on 29 August 1940. The Hall of Heroes, the 72-metre-high tower of the church and the bone chambers of the battle's dead were not built.[17] First because of the war, and later because of the changed political situation, it was no longer possible to complete the plans. The country was occupied first by the Germans and then by the Soviets, and its political and cultural structure changed.

6   Picture of Mohács during the Kádár Era (1956–1988)

In the second half of the 20th century, archaeology gained considerable prestige in the interpretation and validation of historical events, because it provided physical, tangible evidence of past events, as opposed to what critics called subjective and uncertain written sources. Another reason why they have become important is that they serve as *lieu de mémoire*.

The fate of the Battle of Mohács during the communist period was partly to be silenced and partly to be smeared. It could only play a contradictory role in the Marxist interpretation of history. The Christian leaders of the battle were

---

16   The Central European alliance, called the "Little Entente", was a collaboration of states that were partly anti-Hungarian in the post-World War I revisionist period.

17   Hóvári, "A mohácsi csata két emlékéve," [Two commemorative years of the Battle of Mohács] in *Több mint egy csata,* eds. Fodor et al., pp. 539–562.

portrayed as weak and incompetent. The defeat was then justified not only by the Ottoman overwhelming force, but mainly by the fact that the nobility had deprived the country of the possibility of being defended by an armed peasantry by the brutal suppression of the peasant uprising led by György Dózsa in 1514. Thus, the disaster of Mohács served mainly to illustrate that the Hungarian aristocracy was unfit to lead the country.[18]

From the second half of the 1960s, the Mohács issue became the starting point of a debate that lasted for decades, which was essentially no longer about the turbulent history of the first half of the 16th century, but about Hungary's geopolitical position, social structure and political culture, and much more about the Kádár regime, the era of the debate, than about the battle itself.[19] Many Hungarian intellectuals of the time, especially historians, were involved, even those whose field of research was not the 16th century. The papers published were aimed at the academic elite, and were published in the form of books and journal articles.

Looking over the course of the debate, it seems that, although difficult to measure, few have achieved a real mass impact. One of those few was the literary historian István Nemeskürty. Apart from his personal talent and literary vein, two other factors played a role in this. On the one hand, he was undoubtedly supported by the memory policy of the communist state party. On the other hand, he also supported the party's policy: in several of his books at the time, he wrote that he was fighting against Hungarian nationalism, with the aim of creating a kind of internationalist patriotism.

In this way, he opposed both the hard-liner cultural politicians of the communist state and the national intelligentsia (writers, historians, film-makers, visual artists), who primarily wanted to continue the tradition of the folkish writers before the war.

It is noteworthy that Nemeskürty may have been the screenwriter of the 1968 film *Egri csillagok* [The Stars of Eger][20] (a Hungarian historical adventure

---

18 István Nemeskürty, *Ez történt Mohács után. Tudósítás a magyar történelem tizenöt esztendejéről. 1526–1541* [This happened after Mohács. Reporting on fifteen years of Hungarian history. 1526–1541] (Budapest: Szépirodalmi Könyvkiadó, 1966), p. 348. The essay was published for the 400th anniversary of the siege of Szigetvár in 1566. Sultan Süleyman and the castle captain Miklós Zrínyi died in the course of the siege, the latter's self-sacrificing heroism having placed him in the Hungarian (and Croatian) national pantheon.

19 Vilmos Erős, "A Mohács-vita," [Mohacs debate] *Magyar Szemle* 23 (2014), no. 5–6, pp. 55–67.

20 Géza Gárdonyi's novel *Egri csillagok* was published in 1901. The story begins after the Battle of Mohács and continues through the fall of Buda in 1541 to the unsuccessful

film set after the Battle of Mohács, called Lost Talisman in English). The film offered him the opportunity to present his anti-clerical, generally anti-noble elite and anti-Western views through the dialogues of his simple, folk heroes. The film has become one of the most popular Hungarian films of all time,[21] seen and loved by generations of viewers, shown on television countless times, and still broadcast on public television. Its impact on the memory of the era is immeasurable. The film was not about Mohács, but it had a significant impact on the image of Mohács, showing the consequences.

With the development of mass media and its tools, the possibilities for shaping historical memory have increased. From the 1960s onwards, the rise in living standards, the advent of paid holidays and the development of transport boosted domestic tourism in Hungary. There was a massive interest in historical sites such as castles: places needed to be dressed up with accessible stories. This was not only the case in Hungary, but also in Mohács.

Since the early 19th century (after the Napoleonic Wars), the marking of important battle sites with monuments has become common practice in Europe, and they have become places of national self-determination as a kind of modern pilgrimage. Archaeological research on sites of great interest has therefore taken on a political significance that goes beyond the scientific. The hypotheses put forward by historians, based on written accounts, can be confirmed or refuted by archaeological methods, and also generate new ideas, change the way we think about battle, and create new possibilities for political communication.

The battlefield of Mohács can thus no longer be thought of as an "abstract" place – "somewhere on the plain of Mohács" – but as a tangible reality. There is a need to identify the different places on the battlefield: the place where the victims of the battle were buried, the encampment places of the two armies, or the place where the Ottomans executed the 1500–2000 war prisoners. The direction of the research promised both to put an end to the seemingly endless historiographical debates about what happened and where, and to offer new

---

Ottoman siege of Eger Castle in 1552. The film, a Hungarian-Bulgarian co-production of the novel, was released on 19 December 1968. It was directed by Zoltán Várkonyi and written by István Nemeskürty.

21   The film was seen by 9,361,000 viewers in Hungarian cinemas alone. This made it the third most-watched film of all time in Hungary. According to the film version, the protagonist, Gergely Bornemissza, who rises from a peasant background, performs a series of heroic deeds with his fellow soldiers, and in the end, in 1552, his technical ingenuity is largely responsible for the successful defence of Eger from the Ottomans. The actor István Kovács, who played Bornemissza, has received an unimaginable 27,000 fan letters.

ways of reliving and remembering the battle. Thus, through archaeological research, Mohács could become empirically tangible reality.

While in the period between the two world wars, archaeology had played a minor role in the activities surrounding the 400th anniversary, with historians and especially military historians thinking and writing about the battle, after the Second World War archaeologists came into the picture, with the intention of identifying the locations of the troops that were deployed by collecting the battle artifacts.

The background to this is the creation of the concept of the battlefield at Majs as the site of the Battle of Mohács, an intellectual construct from the 1920s.[22] Its main proponents were officers who had become military historians. Shortly before the 400th anniversary commemorations, Gergely, as a kind of amateur archaeologist, dug up Turkish Hill to find Ottoman soldiers buried there, but his venture was unsuccessful: only Roman remains were found. He was the first, but not the only one, to question the already centuries-old tradition of Sátorhely.

The anniversary of 1926 generated unprecedented interest in the battle. It was precisely at this time, partly due to the ineffectiveness of Gergely's research, that several people (Gyalókay, Halmay) suggested that the battle may have taken place somewhere on the western edge of the plain, in the administrative area of the village of Majs, and not at Sátorhely, as tradition had held. However, field investigations in this area had not yet been carried out.

The Gergely-Gyalókay-Halmay hypothesis was tried to be confirmed decades later by the archaeologist László Papp. This archaeological investigation took place between 1959 and 1970, but as Papp himself eventually admitted, he failed to find irrefutable evidence of the battle in Majs.[23] Although he did find artifacts relating to the 1526 fighting, his research yielded no breakthroughs.

László Papp worked actively from 1959 until his retirement in 1964. After that he continued with diminishing energy and almost no money, but slowly his momentum faded, he fell ill, stopped research for good in 1970 and died in 1973.

However, there were important partial results. He uncovered the first two mass graves and carried out valuable investigations at several sites of minor

---

22 Endre Gergely, "Ásatások a mohácsi csatatéren," [Excavations on the battlefield of Mohács] in *Mohácsi emlékkönyv 1526*, ed. Imre Lukinich (Budapest: Királyi Magyar Egyetemi Nyomda, 1926), pp. 349–360.; Jenő Gyalókay, "A mohácsi csata," [The Battle of Mohács] in *Mohácsi emlékkönyv*, ed. Lukinich, p. 218; Barna Halmay, *Az 1526-iki mohácsi csata keletkezése és igazi helye* [The origins and real place of the Battle of Mohács in 1526] (Debrecen: Magyar Nemzeti Könyv- és Lapkiadóvállalat Rt., 1926).

23 See Chapter Nine.

importance.²⁴ As late as 1952, while digging a trench during the fortifications of the (anti-Yugoslav) Southern Defence System, soldiers dug into one grave, but as the communist secret service controlled the area, the information was not made public. It was only later, in 1960, when Papp spoke to a driver, Márton Koller, that the story emerged; he (Koller) told him where he had seen human bones that had been accidentally unearthed in the area. A keen resident of Mohács, a certain József Szűcs (as the archaeologist wrote in his report, "unsolicitedly") joined them when Koller showed Papp where he had seen the bones in question.²⁵ Although the two mass graves became a cornerstone of the archaeological investigations that were then underway, the researcher, based on a hypothesis from the 1920s, believed that the so-called "inner battlefield" (place where the clashes were centred) could have been in the southern area of the village of Majs, in the medieval village of Merse.

As we read in the archaeological chapter of the book,²⁶ Papp started excavations at several sites, and during these he met an ethnic German resident named Jakab Lencz, a tractor driver from Majs, who was ploughing several sites with his machine, while finding archaeological remains. It turned out later, Lencz sold one of these objects for money on at least one occasion. The claims he made about the site he had found were contradictory and could not be proved during the on-the-spot checks. Nevertheless, he provided Papp with the three main finds of the Majs battlefield research.²⁷ The archaeologist then systematically travelled throughout the area and excavated in many places, but no new mass graves, no archaeological evidence of the large quantities of weapons and guns he had expected to find, were found. The mass graves in Sátorhely were thought to contain the remains of Hungarian soldiers massacred by the akıncıs of Bali Bey and the sipahi cavalry.²⁸

In 1967, Papp's life took a turn. During the Horthy era, he had worked as a lawyer and even held a prominent social position, but after the communist takeover he was banned from practising and only rehabilitated during the period of easing of the dictatorial regime. Because of his advanced age, this gesture had no practical, but only moral significance in his life. It is possible, however, that in his last years his thoughts were no longer centred on the

---

24 László Papp, "A mohácsi csatahely kutatása," [Research on the battle site of Mohács] in *A Janus Pannonius Múzeum évkönyve 1960*, ed. János Dombay (Pécs: Janus Pannonius Múzeum, 1961), pp. 197–253.
25 Janus Pannonius Museum, Archaeological Database, 1960, no. 1245–83.
26 See Chapter Nine.
27 See Chapter Nine.
28 Papp, "A mohácsi csatahely kutatása," [Research on the battle site of Mohács] in *A Janus Pannonius Múzeum évkönyve*, ed. Dombay, pp. 197–253.

search for the battlefield of Mohács. This may have been the reason why he did not write a synthesis of his research in Majs (battlefield of Mohács), leaving the process unfinished, and why he died a few years later. The battlefield archaeology programme lost both its coordinator and its face.

In preparation for the approaching 450th anniversary commemorations, a memorial park and military cemetery was built in 1975–1976 near the site of Sátorhely, which serves as a national memorial. During the works, the builders found three more mass graves near the two previously discovered, which were uncovered by Ms Borbála Maráz, archaeologist at the Janus Pannonius Museum, as part of a rescue operation, which was no longer a systematic search. She took the view that the mass graves did not mark the battlefield but the site of the Christian camp to the north of it.[29] The site of the battle was somewhere south and west of the graves. The preparations for the 450th anniversary celebrations were delayed, and the archaeologists could not have been in the way of the completion of the memorial park, which had to be completed on time, so that even if there had been a will to do so, there would have been no possibility of in-depth research. The discovery of new graves at Mohács became a sensation, as did the discovery in 1960.

The commemoration of 29 August 1976 and the nationwide interest in the mass graves presented the communist party-state with a special task: how to integrate the battlefield of Mohács and the mass graves into the political narrative of the communist state? The foundations for this have already been laid in the mentioned István Nemeskürty's work. His efforts were finally summed up in the volume *Önfia vágta sebét*[30] [Wounded by Her Own Son] (1975), which dealt with the situation at the level of the elites of the time.

At the same time, there was a problem that the topic aroused considerable interest among the general public as well as among the relatively narrow circle of intellectuals, historians and literary historians, so it seemed necessary to develop appropriate mass communication. In this case, however, it was not the subtle nuances, the difficult task of presenting a complex historical reality, and the country's international room for manoeuvre at the time and in the past, that had to be dealt with. It was a matter of providing clear answers to simple questions that were understood by all.

---

29   Borbála Maráz, "A mohácsi csatatér régészeti leletei," [Archaeological finds of the battlefield of Mohács] *Honismeret* (1976), no. 4, pp. 23–25.

30   István Nemeskürty, *Önfia vágta sebét. Krónika Dózsa György tetteiről* (Budapest: Magvető Könyvkiadó, 1975), p. 689. The volume covers the events of the first half of the 16th century and captivated a contemporary audience with its highly readable style. Its impact is still felt today.

Press releases focused on the following topics:
- mass graves;
- the site of the battle;
- whose discoveries have made the battlefield a tangible reality.

These themes were in keeping with the spirit of the times.

The concept of Majs, developed by military officers on the occasion of the 400th anniversary, which was not validated by archaeological research in the 1960s, but was not clearly refuted, was embraced and loudly propagated by the party-state controlled press of the time, but somewhat modified to suit ideological needs. The solution to the problem from a communication point of view was to find an all-round suitable candidate to be the face of the 450th anniversary commemorations in the press. He was the József Szűcs who accompanied Papp and Koller, unsolicited, to identify the site where the human bones were found in Sátorhely in 1960.[31]

Szűcs himself was of peasant origin, attended six elementary school classes, and in 1976 worked as a maintenance worker at the Mohács Catering Company. He was thus a member of the "ruling class" of socialist society (in theory at least), a "worker", and thus seemed to be well suited to the job. He certainly had the communication skills to do so.

In the year of the anniversary, the day of the battle fell on a Sunday, a day of rest, and crowds visited the cinemas. In the late August 1976 film newsreel (*Filmhíradó*) "The archaeological exploration of the battlefield of Mohács", and in the print press that followed, he became the hero of the exploration of Mohács.[32] It was reported that Szűcs, the worker, was a man who spent his free time researching, reading Turkish dictionaries, collecting documents, and it was he who led the professional archaeologist to the mass graves. He is also the one who found the battlefield near Majs and even presented the Turkish cannonballs he had collected there as evidence to the cameras.[33]

If we compare his statements with the research documentation preserved in the museum, we can see that almost none of his statements about the battlefield research are true (Table 13.1). Papp had been dead for three years, he

---

[31] See Chapter Nine.

[32] We do not have exact data on the audience for the film report, but we can rely on estimates. The compulsory Filmhíradó screenings before the feature film screenings must have had approximately 700,000–800,000 viewers in the mid-1970s. A newsreel of about 10 minutes consisted of 7 units: Polish-Hungarian economic relations, Open gates at the Tungsram water sports plant, Archaeological research on the battlefield of Mohács, Dam break on the canal linking Hamburg to the Ruhr, Texaco motorbike information service for tourists, Cats of the Colosseum, New Swedish women's fashion.

[33] See Chapter Nine on "non-existent finds".

TABLE 13.1 The truth of József Szűcs' claims in 1976 and 2021

Szűcs' claims	According to the research documentation	Evaluation of his claim
A family history interest[a]	No data	Cannot be justified
Poor, self-conscious worker[a]	In the 1970s and 80s	True
Participated in the Levente movement, good patriot[b]	Around 2021	True
He discovered the mass graves, he led László Papp to the site[a]	Koller took László Papp to the mass graves, Szűcs accompanied them without being asked[c]	Not true
He discovered the village of Földvár and the remains of the battle[a]	László Papp has already identified it as medieval Majsa;[d] and recent research suggests that the traces of clashes observed there date from the late 17th century.[d]	Not true
He found Turkish cannonballs cast in situ at "Earth Castle"[a]	Did not actually exist[d]	Not true

a Extract from the Filmhíradó at the end of August 1976.
b Interview with József Szűcs by Márk Haramza. Szabolcs Varga and Attila Türk eds., *Mohács Szimfónia. Tanulmányok a mohácsi csatával kapcsolatos kutatások eredményeiből* [Mohács Symphony. Studies on the results of research on the Battle of Mohács] (Budapest: Martin Opitz Kiadó, 2022), pp. 9–16.
c Janus Pannonius Museum, Archaeological Database, 1968, no. 1167–83; Janus Pannonius Museum, Archaeological Database, 1962–1963, no. 1157–83.
d See Chapter Nine.

could not speak out, he could not explain how the mass graves were discovered, and what he had found in his research in Majs, but it is also true that the academic historians ignored these statements.

The two local residents of German nationality (Koller, who actually showed Papp the mass graves, and Lencz, to whom the three main "Majsian" finds are linked) were in no position to ask for a correction, if they had even thought of it. The ethnic German community suffered expulsion in 1947, and the displaced German villages were settled by poor peasants from the Hungarian

Great Plain, who formed the new communist elite of these villages, loyal to the regime and rootless in the local area. Among them were settled the ethnic Hungarian refugees from Czechoslovakia, from whom the local leadership expected loyalty, and was able to enforce it through their vulnerable position. For a long time, the Germans' ability to assert their interests was almost non-existent, except, of course, for those who became ardent communists. Lencz, otherwise on good terms with Szűcs, was not one of them, and had clashes with the law (he was trading in finds illegally), and had no interest in putting himself into the limelight.

A contemporary interview also revealed that the relationship between Papp and Szűcs was not cordial, the archaeologist did not let the worker near his excavations, even though – according to him – he would have worked for him for free. Szűcs was a collector, his apartment was full of objects from archaeological sites, human bones. The interview also revealed that he was aware that this practice was not legally permissible, but he overcame this with a peculiar argument typical of the time: the land was his workplace from which he derived special rights as a member of the working (ruling) class.

Based on the surviving documentation, it seems that in 1976 Szűcs appropriated not only Koller's, but also much of Papp's achievements and story. In his statements at the time, Szűcs claimed that he had not only led Papp to the mass graves, but that he had also found the village (the alleged Földvár) that was the site of the 1526 clashes. The archaeological documentation shows that Papp found and surveyed the village in 1968 and identified it as a predecessor of Majs (Nagymajsa).[34] The research report preserved in the museum also shows that the few finds that were recovered were not enough proofs for Pap to believe that the village were identical to Földvár.

It is also worth examining the imagery and the wording of the newsreel. In the film, the half-naked, muscular Szűcs appears like the workers' figures on the labour movement posters... In the film, he exudes a sense of primordial power. He became Someone, a peasant-worker hero: of simple origin, he had to work after the sixth grade, and his father had to work the family farm. Because of his social situation, he could not continue his schooling.[35] His interest in history came from family tradition and environmental influences, as he spent a lot of time in the museum in Mohács. In the film, he speaks in dialect... *"In my family, the love of history was a family tradition. I inherited it instead of title, rank and fortune."* His figure is the icon of the worker of peasant origin. A natural

---

34   See Chapter Nine.
35   Until 1946, elementary school in Hungary had 6 grades, and Szűcs was 19 years old. He finished his schooling in the 1930s.

FIGURE 13.2 József Szűcs in the Filmhíradó of 29 August 1976[a] and a labour movement worker statue.[b]
(A) Extract from the Filmhíradó of late August 1976. (B) Kóthay Nándor's 'Railroad section hand' statue (aluminium), Székesfehérvár, 1956.
SOURCE OF FIGURE 13.2 (A): HTTPS://FILMHIRADOKONLINE.HU/WATCH.PHP?ID= 21817&FBCLID=IWAR3J7GBJPAFOIQTBXZ2QMMIDRWDNILOZOWGWSZ-2YYOKF4LVJ LSCOSJAWLI; (B) PHOTO BY BÁLINT DEÁK

figure, who was not fated to be born in the right place, but who solved the riddles of the battle.

The archaeologist Borbála Maráz, who was excavating in Sátorhely, or any other intellectual, did not speak in the news, only Szűcs spoke, apart from the narrator, who presented the above as expected. His figure is an expression of the working-class perception of the Kádár regime and at the same time of its anti-intellectualism. He is the one who – at least according to the setting – instinctively feels, knows the solution, shows the intellectuals the direction to follow. He is the representative of the working class, the legitimator of its rule: in the simple son of the people shines the power and talent that is the basis of his class' rule. A distant descendant of the idealised peasant figures of the uprising led by György Dózsa (1514).

The Filmhíradó combined Nemeskürty's interpretation of Mohács (the ruling class was divided in 1526, the country could have been defended by the people, but the Hungarian nobility in 1514 made this impossible) with state propaganda aimed at the masses. His tangible "achievements", as presented in the news and narrated in the newspapers, such as the discovery of mass graves, the identification of "Földvár" and the battle site, the presentation of the "Turkish cannonballs", all served to convince viewers and readers with clear, material evidence: the peasant-born worker had achieved results based on his natural intelligence, common sense and hard work, and had interpreted the turn of Hungarian history in his own way.

This is how the "Majs battlefield" became a communist state propaganda product, and the sixth-grade worker and amateur researcher became a reference point for the future. Szűcs's appearance on the news in 1976 and several interviews in the newspapers of the time, which had a large circulation, provided him considerable prestige. He became a well-known, respected and important figure in local public life and in thinking about the Battle of Mohács. For a short while, he achieved national fame, but his "glory" slowly faded away; locally, however, he was recognised and respected for the rest of his life.

In the 1980s, the study of, scholarly activity and publication on the battle declined, the discourse on it temporarily emptied out, and the 19th–20th-century issues gained more space than ever before in Hungarian historical research, which was connected to the Hungarian political thaw. Field research ceased for a time, as the Janus Pannonius Museum in Pécs did not receive proper financial resources to carry out such research. The country, and the municipality of Mohács within it, were for a time preoccupied with other things: the communist regime was in crisis, great changes were maturing, and for a time the Mohács debate lost its public importance and was no longer the focus of interest.

7 The Role of the "Majs Battlefield" after the Change of Regime: Recycling

In the early 1990s, not only was the Kádár party-state dissolved and transformed, but Yugoslavia was also disintegrating, in the immediate vicinity of Mohács. The Hungarian political leadership of the time feared that the country would be drawn into the Croatian-Serbian armed conflict. The heavy fighting took place near the Hungarian border (Eszék/Osijek, Vukovar, Szentlászló, etc.), partly in areas inhabited by the Hungarian minority. Some combat troops were deployed close to the border, and there were also incidents of border violations by military units.

All this served as a basis for the Hungarian Defence Forces to form up in Baranya, along the Croatian border, to repel a possible attack and to drive armed groups that had crossed into Hungarian territory out of the country.

At the same time, a young intelligence officer named Lajos Négyesi was brought to the area. According to him, as a scout he travelled around the border area and started thinking about the Battle of Mohács. He did not do research based on sources but relied mainly on his metal detector. Although the area is vast, Szűcs's discovery, which was propagated in the press, led him to start his metal detecting in the area of Majs, which was already the focus of interest, and he found some archaeological finds, including small arm balls. Based on his investigations, in 1994 he wrote in the prestigious *Hadtörténelmi Közlemények*[36] that he had found Brodarics's "Földvár" and archaeological evidence of the battlefield. The post-1976 press releases linked to Szűcs thus gained scientific legitimacy. However, the evidence cited in the article has no description, photo or drawing in the museum. They have disappeared, and the finds have never been deposited in the museum.[37] Thus, it is no longer possible to verify the results of these investigations.

For Szűcs, this appearance must have been particularly important because it confirmed what he had previously said and what he had been able to transform into public recognition. The concept of the battlefield of Majs with the village identified as Földvár near the Catholic church of Majs was also included in János B. Szabó's 2006 monograph of Battle of Mohács,[38] and at the memorial site in Sátorhely visitors can read and see the interpretation of the battle – unsupported by archaeological data and sources – according to which the battle took place at Majs.

In 2008, József Szűcs was made an Honorary Citizen of Mohács for his research of the Mohács battlefield, his special role in the discovery of the mass graves, the discovery of Földvár and for strengthening the reputation of the town. In the following year, under the leadership of the Pécs archaeologist Gábor Bertók, new research was started on the site near Majs, and the publication of the results began.[39] Year after year, metal detector collections in the

---

36 Lajos Négyesi, "A mohácsi csata," [The Battle of Mohács] *Hadtörténelmi Közlemények* 107 (1994), no. 4, pp. 62–79.

37 According to Balázs Polgár, *Oszmán-török kori csataterek régészeti kutatása Magyarországon. PhD-disszertáció* [Archaeological research of battlefields in Hungary from the Ottoman Turkish era. PhD thesis] (Budapest: ELTE BTK, 2018).

38 János B. Szabó, *A mohácsi csata* [The Battle of Mohács] (Budapest, Corvina, 2006), p. 180.

39 Gábor Bertók, "Nekünk Majs kell? Kutatások a mohácsi csatamezőn," [Do we need Majs? Research on the battlefield of Mohács] in *Régi idők – új módszerek*, eds. Gábor Bertók and Csilla Gáti (Budapest: Archeolingua Alapítvány, 2014), pp. 161–170.

FIGURE 13.3 Colonel Lajos Négyesi (left), János B. Szabó (in the middle), József Szűcs at the Mohács National Memorial.
Note: Négyesi presents the award of the Ministry of Defence to József Szűcs at the Sátorhely memorial site in 2018.
PHOTO: TAMÁS SCHNELL.

area near the village produced a large number of metal objects (6500 by 2022), but only a fraction of these are from the 16th and 17th centuries. Because of the findings resulting from the yearly collection campaigns, the Majs site as a battlefield has received constant attention in the media and public opinion.

The investigations and field results of the research[40] launched in 2018, funded by the Hungarian Academy of Sciences, did not confirm the concept of the Majs site. This led to considerable tensions and public debate[41] in the national press and public opinion.

Presumably not independently of the controversy, on 9 December 2018, on the initiative of Lajos Négyesi, the Ministry of Defence and on the initiative of the Director of the Danube-Drava National Park (DDNP), the Ministry of Agriculture awarded József Szűcs with a diploma of merit. Négyesi presented

---

40 The joint project of the Hungarian Academy of Sciences and the University of Pécs, "Mohács 1526–2025 – Reconstruction and Memory", led by Pál Fodor and Norbert Pap, received 120 million HUF in the framework of the Hungarian Academy of Sciences' Cooperation Programme for Excellence. See at http://mohacs.btk.mta.hu/.
41 The debate can be followed at www.mohacsvita.hu.

the award in public, accompanied by a speech, at the memorial site in Sátorhely, and supported his speech with an excerpt from an article published in Szabad Föld in November 1978.[42] József Szűcs died three years later, in 2021, at the age of 94.

It was also a confirmation of the 1526 battlefield concept of Majs that Colonel Lajos Négyesi, military historian, archaeologist Gábor Bertók and historian Szabolcs Varga received a high state award on 15 March 2021, based on the same justification, on the basis of a nomination by the Danube-Drava National Park, "for their research on the one-time site of the Battle of Mohács", among other merits.

The group, mainly named after Gábor Bertók and Szabolcs Varga, continues to insist on linking the Majs site to the 1526 battle, despite the growing evidence to the contrary since 2018, and relies heavily on Szűcs's local legitimacy.

Already in 2020, their book *"Along the plow, in the footsteps of battle"*[43] announced on the front cover that it was written in honour of József Szűcs, and from the ninth page they published the laudation delivered in his honour at the ceremony when he was awarded the title Honorary Citizen of the Town of Mohács.

The group's next volume went even further. In the collected volume *Mohács Symphony*,[44] published in 2022 and containing the writings of the group's members, a biographical interview with József Szűcs, who had died the previous year, was featured in the opening chapter.[45] The publication of this text is a tribute to Szűcs and a public acknowledgement of his intellectual heritage, as well as a confirmation of the legitimacy of research in Majs.

---

42   The speech of Lajos Négyesi, who presented the award, was preserved by a local internet portal. He argues for Szűcs' merits by quoting an article in *Szabad Föld* (*the national newspaper of agricultural cooperatives*) *from* November 1978. The part of the article read out during the speech perfectly reflects what was said in the 1976 Filmhíradó. Edited under strict party-state control, *Szabad Föld*'s circulation reached 700,000 in the mid 1970s. The number of readers exceeded 1.5–2 million in a country of 10 million. The 2018 laudation is a propaganda piece of the press of the 1970s in the Kádár party-state.

43   Márk Haramza, Gergely Kovaliczky, Gábor Bertók, Béla Simon, István Galambos, and Attila Türk eds., *Eke mentén, csata nyomában. Kötet Szűcs József tiszteletére* [Along the plow, in the footsteps of battle. A volume of studies in honour of József Szűcs] (Budapest: Martin Opitz Kiadó, 2020), p. 247.

44   Varga et al. eds., *Mohács Szimfónia* [Mohács Symphony].

45   Márk Haramza's interview with József Szűcs. Varga et al. eds., *Mohács Szimfónia* pp. 9–16.

8 Concluding Thoughts: Let's See the Battlefield!

The anti-Ottoman struggles in Southeastern and Central Europe had a significant identity-shaping effect in the formation of modern national and historical consciousness in the 19th and 20th centuries. This is also true for Mohács, which was interpreted at European, national and regional levels. The memory of the battle became an essential political issue almost 'the next day', and from the 19th century onwards the 'Mohács topos' became a fundamental issue of Hungarian national self-definition. The actual physical reality of the battlefield attracted special attention only later, from the second half of the 20th century.

Physical objects have played an important role in the associated memory culture from the very beginning, but for a longer period written texts and works of art played a more prominent role. Works such as the *True Account* of Brodarics, Dorffmaister's paintings, Károly Kisfaludy's poem *Mohács*, and folk tradition provided an appropriate means of remembering the battle. The commemorative installations – both on the Hungarian and the Turkish side – were either overtly or covertly sacral in nature, as both sides interpreted the battle as an inevitable religious, civilisational clash, but the emphasis on the civilisational conflict was not constant, and other elements were sometimes present. From time to time, elements of interconnectedness appeared: in 1926, the idea of Hungarian-Turkish unity (*turanism*) was emphasised alongside anti-Westernism. In 1976, the Turkish question almost disappeared in the communication, which concentrated more on domestic affairs, emphasising the Hungarian class conflict and, in the background, anti-Westernism.

To mark the battlefield, the Ottomans chose for sacral reasons a place with a good view of the plain, the Turkish Hill of Sátorhely, which became a Muslim religious site in the 17th century. During the wars of liberation, the Jesuits accompanying the liberating army established a chapel there as an act of sacral reconquest. After its destruction, physical proximity lost its significance in the culture of memory for a time. Visits to the battlefield when visiting Mohács remained a custom, as we can read in the memoirs, but the permanent memorials of the battlefield disappeared.

For those who wanted to get to know the battle, the visual experience was offered by the artwork, not the real environment. This is understandable, since over the centuries the landmarks that had provided a secure orientation have disappeared and been transformed. The two Dorffmaister paintings of the first and second Battles of Mohács, painted for the centenary in 1787, were moved from the bishop's palace in Mohács to the memorial chapel in the public cemetery in 1859. Its tower was intended to serve as a lookout over the battlefield.

A significant milestone was the 400th anniversary commemoration in 1926, and the construction of the Votive Church in the main square of Mohács. The site of the building had no particular role during the battle, but the 72-metre-high tower that was planned for the site was intended to serve as a lookout, just as the tower of the Battle Memorial Chapel had done a century earlier. However, it was not deemed important enough to be built, and the building still stands today as a stump. A view of the battlefield was therefore an attractive idea at the time, but there was no plan to build anything on the battlefield.

Among the venues of the large-scale commemoration series, the monument to Louis II stood out. Governor Horthy's famous "Mohács" speech was delivered here in 1926. It can be seen that it was not primarily the battlefield itself, but the highly symbolic, mythical place of the death of Louis II that stood out in terms of commemorative significance. Among the artistic depictions of the battle, it is his death or the discovery of his body that has remained the most prominent theme practically to the present day.[46]

Although Turkish Hill only played a minor part in the commemorations of 1926, the fact that news footage was taken of the site is an indication of the new type of media interest: it shows that a new, highly visual era in the culture of memory is beginning. From the high ground, the camera moves around to the west, showing that this is where the famous battle took place.

At this point, there is already a debate among historians that perhaps the site of the fighting should not be here, but further west and south, away from Turkish Hill, but for Colonel Jenő Gyalókay – the main expert of the period, who explains to the nobility present what happened – this is not important. He does not consider that there should be a commemorative act at Majs, based on his then newly expressed concept. It was not yet a priority for the culture of remembrance at the time.

The concept of Majs grew out of the concept of military historians and intellectuals in the 1920s. Field studies in the 1960s did not prove its validity by archaeological methods, but the physical battlefield became a focus of attention again because of the discovery of mass graves and the memorialisation of the site. The spirit of the times – the rise of the media, the visual nature of mass culture – demanded a new representation, a new type of commemoration. Visuality is becoming increasingly important at the expense of text: the battlefield and archaeological finds are the best visual record of the battle.

On the 450th anniversary in 1976, the mediatized propaganda of the party-state elevates and exploits Majs, placing him in the dominant narrative of the

---

46 See Chapter Twelve.

era. In 1994, an academic publication subsequently authenticated the site. In 2008, the title of Honorary Citizen of Mohács, and in 2018 and 2021, state honours confirm the "discovery" of József Szűcs, a former maintenance worker who completed six classes, and the preservation of his heritage. In hindsight, we see that the sites promoted in the mass media (Majs and the mass graves) were well suited to the visual needs of the mass media and also to the ideological aspects of the time, but the claims did not correspond to the scientific evidence.

In 2009, researchers at the Janus Pannonius Museum in Pécs resumed the investigations previously carried out by Lajos Négyesi. Their starting point is no longer the 1920s theory of Gyalókay and his contemporaries, but Négyesi's 1994 paper in *Hadtörténelmi Közlemények*. They tried to support the Majs concept with modern archaeological tools and instruments.

Because of the atheism of the communist regime, the military cemetery in Sátorhely was not allowed to have clear religious symbols when it was established in 1976, and Christian representatives were not present at the inauguration, but after the regime change in 1991 a cross was erected there. A close examination of the memorial site, however, reveals hidden references to the religious and civilisational background of the clash. The sculptors who helped found the memorial have hidden a number of stylised crosses and symbols.[47]

The new visitor centre was completed in 2011. This, in turn, is now a strongly religiously charged Catholic symbol, a stylized representation of the Hungarian Holy Crown. The upper level of the building is a dome-shaped room with large glass windows. This is the birth of the newest battlefield lookout, from which it was possible this time to get a real close-up view of one of the scenes of the events, the mass graves.

As the 500th anniversary approaches, a re-evaluation of "Mohács" has begun. In the course of this, the Central European (V4) background of the battle is being highlighted, and in the political discourse the civilisational, religious conflict of the battle in the Huntingtonian sense.[48] In the field of academic research, however, after 2015, a clarifying research and reflection has been launched that cannot be ignored in the longer term. The picture of the battle, its events and its protagonists have taken on a more definite contour than ever before.

---

[47] Hóvári, "A mohácsi csata két emlékéve," [Two commemorative years of the Battle of Mohács] in *Több mint egy csata,* eds. Fodor et al., pp. 539–562.

[48] Mohács Proclamation. The Proclamation was signed on 29 August 2019, at the Sátorhely memorial site, calling for the preparation of a Central European commemoration of the battle of 1526, which will mark its 500th anniversary.

Given the current state of public discourse and political communication, which tries to paint everything black or white, there is a serious chance that the interpretation of the battle and the image of Mohács will return to the early modern narrative: on the plain, the Hungarians were confronting the entire Muslim world, and a clash of global significance was taking place between Islam and Christianity.

We now know that it was not just the Hungarians fighting the Ottomans, but a Central European army led by Hungarians fighting an equally diverse army – although there is no doubt that the fate of Hungary was at stake. Historical facts have not bothered the participants in political discourse for a long time, so we can only rely on education and high-quality historical information to ensure that the not insignificant conclusions of the battle's history can be drawn by mankind, including the Hungarian people, in time.

Rather than interconnection, Mohács is the most important example of civilisational clashes in European–Ottoman context. The battle remains an important cornerstone of thinking about the future of Hungary and Europe today. Representatives of all viewpoints can find arguments in its history to support what they say, but there is now also the opportunity for the researcher, the teacher, the journalist, the citizen interested in history and perhaps the politician to be informed by high-quality treatises and evidence-based claims. And our work had, and could have had, no other purpose than this.

Acknowledgement

This chapter has been produced with the support of the OTKA project, no. K 146585 entitled Hungary and the Western Balkans.

Bibliography

B. Szabó, János. *A mohácsi csata.* [The Battle of Mohács] Budapest, Corvina, 2006.

Bertók, Gábor. "Nekünk Majs kell? Kutatások a mohácsi csatamezőn." [Do we need Majs? Research on the battlefield of Mohács] in *Régi idők – új módszerek,* eds. Gábor Bertók and Csilla Gáti, 161–170. Budapest: Archeolingua Alapítvány, 2014.

Brodarics, István. "Igaz történet a magyarok és Szulejmán török császár mohácsi ütközetéről (1528)." [A true account of the battle between the Hungarians and the Turkish Emperor Süleyman at Mohács (1528)] In *Örök Mohács: Szövegek és értelmezések,* eds. János B. Szabó and Gábor Farkas Farkas, 300–325. Budapest: Bölcsészettudományi Kutatóközpont, 2020.

Erős, Vilmos. "A Mohács-vita." [Mohacs debate] *Magyar Szemle* 23 (2014), 5–6: 55–67.
Fodor, Pál and Szabolcs Varga eds. *Több mint egy csata: Mohács. Az 1526. évi ütközet a magyar tudományos és kulturális emlékezetben*. [More than a battle. Mohács: The battle of 1526 in Hungarian scientific and cultural memory] Budapest: MTA Bölcsészettudományi Kutatóközpont, 2019.
Gergely, Endre. "Ásatások a mohácsi csatatéren." [Excavations on the battlefield of Mohács] In *Mohácsi emlékkönyv 1526*, ed. Imre Lukinich, 349–360. Budapest: Királyi Magyar Egyetemi Nyomda, 1926.
Gyalókay, Jenő. "A mohácsi csata." [The Battle of Mohács] In *Mohácsi emlékkönyv 1526*, ed. Imre Lukinich, 193–276. Budapest: Királyi Magyar Egyetemi Nyomda, 1926.
Halmay, Barna. *Az 1526-iki mohácsi csata keletkezése és igazi helye* [The origins and real place of the Battle of Mohács in 1526] Debrecen: Magyar Nemzeti Könyv- és Lapkiadóvállalat Rt., 1926.
Haramza, Márk, Gergely Kovaliczky, Gábor Bertók, Béla Simon, István Galambos, and Attila Türk eds. *Eke mentén csata nyomában. Kötet Szűcs József tiszteletére* [Along the plow, in the footsteps of battle. A volume of studies in honour of József Szűcs] Budapest: Martin Opitz Kiadó, 2020.
Hóvári, János. "A mohácsi csata két emlékéve: 1926 versus 1976." [Two commemorative years of the Battle of Mohács: 1926 versus 1976] In *Több mint egy csata: Mohács*, eds. Pál Fodor and Szabolcs Varga, 539–562. Budapest: MTA Bölcsészettudományi Kutatóközpont, 2019.
Hóvári, János. "A nagyharsányi csata török szemmel." [The Battle of Nagyharsány through Turkish eyes] In *Előadások és tanulmányok a török elleni visszafoglaló háborúk történetéből: 1686–1688*, ed. László Szita, 63–74. Pécs: Baranya Megyei Levéltár, 1989.
Huntington, Samuel P. *The Clash of Civilizations and the Remaking of World Order*. New York: Simon & Schuster, 1996.
Kitanics, Máté and Norbert Pap. "De-bordering, Re-bordering and Integration of the Croatian Minority of Hungary." *Rocznik Instytutu Europy Srodkowo-Wschodniej/ Yearbook of the Institute of East-Central Europe* 15 (2017), 3: 91–111.
Maráz, Borbála. "A mohácsi csatatér régészeti leletei." [Archaeological finds of the battlefield of Mohács] *Honismeret* (1976), 4: 23–25.
Négyesi, Lajos. "A mohácsi csata." [The Battle of Mohács] *Hadtörténelmi Közlemények* 107 (1994), 4: 62–79.
Nemeskürty, István. *Önfia vágta sebét. Krónika Dózsa György tetteiről*. Budapest: Magvető Könyvkiadó, 1975.
Nemeskürty, István. *Ez történt Mohács után. Tudósítás a magyar történelem tizenöt esztendejéről. 1526–1541*. [This happened after Mohács. Reporting on fifteen years of Hungarian history. 1526–1541] Budapest: Szépirodalmi Könyvkiadó, 1966.

Pap, Norbert and Péter Reményi. "Encounters between Islam and Christianity: Mohács and Kosovo." In *Places of Memory and Legacies in an Age of Insecurities and Globalization. Key Challenges in Geography,* ed. Gerry O'Reilly, 285–305. Springer, 2021.

Papp, Júlia. *The Battle of Mohács and Louis II in the Fine Arts of the 16th–19th centuries.* Manuscript of the MTA Doctoral Thesis (2022).

Papp, László. "A mohácsi csatahely kutatása." [Research on the battle site of Mohács] In *A Janus Pannonius Múzeum évkönyve 1960,* ed. János Dombay, 197–253. Pécs: Janus Pannonius Múzeum, 1961.

Polgár, Balázs. *Oszmán-török kori csataterek régészeti kutatása Magyarországon. PhD-disszertáció.* [Archaeological research of battlefields in Hungary from the Ottoman Turkish era. PhD thesis] Budapest: ELTE BTK, 2018.

Strohmeyer, Arno. "Clash or Go-between? Habsburg-Ottoman Relations in the Age of Süleyman (1520–1566)." In *The Battle for Central Europe: The Siege of Szigetvar and the Death of Süleyman the Magnificent and Nicholas Zrinyi (1566),* ed. Pál Fodor, 213–239. Leiden, Boston, Budapest: Brill, Hungarian Academy of Sciences, Research Centre for the Humanities, 2019.

Todorova, Maria. *Imagining the Balkans.* New York: Oxford University Press, 1997.

Tóth, Ferenc. "A második mohácsi csata mítosza és valósága II." [The myth and reality of the second Battle of Mohács II] In *Több mint egy csata: Mohács,* eds. Pál Fodor and Szabolcs Varga, 413–444. Budapest: MTA Bölcsészettudományi Kutatóközpont, 2019.

Varga, Szabolcs and Attila Türk eds. *Mohács Szimfónia. Tanulmányok a mohácsi csatával kapcsolatos kutatások eredményeiből* [Mohács Symphony. Studies on the results of research on the Battle of Mohács] Budapest: Martin Opitz Kiadó, 2022.

Index

Aczél, István 89, 359, 364–365, 368, 373, 379, 385, 405
Adony 51, 53
Ady, Endre 503
Aeneas Sylvius 114
Ágoston, Gábor 15, 97, 129, 132–133, 136, 148, 155
Ahmed I, Sultan 34
Aidebech, Giovanni 75, 77
Alexander the Great 19, 20
Altinum 243, 249, 256, 432
Andrásfalvy, Bertalan 5, 251, 389
Andrew II, King 277
Arad 310, 502
Athanasio Georgiceo 284

B. Szabó, János 112, 114, 388–389, 418, 442, 518, 519
Babócsa 76, 78
Bach, Márton 473
Bácsfalu 67
Bakics, Pál (Bakić, Pavle) 76, 173
Bali Bey 174, 178–179, 181–182, 184–185, 202, 209, 427, 511
Bán 218, 258
Bánffy, János 92, 95
Bánlaky, József 114
Bár 383–384
Baranyakisfalud (Branjina) 218, 257, 259
Baranyavár 55, 66–67, 176, 181, 258, 428
Bartalits, Mihály 468–472, 476
Barthos, Eduárd 468
Bartoš, Pisař 393
Bartucz, Lajos 309
Báta 50–51, 53–54, 56, 65, 243, 293, 367, 372, 375, 402
Báthori, István 88, 92
Batsányi, János 466
Batthyány, Ferenc 89–91, 95, 173
Battyán (Bezdán) 56
Bátya 274, 275
Bayezid II, Sultan 26, 87, 128, 130–131, 134, 144, 163
Becsei, Imre 277
Bedeő, Pál 470

Bég Stream 57, 255
Behari 20, 205
Behram Pasha 174, 185
Belgrade (Nándorfehérvár) 15, 19, 22, 24–27, 29, 30, 144, 172, 420–421, 427, 450, 452, 455, 498
Bellye 285, 291, 316
Belsy, János 456
Bencsik, István 484
Bende, Lajos 274
Berey, Nicolas 453
Bertók, Gábor 276, 311–312, 321, 347, 348, 351, 518, 520
Bezedek 283, 293
Bicocca 144
Birken, Sigmund 453
Boemo, Antonio 102
Bolgar 126
Borza Stream 183–184, 203, 207–208, 228, 256, 259, 263, 273–276, 279–280, 290, 294–302, 313, 337, 344–346, 418
Borza Valley 66, 183, 257, 278
Borzató Valley 72, 290, 296, 301
Bosics, Radics (Božić, Radič) 76, 106, 173
Bostan Çelebi 27, 203–204, 358, 402
Botlik, Richárd 112
Brandstetter, Maximilian 60, 61, 327
Břetislav Švihovský z Rýzmberka 358
Brodarics, István 6, 10, 50, 56, 59–60, 65–66, 69, 72–73, 75–76, 88–90, 93, 95, 97, 99, 100, 102–104, 106, 111–113, 156, 171, 173, 175–176, 179, 180, 182, 184, 189, 198, 200, 202, 230, 235, 271, 274–275, 278, 287–290, 301–302, 317, 321, 340, 343, 345, 359, 363–364, 367, 369, 372, 374, 383, 386, 391, 403, 431, 501, 518, 521
Bruto (Brutus), Giovanni Michele 396
Bucsánszky, Alajos 470, 472
Buda 21–22, 24, 26–27, 31, 50–51, 53, 57, 62, 75, 77–78, 87–88, 90, 94–95, 98–99, 104, 107–108, 148, 192, 194, 197, 204, 243, 257–259, 307, 366, 370, 372, 396, 423–424, 426, 430, 435, 443, 450, 455, 457, 459, 498–499, 506, 508
Budapest 148, 241–242, 435, 463, 480

Budaszentlőrinc 190–191
Burbery, John 401
Burgio, Antonio Giovanni 60, 75, 77, 89–90, 92, 94–95, 98–99, 103, 104, 107, 113–114, 160, 364, 368, 386
Busbecq, Ogier Ghislain 455–456
Buziglica 67–69, 178, 181, 232–233, 259, 261, 263, 442

C. Tóth, Norbert 112
Cairo 128
Camerarius 102, 358
Cavali, Jacomo 76
Celalzade Mustafa 19, 27, 92, 101, 156, 181, 189, 190
Celalzade Salih 28
Celle 149
Cerignola 142
Chaldiran 11, 129, 144, 174
Charles V, Emperor 17, 20, 22–23, 193, 481
Cividale, Domenico 76
Clement VII, Pope 372
Constantinople (Istanbul) 17, 20, 21, 26, 51, 61, 127, 163, 421, 455, 456, 457, 458, 459, 494, 497
Coronelli, Marco Vincenzo 454
Corvato, Luka 75, 78
Csele Stream 50, 239, 243, 253–254, 328, 333, 359, 369–370, 373–376, 378–379, 384–391, 397–401, 405, 456, 461, 467, 474, 476, 502, 506
Cserei, Mihály 384, 401
Cserna, Károly 476, 477
Csibogád 258
Cureus, Joachimus 190
Cuspinianus, Johannes 372, 450
Cyprus 26, 128
Czettricz, Ulrich (Zetritz, Csetrics) 363–368, 370, 373, 374, 381, 382, 385, 402, 405

Dályok (Duboševica) 48, 67, 181, 205, 257, 260, 275, 286, 290, 293, 295, 312, 329, 436
Damascus 26, 134, 163
Danóc 279, 283, 290, 293, 296–297, 301, 345
Darázs 48, 258, 259
Debreceni Ember, Pál 401
Dernschwam, Hans 421, 455, 456

Dorffmaister, István (Stefan) 455, 460, 463–467, 469, 470, 472, 476, 478–480, 482, 497, 505, 521
Dózsa, György 508, 516
Dubravius, Jan 103, 359
Dudás, Gyula 333
Dunawar (Dunavár) 428

Eisenhut, Georgius 245
Engel, Pál 275
Ercsi 51, 88
Érd 51, 53
Erdődy, Simon 89
Erdősi, Ferenc 6, 242
Este, Annibale Cartagine 95, 188
Esterházy
  László Pál 460, 463
  Pál 401
Eszék (Osijek, Ösek) 31, 51, 55, 57, 60, 257–259, 293, 299, 307, 327, 342, 422, 426, 430, 435, 441, 443, 517
Esztergom 23, 27, 30, 84, 99, 359, 420, 455, 469
Etédi Sós, Márton 400–401
Eugene of Savoy (Savoyai, Jenő), Prince 47, 285, 291, 294, 481
Evliya Çelebi 30, 32, 190, 194, 197, 207, 273, 307, 398, 420, 421, 424

Fekete-kapu (Black Gate, Schwarzes Tor) 101, 208, 307, 314, 316, 319, 320, 345
Ferdinand I, King (Archduke of Austria) 94, 360, 368, 455
Feridun Ahmed Bey 28
Festetich, László 460, 466
Filibe (Plovdiv) 51
Filléres, János 76
Fischer, Béla 482
Fodor, Pál VII, 8, 191
Fogarasi, Pál 76
Földvár 10, 51, 53, 72–73, 158, 159, 162, 165, 177, 178, 182–184, 203, 271–281, 283–288, 290–291, 293–298, 300–302, 317, 321, 339–340, 343, 431, 439, 456, 514, 515, 517, 518
  Dunaföldvár 294
  Tiszaföldvár 294
Forgách, Ferenc 26
Frakno (Forchtenstein) 145
Francis I, King 23

Frangepán, Kristóf 111
Fuess, Albrecht 129
Fuessl, Christoph 454
Fugger, Johann 75, 77, 366–368, 372, 386

Gábris, Gyula 6, 232, 234
Gallipoli 126, 494
Ganz, David 397
Garde (Gardo) 131
Gáti, Csilla 276
Gemelli Careri, Giovanni Francesco 424, 430
George, Friar (Martinuzzi) 22
Gergely, Endre 273–274, 307, 430, 442, 510
Gerlach, Stephan 101, 284, 310, 347, 395, 421, 457, 461
Géta (Ketu) 67–68, 178, 181, 293, 300
Giovanni, Antonio 107
Girk, György 467
Gnoienski, Lenard 64–65, 95, 173
Graz 76, 78, 146, 148, 150–151, 161
Guerin, Balthasar 453
Gül Baba 435
Gyalókay, Jenő 3, 6, 100, 111, 273–274, 276, 280, 288, 333, 386, 510, 522–523
Gyáni, Gábor 6
Győr 364, 370–371, 405, 481
Györffy, György 274, 279
Gyula 23

Hain, Gáspár 399, 408
Halász, Károly 474, 476
Halmay, Barna 111, 273, 288, 510
Hammer-Purgstall, Joseph 425
Hasan Pasha, Governor General of Buda 31, 197, 423–424, 430, 499
Hasslingen, Tobias 344, 425, 442
Heltai, Gáspár 382
Henry VIII, King 94
Hercegmárok (Márok) 259, 260
Herczeg, Miklós 199, 203
Hieronymus of Zara 100
Hild, József 467
Hinz, Walter 132–133
Holló, Barnabás 478, 480–481
Homorúd 247, 380
Horthy, Miklós 7, 506, 511, 522
Hosszúpereszteg 76, 78
Hübschmann, Donát 452
Hummel, Gyula 316

Hunyadi, János 172
Hüsrev Bey 174

Ibn Ḥazm 200
İbrahim Pasha, Grand Vizier 20, 22, 24, 66, 91, 157, 174, 182–183
Idris Baba 435
Illés, Gyula 484
Iovius, Paulus 464
Ipoltlaka 274–278, 283, 295
Istvánffy, Miklós 60, 69, 72, 91, 95–96, 100, 195–196, 383–384, 391, 401
Izsép (Topolje) 48, 58, 222, 226, 247, 250, 259, 260, 279, 293

Jenyei Stream 254
Jiratkó, Albin 478
John I, Szapolyai, King 341, 501
John Sigismund (John II, Szapolyai) 22
Joó, István 222

K. Zoffmann, Zsuzsanna 108, 311, 347
Kállay, János 173
Kalt, József 316
Kanizsai, Dóra (Dorottya) 195, 196–197, 200–202, 484
Kara Mustafa Pasha 36
Kara Osman 283
Karasica Stream 55–57, 67, 108, 176–177, 185, 218, 258
Kaszur, László 322
Katib Mehmed Zaim 358
Kemalpaşazade 19, 24, 29, 69, 90, 93, 98, 126, 156, 185, 190, 201–202, 358
Kerbela 37, 424
Kerekegyháza 275, 280
Keulen, Gerard 454
Király, József 440, 466, 474, 505
Kisfaludy, Károly 439, 474, 502, 521
Kiskőszeg (Batina) 55–57, 66, 108, 245, 247–248, 258, 263, 283, 290–291, 302
Kismajsa 274, 278, 280, 295–296, 302
Kismarton (Eisenstadt) 145
Kiss
   Andrea 241
   Attila 63, 432, 433
   Béla 389
   György 478–481
   Sándor 484

Kneidinger, Andreas   297–298
Kő, Pál   484–486
Koçi Bey   205
Kolçak, Özgür   126
Kölked, Özgür   48, 57–59, 65–66, 176,
    203, 206, 222, 226, 232, 243, 250,
    255–256, 275, 279, 280, 283, 288,
    292–293, 436
Kölled (Kolut)   51, 54–56, 64, 65
Koller, Márton   334, 338, 511, 513–515
Komárom   108
Kopaszi reef   148, 151
Korlátkői, Péter   373
Körmend   145
Kosovo Polje   196, 498
Krassó   51, 54, 56, 59, 64–66, 383–384, 396,
    404
Krenn, Peter   151, 162
Kubinyi, András   111
Kuti, István   442
Kútsebes   322

Lajmér   197, 206, 229, 231–232, 255–257, 260,
    263, 275, 313, 330, 336, 347
Lak   276, 278
Lake Riha   247, 249, 263, 377, 383
Lantieri   76
Lánycsók   59, 67, 221, 226, 228, 254, 255, 261,
    263, 338, 375
Łaski, Hieronymus   392
Laszlovszky, József   241
Lazarus   419, 450
Lazius, Wolfgang   393
Leeds   149
Lehmann, Antal   6, 241
Lencz, Jakab   318, 335, 339, 511, 514
Linz   367
Liszti, László   403
Losonczi, István   384, 401
Louis II, King   1, 3, 8, 10, 21, 25, 50, 52–54,
    63, 85, 88, 94–95, 159, 171–174, 179,
    203, 326–327, 357, 359, 366–368, 373,
    386, 388–401, 402, 440, 448, 450, 453,
    455, 457, 459–461, 463–464, 466–474,
    476, 478–479, 482, 484, 486, 501–503,
    506, 522
Lubenau, Reinhold   459–460, 462
Lutfi Pasha   67, 71, 101, 182, 190, 230
Luttwak, Edward   15

Mágocs   75, 78
Mair, Alexander   452
Majs   59, 66–69, 163, 165–167, 181, 202–203,
    218, 221, 226, 232–234, 257, 259–261,
    271, 275–276, 279, 286, 293, 296, 300,
    307, 314, 317–326, 330–331, 334–340,
    343–345, 350–351, 440, 442, 510–515,
    517–520, 522–523
Majsa   165, 276, 278–279, 314, 317–321, 331,
    338, 514
Makay, György   505
Malán, Mihály   313
Maráz, Borbála   311, 314, 319, 335, 346–348,
    512, 516
Maria, Queen   95, 99, 102
Marj Dabiq   11, 129
Marsigli, Luigi Ferdinando   64, 126, 245, 294
Matrakçı Nasuh   28, 38, 190
Matthias I (Hunyadi, Mátyás), King   127, 160,
    312, 326, 327, 433, 459
Maximilian II, Emperor   31
Mecca   207
Mehmed II, Sultan   172, 494
Mehmed III, Sultan   29–30, 420
Mehmed IV, Sultan   35
Meldeman, Niclas   449
Mercator, Gerard   452
Mércz, András   191
Merse   68, 202, 234, 275, 283, 290, 293, 296,
    307, 317–320, 330, 334–335, 337–339,
    346, 431, 442, 511
Meyerpeck, Wolfgang   453
Mihalovits, János   470, 472–473
Mikoviny, Sámuel   294, 428
Mohács   vii, 1, 3, 5–8, 10, 22, 26, 32, 47, 50,
    51, 53, 55–56, 58–65, 75, 77–78, 83,
    86, 88–89, 92, 97, 99–100, 106–108,
    110, 112–113, 125, 129–130, 142, 144, 148,
    155, 157, 160, 162, 166, 171, 192–194, 197,
    203–204, 210, 232, 238, 243, 247–248,
    250, 254, 255, 263, 288, 291–293,
    302, 306–307, 311, 317–319, 326, 328,
    333–335, 338, 341–342, 362, 370, 375,
    382, 385, 390, 398, 401, 418, 421, 422,
    424, 426, 427, 435, 440–441, 444, 452,
    454–457, 459–463, 467–469, 472–474,
    476, 478, 481–482, 484, 495, 498, 500,
    501, 503–504, 507–510, 512–513, 515,
    517, 520–521, 524

INDEX

Mohács Island   3, 5, 47–48, 50, 105, 180, 218,
    220, 222, 226, 238, 239, 242, 247, 248,
    249, 250, 263, 278, 280, 301, 306, 315,
    319, 320, 322–325, 328, 329, 332, 336,
    344, 358, 367, 377, 383, 385, 391, 404,
    436
Mohács Plain   2, 3, 5, 6, 59, 67, 68, 74, 75, 100,
    160, 181, 188, 217, 218, 220–223, 233, 235,
    238, 240, 249, 253, 259–261, 263, 275,
    287, 291–292, 302, 306, 315, 317–319,
    332, 338, 341, 343–344, 346, 375, 384,
    385, 390, 417, 435, 440, 441, 505
Móré, Fülöp   95
Morello, Ludovico   114
Mula, Agostino   96, 114, 190
Müller
    Ignácz   49
    Philipp Heinrich   454
Murad I, Sultan   494
Murad III, Sultan   147, 148, 458
Murad IV, Sultan   35, 499

N. Ipoly, Márta   271
Nagashino   11, 144
Nagy   327
    Balázs   326
    Géza   161
Nagyharsány   193, 291, 342, 344, 425, 453,
    454, 463, 481–482, 497, 499
Nagymajsa   274, 275, 277–280, 295, 515
Nagynyárád (Nyárád)   59, 70, 218, 221,
    226–228, 233–234, 255, 257, 259,
    263, 279, 286, 296, 299, 307, 338,
    425, 442
Nagyvárad   30
Nagyváty   369
Nándorfehérvár (Beograd)   51, 172, 420, 450
Négyesi, Lajos   101, 276, 320, 340, 350, 518,
    519, 520, 523
Nemes, István   8
Nemeskürty, István   111, 508–509, 512, 516
Németh, Balázs   148–150, 154, 161
Neszmély   75, 77, 363
Nicopol   107, 497
Niš   51
Nuremberg   149, 154, 449, 452–453, 472

Oláh, Miklós   358, 372
Orlai Petrich, Soma   501, 503

Ormány   293
Ortutay, Gyula   504
Osman II, Sultan   35
Osman Cevad Bey   435
Ottendorf, Henrik   57, 63, 401, 423, 432

Paks   51, 53
Paksy, Balázs   481
Palóczi, Edgár   461
Pánya, István   250
Pap, Norbert   8
Papp, László   74, 274, 288, 296, 298, 308–311,
    313–314, 317–321, 333–340, 343–347,
    349–350, 431, 442, 510–511, 513–515
Parker, Geoffrey   15
Parma   142
Partiba, Andrea   370
Pavia   11, 142, 164, 193, 209
Peçevi, İbrahim   29, 67, 159, 432
Pécs   23, 47, 56, 60, 78, 95, 165, 167, 317,
    341, 390, 402, 422, 435, 440, 454, 455,
    463, 466–468, 470, 480, 505, 517, 518,
    523
Pécsi, Márton   6, 241
Pentele   51, 53
Perczel, Imre   468
Perényi
    Ferenc   88, 173, 196
    Imre   195
    Péter   64–65, 89–91, 173
Perjés, Géza   3, 6, 100–111, 274, 276, 418, 462,
    491
Pešina z Čechorodu, Jan Tomáš   401
Pest   23, 242
Pesti, János   260
Péteri Takáts, József   402, 460
Pétervárad (Petrovaradin)   51, 54, 91, 94, 97,
    105, 107, 173
Pethő, Gergely   401
Petőfi, Sándor   503
Petrovics, Péter   22
Phillips, Henry Pratap   142
Pigafetta, Marc'Antonio   457
Pilch, Andor   467
Pócsa   258
Podolya   258
Podvinay, Tamás   105
Polgár, Balázs   316, 319, 321, 336, 441
Pölöskei, József   484

Pozsony (Bratislava)   76, 78–89, 108, 172, 467, 470, 472
Prague   160, 165, 343

Quad, Matthias   453

Radonai, Mátyás   342
Rákosi, Mátyás   338
Ráskai, Gáspár   91, 173, 183
Rhodes   26–27, 128–129, 144
Ridaniya   11, 129
Ridvan Bey Oğlu Hüsrev   435
Rome   20–21, 23, 107, 364
Rudolf II, King   458
Rycaut, Paul   425

Sadoleto, Jacopo   99
Samu, Géza   484
Sandrart, Jacob   453
Sárffy, Ferenc   363–368, 370–374, 377, 381, 402, 405
Sárkány, Ambrus   95
Sárvár   78
Sárvíz   51, 53, 208, 358, 385, 393, 402
Sátorhely (Sátoristye, Šatoršće)   32, 66, 69–70, 72–74, 109–110, 178, 183, 184, 192, 197, 201–202, 206, 208, 223, 227–228, 230–231, 257, 260, 271, 273, 274, 276, 285–286, 288, 290–291, 297, 299, 308, 312–314, 319, 330, 333, 337, 344, 345, 346, 351, 418, 425, 428, 429, 439, 440,–443, 504, 510–513, 516, 518–521, 523
Saturcı Mehmed Pasha   30, 420
Savoia, Fazio   76, 78, 368
Schlick
  Albin   144
  Albrecht   75, 78
  Stefan   92
Schweigger, Salomon   458, 459
Selim I, Sultan   128, 144
Selim II, Sultan   30, 420
Seyyid Lokman   28, 38
Sigismund I
  of Luxembourg   450
  of Poland   320
Siklós   195, 196, 454, 497, 507
Sinan Pasha, Grand Vizier   30, 420
Sintzendorff   458

Solymossy   369
Sudár, Balázs   281, 290, 291
Süleyman I   xi, 19, 24, 37, 53, 144, 210, 419, 450, 455, 484–485, 494, 498
Szabó
  Máté   276
  Pál Zoltán   241
Szajcsán, Éva   276
Szajk   285
Szalkai, László   99, 359
Szapolyai
  György   54, 88, 90, 95, 106, 173, 184, 358, 359
  János (John I, Szapolyai), King   19, 54, 111, 371, 439, 499, 501–502
Szatlóczki, Gábor   112
Szávoszt-Vass, Dániel   249
Szeged   242, 312
Szekcső (Dunaszekcső)   278, 358, 376
Székelyszabar   254
Székesfehérvár   23, 25, 370–371, 405, 457
Szekszárd   51, 53, 276–280, 283, 297, 301, 341
Szerecsen, János   95, 369
Szerémi, György   391
Szigetvár   vii, 15, 23, 26–27, 30, 32, 34, 36, 132, 134, 419–421, 426–427, 442–443, 449, 452, 482, 498
Szilágyi, Sándor   476
Szűcs, József   320, 334, 340, 511, 513–520, 523
Szurmay, Sándor   111, 378

T. Mérey, Klára   250, 253
Tahy, János   95
Tebriz   133
Tekelü, Ahmed   21
Telekpuszta   322
Temesköz   22
Temesvár (Timişoara)   22, 291
Thurzó, Elek   95, 99, 366–368, 372, 386
Tito (Broz, Josip)   338
Töll, László   154
Tolna   51, 53, 88, 90, 95, 111–112, 341, 386
Tolvaj, Balázs   8
Tomicki, Piotr   93, 99, 106, 189
Tomori, Pál   51, 54–57, 59–60, 62, 64–65, 89, 104–105, 112, 114, 157, 173, 179, 183–184, 204, 208–210, 481, 484
Török, Bálint   173
Trencséni, György   359

INDEX

Trepka, András 359, 373, 379
Turbék 32, 419, 426, 433, 443
Turcsányi, Soma 473, 474, 478, 506
Turkish Hill (Törökdomb, Hünkâr Tepesi, Türkenhügel, Turski brig) 10, 32, 72, 197, 206–208, 231, 243, 249, 273, 279–280, 287, 301, 306–307, 312–313, 315–317, 320, 329, 333, 345, 417–419, 421–422, 425–432, 434–438, 441–444, 500, 506, 510, 521–522

Udvar 67, 181, 205, 231, 257, 259–260, 290, 292, 295, 297, 312, 329–330, 335, 338
Uhud 198
Ujházy, Ferenc 476
Újistálló (Manor) 197, 206, 274, 313, 316–317, 329, 333, 345, 347
Újlak (Ilok) 51, 105, 173
Újvári, Antal 335
Ungaro, Thomasso 75, 78
Ungnad, David 457

Vadász, György 484
Vályi, András 425
Vapovius, Bernardus 91, 114
Várdai, Pál 88
Varga, Imre 484
Varthema, Ludovico da Bologna 128
Veleslavína, Daniel Adam 384, 401
Velius, Caspar Ursinus 65, 66, 106, 108, 176, 184, 202
Venice 75, 77, 128, 366
Venier, Domenico 106

Verancsics, Antal 388, 455, 456
Verzelius, Joannes 98
Viczián, István 243
Vidin 126
Vienna 21–23, 26, 30, 35–37, 62, 75, 77–78, 85, 90, 95, 99, 316, 341, 349, 366–367, 420, 449, 451, 455–456, 458, 463, 472, 487, 494, 498
Visy, Zsolt 432
Vizslak Meadow 69–70, 73, 185, 206, 208, 226, 232, 271, 279, 301, 306–307, 312, 314, 316, 320, 329, 336, 337, 344–346, 422, 434, 435, 439
Vladislaus II, King 326, 459
Vötter, Joannes 428, 429

Wallop, John 361
Wit, Frederick 453

Yosef ha-Kohen 395

Zalay, Buda 484
Zaratino, Jacomo 184, 287
Zay, Ferenc 455, 456
Zelesny, Károly 476, 477
Zermegh, János 395, 413
Zrin 78
Zrínyi
    Ádám 283, 482
    Miklós (Nicholas) 132, 134, 342, 449, 508
Zsámboky (Sambucus), János 452
Zündt, Matthias 452

Printed in the United States
by Baker & Taylor Publisher Services